College of Law
T00183

INDEX TO LEGAL CITATIONS AND ABBREVIATIONS

INDEX TO LEGAL CITATIONS AND ABBREVIATIONS

SECOND EDITION

DONALD RAISTRICK
Head of Library Services
Lord Chancellor's Department

Foreword by
The Rt. Hon. LORD JUSTICE NEILL

BOWKER–SAUR
LONDON • MELBOURNE • MUNICH • NEW YORK

Published by Bowker-Saur
60 Grosvenor Street, London W1X 9DA
Tel: 071 493 5841 Fax: 071 580 4089

Bowker-Saur is a division of REED REFERENCE PUBLISHING

British Library Cataloguing-in-Publication Data
A catalogue record for this book is available from the British Library.

Library of Congress Cataloguing-in-Publication Data
A catalogue record for this book is available from the Library of Congress.

ISBN 1-85739-061-X

Typeset by Techset Composition Ltd, Salisbury, Wiltshire
Printed on acid-free paper
Printed and bound in Great Britain by Antony Rowe Ltd, Chippenham, Wiltshire

FOREWORD

It may be that all languages require and develop conventional abbreviations and the use of recognised initial letters.

Certainly Latin is a good example: many a stonemason must have been glad that the economy of SPQR could go a long way to offset the inconvenience of Roman numerals.

Lawyers, however, seem to have acquired an especial taste for abbreviations and acronyms which they use to draw attention to case reports and other legal works. The practice is convenient but in the past it has been the cause of much frustration and time-consuming research.

It was to meet a long-felt need that Donald Raistrick came forward in 1981 with the first edition of his *Index to Legal Citations and Abbreviations*.

Since then on countless occasions lawyers and other readers of legal literature have had good reason to feel grateful for the existence of this work and to admire the skill and industry of its author. A particularly valuable feature of the *Index* is the fact that it includes variants of citations as well as the standard form.

In his Foreword to the first edition of the Index Wallace Breem forecast that it would be found to be 'an invaluable bibliographical tool'. So it has proved. But the introduction of fresh series of law reports and further discoveries by Donald Raistrick have prompted calls for a new edition.

I have no doubt that the second and expanded edition of the Index will place us all even further in the author's debt.

Brian Neill
March 1993

PREFACE

This is the age of the abbreviation and acronym, but in few fields are they more abundant or do they have a longer history than in law. Identifying abbreviations has long been a problem for lawyers and for others using the literature: legal citations span centuries. Authors of books, articles and reports frequently assume that their readers will automatically be able to decipher whatever form of abbreviation is used. There is no standardisation; different people have preferences for different forms, and many abbreviations have more than one meaning.

This index therefore reflects usage. It is not a guide to recommended forms of citation or abbreviation since the unfavoured and incorrect are also included. This second edition has been increased in size to include more than 25,000 entries, from abbreviations with a single meaning to those with more than twenty. The geographical coverage is broader than before. Though the major source of entries is still the United Kingdom and Ireland, the Commonwealth and the USA, the index includes many more entries than before from member countries of the European Communities, from other European countries and also from Africa, Asia and South America. The country of origin, if not England or UK, is indicated unless it is obvious from the title.

The alphabetical arrangement is firstly by single initial letters and subsequently by groups of letters or part-words with the same initial letter. For example, under the letter A, all abbreviations that commence with that letter alone, before a full stop or another capital letter (A.A., A.B.A., A.L.T., ASAL), precede those headed by A forming a part-word (Ab., Acq., Ala., etc.). Where the ampersand appears, that abbreviation is arranged at the end of the sequence of the letter or part-word preceding the ampersand (A.B., A.F., A.Z., A.& B., A.& G., etc. Al., Al.Ser., Al.& N., Al.& Nap., etc.). This arrangement, which is basically a word-by-word approach, has the benefit of grouping together abbreviations with the same root, that would be separated if a strict letter by letter style was adopted. In general, abbreviations headed by a lower case letter precede the same letters in capital form, and those without full stops precede those with.

Preface

I have in most cases given the dates for law report and journal titles. For reports series appearing in the *English Reports*, I have indicated the volume numbers, e.g. 110–3 ER. Those that can be found in the *Revised Reports* show the volume numbers of that series, e.g. 50 RR. Similarly, I have found it possible to include references to some American reports series, e.g. 1–4 U.S., 13 S.C.Eq. Any abbreviations used in the entries in this book are themselves indexed.

In the twelve years that have passed since the publication of the first edition of *Index to Legal Citations and Abbreviations*, many new journals and series of law reports have appeared. I commend the practice of many publishers of printing, in each issue, the approved method of citation for their publication. I hope that many more publishers will follow that example and that those quoting such publications will use the official citation.

I am indebted to many people for the great number of helpful suggestions and comments that I have received over the years. I am, however, particularly grateful to Maureen McCormick, Executive Director of the British Columbia Law Library Society, and Colin Fong, Manager of Library Services at Allen Allen & Hemsley, Sydney, for the invaluable lists of Canadian and Australian abbreviations that they sent to me, and to John Rees, of John Rees Rare Books, who allowed me access to his warehouse, where I was able to check for abbreviations used in a vast range of publications from all over the world. In the preparation and checking of my database, I received a tremendous amount of help, for which I am very grateful, from three people in particular. None of the data from the first edition was held on computer and Sandra Naylor spent many hours helping me to add this material to the database and checking its accuracy. All the entries that I prepared were checked by Paula Nyunt. Stuart Cole also added some of the entries, checked the entire computer printout and corrected some of the page proofs. Without the assistance, so readily given by Paula, Sandra and Stuart, I would not have been able to meet my deadlines. My thanks are also due to Lord Justice Neill for writing the Foreword to this volume, to Fleur and Mark for their understanding, and to Michael Chapman, formerly of Bowker-Saur who secured the editorial board's approval, and Margaret Little, who saw the work through to publication.

Donald Raistrick
March 1993

This volume is dedicated to Fleur and Mark

A

a accession

A. Adam's Justiciary Reports (Scot.) 1893–1906
Affirmed
Alabama
Alberta
All India Reporter, Allahabad Series. 1914–
Amended
Annual
Anonymous
Arkansas
Article
Association
Atlantic Reporter
Buchanan's Reports of the Court of Appeal, Cape (S. Afr.) 1880–1910
Corte di appello (It.)
Louisiana Annuals
Permanent Court of International Justice, Judgments and Orders, Series A. 1923–30
Serie politica, detta A (It.)
United Nations General Assembly Document

AA Ars Aequi: Juridisch Studentenblad (Neth) 1951/2–
Ausführungsanweisung (Ger.) regulatory instructions

A.A. Anglo-American
Annales Africaines
Army Act

A.A.A. American Arbitration Association
Association of Attenders and Alumni of the Hague Academy of International Law
Association of Average Adjusters

A.A.A.I.D. Arab Authority for Agricultural Investment and Development

AAA Yearbook Yearbook of the Association of Attenders and Alumni of the Hague Academy of International Law

A.A.C. Anno ante Christum (Lat.) in the year before Christ

A.A.C.E. Arrêts et avis du Conseil d'État (Belg.) Judgments and opinions of the Council of State

A.A.C.E.R. Articles of Agreement of the Council of Europe Resettlement Fund

A.A.C.N. Anno ante Christum natum (Lat.) the year before the birth of Christ

AAG Area Advisory Group (British Overseas Trade Board)

A.A.I. Associate of the Auctioneers' Institute

A.A.J.E. American Academy of Judicial Education
Anglo-American Judicial Exchange

A.A.L.B. Australian Administrative Law Bulletin. 1985–

A.A.L.Bull. Australian Administrative Law Bulletin. 1985–

A.A.L.C.C. African and Asian Legal Consultative Committee

A.A.L.D. Australian Army Legal Department

A.A.L.L. American Association of Law Libraries

A.A.L.R. Anglo American Law Review. 1972–
Australian Argos Law Reports. 1960–73

A.A.L.S. Association of American Law Schools

A.A.L.S.Proc. Proceedings of the Association of American Law Schools. 1950–

A.A.N. Arquivo da Assembleia Nacional (Port.)

a.a.O. am angeführten Orte (Ger.) at the place quoted

a.a.r. against all risks
aircraft accident report

A.A.R. Administrative Appeals Reports (Aus.) 1984–

A.A.S. Acta Apostolicae Sedis (Lat.) Acts of the Apostolic See

AASE Australian Associated Stock Exchange

A.A.S.M. Associated African States and Madagascar

AAT Administrative Appeals Tribunal (Aus.)

A.A.U.P. American Association of University Professors

A.Ae. Ars Aequi: Juridisch Studentenblad (Neth.) 1951/2–

a.B. auf Bestellung (Ger.) on order

A.B. Anonymous Reports at the end of Benloe (73 ER) 1515–1628
Assembly Bill (USA State Legislatures)
Nederlandse Jurisprudentie – Administratiefrechtelijke Beslissingen (Neth.)

A/B Aktiebolaget (Ger.) limited company
Permanent Court of International Justice, Judgments, Orders and Advisory Opinions, Series A/B. 1931–40

A.B.A. American Bankers' Association
American Bar Association

A.B.A.A. Association of British Adoption Agencies

ABA Antitrust L.J. American Bar Association Antitrust Law Journal. 1966–

A.B.A.F.A. Association of British Adoption and Fostering Agencies

A.B.A.J. American Bar Association Journal. 1915–

A.B.A.Jo. American Bar Association Journal. 1915–

A.B.A.Jour. American Bar Association Journal. 1915–

ABA Rep. American Bar Association Reports

A.B.A.Rep.Int'l.& Comp.L.Sec. American Bar Association, International & Comparative Law Section Reports

ABA Sect Ins N&CL American Bar Association Section of Insurance, Negligence & Compensation Law

ABA Sect Lab Rel L American Bar Association Section of Labor Relations Law

A.B.B. Australian Bankruptcy Bulletin. 1934–

A.B.C. Australian Bankruptcy Cases. 1928–64

A.B.C.C. Association of British Chambers of Commerce

A.B.F. American Bar Foundation

A.B.F.Res.J. American Bar Foundation Research Journal. 1976–

A.B.G.B. Allgemeines Bürgerliches Gesetzbuch. Austrian civil code

A.B.L. Business Law Cases for Australians (CCH) 1978–80
Lag om aktiebolag (Swed.) Corporation law
Law for the Australian Businessman (CCH) 1972–7

A.B.L.A. American Business Law Association

A.B.L.R. Australian Business Law Review. 1973–

ABN Australian Bibliographic Network

A.B.P. Associated Book Publishers

A.B.R. American Bankruptcy Reports. 1889–93

A'B.R.J.N.S.W. A'Beckett, Reserved Judgments, New South Wales (Aus.) 1845

A'B.R.J.P. A'Beckett, Reserved Judgments, Port Phillip, New South Wales (Aus.) 1846–51

A'B.R.J.P.P. A'Beckett, Reserved Judgments, Port Phillip, New South Wales (Aus.) 1846–51

A.B.R.N.S. American Bankruptcy Reports, New Series. 1924–45

A.B.Rep. American Bankruptcy Reports. 1889–93

A'B.Res.Judgm. A'Beckett, Reserved Judgments, Victoria (Aus.) 1846–51

A.B.Rev. American Bankruptcy Review. 1924–37

A.B.S. American Behavioral Scientist
Australian Bureau of Statistics

A.B.S.I.D. Arab Board for Settlement of Investment Disputes

A.B.S.Legal Research Frontiers of Legal Research (American Behavioral Scientist Symposium) 1963

A.B.T. Australian Broadcasting Tribunal

ABTEE Australian Broadcasting Tribunal Fortnightly Newsletter. 1982–

ABWOR (Legal) Assistance by Way of Representation (Legal Aid Act 1988)

A'Beck.Judg.Vic. A'Beckett, Reserved Judgments, Victoria (Aus.) 1846–51

A'Beck.R.J.N.S.W. A'Beckett, Reserved Judgments, New South Wales (Aus.) 1845

A'Beck.R.J.P.P. A'Beckett, Reserved Judgments, Port Phillip (Aus.) 1846–51

A'Beck.Res. A'Beckett, Reserved Judgments, Port Phillip (Aus.) 1846–51

A'Beck.Res.Judgm. A'Beckett, Reserved Judgments, New South Wales (Aus.) 1845

A'Beckett Res.Judg. A'Beckett, Reserved Judgments, Victoria (Aus.) 1846–51

ABl. Amtsblatt (Ger.) Official gazette

A.Bus.L.Rev. Australian Business Law Review. 1973–

A.C. action civile (Fr.) civil action
Advance California Reports
anno Christi (Lat.) in the year of Christ
ante Christum (Lat.) before Christ
Appeal Cases
Appeal Cases (Sri L.)
Appellate Court
Arbitration Court (N.Z.)
Assemblée consultative du Conseil de l'Europe
Buchanan, Court of Appea
Cape Colony (S.Afr.) 1880
Canadian Reports, Appeal Cases. 1828–1913
Law Reports Appeal Cases. 1891–

a/c account

A.C.A. Accident Compensation Appeal Authority (N.Z.)
Advance California Appellate Reports. 1940–
Australian Corporate Affairs Reporter (CCH) 1971–82

A.C.A.A. Accident Compensation Appeal Authority (N.Z.)

A.C.A.B.Q. Advisory Committee on Administrative and Budgetary Questions

ACAS Advisory, Conciliation and Arbitration Service

A.C.C. Accident Compensation Commission (later Corporation) (N.Z.)
Allahabad Criminal Cases (India)
American Corporation Cases, by Withrow. 1868–87
Australian Company Law Cases (CCH) 1982–
Australian Copyright Council

A.C.C.B. Australian Copyright Council Bulletin. 1973–

A.C.C.J. American Chamber of Commerce in Japan

A.A.C.C.L.A. Association of American Chambers of Commerce in Latin America

A.C.C.Report Accident Compensation Commission Report (N.Z.) 1976–80

A.C.D.C. Australian Commercial Disputes Centre (Sydney)

A.C.D.D. Advisory Committee of Drug Dependence

ACF Arrête du Conseil fédéral (Switz.)

A.C.H.R. American Convention on Human Rights

ACI International Exchangers Association

A.C.I.C.A. Australian Centre for International Commercial Arbitration (Melbourne)

A.C.I.L.L. Australian Construction Industry Law Letter. 1988–

A.C.J. Acting Chief Justice
Alternative Criminology Journal (Aus.) 1975–
Judgments, etc. of the Arbitration Court of New Zealand. 1978–

A.C.J.A. American Criminal Justice Association

A.C.J.(Mad.Pr.) Accident Compensation Journal, Madhya Pradeṣh (India)

A.C.L. Australian Companies and Securities Legislation (CCH) 1987–
Australian Companies Legislation (CCH) 1982–86
Australian Current Law. 1963–

ACL AT Australian Current Law Articles. 1980–

ACL Bull. Australian Current Law Bulletin

A.C.L.C. Australian Company Law Cases (CCH) 1982–

A.C.L.D. Australian Current Law Digest

A.C.L.J. American Civil Law Journal. 1873

A.C.L.R. Australian Company Law Reports. 1974–
Australian Construction Law Reporter. 1982–
Australian Current Law Review. 1969–71

A.C.L.Rev. Australian Current Law Review. 1969–71

A.C.L.U.Leg.Act.Bull. American Civil Liberties Union Legislative Action Bulletin

A.C.M. Court Martial Reports, Air Force Cases (USA)

ACMB Appellate Court Minute Book (Maori Appellate Court) (N.Z.)

A.C.M.S. Special Air Force Court Martial (USA)

A.C.N. ante Christum natum (Lat.) before the birth of Christ
Australian Customs Notice

ACOM Arbitration Commission (New Zealand)

AcP Archiv für die civilistische Praxis (Ger.) 1818–1944, 1948/9–

ACP African, Caribbean and Pacific States
Australian Company Law and Practice (CCH) 1981–

A.C.P.C. Australian Crime Prevention Council

ACPC Forum Australian Crime Prevention Council Forum. 1978–

ACPCQJ Australian Crime Prevention Council Quarterly Journal. 1978–

A.C.P.O. Association of Chief Police Officers

A.C.P.S. Advisory Council on the Penal System

A.C.R. American Criminal Reports, by Hawley. 1877–1903
Appeal Court Reports (Sri L.) 1903–10
Australian and New Zealand Conveyancing Report (CCH) 1978–
Australian Criminal Reports. 1978–

ACS Archivio Centrale dello Stato (It.)

ACSCC Australian Consumer Sales and Credit Cases (in Australian Consumer Sales and Credit Law Reporter) (CCH) 1981–

A.C.S.L. Australian Company Secretary's Letter (CCH) 1982–

A.C.T. Australian Capital Territory

A.C.T.R. Australian Capital Territory Reports. 1973–

ACTLRC Australian Capital Territory Law Reform Commission

ACTLS Australian Capital Territory Law Society

ACTLS Newsl. Australian Capital Territory Law Society Newsletter

ACTP Australian Accounts Preparation Manual (CCH) 1985–

A.C.T.R. Australian Capital Territory Reports. 1973–

A.C.T.U. Australian Council of Trade Unions

A.C.W.S. All Canada Weekly Summaries. 1977–

A.C.& S.J. Australian Conveyancer and Solicitors Journal. 1948–59

A.Cr.C. Allahabad Criminal Cases (India)
A.Cr.R. Allahabad Criminal Reports (India) 1928–
A.Crim.R. Australian Criminal Reports. 1979–
A.D. American Decisions
Anno Domini (Lat.) in the year of our Lord
Annual Digest and Reports of Public International Law Cases. 1919–49
Australian Digest. 1825–
New York Supreme Court Appellate Division Reports
South African Supreme Court Appellate Division Reports. 1910–46
A.D.2d. New York Supreme Court Appellate Division Reports, Second Series
A.D.A.S. Agricultural Development and Advisory Service
A.D.B. Anti-Discrimination Board
Asian Development Bank
Australian Digest Bulletin
ADB–INK Newsletter Anti-Discrimination Board Newsletter, New South Wales (Aus.)
A.D.C. Acta Dominorum Concilii (Scot.) 1839–1943
ADELA Atlantic Community Development Group for Latin America
ADHGB Allgemeines Deutches Handelsgesetzbuch von 1861 (Ger.) German commercial code
ADIG CCH Tax Action Digest (Aus.) 1984–
A.D.I.L. Annual Digest and Reports of Public International Law. 1919–49
A.D.L. Lag om arbetsdomstol (Swed.) Labour court law
ADL Bull. Australian Administrative Law Bulletin. 1985–
ADLS Auckland District Law Society (N.Z.)
ADP Automatic Data Processing
ADR Alternative Dispute Resolution
Australian De Facto Relationships Law (CCH) 1985–
European Agreement concerning the International Carriage of Dangerous Goods by Road
A.D.R.L.J. Arbitration and Dispute Resolution Law Journal. 1992–
A.d.V. Archiv des Völkerrechts (Ger.)
A.Di.I. Annali di diritto internazionale (It.)
A.E. Annuaire Européen. European Yearbook. 1955–
AEB Australian Business and Estate Planning Reporter (CCH) 1979–
A.E.C. American Electrical Cases. 1873–1908
Atomic Energy Commission (USA)
Atomic Energy Commission Reports (USA) 1956–75
A.E.C.U. African Economic and Customs Union
AEDC Australian Electronics Development Corporation
AEG Australian Estate and Gift Duty Reporter (CCH) 1971–80
AEGR Australian Estate and Gift Duty Reporter (CCH) 1971–80
AEL Australian Employment Legislation (CCH) 1984–
A.E.L.E. Association européene de libre-échange. European Free Trade Association
A.E.L.R. All England Law Reports. 1936–
AEM Australian Employment Law Guide (CCH) 1984–
AEOP Australian and New Zealand Equal Opportunity Law and Practice (CCH) 1984–
A.E.R. All England Law Reports. 1936–
A.E.R.Rep. All England Law Reports Reprint. 1558–1935
A.E.R.Rep.Ext. All England Law Reports Reprint Extension Volumes, Australia. 1861–1935
AETR European Agreement on the Work of Crews of Vehicles Engaged in International Road Transport
a.f. anno futuro (Lat.) next year
A.F. Air Force

Arrête fédéral (Switz.)
AFAM Australian Family Law Guide (CCH) 1985–
A.F.A.R. Australian Foreign Affairs Record. 1930–
AFB Australian Fringe Benefits Tax Guide for Employers (CCH) 1986–
A.F.C.O. Admiralty Fleet Confidential Order
AFDB African Development Bank
A.F.D.I. Annuaires français de droit international (Fr.) 1955–
AFIN Australian Finance Availability Guide (CCH) 1987–
A.F.JAG L.Rev. Air Force JAG Law Review (USA) 1965–73
A.F.L. American Federation of Labor
Australian Family Law and Practice (CCH) 1975–
Australian Family Lawyer. 1985–
A.F.L.A. Association of Fire Loss Adjusters
A.F.L.B. Australian Family Law Bulletin. 1987–
A.F.L.–C.I.O. American Federation of Labor and Congress of Industrial Organizations
A.F.L.R. Air Force Law Review (USA) 1974–
A.F.L.Rev. Air Force Law Review (USA) 1974–
A.F.O. Admiralty Fleet Order
A.F.P. Australian Federal Police
A.F.P.M. Arquivo da Familia Pinto de Mesquita (Port.)
A.F.R. Australian Financial Review
A.F.Rep. Alaska Federal Reports (USA) 1869–1937
AFT Act on Foreign Trade
Australian Federal Tax Reporter (CCH) 1969–
AFTR American Federal Tax Reports. 1796–
Australian Federal Tax Reporter (CCH) 1969–
AG Aktiengesellschaft (Ger.) joint stock company
Amtsgericht (Ger.) District Court
Attorney General's Opinions (USA)
A.G. Adjutant General
Agent General
Attorney General
A-G Attorney-General
AGB Allgemeine Geschaftsbedingungen (Ger.) general conditions (of contracts, transactions, etc.)
AGBGB Ausführungsgesetz z. Burgerlichen Gesetzbuch (Ger.) implementing law to the civil code
AGG Arbeitsgerichtsgesetz (Ger.) law on labour courts
AGCAS Association of Graduate Careers Advisory Services
A.G.D.L. Attorney General of the Duchy of Lancaster
A.G.Dec. Attorney General's Decisions (USA)
AGIS Attorney-General's Information Service (Aus.)
A.G.L.A. Australian Government Lawyers' Association
AGLA Bull. AGLA Bulletin: Journal of the Australian Government Lawyers' Association. 1986–
A.G.M. Annual General Meeting
A-G Newsl. Attorney-General's Newsletter, Victoria (Aus.) 1985–
A.G.O. Attorney General's Opinions (USA) 1789–
AGPS Australian Government Publishing Service
A.G.S. Australian Government Solicitors' Office
AGVE Aargauische Gerichts–und Verwaltungsentscheide (Switz.)
A.H.A. Area Health Authority
AHCA Additional Housing Costs Allowance
AHF Australian High Court and Federal Court Practice (CCH) 1978–
a.h.l. ad hunc locum (Lat.) at this place
A.H.R. Academy of Human Rights
a.h.s. anno humanae salutis (Lat.) in the year of human salvation
a.h.v. ad hunc vocem (Lat.) at this word

AHVG Bundesgesetz über die Alters- und Hinterlassenenversicherung (Switz.)

A.I. Admiralty Instruction
Amnesty International
Artificial Insemination

A.I.Arb. Associate of the Institute of Arbitrators

A.I.B. Accidents Investigation Branch

A.I.C. Australian Institute of Criminology

A.I.Cr.D. All India Criminal Decisions. 1947–

A.I.D. Agency for International Development
Artificial insemination by donor

A.I.D.A. Association internationale de droit africain. International African Law Association
Association internationale du droit de l'assurance. International Association for Insurance Law

A.I.D.I. Annuaire de l'Institut de Droit International

A.I.D.P. Association internationale de droit pénal. International Association of Penal Law

AIDS Acquired immune deficiency syndrome

A.I.E.A. Agence internationale de l'énergie atomique

A.I.E.E. Association des instituts d'études européennes. Association of Institutes for European Studies

AIFC Agreement on International Freight Railway Communication

A.I.F.S. Australian Institute of Family Studies
Australian Institute of Forensic Sciences

A.I.H. Artificial insemination by husband

A.I.I.A. Australian Information Industry Association
Australian Institute of International Affairs

A.I.J.A. Australian Institute of Judicial Administration

A.I.J.D. Association internationale des juristes démocrates. International Association of Democratic Lawyers

A.I.L.A. Australian Insurance Law Association

A.I.L.N. Australian International Law News. 1984–

AILR Australian Industrial Law Review (CCH) 1959–

AIM Asian Institute of Management

AIN Australian and New Zealand Insurance Reporter (CCH) 1979–

A.I.O.C. Anglo-Iranian Oil Company

AIPC Australian Intellectual Property Cases (in Australian Industrial and Intellectual Property) (CCH) 1982–

A.I.P.L. Annual of Industrial Property Law. 1975–9

AIPPI International Association for the Protection of Industrial Property

A.I.R. All India Reporter. 1914–

A.I.R.A. All India Reporter, Allahabad Series. 1914–

A.I.R.Aj. All India Reporter, Ajmer Series. 1949–57

A.I.R.All. All India Reporter, Allahabad Series. 1914–

A.I.R.And. All India Reporter, Andhra Series. 1954–6

A.I.R.Andh. All India Reporter, Andhra Series. 1954–6

A.I.R.Andh.Pra. All India Reporter, Andhra Pradesh Series. 1957–

A.I.R.Asm. All India Reporter, Assam Series. 1949–

A.I.R.Assam All India Reporter, Assam Series. 1949–

A.I.R.B. All India Reporter, Bombay Series. 1914–

A.I.R.Bhop. All India Reporter, Bhopal Series. 1951–6

A.I.R.Bilas. All India Reporter, Bilaspur Series. 1952–5

A.I.R.Bom. All India Reporter, Bombay Series. 1914–

A.I.R.C. All India Reporter, Calcutta Series. 1914–

A.I.R.Cal. All India Reporter, Calcutta Series. 1914–

A.I.R.Dacca All India Reporter, Dacca Series. 1949–50

A.I.R.East Punjab All India Reporter, East Punjab Series. 1948–50

A.I.R.F.C. All India Reporter, Federal Court Series. 1947–50

A.I.R.H.P. All India Reporter, Himachal Pradesh Series. 1949–

A.I.R.Him.Pra. All India Reporter, Himachal Pradesh Series. 1949–

A.I.R.Hy. All India Reporter, Hyderabad Series. 1950–7

A.I.R.Hyd. All India Reporter, Hyderabad Series. 1950–7

A.I.R.Ind.Dig. All India Reporter, Indian Digest. 1946–52

A.I.R.J.& K. All India Reporter, Jammu and Kashmir Series. 1951–

A.I.R.Kerala All India Reporter, Kerala Series. 1957–

A.I.R.Kutch All India Reporter, Kutch Series. 1949–56

A.I.R.Lahore All India Reporter, Lahore Series. 1914–50

A.I.R.M. All India Reporter, Madras Series. 1914–

A.I.R.M.B. All India Reporter, Madhya Bharat Series. 1950–7

A.I.R.M.P. All India Reporter, Madhya Pradesh Series. 1957–

A.I.R.Mad. All India Reporter, Madras Series. 1914–

A.I.R.Madh.Pra. All India Reporter, Madhya Pradesh Series. 1957–

A.I.R.Manip. All India Reporter, Manipur Series. 1952–

A.I.R.My. All India Reporter, Mysore Series. 1950–

A.I.R.N. All India Reporter, Nagpur Series. 1914–57

A.I.R.Nag. All India Reporter, Nagpur Series. 1914–57

A.I.R.Oris. All India Reporter, Orissa Series. 1949–

A.I.R.Oudh All India Reporter, Oudh Series. 1914–49

A.I.R.P. All India Reporter, Patna Series. 1916–

A.I.R.P.C. All India Reporter, Privy Council. 1914–50

A.I.R.Pat. All India Reporter, Patna Series. 1916–

A.I.R.Pep. All India Reporter, Patiala and East Punjab States Union Series. 1950–7

A.I.R.Pepsu. All India Reporter, Patiala and East Punjab States Union Series. 1950–7

A.I.R.Pesh. All India Reporter, Peshawar Series. 1933–50

A.I.R.Pun. All India Reporter, Punjab Series. 1951–

A.I.R.R. All India Reporter, Rajasthan Series. 1950–

A.I.R.Raj. All India Reporter, Rajasthan Series. 1950–

A.I.R.S.C. All India Reporter, Supreme Court. 1950–

A.I.R.Sau. All India Reporter, Saurashtra Series. 1950–7

A.I.R.Simla All India Reporter, Simla Series. 1951–

A.I.R.Sind All India Reporter, Sind Series. 1914–50

A.I.R.T.C. All India Reporter, Travancore–Cochin Series. 1950–7

A.I.R.Trip. All India Reporter, Tripura Series. 1952–

A.I.R.V.P. All India Reporter, Vindhya Pradesh Series. 1951–7

A.I.S.A.M. International Association of Mutual Insurance Societies

AISHWC Australian Industrial Safety, Health and Welfare Cases (in Australian Industrial Safety, Health and Welfare Reporter) (CCH) 1979–

A.I.S.J. Association internationale des sciences juridiques. International Association of Legal Science

AISP Australian Insolvency Management Practice (CCH) 1984–

AITG Australian Income Tax Guide (CCH)

A.I.T.L.& P. Australian Income Tax Law and Practice

A.I.T.R. Australian and New Zealand

Income Tax Reports. 1937, 1940–69
AIX Australian International Tax Agreements (CCH) 1982–
A.Ins.R. American Insolvency Reports. 1878–83
A.J. Acta Juridica (S.Afr.) 1958–
Acting Justice or Judge
L'Actualité Juridique (Fr.)
Alberta Judgments (unreported decisions available on QL) 1986–
American Journal of International Law. 1907–
American Jurist. 1829–43
Aranzadi Jurisprudencia (Sp.) Law journal
Associate Judge
British Guiana Supreme Court, Appellate Jurisdiction
A.J.A.G. Assistant Judge Advocate General
A.J.C.L. American Journal of Comparative Law. 1952–
AJCompL American Journal of Comparative Law. 1952–
A.J.F.L. Australian Journal of Family Law. 1986–
A.J.F.S. Australian Journal of Forensic Sciences. 1968–
AJHR Appendix to the Journals of the House of Representatives (N.Z.) 1858–
A.J.I.L. American Journal of International Law. 1907–
A.J.L.L. Australian Journal of Labour Law. 1988–
A.J.L.S. Australian Journal of Law and Society (Macquarie University) 1982
A.J.P. Annales des justices de paix (Fr.) 1792–
A.J.P.A. Australian Journal of Public Administration. 1942–
A.J.R. Australian Jurist Reports. 1870–4
AJRBP Access to Justice in Rural Britain Project (University of Essex)
A.J.R.(N.C.) Australian Jurist Reports (Notes of Cases) 1870–4
A.J.S. American Judicature Society
AJSH Journal of Occupational Health and Safety – Australia and New Zealand (CCH) 1985–
A.Jur.Rep. Australian Jurist Reports. 1870–4
A.K. Kaartsysteem T.M.C.Asser Instituut (Neth.)
a.k.a. also known as
A.K.Marsh. A.K. Marshall, Kentucky Supreme Court Reports (8–10 Ky) 1817–21
AKtG Aktiengesetz (Ger.)
A.L. Aranzadi Legislacion (Sp.) Spanish legislation
A.L.A. American Library Association
Associate of the Library Association (UK)
A.L.A.A. American Labor Arbitration Awards (P–H) 1946–
Aviation Law Association of Australia
A.L.A.C. Alcoholic Liquor Advisory Council (N.Z.)
A.L.B. Aboriginal Law Bulletin (Aus.) 1981–
A.L.C. American Labor Cases (P–H) 1946–
American Leading Cases
A.L.C.A. Arts Law Centre of Australia
A.L.C.F. Australian Law Council Foundation
ALD Administrative Law Decisions (in Australian Administrative Law Service) 1976–
ALEC Australian Industrial and Intellectual Property (CCH) 1983–
A.L.I. American Law Institute
ALIABA American Law Institute–American Bar Association Committee on Continuing Professional Education
A.L.J. Albany Law Journal. 1870–1908
Allahabad Law Journal (India) 1904–
American Law Journal. 1884–5
Australian Law Journal. 1927–
A.L.J.N.S. American Law Journal, New Series. 1848–52
A.L.J.R. Australian Law Journal Reports. 1958–
ALLG Australian Law Librarians' Group

A.L.L.G.Newsl. Australian Law Librarians' Group Newsletter. 1973–
ALLR Australian Labour Law Reporter (CCH)
A.L.M. American Law Magazine. 1843–46
A.L.M.D. Australian Legal Monthly Digest. 1967–
ALN Administrative Law Notes (in Australian Administrative Law Service) 1977–86
Australian Law News (Law Council of Australia) 1977–
ALPD Australian Legal Profession Digest (Law Council of Australia)
A.L.Q. Arab Law Quarterly
A.L.R. Adelaide Law Review. 1960–
Aden Law Reports. 1937–
Alberta Law Reports (Can.) 1908–32
American Labor Cases (P–H) 1947–
American Law Register. 1852–1907
American Law Reports
American Law Reports, Annotated. 1913–47
Argus Law Reports, Victoria (Aus.) 1895–1959
Australian Argus Law Reports. 1960–73
Australian Law Reports. 1973–
ALR 2d American Law Reports Annotated, Second Series. 1948–65
ALR 3d American Law Reports Annotated, Third Series. 1965–80
ALR 4th American Law Reports Annotated, Fourth Series. 1980–
A.L.R.A. Abortion Law Reform Association
A.L.R.A.C. Australian Law Reform Agencies Conference
A.L.R.A.N.L. Abortion Law Reform Association News Letter
A.L.R.C. Australian Law Reform Commission
A.L.R.(C.N.) Argus Law Reports, Current Notes (Aus.) 1895–1958
A.L.R.Comm. African Law Reports, Commercial Series
A.L.R.Fed. American Law Reports Annotated, Federal
A.L.R.Mal. African Law Reports, Malawi Series
A.L.R.N.S. American Law Register, New Series. 1908–10
A.L.R.S.L. African Law Reports, Sierra Leone Series
A.L.Rec. American Law Record (Cincinnati) 1872–87
A.L.Reg. American Law Register (Philadelphia) 1852–1907
A.L.Reg.(N.S.) American Law Register, New Series. 1908–10
A.L.Reg.(O.S.) American Law Register, Old Series. 1852–1907
A.L.Rep. American Law Reporter
A.L.Rev. American Law Review. 1866–1929
ALSA American Legal Studies Association
Australasian Law Students' Association
ALSA Forum American Legal Studies Association Forum
ALSAJ Australasian Law Students' Association Journal. 1986–
A.L.T. American Law Times. 1868–77
Association of Law Teachers
Australian Law Times. 1879–1928
A.L.T.Bankr. American Law Times, Bankruptcy Reports
A.L.T.R. American Law Times Reports. 1868–73, 1874–7
A.L.T.S. Automated Land Titles System
ALVE Australian Leave and Holidays Practice Manual (CCH) 1981–
ALWG Australian Legal Workers Group, New South Wales
ALWG Newsl. Australian Legal Workers Group Newsletter, New South Wales. 1980–
A.M.A. American Management Association
American Medical Association
AMAS African and Malagasy Associated States
A.M.C. American Maritime Cases. 1923–
AML Anti-Monopoly Law

A.M.L.B. Advertising and Marketing Law Bulletin (Aus.) 1984–6
Trade Practices Advertising and Marketing Law Bulletin (Aus.) 1987–

A.M.L.J. Akmer-Merwara Law Journal (India) 1927–

AMM Archivio Storico del Ministero della Marina (It.)

A.M.P.L.A. Australian Mining and Petroleum Law Association

A.M.P.L.A.Bull. Australian Mining and Petroleum Law Association Bulletin. 1982–

AMPLA Journal Australian Mining and Petroleum Law Journal. 1977–82

AMPLA Yearbook Australian Mining and Petroleum Law Association Yearbook. 1983–

A.M.P.L.J. Australian Mining and Petroleum Law Journal. 1977–82

AMT Air Mail Transfer (Banking)

A.M.v.B. Algemene Maatregel van bestuur (Neth.) Order in Council

A.M.& O. Armstrong, Macartney & Ogle, Nisi Prius Reports (Ire.) 1840–2

A.Moo. A. Moore's Reports, in 1 Bosanquet & Puller p.471ff (126 ER) 1796–7

A.N. Abbott's New Cases, New York
Assemblée Nationale (Fr.) National Assembly

ANA Article Number Association

ANB Australian National Bibiliography. 1961–

A.N.–B. Arrêts du Nouveau–Brunswick (unreported decisions available on QL) (Can.) 1986–

A.N.C. Abbott's New Cases, New York
African National Congress (S.Afr.)
American Negligence Cases. 1789–1897
New South Wales Conveyancing Law and Practice (CCH) (Aus.) 1980–

ANLX New South Wales Land Tax (CCH) 1984–

A.N.R. American Negligence Reports. 1897–1909

ANRU New South Wales Revenue Rulings (CCH) (Aus.) 1980–

A.N.S.A. Association Nationale des Sociétés par Actions (Fr.)

ANST New South Wales Strata Title Law and Practice (CCH) (Aus.) 1979–

A.N.T.T. Arquivo Nacional da Torre do Tombo (Port.)

A.N.W.T.& Y.Tax R. Alberta, Northwest Territories & Yukon Tax Reporter (Can.) 1973–

A.N.Z.A.L.S. Australian and New Zealand Association of Law Schools

A.N.Z.A.P.P.L. Australian and New Zealand Association of Psychiatry, Psychology and Law

ANZCERTA Australia New Zealand Closer Economic Relations – Trade Agreement

ANZC Hals Australian and New Zealand Commentary on Halsbury's Laws of England

ANZ ConvR Australian and New Zealand Conveyancing Report (CCH) 1979–

ANZ Insurance Cases Australian and New Zealand Insurance Cases (in Australian and New Zealand Insurance Reporter) (CCH) 1979–

ANZJC Australian and New Zealand Journal of Criminology. 1968–

ANZJ Crim Australian and New Zealand Journal of Criminology. 1968–

ANZJ of Crim Australian and New Zealand Journal of Criminology. 1968–

ANZUS Treaty signed by Australia, New Zealand and the United States

AO Anordnung (Ger.) direction, instruction
Reichsabgabenordnung (Ger.) Imperial Taxation Act

A.O. Administrative order
Army Order

A.O.A. Accident Offices' Association

A.O.J.P. Australian Official Journal of Patents, Trade Marks and Designs. 1904–

A.O.J.P.T.M.D. Australian Official Journal of Patents, Trade Marks and Designs. 1904–

AoR Archiv des öffentlichen Rechts (Ger.)
A.O.S.W. Association of Official Shorthandwriters
A.P. Additional Premium
Annual Practice
Arios Pagos (Supreme Court of Greece)
A.P.A. Additional personal allowance
Australian Planning Appeal Decisions. 1982–
APACS Association for Payment Clearing Services
APAD Australian Planning Appeal Decisions. 1982–
A.P.A.I.S. Australian Public Affairs Information Service. 1945–
A.P.B. Ashurst's Paper Books, in Lincoln's Inn Library
Association Professionnelle des Banques (Fr.)
APC Acts of the Privy Council of England, ed. by J.R. Dasent. 1890–95
AP, CD Atti Parlamentari della Camera dei Deputati (It.) 1860
A.P.C.L. Asian Pacific Commercial Lawyer. 1984–
A.P.C.N. anno post Christum (Lat.) in the year after the birth of Christ
A.P.D. Archives de philosophie du droit (Fr.) 1931–40, 1952–
APEX Association of Professional, Executive, Clerical and Computer Staff
A.P.I.C. Arab Petroleum Investment Corporation
APLA American Patent Law Association
Asia-Pacific Lawyers' Association
APLA Bull. Bulletin of the American Patent Law Association. 1952–
APLA Journal Asia-Pacific Lawyers' Association Journal (Korea) 1987–
APLA Q. American Patent Law Association Quarterly. 1972–
APLB Australian Property Law Bulletin. 1986–
A.P.L.Cas. Archbold's Poor Law Cases. 1842–58
A.P.L.T.R. Asian Pacific Law and Tax Review. 1984–
APM Australian Personnel Management (CCH) 1977–
A.P.O. Arbeidsplaatsenovereenkomst (Neth.) Agreement on job protection
A.P.R. Atlantic Provinces Reports (Can.) 1975–
A.P.R.C.T.L. Asian Pacific Review of Computers, Technology and the Law. 1984–5
AP, S Atti Parlamentari della Camera dei Senatori (It.) 1861
A.P.S. The Acts of the Parliaments of Scotland, 1124–1707. 1814–75
A.P.S.R. American Political Science Review
A.P.T.I.R.C. Asian-Pacific Tax and Investment Research Centre, Singapore
APTIRC Bulletin Asian-Pacific Tax and Investment Bulletin (Singapore) 1983–
A.P.Tax & Invest.Bull. Asian-Pacific Tax and Investment Bulletin (Singapore) 1983–
APVO Ausländerpolizeiverordnung (Ger.) Police (Aliens) Order
APY Australian Pay-roll Tax Manual (CCH) 1979–
A.Pol.J. Australian Police Journal
A.Q. Advocates' Quarterly (Can.) 1977–
Australian Quarterly (Australian Institute of Political Science) 1929–
AQC Queensland Conveyancing Law and Practice (CCH) (Aus.) 1982–
AR Additional requirements
A.R. Alberta Reports (Can.) 1977–
All Risks
American Reports
Anno Regni (Lat.) in the year of the reign
Annual Register
Annual Return
Appeal Reports, Upper Canada. 1846–66
Argus Reports, Victoria (Aus.) 1895–1959
Army Regulations
Arrêté royal (Belg.) Royal decree

Atlantic Reporter
Industrial Arbitration Reports, New South Wales (Aus.) 1902–
Ontario Appeal Reports. 1876–1900

A.R.Austrl. Industrial Arbitration Reports, New South Wales (Aus.) 1902–

A.R.B. Air Registration Board

ARBA Arkansas Bar Association

A.R.C. Agricultural Research Council
American Railway Cases. 1854–6
American Ruling Cases

ARE Arab Republic of Egypt

A.R.M. Memorandum of the Internal Revenue Bureau Committee on Appeals and Review (USA)

A.R.(N.S.W.) Industrial Arbitration Reports, New South Wales (Aus.) 1902–

A.R.O. Army Routine Order

AROB Administratieve rechtspraak overheidsbeschikkingen (Neth.) 1976–

A.R.(Ont.) Ontario Appeal Reports. 1876–1900

A.R.P. Appeal Rules Precedents (British Columbia Practice), cases to Nov. 1971 (Can.)

A.R.R. American Railway Reports
Anno Regni Regis/Reginae (Lat.) in the year of the King's/Queen's reign
Recommendation of the Internal Revenue Bureau Committee on Appeals and Review (USA)

ARS Agreement relating to Refugee Seamen
Entscheidungen des Reichsarbeitsgerichts und der Landesarbeitsgerichte (Ger.) Labour court reports

A.R.S. Advanced Record System
Anno Reparatae Salutis (Lat.) in the year of redemption
Arizona Revised Statutes

ARSP Archiv für Rechts–und Sozialphilosophie (Ger.) 1933–44, 1949–

ARUNA Annual Review of United Nations Affairs

A.Rep. American Reports
Atlantic Reporter

AS Amtliche Sammlung der Bundesgesetz und Verordnungen (Switz.) legislative series

A.S. Act of Sederunt (Scot.)
American Samoa
Anglo Saxon
Assistant Solicitor

A/S Account sales
Joint-stock company

ASA Advertising Standards Authority

A.S.A.L. Annual Survey of African Law. 1967–
Annual Survey of American Law. 1942–
Annual Survey of Australian Law. 1976–

A.S.A.Newsl. Association for the Study of Abortion Newsletter (USA)

a.s.a.p. as soon as possible

A.S.A.R. All South Africa Law Reports. 1947–

A.S.B. Air Safety Board (USA)

A.S.B.L. Association sans but lucratif (Belg.) non–profit making corporation or association

ASC Australian Consumer Sales and Credit Law Reporter. 1978–
Australian Securities Commission

A.S.C.A.P.Cop.L.Symp. Copyright Law Symposium (American Society of Composers, Authors and Publishers)

A.S.C.L. Annual Survey of Commonwealth Law. 1965–75

A.S.Code American Samoa Code

ASD Australian Sentencing Digest. 1985–

ASDI Annuaire suisse de droit international (Switz.)

ASE Archivio Storico del Ministero degli Affari Esteri (It.)

ASEAN Association of Southeast Asian Nations

ASEAN–CCI The ASEAN Chambers of Commerce and Industry

A.S.E.L. Annual Survey of English Law. 1928–40, 1945

ASFL Australian State Family Law Legislation (CCH) 1986–

ASH Action on Smoking and Health

Australian Industrial Safety, Health and Welfare (CCH) 1979–

A.S.I.L. American Society of International Law
Annual Survey of Indian Law. 1965–

A.S.I.L.Proc. Proceedings of the American Society of International Law

A.S.I.L.Procgs. Proceedings of the American Society of International Law

ASJG Acta Scandinavica Juris Gentium

A.S.L. Advanced Student in Law
Annual Survey of Law (Aus.) 1976–80

ASLC Australian Securities Law Cases (in Australian Securities Law Reporter) 1971–

A.S.L.I.B. Association of Special Libraries and Information Bureaux, now Aslib the Association for Information

A.S.L.O. Associated Scottish Life Offices

A.S.L.P. Australian Society of Legal Philosophy

A.S.L.P.Bull. Australian Society of Legal Philosophy Bulletin. 1977–

A.S.L.P.Proc. Australian Society of Legal Philosophy Proceedings. 1960–65

A.S.M.A. Australian Stipendiary Magistrates' Association
Journal of the Australian Stipendiary Magistrates' Association. 1978–

A.S.M.L. Annual Survey of Massachusetts Law. 1954–

ASP Australian Superannuation and Employment Benefits Guide (CCH) 1978–

ASPAC Asian and Pacific Council

A.S.Proceedings Proceedings of the American Society of International Law

A.S.R. American State Reports
Australian Securities Law Reporter (CCH) 1972–

ASS Australian Social Security Guide (CCH) 1984–

A.S.S.A.L. Annual Survey of South African Law. 1947–

ASSC Australian Social Security Cases (in Australian Social Security Guide) (CCH) 1984–

ASTC Australian Sales Tax Cases (in Australian Sales Tax Guide)

ASTE Association for the Study of Soviet-type Economies (USA)

ASTM Australian Stamp Duties (CCH) 1985–

A.S.T.M.S. Association of Scientific, Technical and Managerial Staffs

ASX Australian Stock Exchange

ASt Ausgleichssteuer (Ger.) Adjustment Tax

A.T. Appeal Tribunal
Australian Current Law Digest. 1980–

ATA Temporary Admission (Admission temporaire)

A.T.C. Annotated Tax Cases. 1922–76
Assessed Tax Case
Australian Tax Cases (CCH) 1969–

A.T.D. Accession Treaty and Decision concerning the ECSC
Australasian Tax Decisions. 1943–69
Australian Tax Decisions. 1930–42

ATEA Australian Telecommunications Employees Association

A.T.F. Arrêts du Tribunal fédéral (Switz.)
Australian Tax Forum. 1984–
Recueil officiel des arrêts du Tribunal fédéral (Lausanne, Switz.)

ATG Australian Income Tax Guide (CCH) 1969–

ATL Australian Income Tax Legislation (CCH) 1976–

A.T.L.A. Association of Trial Lawyers of America

A.T.L.A.J. American Trial Lawyers Association Journal. 1965–

A.T.M. Australian Tax Monitor. 1984–

A.T.O. Australian Taxation Office

ATOP Australian Taxation Office Practice. 1986–

ATOR Australian Torts Reporter (CCH) 1984–

ATP Aid and Trade Provision
Australian Trade Practices Reporter (CCH) 1972–

ATPR Australian Trade Practices

Reports (in Australian Trade Practices Reporter) (CCH) 1974–

ATPR (Com) Australian Trade Practices Reporter Commission Decisions (CCH) 1974–

ATPR (Digest) Australian Trade Practices Reporter Cases and Decisions Digest (CCH) 1985–

A.T.R. Australasian Tax Reports. 1969–

A.T.R.F. Australian Tax Research Foundation

ATRU Australian Income Tax Rulings (CCH) 1983–

A.T.Rev. Australian Tax Review. 1971–

A.T.S. Australian Treaty Series. 1948–

ATUG Australian Telecommunications Users' Group

A.U.C. Anno Urbis Conditae (Lat.) in the year of the founding of the city
Arquivo da Universidade de Coimbra (Port.)

AUDI Anuario Uruguayo de Derecho Internacional

A.U.L.R. American University Law Review. 1957–
Auckland University Law Review (N.Z.) 1967–

A.U.L.S.A. Australasian Universities Law Schools Association

AUSDOC Australian Document Exchange Pty Ltd

AUSTEL Australian Telecommunications Authority

a.v. annos vixit (Lat.) he/she lived for...years

AV Allgemeine Verwaltungsvorschrift, Allgemeine Vorschrift (Ger.) general administrative regulation

AVB Allgemeine Versicherungsbedingungen (Ger.) general conditions of insurance

AVC Victorian Conveyancing Law and Practice (CCH) 1981–

AVCC Australian Vice-Chancellors' Committee

AVCP Victoria Civil Procedure Updater (CCH) 1987–

AVMA Action for Victims of Medical Accidents

AVMA M.& L.J. Action for Victims of Medical Accidents Medical and Legal Journal

AVR Archiv des Völkerrechts (Ger.)

AVST Australian Investment Planning Guide (CCH) 1985–

A.V.T. Added Value Tax

AVW Victorian Accident Compensation Practice Guide (CCH) 1985–

AWCCD Australian Workers Compensation Case Digests (in Australian Workers Compensation Guide) (CCH)

AWD Außenwirtschaftsdienst des Betriebs–Beraters (Ger.) 1954–

AWG Außenwirtschaftsgesetz (Ger.) Foreign Trade Act

AWK Australian Workers Compensation Guide (CCH) 1984–

A.W.L.D. Alberta Weekly Law Digest (Can.) 1982–

A.W.N. Allahabad Weekly Notes (India) 1880–1908

A.W.O.L. absent without leave

A.W.R. Allahabad Weekly Reporter (India) 1933–

AWW Algemene Weduwen–en Wezenwet (Neth.) General Widows and Orphans Act

AXT Australian Sales Tax Guide (CCH) 1973–

A.Y.B.I.L. Australian Yearbook of International Law. 1965–

AZO Allgemeine Zollordnung (Ger.) General customs regulations

AZP Archiv für die civilistische Praxis (Ger.) 1818–1944, 1948/9–

A.& A. Amendments and additions

A.& A.Corp. Angell & Ames, Corporations

A.& C. Addenda & corrigenda

A.& E. Admiralty and Ecclesiastical
Adolphus & Ellis' Reports (110–3 ER) 1834–40

A.& E.A.C. American and English Annotated Cases

A.& E.Ann.Cas. American and English Annotated Cases

A.& E.Anno. American and English Annotated Cases

A.& E.Cas. American and English Annotated Cases

A.& E.Corp.Cas. American and English Corporation Cases. 1893–4

A.& E.Corp.Cas.N.S. American and English Corporation Cases, New Series. 1896–1904

A.& E.Enc. American and English Encyclopedia of Law and Practice

A.& E.Ency. American and English Encyclopedia of Law and Practice

A.& E.Ency.Law American and English Encyclopedia of Law and Practice

A.& E.(N.S.) Adolphus & Ellis' Queen's Bench Reports, New Series (113–8 ER) 1841–52

A.& E.P.& P. American and English Pleading and Practice

A.& E.Pat.Cas. American and English Patent Cases. 1662–1890

A.& E.R.Cas. American and English Railroad Cases. 1879–95

A.& E.R.Cas.N.S. American and English Railroad Cases, New Series. 1894–1913

A.& E.R.R.C. American and English Railroad Cases. 1879–95

A.& E.R.R.Cas. American and English Railroad Cases. 1879–95

A.& E.R.R.Cas.N.S. American and English Railroad Cases, New Series. 1894–1913

A.& F.Fix. Amos & Ferard on Fixtures. 3ed. 1893

A.& H. Arnold & Hodges' Practice Cases, Queen's Bench. 1840–1

A.& N. Alcock & Napier's King's Bench Reports (Ire.) 1831–3

A.& O.P.& E.L.U. Allen & Overy Pensions and Employment Law Update

A.& P. Accounts and Papers

Aanh.Hand.I (II) Aanhangsel tot het Verslag der Handelingen van de Eerste (Tweede) Kamer der Staten–Generaal (Neth.) Addenda to the Report of the Proceedings of the First (Second) Chamber of the States–General

aant. aantekening (Neth.) note

Aarvold Report Report of the Interdepartmental Committee on Magistrates' Courts in London (Cmnd. 1606) 1962

Ab. Abridgement
Abstract
Abstracts of Treasury Decisions (USA)

Ab.Ca. Crawford & Dix's Abridged Cases (Ire.) 1837–8

Ab.Eq.Cas. Equity Cases Abridged (21–2 ER) 1667–1744

ab init. ab initio (Lat.) from the beginning

Ab.N. Abstracts of Treasury Decisions, New Series (USA)

Aband.Prop. Abandoned property

Abb. Abbott, United States Circuit and District Court Reports. 1863–71

Abb.Adm. Abbott, Admiralty Reports (USA) 1847–50

Abb.App.Dec. Abbott, Court of Appeals Decisions, New York. 1850–69

Abb.C.C. Abbott, Circuit Court Reports (USA) 1863–71

Abb.Cl.Ass. Abbott, Clerks' and Conveyancers' Assistant

Abb.Ct.App. Abbott, Court of Appeals Decisions, New York. 1850–69

Abb.Dec. Abbott, Court of Appeals Decisions, New York. 1850–69

Abb.Dig. Abbott, New York Digest

Abb.Dig.Corp. Abbott, Digest of the Law of Corporations

Abb.F. Abbott, Forms of Pleading

Abb.F.Supp. Abbott, Forms of Pleading, Supplement

Abb.Int. Abbott, Introduction to Practice under the Codes

Abb.Law Dict. Abbott, Law Dictionary. 1879

Abb.Leg.Rem. Abbott, Legal Remembrancer

Abb.Mo.Ind. Abbott, Monthly Index

Abb.N.C. Abbott, New Cases, New York. 1876–94

Abb.N.Cas. Abbott, New Cases, New York. 1876–94

Abb.N.S. Abbott, Practice Reports, New Series. 1865–75

Abb.N.Y.App. Abbott, Court of Appeals Decisions, New York. 1850–69

Abb.N.Y.Dig. Abbott, New York Digest

Abb.Nat.Dig. Abbott, National Digest

Abb.Pl. Abbott, Pleading under the Code

Abb.Pr. Abbott, New York Practice Reports. 1854–75

Abb.Pr.N.S. Abbott, New York Practice Reports, New Series. 1865–75

Abb.Sh. Abbott, Merchant Ships. 14ed. 1901

Abb.Ship. Abbott, Merchant Ships. 14ed. 1901

Abb.Tr.Ev. Abbott, Trial Evidence

Abb.U.S. Abbott, Circuit Court Reports (USA) 1863–71

Abb.Y.Bk. Abbott, Yearbook of Jurisprudence

Abbott Abbott, Law Dictionary. 1879
Abbott, Merchant Ships. 14ed. 1901

Abbott Civ.Jur.Tr. Abbott, Civil Jury Trials

Abbott Crim.Tr.Pr. Abbott, Criminal Trial Practice

Abbrev.Plac. Placitorum Abbreviatis (Record Commissioner)

Abdy R.Pr. Abdy, Roman Civil Procedure

Abdy & W.Gai. Abdy & Walker, Gaius and Ulpian

Abdy & W.Just. Abdy & Walker, Justinian

A'Beck.Judg.Vict. A'Beckett, Reserved Judgments, Victoria (Aus.) 1846–51

A'Beck.R.J.N.S.W. A'Beckett, Reserved Judgments, New South Wales (Aus.) 1845

A'Beck.R.J.P.P. A'Beckett, Reserved Judgments, Port Phillip, New South Wales (Aus.) 1846–51

A'Beck.Res.Judg. A'Beckett, Reserved Judgments

Abh. Abhandlungen (Ger.) treatises

Abney, Reports Reports of Cases by Sir Thomas Abney. 1750

abr. abridged
abridgement

Abr.Ca.Eq. Abridgement of Cases in Equity (21–2 ER) 1667–1744

Abr.Cas. Crawford & Dix, Abridged Cases (Ire.) 1837–8

Abr.Cas.Eq. Abridgement of Cases in Equity (21–2 ER) 1667–1744

Abs. Absatz (Ger.) paragraph
Absent
Absolute
Abstain
Abstract
Abstracts of Treasury Decisions (USA)
Ohio Law Abstract

Abs.Crim.Pen. Abstracts on Criminology and Penology (USA) 1969–

Abs.(N.S.) Abstracts of Treasury Decisions, New Series (USA)

Abschn. Abschnitt (Ger.) paragraph or chapter

abse.re. absente rea (Lat.) the defendant being absent

abstr. abstract

Abt. Abteilung (Ger.)
AEthelbert

abv. above

AbzG Abzahlungsgesetz (Ger.) law on hire purchase agreements

AcP Archiv für die civilistische Praxis (Ger.) 1818–1944, 1948/9–

Acad. Academy

Acad.Pol.Sci.Proc. Academy of Political Science Proceedings (USA)

Acc. Accord

Accioly Accioly, Tratado de Direito internacional publico. 1933–5

acct. account

Acct. The Accountant. 1874–

Acct.L.Rep. Accountant Law Reports

Acct.Rec. Accountants Record

Accty. Accountancy

acq. acquittal
acquitted
acq.in result acquitted in result
Act. Action
Acton's Prize Cases (12 ER) 1809–11
Act.Ass. Acts of the General Assembly of the Church of Scotland. 1638–1842
Act.Can. Acta Cancellariae, by Monro
Act.Cur.Ad.Sc. Acta Curiae Admiralatus Scotiae, by Wade
Act.écon. Actualité économique (Fr.)
Act.Jur. L'Actualité Juridique: droit administratif (Fr.) 1945–
Act.Jur.D.A. L'Actualité Juridique: droit administratif (Fr.) 1945–
Act.Lawt.Ct. Acts of Lawting Court (Scot.)
Act.Ld.Aud.C. Acts of the Lords Auditors of Causes (Scot.)
Act.Ld.Co.C.C. Acts of the Lords of Council in Civil Causes (Scot.) 1478–1501
Act.Ld.Co.Pub.Aff. Acts of the Lords of Council in Public Affairs (Scot.)
Act of Sed. Act of Sederunt (Scot.)
Act.P.C. Acts of the Privy Council, by Dasent
Act.P.C.N.S. Acts of the Privy Council, New Series
Act.Pr.C. Acton's Prize Cases (12 ER) 1809–11
Act.Pr.C.Col.S. Acts of the Privy Council, Colonial Series
Act.Reg. Acta Regia
Act.Scand.Juris.Gent. Acta Scandinavica Juris Gentium (Den.)
Act.Sed. Act of Sederunt (Scot.)
Acta Acta Academiae Universalis Jurisprudentiae Comparativae (Ger.)
Acta Crim. Acta Criminologia (Can.) 1968–74
Acta Jur. Acta Juridica (S.Afr.) 1958–
Acta Jur.Hung. Acta Juridica Academiae Scientiarum Hungaricae (Hungary)
Acta Med.Leg.Soc. Acta Medicinae Legalis et Socialis (Belg.) 1948–
Acta Pol. Acta Politica (Neth.)
Acta U.Carol.Jur. Acta Universitatis Carolinae: Juridica (Czechoslovakia)
Acta U.Carol.Jur.Mono. Acta Universitatis Carolinae: Juridica Monographia (Czechoslovakia)
Acton Acton's Prize Cases (12 ER) 1809–11
Acts Austl.Parl. Acts of the Australian Parliament
Acts S.Austl. Acts of South Australia
Acts Tasm. Acts of Tasmania
Acts Van Diem.L. Acts of Van Dieman's Land (Aus.)
Acts Vict. Acts of Victoria (Aus.)
Acts & Ords.Interreg. Acts and Ordinances of the Interregnum. 1642–60
Ad. Addam's Ecclesiastical Reports (162 ER) 1822–26
Addendum
Administration
Administrator
Ad.Con. Addison, Contract. 11ed. 1911
Ad.Eq. Adams' Equity. 1850
ad init. ad initium (Lat.) at, or to, the beginning
ad int. ad interim (Lat.) in the meantime
Ad.Jus. Adam's Justiciary Court Reports (Scot.) 1893–1916
Ad.L. Administrative Law
Ad.L.2d Pike & Fischer, Administrative Law Reporter, Second Series (USA)
Ad.L.2d(P&F) Pike & Fischer, Administrative Law Reporter, Second Series (USA)
Ad.L.Bull. Administrative Law Bulletin (USA) 1949–50
Ad.L.Rev. Administrative Law Review (USA) 1960–
ad loc. ad locum (Lat.) at the place
Ad.op. Advisory opinion
ad us. ad usum (Lat.) according to custom
ad val. ad valorum (Lat.) in proportion to the value of goods/according to the value
Ad.& E. Adolphus & Ellis' Reports (110–3 ER) 1834–40

Ad.& El. Adolphus & Ellis' Reports (110–3 ER) 1834–40
Ad.& El.N.S. Adolphus & Ellis' Reports, New Series (113–8 ER) 1841–52
Ad.& Fos. Adoption and Fostering
Ad.& Mar.L.L. Advertising and Marketing Law Letter
Ad.& Mar.L.& P. Advertising and Marketing Law and Practice
Adam Adam's Justiciary Court Reports (Scot.) 1893–1916
Adams Adams' Reports (41–2 Maine)
Adams' Reports (1 New Hampshire)
Adams Eq. Adams' Equity. 1850
Adams L.J. Adams County Legal Journal, Philadelphia (USA)
Add. Addams' Ecclesiastical Reports (162 ER) 1822–6
Addison's Reports, Philadelphia Supreme Court (USA)
Additional
Add.C. Addison, Contract. 11ed. 1911
Add.Con. Addison, Contract. 11ed. 1911
Add.Cont. Addison, Contract. 11ed. 1911
Add.E.R. Addams' Ecclesiastical Reports (162 ER) 1822–6
Add.Ecc. Addams' Ecclesiastical Reports (162 ER) 1822–6
Add.Eccl. Addams' Ecclesiastical Reports (162 ER) 1822–6
Add.Eccl.Rep. Addams' Ecclesiastical Reports (162 ER) 1822–6
Add.Pa. Addison's County Court Reports, Philadelphia (USA)
Add.Rep. Addison's County Court Reports, Philadelphia (USA)
Add.T. Addison, Torts. 8ed. 1906
Add.Tor. Addison, Torts. 8ed. 1906
Add.Torts Addison, Torts. 8ed. 1906
Addams Addams' Ecclesiastical Reports (162 ER) 1822–6
Addis. Addison's County Court Reports, Philadelphia (USA)
Addison(Pa.) Addison's County Court Reports, Philadelphia (USA)
addit. additional
Adel. Adelaide
Adel.L.R. Adelaide Law Review (Aus.) 1960–
Adel.L.Rev. Adelaide Law Review (Aus.) 1960–
Adel.Law Rev. Adelaide Law Review (Aus.) 1960–
Adelaide L.R. Adelaide Law Review (Aus.) 1960–
Adelaide L.Rev. Adelaide Law Review (Aus.) 1960–
Adelphia L.J. Adelphia Law Journal (USA)
Aden L.R. Aden Law Reports. 1937–
Adj. Adjourned
Adjudged
Adjust
Adjustment
Adj.Sess. Adjourned Session
Adjournal, Books of Records of the Court of Justiciary (Scot.)
Adm. Administrative
Administrator
Admiralty
Admission
Admitted
High Court of Admiralty
Adm.& Ecc. Law Reports, Admiralty and Ecclesiastical
Adm.& Eccl. Law Reports, Admiralty and Ecclesiastical
Adm.Interp. Administrative Interpretations
Adm.L.Rev. Administrative Law Review (USA)
Admin. Administration
Administrator
Admin.App.Trib. Administrative Appeals Tribunal (Aus.)
Admin.Cd. Administrative Code
Admin.Dec. Administrative Decisions
Admin.(Ireland) Administration (Ire.)
Admin.L.Conf. Proceedings of the Administrative Law Conference (Can.)
Admin.L.J. Administrative Law Journal (Can.) 1985–
Admin.L.R. Administrative Law Reports (Can.) 1983–

Admin.L.Rev. Administrative Law Review (USA)
Admin.pub. Administration publique (Belg.) 1976–
Admin Rev. Admin Review, Administrative Review Council (Aus.) 1984–
Admin.Sci.Q. Administrative Science Quarterly (USA)
Admin.& Soc'y. Administration and Society (USA)
administr. administrator
administrn. administration
administrv. administrative
Admir. Admiralty
Admix. Administratix
Admn. Administrative Appeals Tribunals Decisions (Aus.) 1984–5
admon administration (of a deceased person's estate)
Admr. Administrator
Admty. Admiralty
Admx. Administratix
Adol.& E. Adolphus & Ellis' Reports (110–3 ER) 1834–40
Adol.& El.N.S. Adolphus & Ellis' Reports, New Series (113–8 ER) 1841–52
Adolph.& E. Adolphus & Ellis' King's Bench Reports (110–3 ER) 1834–40
adv. advisory
advocaat (Neth.) barrister
advocate
Adv. Advocate (Can.) 1943–
Advocate (Cleveland, USA) 1929
Advocate (Ife, Nigeria) 1968–
Advocate (London) 1875
Advocate (Minneapolis) 1889–90
Adv.Bl. Advokatbladet (Den.) 1921–
Adv.Chron. The Advocates' Chronicle (India) 1932–
Adv.O. Advance Opinions in Lawyers' Edition of United States Reports
Adv.Op. Advisory Opinion
Adv.Ops. Advance Opinions in Lawyers' Edition of United States Reports
Adv.Rep.N.J. New Jersey Advance Reports and Weekly Review
advert. advertisement
Advert.L.Anth. Advertising Law Anthology (USA) 1973–
Advoc.Q. The Advocates' Quarterly (USA)
Advocate (Tor.) The Advocate (University of Toronto) (Can.)
Advocate (Van.) The Advocate (Vancouver Bar Association) (Can.) 1943–
Advocates' Q. The Advocates' Quarterly (Can.) 1979–
Advocates' Soc.J. The Advocates' Society Journal (Can.)
advt. advertisement
advertising
Adye C.M. Adye, Courts-Martial. 8ed. 1810
Aelf.C. Canons of Aelfric
AfDB African Development Bank
AfDF African Development Fund
AfR Archiv för retsvidenskaben og dens anvendelse (Den.) 1824–31
aff. affair(s)
affirmed
affirming
Aff.Priv. Archivo Centrale dello Stato (It.)
aff'd affirmed
aff'g affirming
afft. affidavit
Afr. Africa
African
Afrikaans
Afr.Aff. African Affairs
Afr.J.Intl.L. African Journal of International Law
Afr.L.Digest African Law Digest
Afr.L.Stud. African Legal Studies
Afr.Q. Africa Quarterly, New Delhi
Afr.Stud.Rev. African Studies Review
African J.Int.L. African Journal of International Law
African L.D. African Law Digest. 1966–
African L.R.Comm. African Law Reports, Commercial Series
African L.R.Mal. African Law Reports,

Malawi Series
African L.R.S.L. African Law Reports, Sierra Leone Series
African L.S. African Law Studies (USA) 1969–
afsd. aforesaid
Ag. Agency
Agree(s)
Agreement
Agcy. Agency
Agn.Fr. Agnew, Statute of Frauds. 1876
Agn.Pat. Agnew, Patents. 1874
Agr. Agree(s)
Agreement
Agriculture
Agra Agra High Court Reports (India) 1866–8
Agra F.B. Agra Full Bench Rulings (India) 1866–8
Agra H.C. Agra High Court Reports (India) 1866–8
agric. agricultural
agriculture
Agric.C. Agricultural Code
Agric.Conserv.& Adj. Agricultural Conservation and Adjustment
Agric.Dec. Agricultural Decisions (USA) 1942–
Agric.& Mkts. Agriculture and Markets
agt. agent
agy. agency
Aik. Aiken's Supreme Court Reports, Vermont (USA) 1825–8
Aik.Dig. Aiken's Alabama Digest
Aik.Stat. Aiken's Alabama Digest
Air Aff. Air Affairs (USA)
Air L. Air Law (Neth.) 1976–
Air Law (USA) 1975–
Air L.R. Air Law Review (USA) 1930–41
Air L.Rev. Air Law Review (USA) 1930–41
Aird Black. Aird, Blackstone Economised. 2ed. 1873
Aird Civ.Law Aird, Civil Laws of France
Aitchison Aitchison, A Collection of Treaties, Engagements and Sanads Relating to India and Neighbouring Countries. 1933
Aiyar Aiyar, Company Cases (India)
Aiyar C.C. Aiyar, Company Cases (India)
Aiyar L.P.C. Aiyar, Leading Privy Council Cases (India)
Aiyar Unrep.D. Aiyar, Unreported Decisions (India)
Aj. All India Reporter, Ajmer Series. 1949–57
Ajmer-Merwara L.J. Ajmer-Merwara Law Journal (India)
Ak. Alaska
Arkansas Supreme Court Reports. 1837–
Akron L.Rev. Akron Law Review (USA) 1967–
Akron Tax J. Akron Tax Journal (USA)
AktG Aktiengesetz (Ger.) law governing public companies
al. alinea (Switz.)
Al. Alabama
Aleyn's Reports, King's Bench (82 ER) 1646–9
Alinea (It. & Neth.) paragraph
Alinéa (Belg. & Fr.) paragraph
Al.Pr. Alison, Principles of the Criminal Law of Scotland. 1832
Al.Ser. Indian Law Reports, Allahabad Series. 1876–
Al.& N. Alcock & Napier's King's Bench Reports (Ire.) 1831–3
Al.& Nap. Alcock & Napier's King's Bench Reports (Ire.) 1831–3
Ala. Alabama
Alabama Supreme Court
Alabama Supreme Court Reports (USA) 1840–
Minor's Alabama Reports. 1820–6
Ala.A. Alabama Appellate Court
Ala.Acts Acts of Alabama
Ala.App. Alabama Appellate Court Reports (USA) 1910–
Alabama Court of Appeals
Ala.Bar Bull. Alabama Bar Bulletin (USA) 1939
Ala.C. Code of Alabama
Ala.Code Code of Alabama

Ala.L.J. Alabama Law Journal (USA) 1925–30
Ala.L.Rev. Alabama Law Review (USA) 1948–
Ala.Law. Alabama Lawyer (USA) 1940–
Ala.N.S. Alabama Reports, New Series (USA) 1840–
Ala.S.B.A. Alabama State Bar Association
Ala.Sel.Cas. Shepherd's Alabama Select Cases (37–9 Ala)
Ala.St.B.A. Alabama State Bar Association
Ala.St.Bar Assn. Alabama State Bar Association
Ala.St.Found.Bull. Alabama State Foundation Bulletin (USA) 1966–
Alas. Alaska
Alaska Alaska Reports
Alaska B.B. Alaska Bar Brief (USA) 1972–
Alaska Co. Alaska Code
Alaska Fed. Alaska Federal Reports
Alaska Fed.Rep. Alaska Federal Reports
Alaska L.J. Alaska Law Journal (USA) 1963–71
Alaska L.Rev. Alaska Law Review
Alaska Sess.Laws Alaska Session Laws
Alaska Stat. Alaska Statutes
Alb. Albany
Alb.Arb. Albert Insurance Arbitration (Lord Cairns' Decisions) 1871–5
Alb.L.J. Albany Law Journal (USA) 1870–1908
Alb.L.Q. Alberta Law Quarterly (Can.) 1934–45
Alb.L.R. Alberta Law Reports
Alb.L.Rev. Albany Law Review (USA) 1948–
Alb.L.S.Jour. Albany Law School Journal (USA) 1875–6
Alb.Law J. Albany Law Journal (USA) 1870–1908
Albany L.Rev. Albany Law Review (USA) 1948–
Alberta L.(Can.) Alberta Law Reports
Alberta L.Q. Alberta Law Quarterly (Can.) 1934–45
Alberta L.R.R. Alberta Institute of Law Research and Reform
Alberta L.Rev. Alberta Law Review (Can.) 1955–
Alc.Reg. Alcock, Registration Cases (Ire.) 1832–41
Alc.Reg.C. Alcock, Registration Cases (Ire.) 1832–41
Alc.& N. Alcock & Napier's King's Bench Reports (Ire.) 1831–3
Alc.& Nap. Alcock & Napier's King's Bench Reports (Ire.) 1831–3
Alco.Bev. Alcoholic Beverage
Alco.Bev.Cont. Alcoholic Beverage Control
Alcock & N. Alcock & Napier's King's Bench Reports (Ire.) 1831–3
Ald. Alden's Condensed Reports, Philadelphia (USA)
Aldridge, History and Jurisdiction of the Courts of Law. 1835
Alex.Br.Sta. Alexander's British Statutes in Force in Maryland
Alexander Alexander's Reports (66–72 Mississippi)
Aleyn Aleyn's Reports, King's Bench (82 ER) 1646–9
Alis.Princ.Scot.Law Alison's Principles of the Criminal Law of Scotland
Alk. Alaska
Alaska Reports
all. allegata (It.) schedules, enclosures
All. All India Reporter, Allahabad Series. 1914–
Allen's Massachusetts Reports (83–96 Mass) 1861–7
Allen's New Brunswick Reports (Can.) 1848–66
India Law Reports, Allahabad Series. 1876–
Indian Rulings, Allahabad. 1929–47
All.Cr.Cas. Allahabad Criminal Cases–
All E.R. All England Law Reports. 1936–
All E.R.Rep. All England Law Reports Reprint. 1558–1935
All E.R.Rep.Ext. All England Law Reports Reprint, Australian Extension Volumes. 1865–1935

All E.R.Rev. All England Law Reports Annual Review

All Eng. All England Law Reports. 1936–

All I.C.R. All Indian Criminal Reports

All I.R. All India Reporter. 1914–

All Ind.Cr.R. All Indian Criminal Reports

All Ind.Cr.T. All India Criminal Times

All Ind.Crim.Dec. All India Criminal Decisions. 1947–

All Ind.Rep. All India Reporter. 1914–

All Ind.Rep.N.S. All India Reporter, New Series

All India Crim.Dec. All India Criminal Decisions. 1947–

All India Rptr. All India Reporter. 1914–

All.L.D.of Mar. Alleyne, Legal Decrees of Marriage. 1810

All.L.J.& Rep. Allahabad Law Journal and Reports (India) 1904–

All.L.R. Allahabad Law Review (India) 1969–

All.L.T. Allahabad Law Times (India) 1923–

All.N.B. Allen's New Brunswick Reports (Can.) 1848–66

All N.L.R. All Nigeria Law Reports. 1961–2

All Pak.Leg.Dec. All Pakistan Legal Decisions. 1948–

All.Ser. India Law Reports, Allahabad Series. 1876–

All.Tel.Cas. Allen's Telegraph Cases (American and English)

All.W.N. Allahabad Weekly Notes (India)

All.W.R. Allahabad Weekly Reporter (India)

Alla.L.J. Allahabad Law Journal (India)

Allam-es Jog. Allam-es Jogtudomany (Hungary)

Allen Allen, Law in the Making. 7ed. 1964
Allen's Massuchusetts Reports (83–96 Mass) 1861–7
Allen's New Brunswick Reports (Can.) 1848–66
Allen's Reports, Washington Territory (USA) 1854–85

AllgGeschBed. Allgemeine Geschaftsbedingungen (Ger.) general conditions (of contracts, transactions, etc.)

AllgVersBed. Allgemeine Versicherungsbedingungen (Ger.) general conditions of insurance

Allin. Allinson's Pennsylvania Superior and District Court Reports

Alln.Part. Allnat, Law of Partition. 1820

Allwood Allwood's Appeal Cases under the Weights & Measures Act. 1906

Almond–Coleman, Developing Areas Almond & Coleman, The Politics of Developing Areas. 1960

alt. alternative

Alta. Alberta
Alberta Law Reports (Can.) 1908–32

Alta.Dec. Alberta Decisions (Can.) 1974–

Alta.L. Alberta Law Reports (Can.) 1908–32

Alta.L.Q. Alberta Law Quarterly (Can.) 1934–45

Alta.L.R. Alberta Law Reports (Can.) 1908–32

Alta.L.Rev. Alberta Law Review (Can.) 1955–

Alta.Rev.Stat. Alberta Revised Statutes (Can.)

Alta.Stat. Alberta Statutes (Can.)

Alternatives Canadian Alternatives for the Delivery of Legal Services

Alves Dampier & Maxwell's British Guiana Reports

Am. Amended
Amendment
American

Am.Acad.Matri. Law.J. American Academy of Matrimonial Lawyers Journal

Am.Acad.Pol.& Soc.Sci. American Academy of Political and Social Science

Am.Ann.Cas. American Annotated Cases. 1904–12

Am.Anthrop. American Anthropologist

Am.Assoc.Univ.Prof.Bull. American

Association of University Professors Bulletin

Am.B.A. American Bar Association

Am.B.R. American Bankruptcy Reports. 1889–1923

Am.B.R.(N.S.) American Bankruptcy Reports, New Series. 1924–45

Am.Bank.Rev. American Bankruptcy Review. 1924–37

Am.Bankr.L.J. American Bankruptcy Law Journal. 1971–

Am.Bankr.N.S. American Bankruptcy Reports, New Series. 1924–45

Am.Bankr.R. American Bankruptcy Reports. 1889–1923

Am.Bankr.R.(N.S.) American Bankruptcy Reports, New Series. 1924–45

Am.Bankr.Reg. American Bankruptcy Register

Am.Bankr.Rep. American Bankruptcy Reports. 1889–1923

Am.Bankr.Rep.N.S. American Bankruptcy Reports, New Series. 1924–45

Am.Bankr.Rev. American Bankruptcy Review. 1924–37

Am.Bar Ass.J. American Bar Association Journal. 1915–

Am.Bar Asso.Jour. American Bar Association Journal. 1915–

Am.Bar Asso.Rep. American Bar Association Reports

Am.Bar Found.Res.J. American Bar Foundation Research Journal. 1976–

Am.Bar N. American Bar News. 1956–76

Am.B'kc'y Rep. American Bankruptcy Reports. 1889–1923

Am.Bus.L.J. American Business Law Journal. 1963–

Am.C.L.J. American Civil Law Journal. 1873

Am.Cent.Dig. American Digest (Century Edition)

Am.Ch.Dig. American Chancery Digest

Am.Civ.L.J. American Civil Law Journal. 1873

Am.Consul.Bul. American Consular Bulletin. 1919–24

Am.Corp.Cas. American Corporation Cases (Withrow) 1868–87

Am.Cr. American Criminal Reports. 1877–1903

Am.Cr.Rep. American Criminal Reports. 1877–1903

Am.Cr.Tr. American Criminal Trials

Am.Crim.L.Q. American Criminal Law Quarterly. 1963–70

Am.Crim.L.Rev. American Criminal Law Review. 1971–

am.cur. amicus curiae (Lat.) friend of the court

Am.Dec. American Decisions (Select Cases)

Am.Dig. American Digest

Am.Dig.Cent.Ed. American Digest (Century Edition)

Am.Dig.Dec.Ed. American Digest (Decennial Edition)

Am.Ec.Rev. American Economic Review

Am.Econ.Rev. American Economic Review

Am.El.Cas. American Electrical Cases. 1873–1908

Am.Elec.Ca. American Electrical Cases. 1873–1908

Am.Elect.Cas. American Electrical Cases. 1873–1908

Am.Electl.Cas. American Electrical Cases. 1873–1908

Am.Electr.Cas. American Electrical Cases. 1873–1908

Am.Fed.Tax R. American Federal Tax Reports (P–H) 1796–

Am.Fed.Tax R.2d American Federal Tax Reports, Second Series (P–H)

Am.Hist.Rev. American Historical Review

Am.Ind.L.R. American Indian Law Review. 1973–

Am.Indian L.Rev. American Indian Law Review. 1973–

Am.Ins.Rep. American Insolvency Reports. 1878–83

Am.Insolv.Rep. American Insolvency Reports. 1878–83

Am.J.Comp.L. American Journal of Comparative Law. 1952–
Am.J.Comp.Law American Journal of Comparative Law. 1952–
Am.J.Crim.L. American Journal of Criminal Law. 1972–
Am.J.Fam.L. American Journal of Family Law
Am.J.Int.Law American Journal of International Law. 1907–
Am.J.Int'l.L. American Journal of International Law. 1907–
Am.J.Juris. American Journal of Jurisprudence. 1969–
Am.J.Jurisprud. American Journal of Jurisprudence. 1969–
Am.J.L.& Med. American Journal of Law and Medicine. 1975–
Am.J.Law & Med. American Journal of Law and Medicine. 1975–
Am.J.Leg.Forms Anno. American Jurisprudence Legal Forms Annotated
Am.J.Legal Hist. American Journal of Legal History. 1957–
Am.J.Philol. American Journal of Philology
Am.J.Pl.& Pr.Forms Anno. American Jurisprudence Pleading & Practice Forms Annotated
Am.J.Proof of Facts American Jurisprudence Proof of Facts
Am.J.Psych. American Journal of Psychology
Am.J.Soc. American Journal of Sociology
Am.J.Soc.Sci. American Journal of Social Sciences
Am.J.Tax Pol'y American Journal of Tax Policy
Am.J.Trial Advoc. American Journal of Trial Advocacy
Am.J.Trials American Jurisprudence Trials
Am.Jour.Pol. American Journal of Politics
Am.Jud.Soc. American Judicature Society
Journal of American Judicature Society
Am.Jur. American Jurisprudence
American Jurist & Law Magazine. 1829–43
Am.Jur.Leg.Forms Anno. American Jurisprudence Legal Forms Annotated
Am.Jur.Pl.& Pr.Forms Anno. American Jurisprudence Pleading & Practice Forms Annotated
Am.Jur.Proof of Facts Anno. American Jurisprudence Proof of Facts Annotated
Am.Jur.Trials American Jurisprudence Trials
Am.Jurist American Jurist and Law Magazine. 1829–43
Am.L.Cas. American Leading Cases
Am.L.Ins. American Law Institute
American Law Institute, Restatement of the Law
Am.L.Inst. American Law Institute
Am.L.J. American Law Journal (Ohio) 1884–5
Hall's American Law Journal (Philadelphia) 1808–17
Am.L.J.N.S. American Law Journal, New Series (Philadelphia) 1848–52
Am.L.J.(O) American Law Journal (Ohio) 1884–5
Am.L.J.(O.S.) American Law Journal (Hall's) (Philadelphia) 1808–17
Am.L.M. American Law Magazine (Philadelphia) 1843–6
Am.L.Rec. American Law Record. 1872–87
Am.L.Reg. American Law Register (Philadelphia) 1852–1907
Am.L.Reg.(N.S.) American Law Register, New Series. 1908–10
Am.L.Reg.(O.S.) American Law Register, Old Series. 1852–1907
Am.L.Reg.& Rev. American Law Register and Review
Am.L.Rep. American Law Reporter, Davenport (Iowa)
Am.L.Rev. American Law Review. 1866–1929
Am.L.S.Rev. American Law School Review. 1902–47

Am.L.T. American Law Times, New York. 1905–6
American Law Times, Washington. 1868–77

Am.L.T.Bankr. American Law Times Bankruptcy Reports

Am.L.T.Bankr.Rep. American Law Times Bankruptcy Reports

Am.L.T.R. American Law Times Reports. 1868–73

Am.L.T.R.N.S. American Law Times Reports, New Series. 1874–77

Am.L.T.Rep. American Law Times Reports. 1868–73

Am.Lab.Arb.Cas. American Labor Arbitration Cases (P–H) 1946–

Am.Lab.Cas. American Labor Cases (P–H) 1947–

Am.Lab.Leg.Rev. American Labor Legislation Review. 1911–42

Am.Labor Legis.Rev. American Labor Legislation Review. 1911–42

Am.Law. American Lawyer. 1893–1908

Am.Law Inst. American Law Institute, Restatement of the Law

Am.Law J. American Law Journal. 1808–17

Am.Law J.N.S. American Law Journal, New Series. 1848–52

Am.Law Mag. American Law Magazine. 1843–6

Am.Law Rec. American Law Record. 1872–87

Am.Law Reg. American Law Register. 1852–1907

Am.Law Reg.N.S. American Law Register, New Series. 1908–10

Am.Law Reg.O.S. American Law Register, Old Series. 1852–1907

Am.Law Rev. American Law Review. 1866–1929

Am.Law S.Rev. American Law School Review. 1902–47

Am.Law T.Rep. American Law Times Reports. 1868–73

Am.Lawy. American Lawyer. 1893–1908

Am.Lead.Cas. Hare & Wallace, American Leading Cases

Am.Lead.Cas.(H.& W.) Hare & Wallace, American Leading Cases

Am.Leg. American Legislator. 1971–

Am.Leg.N. American Legal News
American Legal Notes

Am.Mar.Cas. American Maritime Cases. 1923–

Am.Mo.Rev. American Monthly Review

Am.Neg.Ca. American Negligence Cases. 1789–1897

Am.Neg.Cas. American Negligence Cases. 1789–1897

Am.Neg.Dig. American Negligence Digest

Am.Neg.Rep. American Negligence Reports. 1897–1909

Am.Negl.Cas. American Negligence Cases. 1789–1897

Am.Negl.R. American Negligence Reports. 1897–1909

Am.Negl.Rep. American Negligence Reports. 1897–1909

Am.Oriental Soc'y American Oriental Society Journal

Am.Pat.L.Assoc.Bull. American Patent Law Association Bulletin

Am.Pat.L.Q.J. American Patent Law Association Quarterly Journal

Am.Phil.Q. American Philosophical Quarterly

Am.Pol.Q. American Politics Quarterly

Am.Pol.Sc.R. American Political Science Review

Am.Pol.Sci.J. American Political Science Journal

Am.Pol.Sci.Rev. American Political Science Review

Am.Pr. American Practice

Am.Pr.Rep. American Practice Reports. 1897–8

Am.Pr.Rep.N.S. American Practice Reports, New Series

Am.Prob. American Probate Reports. 1875–95

Am.Prob.N.S. American Probate Reports, New Series

Am.Prob.Rep. American Probate Reports. 1875–95

Am.Q.Reg. American Quarterly Register
Am.Q.Rev. American Quarterly Review
Am.R. American Reports
Am.R.Cas. American Railway Cases. 1854–6
Am.R.R.Cas. American Railway Cases. 1854–6
Am.R.R.& C.Rep. American Railroad and Corporation Reports. 1888–96
Am.R.Rep. American Railway Reports. 1872–81
Am.Rail.Cas. American Railway Cases. 1854–6
Am.Rail.R. American Railway Reports. 1872–81
Am.Railw.Cas. American Railway Cases. 1854–6
Am.Rep. American Reports.
Am.Rev.of Hist.& Politics American Review of History and Politics
Am.Ry.Cas. American Railway Cases. 1854–6
Am.Ry.Rep. American Railway Reports. 1872–81
Am.S.R. American State Reports. 1886–1911
Am.Soc.Int.L.Proc. Proceedings of the American Society of International Law
Am.Soc.Int.Law American Society of International Law
Am.Soc.Int.Law Proceed. Proceedings of the American Society of International Law
Am.Soc.Rev. American Sociological Review
Am.Sociolog.Rev. American Sociological Review
Am.St.P. American State Papers
Am.St.R. American State Reports. 1886–1911
Am.St.R.D. American Street Railway Decisions
Am.St.Rep. American State Reports. 1886–1911
Am.St.Ry.Dec. American Street Railway Decisions
Am.St.Ry.Rep. American Street Railway Reports
Am.Stock Ex.Guide American Stock Exchange Guide (CCH)
Am.Them. American Themis. 1844
Am.Tr.M.Cas. Cox, American Trade Mark Cases. 1825–71
Am.Trade Mark Cas. Cox, American Trade Mark Cases. 1825–71
Am.Trial Law.L.J. American Trial Lawyers Law Journal
Am.U.Int.L.Rev. American University, Intramural Law Review. 1952–
Am.U.Intra.L.Rev. American University, Intramural Law Review. 1952–
Am.U.J.Int'l L.& Pol'y American University Journal of International Law and Policy
Am.U.L.R. American University Law Review. 1957–
Am.U.L.Rev. American University Law Review. 1957–
Am.Univ.L.Rev. American University Law Review. 1957–
Am.Whig Rev. American Whig Review
Am.& E.Corp.Cas. American and English Corporation Cases. 1883–94
Am.& E.Corp.Cas.N.S. American and English Corporation Cases, New Series. 1896–1904
Am.& E.Eq.D. American and English Decisions in Equity. 1894–1904
Am.& E.R.Cas. American and English Railroad Cases. 1879–95
Am.& E.R.Cas.N.S. American and English Railroad Cases, New Series. 1894–1913
Am.& Eng.Ann.Cas. American and English Annotated Cases
Am.& Eng.Corp.Cas. American and English Corporation Cases. 1883–94
Am.& Eng.Corp.Cas.N.S. American and English Corporation Cases, New Series. 1896–1904
Am.& Eng.Dec.Eq. American and English Decisions in Equity. 1894–1904
Am.& Eng.Dec.in Eq. American and English Decisions in Equity. 1894–1904
Am.& Eng.Enc.Law American and English Encyclopedia of Law

Am.& Eng.Enc.Law Sup. American and English Encyclopedia of Law, Supplement

Am.& Eng.Enc.Law & Pr. American and English Encyclopedia of Law and Practice

Am.& Eng.Ency.Law American and English Encyclopedia of Law

Am.& Eng.Eq.D. American and English Decisions in Equity. 1894–1904

Am.& Eng.Pat.Cas. American and English Patent Cases. 1882–1890

Am.& Eng.R.Cas. American and English Railroad Cases. 1879–95

Am.& Eng.R.Cas.N.S. American and English Railroad Cases, New Series. 1894–1913

Am.& Eng.R.R.Cas. American and English Railroad Cases. 1879–95

Am.& Eng.Ry.Cas. American and English Railway Cases. 1879–95

Am.& Eng.Ry.Cas.N.S. American and English Railway Cases, New Series. 1894–1913

Amb. Ambler's Chancery Reports (27 ER) 1737–84

Ambl. Ambler's Chancery Reports (27 ER) 1737–84

Ambrosetti,Riforma Ambrosetti, Il Diritto Naturale della Riforma Cattolica (It.) 1951

Amdt. amendment

amend. amended
amending
amendment

Amer. America
American
Amerman's Reports (111–5 Pennsylvania)

Amer.Anthrop. American Anthropologist

Amer.Econ.Rev. American Economic Review

Amer.Fed.Tax Rep. American Federal Tax Reports (P–H) 1796–

Amer.J.Comp.L. American Journal of Comparative Law. 1952–

Amer.J.Int'l.L. American Journal of International Law. 1907–

Amer.Journ.Int.Law American Journal of International Law. 1907–

Amer.Jur. American Jurist. 1829–43

Amer.Law. American Lawyer, New York. 1893–1908

Amer.Law Reg.(N.S.) American Law Register, New Series. 1908–10

Amer.Law Reg.(O.S.) American Law Register, Old Series. 1852–1907

Amer.Law Rev. American Law Review. 1866–1929

Amer.Lawy. American Lawyer. 1893–1908

Amer.Rev. American Review

Amer.Univ.Law Rev. American University Law Review

Amer.& Eng.Enc.Law American and English Encyclopedia of Law

Ames Ames' Reports (1 Minnesota)
Ames' Reports (4–7 Rhode Island)

Ames Cas.B.& N. Ames' Cases on Bills and Notes

Ames Cas.Par. Ames' Cases on Partnership

Ames Cas.Pl. Ames' Cases on Pleading

Ames Cas.Sur. Ames' Cases on Suretyship

Ames Cas.Trusts Ames' Cases on Trusts

Ames K.& B. Ames, Knowles & Bradley's Reports (8 Rhode Island)

Amos & F.Fixt. Amos & Ferrard on Fixtures

Amtl.S. Entscheidungen des k.k. Obersten Gerichtshofs in Zivil – und Justizverwaltungssachen veröffentlicht von diesem Gerichtshofe, Fortsetzung der von Nowak begründeten Sammlung (Austria)

an. annual

An. Anonymous, at end of Benloe's, or Bendloe's, Reports

An.ad. Annuaire administratif et judiciaire de Belgique (Belg.)

An.Argentino Der.Intern. Anuario Argentino de Derecho Internacional

An.B. Anonymous Reports at end of Benloe's, or Bendloe's, Reports

An.Der.Civ. Anuario de Derecho Civil (Sp.)
An.Der.Hum. Anuario de Derechos Humanos (Sp.)
An.Der.Intern. Anuario de Derecho Internacional (Sp.)
An.Der.(Panama) Anuario de Derecho (Panama)
An.Hisp.–Luso.–Am. Anuario Hispano–Luso–Americano de Derecho Internacional (Sp.)
An.Jur.Interam. Anuario Juridico Interamericano (USA)
AnO Anordnung (Ger.) direction, instruction
An.W.R. Andhra Weekly Reporter (India) 1955–
Anal. Analysis
Anal.Prav.Fak.Beograd Anali Pravnog Fakulteta u Beogradu (Yugoslavia)
Anales Jud. Anales Judiciales de la Corte Suprema de Justicia (Peru)
anc. ancient
Anc.Charters Ancient Charters. 1692
Anc.Correspondence Public Record Office, Ancient Correspondence of the Chancery and Exchequer
Anc.Petitions Public Record Office, Ancient Petitions of the Chancery and Exchequer
And. All India Reporter, Andhra Series. 1954–6
Anderson's Agricultural Decisions (Scot.) 1800–83
Anderson's Common Pleas Reports (123 ER) 1534–1605
Andrew's King's Bench Reports (95 ER) 1738–9
Andrews' Reports (63–73 Conn.)
Indian Law Reports, Andhra Series. 1959–
And.Agr.Dec. Anderson's Agricultural Decisions (Scot.) 1800–83
And.Dig. Andrews, Digest of the Opinions of the Attorneys-General
And.Ind. Andhra, India
And.& Ston.J.A. Andrews & Stoney's Supreme Court of Judicature Acts
And.W.R. Andhra Weekly Reporter (India) 1955–
Ander. Anderson's Reports, Court of Common Pleas (123 ER) 1534–1605
Anders. Anderson's Reports, Court of Common Pleas (123 ER) 1534–1605
Anderson Anderson's Reports, Court of Common Pleas (123 ER) 1534–1605
Anderson, Reports Sir Edmund Anderson, Les Reports des mults principals cases. 1664–5
Anderson UCC Anderson's Uniform Commercial Code (USA)
Andh. All India Reporter, Andhra Series. 1954–6
Andh.Pra. All India Reporter, Andhra Pradesh Series. 1957–
Andh.W.R. Andhra Weekly Reporter (India) 1955–
Andhra W.R. Andhra Weekly Reporter (India) 1955–
Andr. Andrew's King's Bench Reports (95 ER) 1738–9
Andrews Andrew's King's Bench Reports (95 ER) 1738–9
Ang. Angell & Durfee's Reports (1 Rhode Island)
Ang.& Dur. Angell & Durfee's Reports (1 Rhode Island)
Anglo-Am.L.R. Anglo-American Law Review. 1972–
Anh. Anhang (Ger.) supplement, schedule
Anl. Anlage (Ger.) enclosure
Anm. Anmerking (Ger.) note, comment, annotation
Ann. Annotated
Annual
Cunningham's Reports, King's Bench
King's Bench Cases tempore Hardwicke (95 ER) 1733–38
Queen Anne
Ann.Air & Space L. Annals of Air and Space Law (Can.)
Ann.Am.Acad. Annals of the American Academy of Political and Social Science
Ann.Bari. Annali della Facolta giuridica della Universita di Bari (It.) 1927–

Ann.Cal.Codes West's Annotated California Codes

Ann.can.d.int. Annuaire canadien de droit international (Canadian Yearbook of International Law) 1962–

Ann.can.droits de la personne Annuaire canadien des droits de la personne (Canadian Human Rights Yearbook) 1983–

Ann.Cas. American and English Annotated Cases
American Annotated Cases
New York Annotated Cases

Ann.Code Annotated Code

Ann.Codes & St. Bellinger & Cotton's Annotated Codes and Statutes (Oregon)

Ann.Conf.on Intell.Prop. Annual Conference on Intellectual Property

Ann.Cong. Annals of Congress

Ann.de l'Inst.de Droit Int'l Annuaire de l'Institut de Droit International (Fr.)

Ann.dir.comp. Annuario di diritto comparato e di studi legislativi (It.) 1927–

Ann.Dir.Comp.& Stud.Legis. Annuario di diritto comparato e di studi legislativi (It.) 1927–

Ann.Dig. Annual Digest and Reports of International Law Cases

Ann.Dr. Annales de droit (Belg.) 1965–

Ann.Dr.com. Annales de Droit commercial (Fr.)

Ann.Dr.Louvain Annales de Droit du Louvain, Revue Trimestrielle de Droit Belge (Belg.)

Ann.Dr.Marit.& Aéro-Spat. Annuaire de Droit Maritime et Aéro-Spatial (Fr.)

Ann.Européen Annuaire Européen (Neth.)

Ann.Fac.Dr.Kinshasa Annales de la Faculté de droit de Kinshasa (Zaire)

Ann.Fac.droit Liège Annales de la Faculté de droit de Liège (Belg.)

Ann.Fr.Dr.Int. Annuaire Français de Droit International (Fr.)

Ann.Giur.Ital. Annali di giurisprudenza italiana

Ann.Hist.Fac.Dr.& Sci.Jur. Annales d'Histoire des Facultés de Droit et de la Science Juridique (Fr.)

Ann.I.D.I. Annuaire de l'Institut de Droit International (Fr.)

Ann.Ind.Prop.L. Annual of Industrial Property Law. 1975–

Ann.Inst.Dr.Intern. Annuaire de l'Institut de Droit International (Switz.)

Ann.J.P. Annales des justices de paix (Fr.) 1792–

Ann.L.Rep. Annotated Law Reporter (India) 1932–5

Ann.Law Reg. Annual Law Register of the United States

Ann.Law Rev. Annual Law Review (Aus.) 1948–59

Ann.Leg.Bibliog. Annual Legal Bibliography (USA) 1961–

Ann.Leg.Forms Mag. Annotated Legal Forms Magazine

Ann.parl. Annales parlementaires (Belg.)

Ann.Pr. Annual Practice

Ann.Prac. Annual Practice

Ann.Reg. Annual Register, London

Ann.Rep. Annual Report

Ann.Rev.Banking L. Annual Review of Banking Law (USA)

Ann.Sachs.OLG Annalen des Sachsischen Oberlandesgerichts

Ann.sem.giur.Catania Annali seminario giuridico della Universita di Catania (It.) 1946–53

Ann.sem.giur.Palermo Annali del seminario giuridico della Universita di Palermo (It.) 1916–

Ann.St. Annotated Statutes

Ann.st.dir. Annali di storia del diritto (It.) 1957–

Ann.stat.guid. Annuario di statistiche guidiziarie (It.) 1949–

Ann.Surv.Am.L. Annual Survey of American Law

Ann.Surv.Austl.L. Annual Survey of Australian Law

Ann.Surv.of Aust.Law Annual Survey of Australian Law. 1981–

Ann.Surv.of Law Annual Survey of Law (Aus.) 1977–80

Ann.Tax Cas. Annotated Tax Cases. 1922–

Ann.U.Sci.Budapest Jur. Annales Universitatis Scientiarum Budapestinensis de Rolando Eotvos Nominatae, Sectio Juridica (Hungary)

Ann.U.Sci.Soc.Toulouse Annales de l'Université des Sciences Sociales de Toulouse (Fr.)

Annales Int'l de Crimin. Annales internationales de criminologie (Fr.)

Annales Lond. Annales Londonienses (in Chronicles of the Reigns of Edward I and Edward II, edited by Stubbs) 1882

Annales Paulini Annales Paulini (in Chronicles of the Reigns of Edward I and Edward II, edited by Stubbs) 1882

Annals Annals of the American Academy of Political and Social Sciences

Annals of Burton Annales de Burton (in Annales Monastici, edited by Luard) 1864

Annals of Dunstable Annales Prioratus de Dunstaplia (in Annales Monastici, edited by Luard) 1864

Annals of Tewsbury Annales de Theokesberia (in Annales Monastici, edited by Luard) 1864

Annaly Lee's King's Bench Reports tempore Hardwicke. Annaly edition (95 ER) 1733–8

Anno. Annotated

Annuaire Annuaire de l'Institut de droit international

Annuaire de l'Institut Annuaire de l'Institut de droit international

Annuaire français Annuaire français de droit international (Fr.)

Annuaire suisse Annuaire suisse de droit international (Switz.)

Annual Digest Annual Digest and Reports of International Public Law Cases

Annual L.Rev. Western Australian Annual Law Review

Annual Survey Annual Survey of South African Law. 1947–

Annuario Dir.Comp. Annuario di diritto comparato e di studi legislativi

anny. annuity

anon. anonymous

anr. another

Ans.Con. Anson on Contracts

Anson,Cont. Anson on Contracts

Anspr. Anspruch (Ger.) claim, title, right

Anst. Anstruther's Exchequer Reports (145 ER) 1792–7

Anstr. Anstruther's Exchequer Reports (145 ER) 1792–7

Anth. Anthon's New York Nisi Prius Reports. 1807–51

Anth.Shep. Anthony's edition of Shephard's Touchstone

Anthon N.P.(N.Y.) Anthon's New York Nisi Prius Reports. 1807–51

Antitrust Bull. Antitrust Bulletin (USA) 1955–

Antitrust L.J. Antitrust Law Journal. 1966–

Antitrust L.Sym. Antitrust Law Symposium. 1949–

Antitrust L.& Econ.Rev. Antitrust Law and Economic Review. 1967–

Antitrust L.& Trade Reg.Rep. Antitrust Law and Trade Regulations Report (BNA)

Anti-Trust Report Report of the Attorney-General's National Committee to Study the Anti-Trust Laws (USA) 1955

Anzilotti,Corso Anzilotti, Corso di diritto internazionale. 3ed. 1928 (It.)

ap. apud (Lat.) in the works of (an author)

Ap. New York Supreme Court Appellate Division Reports

Ap.2d New York Supreme Court Appellate Division Reports, Second Series

Ap.Bre. Appendix to Breese's Reports (Illinois)

Ap.Just. Apud Justinianum (in Justinian's Institutes)

Ap.Justin. Apud Justinianum (in Justinian's Institutes)
App. Appeal Cases
Appendix
Appleton's Reports (19, 20 Maine)
Ohio Appellate Reports
App.Ca. Buchanan, Reports of Courts of Appeal, Cape Colony (S.Afr.)
App.Cas. Appeal Cases
Law Reports Appeal Cases, House of Lords. 1875–90
App.Cas.Beng. Marshall & Sevestre's Appeal Reports, Bengal (India) 1862–4
app.Cha. appearance in Chancery
appeared in Chancery
App.Civ. Appellacao Civil (Brazil)
App.Comp.& Comm.L. Applied Computer and Communications Law
App.Ct.Rep. Court of Appeal Reports, New Zealand. 1867–77
Bradwell's Illinois Appeal Court Reports
App.D. Law Reports Appellate Division (S.Afr.)
App.D.C. Appeals Cases, District of Columbia. 1893–1941
app.den. appeal denied
App.Dep't Appellate Department
App.Dep't Super.Ct. Appellate Department of the Superior Court, California (USA)
app.dism. appeal dismissed
App.Div. Appellate Division
New York Supreme Court Appellate Division Reports. 1896–
Supreme Court, Appellate Division Reports (S.Afr.) 1910–46
App.Div.(N.Y.) New York Supreme Court Appellate Division Reports. 1896–
App.Div.2d. New York Supreme Court Appellate Division Reports, Second Series
App.Exam. Appeal(s) Examiner (USA)
App.Fish.Com. Appeals from Fisheries Commission (Ire.) 1861–93
App.J.H.R. Appendix to the Journals of the House of Representatives (N.Z.) 1858–
App.N.Z. Court of Appeal Reports, New Zealand. 1867–77
App.R.N.Z. Court of Appeal Reports, New Zealand. 1867–77
App.Ref. Appeal(s) Referee
App.Rep. Ontario Appeal Reports (Can.) 1876–1900
App.Rep.Ont. Ontario Appeal Reports (Can.) 1876–1900
App.T. Supreme Court Appellate Term
App.Tax Serv. Appeals Relating to Tax on Servants. 1781
App.Trib. Appeal(s) Tribunal
Appd. Approved
Append. Appendix
appl. applied
Appl. Applicable
Appleton Appleton's Reports (19, 20 Maine)
appr. approved in, or approving
Approp. Appropriation(s)
apprvd. approved
apps. appendixes
apptd. appointed
appx. appendix
Appx.Bre. Appendix to Breese's Reports, Illinois
Ar Archives
Ar F Archives fédérales (Switz.)
Ar.J. Arbitration Journal, New Series (USA) 1945–
Ar.Rep. Argus Reports, Victoria (Aus.) 1895–1959
Arab L.Q. Arab Law Quarterly
Arabin Decisions of Sergeant Arabin
Aram. Aramaic
Arb. Arbitration
Arbitration. 1954–
Arbitrator
Labor Arbitration Awards (CCH) 1946–
ArbAusglG Gesetz u.d. Ausgleichs – und Schiedsverfahren Arbeitsstreitigkeiten (Ger.) law on labour arbitration
Arb.Ct. Judgments, etc. of the

Arbitration Court of New Zealand. 1978–

ArbG. Arbeitsgericht (Ger.) Labour Tribunal

ArbGG Arbeitsgerichtsgesetz (Ger.) law on labour courts

Arb.Int. Arbitration International

Arb.J. Arbitration Journal (UK) 1953–54
Arbitration Journal (USA) 1937–42

Arb.J.(N.S.) Arbitration Journal, New Series (USA) 1945–

Arb.J.(O.S.) Arbitration Journal, Old Series (USA) 1937–42

Arb.L.Dig. Arbitration Law: A Digest of Court Decisions

ArbRSamml. Entscheidungen des Reichsarbeitsgericht und der Landesarbeitsgerichte (Ger.) Labour Court Reports

ArbRSlg Entscheidungen des Reichsarbeitsgericht und der Landesarbeitsgerichte (Ger.) Labour Court Reports

ArbRspr. Rechtsprechung in Arbeitssachen (Ger.) Labour Court Reports

Arbitr. Arbitration

Arbitration Int. Arbitration International

Arbuth. Arbuthnot's Select Criminal Cases, Madras (India) 1826–50

Arch. Court of Arches

Arch.Bank. Archbold on Bankruptcy. 11ed. 1956

Arch.C.P. Archbold's Practice in Common Pleas. 1834

Arch.C.S.Pr. Archibald, Country Solicitor's Practice in the Queen's Bench. 1881

Arch.Civ.Pl. Archbold's Civil Pleading and Evidence. 2ed. 1837

Arch.civ.Pr. Archiv für die civilistische Praxis (Ger.)

Arch.Civ.Prax. Archiv für die civilistische Praxis (Ger.)

Arch.Cr. Archbold's Pleading and Evidence in Criminal Cases

Arch.Cr.L. Archbold J.F. – Applied to a number of titles relating to criminal law

Arch.Cr.Pl. Archbold's Pleading and Evidence in Criminal Cases

Arch.Cr.Prac. Archbold's Pleading and Evidence in Criminal Cases

Arch.de Phil.du Droit Archives de Philosophie du Droit, New Series. 1952–

Arch.de Phil.et Soc.Jur. Archives de Philosophie du Droit et de Sociologie Juridique (to 1940)

Arch.d'Hist.du Droit Archives d'Histoire du Droit

Arch.d'Hist.du Droit Orient. Archives d'Histoire du Droit Oriental (Belg.)

Arch.Forms Archbold, Indictments, with Forms. 1916

Arch.G. Archivio giuridico (It.) 1868–

Arch.giur. Archivio giuridico (It.) 1868–

Arch.Giur.Serafini Archivio Giuridico Filippo Serafini (It.)

Arch.Hist.Dr.Oriental Archives d'Histoire du Droit Oriental (Belg.)

Arch.Hist.Port. Archivo Historico Portiguez

Arch.Idiotikou Dikaiou Archeion Idiotikou Dikaiou, Athens (Gr.)

Arch.J.C.Pr. Archibald, Practice of Judges Chambers. 2ed. 1886

Arch.J.P. Archbold, Justice of the Peace. 7ed. 1859

Arch.Jud. Archivo Judiciario (Brazil)

Arch.K.B.Forms Archbold, Forms in King's Bench and Common Pleas. 3ed. 1828

Arch.K.B.Pr. Archbold, King's Bench Practice. 14ed. 1885

Arch.L.R. Architects Law Reports. 1904–9

Arch.L.& T. Archbold, Law of Landlord and Tenant. 3ed. 1864

Arch.Lun. Archbold, Lunacy Laws. 5ed. 1915

Arch.Mun.Corp. Archbold, Municipal Corporations Act. 1836

Arch.N.P. Archbold, Law Of Nisi Prius. 2ed. 1845

ArchöR Archiv des öffentlichen Rechts (Ger.) 1886–1944, 1948–

ArchÖffR Archiv des öffentlichen Rechts (Ger.) 1886–1944, 1948–
Arch.P.C. Archbold, Pleas of the Crown. 1813
Arch.P.C.P. Archbold, Practice of the Court of Common Pleas. 1829
Arch.P.Ch. Archbold, Practice by Chitty
Arch.P.K.B. Archbold, Practice in the King's Bench. 14ed. 1885
Arch.P.L. Archbold, Poor Law. 16ed. 1930
Arch.P.L.C. Archbold, Poor Law Cases. 1842–58
Arch.P.L.Cas. Archbold, Poor Law Cases. 1842–58
Arch.Part. Archbold, Law of Partnership. 2ed. 1857
Arch.Phil.Dr. Archives de Philosophie du Droit (Fr.)
Arch.Pr.Q.S. Archbold, Practice in Quarter Sessions. 6ed. 1908
ArchRSozPhil Archiv für Rechts- und Sozialphilosophie (Ger.) 1933/4–1944, 1949/50–
Arch.R.–und Sozialph. Archiv für Rechts und Sozialphilosophie (Ger.) 1933/4–1944, 1949/50–
Arch.R.–und Wirtschaftsph. Archiv für Rechts- und Wirtschaftsphilosophie (Ger.)
Arch.Sozialw.und Sozialph. Archiv für Sozialwissenschaften und Sozialphilosophie
Arch.Sozialw.und Sozialpol. Archiv für Sozialwissenschaft und Sozialpolitik
Arch.Sum. Archbold, Summary of the Laws of England. 1848–9
ArchVR Archiv des Völkerrechts (Ger.)
ArchZivPr Archiv für zivilistische Praxis (Ger.) 1818–1944, 1948/9–
Archb.Civ.Pl. Archbold, Civil Pleading and Evidence. 2ed. 1837
Archb.Cr.Law Archbold, Pleading and Evidence in Criminal Cases
Archb.Cr.Prac. Archbold, Pleading and Evidence in Criminal Cases
Archb.Crim.Pl. Archbold, Pleading and Evidence in Criminal Cases
Archb.Landl.& Ten. Archbold, Law of Landlord and Tenant. 3ed. 1864
Archb.N.P. Archbold, Law of Nisi Prius. 2ed. 1845
Archb.N.Prac. Archbold, New Practice, Pleading and Evidence in the Courts of Common Law at Westminster. 2ed. 1855
Archb.New Pr. Archbold, New Practice, Pleading and Evidence in the Courts of Common Law at Westminster. 2ed. 1855
Archb.Pr.K.B. Archbold, Practice in the King's Bench. 14ed. 1885
Archer Archer's Reports (2 Florida) (USA)
Archer & H. Archer & Hogue's Reports (2 Florida) (USA)
Archer & Hogue Archer & Hogue's Reports (2 Florida) (USA)
Architects L.R. Architects' Law Reports. 1904–9
Archives Archives de philosophie du droit et de sociologie juridique
Arg. Arguendo (Lat.) in arguing
Arg.L.R. Argus Law Reports (Aus.) 1895–1959
Arg.Mo. Moore's King's Bench Reports (Arguments of Moore) (72 ER) 1512–1621
Arg.Rep. Argus Law Reports (Aus.) 1895–1959
Argus L.R. Argus Law Reports (Aus.) 1895–1959
Argus L.R.(C.N.) Argus Law Reports (Current Notes) (Aus.) 1895–1959
Arh.Prav.Drust.Nauk. Arhiv za Pravne i Drustvene Nauke (Yugoslavia)
Arist. Aristotle
Ariz. Arizona
Arizona Supreme Court Reports. 1866–
Ariz.App. Arizona Appeals Reports. 1965–
Ariz.B.J. Arizona Bar Journal. 1965–
Ariz.J.Int'l & Comp.L. Arizona Journal of International and Comparative Law
Ariz.L.Rev. Arizona Law Review. 1959–
Ariz.Legis.Serv. West's Arizona

Legislative Service
Ariz.Rev.Stat. Arizona Revised Statutes
Ariz.Rev.Stat.Ann. Arizona Revised Statutes Annotated
Ariz.Sess.Laws Arizona Session Laws
Ariz.St.L.J. Arizona State Law Journal. 1974–
Ark. Arkansas
Arkansas Supreme Court Reports. 1837–
Arkley's Justiciary Reports (Scot.) 1846–8
Ark.Acts General Acts of Arkansas
Ark.B.A. Arkansas Bar Association
Ark.Just. Arkley's Justiciary Reports (Scot.) 1846–8
Ark.L.J. Arkansas Law Journal. 1877
Ark.L.Notes Arkansas Law Notes
Ark.L.Rev. Arkansas Law Review. 1946–
Ark.Stat.Ann. Arkansas Statutes Annotated
Arkiv f.Luftrett Arkiv for Luftrett (Norway)
Arkiv f.Sjorett Arkiv for Sjorett (Norway)
Arkl. Arkley's Justiciary Reports (Scot.) 1846–8
Arkley Arkley's Justiciary Reports (Scot.) 1846–8
Arm.M.& O. Armstrong, Macartney and Ogle's Nisi Prius Reports (Ire.) 1840–2
Arm.Mac.& Og. Armstrong, Macartney and Ogle's Nisi Prius Reports (Ire.) 1840–2
Arm.& O. Armstrong, Macartney and Ogle's Nisi Prius Reports (Ire.) 1840–2
Armitage Report Report of the Committee on Political Activities of Civil Servants (Cmnd. 7057) 1977
Armour Armour's Manitoba Queen's Bench Reports tempore Wood (Can.) 1875–83
Arms.Br.P.Cas Armstrong's Breach of Privilege Cases, New York
Arms.Con.El. Armstrong's Contested Election Cases, New York
Arms.Con.Elec. Armstrong's Contested Election Cases, New York
Arms.Elect.Cas. Armstrong's Contested Election Cases, New York
Arms.M.& O. Armstrong, Macartney and Ogle's Nisi Prius Reports (Ire.) 1840–2
Arms.Mac.& Og. Armstrong, Macartney and Ogle's Nisi Prius Reports (Ire.) 1840–2
Arms.Tr. Armstrong's Limerick Trials (Ire.)
Armstrong M.& O. Armstrong, Macartney and Ogle's Nisi Prius Reports (Ire.) 1840–2
Army Lawy. Army Lawyer (USA) 1971–
Arn. Arnold's Common Pleas Reports (50 RR) 1838–9
Arnot's Criminal Trials (Scot.) 1536–1784
Arnould, Marine Insurance
Arn.El.Cas. Arnold's Election Cases
Arn.Ins. Arnould, Marine Insurance
Arn.Mun.Car. Arnold, Municipal Corporations. 7ed. 1935
Arn.Pub.M. Arnold, Public Meetings and Political Societies. 1833
Arn.& H. Arnold & Hodges' Practice Cases, Queen's Bench. 1840–1
Arn.& H.B.C. Arnold & Hodges' Bail Court Reports
Arn.& Hod. Arnold & Hodges' Practice Cases, Queen's Bench. 1840–1
Arn.& Hod.B.C. Arnold & Hodges' Bail Court Reports
Arn.& Hod.P.C. Arnold & Hodges' Practice Cases, Queen's Bench. 1840–1
Arn.& Hod.Pr.Cas. Arnold & Hodges' Practice Cases, Queen's Bench. 1840–1
Arnold Arnold's Common Pleas Reports (50 RR) 1838–9
Arnold & H. Arnold & Hodges' Practice Cases, Queen's Bench. 1840–1
Arnot Cr.C. Arnot's Criminal Cases (Scot.) 1536–1784
Arr. arrêté (Fr.) decision, order (of a court), decree
Arrang. arrangement
Art. Article(s)

Artic.Cl. Articled Clerk. 1867–8
Artic.Cl.Deb. Articled Clerk and Debater. 1866
Artic.Cl.J.Exam. Articled Clerks' Journal and Examiner. 1879–81
Artic.Cleri Articuli Cleri (Lat.) Articles of the Clergy
Artic.sup.Chart. Articuli super Chartas (Lat.) Articles upon the charters
arts. articles
artt. artikelen (Neth.) articles
Arun.Mines Arundell, Mines and Mining Companies. 1863
As. Æthelstan
Asia
AsDB Asian Development Bank
Ash. Ashmead's Pennsylvania Reports. 1808–41
Ashb. Ashburner, Principles of Equity. 2ed. 1933
Ashe Ashe's Tables to the Year Books, Coke's Reports, or Dyer's Reports
Ashm. Ashmead's Pennsylvania Reports. 1808–41
Ashm.(Pa.) Ashmead's Pennsylvania Reports. 1808–41
Ashton Ashton's Opinions of the United States Attorneys General (9–12 Opinions)
Ashurst Ashurst's Paper Books
Ashurst's Manuscript Reports (printed in 2 Chitty)
Asia Q. Asia Quarterly
Asian-Pac.Tax & Invest.Bull. Asian-Pacific Tax and Investment Bulletin (Singapore)
Asian Surv. Asian Survey
Asian & Afr.Stud. Asian and African Studies
Aslib formerly the Association of Special Libraries and Information Bureau
Asm. All India Reporter, Assam Series. 1949–
Asp. Aspinall's Maritime Cases. 1870–1940
Asp.Cas. Aspinall's Maritime Cases. 1870–1940
Asp.M.C. Aspinall's Maritime Cases. 1870–1940
Asp.M.C.L. Aspinall's Maritime Cases. 1870–1940
Asp.M.L.C. Aspinall's Maritime Cases. 1870–1940
Asp.Mar.L.Cas. Aspinall's Maritime Cases. 1870–1940
Asp.Mar.Law Cas. Aspinall's Maritime Cases. 1870–1940
Asp.Rep. Aspinall's Maritime Cases. 1870–1940
Aspin. Aspinall's Maritime Cases. 1870–1940
Ass. Assemblée générale du contentieux (Conseil d'État) (Fr.)
Assembly
Assizes
Assurance (Fr.) insurance
Liber Assisarum (Book of Assizes) (Year Books Part V) 1327–77
Ass.féd. Assemblée fédérale (Switz.)
Ass.Ind. Assam (India)
Assam All India Reporter, Assam Series. 1949–
Indian Law Reports, Assam Series. 1949–
Assd. Assigned
Assem. Assembly, USA State Legislature
Assess.Ct. Assessment Court (N.Z.)
Assn. Association
assoc. associate
association
asst. assistant
Ast.Ent. Ashton's Entries. 1673
At. Atlantic Reporter (USA)
AtG Bundesgesetz über die friedliche Verwendung der Atomenergie und den Strahlenschutz (Ger.) 1959
Atch. Atchison, Navigation and Trade Reports
Atch.E.C. Atcheson, Election Cases
Ateneo L.J. Ateneo Law Journal (Philippines)
Ath.Mar.Set. Atherley, Marriage Settlements. 1813
Athlr. Æthelred
Atk. Atkinson's Quarter Sessions

Records, Yorkshire
Atkyns' Chancery Reports (26 ER) 1736–55

Atk.P.T. Atkyn's Parliamentary Tracts

Atk.Sher. Atkinson, Sheriffs. 6ed. 1878

Atkinson Atkinson, Law of Solicitors' Liens. 1905

Atl. Atlantic Reporter (USA)

Atl.2d Atlantic Reporter, Second Series

Atl.Mo. Atlantic Monthly

Atl.R. Atlantic Reporter (USA)

Atlan. Atlantic Monthly (USA)

Atom.En.L.Rep.(CCH) Atomic Energy Law Reporter (CCH) (USA)

Atomic Energy L.J. Atomic Energy Law Journal (USA) 1959–

Att. Attorney

Att.-Gen. Attorney-General

Attenborough Attenborough, The Laws of the Earliest English Kings

Atti del Governo Raccolta degli Atti del Governo di Sua Maesta il Re di Sardegna (It.) 1814

Atti parl. Atti parlamentari (It.) Parliamentary Acts

Atty. Attorney

Atty.Gen. Attorney-General

Atty.Gen.Op. Attorney General's Opinions (USA) 1789–

Atty.Gen.Op.N.Y. Attorney General's Opinions, New York (USA)

Att'y.Gen.Rep. United States Attorneys General Reports

Atw. Atwater's Reports (1 Minnesota)

Atwater Atwater's Reports (1 Minnesota)

Auch. Auchinleck's Manuscript Cases, Court of Session (Scot.)

Auck.U.L.Rev. Auckland University Law Review (N.Z.) 1968–

Auckland U.L.Rev. Auckland University Law Review (N.Z.) 1968–

Auct.Reg.& L.Chron. Auction Register & Law Chronicle (USA)

Aud. Audit
Auditor

Aud.-Gen. Auditor-General

Aufl. Auflage (Ger.) edition

Auftr. Auftrag (Ger.) Commission

Ault. Court Rolls of Ramsey Abbey. 1928

Aus. Australia

Aus.Quart. Australian Quarterly. 1929–

Aus.Rep. Austin's Appeal Reports (Sri L.) 1833–95

Aus.Y.I.L. Australian Yearbook of International Law

Ausg. Ausgabe (Ger.) edition

AuslG Ausländergesetz (Ger.) Aliens Act

Ausländ.Wirt.& Steuer. Ausländisches Wirtschafts – und Steuerrecht (Ger.)

Aust. Austin's Appeal Reports (Sri L.) 1833–95
Austin's County Court Cases. 1867–9
Australia
Austria

Aust.Acc. Australian Accountant (Journal of the Australian Society of Accountants) 1931–

Aust.Bankr.Cas. Australian Bankruptcy Cases. 1928–64

Aust.Bar Gaz. Australian Bar Gazette. 1961–70

Aust.Bar Rev. Australian Bar Review. 1985–

Aust.Bus.L.Rev. Australian Business Law Review. 1973–

Aust.Bus.Lawyer Australian Business Lawyer. 1986–

Aust.Bus.Rev. Australian Business Law Review. 1973

Aust.C.L.Rev. Australian Current Law Review. 1969–71

Aust.(Ceylon) Austin's Appeal Reports (Sri L.) 1833–95

Aust.Comp.Law Cases Australian Company Law Cases. 1982–

Aust.Conv.Sol.J. Australian Conveyancer and Solicitors' Journal. 1948–59

Aust.Copyright Cncl.Bull. Australian Copyright Council Bulletin. 1973–

Aust.Crim.& N.Z.J. Australian and New Zealand Journal of Criminology. 1968–

Aust.D.F.A. Australian Department of Foreign Affairs

Aust.Digest Australian Digest. 2ed. 1963–88, 3ed. 1988–
Aust.Director Australian Director
Aust.Ind.L.R. Australian Industrial Law Review. 1959–
Aust.J.For.Sci. Australian Journal of Forensic Sciences. 1968–
Aust.J.L.& Soc. Australian Journal of Law and Society. 1982–
Aust.J.Psych.Phil. Australasian Journal of Psychology and Philosophy
Aust.J.Pub.Admin. Australian Journal of Public Administration. 1976–
Aust.Jnl.of Forensic Sciences Australian Journal of Forensic Sciences. 1968–
Aust.Jnl.of Social Issues Australian Journal of Social Issues. 1966–
Aust.Jur. Austin, Lectures on Jurisprudence.
Australian Jurist. 1870–4
Australian Jurist Reports. 1870–4
Aust.Jur.Abr. Austin, Lectures on Jurisprudence, Abridged
Aust.Jur.R. Australian Jurist Reports. 1870–4
Aust.Jur.Rep. Australian Jurist Reports. 1870–4
Aust.K.A. Austin's Kandran Appeals (Sri L.)
Aust.L.J. Australian Law Journal. 1927–
Aust.L.J.Rep. Australian Law Journal Reports. 1958–
Aust.L.N. Australian Law News. 1977–
Aust.L.T. Australian Law Times. 1879–1928
Aust.Law. Australian Lawyer. 1960–9
Aust.Law News Australian Law News. 1977–
Aust.Lawyer Australian Lawyer. 1960–9
Aust.N.Z.J.Criminol. Australian and New Zealand Journal of Criminology. 1968–
Aust.Pol.J. Australian Police Journal
Aust.Q. Australian Quarterly. 1929–
Aust.Quart. Australian Quarterly. 1929–
Aust.Tax D. Australian Tax Decisions. 1930–69
Aust.Tax Rev. Australian Tax Review. 1971–
Aust.Torts Rep. Australian Torts Reporter (CCH) 1984–
Aust.Yr.Bk.I.L. Australian Yearbook of International Law. 1965–
Aust.& N.Z.J.Crim. Australian and New Zealand Journal of Criminology. 1968–
Aust.& N.Z.J.Criminol. Australian and New Zealand Journal of Criminology. 1968–
Austin Austin's Appeal Reports (Sri L.) 1833–95
Austin C.C. Austin's County Court Cases. 1867–9
Austin (Ceylon) Austin's Appeal Reports (Sri L.) 1833–95
Austin, Lectures J. Austin, Lectures on Jurisprudence. 3ed. 1863
Austin, Province Determined J. Austin, The Province of Jurisprudence Determined, ed. H.L.A. Hart, 1954
Austl. Australia
Austl.Argus L.R. Australian Argus Law Reports. 1960–
Austl.B.Rev. Australian Bar Review. 1985–
Austl.Bankr.Cas. Australian Bankruptcy Cases
Austl.Bus.L.Rev. Australian Business Law Review. 1973
Austl.Com.J. Australian Commerical Journal
Austl.J.Fam.L. Australian Journal of Family Law
Austl.J.For.Sci. Australian Journal of Forensic Sciences. 1968–
Austl.J.L.& Soc'y Australian Journal of Law and Society. 1982–
Austl.J.Lab.L. Australian Journal of Labour Law
Austl.Jur.R. Australian Jurist Reports. 1870–4
Austl.L.J. Australian Law Journal. 1927–
Austl.L.J.Rep. Australian Law Journal Reports. 1958–

Austl.Stat.R.Consol. Statutory Rules Consolidation, Australian Parliament
Austl.Tax Australian Tax Decisions
Austl.Tax Rev. Australian Tax Review. 1971–
Austl.Y.B.Int'l.L. Australian Yearbook of International Law. 1965–
Austl.Yrbk.Int.L. Australian Yearbook of International Law. 1965–
Austr.B.C. Australian Bankruptcy Cases
Austr.C.L.R. Commonwealth Law Reports (Aus.) 1903–
Austr.Jur. Australian Jurist. 1870–4
Austr.L.J. Australian Law Journal. 1927–
Austr.L.T. Australian Law Times. 1879–1928
Austr.Tax D. Australian Tax Decisions
Austr.Tax R. Australian Tax Review. 1971–
Austral. Australia
Austral.Off.J.Pat. Australian Official Journal of Patents, Trade Marks and Designs. 1904–
Australian YIL Australian Yearbook of International Law
Auth. Authentica
Authorised
Authorities
Authority
Auto. Automobile
Auto.Cas. Automobile Cases (CCH) (USA) 1938–
Auto.Cas.2d Automobile Cases, Second Series (CCH) (USA)
Auto.Ins.Cas. Automobile Insurance Cases (CCH) (USA) 1938–
Auto.L.Rep. Automobile Law Reporter (CCH) (USA)
Av. Average
Aviation
Av.Adj.Assoc.Dig. Digest of Reports of the Average Adjusters Association. 1895
Av.Cas. Aviation Cases (CCH) (USA)
Av.gén. avocat général (Fr.) district attorney
Av.L.Rep. Aviation Law Reporter (CCH) (USA)
AvbetL Lag om avbetalningskop (Swed.) Law on instalment purchase contracts
Ave. Avenue
Avv. Avvocato (It.) barrister
Ayl.Char. Ayliffe, Calendar of Ancient Charters. 1774
Ayl.Pan. Ayliffe, Pandect of the Roman Civil Law. 1734
Ayl.Pand. Ayliffe, Pandect of the Roman Civil Law. 1734
Ayl.Par. Ayliffe, Parergon Juris Canonici Anglicani. 1726, 1734
Ayliffe Ayliffe, Pandect of the Roman Civil Law. 1734
Ayliffe, Parergon Juris Canonici Anglicani. 1726, 1734
Ayr Ayr's Registration Cases (Scot.) 1835–6
Ayr & Wig. Ayr & Wigton's Registration Cases (Scot.) 1839–41
Az. Arizona
Arizona Reports
Az.A. Arizona Court of Appeals Reports
Az.L. Arizona Law Review. 1959–
Az.L.R. Arizona Law Review. 1959–
Az.Mar.Law Azuni, Maritime Law. 1805
Azuni Mar.Law Azuni, Maritime Law. 1805

B

b. book
born
brother

B. All India Reporter, Bombay Series. 1914–
Bar
Barber's Gold Law Cases (S.Afr.) 1883–1903
Barbour's New York Reports. 1847–77
Baron
Beavan's Rolls Court Reports (48–55 ER) 1838–66
Boston
Buchanan's Supreme Court Reports, Cape (S.Afr.) 1868–79
Burgerlijk Wetboek (Neth.) civil code
Common Bench
Indian Law Reports, Bombay Series. 1876–
Series B, containing the Advisory Opinions of the Permanent Court of International Justice. 1922–30
Weekly Law Bulletin (Ohio) 1885–1901

BA Book of Awards (made under the Industrial Conciliation and Arbitration Act, New Zealand). 1894–
Bundesanwalt (Ger.) public prosecutor or attorney general
Bundesanwaltschaft (Ger.) the office of public prosecutor

B.A. Bulletin des assurances (Belg.)

B.A.Bull.L.A. Bar Association Bulletin, Los Angeles. 1925–

B.A.C. Buchanan's Appeal Court Reports, Cape (S.Afr.) 1880–1909

BACS Bankers Automated Clearing Services Ltd.

BAG Bundesarbeitsgericht (Ger.) Federal Labour Court, Reports of the Federal Labour Court

BAGE Entscheidungen des Bundesarbeitsgerichts (Ger.) Reports of the Decisions of the Federal Labour Court. 1954–

BAGG Arbeitsgerichtsgesetz (Ger.) law on labour courts

BALGPS Bar Association for Local Government and the Public Service

B.A.L.O. Bulletin des annonces legales obligatoires (Fr.) Official gazette for legal notices

B.A.O. Bankruptcy Annulment Order

BASATA The British and South Asian Trade Association

B.A.S.F. The Bar Association of San Francisco

B.A.S.L.P. Bulletin of the Australian Society of Legal Philosophy. 1977–

B.A.S.W. British Association of Social Workers

BAnz Bundesanzeiger (Ger.) Federal Reporter. 1949–

BArbG Bundesarbeitsgericht (Ger.) Federal Labour Court, Reports of the Federal Labour Court

BB Brottsbalk (Swed.) Criminal Code

B.B. Bail Bond
Beslissingen in Belastingzaken (Neth) Reports of tax cases

BBA British Business Association (Singapore)
Buitengewoon Besluit Arbeidsverhoudingen (Neth.)

BBG Bundesbeamtengesetz (Ger.) law on federal civil servants

B.B.L.I. Records of the Honourable

Society of Lincoln's Inn (The Black Books) ed. by J.D. Walker & R. Roxburgh. 1897–1968

B.B.T.C. Banca, Borsa e Titoli di Credito (It.)

B.B.& F.L.R. Butterworths Banking and Financial Law Review

B.Bar Bench & Bar (Chicago) 1869–74
Bench & Bar (Detroit) 1921–6
Bench & Bar (Missouri) 1935–42
Bench & Bar (Montreal) 1931–45
Bench & Bar (New York) 1905–20

B.Bl. Bundesblatt der Schweizerischen Eidgenossenschaft (Switz.)
Henry Blackstone's Common Pleas Reports (126 ER) 1788–96

B.C. Bail Court
Bankruptcy Cases
Before Christ
Bell, Commentaries on the Laws of Scotland. 1870
Board of Control
British Columbia
British Columbia Reports (Can.) 1867–1947
British Council
New South Wales Bankruptcy Cases (Aus.) 1890–99

B.C.A. Board of Contract Appeals Decisions (USA)

B.C.B. Butterworths Conveyancing Bulletin (N.Z.) 1982–

B.C.C. Bail Court Cases (Lowndes & Maxwell) 1852–4
Bail Court Reports, Saunders & Cole (82 RR) 1846–8
British Chamber of Commerce
British Company Law Cases. 1983–
British Copyright Council
W. Brown's Chancery Cases (28–9 ER) 1778–94

B.C.C.L.G. British Columbia Corporations Law Guide (Can.) 1974–

B.C.Corp.L.J. British Columbia Corporations Law Journal

B.C.D. Bankruptcy Court Decisions

B.C.Dec. British Columbia Decisions (Can.) 1972–

B.C.Envtl.Aff.Rev. Boston College Environmental Affairs Law Review (USA)

B.C.F.L.Q. British Columbia Family Law Quantum Service (Can.) 1986–

B.C.Human Rights Comm.Newsl. The Human Rights Commission Newsletter (Can.)

B.C.Ind.& Com.L.Rev. Boston College Industrial and Commercial Law Review (USA) 1959–

B.C.Int'l & Comp.L.Rev. Boston College International and Comparative Law Review (USA)

B.C.J. British Columbia Judgments (unreported decisions available on QL) (Can.) 1986–

B.C.L. Bachelor of Canon Law
Bachelor of Civil Law
Building and Construction Law (Aus.) 1985–
Butterworths Current Law (N.Z.) 1969–

B.C.L.B. Butterworths Company Law Bulletin (Aus.) 1986–

B.C.L.C. Butterworths Company Law Cases. 1983–

B.C.L.R. British Columbia Law Reports (Can.) 1977–

B.C.L.R.C. British Columbia Law Reform Commission

B.C.L.R.S. Building and Construction Legal Reporting Service (Aus.) 1978–

B.C.L.Rev. Boston College Law Review (USA)

B.C.(N.S.W.) New South Wales Bankruptcy Cases (Aus.) 1890–99

B.C.R. Bail Court Cases, Lowndes & Maxwell. 1852–4
Bail Court Reports, Saunders & Cole (82 RR) 1846–8
British Columbia Reports (Can.) 1867–1947
W. Brown's Chancery Cases (28–9 ER) 1778–94
Butterworths Company Reports (N.Z.) 1970–

B.C.R.D. British Columbia Recent Decisions (Can.) 1980–

B.C.Rep. Bail Court Cases, Lowndes & Maxwell. 1852–4
Bail Court Reports, Saunders & Cole (82 RR) 1846–8
British Columbia Reports (Can.) 1867–1947
W. Brown's Chancery Cases (28–9 ER) 1778–94

B.C.Rev.Stat. British Columbia Revised Statutes (Can.)

B.C.Stat. British Columbia Statutes (Can.)

B.C.Studies British Columbia Studies

B.C.T.S. British Columbia Taxation Service (Can.) 1969–

B.C.Third World L.J. Boston College Third World Law Journal (USA)

B.C.W.L.D. British Columbia Weekly Law Digest (Can.) 1982–

B.C.W.S. British Columbia Securities Commission Weekly Summary (Can.) 1987–

B.Ch. Barbour's Chancery Reports, New York

B.Col. British Columbia

B.D.I.L. British Digest of International Law. 1965–

B.D.V. Brussels Definition of Values

B.D.& O. Blackham, Dundas & Osborne's Nisi Prius Reports (Ire.) 1846–8

B.Dig. Bose's Digest (India)

b.e. bill of exchange

B.E. Baron of the Court of Exchequer
British Embassy

B.E.A. British East Africa
British European Airways

BENELUX Belgium, Netherlands, Luxembourg Economic Union

B.E.Q.B. Bank of England Quarterly Bulletin. 1960–

BESO British Executive Service Overseas

B.E.U. Benelux Economic Union

BEWT Bureau of East–West Trade

B.en Dr. Bachelier en Droit (Fr.) Bachelor of Law

B.Ex. Baron of the Exchequer

b.f. bankruptcy fee
brought forward

BFH Bundesfinanzhof (Ger.) Federal Supreme Tax Court

BFHE Entscheidungen des Bundesfinanzhofs (Ger.) Reports of the Federal Supreme Tax Court

B.F.L.R. Banking and Finance Law Review (Can.) 1986–

BFM Beambtenfonds voor het Mijnbedriff (Neth.) Social security organisation

B.F.N. Butterworths Fortnightly Notes (N.Z.) 1925–7

b.f.p. bona fide purchaser

B.F.S.P. British and Foreign State Papers

b/g bonded goods

BG Bundesgericht (Ger.) Federal Supreme Court
Bundesgesetz (Ger. & Switz.) Federal Act or Statute
Berufungsgericht (Ger.) Court of Appeal

B.G. British Guiana Law Reports. 1890–6

BGB Bürgerliches Gesetzbuch (Ger. & Switz.) Civil Code

BGBl Bundesgestzblatt (Ger.) Federal Law Gazette

BGE Amtliche Sammlung der Entscheidungen des Schweizerischen Bundesgerichtes (Switz.)
Entscheidungen des Bundesgerichts (Ger.)

BGH Bundesgerichtshof (Ger.) Federal Supreme Court

BGHSt Entscheidungen des Bundesgerichtshof in Strafsachen (Ger.) Reports of the Supreme Federal Court in Criminal Matters. 1951–

BGHZ Entscheidungen des Bundesgerichtshof in Zivilsachen (Ger.) Reports of the Federal Supreme Court in Civil Cases. 1951–

B.G.L. Bachelor of General Laws

B.G.L.R. Reports of the Supreme Court (British Guiana) 1914–

B.H.C. Bombay High Court Reports

(India) 1862–75
British High Commission
B.H.C.P.J. Bombay High Court Printed Judgments (India) 1869–1900
B.H.C.R. Bombay High Court Reports (India) 1862–75
B.I.A. British Insurance Association
BIAC Business and Industry Advisory Committee (to the OECD)
B.I.A.L.L. British and Irish Association of Law Librarians
B.I.B. Board of International Broadcasting
B.I.B.A. British Insurance Brokers' Association
B.I.C. Bureau of International Commerce
B.I.F.D. Bulletin for International Fiscal Documentation (Neth.) 1947–
B.I.H.R. British Institute of Human Rights
Bulletin of the Institute of Historical Research
B.I.I.C.L. British Institute of International and Comparative Law
B.I.L.A. British Insurance Law Association
B.I.L.A.Bull. British Insurance Law Association Bulletin. 1964–
B.I.L.C. British International Law Cases
B.I.L.E.T.A. British & Irish Legal Education Technology Association
BILETA Newsl. B.I.L.E.T.A. Newsletter
B.I.L.S. British International Law Society
BIMCO Baltic and International Maritime Conference
B.I.R. Board of Inland Revenue
BIRD International Bank for Reconstruction and Development
BIRPI United International Bureaux for the Protection of Intellectual Property
B.I.S. Bank for International Settlements
BISD Basic Instruments and Selected Documents (of the GATT)
B.I.T. Bureau International du Travail (International Labour Organisation)
B.J. Bachelor of Jurisprudence
Belgique judiciaire (Belg.) 1842–
B.J.A.L. British Journal of Administrative Law. 1954–
B.J.Crim. British Journal of Criminology. 1960–
B.J.Delinq. British Journal of Delinquency. 1950–60
B.J.I.B.& F.L. Butterworths Journal of International Banking and Financial Law. 1986–
B.J.I.R. British Journal of Industrial Relations. 1963–
B.J.Ind.Rel. British Journal of Industrial Relations. 1963–
B.J.L.S. British Journal of Law and Society. 1974–
BJM Basler Juristische Mitteilungen (Switz.)
B.J.R.L. The Bulletin of the John Rylands Library
B.Jur. Baccalaureus Juris (Lat.)
Bachelor of Jurisprudence
B.Jur.& Soc.S. Bachelor of Juridical and Social Sciences
BK Bundeskanzler (Ger.) Federal Chancellor
Bundeskanzleramt (Ger.) Federal Chancery
BKA Bundeskartellamt (Ger.) Federal Cartel Office
b.l. bill of lading
B.L. Bachelor of Laws
Bachelor of Letters
Barrister-at-Law
Bill of Lading
Black Letter
British Library
B.L.A. Bachelor of Law and Administration
British Legal Association
B.L.B. Banking Law Bulletin (Aus.) 1985–
Business Law Brief
B.L.C. Bollettino de legislazione comparata (It.) 1966–
B.L.D. Bulletin legislatif Dalloz (Fr.)
Bulletin of Legal Developments. 1966–

B.L.E.C. Business Law Education Centre (Melbourne, Aus.)
BLEU Belgium–Luxembourg Economic Union
B.L.I.J. Burma Law Institute Journal. 1958–60
B.L.J. Banking Law Journal (USA) 1889–
Bihar Law Journal Reports (India) 1953–
Burma Law Journal. 1922–7
B.LL. Bachelor of Laws
B.L.R. Bahamas Law Reports
Barbados Law Reports. 1894–1903
Baylor Law Review (Texas) 1948–
Bengal Law Reports, High Court (India) 1868–75
Bermuda Law Reports. 1904–26
Bombay Law Reporter (India) 1899–
Building Law Reports. 1971–
Business Law Review. 1954–
B.L.R.A.C. Bengal Law Reports, Appeal Cases
B.L.R.P.C. Bengal Law Reports, Privy Council
B.L.R.Sup.Vol. Bengal Fuel Bench Rulings, Supplementary Volume (India) 1863–8
B.L.S.A. British Legal Services Agency
B.L.T. Bacon, Lettuce and Tomato (Can. & USA)
Baltimore Law Transcript
Burma Law Times. 1907–20
B.L.W.A. Black Legal Workers' Association
B.Leg.S. Bachelor of Legal Science (Macquarie University, Aus.)
B.M. Bayly Moore's Reports, Common Pleas (19–29 RR) 1817–27
Ben Monroe's Kentucky Reports (40–57 Ky) 1840–57
British Museum
Burrow's Reports tempore Mansfield (97–8 ER) 1757–71
B.M.A. British Medical Association
BMITA British Malaysian Industry and Trade Association
BMJ Bundesminister(ium) der Justiz (Ger.) Federal Minister (Ministry) of Justice
B.M.J. British Medical Journal. 1857–
B.M.L. Businessman's Law
B.M.L.A. British Maritime Law Association
B.Mon. Ben Monroe's Kentucky Reports (40–57 Ky) 1840–57
B.Mon.(Ky.) Ben Monroe's Kentucky Reports (40–57 Ky) 1840–57
B.Monr. Ben Monroe's Kentucky Reports (40–57 Ky) 1840–57
B.Moore Bayly Moore's Reports, Common Pleas (19–29 RR) 1817–27
B.N. Blue Notes (Ontario Court of Appeal) (Can.)
Brussels Nomenclature (or Customs Co-operation Council Nomenclature)
B.N.A. Bureau of National Affairs (USA)
B.N.A.Act British North America Act
BNB Beslissingen in Belastingzaken (Neth.)
Beslissingen Nederlandse Belastingrechtspraak (Neth.) Tax case reports
B.N.B. Bracton's Note Book
British National Bibliography. 1950–
B.N.C. Bingham's New Cases, Common Pleas (131–3 ER) 1834–40
Brasenose College, Oxford
Brooke's New Cases, King's Bench (73 ER) 1515–58
Bushbee's North Carolina Law Reports (44–5 NC)
B.N.O.C. British National Oil Corporation
B.N.P. Buller, Nisi Prius
B.N.T. Brussels Tariff Nomenclature
B.O.A.C. Butterworths' Ontario Appeal Cases (Can.)
BOAG British Overseas Aid Group
B.O.C.D. Bulletin officiel des contributions directes (Fr.)
B.O.D. Butterworths' Ontario Digest
B.O.E. Bulletin officiel de l'enregistrement et du domaine (Fr.)
B.O.E.D. Bulletin officiel de l'enregistrement et du domaine (Fr.)

B.O.Estado Boletin Oficial del Estado (Sp.) legislative series
BOP Balance of Payments
B.o.T. Board of Trade
BOTAC British Overseas Trade Advisory Council (disbanded 1982)
BOTB British Overseas Trade Board (Department of Trade)
B.O.T.Jo. Board of Trade Journal
BPAS British Pregnancy Advisory Service
B.P.B. Buller's Paper Book
B.P.C. Brown's Cases in Parliament (1–3 ER) 1702–1801
B.P.I.L. British Practice in International Law. 1963–
B.P.L. Bott's Poor Law Cases. 1560–1833
British Pension Lawyer
B.P.L.Cas. Bott's Poor Law Cases. 1560–1833
B.P.N.R. Bosanquet & Puller's New Reports, Common Pleas (127 ER) 1804–7
B.P.R. Brown's Cases in Parliament (1–3 ER) 1702–1801
Butterworths Property Reports (in Charlebois, Conveyancing Service, N.S.W.) (Aus.) 1950–
b.r. bills receivable
B.R. Baltimore City Reports
Bancus Reginae (Queen's Bench)
Bancus Regis (King's Bench)
Bankruptcy Register (USA) 1867–9
Bankruptcy Reporter (available on Westlaw) (USA) 1979–
Bankruptcy Reports (USA)
Board of Review Reports, U.S. Army. 1929–49
Broadcasting Reports (in Durie & Catterns, Broadcasting Law and Practice) (Aus.) 1979–
Brooklyn Law Review, New York. 1932–
Quebec Official Reports, Queen's Bench (Can.) 1892–1900
BRÅ Brottsförebyggande rådet (Swed.) The National Council for Crime Prevention
B.R.A. Butterworth's Rating Appeals. 1913–31
B.R.C. British Ruling Cases
BRD Bundesrepublik Deutschland. Federal Republic of Germany
B.R.H. Cases in King's Bench tempore Hardwicke (95 ER) 1733–8
B.R.J. Bill of Rights Journal (USA) 1968–
B.R.W. Business Review Weekly (Aus.) 1979–
b.rec. bill(s) receivable
B.Reg. Bankruptcy Register (USA) 1867–9
b.s. balance sheet
bill of sale
B.S. Bancus Superior (Upper Bench)
British Standard
Brown's Supplement to Morison's Dictionary of Decisions, Court of Session (Scot.) 1622–1780
Bulletin officiel de l'Assemblée fédérale (Switz.)
BSBDI Boletin de la Sociedade brasileira de direito internacional (Brazil)
BSD Busy Solicitor's Digest
BSG Bundessozialgericht (Ger.) Federal Court of Social Security
Entscheidungen des Bundessozialgerichts (Ger.) Reports of the Federal Court of Social Security. 1955–
b.s.g.d.g. breveté sans garantie du gouvernement (Fr.) patented without government guarantee
B.S.I. British Standards Institution
BSozG Bundessozialgericht (Ger.) Federal Court of Social Security
Entscheidungen des Bundessozialgerichts (Ger.) Reports of the Federal Court of Social Security. 1955–
BStBl Bundessteuerblatt (Ger.) Federal Tax Gazette. 1951–
B.T. Bosworth & Toller, Anglo-Saxon Dictionary

B.T.A. Board of Tax Appeals Reports (USA) 1924–42

B.T.A.C.C.H. Board of Tax Appeals Decisions (CCH) (USA)

B.T.A.P.H. Board of Tax Appeals Decisions (P–H) (USA)

BTCE Bureau of Transport & Communications Economics (Aus.)

BTN Brussels Tariff Nomenclature

BTPD Busy Tax Practitioners Digest (Aus.) 1984–5

B.T.R. Brewing Trade Review Licensing Law Reports. 1913–53
British Tax Review. 1956–

B.T.R.L.R. Brewing Trade Review Licensing Law Reports. 1913–53

B.T.Suppl. Bosworth & Toller, Anglo-Saxon Dictionary, Supplement

B.Tr. Bishop's Trial

B.U.A. Bollettino Ufficiale della Valle d'Aosta (It.) Official Gazette of the Valle d'Aosta

B.U.Int'l L.J. Boston University International Law Journal (USA)

B.U.J.Tax L. Boston University Journal of Tax Law (USA)

B.U.L.Rev. Boston University Law Review. 1921–

B.U.S.L. Boston University School of Law

B.U.Sa. Bollettino Ufficiale Regione Sarda (It.) Official Bulletin of the Regione Sarda

B.U.T. Bollettino Ufficiale Trentino Alto-Adige (It.) Official Gazette of the Trentino Alto-Adige

b/v book value

BV Besloten Vennootschap met Beperkte Aansprakelijkheid (Neth.) Private company
Bundesverfassung (Switz.)

BVM Business Visitors Memorandum (British Overseas Trade Board)

BVP British Volunteers Programme

BVerfG Bundesverfassungsgericht (Ger.) Federal Constitutional Court

BVerfGE Entscheidungen des Bundesverfassungsgerichts (Ger.) Reports of Decisons of the Federal Constitutional Court. 1952–

BVerwG Bundesverwaltungsgericht (Ger.) Federal Supreme Administrative Court; Reports of the Decisions of the Federal Supreme Administrative Court. 1954–

BW Burgerlijk Wetboek (Neth.) civil code

B.W.B. British Waterways Board

B.W.C.C. Butterworth's Workmen's Compensation Cases. 1908–47

B.W.T.Bull. Butterworths Weekly Tax Bulletin (Aus.) 1985–

B.Y. Brigham Young
British Yearbook of International Law

B.Y.B. British Yearbook of International Law. 1920–

B.Y.B.I.L. British Yearbook of International Law. 1920–

B.Y.I.L. British Yearbook of International Law. 1920–

B.Y.U.J.Pub.L. Brigham Young University Journal of Public Law

B.Y.U.L.R. Brigham Young University Law Review (USA) 1975–

B.Y.U.L.Rev. Brigham Young University Law Review (USA) 1975–

BZBl Bundeszollblatt (Ger.) Federal Customs Gazette. 1950–

B.& A. Banning & Arden's Patent Reports (USA) 1874–81
Barnewall & Adolphus' King's Bench Reports (109–110 ER) 1830–4
Barnewall & Alderson's King's Bench Reports (106 ER) 1817–22
Barron & Arnold's Election Cases. 1843–6
Barron & Austin's Election Cases. 1842

B.& Ad. Barnewall & Adolphus' King's Bench Reports (109–110 ER) 1830–4

B.& Ald. Barnewall & Alderson's King's Bench Reports (106 ER) 1817–22

B.& Arn. Barron & Arnold's Election Cases. 1843–6

B.& Aust. Barron & Austin's Election Cases. 1842

B.& B. Ball & Beatty's Chancery Reports (12 RR) (Ire.) 1807–14
Bench & Bar (Chicago) 1869–74
Bench & Bar (Detroit) 1921–6
Bench & Bar (Missouri) 1935–42
Bench & Bar (Montreal) 1931–45
Bench & Bar (New York) 1905–20
Bowler & Bowers' Reports (2, 3 U.S. Comptroller's Decisions)
Broderip & Bingham's Common Pleas Reports (129 ER) 1819–22

B.& Bar Bench & Bar (Chicago) 1869–74
Bench & Bar (Detroit) 1921–6
Bench & Bar (Missouri) 1935–42
Bench & Bar (Montreal) 1931–45
Bench & Bar (New York) 1905–20

B.& C. Barnewall & Cresswell's King's Bench Reports (107–9 ER) 1822–30

B.& C.Comp. Bellinger & Cotton's Annotated Codes and Statutes (Oregon)

B.& C.Int. Benefits and Compensation International

B.& C.Pr.Cas. British and Colonial Prize Cases. 1914–19

B.& C.R. Reports of Bankruptcy and Companies (Winding Up) Cases. 1918–41

B.& D. Benloe & Dalison's Common Pleas Reports (123 ER) 1486–1580

B.& F. Broderick & Fremantle's Ecclesiastical Reports. 1840–64

B.& G. Brownlow & Goldesborough's Common Pleas Reports (123 ER) 1569–1624

B.& H. Blatchford & Howland's United States District Court Reports

B.& H.Cr.Cas. Bennett & Heard's Leading Criminal Cases

B.& H.Dig. Bennett & Heard's Massachusetts Digest

B.& H.Lead.Ca. Bennett & Heard's Leading Criminal Cases

B.& H.Lead.Cas. Bennett & Heard's Leading Criminal Cases

B.& I. Bankruptcy and Insolvency Cases. 1853–55

B.& L. Browning & Lushington's Admiralty Reports (167 ER) 1864–5
Bullen & Leake's Precedents of Pleading

B.& L.Pr. Bullen & Leake's Precedents of Pleading

B.& M. Brown & Macnamara's Railway Cases

B.& M.E.L. Baker & McKenzie Employment Law

B.& M.P.L.& E.B. Baker & Mackenzie Pensions Law and Employee Benefits

B.& Mac. Brown & Macnamara's Railway Cases

B.& O.Bd.of Rev. Selected Decisions of the Board of Review, Bihar and Orissa (India)

B.& P. Bosanquet & Puller's Reports (126–7 ER) 1796–1804

B.& P.N.R. Bosanquet & Puller's New Reports (127 ER) 1804–7

B.& S. Best & Smith's Queen's Bench Reports (121–2 ER) 1861–5
Beven & Siebel's Ceylon Reports (Sri L.) 1859–75

B.& V. Beling & Vanderstraaten's Reports (Sri L.) 1846–69

B.& W. Burgemeester en Wethouders (Neth.) Municipal Board

Ba.L.R. University of Baltimore Law Review. 1971–

Ba.& B. Ball & Beatty's Irish Chancery Reports (12 RR) 1807–14

Ba.& Be. Ball & Beatty's Irish Chancery Reports (12 RR) 1807–14

Bab.Auc. Babington's Law of Auctions. 1826

Bab.Set-off Babington's Law of Set-off

Bac. Baccalaureus (Lat.) degree of Bachelor

Bac.Ab. Bacon's Abridgement. 7ed. 1832

Bac.Abr. Bacon's Abridgement. 7ed. 1832

Bac.Aph. Bacon (F), Aphorisms

Bac.Aphorisms Bacon (F), Aphorisms

Bac.Ca. Bacon, Case of Treason. 1641

Bac.Chanc. Bacon's Decisions, by Ritchie, Chancery. 1617–21

Bac.Comp.Arb. Bacon, Complete Arbitration

Bac.Dig. Bacon's Georgia Digest. 1942
Bac.Gov. Bacon on Government. 1760
Bac.Law Tr. Bacon, Law Tracts. 1741
Bac.Law Tracts Bacon, Law Tracts. 1741
Bac.Lease Bacon, Leases and Terms of Years. 1798
Bac.Lib.Reg. Bacon, Liber Regis. 1786
Bac.Max. Bacon, Rules and Maxims
Bac.Read.Uses Bacon, Readings on the Statute of Uses. 2ed. 1741
Bac.Rep. Bacon's Decisions, by Ritchie, Chancery. 1617–21
Bac.St.Uses Bacon, Readings on the Statute of Uses. 2ed. 1741
Bac.Tr. Bacon, Law Tracts. 1741
Bac.Uses Bacon, Readings on the Statute of Uses. 2ed. 1741
Bach Bach's Reports (19–21 Montana)
Bacon Bacon, A New Abridgement of the Law. 7ed. 1832
Bacon, Aphorisms
Bacon, Arguments in Law
Bacon, Complete Arbitrator
Bacon, Elements of the Common Law
Bacon, Government
Bacon, Law Tracts
Bacon, Leases and Terms of Years
Bacon, Liber Regis
Bacon, Maxims
Bacon, Readings on the Statute of Uses
Bacon, Abridgement Bacon, A New Abridgement of the Law. 7ed. 1832
Bag.Ch.Pr. Bagley, Practice at Chambers. 1834
Bag.Eng.Const. Bagehot, English Constitution. 8ed. 1904
Bag.& Har. Bagley & Harman's Reports (17–19 California)
Bagl.(Cal.) Bagley's Reports (16 California)
Bagl.& H. Bagley & Harman's Reports (17–19 California)
Bagl.& Har. Bagley & Harman's Reports (17–19 California)
Bah.L.R. Bahamas Law Reports. 1900–6
Bahamas L.R.C. Law Revision Committee, Bahamas
Bahawalpur,Pak. Bahawalpur, Pakistan
Bai. Bailey's Law Reports, South Carolina (17–18 SCL) 1828–32
Bai.Eq. Bailey's Equity Reports, South Carolina (8 SCEq) 1830–1
Bail. Bailey's Law Reports, South Carolina (17–18 SCL) 1828–32
Bail C.C. Lowndes & Maxwell's Bail Court Cases. 1852–4
Bail Cr.Rep. Lowndes & Maxwell's Bail Court Cases. 1852–4
Bail Ct.Cas. Lowndes & Maxwell's Bail Court Cases. 1852–4
Bail Ct.R. Saunders & Cole's Bail Court Reports (82 RR) 1846–8
Bail Ct.Rep. Lowndes & Maxwell's Bail Court Cases. 1852–4
Saunders & Cole's Bail Court Reports (82 RR) 1846–8
Bail.Dig. Bailey's North Carolina Digest. 1937
Bail.Eq. Bailey's Equity Reports, South Carolina (8 SCEq) 1830–1
Bail.Eq.(S.C.) Bailey's Equity Reports, South Carolina (8 SCEq) 1830–1
Bail.L. Bailey's Law Reports, South Carolina (17–18 SCL) 1828–32
Bail.L.(S.C.) Bailey's Law Reports, South Carolina (17–18 SCL) 1828–32
Baild. Baildon's Select Cases in Chancery (Selden Society Pubn. vol. 10) 1364–1471
Bailey Bailey's Equity Reports, South Carolina (8 SCEq) 1830–1
Bailey's Law Reports, South Carolina (17–18 SCL) 1828–32
Bailey Ch. Bailey's Equity Reports, South Carolina (8 SCEq) 1830–1
Bailey Eq. Bailey's Equity Reports, South Carolina (8 SCEq) 1830–1
Bailey Mast.Liab. Bailey, Law of Master's Liability for Injuries to Servants
Bailm. Bailment
Bainb.Mines Bainbridge, Mines and Minerals. 5ed. 1900
Baker Quar. Baker, Law of Quarantine
Bal. Balasingham's Notes of Cases (Sri L.) 1911–14

Balasingham's Reports of Cases (Sri L.) 1904–9

Bal.Ann.Codes Ballinger's Annotated Codes and Statutes (Washington)

Bal.Notes Balasingham's Notes of Cases (Sri L.) 1911–14

Bal.Pak. Baluchistan, Pakistan

Bal.R.D. Baldeva Rame Dave, Privy Council Judgment (India)

Bal.Rep. Balasingham's Reports of Cases (Sri L.) 1904–9

Balas. Balasingham's Notes of Cases (Sri L.) 1911–14
Balasingham's Reports of Cases (Sri L.) 1904–9

Balas.N.C. Balasingham's Notes of Cases (Sri L.) 1911–14

Balas.R.C. Balasingham's Reports of Cases (Sri L.) 1904–9

Balasingham Rep. Balasingham's Reports of Cases (Sri L.) 1904–9

Bald. Baldwin's United States Circuit Court Reports

Bald.Bank. Baldwin, Law of Bankruptcy. 11ed. 1915

Bald.C.C. Baldwin's United States Circuit Court Reports

Bald.Pat.Cas. Baldwin's Patent, Copyright and Trade-Mark Cases (USA) 1930

Bald.U.S.Sup.Ct.Rep. Baldwin's United States Supreme Court Reports

Baldev.P.C. Baldeva Ram Dave, Privy Council Judgment (India)

Baldw. Baldwin's United States Circuit Court Reports

Baldw.Dig. Baldwin's Connecticut Digest

Balf. Balfour, Practicks of the Law of Scotland. 1754

Balf.Pr. Balfour, Practicks of the Law of Scotland. 1754

Ball. Ballard's Somerton Court Rolls

Ball.Ind. Ball's Index to Irish Statutes

Ball.Lim. Ballantine, Statute of Limitations. 1810

Ball & B. Ball & Beatty's Chancery Reports, Ireland (12 RR) 1807–14

Ball & B.(Ir.) Ball & Beatty's Chancery Reports, Ireland (12 RR) 1807–14

Ball & Beatty Ball & Beatty's Chancery Reports, Ireland (12 RR) 1807–14

Balladore Pallieri Balladore Pallieri, Diritto internazionale pubblico (It.) 1937

Ballentine Ballentine's Law Dictionary

Ballinger's Ann.Codes & St. Ballinger's Annotated Codes and Statutes (Washington)

Balt. Baltimore

Balt.C.Rep. Baltimore City Reports

Balt.L.T. Baltimore Law Transcript. 1868–70

Balt.L.Tr. Baltimore Law Transcript. 1868–70

Bamber Report of Mining Cases decided by the Railway and Canal Commission. 1923–4

Bamford B. Bamford, Law of Partnerships and Voluntary Associations in South Africa

Ban.Br. Sir Orlando Bridgman's Common Pleas Reports, ed. by Bannister (124 ER) 1660–7

Ban.L.J. Banaras Law Journal (India) 1965–

Ban.& A. Banning & Arden's Patent Cases (USA) 1874–81

Banaras L.J. Banaras Law Journal (India) 1965–

Banc.Sup. Bancus Superior (Lat.) Upper Bench

Banca,borsa tit.cred. Banca, borsa e titoli di credito (It.) 1934–

Banca Naz.del Lavoro Banca nazionale del lavoro (It.)

Banco di Roma Rev. Banco di Roma, Review of the Economic Conditions in Italy

Bang. Bangladesh

Bang.L.R. Bangala Law Reports (India)

Bank. Bankruptcy
Bankruptcy Court

Bank.C. Banking Code

Bank.Cas. Banking Cases (USA) 1898–1903

Bank.Ct.Rep. American Law Times Bankruptcy Reports
Bankrupt Court Reporter (New York)

Bank Eng.Q.B. Bank of England Quarterly Bulletin. 1960–

Bank.Gaz. Bankruptcy Gazette (USA)

Bank.I. Bankton's Institutes of Scottish Law. 1751–3

Bank.Insol.Rep. Bankruptcy and Insolvency Cases. 1853–5

Bank.Inst. Bankton's Institutes of Scottish Law. 1751–3

Bank.L.J. Banking Law Journal (USA) 1889–

Bank.L.R. Banking Law Reports. 1991–

Bank.Mag. Banker's Magazine (USA)

Bank.Reg. National Bankruptcy Register (USA) 1867–82

Bank.Rep. American Law Times Bankruptcy Reports

Bank.& Ins. Bankruptcy and Insolvency Reports. 1853–5

Bank.& Ins.R. Bankruptcy and Insolvency Reports. 1853–5

Bank.& Insol.Rep. Bankruptcy and Insolvency Reports. 1853–5

Banker's L.J. Banker's Law Journal (USA)

Banking L.J. Banking Law Journal (USA) 1889–

Bankr. Bankruptcy

Bankr.Dev.J. Bankruptcy Developments Journal (USA)

Bankr.Ins.R. Bankruptcy and Insolvency Reports. 1853–5

Bankr.L.Rep. Bankruptcy Law Reporter (CCH) (USA)

Bankr.Reg. National Bankruptcy Register (New York) 1867–82

Bankr.& Ins.R. Bankruptcy and Insolvency Reports. 1853–5

Banks Banks' Reports (1–5 Kansas)

Banks Report Report of the Committee to Examine the Patent System and Patent Law (Cmnd. 4407) 1970

Banks.& Ins. Bankruptcy and Insolvency Reports. 1853–5

Bankt. Bankton's Institutes of the Laws of Scotland, by MacDougall. 1751–3

Bann. Bannister's edition of O. Bridgman's Common Pleas Reports (124 ER) 1660–7

Bann.Br. Bannister's edition of O. Bridgman's Common Pleas Reports (124 ER) 1660–7

Bann.Lim. Banning, Limitation of Actions. 3ed. 1906

Bann.& A. Banning & Arden's Patent Cases (USA) 1874–81

Bann.& A.Pat.Cas. Banning & Arden's Patent Cases (USA) 1874–81

Bann.& Ard. Banning & Arden's Patent Cases (USA) 1874–81

Banz. Bundesanzeiger (Ger.) Federal Reporter. 1949–

Bar. Bar Reports in all the Courts (12–23 Law Times Reports) 1865–71
Barbour's Reports (New York) 1847–77
Barnardiston's Chancery Reports (27 ER) 1740–1
Barnardiston's King's Bench Reports (94 ER) 1726–35
Barrow's Reports (18 Rhode Island)

Bar.Anc.Stat. Barrington, Observations upon the Statutes. 5ed. 1796

Bar Bull.(N.Y.County L.A.) Bar Bulletin, New York County Lawyers' Association. 1943–

Bar.Ch. Barnardiston's Chancery Reports (27 ER) 1740–1

Bar.Chy. Barnardiston's Chancery Reports (27 ER) 1740–1

Bar.Dig. Barclay, Digest of the Law of Scotland. 1894

Bar.Eq. Barton, Suit in Equity

Bar Ex.Ann. Bar Examination Annual. 1893–4

Bar Ex.Guide Bar Examination Guide. 1895–9

Bar Ex.J. Bar Examination Journal. 1871–92

Bar Ex.Jour. Bar Examination Journal. 1871–92

Bar Exam. Bar Examiner (Denver, USA) 1931–

Bar Gaz. Bar Gazette (N.S.W., Aus.) 1961–3
Bar.Mag. Barrington, Magna Charta. 2ed. 1900
Bar.N. Barnes' Notes of Practice, Common Pleas Reports (94 ER) 1732–60
Bar News Bar News – Journal of the New South Wales Bar Association (Aus.) 1985–
Bar.Obs.St. Barrington's Observations upon the Statutes. 5ed. 1796
Bar Re. Bar Reports in all the Courts (12–23 Law Times Reports) 1865–71
Bar Rep. Bar Reports in all the Courts (12–23 Law Times Reports) 1865–71
Bar.& Ad. Barnewall & Adolphus' King's Bench Reports (109–110 ER) 1830–4
Bar.& Al. Barnewall & Alderson's King's Bench Reports (106 ER) 1817–22
Bar.& Arn. Barron & Arnold's Election Cases. 1843–6
Bar.& Au. Barron & Austin's Election Cases. 1842
Bar.& Aust. Barron & Austin's Election Cases. 1842
Bar.& Cr. Barnewall & Cresswell's King's Bench Reports (107–9 ER) 1822–30
Bar & Leg.W. Bar and Legal World. 1903
Barb. Barber's Gold Law Cases (S.Afr.) 1883–1903
Barber's Reports (14–24 Arkansas)
Barbour's Supreme Court Reports (New York) 1847–77
Barb.Abs. Barbour's Abstracts of Chancellor's Decisions (New York)
Barb.App.Dig. Barber's Digest (New York)
Barb.Ark. Barber's Reports (14–24 Arkansas)
Barb.Ch. Barbour's Chancery Reports (New York) 1845–8
Barb.Ch.(N.Y.) Barbour's Chancery Reports (New York) 1845–8
Barb.Ch.Pr. Barbour's Chancery Practice (New York)
Barb.Cr.Law Barbour's Criminal Law
Barb.Cr.P. Barbour's Criminal Practice
Barb.Dig. Barbour's Kentucky Digest
Barb.L.R. Barbados Law Reports
Barb.S.C. Barbour's Supreme Court Reports (New York) 1847–77
Barb.& C.Ky.St. Barbour & Carroll's Kentucky Statutes
Barbe. Barber's Reports (14–24 Arkansas)
Barber Barber's Gold Law Cases (S.Afr.) 1883–1903
Barber's Reports (14–24 Arkansas)
Barc.Dig. Barclay's Missouri Digest
Barc.Dig.Law Sc. Barclay's Digest of the Law of Scotland
Barl.Just. Barlow, Justice of the Peace. 1745
Barn. Barnardiston's Chancery Reports (27 ER) 1740–1
Barnardiston's King's Bench Reports (94 ER) 1726–35
Barnes' Common Pleas Reports (94 ER) 1732–60
Barnfield's Reports (19–20 Rhode Island)
Barn.C. Barnardiston's Chancery Reports (27 ER) 1740–1
Barn.Ch. Barnardiston's Chancery Reports (27 ER) 1740–1
Barn.K.B. Barnardiston's King's Bench Reports (94 ER) 1726–35
Barn.No. Barnes' Notes of Cases, Common Pleas (94 ER) 1732–60
Barn.Pr.M. Barnstaple, Printed Minutes and Proceedings
Barn.Sh. Barnes, Exposition of the Law respecting Sheriffs. 1816
Barn.& Ad. Barnewall & Adolphus' King's Bench Reports (109–110 ER) 1830–4
Barn.& Adol. Barnewall & Adolphus' King's Bench Reports (109–110 ER) 1830–4
Barn.& Ald. Barnewall & Alderson's King's Bench Reports (106 ER) 1817–22
Barn.& C. Barnewall & Cresswell's

King's Bench Reports (107–109 ER) 1822–30

Barn.& Cr. Barnewall & Cresswell's King's Bench Reports (107–109 ER) 1822–30

Barn.& Cress. Barnewall & Cresswell's King's Bench Reports (107–109 ER) 1822–30

Barnard. Barnardiston's King's Bench Reports (94 ER) 1726–35

Barnard.Ch. Barnardiston's Chancery Reports (27 ER) 1740–1

Barnard.Ch.Rep. Barnardiston's Chancery Reports (27 ER) 1740–1

Barnard.K.B. Barnardiston's King's Bench Reports (94 ER) 1726–35

Barnardiston C.C. Barnardiston's Chancery Reports (27 ER) 1740–1

Barnes Barnes' Notes of Cases of Practice in Common Pleas (94 ER) 1732–60

Barnes,N.C. Barnes' Notes of Cases of Practice in Common Pleas (94 ER) 1732–60

Barnes Notes Barnes' Notes of Cases of Practice in Common Pleas (94 ER) 1732–60

Barne's Fed.Code Barne's Federal Code

Barnet Barnet, Central Criminal Courts Reports

Barnf.& S. Barnfield & Stiness' Reports (20 Rhode Island)

Barnw.Dig. Barnwall's Digest of the Year Books

Baroda L.R. Baroda Law Reports (India)

Baron. Barony of Urie Court Records (Scot.) 1604–1747

Barr. Barr's Reports (1–10 Pennsylvania)
The Barrister (Can.) 1894–7
The Barrister (USA) 1974–
Barrows' Reports (18 Rhode Island)

Barr.Ch.Pr. Barroll, Chancery Practice (Maryland)

Barr.M. Barradall, Manuscript Reports (Virginia)

Barr.Obs.St. Barrington's Observations upon the Statutes. 5ed. 1796

Barr.(Pa.) Barr's Reports (1–10 Pennsylvania)

Barr.St. Barrington's Observations upon the Statutes. 5ed. 1796

Barr.& Arn. Barron & Arnold's Election Cases. 1843–6

Barr.& Aus. Barron & Austin's Election Cases. 1842

Barrera Graf J. Barrera Graf, Estudios de Derecho Mercantil (Mexico) 1958

Barring.Obs.St. Barrington's Observations upon the Statutes. 5ed. 1796

Barring.St. Barrington's Observations upon the Statutes. 5ed. 1796

Barrows Barrows' Reports (18 Rhode Island)

Barrows(R.I.) Barrows' Reports (18 Rhode Island)

Barry Ch.Pr. Barry, Statutory Jurisdiction of Chancery. 1861

Barry Conv. Barry, Practice of Conveyancing. 1865

Bart. Baronet
Bartholomew

Bart.Conv. Barton, Science of Conveyancing. 2ed. 1810–22

Bart.El.Cas. Bartlett, Congressional Election Cases (USA) 1834–65

Bart.Eq. Barton, Suit in Equity

Bart.L.Pr. Barton, Law Practice

Bart.Mines Bartlett, Law of Mining. 1850

Bart.Prec.Conv. Barton, Modern Precedents in Conveyancing. 3ed. 1826

Bartholoman Bartholoman's Reports at the Yorkshire Lent Assize, March 9, 1811

Bat.Dig. Battle's North Carolina Digest

Bat.Sp.Perf. Batten, Specific Performance on Contracts. 1849

Bat.Stat. Battle's Revised Statutes of North Carolina. 1873

Bate.Auct. Bateman, Law of Auctions. 11ed. 1953

Bate.Exc. Bateman, General Laws of Excise. 2ed. 1840

Bates Bates' Delaware Chancery Reports

Bates Dig. Bates' Digest (Ohio)
Bates Part. Bates, Law of Partnership
Bateson Leicester Records (Municipal Courts) 1103–1603
Batt. Batty's King's Bench Reports (Ire.) 1825–46
Batts' Ann.St. Batts' Annotated Revised Civil Statutes (Texas)
Batts' Rev.St. Batts' Annotated Revised Civil Statutes (Texas)
Batty(Ire.) Batty's King's Bench Reports (Ire.) 1825–46
Baty Baty, The Canons of International Law. 1930
Baumgardt, Bentham D. Baumgardt, Bentham and the Ethics of Today. 1952
Bax. Baxter's Reports (60–68 Tennessee)
Baxt.(Tenn.) Baxter's Reports (60–68 Tennessee)
Baxter Baxter's Reports (60–68 Tennessee)
Bay Bay's Reports (1–3, 5–8 Missouri) Bay's South Carolina Law Reports (1–2 SCL) 1783–1804
Bay.ObLGZ Sammlung von Entscheidungen des Bayerischen Obersten Landesgerichts in Zivilsachen (Ger.)
Bayley Bills Bayley, Bills of Exchange. 6ed. 1849
Baylles Sur. Baylles, Sureties and Guarantors
Baylor L.Rev. Baylor Law Review (USA) 1948–
Bcy. Bankruptcy
Bd. Band (Ger.) volume
Board
Bd.Cont.App.Dec. Board of Contract Appeals Decisions (USA)
BdG Bundesgesetz (Ger.) Federal Act or Statute
BdGes Bundesgesetz (Ger.) Federal Act or Statute
Bde Bande (Ger.) volumes
Bea. Beavan's Reports of Cases in the Rolls Court (48–55 ER) 1838–66
Bea.C.E. Beames' Costs in Equity. 2ed. 1840
Bea.Costs Beames' Costs in Equity. 2ed. 1840
Bea.Eq.Pl. Beames' Equity Pleading. 1818
Bea.Ne Ex. Beames, Writ of Ne Exeat Regno. 2ed. 1824
Bea.Ord. Beames, Orders in Chancery, 1600–1815. 1815
Bea.Pl.Eq. Beames, Pleas in Equity. 1818
Beach Contrib.Neg. Beach, Contributory Negligence
Beach Eq.Prac. Beach, Modern Practice in Equity
Beach Mod.Eq.Jur. Beach, Commentaries on Modern Equity Jurisprudence
Beach Priv.Corp. Beach, Private Corporations
Beach Pub.Corp. Beach, Public Corporations
Beach Rec. Beach, Law of Receivers
Bear.Tithes Bearblock, Treatise upon Tithes. 6ed. 1832
Beas. Beasley's New Jersey Equity Reports (12–13 NJEq)
Beasl. Beasley's New Jersey Equity Reports (12–13 NJEq)
Beat. Beatty's Irish Chancery Reports. 1813–30
Beatt. Beatty's Irish Chancery Reports. 1813–30
Beatty Beatty's Irish Chancery Reports. 1813–30
Beatty Ir.Ch. Beatty's Irish Chancery Reports. 1813–30
Beau.Bills Beaumont, Bills of Sale. 1855
Beau.Ins. Beaumont, Life and Fire Insurance. 2ed. 1846
Beav. Beavan's Rolls Court Reports (48–55 ER) 1838–66
Beav.O.C. Beavan, Ordines Cancellariae. 2ed. 1853
Beav.R.& C. Beavan & Walford's Railway and Canal Parliamentary Cases. 1846
Beav.R.& C.Cas. Beavan & Walford's Railway and Canal Parliamentary Cases. 1846

Beav.& W. Beavan & Walford's Railway and Canal Parliamentary Cases. 1846

Beav.& W.Ry.Cas. Beavan & Walford's Railway and Canal Parliamentary Cases. 1846

Beav.& Wal. Beavan & Walford's Railway and Canal Parliamentary Cases. 1846

Beav.& Wal.Ry.Cas. Beavan & Walford's Railway and Canal Parliamentary Cases. 1846

Beavan Ch. Beavan's Rolls Court Reports (48–55 ER) 1836–66

Beaver Beaver County Legal Journal (Pennsylvania)

Beaver Co.L.J. Beaver County Legal Journal (Pennsylvania)

Beaw. Beawes, Lex Mercatoria. 6ed. 1813

Beaw.Lex Mer. Beawes, Lex Mercatoria. 6ed. 1813

Beaw.Lex Merc. Beawes, Lex Mercatoria. 6ed. 1813

Beawes Lex Merc. Beawes, Lex Mercatoria. 6ed. 1813

Bec.Cr. Beccaria, Crimes and Punishment

Beck Beck's Colorado Reports (12–16 Colorado, 1 Colorado Appeals)
Beck's Theory and Principles of Pleading in Civil Actions

Beck (Colo.) Beck's Colorado Reports (12–16 Colorado, 1 Colorado Appeals)

Beck Med.Jur. Beck, Medical Jurisprudence. 7ed. 1842

Bedell Bedell's New York Reports (163–191 NY)

Bee Bee's United States District Court Reports

Bee Adm. Bee's Admiralty (Appendix to Bee's U.S. District Court Reports)

Bee.Anal. Beebee, Analysis of Common Law Practice

Bee C.C.R. Bee's Crown Cases Reserved

Beebe Cit. Beebe's Ohio Citations

bef. before

Begg Code Begg, Conveyancing Code (Scot.)

Begg L.Ag. Begg, Law Agents (Scot.)

Behari Revenue Reports of Upper Provinces (India)

Bel. Beling & Vanderstraaten's Reports (Sri L.) 1846–69
Belize
Bellasis' Civil Cases, Bombay (India) 1840–8
Bellasis' Criminal Cases, Bombay (India) 1827–46
Bellewe's King's Bench Reports (72 ER) 1378–1400
Bellinger's Oregon Reports (4–8 Or)

Bel.Cas.t.H.VIII Bellewe's Cases tempore Henry VIII, Brooke s New Cases (73 ER) 1515–58

Bel.Cas.t.R.II Bellewe's Cases tempore Richard II (72 ER) 1378–1400

Bel.Prob. Belknap's Probate Law of California

Belg. Belgian
Belgium

Belg.Jud. Belgique judiciaire (Belg.) 1842–

Beling Beling & Vanderstraaten's Reports (Sri L.) 1846–69

Beling & Van. Beling & Vanderstraaten's Reports (Sri L.) 1846–69

Bell Bell's Crown Cases Reserved (169 ER) 1858–60
Bell's House of Lords Appeal Cases (Scot.) 1842–50
Bell's Reports, Calcutta High Court (India) 1858–1906
Bell's Session Cases (Scot.) 1790–5
Bellasis' Civil Cases, Bombay (India) 1840–8
Bellasis' Criminal Cases, Bombay (India) 1827–46
Bellewe's King's Bench Reports (72 ER) 1378–1400
Bellinger's Oregon Reports (4–8 Or)
Brooke's New Cases, by Bellewe (73 ER) 1515–58

Bell Ap.Ca. Bell's House of Lords Appeal Cases (Scot.) 1842–50

Bell App. Bell's House of Lords Appeal

Cases (Scot.) 1842–50

Bell App.Cas. Bell's House of Lords Appeal Cases (Scot.) 1842–50

Bell App.(Sc.) Bell's House of Lords Appeal Cases (Scot.) 1842–50

Bell Arb. Bell, Law of Arbitration in Scotland

Bell C. Bell (C.) Court of Session Cases (Scot.) 1790–5

Bell C.C. Bell's Crown Cases Reserved (169 ER) 1858–60
Bell's Reports, Calcutta High Court (India) 1858–1906
Bellasis' Civil Cases, Bombay (India) 1840–8
Bellasis' Criminal Cases, Bombay (India) 1827–46

Bell C.H.C. Bell's Reports, Calcutta High Court (India) 1858–1906

Bell C.T. Bell, Completing Titles (Scot.)

Bell Cas. Bell's Session Cases (Scot.) 1790–5

Bell.Cas.t.H.VIII Bellewe's Cases tempore Henry VIII, Brooke's New Cases (73 ER) 1515–58

Bell.Cas.t.Hen.VIII Bellewe's Cases tempore Henry VIII, Brooke's New Cases (73 ER) 1515–58

Bell.Cas.t.R.II Bellewe's Cases tempore Richard II (72 ER) 1378–1400

Bell.Cas.t.Rich.II Bellewe's Cases tempore Richard II (72 ER) 1378–1400

Bell Comm. Bell's Commentaries on the Law of Scotland

Bell Convey. Bell, Lecture on Conveyancing (Scot.)

Bell Cr.C. Bell's Crown Cases Reserved (169 ER) 1858–60
Bellasis' Criminal Cases, Bombay (India) 1827–46

Bell Cr.Ca. Bell's Crown Cases Reserved (169 ER) 1858–60
Bellasis' Criminal Cases, Bombay (India) 1827–46

Bell Cr.Cas. Bell's Crown Cases Reserved (169 ER) 1858–60
Bellasis' Criminal Cases, Bombay (India) 1827–46

Bell Ct.of Sess. Bell's Session Cases (Scot.) 1790–5

Bell Ct.of Sess.fol. R. Bell's Decisions, Session Cases (Scot.) 1794–5

Bell Deeds Bell, System of the Forms of Deeds (Scot.)

Bell.Del. Beller's Delineation of Universal Law. 3ed. 1754

Bell Dict. Bell, Dictionary and Digest of the Laws of Scotland

Bell Dict.Dec. Bell, Dictionary of Decisions, Court of Session (Scot.) 1808–33

Bell Elec. Bell, Election Law of Scotland

Bell Fol. R. Bell's Decisions, Session Cases (Scot.) 1794–5

Bell folio R. Bell's Decisions, Session Cases (Scot.) 1794–5

Bell H.C. Bell's Reports, Calcutta High Court (India) 1858–1906

Bell H.L. Bell's House of Lords Appeal Cases (Scot.) 1842–50

Bell H.L.Sc. Bell's House of Lords Appeal Cases (Scot.) 1842–50

Bell H.W. Bell, Property as arising from the Relation of Husband and Wife. 1849

Bell(In.) Bell's Reports, High Court of Calcutta (India) 1858–1906

Bell Med.L.J. Bell's Medico Legal Journal

Bell Oct.R. Bell's Decisions (Octavo Reports), Court of Session (Scot.) 1790–2

Bell.(Or.) Bellinger's Oregon Reports (4–8 Or)

Bell P.C. Bell's Cases in Parliament (House of Lords Appeals) (Scot.) 1842–50

Bell Prin. Bell, Principles of the Law of Scotland. 10ed. 1899

Bell Put.Mar. Bell, Putative Marriage Cases (Scot.)

Bell Sale Bell, Sale of Food and Drugs

Bell Sc.App. Bell's House of Lords Appeal Cases (Scot.) 1842–50

Bell Sc.App.Cas. Bell's House of Lords Appeal Cases (Scot.) 1842–50

Bell Sc.Cas. Bell's Session Cases (Scot.) 1790–5
Bell Sc.Dig. Bell, Scottish Digest
Bell Ses.Cas. Bell's Session Cases (Scot.) 1790–5
Bell Sty. Bell, System of the Forms of Deeds (Styles) (Scot.)
Bell T.D. Bell, Testing of Deeds (Scot.)
Bellas. Bellasis' Civil Cases, Bombay (India) 1840–8
Bellasis' Criminal Cases, Bombay (India) 1827–46
Bellasis Bellasis' Civil Cases, Bombay (India) 1840–8
Bellasis' Criminal Cases, Bombay (India) 1827–46
Bellewe Bellewe's King's Bench Reports tempore Richard II (72 ER) 1378–1400
Bellewe t.H.VIII Bellewe's Cases tempore Henry VIII, Brooke's New Cases (73 ER) 1515–58
Bellewe's Ca.temp.Hen.VIII Bellewe's Cases tempore Henry VIII, Brooke's New Cases (73 ER) 1515–58
Bellewe's Ca.temp.R.II Bellewe's King's Bench Reports tempore Richard II (72 ER) 1378–1400
Bellinger Bellinger's Oregon Reports (4–8 Or)
Bellingh.Tr. Report of Bellingham's Trial
Bell's App. Bell's House of Lords Appeal Cases (Scot.) 1842–50
Bell's Comm. Bell's Commentaries on the Laws of Scotland. 7ed. 1870
Bell's Dict. Bell's Dictionary of Decisions, Court of Session (Scot.) 1808–33
Belt Bro. Belt's edition of Browne's Chancery Cases (28–9 ER) 1778–94
Belt Sup. Belt's Supplement to Vesey Senior's Chancery Reports (28 ER) 1746–56
Belt Sup.Ves. Belt's Supplement to Vesey Senior's Chancery Reports (28 ER) 1746–56
Belt Supp. Belt's Supplement to Vesey Senior's Chancery Reports (28 ER) 1746–56
Belt Ves.Sen. Belt's Supplement to Vesey Senior's Chancery Reports (28 ER) 1746–56
Belt's Supp. Belt's Supplement to Vesey Senior's Chancery Reports (28 ER) 1746–56
Ben. Benedict's United States District Court Reports
Bengal Law Reports (India) 1868–75
Benloe's King's Bench Reports (73 ER) 1531–1628
Ben.Adm. Benedict's American Admiralty Practice
Ben.Adm.Prac. Benedict's American Admiralty Practice
Ben.F.B. Bengal Full Bench Rulings (India) 1863–8
Ben.F.I.Cas. Bennett, Fire Insurance Cases
Ben.File Benefits File
Ben.in Keil. Benloe or Bendloe in Keilway's Reports, King's Bench (73 ER) 1531–1628
Ben Monroe Ben Monroe's Kentucky Reports (40–57 Ky) 1840–57
Ben.Ord. Benevolent Orders
Ben.& D. Benloe & Dalison's Common Pleas Reports (123 ER) 1486–1580
Ben.& Dal. Benloe & Dalison's Common Pleas Reports (123 ER) 1486–1580
Ben.& H.L.C. Bennett & Heard, Leading Criminal Cases
Ben.& S.Dig. Benjamin & Slidell's Louisiana Digest
Bench & B. Bench & Bar (Chicago) 1869–74
Bench & Bar (Detroit) 1921–6
Bench & Bar (Missouri) 1935–42
Bench & Bar (Montreal) 1931–45
Bench & Bar (New York) 1905–20
Bendl. Benloe's (or Bendloe's) King's Bench Reports (73 ER) 1531–1628
Bendloe Benloe's (or Bendloe's) King's Bench Reports (73 ER) 1531–1628
Bened. Benedict's United States District Court Reports
Benedict Benedict's United States

District Court Reports
benef. beneficiary
Beng. Bengal
Bengal Law Reports (India) 1868–75
Beng.Ind. Bengal, India
Beng.L.R. Bengal Law Reports (India) 1868–75
Beng.L.R.App.Cas. Bengal Law Reports,Appeal Cases (India)
Beng.L.R.P.C. Bengal Law Reports, Privy Council Cases (India)
Beng.L.R.Supp. Bengal Law Reports, Supplement (India)
Beng.S.D.A. Bengal Sudder Dewanny Adawlut Cases (India) 1845–62
Beng.Zillah Decisions of the Zillah Courts, Lower Provinces (India) 1846–61
Benj. Benjamin, Sale of Goods
Benjamin's New York Annotated Cases
Benj.Chalm.Bills & N. Benjamin's Chalmer's Bills and Notes
Benj.Sa. Benjamin, Sale of Goods
Benj.Sales Benjamin, Sale of Goods
Benl. Benloe's (or Bendloe's) King's Bench Reports (73 ER) 1531–1628
Benloe & Dalison's Common Pleas Reports (123 ER) 1486–1580
Benl.in Ashe Benloe at the end of Ashe's Tables
Benl.in Keil. Benloe or Bendloe in Keilway's Reports (73 ER) 1531–1628
Benl.K.B. Benloe's King's Bench Reports (73 ER) 1531–1628
Benl.New Benloe's King's Bench Reports (73 ER) 1531–1628
Benl.Old Benloe & Dalison's Common Pleas Reports (123 ER) 1486–1580
Benl.& D. Benloe & Dalison's Common Pleas Reports (123 ER) 1486–1589
Benl.& Dal. Benloe & Dalison's Common Pleas Reports (123 ER) 1486–1580
Benloe Benloe or New Benloe's Reports (73 ER) 1531–1628
Benn. Bennett's Reports (1 California)
Bennett's Reports (1 Dakota)
Bennett's Reports (16–21 Missouri)
Benn.Cal. Bennettt's Reports (1 California)
Benn.(Dak.) Bennett's Reports (1 Dakota)
Benn.F.I.Cas. Bennett's Fire Insurance Cases
Benn.(Mo.) Bennett's Missouri Cases (16–21 Mo)
Benn.& H.Cr.Cas. Bennett & Heard's Leading Criminal Cases
Benn.& H.Dig. Bennett & Heard's Massachusetts Digest
Benn & Peters, Principles S.I. Benn & R.S. Peters, Social Principles of the Democratic State. 1959
Benne Benne's Reports, 7 Modern Reports (87 ER) 1702–45
Bennett Bennett's Reports (1 California)
Bennett's Reports (1 Dakota)
Bennett's Reports (16–21 Missouri)
Benson Report Report of the Royal Commission on Legal Services (Cmnd. 7648) 1979
Bent. Bentley's Irish Chancery Reports
Bent.Cod. Bentham's Codification
Bent.Const.Code Bentham's Constitutional Code for All Nations. 1830
Bent.Ev. Bentham's Judicial Evidence. 1825
Bent.Jud.Ev. Bentham's Judicial Evidence. 1825
Bent.Mor.Leg. Bentham's Principles of Morals and Legislation. 3ed. 1876
Bent.Pack.Jur. Bentham, Act of Packing as applied to Special Juries. 1821
Bent.Pun. Bentham's Rationale of Punishment. 1830
Bent.The.Leg. Bentham's Theory of Legislation. 8ed. 1894
Benth.Ev. Bentham's Rationale of Judicial Evidence. 1827
Benth.Jud.Ev. Bentham's Rationale of Judicial Evidence. 1827
Bentham, Limits Bentham, Limits of Jurisprudence. 1945

Bentham, Theory Bentham, Theory of Legislation. 8ed. 1894

Bentl.Atty.-Gen. Bentley's Reports, vols. 13–19 Attorneys-General's Opinions

Beor. Queensland Law Reports (Aus.) 1876–78

bep. bepaling (Neth.) provision (in statute or contract)

beqd. bequeathed

beqt. bequest

Ber. Berichtigung (Ger.) correction
Berton's Reports, New Brunswick (2 New Brunswick Reports) 1835 39

Berar Berar Law Journal (India)

Berk Co.L.J. Berk's County Law Journal (Pennsylvania)

Berkeley Women's L.J. Berkeley Women's Law Journal (USA)

Berle–Means, Modern Corporation A.A. Berle & G. Means, The Modern Corporation and Private Property. 1932

Bermuda L.R.C. Law Reform Committee, Bermuda

Bern. Bernard's Church Cases (Ire.) 1870–75

Bern.Ch.Cas. Bernard's Church Cases (Ire.) 1870–75

Bernstein, Independent Commission M.H. Bernstein, Regulating Business by Independent Commission. 1955

Berry Berry's Reports (1–28 Missouri Appeals)

Bert. Berton's New Brunswick Reports (Can.) 1835–9

besch. beschikking (Neth.) decree

besl. besluit (Neth.) decree or resolution

Best Beg.& Rep. Best on the Right to Begin and Reply. 1837

Best Ev. Best on Evidence. 12ed. 1922

Best Jur.Tr. Best on Trial by Jury. 1837

Best Pres. Best on Presumptions of Law and Fact. 1844

Best Presumptions Best on Presumptions of Law and Fact. 1844

Best & S. Best & Smith's Queen's Bench Reports (121–2 ER) 1861–65

Best & Sm. Best & Smith's Queen's Bench Reports (121–2 ER) 1861–65

BetrRG Betriebsrategesetz (Ger.) Law on works' councils

BetrVG Betriebsverfassungsgesetz (Ger.) Law on the representation of workers and works' councils

Betts'Adm.Pr. Betts' Admiralty Practice

Betts'Dec. Blatchford & Howland's United States District Court Reports
Olcott's United States District Court Reports

Bev. Beven's Reports (Sri L.)

Bev.Emp.L. Bevin on Employer's Liability for Negligence of Servants. 1881

Bev.Pat. Bevill's Patent Cases

Bev.& M. Beven & Mill's Reports (Sri L.) 1820–67

Bev.& Sieb. Beven & Siebel's Reports (Sri L.) 1859–75

Beven Beven, Principles of Law. 4ed. 1928
Beven's Ceylon Reports (Sri L.)

Beveridge Report Report on Social Insurance (Cmd. 6404) 1942–3

Bew.& N.Pr. Bewley & Naish on Common Law Procedure

BezG. Bezirksgericht (Ger.) District Court

Bez.Ger. Bezirksgericht (Ger.) District Court

Bgt. Bought

Bhd. Brotherhood

Bhop. All India Reporter, Bhopal. 1951–6

Bibb Bibb's Kentucky Reports (4–7 Kentucky) 1808–17

Bibb(Ky.) Bibb's Kentucky Reports (4–7 Kentucky) 1808–17

Bick. Bicknell & Hawley's Reports (10–20 Nevada)

Bick.(In.) Bicknell's Reports (India)

Bick.& H. Bicknell & Hawley's Reports (10–20 Nevada)

Bick.& Hawl. Bicknell & Hawley's Reports (10–20 Nevada)

Bid. Bidder's Court of Referees Reports
Bidder's Locus Standi Reports. 1920–36

Bid.Ins. Biddle on Insurance

Bid.War.Sale Chat. Biddle on Warranties in Sale of Chattels
Bidd. Bidder's Locus Standi Reports. 1920–36
Big. Bignell's Reports (Bengal, India) 1830–31
Big.Cas. Bigelow's Cases tempore William I to Richard I
Big.Cas.B.& N. Bigelow's Cases on Bills and Notes
Big.Cas.Torts Bigelow's Leading Cases in Torts. 1889
Big.Enc.Proc. Bigelow's English Procedure
Big.Eq. Bigelow on Equity
Big.Est. Bigelow on Estoppel
Big.Fr. Bigelow on Frauds
Big.Jarm.Wills Bigelow's edition of Jarman on Wills
Big.L.I.Cas. Bigelow's Life and Accident Insurance Cases
Big.Lead.Cas. Bigelow's Leading Cases in Bills and Notes (or Torts, or Wills)
Big.Ov.Cas. Bigelow's Overruled Cases
Big.Plac. Bigelow's Placita Anglo-Normanica. 1066–1195
Big.Proc. Bigelow's English Procedure
Big.Torts Bigelow on Torts. 1889
Bign. Bignell's Reports (Bengal, India) 1830–1
Bih.Ind. Bihar, India
Bih.L.J.Rep. Bihar Law Journal Reports (India) 1953–
Bih.Rep. Bihar Reports (India)
bijl. bijlage (Neth.) annex
Bijl.Hand.I (II) Bijlagen bij het Verslag der Handelingen van de Eerste (Tweede) Kamer de Staten-Generaal (Neth.) Annexes to the Report of the Proceedings of the First (Second) Chamber of the States-General
Bil.Aw. Billing, Law of Awards and Arbitration. 1845
Bil.Pews Billing, Law relating to Pews. 1845
Bilas. All India Reporter, Bilaspur. 1952–5
Bilb.Ord. Ordinances of Bilboa
Bill of Rights J. Bill of Rights Journal (USA) 1968–
Billot Extrad. Billot, Traité de l'Extradition
Bi-Mo.L.Rev. Bi–Monthly Law Review, University of Detroit
Bin. Binney's Pennsylvania Reports (USA) 1799–1814
Bin.Dig. Binmore's Digest, Michigan
Bing. Bingham's Common Pleas Reports (130–1 ER) 1822–34
Bing.Act.& Def. Bingham's Actions and Defences in Real Property
Bing.Ex. Bingham, Judgments and Executions. 1815
Bing.Inf. Bingham, Infancy and Coveture. 1826
Bing.Judg. Bingham, Judgments and Executions. 1815
Bing.L.& T. Bingham, Landlord and Tenant. 1820
Bing.N.C. Bingham, New Cases, English Common Pleas (131–3 ER) 1834–40
Bing.N.Cas. Bingham, New Cases, English Common Pleas (131–3 ER) 1834–40
Bing.R.P. Bingham on the Law of Real Property
Binm.Ind. Binmore's Index–Digest of Michigan Reports
Binn. Binney's Pennsylvania Reports. 1799–1814
Binn Jus. Binn's Pennsylvania Justice (USA)
Binn.(Pa.) Binney's Pennsylvania Reports. 1799–1814
Biog. Biographical Biography
Bird Conv. Bird, New Pocket Conveyancer. 5ed. 1830
Bird L.& T. Bird, Laws respecting Landlords, Tenants and Lodgers. 11ed. 1833
Bird Sol.Pr. Bird, Solution of Precedents of Settlements. 1800
Bird Supp. Bird's Supplement to Barton's Conveyancing. 2ed. 1817

Birds.St. Birdseye's Statutes (New York)
Birdw. Birdwood's Printed Judgments (India)
Biret Vocab. Biret, Vocabulaire des Cinq Codes, ou definitions simplifées des termes de droit et de jurisprudence exprimé dans ces codes. 1862
Birk.J. Birkenhead's Judgments, House of Lords. 1919–22
Birmingham I.J.A. Institute of Judicial Administration, Birmingham
Bis. Bissell's United States Circuit Court Reports
Bish.Burr. Bishop's edition of Burrill on Assignments
Bish.Con. Bishop on Contracts
Bish.Cont. Bishop on Contracts
Bish.Cr.Law Bishop on Criminal Law
Bish.Cr.Proc. Bishop on Criminal Procedure
Bish.First Bk. Bishop, First Book of the Law
Bish.Ins. Bishop on Insolvent Debtors
Bish.Mar.Div.& Sep. Bishop on Marriage, Divorce and Separation
Bish.Mar.Wom. Bishop on Married Women
Bish.Mar.& Div. Bishop on Marriage and Divorce
Bish.New Cr.Law Bishop's New Criminal Law
Bish.New Cr.Proc. Bishop's New Criminal Procedure
Bish.Noll.Pros. Bishop's Law of Nolle Prosequi
Bish.Non-Cont.Law Bishop on Non-Contract Law, Rights and Torts
Bish.St.Crimes Bishop on Statutory Crimes
Bish.Stat.Cr. Bishop on Statutory Crimes
Bish.Wr.L. Bishop on Written Law
Bishop Dig. Bishop's Digest, Montana
Bisp.Eq. Bispham's Principles of Equity
Bisph.Eq. Bispham's Principles of Equity
Biss. Bissell's United States Circuit Court Reports
Biss.Est. Bisset's Estates for Life. 1842
Biss.Part. Bisset's Partnership and Joint Stock Companies. 1847
Biss.Stat. Bissell's Minnesota Statutes
Biss.& Sm. Bissett & Smith's Digest (S.Afr.)
Bissett Est. Bissett on Estates for Life. 1842
Bit.& Wise Bittleston and Wise's New Magistrates' Cases
Bitt. Bittleston's Reports in Chambers, Queen's Bench Division. 1875–6, 1883–4
Bitt.Ch. Bittleston's Reports in Chambers, Queen's Bench Division. 1875–6, 1883–4
Bitt.Ch.Cas. Bittleston's Reports in Chambers, Queen's Bench Division. 1875–6, 1883–4
Bitt.Cha.Cas. Bittleston's Reports in Chambers, Queen's Bench Division. 1875–6, 1883–4
Bitt.Chamb.Rep. Bittleston's Reports in Chambers, Queen's Bench Division. 1875–6, 1883–4
Bitt.P.C. Bittleston's Practice Cases under Judicature Act. 1844–8
Bitt.Pr.Cas. Bittleston's Practice Cases under Judicature Act. 1844–8
Bitt.Pr.Case Bittleston's Practice Cases under Judicature Act. 1844–8
Bitt.Prac.Case Bittleston's Practice Cases under Judicature Act. 1844–8
Bitt.Rep.in Ch. Bittleston's Reports in Chambers, Queen's Bench Division. 1875–6, 1883–4
Bitt.W.& P. Bittleston, Wise & Parnell's New Magistrates' Cases. 1844–50
Bittner Bittner, Die Lehre von völkerrechtlichen Urkunden. 1924
Bjorkman Bjorkman, Nordische Personennamen in England in alt– und frühmittelenglischer Zeit
Bk. Black, United States Supreme Court Reports (66–67 US) 1861–2
Book
Bk.Aw. Book of Awards (made under the Industrial Conciliation and Arbitration Act, New Zealand) 1984–
Bk.Judg. Book of Judgments by

Townshend
Bk.L.J. Banking Law Journal (USA) 1889–
Bkg. Banking
bkrupt. bankrupt
bks. books
Bky. Bankruptcy
Bl. Black's United States Supreme Court Reports (66–7 US) 1861–2
Blackford's Indiana Reports. 1817–47
Blackstone's Commentaries on the Laws of England
Blatchford's United States Circuit Court Reports
Blount's Law Dictionary
Henry Blackstone's Common Pleas Reports (126 ER) 1788–96
William Blackstone's King's Bench Reports (96 ER) 1746–80
Bl.B.Adm. Twiss, Black Book of the Admiralty
Bl.C.C. Blatchford's United States Circuit Court Reports
Bl.Chy.Pr. Blake, Chancery Practice
Bl.Com. Blackstone's Commentaries on the Laws of England
Bl.Comm. Blackstone's Commentaries on the Laws of England
Bl.D. Blount, Law Dictionary
Bl.D.& O. Blackham, Dundas & Osborne's Irish Nisi Prius Reports. 1846–8
Bl.D.& Osb. Blackham, Dundas & Osborne's Irish Nisi Prius Reports. 1846–8
Bl.Dict. Black's Law Dictionary
Bl.Emp.L. Black, Employer's Liability
Bl.f.Zurch.Rspr. Blätter für Zurcherische Rechtsprechung
Bl.H. Henry Blackstone's Common Pleas Reports (126 ER) 1788–96
Bl.Judgm. Black on Judgments
Bl.L.D. Black's Law Dictionary
Blount's Law Dictionary
Bl.L.J. Black Law Journal (USA) 1971–
Bl.L.T. Blackstone's Law Tracts
Bl.Law Tracts Blackstone's Law Tracts
Bl.N.S. Bligh, House of Lords Reports, New Series (4–6 ER) 1827–37
Bl.Pr.Cas. Blatchford's Prize Cases (USA)
Bl.Prize Blatchford's Prize Cases
Bl.R. Sir William Blackstone's King's Bench Reports (96 ER) 1746–80
Bl.W. Sir William Blackstone's King's Bench Reports (96 ER) 1746–80
Bl.Zu.R. Blätter für Zurcherische Rechtsprechung
Bl.& H. Blake & Hedges Reports (2–3 Montana)
Blatchford & Howland's United States District Court Reports
Bl.& How. Blatchford & Howland's United States District Court Reports
Bl.& W.Mines Blanchard & Weeks' Leading Cases on Mines
Bla. Black's U.S. Supreme Court Reports (66–7 US) 1861–2
Blackstone's King's Bench Reports (96 ER) 1746–80
Bla.Ch. Bland's Maryland Chancery Reports
Bla.Com. Blackstone's Commentaries on the Laws of England
Bla.Comm. Blackstone's Commentaries on the Laws of England
Bla.H. Henry Blackstone's Common Pleas Reports (126 ER) 1788–96
Bla.Life Ass. Blayney, Life Assurance. 1837
Bla.W. Sir William Blackstone's King's Bench Reports (96 ER) 1746–80
Black Black's Reports (30–53 Indiana)
Black's Supreme Court Reports (66–7 US) 1861–2
Blackerby's Magistrates' Reports. 1327–1716
Blackford's Indiana Reports. 1817–47
H. Blackstone's Common Pleas Reports (126 ER) 1788–96
Sir W. Blackstone's King's Bench Reports (96 ER) 1746–80
Black.Anal. Blackstone's Analysis of the Laws of England
Black.Com. Blackstone's Commentaries on the Laws of England

Black.Cond. Blackwell's Condensed Illinois Reports
Black.Cond.Rep. Blackwell's Condensed Illinois Reports
Black Const.Law Black on Constitutional Law
Black Const.Prohib. Black's Constitutional Prohibitions
Black D.& O. Blackham, Dundas & Osborne's Irish Nisi Prius Reports. 1846–8
Black Dict. Black's Law Dictionary
Black.H. Henry Blackstone's Common Pleas Reports (126 ER) 1788–96
Black Interp.Laws Black on the Construction and Interpretation of Laws
Black Intox.Liq. Black on the Laws Regulating the Manufacture and Sale of Intoxicating Liquors
Black Judg. Black on Judgments
Black Judgm. Black on Judgments
Black.Jus. Blackerby's Justices' Cases (Magistrates' Reports) 1327–1716
Black L.J. Black Law Journal (USA) 1971–
Black Law Dict. Black's Law Dictionary
Black.Mag.Ch. Blackstone on Magna Charta
Black R. Black's United States Supreme Court Reports (66–7 US) 1861–2
W. Blackstone's King's Bench Reports (96 ER) 1746–80
Black.Sal. Blackburn on Sale. 3ed. 1910
Black Ship.Ca. Black's Decisions in Shipping Cases
Black St.Const. Black on Construction and Interpretation of Laws
Black.Tax Tit. Blackwell's Tax Titles
Black.W. Sir William Blackstone's King's Bench Reports (96 ER) 1746–80
Blackb. Blackburn on Sales. 3ed. 1910
Blackb.Sales Blackburn on Sales. 3ed. 1910
Blackf. Blackford's Indiana Reports. 1817–47
Blackf.(Ind.) Blackford's Indiana Reports. 1817–47
Black's Law Dict. Black's Law Dictionary
Blackst. H. Blackstone's Common Pleas Reports (126 ER) 1788–96
Sir William Blackstone's King's Bench Reports (96 ER) 1746–80
Blackst.R. Sir William Blackstone's King's Bench Reports (96 ER) 1746–80
Blackstone's Commen. Blackstone's Commentaries on the Laws of England
Blackw. Blackwood's Magazine
Blackw.Cond. Blackwell's Condensed Reports (Illinois)
Blackw.Sc.Atc. Blackwell's Scotch Acts
Blackw.Tax Titles Blackwell's Tax Titles
Blair Blair, Manual for Scotch Justices of the Peace
Blair Co. Blair County Law Reports, Pennsylvania
Blair Co.L.R. Blair County Law Reports, Pennsylvania
Blair Co.L.R.(Pa.) Blair County Law Reports, Pennsylvania
Blake Blake's Reports (1–3 Montana)
Blake Ch.Pa. Blake's Chancery Practice, New York
Blake & H. Blake & Hedges' Reports (2–3 Montana)
Blan.Lim. Blanshard on Statutes of Limitations. 1826
Blan.& W.Lead.Cas. Blanchard & Weeks' Leading Cases on Mines
Blanc.& W.L.C. Blanchard & Weeks' Leading Cases on Mines
Bland Bland's Maryland Chancery Reports. 1811–32
Bland Ch.(Md.) Bland's Maryland Chancery Reports. 1811–32
Bland's Ch. Bland's Maryland Chancery Reports. 1811–32
Blansh.Lim. Blanshard on Statutes of Limitations. 1826
Blash.Juries Blashfield, Instructions to Juries
Blatchf. Blatchford's United States Circuit Court Reports
Blatchf.C.C. Blatchford's United States Circuit Court Reports

Blatchf.Pr.Cas. Blatchford, Prize Cases (USA) 1789–1918
Blatchf.Prize Cas. Blatchford, Prize Cases (USA) 1789–1918
Blatchf. & H. Blatchford & Howland's United States District Court Reports
Blätter f.IPR. Blätter für Internationales Privatrecht (Ger.)
Blax.Eng.Co. Blaxland's Codex Legum Anglicanarum. 1839
Blay.Ann. Blayney, Life Annuities. 1817
Blay.Life Ins. Blayney, Life Assurance. 1837
Bldg. Building
Bldg.& Constr.L. Building and Construction Law
Bleck. Bleckley's Reports (34–5 Georgia)
Bleckley Bleckley's Reports (34–5 Georgia)
Blennerhasset Report Department of the Environment, Report on Drinking and Driving. 1976
Bli. Bligh's House of Lords Reports (4 ER) 1818–21
Bli.N.S. Bligh's House of Lords Reports, New Series (4–6 ER) 1827–37
Bli.(N.S.) Bligh's House of Lords Reports, New Series (4–6 ER) 1827–37
Bli.(O.S.) Bligh's House of Lords Reports, Old Series (4 ER) 1818–21
Blick.Rev. Blickenaderfer, Law Students' Review
Bligh Bligh's House of Lords Reports (4 ER) 1818–21
Bligh N.S. Bligh's House of Lords Reports, New Series (4–6 ER) 1827–37
Bliss. Delaware County Reports, Pennsylvania
Bliss Co.Pl. Bliss on Code Pleading
Bliss Ins. Bliss on Life Insurance
Bliss N.Y.Co. Bliss's Annotated New York Code
Blk. Block
Bloom.Man. Bloomfield's Manumission Cases (New Jersey)
Bloom.Neg.Cas. Bloomfield's Negro Cases (New Jersey)
Blount Frag.Ant. Blount, Fragmenta Antiquitatis
Blount L.D. Blount's Law Dictionary
Blount Tr. Blount's Impeachment Trial
Blu. Bluett's Advocate's Note Book (Isle of Man) 1720–1846
Blue Sky L.Rep. Blue Sky Law Reporter (CCH) (USA)
Bluett Bluett's Advocate's Note Book (Isle of Man) 1720–1846
Blum.B'k'cy. Blumenstiel, Bankruptcy
Bluntschli Bluntschli, Das moderne Völkerrecht der civilisiten Staaten als Rechtsbuch dargestellt. 1878
Bly.Us. Blydenburgh, Law of Usury. 1844
blz. bladzijde (Neth.) page
Bn. Baron
Board of Review Decisions Decisions of the Income Tax Board of Review (Aus.) 1936–50
Boberg P.Q.R. Boberg, The Law of Persons and the Family (S.Afr.) 1977
Bodenheimer E. Bodenheimer, Jurisprudence: the Philosophy and Method of the Law (USA)
Bogert Trusts Bogert on Trusts and Trustees
Boh.Att. Bohun, Practising Attorney
Boh.Curs.Can. Bohun, Cursus Cancellariae
Boh.Dec. Bohun's Declarations and Pleadings
Boh.Eccl.Jur. Bohun, Ecclesiastical Jurisdiction
Boh.Eng.L. Bohun, English Lawyer
Boh.Inst.Leg. Bohun, Institutio Legalis
Boh.Priv.Lond. Bohun, Privilegia Londini
Boh.Ti. Bohun, Tithes
Bohun Bohun's Election Cases
Bohun Curs.Canc. Bohun's Cursus Cancellariae
Bohun Inst.Leg. Bohun's Institutio Legalis
Bol.Fac.Der.Cordoba Boletin de la Facultad de Derecho y Ciencias Sociales, Cordoba (Argentina)
Bol.Fac.Dir. Boletim da Faculdade de

Direito da Universidade de Coimbra (Port.)
Bol.Mex.Der.Comp. Boletin Mexicano de Derecho Comparado (Mexico)
Bol.Min.Just.(Suppl.) Boletim do Ministéro da Justiça, Legislaçao (Port.) Law reports, legislative supplement
Bol.Min.Justica Boletim do Ministéro da Justiça (Port.) Law reports. 1940–
Boll. Bolletino del Tribunale delle Prede (It.) 1941–2
Boll.dell'Ist.di Diritto Romano Bolletino dell'Istituto de Diritto Romano (It.)
Bolland Select Bills in Eyre (Selden Society pub. vol. 30)
Bolletino Ufficiale Demanio Ministero delle Finanze, Bolletino Ufficiale della Direzione Generale del Demanio e delle tasse sugli affari (It.)
Bolletino Ufficiale Giustizia Ministero di Grazia e Giustizia e dei Culti, Bolletino Ufficiale (It.)
Bolletino Ufficiale Interno Ministero dell'Interno, Bolletino Ufficiale (It.)
Bom. All India Reporter, Bombay. 1914–
Indian Law Reports, Bombay. 1876–
Indian Rulings, Bombay. 1929–47
Bombay High Court Reports (India) 1862–75
Bom.A.C. Bombay Reports, Appellate Jurisdiction (India)
Bom.Cr.Cas. Bombay Reports, Crown Cases (India)
Bom.H.C.R. Bombay High Court Reports (India) 1862–75
Bom.India Bombay, India
Bom.L.J. Bombay Law Journal (India) 1923–46
Bom.L.R. Bombay Law Reporter (India) 1899–
Bom.L.R.J. Bombay Law Reporter (India) 1899–
Bom.O.C. Bombay Reports, Original Civil Jurisdiction (India)
Bombay Reports, Oudh Cases (India)
Bom.Unrep.Cr.C. Bombay Unreported Criminal Cases (India) 1862–98
Bomb. Indian Law Reports, Bombay Series. 1876–
Bomb.Cr.Rul. Bombay High Court Criminal Rulings (India)
Bomb.H.C. Bombay High Court Reports (India) 1862–75
Bomb.H.Ct. Bombay High Court Reports (India) 1862–75
Bomb.Hg.Ct. Bombay High Court Reports (India) 1862–75
Bomb.L.R. Bombay Law Reporter (India) 1899–
Bomb.Ser. Indian Law Rcports, Bombay Series. 1876–
Bombay Selections Selections from the Records of the Bombay Government. 1856
Bon.Ins. Bonney, Insurance
Bon.R.R.Car. Bonney, Railway Carriers
Bond Bond's United States Circuit Court Reports
Bond L.Rev. Bond Law Review
Bond Md.App. Proceedings of the Court of Appeal of Maryland
Bone Prec. Bone, Precedents in Conveyancing. 1838–40
Boo.R.Act. Booth, Real Actions
Book of Judg. Book of Judgments
Books Sed. Books of Sederunt
Boor. Booraem's Reports (6–8 California)
Booraem Booraem's Reports (6–8 California)
Boote Boote's Suite at Law
Boote Act. Boote, Action at Law
Boote Ch.Pr. Boote, Chancery Practice
Boote S.L. Boote's Suite at Law
Booth Chester Palatine Courts. 1811
Booth In.Of. Booth, Indictable Offences
Booth R.Act. Booth on Real Actions
Booth Report Report of the Matrimonial Causes Procedure Committee. 1985
Borchard Borchard, The Diplomatic Protection of Citizens Abroad. 1915
Borr. Borradaile's Civil Cases, Bombay (India) 1800–24
Borth. Borthwick, Modes of

Prosecuting for Libel. 1830

Bos. Bosworth's Superior Court Reports (New York)

Bos.N.R. Bosanquet & Puller's New Reports, Common Pleas (127 ER) 1804–7

Bos.Pl. Bosanquet's Rules of Pleading. 1835

Bos.Pol.Rep. Boston Police Court Reports

Bos.& D.Lim. Bosanquet & Darby's Limitations

Bos.& P. Bosanquet & Puller's Common Pleas Reports (126–7 ER) 1796–1804

Bos.& P.N.R. Bosanquet & Puller's New Reports, Common Pleas (127 ER) 1804–7

Bos.& Pu. Bosanquet & Puller's Common Pleas Reports (126–7 ER) 1796–1804

Bos & Pul. Bosanquet & Puller's Common Pleas Reports (126–7 ER) 1796–1804

Bos.& Pul.N.R. Bosanquet & Puller's New Reports, Common Pleas (127 ER) 1804–7

Bosc.Con. Boscawen on Convictions

Bost.B.J. Boston Bar Journal

Bost.Coll.Ind.L.Rev. Boston College Industrial and Commercial Law Review (USA)

Bost.L.R. Boston Law Reporter

Bost.Law Rep. Boston Law Reporter

Bost.Pol.Rep. Boston Police Court Reports

Bost.U.L.Rev. Boston University Law Review. 1921–

Boston B.J. Boston Bar Journal

Boston Coll.Ind.L.Rev. Boston College Industrial and Commercial Law Review (USA)

Boston Coll.Int'l & Comp.L.J. Boston College International and Comparative Law Journal (USA)

Boston Coll.L.Rev. Boston College Law Review (USA)

Boston Coll.Third World L.J. Boston College Third World Law Journal (USA)

Boston U.L.R. Boston University Law Review. 1921–

Boston U.L.Rev. Boston University Law Review. 1921–

Bosw. Boswell's Reports on Literary Property (Scôtch Court of Sessions) 1773
Bosworth, New York Superior Court Reports

Bot. Botswana

Botswana L.R.C. Botswana Law Reform Committee

Bott Bott's Poor Law Settlement Cases. 1761–1827

Bott P.L. Bott's Poor Law Cases. 1560–1833

Bott P.L.Cas. Bott's Poor Law Cases. 1560–1833

Bott P.L.Const. Const's Edition of Bott's Poor Law Cases. 1560–1833

Bott Poor Law Cas. Bott's Poor Law Cases. 1560–1833
Bott's Poor Law Settlement Cases. 1761–1827

Bott Set.Cas. Bott's Poor Law Settlement Cases. 1761–1827

Bott's P.L. Bott's Poor Law Cases. 1560–1833

Bou.Dic. Bouvier, Law Dictionary

Bou.Inst. Bouvier's Institutes of American Law

Bouch.Inst. Boucher's Instituts au Droit Maritimes

Boul.P.Dr.Com. Boulay–Paty, Cours de Droit Commercial Maritime

Bould. Bouldin's Reports (119 Alabama)

Bouln. Boulnois' Supreme Court Reports (Bengal, India) 1856–9

Boulnois Boulnois' Supreme Court Reports (Bengal, India) 1856–9

Bourke Bourke's Reports, Calcutta High Court (India) 1864–6

Bourke P.P. Bourke's Parliamentary Precedents. 1842–56

Bousq.Dict.de Dr. Bousquet, Dictionnaire de Droit

Bouv. Bouvier, Law Dictionary
Bouv.L.Dict. Bouvier, Law Dictionary
Bouv.Law Dict. Bouvier, Law Dictionary
Bouvier Bouvier, Law Dictionary
Bouwer A.P.J. Bouwer, Die Beredderingsproses van Bestorwe Boedels (S.Afr.)
Bov.Pat.Ca. Bovill's Patent Cases
Bow. Bowler & Bowers (2–3 US Comptroller's Decisions)
Bowler's London Session Records. 1605–85
Bow.Com. Bowyer, Commentaries on Universal Public Law. 1854
Bow.Civ.Law Bowyer, Modern Civil Law. 1848
Bow.Cons.Law Bowyer, Commentaries on the Constitutional Law of England. 2ed. 1846
Bow.Int. Bowyer, Introduction to the Study and Use of the Civil Law. 1874
Bow.Pub.Law Bowyer, Commentaries on Universal Public Law. 1854
Bowen Pol.Econ. Bowen's Political Economy
Bowstead Bowstead on Agency
Boy.Char. Boyle, Charities. 1837
Boyce Boyce's Delaware Supreme Court Reports (24–30 Del) 1909–19
Boyd Adm. Boyd's Admiralty Law (Ire.)
Boyd Jus. Boyd, Justice of the Peace
Boyd Sh. Boyd, Merchant Shipping Laws. 1876
Boyle Act. Boyle's Precis of an Action at Common Law
Bp. Bishop
br. branch
Br. Bracton
Bradford
Bradwell
Brayton
Breese
Brevard
Brewster
Bridgman
Brightly
British
Britton
Brockenbrough
Brooke
Broom
Brown
Browne
Brownlow
Bruce
Br.Abr. Brooke's Abridgment
Br.Brev.Jud. Brownlow's Brevia Judicialia, etc. 1662
Br.Brev.Jud.& Ent. Brownlow's Brevia Judicialia, etc. 1662
Br.Bur. British Burma
Br.C.C. British Crown Cases (American reprint)
Brown's Chancery Cases (28–9 ER) 1778–94
Br.Col. British Columbia
Br.Com. Broom, Common Law. 9ed. 1896
Br.Cons.Law Broom, Constitutional Law. 3ed. 1885
Br.Cr.Cas. British Crown Cases
Br.Ent. Brownlow, Entries
Br.Fed.Dig. Brightly's Federal Digest
Br.J.Admin.L. British Journal of Administrative Law. 1954–
Br.J.Delinq. British Journal of Delinquency. 1950–60
Br.J.Soc. British Journal of Sociology
Br.Jo.Soc. British Journal of Sociology
Br.L.R. Brooklyn Law Review. 1932–
Br.Leg.Max. Broom's Legal Maxims. 10ed. 1939
Br.Max. Broom's Legal Maxims. 10ed.1939
Br.N.B. Bracton's Note Book. 1217–40
Br.N.C. Brooke's New Cases, King's Bench (73 ER) 1515–58
Br.N.Cas. Brooke's New Cases, King's Bench (73 ER) 1515–58
Br.Not. Brooke's Office and Practice of a Notary. 9ed. 1939
Br.P.C. Brown's Parliamentary Cases (1–3 ER) 1702–1800
Br.Phil.Law Broom, Philosophy of Law. 3ed. 1883
Br.R. Browne's Reports (Sri L.) 1901–2

Br.Reg. Braithwaite's Register
Br.Rul.Cas. British Ruling Cases
Br.Sup. Brown's Supplement to Morison's Dictionary of Decisions, Session Cases (Scot.) 1622–1780
Br.Syn. Brown's Synopsis of Decisions, Scotch Court of Session. 1540–1827
Br.& B. Broderip & Bingham's Common Pleas (129 ER) 1819–22
Br.& Col. British and Colonial Prize Cases. 1914–19
Br.& Col.Pr.Cas. British and Colonial Prize Cases. 1914–19
Br.& F.Ecc. Broderick & Fremantle's Ecclesiastical Cases. 1840–64
Br.& For.St.Papers British and Foreign State Papers
Br.& Fr. Broderick & Fremantle's Ecclesiastical Cases. 1840–64
Br.& G. Brownlow & Goldesborough's Common Pleas Reports (123 ER) 1569–1624
Br.& Had. Broom & Hadley, Commentaries on the Laws of England. 2ed. 1875
Br.& L. Browning & Lushington's Admiralty Reports (167 ER) 1863–65
Br.& Lush. Browning & Lushington's Admiralty Reports (167 ER) 1863–65
Br.& R. Brown & Rader's Reports (137 Missouri)
Bra. Bracton, de Legibus et Consuetudinibus Angliae
Bra.Ind.Soc. Brabrook, Industrial and Provident Societies. 1869
Brac. Bracton, de Legibus et Consuetudinibus Angliae
Bracton's Note Book, King's Bench. 1217–40
Brac.L.J. Bracton Law Journal. 1965–
Bract. Bracton, de Legibus et Consuetudinibus Angliae
Bracton Bracton, de Legibus et Consuetudinibus Angliae
Bracton L.J. Bracton Law Journal. 1965–
Brad. Bradford's Reports (Iowa) 1839–41
Bradford's New York Surrogate Court Reports. 1849–57
Bradford's Proceedings in the Court of Star Chamber
Bradwell's Reports (1–20 Illinois Appeals)
Bradb. Bradbury's Pleading and Practice Reports (New York)
Bradf. Bradford's Iowa Reports. 1839–41
Bradford's New York Surrogate Court Reports. 1849–57
Bradford's Proceedings in the Court of Star Chamber
Bradf.Sur. Bradford's New York Surrogate Court Reports. 1849–57
Bradf.Surr. Bradford's New York Surrogate Court Reports. 1849–57
Bradford Bradford's Iowa Supreme Court Reports. 1839–41
Bradl. Bradley's Rhode Island Reports
Bradl.(R.I.) Bradley's Rhode Island Reports
Bradw. Bradwell's Illinois Appellate Reports (1–20 Ill. App.)
Brady Ind. Brady's Index, Arkansas Reports
Brain.L.P. Brainard's Legal Precedents in Land and Mining Cases (USA)
Braith. Jamaica Law Reports (Braithwaite)
Braith.Chy. Braithwaite, Times of Procedure in Chancery. 1864
Braith.Oaths Braithwaite, Oaths in Chancery. 2ed. 1864
Braithwaite, Oaths in the Supreme Court. 4ed. 1881
Braith.Pr. Braithwaite, Record and Writ of Practice of the Court of Chancery. 1858
Brame Brame's Reports (66–72 Mississippi)
Branch Branch's Reports (1 Florida)
Branch Max. Branch's Maxims
Branch Pr. Branch's Principia Legis et Equitatis (Maxims)
Branch Princ. Branch's Principia Legis et Equitatis (Maxims)

Brand.F.Attachm. Brandon on Foreign Attachment
Brand.For.Att. Brandon on Foreign Attachment
Brand.May.Ct. Brandon, Practice of the Mayor's Court. 1864
Brandt Sur. Brandt, Suretyship and Guaranty
BranntwMonG Branntweinmonopolgesetz (Ger.) Act on Spirit Beverages Monopoly
Brans.Dig. Branson's Digest of Reports, Bombay (India)
Brant. Brantly's Reports (80–90 Maryland)
Brantly Brantly's Reports (80–90 Maryland)
Brayt. Brayton's Vermont Reports. 1815–19
Brayton (Vt.) Brayton's Vermont Reports. 1815–19
Brd. Board
Bresse Bresse's Illinois Supreme Court Reports (1 Ill.) 1819–31
brev. brevet(é) (Fr.) patent(ed)
Brev. Brevard's South Carolina Reports (3–5 SCL) 1793–1816
Brev.Dig. Brevard's Digest of the Public Statute Law, South Carolina
Brev.Ju. Brevia Judicialia (Judicial Writs)
Brev.Sel. Brevia Selecta (Choice Writs)
Brew. Brewer's Reports (19–26 Maryland)
Brew.(Md.) Brewer's Reports (19–26 Maryland)
Brewer Brewer's Reports (19–26 Maryland)
Brewst. Brewster's Pennsylvania Reports (4 Pa.) 1856–73
Bri.Pub.Wor. Brice, Law relating to Public Worship. 1875
Bri.Ult.V. Brice, Ultra Vires. 3ed. 1893
Brick.Dig. Brickell's Digest (Alabama)
Bridg. Sir J. Bridgman's Reports, Common Pleas (123 ER) 1613–21
Bridg.Dig.Ind. Bridgman's Digested Index of Reported Cases in the Laws of Equity
Bridg.Eq.Ind. Bridgman's Index to Equity Cases
Bridg.J. Sir J. Bridgman's Common Pleas Reports (123 ER) 1613–21
Bridg.Leg.Bib. Bridgman, Legal Bibliography. 1801
Bridg.O. Sir Orlando Bridgman's Common Pleas Reports (124 ER) 1660–67
Bridg.Ref. Bridgman, Reflections on the Study of the Law. 1804
Brief Brief (Law Society of Western Australia) 1974–
Briefnotes Briefnotes (Public Solicitor's Office, New South Wales) (Aus.) 1978–
Brierly J.L. Brierly, The Law of Nations
Brig.Yo.U.L.R. Brigham Young University Law Review (USA) 1975–
Brigham Y.U.L.R. Brigham Young University Law Review (USA) 1975–
Bright. Brightly, Pennsylvania Nisi Prius Reports. 1809–51
Bright.Dig. Brightly's Analytical Digest of the Laws of the United States
Brightly's Digest (New York)
Brightly's Digest (Pennsylvania)
Bright.E.C. Brightly's Leading Election Cases (Pennsylvania)
Bright.Elec.Cas. Brightly's Leading Election Cases (Pennsylvania)
Bright H.& W. Bright, Husband and Wife. 3ed. 1849
Bright.N.P. Brightly's Pennsylvania Nisi Prius Reports. 1809–51
Bright.Pur.Dig. Brightly's Edition of Purdon's Digest of Pennsylvania Laws
Bright.Purd. Brightly's Edition of Purdon's Digest of Pennsylvania Laws
Brightly Dig. Brightly's Analytical Digest of the Laws of the United States
Brightly's Digest (New York)
Brightly's Digest (Pennsylvania)
Brightly Elect.Cas. Brightly's Leading Election Cases (Pennsylvania)
Brightly N.P. Brightly's Pennsylvania Nisi Prius Reports. 1809–51

Brisb.Minn. Brisbin's Reports (1 Minnesota)
Brisbin Brisbin's Reports (1 Minnesota)
Brit. Britain
Britannia
Britannica
British
Britton's Ancient Pleas of the Crown
Brit.Adm.Rev. British Administrative Review
Brit.Burm. British Burma
Brit.Col.(Can.) British Columbia
Brit.Cr.Cas. British Crown Cases
Brit.Gui. British Guiana
Brit.Hond. British Honduras
Brit.J.Admin.Law British Journal of Administrative Law. 1954–
Brit.J.Criminol. British Journal of Criminology. 1960–
Brit.J.Delinq. British Journal of Delinquency. 1950–60
Brit.J.Ind.Rel. British Journal of Industrial Relations. 1963–
Brit.J.Int'l L. British Journal of International Law
Brit.J.L.& Soc'y British Journal of Law and Society. 1974–
Brit.J.Law & Soc. British Journal of Law and Society. 1974–
Brit.J.of Crimin. British Journal of Criminology. 1960–
Brit.J.of Delinquency British Journal of Delinquency. 1950–60
Brit.J.Pol.Sci. British Journal of Political Science
Brit.Quar.Rev. British Quarterly Review
Brit.Rul.Cas. British Ruling Cases
Brit.Tax Rev. British Tax Review. 1956–
Brit.Y.B.Int.L. British Yearbook of International Law. 1920–
Brit.Y.B.Int'l.L. British Yearbook of International Law. 1920–
Brit.Yrbk.Intl.L. British Yearbook of International Law. 1920–
Brit.& Col.Pr.Cas. British and Colonial Prize Cases
Britt. Britton's Ancient Pleas of the Crown
Brn. Brownlow and Goldesborough's Common Pleas Reports (123 ER) 1569–1624
Bro. Brother
Brown's Chancery Reports (28–9 ER) 1778–94
Brown's Michigan Nisi Prius Reports. 1869–71
Brown's Parliamentary Cases (1–3 ER) 1702–1801
Brown's Reports (53–65 Mississippi)
Brown's Reports (80–136 Missouri)
Brown's Reports (Pennsylvania) 1801–14
Browne's Reports (Sri L.) 1872–1902
Brownlow & Goldesborough's Common Pleas Reports (123 ER) 1569–1624
W.G. Brooke's Ecclesiastical Reports. 1850–72
Bro.A.& R. Brown, United States District Court Reports (Admiralty and Revenue Cases)
Bro.Ab. Brooke's Abridgement (1573, 1576, 1586 editions)
Bro.Abr. Brooke's Abridgement (1573, 1576, 1586 editions)
Bro.Abr.in Eq. Browne's New Abridgement of Cases in Equity
Bro.Ac. Browne, Actions at Law. 1843
Bro.Adm. Brown's United States Admiralty Reports
Bro.Ag. Brown, Agency and Trusts. 1868
Bro.C.C. W. Brown's Chancery Reports (28–9 ER) 1778–94
Bro.Car. Browne, Law of Carriers. 1873
Bro.Ch. W. Brown's Chancery Reports (28–9 ER) 1778–94
Bro.Ch.Cas. W. Brown's Chancery Reports (28–9 ER) 1778–94
Bro.Ch.Pr. Browne's Practice of the High Court of Chancery. 1830
Bro.Ch.R. Brown's Chancery Reports (28–9 ER) 1778–94
Bro.Civ.Law Browne's Civil and Admiralty Law
Bro.Div.Pr. Browne's Divorce Practice. 11ed. 1931

Bro.Ecc. Brooke's Ecclesiastical Cases. 1850–72

Bro.Ent. Brown's Entries. 1693
Brownlow's Latine Redivivus (or Entries)

Bro.Fr. Browne, Statute of Frauds

Bro.Hered. Browne, Law of Rating of Hereditaments. 2ed. 1886

Bro.Just. Brown's Justiciary Reports (Scot.) 1842–5

Bro.Law Dic. Brown, Law Dictionary. 2ed. 1880

Bro.Leg.Max. Brooms' Legal Maxims. 10ed. 1939

Bro.Lim. Brown, Limitations as to Real Property. 1869

Bro.Max. Brooms' Legal Maxims. 10ed. 1939

Bro.N.B.Cas. Browne's National Bank Cases (USA) 1878–89

Bro.N.C. Brooke's New Cases, King's Bench (73 ER) 1515–58

Bro.N.P. Brown's Michigan Nisi Prius Reports (USA) 1869–71

Bro.P.C. J. Brown's Parliamentary Cases (1–3 ER) 1702–1800

Bro.Pa. Browne's Pennsylvania Reports. 1801–14

Bro.(Pa.) Browne's Pennsylvania Reports. 1801–14

Bro.Parl.Cas. J. Brown's Cases in Parliament (1–3 ER) 1702–1800

Bro.Prac. Brown's Practice (Praxis) or Precedents in Chancery

Bro.Prob.Pr. Browne's Probate Practice. 2ed. 1881

Bro.Sal. Brown, Treatise on Law of Sale (Scot.)

Bro.St. Brodie, Notes and Supplement to Stair's Institutions (Scot.)

Bro.St.Fr. Browne, Statute of Frauds

Bro.Stair Brodie's Notes and Supplement to Stair's Institutions (Scot.)

Bro.Sup.to Mor. Brown's Supplement to Morison's Dictionary of Decisions (Scot.) 1622–1780

Bro.Supp. Brown's Supplement to Morison's Dictionary of Decisions (Scot.)

Bro.Syn. Brown's Synopsis of Decisions, Court of Session (Scot.) 1532–1827

Bro.Synop. Brown's Synopsis of Decisions, Court of Session (Scot.) 1532–1827

Bro.Tr.M. Browne, Trade Marks

Bro.Us.& Cus. Browne, Law of Usages and Customs

Bro.V.M. Brown, Vade Mecum

Bro.& F. Broderick & Fremantle's Ecclesiastical Cases. 1840–64

Bro.& Fr. Broderick & Fremantle's Ecclesiastical Cases. 1840–64

Bro.& G. Brownlow & Goldesborough's Common Pleas Reports (123 ER) 1569–1624

Bro.& H. Brown & Hemingway's Reports (53–65 Mississippi)

Bro.& L. Browning & Lushington's Admiralty Reports (167 ER) 1863–65

Bro.& Lush. Browning & Lushington's Admiralty Reports (167 ER) 1863–65

Bro.& M. Brown & Macnamara's Railway Cases. 1855
Brown & McCall's Yorkshire Star Chamber Cases

Bro.& Mac. Brown & Macnamara's Railway Cases. 1855

Brock. Brockenborough's Marshall's Decisions, United States Circuit Court

Brock.C.C. Brockenborough's Marshall's Decisions, United States Circuit Court

Brock.Cas. Brockenborough's Virginia Cases

Brock.Marsh. Brockenborough's Marshall's Decisions, United States Circuit Court

Brock.& H. Brockenborough & Holmes' Virginia Cases

Brock.& Ho. Brockenborough & Holmes' Virginia Cases

Brod. Brodrick & Fremantle's Ecclesiastical Cases. 1840–64

Brod.Stair Brodie's Notes to Stair's Institutes (Scot.)

Brod.& B. Broderip & Bingham's

Common Pleas Reports (129 ER) 1819–22
Brod.& Bing. Broderip & Bingham's Common Pleas Reports (129 ER) 1819–22
Brod.& F. Broderick & Fremantle's Ecclesiastical Cases. 1840–64
Brod.& Fr. Broderick & Fremantle's Ecclesiastical Cases. 1840–64
Brod.& Frem. Broderick & Fremantle's Ecclesiastical Cases. 1840–64
Brodix Am.& E.Pat.Cas. Brodix's American and English Patent Cases (USA) 1662–1890
Brodix Am.& Eng.Pat.Cas. Brodix's American and English Patent Cases (USA) 1662–1890
Brodrick Report Report of the Home Office Committee on Death Certification and Coroners (Cmnd. 4810) 1971
Broed.Cand.Not. Broederschap der Candidaat–Notarissen (Neth.)
Brook.J.Int'l L. Brooklyn Journal of International Law (USA)
Brook.L.Rev. Brooklyn Law Review (USA)
Brooke Brooke's Ecclesiastical Reports. 1850–72
Brooke's New Cases, King's Bench (73 ER) 1515–58
Brooke,Abr. Brooke's Abridgment (1573, 1576, 1586 editions)
Brooke Eccl. Brooke's Six Ecclesiastical Judgments. 1850–72
Brooke Eccl.Judg. Brooke's Six Ecclesiastical Judgments. 1850–72
Brooke N.C. Brooke's New Cases, King's Bench Reports (73 ER) 1515–58
Brooke Not. Brooke on the Office and Practice of a Notary. 9ed. 1939
Brooke(Petit) Brooke's New Cases, King's Bench (73 ER) 1515–58
Brooke Six Judg. Brooke's Six Ecclesiastical Judgments. 1850–72
Brookl.Bar. Brooklyn Barrister. 1950– Brooklyn Bar Association
Brookl.J.Int.L. Brooklyn Journal of International Law. 1975–
Brookl.L.Rev. Brooklyn Law Review. 1932–43, 1947–
Brookl.Rec. Brooklyn Daily Record, New York
Brooklyn Bar. Brooklyn Barrister. 1950–
Brooklyn Daily Rec. Brooklyn Daily Record, New York
Brooklyn J.Int.L. Brooklyn Journal of International Law. 1975–
Brooklyn L.Rev. Brooklyn Law Review. 1932–43, 1947–
Brooks Brooks' Reports (106–119 Michigan)
Broom Com.Law Broom's Commentaries on the Common Law. 9ed. 1896
Broom Leg.Max. Broom's Legal Maxims. 10ed. 1939
Broom Max. Broom's Legal Maxims. 10ed. 1939
Broom & H.Comm. Broom & Hadley's Commentaries on the Law of England. 2ed. 1875
Bros. Brothers
Brough.Civ.Pro. Broughton's Indian Civil Procedure
Broun Broun's Justiciary Reports (Scot.) 1842–45
Broun Just. Broun's Justiciary Reports (Scot.) 1842–45
Brown. Brownlow & Goldesborough's Common Pleas Reports (123 ER) 1569–1624
J. Brown's Cases in Parliament (1–3 ER) 1702–1801
Brown's Chancery Reports (28–9 ER) 1778–94
Brown's Law Dictionary and Institute. 2ed. 1880
Brown's Michigan Nisi Prius Reports. 1869–71
Brown's Reports (53–65 Mississippi)
Brown's Reports (80–137 Missouri)
Brown's Reports (4–25 Nebraska)
Brown's Synopsis of Decisions, Court of Session (Scot.) 1532–1827
Brown's United States Admiralty

Reports
Brown's United States District Court Reports

Brown A.& R. Brown's United States District Court Reports (Admiralty and Revenue Cases)

Brown Adm. Brown's Admiralty Reports (USA)

Brown C. Brown's Chancery Cases or Reports (28–9 ER) 1778–94

Brown,C.C. Brown's Chancery Cases or Reports (28–9 ER) 1778–94

Brown Ch. Brown's Chancery Cases or Reports (28–9 ER) 1778–94

Brown Ch.C. Brown's Chancery Cases or Reports (28–9 ER) 1778–94

Brown Civ.& Adm.Law Brown's Civil and Admiralty Law

Brown Dict. Brown's Law Dictionary. 2ed. 1880

Brown Ecc. Brown's Ecclesiastical Cases. 1850–72

Brown Ga.Pl.& Pr.Anno. Brown, Georgia Pleading and Practice and Legal Forms Annotated

Brown, Modern Legislation J. Brown, Underlying Principles of Modern Legislation. 1912

Brown N.P. Brown's Michigan Nisi Prius Reports. 1869–71

Brown P.C. Brown's Parliamentary Cases (1–3 ER) 1702–1800

Brown Parl. Brown's Parliamentary Cases (1–3 ER) 1702–1800

Brown Sup. Brown's Supplement to Morison's Dictionary of Decisions, Session Cases (Scot.) 1622–1780

Brown Sup.Dec. Brown's Supplement to Morison's Dictionary of Decisions, Session Cases (Scot.) 1622–1780

Brown Syn. Brown's Synopsis of Decisions, Court of Session (Scot.) 1532–1827

Brown.& G. Brownlow & Goldesborough's Common Pleas Reports (123 ER) 1569–1624

Brown & H. Brown & Hemingway's Reports (53–58 Mississippi)

Brown & Hemingway Brown & Hemingway's Reports (53–58 Mississippi)

Brown.& L. Browning & Lushington's Admiralty Reports (167 ER) 1863–5

Brown.& Lush. Browning & Lushington's Admiralty Reports (167 ER) 1863–5

Brown.& Lush.M.& D. Browning & Lushington on Marriage and Divorce

Brown & MacN. Brown & MacNamara, Railway Cases. 1855

Brown & R. Brown & Rader's Missouri Reports

Browne Browne's Civil Procedure Reports (New York)
Browne's Reports (97–109 Massachusetts)
Browne's Reports (Pennsylvania) 1801–1814
Browne's Reports (Sri L.) 1901–2

Browne Bank Cas. Browne's National Bank Cases (USA) 1878–89

Browne Act. Browne, Actions at Law. 1843

Browne Civ.Law Browne, Civil and Admiralty Law

Browne Div. Browne, Practice in Divorce. 11ed. 1931

Browne Div.Pr. Browne, Practice in Divorce. 11ed. 1931

Browne Jud.Interp. Browne, Judicial Interpretation of Common Words and Phrases

Browne N.B.C. Browne's National Bank Cases (USA) 1878–89

Browne Prob. Browne, Probate Practice. 2ed.1881

Browne Prob.Pr. Browne, Probate Practice. 2ed. 1881

Browne St.Frauds Browne, Statute of Frauds

Browne Us. Browne, Usages and Customs. 1875

Browne & G. Browne & Gray's Reports (110–114 Massachusetts)

Browne & Gray Browne & Gray's Reports (110–114 Massachusetts)

Browne & H. Browne & Hemingway's Reports (Mississippi)
Browne & Macn. Browne & Macnamara's Railway and Canal Cases. 1855
Browne & Th.Railw. Browne & Theobald, Railways. 4ed. 1911
Browne's Rep. Browne's Reports (Sri L.) 1901–2
Brownl. Brownlow & Goldesborough's Common Pleas Reports (123 ER) 1569–1624
Brownl.Ent. Brownlow's Entries
Brownl.Redv. Brownlow's Latine Redivivus (or Entries)
Brownl.& G. Brownlow & Goldesborough's Common Pleas Reports (123 ER) 1569–1624
Brownl.& Gold. Brownlow & Goldesborough's Common Pleas Reports (123 ER) 1569–1624
Brownlie I. Brownlie, Principles of Public International Law
Brown's Roman Law Brown's Epitome and Analysis of Savigny's Treatise on Obligations in Roman Law
Bru. Bruce's Decisions, Court of Session (Scot.) 1714–15
Bruce, Military Law (Scot.)
Bru.Princip. Bruce, Principia Juris Feudalis
Bru.& Wil.Adm. Bruce & Williams, Admiralty Jurisdiction
Brun.Col.Cas. Brunner's Collected Cases (USA)
Brun.Sel.Cas. Brunner's Selected Cases (USA)
Brunk.Ir.Dig. Brunker's Irish Common Law Digest
Brunn.Coll.Cas. Brunner's Collected Cases (USA)
Brunn.Sel.Cas. Brunner's Selected Cases (USA)
Brunner Col.Cas. Brunner's Collected Cases (USA)
Brunner Sel.Cas. Brunner's Selected Cases (USA)
Bruns.L.C. Brunskill's Land Cases (Ire.) 1891–5
Brunskill Brunskill's Land Cases (Ire.) 1891–5
Brux. Bruxelles (Brussels)
Bruzard Mauritius Reports by Bruzard. 1842–5
Bry.& Str.Com.L. Bryant & Stratton, Commercial Law
Bryce Civ.L. Bryce's Study of the Civil Law
Bryce, Studies Bryce, Studies in History and Jurisprudence. 1901
Bryce Tr.M. Bryce, Registration of Trade Marks
Bs.L. Bills of Lading
Bs/L Bills of Lading
Bt. Baronet
Benedict's United States District Court Reports
Bu.L.R. Buffalo Law Review. 1951–
Buch. Buchanan's Appeal Court Reports, Cape of Good Hope (S.Afr.) 1880–1910
Buchanan's New Jersey Equity Reports (71–85 NJEq)
Buchanan's Remarkable Cases (Scot.) 1806–13
Buchanan's Supreme Court Reports, Cape of Good Hope (S.Afr.) 1868–79
Buch.A.C. Buchanan's Appeal Court Reports, Cape of Good Hope (S.Afr.) 1880–1910
Buch.App.Cas. Buchanan's Appeal Court Reports, Cape of Good Hope (S.Afr.) 1880–1910
Buch.Cas. Buchanan's Remarkable Cases (Scot.) 1806–13
Buch.Ct.App.Cape G.H. Buchanan's Appeal Court Reports, Cape of Good Hope (S.Afr.) 1880–1910
Buch.E.Cape G.H. E. Buchanan's Supreme Court Reports, Cape of Good Hope (S.Afr.) 1868–79
Buch.E.D.Cape G.H. Buchanan's Eastern District Reports, Cape of Good Hope (S.Afr.) 1880–1909
Buch.Eq.(N.J.) Buchanan's New Jersey Equity Reports (71–85 NJEq)

Buch.J.Cape G.H. J. Buchanan's Reports, Cape of Good Hope

Buch.Rep. Buchanan's Reports, Cape of Good Hope

Buch.S.C.Rep. Buchanan's Supreme Court Reports, Cape of Good Hope (S.Afr.) 1868–79

Buchanan Buchanan's Reports, Court of Session and Justiciary (Scot.) 1806–13

Buck Buck's Cases in Bankruptcy. 1816–20
Buck's Reports (7–8 Montana)

Buck Bankr. Buck's Cases in Bankruptcy. 1816–20

Buck Cas. Buck's Cases in Bankruptcy. 1816–20

Buck.Cooke Bucknill's Cooke's Cases of Practice, Common Pleas

Buck.Dec. Buckner's Decisions (in Freeman's Mississippi Chancery Reports) 1839–43

Buck.Ins. Bucknill, Care of the Insane. 1880

Buckl. Buckley on the Companies Acts

Bucks Bucks County Law Reporter (Pennsylvania)

Bucks Co.L.Rep. Bucks County Law Reporter (Pennsylvania)

Buff.L.R. Buffalo Law Review (USA) 1951–

Buff.L.Rev. Buffalo Law Review (USA) 1951–

Buff.Super.Ct. Sheldon's Superior Court Reports (Buffalo, New York)

Buff.Super.Ct.(N.Y.) Sheldon's Superior Court Reports (Buffalo, New York)

Buffalo L.Rev. Buffalo Law Review (USA) 1951–

Build.L.M. Building Law Monthly

Build.L.R. Building Law Reports. 1976–

Bul. Bulletin

Bull. Bulletin
Weekly Law Bulletin (Ohio) 1885–1901

Bull.Anglo-Sov.L.A. Bulletin of the Anglo-Soviet Law Association. 1947–53

Bull.Argent.de Droit Int.Privé Bulletin Argentin de droit international privé

Bull.C.E. Bulletin des communautés européennes

Bull.Can.Welfare L. Bulletin of the Canadian Welfare Law. 1972–

Bull.Coll.Wm.& Mary William and Mary College, Bulletin (USA)

Bull.Comp.L. American Bar Association Comparative Law Bureau, Bulletin

Bull.Comp.Lab.Rel. Bulletin of Comparative Labour Relations (USA) 1970–

Bull.Civ. Bulletin des arrêts de la Chambre Civile de la Cour de Cassation (Fr.) 1792–

Bull.Copyright Soc'y. Bulletin of the Copyright Society of the USA. 1953–

Bull.Cr.Soc. Bulletin of the Copyright Society of the USA. 1953–

Bull.C'right Soc'y. Bulletin of the Copyright Society of the USA. 1953–

Bull.Crim. Bulletin arrêts de la Chambre Criminelle de la Cour de Cassation (Fr.) 1798–

Bull.Czech.L. Bulletin of Czechoslovak Law. 1960–

Bull.E.C. Bulletin of the European Communities

Bull.Études Jur.Écon.& Soc.Cairo Bulletin du Centre de Documentation d'Études Juridiques, Économiques et Sociales (Egypt)

Bull.Europ.Commun. Bulletin of the European Communities

Bull.for Int'l Fisc.Doc. Bulletin for International Fiscal Documentation (Neth.)

Bull.I.B.A. Bulletin of the International Bar Association. 1947–

Bull.I.C.J. Bulletin of the International Commission of Jurists. 1954–68

Bull.Inst.Belge Institut Belge de droit comparé, Bulletin trimestriel (Belg.)

Bull.Inst.Int. Bulletin de l'Institut juridique international (Belg.)

Bull.Int.Fisc.Doc. Bulletin for International Fiscal Documentation (Neth.) 1946–

Bull.ist.dir.rom. Bulletino dell'istitutio di

diritto romano (It.) 1888–
Bull.J.A.G. Bulletin of Judge Advocate General of the Army (USA)
Bull.J.S.B. Bulletin of the Judicial Studies Board
Bull.leg. Bulletin legislatif belge (Belg.) periodical collection of legislation
Bull.Leg.Dev. Bulletin of Legal Developments. 1966–
Bull.Med.E. Bulletin of Medical Ethics
Bull.Mediev.Canon L. Bulletin of Medieval Canon Law
Bull.N.P. Buller's Law of Nisi Prius
Bull.Nat.Tax Assoc. Bulletin of the National Tax Association (USA)
Bull.O. Weekly Law Bulletin (Ohio) 1885–1901
Bull.of Peace Proposals Bulletin of Peace Proposals (Norway)
Bull.(Ohio) Weekly Law Bulletin (Ohio) 1885–1901
Bull.Ostrechtsforschung Bulletin der Ostrechtsforschung in den Ländern des Europarates (Ger.)
Bull.Pan-Am.Union Bulletin of the Pan-American Union (USA)
Bull.Que.Soc.Crim. Bulletin of the Quebec Society of Criminology (Can.)
Bull.S.O.A.S. Bulletin of the School of Oriental and African Studies
Bull.Soc.d'Études Leg. Bulletin de la Societé d'études législatives (Fr.)
Bull.Soc.et.législ. Bulletin de la Societé d'études législatives (Fr.) 1901–
Bull.Soc.int.crimin. Bulletin de la Societé internationale de criminologie (Fr.)
Bull.Soc.Legisl.Comp. Bulletin de la Societé de législation comparée (Fr.)
Bull.us. Bulletin usuel des lois et arrêtes (Belg.) periodical collection of legislation
Bull.Waseda Univ.Inst.of Comp.Law Bulletin of the Waseda University Institute of Comparative Law (Japan)
Bull.& L. Bullen & Leake's Precedents of Pleading in Queen's Bench Decisions
Buller MSS. J. Buller's Paper Books, Lincoln's Inn Library
Buller N.P. Buller's Nisi Prius
Bulletin Comp.L. Bulletin of the Comparative Law Bureau
Bulletino Scialoja Bulletino dell'Istituto di Diritto Romano 'Vittorio Scialoja' (It.)
Bulst. Bulstrode's King's Bench Reports (80–1 ER) 1609–25
Bulstr. Bulstrode's King's Bench Reports (80–1 ER) 1609–25
Bump Const.Dec. Bump, Notes of Constitutional Decisions (USA)
Bump Fed.Pr. Bump, Federal Procedure (USA)
Bump Fr.Conv. Bump, Fraudulent Conveyances (USA)
Bump St.L. Bump, United States Stamp Laws
Bump's Int.Rev.Law Bump, Internal Revenue Laws (USA)
Bunb. Bunbury's Exchequer Reports (145 ER) 1713–41
Bunbury Bunbury's Exchequer Reports (145 ER) 1713–41
Buny.Dom.L. Bunyon, Domestic Law. 1875
Buny.Fire Ins. Bunyon, Fire Insurance. 7ed. 1923
Buny.Life Ins. Bunyon, Life Insurance. 5ed. 1914
Bur. Bureau
Burnett's Wisconsin Supreme Court Reports. 1841–3
Burrow's King's Bench Reports tempore Mansfield (97–8 ER) 1757–71
Bur.L.J. Burma Law Journal. 1922–27
Bur.L.R. Burma Law Reports. 1948–
Bur.L.T. Burma Law Times. 1907–20
Bur.M. Burrow's King's Bench Reports tempore Mansfield (97–8 ER) 1757–71
Bur.S.C. Burrow's Settlement Cases. 1733–76
Bur.& Gres.Eq.Pl. Burroughs & Gresson's Irish Equity Pleader
Burchell & Hunt E.M. Burchell & P.M.A. Hunt, South African Criminal Law and Procedure
Burf. Burford's Reports (6–18 Oklahoma)

Burg.Dig. Burgwyn's Digest, Maryland Reports
Burge App. Burge, Appellate Jurisdiction. 1841
Burge Col.Law Burge, Colonial and Foreign Law. 2ed. 1907–8
Burge Sur. Burge, Suretyship. 1869
Burgess Burgess' Reports (16–49 Ohio State)
Burgw.Md.Dig. Burgwyn's Maryland Digest
Burke Cel.Tr. Burke's Celebrated Trials
Burke Cop. Burke, Copyright. 1842
Burke Cr.L. Burke, Criminal Law. 2ed. 1845
Burke Int.Cop. Burke, International Copyright. 1852
Burke Tr. Burke's Celebrated Trials
Burks Burks' Reports (91–8 Virginia)
Burl.Nat. Burlamaqui's Natural and Political Law
Burlamaqui Burlamaqui's Natural and Political Law
Burlesque Reps. Skillman's New York Police Reports
Burm.L.J. Burma Law Journal. 1922–7
Burm.L.R. Burma Law Reports. 1948–
Burm.L.T. Burma Law Times. 1907–20
Burma L.Inst.J. Burma Law Institute Journal. 1958–60
Burma L.R. Burma Law Reports. 1948–
Burma Law Inst.J. Burma Law Institute Journal. 1958–60
Burn. High Commission Court. 1865
Star Chamber Proceedings
Burnett's Reports (Wisconsin) 1841, 1842–3
Burn.Cr.L. Burnet, Criminal Law of Scotland
Burn Dict. Burn's Law Dictionary
Burn Eccl.Law Burn's Ecclesiastical Law. 9ed. 1842
Burn J.P. Burn's Justice of the Peace. 30ed. 1869
Burnet Burnet, Manuscript Decisions, Court of Session (Scot.)
Burnett Burnett's Reports (20–2 Oregon)
Wisconsin Reports. 1841, 1842–3
Burnett (Wis.) Burnett's Wisconsin Reports. 1841, 1842–3
Burns'Ann.St. Burns' Annotated Statutes (Ind.)
Burns-Begg Southern Rhodesia High Court Reports by Burns-Begg. 1899
Burn's Eccl.Law Burn's Ecclesiastical Law. 9ed. 1842
Burn's J.P. Burn's Justice of the Peace. 30ed. 1869
Burns Pract. Burns, Conveyancing Practice (Scot.)
Burns'Rev.St. Burns' Annotated Statutes (India)
Burr. Burrow's King's Bench Reports tempore Mansfield (97–8 ER) 1757–71
Burr.Adm. Burrell's Admiralty Cases (167 ER) 1584–1774
Burr.Dict. Burrill's Law Dictionary
Burr.Law Dict. Burrill's Law Dictionary
Burr.Pr. Burrill's New York Practice
Burr.S.C. Burrow's Settlement Cases. 1733–76
Burr.t.M. Burrow's King's Bench Reports tempore Mansfield (97–8 ER) 1757–71
Burr.Tr. Burr's Trial, reported by Robertson
Burr.Tr.Rob. Burr's Trial, reported by Robertson
Burr.& Gr.Eq.Pl. Burroughs & Gresson's Irish Equity Pleader
Burrell Burrell's Admiralty Reports ed. by Marsden (167 ER) 1584–1774
Burrill Burrill's Law Dictionary
Burrill Ass. Burrill, Voluntary Assignments
Burrill Circ.Ev. Burrill, Circumstantial Evidence
Burrill Pr. Burrill, New York Practice
Burrow Sett.Cas. Burrow's Settlement Cases. 1733–76
Burt.Cas. Burton's Cases with Opinions. 1700–95
Burt.Man. Burton, Manual of the Laws of Scotland
Burt.Parl. Burton, Parliamentary Diary

Burt.R.P. Burton, Real Property. 8ed. 1856
Burt.Real Prop. Burton, Real Property. 8ed. 1856
Burt.Sc.Tr. Burton's Scotch Trials
Bus. Business
Bus.Corp. Business Corporation
Bus.Hist. Business History
Bus.L. Business and Law (N.Z.) 1966
The Business Lawyer (USA) 1946–
Bus.L.J. Business Law Journal (USA) 1923–32
Bus.L.R. Business Law Review. 1954–8
Business Law Review. 1980–
Bus.L.Rev. Business Law Review. 1954–8
Business Law Review. 1980–
Bus.Law. Business Lawyer (USA) 1946–
Bus.Reg. Business Regulation
Bus.& Com. Business and Commerce
Bus.& Law Business and the Law (Can.) 1985–
Bus.& Prof. Business and Professions
Bus.& Prof.C. Business and Professions Code
Busb. Busbee's North Carolina Reports (44 NC) 1852–3
Busb.Cr.Dig. Busbee's Criminal Digest (North Carolina)
Busb.Eq. Busbee's Equity Reports (45 NC) 1852–3
Busb.L. Busbee's Law Reports (44 NC) 1852–3
Busbee Eq.(N.C.) Busbee's Equity Reports (45 NC) 1852–3
Bush Bush's Kentucky Reports (64–77 Kentucky) 1866–79
Bush Dig. Bush's Digest of Florida Laws
Bush.Elec. Bushby, Parliamentary Elections. 5ed. 1880
Bush (Ky.) Bush's Kentucky Reports (64–77 Kentucky) 1866–79
Business L.J. Business Law Journal (USA) 1923–32
Business L.R. Business Law Review. 1954–8
Business Law Review. 1980–
Business Q. Business Quarterly
Busk.Pr. Buskirk, Indiana Practice
Bustamante Bustamante, Derecho internacional publico. 1933–5
Busw.& Wol.Pr. Buswell & Wolcott, Massachusetts Practice
Butler Co.Litt. Butler's Notes to Coke on Littleton
Butler Hor.Jur. Butler's Horae Juridicae Subsecivae
Butler Report Report of the Home Office Committee on Mentally Abnormal Offenders (Cmnd. 6244) 1975
Butt.R.A. Butterworth's Rating Appeals. 1913–31
Butt.Rat.App. Butterworth's Rating Appeals. 1913–31
Butt.S.A.Law Rev. Butterworth's South African Law Review. 1954–7
Butt.W.C.C. Butterworth's Workmen's Compensation Cases. 1908–47
Butt.Work.Comp.Cas. Butterworth's Workmen's Compensation Cases. 1908–47
Butterworth's S.A.Law Review Butterworth's South African Law Review. 1954–7
Butts Sh. Butts' edition of Shower's King's Bench Reports
Buxton Buxton's Reports (123–9 North Carolina)
Buxton (N.C.) Buxton's Reports (123–9 North Carolina)
By.L.R. Baylor Law Review (Texas) 1948–
Byl.Bills Byles on Bills of Exchange
Byl.Us.L. Byles on the Usuary Laws. 1845
Byles Byles on Bills of Exchange
Byn.War Bynkershoek's Law of War
Bynk. Bynkershoek's Quaestionum Juris Publici
Bynk.Obs.Jur.Rom. Bynkershoek's Observationum Juris Roman Libri
Byrne B.S. Byrne, Bills of Sale. 2ed. 1870
Byth.Conv. Bythewood, Precedents in Conveyancing. 4ed. 1884–90
Byth.Prec. Bythewood, Precedents in Conveyancing. 4ed. 1884–90

C

c. case(s)
chapter
circa (Lat.) about
civil
contre (Fr.) against, versus
criticised

C. All India Reporter, Calcutta Series. 1914–
Calcutta
California
California Reports
Canada
Cape Provincial Division Reports (S.Afr.) 1910–46
Cassazione civile (It.)
Catholic
Century
Chancellor
Chancery
Chapter
Circuit
Codex Juris Civilis
College
Colorado
Command Papers, 2nd series (C.1–9550) 1870–99
Congress
Connecticut
Conservative Party
Copyright
Court
Cowen's New York Reports
Indian Law Reports, Calcutta Series. 1876–

C.2d California Supreme Court Reports, Second Series

C.3d California Supreme Court Reports, Third Series

C33 Public Record Office, Chancery decree and order books

C53 Public Record Office, close rolls

C62 Public Record Office, liberate rolls

C66 Public Record Office, patent rolls

C82 Public Record Office, warrants for the Great Seal

C139–142 Public Record Office, Chancery inquisitions, post mortem

C184 Public Record Office, oath books and rolls of the Clerk of the Crown in Chancery. 1700–

C193/9 Public Record Office, oath book of the Clerk of the Crown in Chancery. 1637–40, 1660–1700

C202 Public Record Office, writs filed in the Petty Bag Office (including Serjeants' writs from 1634)

C216/17–19 Public Record Office, rolls of appearances of Serjeants at Law. 1648–9, 1692–1715, 1740–86

C231 Public Record Office, docket books of the Clerk of the Crown in Chancery

C255/8/6 Public Record Office, file of writs from the Petty Bag records 8–10 Jas. I

C255/13 Public Record Office, Serjeants' writs (down to 1631) formerly filed in the Petty Bag office; continued in C202

C.A. California Appellate Reports
Chartered Accountant
Chief Accountant
Commercial Agent
Consumers' Association
Court of Appeal
Court of Appeals

Court of Appeals Reports (N.Z.)
Crown Agent
Customs Appeals Reports (USA)
Recueils de Jurisprudence, Cour d'Apel (Québec, Can.) 1970–

C.A.2d California Appellate Reports, Second Series

C.A.3d California Appellate Reports, Third Series

C.A.A. Civil Aeronautics Administration (USA)
Civil Aeronautics Authority (USA)
Civil Aeronautics Authority Reports (USA)
Civil Aviation Authority
Commonwealth Arbitration Awards and Determination (Aus.) 1923–36

C.A.A.J. Civil Aeronautics Administration Journal (USA) 1940–

C.A.A.Op. Civil Aeronautics Authority Opinions (USA)

C.A.B. Citizens' Advice Bureau
Civil Aeronautics Board (USA)
Civil Aeronautics Board Reports (USA) 1940–
Civil Aviation Board
Current Affairs Bulletin (Aus.) 1947–

CABEI Central American Bank for Economic Integration

CABx Citizens' Advice Bureaux

C.A.C. Central Arbitration Committee
Code of Advertising Committee
Convention on International Civil Aviation. 1944
Corporate Affairs Commission (Aus.)

C.A.C.M. Central American Common Market

c.-à.-d. c'est-à-dire (Fr.) that is to say

C.A.D. Canadian Annual Digest
Comité d'Aide au Developpement (OECD)
Computer assisted design

C.A.D.C. District of Columbia Court of Appeals (USA)

c.a.f. cost and freight

C.A.F. Colecçao Amarai de Figueiredo (Port.)

CAFOD Catholic Fund for Overseas Development

CAJR Report of New York State Commission on Administration of Justice

C.A.L. Copyright Agency Limited (Aus.)

C.A.L.A. Civil Aviation Licensing Act

C.A.L.Bull. Bulletin of the City of New York Association of the Bar's Committee on Amendment of the Law

C.A.L.L. Canadian Association of Law Libraries

CALS Customs Acts Legislation Service (Aus.) 1984–

C.A.M. Church Assembly Measure
Civil Aeronautics Manual (USA)

C.A.M.E. Conseil d'Assistance Mutuelle Économique

C.A.M.L.A. Communications and Media Law Association (Aus.)

C.A.Mag. C.A. Magazine (Can.) 1867–

CANZLLI Current Australian and New Zealand Legal Literature Index. 1973–

CAO Collectieve Arbeids Overeenkomst (Neth.) Collective Labour Agreement

C.A.P. Code of Advertising Practice. 1962
Common Agricultural Policy (European Communities)

C.A.R. Civil Air Regulations (USA)
Commonwealth Arbitration Reports (Aus.) 1905–
Criminal Appeal Reports. 1908–

CARALL Caribbean Association of Law Libraries

C.A.R.(Aust.) Commonwealth Arbitration Reports (Aus.) 1905–

CARICOM Caribbean Common Market

CARIFTA Caribbean Free Trade Association

CARJIP Caribbean Justice Improvement Project

C.A.S. Codifying Act of Sederunt (Scot.)

C.A.Supp. California Appellate Reports Supplement

C.A.T. Court of Appeal Transcript

CATx Texas Civil Appeals
CAUL Committee of Australian University Librarians
c.a.v. curia advisari vult (Lat.) the court wishes to consider the matter
C.App. Sentenza della Corte di Appello (It.) Decision of the Court of Appeal
C.App.R. Criminal Appeal Reports. 1908–
C.Ass. Sentenza della Corte d'Assise (It.) Decision of the Corte d'Assise
C.B. Butterworths Conveyancing Bulletin (N.Z.) 1982–
Cape Breton
Chief Baron
Citizens' Band Radio
Common Bench Reports by Manning, Granger & Scott (135–9 ER) 1845–56
Cumulative Bulletin of the Internal Revenue Bureau (USA) 1919–
C.B.A. Connecticut Bar Association
C.B.E.S. Recueils de Jurisprudence, Cour de Bien-être Social (Québec, Can.) 1976–9
CBEx Chief Baron of the Exchequer
C.B.I. Confederation of British Industry
C.B.J. Connecticut Bar Journal. 1927–
C.B.L.J. Canadian Business Law Journal. 1975–
C.B.(N.S.) Common Bench Reports by Manning, Granger & Scott, New Series (140–4 ER) 1856–65
C.B.R. Canadian Bankruptcy Reports. 1920–
Canadian Bar Review
Cour du Banc de la Reine (Québec)
Court of Queen's Bench
C.B.R.N.S. Canadian Bankruptcy Reports, New Series. 1960–
C.B.R.P.T. Confederation of British Road Passenger Transport
cc connected case
C.C. Caius College (Cambridge)
California Compensation Cases
Cases in Chancery
Causes Célèbres
Central Committee
Cepi Corpus
Chamber of Commerce
Charity Commission
Circuit Court
City Council
City Court
Civil Code
Civil Court
Close Corporation
Code civil (Fr.) civil code
Codice civile (It.) civil code
Codigo civil
Coleman's New York Cases
Common Council
Contract Clauses (Can.) 1977–
County Council
County Court
Crown Cases
Crown Court
Current Cases (Ghana) 1965–71
Ohio Circuit Court Reports
C.C.A. Cargo Claims Analysis
Caribbean Conservation Association
Circuit Court of Appeals (USA)
Company Labour Agreements (It.)
County Court Appeals
Court of Criminal Appeal
C.C.A.(U.S.) Circuit Court of Appeals (USA)
C.C.B. Code de commerce belge
C.C.B.E. Consultative Committee of the Bars and Law Societies of the European Community
C.C.B.& E.B. Clifford Chance Benefits and Employment Bulletin
C.C.C. Canadian Criminal Cases. 1898–
Central Criminal Court (Old Bailey)
Choyce Cases in Chancery (21 ER) 1557–1606
Commercial Court Committee
Cox's Criminal Cases. 1843–1945
Customs Co-operation Council
C.C.C.(2d) Canadian Criminal Cases, Second Series. 1971–83
C.C.C.(3d) Canadian Criminal Cases, Third Series. 1983–
C.C.C.Cas. Central Criminal Court Session Papers. 1834–1913
CCCN Customs Co-operation Council

Nomenclature

C.C.C.Sess.Pap. Central Criminal Court Session Papers. 1834–1913

CCFTD Convention on the Conflicts of Laws relating to the Form of Testamentary Dispositions. 1961

C.C.I.A. Commission of the Churches on International Affairs

C.C.P. Canadian Competition Policy

CCT Common Customs Tariff of the E.E.C.

C.C.Chr. Chancery Cases Chronicle (Ontario)

C.C.Chron. Chancery Cases Chronicle (Ontario)
County Courts Chronicle. 1847–1920

C.C.Ct.Cas. Central Criminal Court Cases. 1834–1913

CCD Commonwealth Employees' Compensation Decisions (in Australian Administrative Law Service) 1974–81

C.C.E. Caines' Cases in Error, New York
Cases of Contested Elections (USA) 1789–1834

CCEB Continuing Legal Education of the Bar, University of California Extension

C.C.E.L. Canadian Cases on Employment Law. 1983–

C.C.E.R. Canadian Customs and Excise Reports. 1980–

C.C.F. Contract Cases Federal (CCH) 1942–4

CCH Commerce Clearing House, Inc.

CCH Atom.En.L.Rep. Atomic Energy Law Reporter (CCH)

CCH CLC CCH Company Law Cases (Aus.) 1969–81

CCH Comm.Mkt.Rep. Common Market Reporter (CCH)

CCH Fed.Banking L.Rep. Federal Banking Law Reporter (CCH)

CCH Fed.Sec.L.Rep. Federal Securities Law Reporter (CCH)

CCH Inh.Est.& Gift Tax Rep. Inheritance, Estate and Gift Tax Reporter (CCH)

CCH L.L.R. Labor Law Reporter (CCH) 1946–

CCH Lab.Cas. Labor Cases (CCH) 1937–

CCH Lab.L.Rep. Labor Law Reporter (CCH) 1946–

CCH N.S.W.Conv.R. New South Wales Conveyancing Law and Practice (Aus.) 1980–

CCH Q.Conv.R. Queensland Conveyancing Law and Practice. 1982–

CCH Stand.Fed.Tax Rep. Standard Federal Tax Reporter (CCH)

CCH State Tax Cas.Rep. State Tax Cases Reporter (CCH) 1918–44

CCH State Tax Rev. State Tax Review (CCH) 1941–

CCH Tax Ct.Mem. Tax Court Memorandum Decisions (CCH) 1942–

CCH Tax Ct.Rep. Tax Court Reporter (CCH)

CCH.V.Conv.R. Victorian Conveyancing Law and Practice (Aus.) 1981–

C.C.I. Chambre de Commerce International

CCIR International Radio Consultative Committee (International Telecommunication Union)

CCITT International Telegraph and Telephone Consultative Committee (International Telecommunication Union)

C.C.J. County Court Judge

C.C.L. Canadian Current Law. 1957–
Council for Civil Liberties (Aus.)

C.C.L.C. Civil Code (Québec)

C.C.L.I. Canadian Cases on the Law of Insurance. 1983–

C.C.L.R. Canadian Computer Law Reporter
Consumer Credit Law Reports

C.C.L.T. Canadian Cases on the Law of Torts. 1976–

C.C.N. Commonwealth Employees' Compensation Notes (in Australian Administrative Law Service) 1974–81

CCNL National Collective Labour Contracts (It.)

C.C.N.S. Ohio Circuit Court Reports, New Series
C.C.O. Code of Court Organisation (Neth.)
C.C.P. Code of Civil Proceedings (Neth.)
Code of Civil Procedure
County Court Practice
Court of Common Pleas
C.C.P.A. Court of Customs and Patent Appeals (USA)
Reports of the Court of Customs and Patent Appeals (USA) 1929–
CCPIT China Committee (Council) for the Promotion of International Trade
C.C.Q. Civil Code of Quebec
C.C.R. Calendar of the Close Rolls
Circuit Court Reports (USA)
City Courts Reports (USA)
County Court Reports. 1860–1920
County Court Rules
Court for Crown Cases Reserved
Crown Cases Reserved. 1865–75
CCRC County Court Rules Committee
C.C.R.E.M. Canadian Commercial Real Estate Manual. 1986–
C.C.R.Vic. County Court Reports, Victoria (Aus.)
C.C.Rep. County Courts Reporter (in Law Journal)
CCS Code civil suisse (Switz.)
C.C.S.M. Continuing Consolidation of the Statutes of Manitoba (Can.) 1970–
C.C.Supp. City Court Reports, Supplement (New York)
C.C.T. Common customs tariff
C.C.U.S. Circuit Courts of the United States
C.C.W. Council for Children's Welfare
C.C.& B.B. Cepi Corpus and Bail Bond
C.C.& C. Cepi Corpus and Committitur
C.civ. Code civil (Fr.) civil code
C.civ.ann. Code civil annoté Dalloz (Fr.) annotated civil code
C.Civ.Proc. Code of Civil Procedure
C.Cl. Court of Claims Reports (USA)
C.com. Code de commerce (Fr.) commercial code
C.comm. Codice commerciale (It.) commercial code
C.Cost. Corte Costituzionale (It.) Constitutional Court
C.Cr.Pr. Code of Criminal Procedure
c.d. compact disk
cum dividendo (Lat.) with dividend
c/d certificate of deposit
C.D. Application for certiorari denied
Century Digest (USA)
Chancery Division
Circuit Decisions
Commissioner's Decisions, U.S. Patent Office
Compact Disk
Comyn's Digest of the Laws of England. 1762–1882
Corps Diplomatique
Customs Court Decisions (USA)
Customs Decisions (U.S. Treasury Department)
Ohio Circuit Decisions
CDA Central Dispatching Administration of the Unified Grid Systems
CDB Caribbean Development Bank
C.D.C. Cahiers de Droit Comparé (Belg.) 1964–
Commonwealth Development Corporation
Control Data Corporation
C.D.E. Cahiers de Droit Européen (Belg.) 1965–
C.D.F. Cahiers de Droit Familial (Belg.) 1973–
C.D.F.C. Commonwealth Development Finance Company Ltd.
C.D.I. Commission du droit international des Nations Unies
CDIU Centrale Dienst In– en Uitvoer (Neth.) Central Bureau for Import and Export
CDR Centre for Dispute Resolution
CDRG Construction Disputes Resolution Group
C.de D. Cahiers de Droit (Can.) 1954–
C.douanes Code des douanes (Fr.) Customs (excise) code

c.e. caveat emptor (Lat.) let the buyer beware
C.E. Arrêt du Conseil d'État
Commisaire Enqueteur (Québec, Can.)
Conseil d'État (Belg., Fr.) Council of State, Supreme Administrative Court
Council of Europe
Customs & Excise
C.E.A. Comité Européen d'Assurances (European Insurance Committee)
CEAO West African Economic Community
C.E.B.& P.G.R. Canadian Employment Benefits and Pension Guide Reports
C.E.C.A. Communauté européenne du charbon et de l'acier (European Coal and Steel Community)
C.E.D. Canadian Encyclopedic Digest
CEDR Centre for Dispute Resolution
C.E.E. Communauté économique européenne (European Economic Community)
CEFA Convention on the Execution of Foreign Arbitral Awards. 1927
C.E.Gr. C.E. Greene's New Jersey Equity Reports (16–27 NJEq)
C.E.Greene C.E. Greene's New Jersey Equity Reports (16–27 NJEq)
CELA Newsletter Canadian Environmental Law Association Newsletter. 1975–
CELI Caribbean Environmental Law Index
C.E.L.R. Canadian Environmental Law Reports. 1972–
C.E.M.A. Council for Economic Mutual Assistance
C.E.N. European Standards Co-ordination Committee
CENTO Central Treaty Organisation (Baghdad Pact)
C.E.P. Community Enterprise Programme
C.E.P.C. Comité européen pour les problèmes criminels (European Committee on Crime Problems)
CEPT European Conference of Postal and Telecommunications Administrations
C.E.R. Canadian Customs and Excise Reports. 1980–
Closer Economic Relations
CERD Convention on the Elimination of all Forms of Racial Discrimination. 1966
C.E.R.D.S. Charter of Economic Rights and Duties of States
C.E.R.N. Centre Européen de Recherche Nucléaire
C.E.S. Court of Exchequer (Scot.)
CESI Centre for Economic and Social Information (U.N.)
C.E.T. Common external tariff
C.Environ.L.N. Canadian Environmental Law News. 1972–
C.F. Code forestier (Fr.) Forestry code
Conseil fédéral suisse (Switz.)
C.F.A. Communauté financière africaine
Consumer Federation of America
C.F.F. Chemins de fer fédéraux
c.f.i. cost, freight and insurance
CFIMT Convention on the Facilitation of International Maritime Traffic. 1965
C.F.L.Q. Canadian Family Law Quarterly. 1986–
C.F.R. Calendar of Fine Rolls
Code of Freight Regulations (USA)
CFW Convention concerning Frontier Workers. 1950
c.f.& i. cost, freight and insurance
C.for. Code forestier (Fr.) Forestry code
CG Consultative Group
CGCE Corte di giustizia delle Comunita Europee (It.) Court of Justice of the European Communities
CGCM Court Martial Reports, Coast Guard Cases (New York)
CGCMM Coast Guard Court Martial Manual (USA)
C.G.H. Cape of Good Hope (S.Afr.)
C.G.I. Code général des impôts (Fr.)
C.G.O. Comptroller General's Opinions, Treasury Department (USA)
C.G.P.M. General Conference on Weights and Measures
CGR Coast Guard Regulations (USA)

C.G.S. Commissioner of the Great Seal
C.G.S.A. Connecticut General Statutes Annotated
C.G.T. Capital Gains Tax
C.gen.imp. Code général des impôts (Fr.) general code of taxes
C.H. W. Stubbs, The Constitutional History of England. 5ed. 1891
CHAPS Clearing House Automated Payments System
CHAR Campaign for the Homeless and Rootless
CHAS Catholic Housing Aid Society
C.H.C. Clerk to the House of Commons
CHESS Support Scheme for Higher Education throughout the Commonwealth
C.H.O.G.M. Commonwealth Heads of Government Meeting
C.H.R.R. Canadian Human Rights Reporter. 1980–
C.H.Rec. City Hall Recorder (New York)
C.H.Rep. City Hall Reporter (New York)
C.H.R.Y.B. Canadian Human Rights Yearbook. 1983–
C.H.& A. Carrow, Hamerton & Allen's Session Cases (Scot.) 1844–51
C.Home Clerk Home's Decisions, Court of Session (Scot.) 1844–51
C.I. Channel Islands
Committee of Inspection
La Communita Internazionale
Constitutional Instrument (Ghana)
Criminal Investigation Branch (Aus.)
Cumulative Index
Decisions of the Commissioner under the National Insurance (Industrial Injuries) Acts. 1948–
C.I.A. Central Intelligence Agency
C.I.B. Commercial and Industrial Bulletin (Ghana) 1960–
Customs Acts Legislation Service Information Bulletin (Aus.) 1984–
C.i.c. Code d'instruction criminelle (Fr.) Code of criminal procedure
C.I.C. Cost, Insurance, Commission
Current Indian Cases (India) 1912–15
CICES Convention for the International Council for the Exploration of the Sea. 1964
C.I.D. Centre for Industrial Development (E.E.C./A.C.P.)
Criminal Investigation Department
CIDA Canadian International Development Agency
C.I.E.C. Centre international d'études criminologiques (International Centre for Criminological Studies)
Commission Internationale de l'État Civil
c.i.f. cost, insurance, freight
c.i.f.c.i. cost, insurance, freight, commission and interest
c.i.f.e. cost, insurance, freight and exchange
c.i.f.i. cost, insurance, freight and interest
c.i.f.& c. cost, insurance, freight and commission
C.I.I. Chartered Insurance Institute
C.I.J. Cour internationale de Justice
C.I.J.Annuaire Annuaire de la Cour international de Justice
C.I.J.L.Bulletin Centre for the Independence of Judges and Lawyers Bulletin (Switz.)
C.I.J.Rec. Cour international de Justice, Recueil des arrêts, avis consultatifs et ordonnances
C.I.J.Mémoires Cour international de Justice, Mémoires, Plaidoiries et Documents
C.I.L.L. Construction Industry Law Letter
C.I.L.S. Center for International Legal Studies (USA)
C.I.L.S.A. The Comparative and International Law Journal of Southern Africa. 1968–
CIM Chief Industrial Magistrate (Aus.)
Convention internationale concernant le transport des merchandises par chemins de fer (International Convention concerning the Carriage of Goods by Rail)
CIME Committee for International

Investment and Multinational Enterprises
C.I.O. Congress of Industrial Organisations
C.I.P.A. Chartered Institute of Patent Agents
The Journal of the Chartered Institute of Patent Agents
CIPEC Intergovernmental Council of Copper Exporting Countries
C.I.P.M. Calendar of Inquisitions post Mortem
C.I.P.R. Canadian Intellectual Property Reports. 1984–
C.I.R. Commission on Industrial Relations
CIRCE European Communities Information and Documentary Research Centre
CIRCIT Centre for International Research on Communication and Information Technologies
C.I.R.D.I. Centre International pour le Règlement des Différends Relatifs aux Investissements
CIRIB International Commission for Rationalisation in Banking
C.I.T.C.M. Canberra Income Tax Circular Memorandum. 1930–82
CITEJA International Technical Committee of Aerial Legal Experts
C.I.T.R. Calendar of Inner Temple Records, ed. by Inderwick & Roberts. 1896–1936
C.I.T.T. Canadian International Trade Tribunal. Bulletin. 1989–
CIV Convention internationale concernant le transport des voyageurs et des bagages par chemins de fer (International Convention concerning the Carriage of Passengers and Baggage by Rail)
C.inst.crim. Code d'instruction criminelle (Belg. & Fr.) Code of criminal procedure
C.instr.cr. Code d'instruction criminelle (Belg. & Fr.) Code of criminal procedure
C.instr.crim. Code d'instruction criminelle (Belg. & Fr.) Code of criminal procedure
C.J. Chief Justice or Judge
Circuit Judge
Corpus Juris
Journal of the House of Commons
Lord Chief Justice
C.J.A.L.P. Canadian Journal of Administrative Law and Practice. 1987–
C.J.Ann. Corpis Juris Annotations
C.J.B. Chief Judge in Bankruptcy
C.J.C. Community Justice Centre (Aus.)
Corpus Juris Civilis
Couper's Justiciary Cases (Scot.) 1868–85
C.J.C.P. Chief Justice of the Common Pleas
C.J.Can. Corpus Juris Canonici
C.J.Civ. Corpus Juris Civilis
C.J.D. Campaign for Justice in Divorce
CJEC Court of Justice of the European Communities
C.J.F. Chief Justice of the Federation (Nigeria)
C.J.in Eq. Chief Judge in Equity (New South Wales, Aus.)
C.J.K.B. Chief Justice of the King's Bench
C.J.L. Columbia Journal of Law and Social Problems. 1965–
C.J.L.J. Canadian Journal of Law and Jurisprudence. 1988–
C.J.M.B. Chief Judge's Minute Book (Maori Land Court) (N.Z.)
C.J.N. Chief Justice of Nigeria
C.J.Q. Civil Justice Quarterly
C.J.Q.B. Chief Justice of the Queen's Bench
C.J.S. Corpus Juris Secundum
C.J.U.B. Chief Justice of the Common (Upper) Bench
C.K. Chicago-Kent Law Review (Illinois) 1923–38, 1938–
C.K.L.R. Chicago-Kent Law Review (Illinois) 1923–38, 1938–
C.L. Butterworths Current Law (N.Z.) 1969–
Civil Law

Civil Liberties
Les codes Larcier (Belg.) collection of legislation
Commercial List
Common Law
Common Law Reports. 1853–5
Current Law. 1947–
Irish Common Law Reports
C.L.A. Computer Law Association (USA)
Copyright Licensing Agency
University of California at Los Angeles Law Review. 1953–
C.L.A.A.B. Commercial Law Association of Australia Bulletin. 1983–6
C.L.A.A.Bull. Commercial Law Association of Australia Bulletin. 1983–6
C.L.A.B. Commercial Law Association Bulletin (Aus.) 1968–83
C.L.A.Bull. Commercial Law Association Bulletin (Aus.) 1968–83
C.L.B. Commonwealth Law Bulletin. 1974–
Communications Law Bulletin (Aus.) 1981–
C.L.B.U. China Law and Business Update (Aus.)
C.L.C. Australian Company Law Cases (in Australian Corporate Affairs Reporter) (CCH) 1971–81
Current Law Consolidation
C.L.Ch. Common Law Chamber Reports, Ontario (Can.)
C.L.Chamb. Common Law Chamber Reports, Ontario (Can.)
C.L.Chamb.Rep. Common Law Chamber Reports, Ontario (Can.)
CLD CompuLaw Digest (Aus.) 1985–
C.L.D. Case Law Digest (Canadian Abridgment)
Company Lawyer Digest
Criminal Law Digest (USA) 1965–70, 1983–
C.L.E. Commercial Laws of Europe
Continuing Legal Education
Council of Legal Education
C.L.E.A. Commonwealth Legal Education Association
C.L.E.A.Newsl. Commonwealth Legal Education Association Newsletter
C.L.E.Bull. Continuing Legal Education Bulletin (Queensland Law Society) (Aus.) 1985–
C.L.E.O. Community Legal Education Office (Victoria, Aus.)
CLG Chinese Law and Government
C.L.G.A.Newsl. Customary Law Group of Australia Newsletter. 1977–
C.L.I. Caribbean Law Institute
Commodity Law International
CLIC Canadian Law Information Council
C.L.I.P. Centre for Legal Information and Publications (College of Law, St Leonards, New South Wales, Aus.)
C.L.J. Calcutta Law Journal (India) 1905–
California Law Journal. 1862–3
Cambridge Law Journal. 1921–
Canada Law Journal. 1855–1922
Cape Law Journal (S.Afr.) 1884–1900
Central Law Journal (USA) 1874–1927
Ceylon Law Journal (Sri L.) 1885–92
Chicago Law Journal. 1883–1907
Colonial Law Journal (N.Z.) 1865, 1874–5
Colonial Law Journal Reports (N.Z.) 1865, 1874–75
Criminal Law Journal (Aus.) 1977–
Criminal Law Journal (India) 1904–
C.L.J.N.S. Canada Law Journal, New Series. 1865–1922
C.L.J.O.S. Canada Law Journal, Old Series. 1855–64
C.L.J.& Lit.Rev. California Law Journal and Literary Review. 1862–3
C.L.L. Canadian Law Libraries. 1975–
Commonwealth Law Librarian. 1992–
Corporate Legal Letter
C.L.L.C. Canadian Labour Law Cases
C.L.L.R. Crown Lands Law Reports (Queensland, Aus.) 1859–1973
C.L.M. Current Law Monthly. 1947–
C.L.N. Chicago Legal News. 1868–1925

C.L.P. Common law procedure
Current Legal Problems. 1948–
C.L.P.A. Common Law Procedure Acts
C.L.P.Act Common Law Procedure Acts
CLPD Convention abolishing the Requirement of Legislation for Foreign Public Documents. 1961
C.L.Q. Commercial Law Quarterly (Aus.) 1987–
Cornell Law Quarterly (New York) 1915–67
Criminal Law Quarterly (Can.) 1957–
C.L.(Q.) Crown Lands Law Reports (Queensland, Aus.) 1859–1973
C.L.R. Calcutta Law Reports (India) 1877–84
Canada Law Reports. 1923–
Cape Law Reports (S.Afr.)
Ceylon Law Reports (Sri L.)
Cleveland Law Record (USA)
Columbia Law Review (USA) 1901–
Common Law Reports. 1853–55
Commonwealth Law Reports (Aus.) 1903–
Commonwealth Law Review
Construction Law Reports (Can.) 1983–
Cornell Law Review. 1967–
Criminal Law Review. 1954–
Crown Lands Law Reports (Queensland, Aus.) 1859–
Cyprus Law Reports. 1883–
C.L.R.Aust. Commonwealth Law Reports (Aus.) 1903–
C.L.R.B. Canadian Labour Relations Board
C.L.R.B.R. Canadian Labour Relations Board Reports. 1974–82
C.L.R.B.R.(N.S.) Canadian Labour Relations Board Reports, New Series. 1983–
C.L.R.C. Canada Law Reform Commission
Copyright Law Review Committee (Aus.)
Criminal Law Revision Committee
C.L.R.(Can.) Canada Law Reports. 1923–
Common Law Reports (Can.) 1835–55
C.L.Rec. Cleveland Law Record (USA)
C.L.Reg. Cleveland Law Register (USA)
C.L.Rep. Cleveland Law Reporter (USA) 1878–9
C.L.S. Canada Labour Service. 1945–
Christian Lawyers' Society (Victoria, Aus.)
CLSR The Computer Law and Security Report. 1985–
C.L.S.R.C. Company Law and Securities Review Committee (Aus.)
C.L.Stats. Current Law Statutes Annotated
C.L.T. Canadian Law Times. 1881–1922
Cuttack Law Times (Orissa, India) 1935–
C.L.T.Occ.N. Canadian Law Times Occasional Notes. 1881–1909
C.L.W. Ceylon Law Weekly (Sri L.) 1932–
C.L.Y. Current Law Year Book. 1947–
C.L.Y.B. Current Law Year Book. 1947–
C.L.& P. Computer Law and Practice
C.L.& P.R. Charity Law and Practice Review
C.Lar. Les codes Larcier (Belg.) collection of legislation
C.Leg.Rec. California Legal Record. 1878–9
c.m. causa mortis (Lat.) by reason of death
C.M. Camden Miscellany
Canberra Income Tax Circular Memorandum (Aus.) 1930–82
Cleveland State Law Review. 1969–
Cleveland-Marshall Law Review (Ohio) 1951–69
Compliance Monitor
Council of Ministers
Court Martial Reports, Army Cases (USA)
C.M.A. Court of Military Appeals Reports (USA) 1951–
C.-M.A.C. Courts Martial Appeal Court
C.M.C. Collective Measures Commission (UN)

C.M.E.A. Council for Mutual Economic Assistance
C.M.H. Cambridge Medieval History
C.M.J. Canadian Municipal Journal. 1891–2
C.M.L.R. Cleveland-Marshall Law Review (Ohio) 1951–69
Common Market Law Reports. 1962–
Common Market Law Review. 1963–
C.M.L.Rev. Common Market Law Review. 1963–
C.M.P.R. Canadian Mortgage Practice Reporter. 1979–86
CMR Convention on the Contract for the International Carriage of Goods by Road
C.M.R. Common Market Reporter (CCH)
Court-Martial Reports (USA) 1951–
Court of Military Review (USA)
CMT Cellular mobile telephony
CMTR Calendar of the Middle Temple Records, ed. by C.H. Hopwood. 1903
C.M.& H. Cox, Macrae & Hertslet's County Court Reports. 1847–57
C.M.& R. Crompton, Meeson & Roscoe's Exchequer Reports (149–50 ER) 1834–5
C.N. Code Napoléon (Fr.) civil code
Conseil National (Switz.)
CNAF International Convention for the Northwest Atlantic Fisheries. 1949
C.N.Conf. Cameron & Norwood's North Carolina Conference Reports
C.N.L.B. Canadian Native Law Bulletin. 1977–8
C.N.L.R. Canadian Native Law Reporter. 1979–
C.N.P. Cases at Nisi Prius
C.N.P.C. Campbell's Nisi Prius Cases (170–1 ER) 1808–16
C.N.U.C.E.D. Conference des Nations Unies sur le Commerce et le Developpement
C.N.U.D.C.I. Commission des Nations Unies pour le Droit Commercial International
CNV Christelijk Nationaal Vakverbond (Neth.) National Federation of Christian Democratic Workers
c/o care of
carried over
certificate of origin
C.O. Code des obligations (Switz.)
Colonial Office
Common Orders
Criminal Office
Crown Office
COCOM Consultative Group Co-ordinating Committee
C.O.D. Cash on delivery
Collect on delivery
Crown Office Digest
CODI Customers of Dynix Inc.
COFACE Compagnie français d'assurance pour le commerce extérieur
COFI Committee on Fisheries (FAO)
C.O.H.S.C. Canadian Occupational Health and Safety Cases. 1989–
C.O.I. Central Office of Information
COIE Committee on Invisible Exports
COM Council of Ministers (E.E.C.)
Council of Ministers document
COMECON Council of Mutual Economic Assistance
C.O.M.S.A.T. Communications Satellite Corporation (USA)
C.O.R. Crown Office Rules
COREPER European Communities Committee of Permanent Representatives
CORFO Corporacion de Fomento de la Produccion de Chile (Chilean Development Corporation)
COSIRA Council for Small Industries in Rural Areas
COST European Co-operation in Science and Technology
C.O.T. Council on Tribunals
C.of C.E. Cases of Contested Elections (USA) 1789–1834
C.of E. Church of England
Council of Europe
C.of E.Agr.P.I. General Agreement on Privileges and Immunities of the Council of Europe

C.of I.R. Commissioner of Inland Revenue (N.Z.)
C.of S.Ca. Court of Session Cases (Scot.)
C.of S.Ca.1st Series Court of Session Cases, First Series, by Shaw, Dunlop & Bell (Scot.) 1821–38
C.of S.Ca.2nd Series Court of Session Cases, Second Series, by Dunlop, Bell & Murray (Scot.) 1838–62
C.of S.Ca.3rd Series Court of Session Cases, Third Series, by Macpherson, Lee & Bell (Scot.) 1862–73
C.of S.Ca.4th Series Court of Session Cases, Fourth Series, by Rettie, Crawford & Melville (Scot.) 1873–98
C.of S.Ca.5th Series Court of Session Cases, Fifth Series, by Fraser (Scot.) 1898–1906
C.p. Code pénal (Belg. & Fr.) criminal code
Codice penale (It.) criminal code
C.P. Cape Province (S.Afr.)
Central Provinces (Madhya Pradesh, India)
Charter Party
Chief Prosecutor (Swed.)
Civil Power
Civil Procedure
Civil Procedure Reports (New York)
Clerk of the Peace
Code of Practice
Code of Procedure
Code Pénal
Code pénal suisse
Common Pleas
Commonwealth Preference
Complete Peerage. 1910–59
Convicted Poacher
Court of Common Pleas
Court of Probate
Crown Pleas
Law Reports, Common Pleas. 1865–75
Recueil de Jurisprudence, Cour provinciale (Québec, Can.) 1976–
Upper Canada, Common Pleas Reports. 1850–82
C.P.A. Commonwealth Parliamentary Association
Cour permanent d'arbitrage
C.P.A.C. Consumer Protection Advisory Committee
CPAG Child Poverty Action Group
C.P.A.M. Caisse Primaire d'Assurance Maladie (Fr.)
c.p.c. code de procédure civile (Fr.) code of civil procedure
codice di procedura civile (It.) code of civil procedure
C.P.C. Carswell's Practice Cases (Can.) 1976–
Cooper's Chancery Practice Cases (47 ER) 1837–8
Clerk of the Privy Council
Code de Procédure Civil (code of civil procedure)
Code of Civil Procedure (Québec)
C.P.C.t.Br. C.P. Cooper's Chancery Reports tempore Brougham (47 ER) 1833–4
C.P.C.t.Cott. C.P. Cooper's Chancery Reports tempore Cottenham (47 ER) 1846–8
C.P.Coop. C.P. Cooper's Chancery Practice Cases (47 ER) 1837–8
C.P.Cooper C.P. Cooper's Chancery Practice Cases (47 ER) 1837–8
C.P.D. Law Reports, Common Pleas Division. 1875–80
South African Law Reports, Cape Provincial Division. 1910–46
C.P.Div. Law Reports, Common Pleas Division. 1875–80
C.P.E. Centrally Planned Economies
Chronique de politique etrangère
Common Professional Examination
Customer premises equipment
C.P.F.I. Caisse de Péréquation de la Ferraille Importée
C.P.I. Consumer Price Index
Court Practice Institute (USA)
C.P.Ind. Central Provinces, India
C.P.J.I. Cour permanent de justice internationale (Permanent Court of International Justice)
C.P.J.I.,Serie A Cour permanent de justice internationale: Arrêts

C.P.J.I.,Serie B Cour permanent de justice internationale: Avis consultatifs
C.P.J.I.,Serie A/B Cour permanent de justice internationale: Arrêts, ordonnances et avis consultatifs depuis 1931
C.P.J.I.,Serie C Cour permanent de justice internationale: Actes et documents concernant les arrêts et avis consultatifs
C.P.J.I.,Serie D Cour permanent de justice internationale: Collection des textes concernant le compétence de la Cour
C.P.J.I.,Serie E Cour permanent de justice internationale: Rapports annuels
C.P.L. Conveyancer and Property Lawyer. 1936–
Current Property Law. 1952–3
C.P.L.R. Central Provinces Law Reports (India) 1886–1904
Civil Practice Law and Rules (USA)
C.P.O.R. Canadian Patents Office Record. 1950–69
c.p.p. codice di procedure penale (It.) code of criminal procedure
C.P.P. Canadian Public Policy
Code de procédure pénale
Craig–Park–Paulsson, International Chamber of Commerce Arbitration (USA) 1983
C.P.Q. Code of Civil Procedure, Quebec
C.P.R. Calendar of the Patent Rolls preserved in the Public Record Office. 1891–
Canadian Patent Reporter. 1941–
C.P.Rep. Common Pleas Reporter, Scranton, Pennsylvania
C.P.S. Clerk of Petty Sessions (Aus.)
Code pénal suisse
Crown Prosecution Service
Custos Privati Siglii (Lat.) Keeper of the Privy Seal
C.P.S.A.R. Commonwealth Public Service Arbitration Reports (Aus.) 1920–
C.P.S.C. Consumer Product Safety Commission (USA)
CPS Commission Consumer Product Safety Commission (USA)
C.P.T. Code des Postes et Télécommunications (Fr.)
CPU Central processing unit
C.P.U.C. Common Pleas Reports, Upper Canada. 1850–82
C.pen. Code pénal (Fr.) criminal code
Codice penale (It.)
C.Pr. Code of Procedure
C.pr.civ. Code de Procédure civile (Belg. & Fr.) code of civil procedure
C.pr.pén. Code de procédure pénale (Belg. & Fr.) code of criminal procedure
C.Priv. Committee for Privileges, House of Commons/Lords
C.proc.civ. Code de procédure civile (Belg. & Fr.) code of civil procedure
C.Q.A. Congressional Quarterly Almanac (USA)
C.Q.S. Chartered Quantity Surveyor
C.R. Canadian Reports, Appeal Cases. 1828–1913
Carolina Regina (Queen Caroline)
Carolus Rex (King Charles)
Central Reporter
Chancery Reports
Close Rolls
Code Reporter
Columbia Law Review. 1901–
Commonwealth Record (Aus.) 1976–87
Compte rendu des séances, Chambre des députés (Lux.) annual publication
Conseil de la République (Fr.)
Conveyancing Review (Scot.) 1957–
Criminal Reports (Can.) 1946–67, 1978–
Curia Regis (King's Court)
Custos Rotulorum (Keeper of the Rolls)
C.R.(3d) Criminal Reports, Third Series (Can.) 1978–
C.R.A.C. Canadian Reports, Appeal Cases. 1828–1913
C.R.C. Canadian Railway and Transport Cases. 1902–
Consolidated Regulations of Canada
C.R.D. Charter of Rights Decisions (Can.) 1982–
C.R.E. Commission for Racial Equality
CREFA Convention on the

Recognition and Enforcement of Foreign Arbitral Awards. 1958

C.R.E.News. Charles Russell Employment Newsletter

CRFF Convention on the Rights and Obligations of Foreign Forces and their Members in the Federal Republic of Germany. 1952

CRMN European Convention on the Reduction of Multiple Nationality. 1963

C.R.N.S. Code Reports, New Series (New York)
Criminal Reports, New Series (Can.) 1967–78

C.R.N.Z. Criminal Reports of New Zealand. 1983–

C.R.O. Central Records Office (USA)
Companies Registration Office

C.R.P. Calendarium Rotulorum Patentium (Calendar of the Patent Rolls)

CRPG Convention on Relations between the Three Powers and the Federal Republic of Germany. 1952

C.R.R. Canadian Rights Reporter. 1982–
Chief Registrar's Reports of Friendly Societies
Curia Regis Roll

C.R.T.C. Canadian Railway and Transport Cases. 1902–

C.Rev. Criminal Review (USA)

C.Rob. Christopher Robinson's Admiralty Reports (165 ER) 1799–1808

C.Rob.Adm. Christopher Robinson's Admiralty Reports (165 ER) 1799–1808

C.S. Civil Servant
Civil Service
Civil Suit
Clerk of Session
Clerk to the Signet (Scot.)
Common Serjeant
Compiled Statutes
Comunicazioni e Studi dell'Istituto di Diritto Internazionale e Straniero dell'Universita di Milano (It.)
Connecticut Supplement (USA)
Consolidated Statutes
Court of Session (Scot.)
Customer Support
Custos Sigilli (Keeper of the Seal)
Quebec Reports, Supreme Court (Can.) 1942–

C.S.A.A. Civil Service Arbitration Awards

C.S.B. Companies and Securities Bulletin (Aus.) 1982–

C.S.B.C. Consolidated Statutes, British Columbia

C.S.C. Canada Supreme Court
Civil Service Commission (UK & USA)
Court of Session Cases (Scot.)

C.S.C.R. Cincinnati Superior Court Reporter (USA)

C.S.D. Civil Service Department
Commissioner of Stamp Duties (Aus.)

CSE Convention on Student Employees. 1950

C.S.F.O. Corporate Structure, Finance and Operations: essays on the law and business practice (Can.) 1980–

CSFT Convention and Statute on Freedom of Transit. 1921

C.S.I. Decisions of the Commissioners under the National Insurance (Industrial Injuries) Acts, relating to Scotland. 1948–

C.S.J. Crime and Social Justice (Aus.) 1974–

C.S.L.C. Consolidated Statutes of Lower Canada

C.S.L.R. Cleveland State Law Review. 1969–

C.S.L.R.C. Companies and Securities Law Review Committee (Aus.)

CSLS International Convention for the Safety of Life at Sea. 1960

C.S.M. Chief Stipendiary Magistrate
Consolidated Statutes of Manitoba (Can.)

CSMW Convention on the Settlement of Matters arising out of the War and the Occupation. 1954

C.S.N.B. Consolidated Statutes of New Brunswick (Can.)

C.S.O. Central Statistical Office
Community service obligation

C.S.P. Recueils de Jurisprudence, Cour des Sessions de la Paix (Québec, Can.) 1976–

CSPD Calendar of State Papers (Domestic)

C.S.P.R.U. Civil Service Pay Research Unit

C.S.U.C. Consolidated Statutes, Upper Canada

C.S.U.L.A. California State University, Los Angeles

C.S.V.S. Chartered Surveyors Voluntary Service

C.S.W. Chartered Surveyor Weekly

C.S.& J. Cushing, Storey & Joselyn's Election Cases (Massachusetts)

C.S.& P. Craigie, Stewart & Paton's Appeal Cases (Scot.) 1726–1821

C.Sess. Court of Session (Scotland)

C.Stato Consiglio di Stato (It.)

C.T. Cape Times (S.Afr.)
Constitutiones Tiberii
Corporation Tax
Council on Tribunals
Court Trust

c.t.a. cum testamento annexo (Lat.) with will annexed

C.T.B.R. Commonwealth Taxation Board of Review Decisions, Old Series (Aus.) 1925–51

C.T.B.R.(N.S.) Taxation Board of Review Decisions, New Series (Aus.) 1950–86

C.T.B.R.(N.S.)V.T.B.R.Case Victorian Taxation Board of Review Case

C.T.C. Canada Tax Cases. 1917–
Canadian Transport Cases. 1966–
Centre on Transnational Corporations
Commission on Transnational Corporations
Cuban Labor Confederation

C.T.C.L.R. Cape Times Common Law Reports (S.Afr.) 1891–1910

C.T.E.C. Canadian Temporary Economic Controls

C.t.K. Select Cases tempore King, Chancery (25 ER) 1724–33

C.t.N. Eden's Chancery Reports tempore Northington (28 ER) 1757–66

C.T.N. Cases in the time of L.C. Northington

C.T.News & Reps. Capital Taxes News and Reports

C.T.P. Capital Tax Planning Convention containing the Transitional Provisions (E.C.S.C.)

C.T.R. Cape Times Reports (S.Afr.) 1891–1910

C.T.S. Concise Tax Service (Aus.) 1980–
Consolidated Treaty Series (ed. by C. Parry)

C.t.T. Cases in Equity tempore Talbot (25 ER) 1733–8

C.T.T. Capital Transfer Tax

C.T.T.News C.T.T. News: a Monthly Review of Capital Transfer Tax Law. 1979–

C.T.& E.P.Q. Capital Taxes and Estate Planning Quarterly

C.Tax C. Canada Tax Cases. 1917–

C.Theod. Codex Theodosianus (Lat.) The Theodosian Code

C.Tr. Corporate Trust

C.trav. code du travail (Fr.) labour code

C.U. California Unreported Cases

C.U.A.L.R. Catholic University of America Law Review. 1950–75

C.U.A.L.S. Catholic University of America Law School

C.U.B. Canadian Unemployment Benefits

C.U.L. Cambridge University Library

C.U.L.R. Catholic University Law Review (USA) 1975–

CUN Charter of the United Nations

C.U.R. University of Colorado Law Review. 1962–

c.v. commanditaire vennootschap (Neth.) limited partnership

C.Vict. Dominion of Canada Statutes in the Reign of Victoria

C.W. Copyright World

C.W.C.L. Conspectus of Workers' Compensation Legislation (Aus.) 1964–79

CWDE Centre for World Development Education

C.W.Dud. C.W. Dudley's Law Reports, South Carolina

C.W.Dud.Eq. C.W. Dudley's Equity Reports, South Carolina

C.W.H. Committee of the Whole House, House of Lords

C.W.I. Decisions of the Commissioners under the National Insurance (Industrial Injuries) Acts relating to Wales. 1948–

C.W.L. Case Western Reserve Law Review (Ohio) 1967–

C.W.N. Calcutta Weekly Notes (India) 1896–

C.W.R. Ceylon Weekly Reporter (Sri L.) 1915–20

C.Y.C. Cyclopedia of Law and Procedure, New York

C.Y.P.A. Children and Young Persons Act

C.Z. Canal Zone

C.Z.Code Canal Zone Code

C.Z.Rep. Canal Zone Reports, Supreme and District Courts

C.& A. Cooke & Alcock's King's Bench Reports (Ire.) 1833–4

C.& C. Case and Comment
Coleman & Caine's Cases (New York)

C.& D. Corbett & Daniell's Election Cases. 1819–
Crawford & Dix's Circuit Cases (Ire.) 1839–46

C.& D.A.C. Crawford & Dix's Abridged Cases (Ire.) 1839–46

C.& D.C.C. Crawford & Dix's Circuit Cases (Ire.) 1839–46

C.& E. Cababe & Ellis' Queen's Bench Reports. 1882–5

c.& f. cost and freight

C.& F. Clark & Finnelly's House of Lords Cases (6–8 ER) 1831–46

C.& F.L. Credit and Finance Law

C.& H.Char.Tr. Cooke & Harwood, Charitable Trusts. 2ed. 1867

C.& H.Dig. Coventry & Hughes' Digest

C.& H.Elec.Cas. Clarke & Hall's Cases of Contested Elections in Congress (USA) 1789–1834

C.& J. Crime and Justice Bulletin (New South Wales Attorney-General's Department) (Aus.)
Crompton & Jervis's Exchequer Reports (148–9 ER) 1830–2

C.& K. Carrington & Kirwan's Nisi Prius Reports (174–5 ER) 1843–50

C.& L. Connor & Lawson's Chancery Reports (Ire.) 1841–3

C.& L.C.C. Caines & Leigh's Crown Cases

C.& L.Dig. Cohen & Lee's Maryland Digest

C.& M. Carrington & Marshman's Nisi Prius Reports (174 ER) 1840–2
Crompton & Meeson's Exchequer Reports (149 ER) 1832–4

C.& Mar. Carrington & Marshman's Nisi Prius Reports (174 ER) 1840–2

C.& N. Cameron & Norwood's North Carolina Conference Reports (1 NC) 1800–4

C.& O.R.Cas. Carrow & Oliver's Railway and Canal Cases. 1835–54

C.& P. Carrington & Payne's Nisi Prius Reports (171–3 ER) 1823–41
Craig & Phillips' Chancery Reports (41 ER) 1840–1

C.& R. Clifford & Rickard's Locus Standi Reports. 1873–84
Cockburn & Rowe's Election Cases. 1833

C.& S. Clark & Scully's Drainage Cases, Ontario (Can.) 1891–1900
Clifford & Stephen's Locus Standi Reports. 1867–72

C.& S.App. Clifford & Stephen's Locus Standi Reports, Appendix

C.& S.Dig. Connor & Simonton's South Carolina Digest

C.& S.L.J. Company and Securities Law Journal (Aus.) 1982–

Ca. California
Case(s)

Ca.2d California Supreme Court Reports, Second Series

Ca.A. California Appellate Reports
Ca.A.2d California Appellate Reports, Second Series
Ca.A.3d California Appellate Reports, Third Series
Ca.Céléb. Causes Célèbres (Québec Provincial Reports)
Ca.L.R. California Law Review. 1912–
Ca.P. Cases in Parliament (Shower) 1694–9
Ca.Parl. Cases in Parliament (Shower) 1694–9
Ca.Prac.C.P. Cooke's Practice Cases, Common Pleas (125 ER) 1706–47
Ca.R. California Reporter
Ca.resp. Capias ad satisfaciendum (Lat.) writ of execution
Ca.Sett. Cases of Settlements and Removals. 1710–42
Ca.t.Ch.2 Cases tempore Charles 2. 1681–98
Ca.t.F. Finch's Chancery Reports (23 ER) 1673–81
Ca.t.Geo.I Cases tempore George I (8 & 9 Modern Reports) 1721–6
Ca.t.H. Cases tempore Hardwicke, King's Bench (95 ER) 1733–8
Cases tempore Holt, 11 Modern Reports (88 ER) 1702–10
Ca.t.Hard. Cases tempore Hardwicke, King's Bench (95 ER) 1733–8
Ca.t.Holt Cases tempore Holt, 11 Modern Reports (88 ER) 1702–10
Ca.t.K. Select Cases tempore King, Chancery (25 ER) 1724–33
Ca.t.King Select Cases tempore King, Chancery (25 ER) 1724–33
Ca.t.Lee Ecclesiastical Cases tempore Lee. 1752–8
Ca.t.Mac. Cases in Law and Equity, 10 Modern Reports (88 ER) 1710–24
Ca.t.N. Eden's Chancery Reports tempore Northington (28 ER) 1757–66
Ca.t.Nap. Drury's Chancery Reports tempore Napier (Ire.) 1858–9
Ca.t.North. Eden's Chancery Reports tempore Northington (28 ER) 1757–66
Ca.t.Plunk. Cases in Chancery tempore Court Cases, Pennsylvania Eastern District (USA)
Ca.t.Q.A. Cases tempore Holt, 11 Modern Reports (88 ER) 1702–10
Ca.t.Sugd. Drury's Chancery Reports tempore Sugden (Ire.) 1841–4
Ca.t.Talb. Cases in Equity tempore Talbot, Forrester's Reports (25 ER) 1733–8
Ca.t.Wm.3 Cases tempore William 3, 12 Modern Reports (88 ER) 1690–1732
Ca.temp.F. Finch's Chancery Reports (23 ER) 1673–81
Ca.temp.H. Cases tempore Hardwicke, King's Bench (95 ER) 1733–8
Ca.temp.Hard. Cases tempore Hardwicke, King's Bench (95 ER) 1733–8
Ca.temp.Holt Cases tempore Holt, King's Bench, 11 Modern Reports (88 ER) 1702–10
Ca.temp.K. Cases in Chancery tempore King (25 ER) 1724–33
Ca.temp.King Cases in Chancery tempore King (25 ER) 1724–33
Ca.temp.Talb. Cases in Equity tempore Talbot, Forrester's Reports (25 ER) 1733–8
Ca.temp.Talbot Cases in Equity tempore Talbot, Forrester's Reports (25 ER) 1733–8
Ca.U. California Unreported Cases
Ca.W.I.L.J. California Western International Law Journal. 1970–
Ca.W.L.R. California Western Law Review. 1965–
Cab.Int. Cababe, Interpleader and Attachment of Debts. 3ed. 1900
Cab.Lawy. Wade, Cabinet Lawyer
Cab.& E. Cababe & Ellis' Queen's Bench Reports. 1882–5
Cab.& El. Cababe & Ellis' Queen's Bench Reports. 1882–5
Cab.& Ell. Cababe & Ellis' Queen's Bench Reports. 1882–5
Cadw.Dig. Cadwalader's Digest of Attorney-General's Opinions (USA)
Cadwalader Cadwalader's District

Cah.dr.europ. Cahiers de droit européen (Belg.)
Cah.dr.fisc.int. Cahiers de droit fiscal international
Cah.Int.de Soc. Cahiers Internationaux de Sociologie
Cahiers Dr. Les Cahiers de Droit (Can.)
Cahiers Dr.Euro. Cahiers de droit européen (Belg.)
Cahiers Dr.Fisc.Intern. Cahiers de droit fiscal international
Cahill's Ill.St. Cahill's Illinois Statutes Plunkett (Ire.) 1834–9
Cai. Caines' New York Cases in Error. 1796–1805
Caines' New York Supreme Court Reports. 1803–5
Caines' Term Reports, New York Supreme Court
Cai.Cas. Caines' New York Cases in Error. 1796–1805
Caines' New York Supreme Court Reports. 1803–5
Caines' Term Reports, New York Supreme Court
Cai.Cas.Err. Caines' New York Cases in Error. 1796–1805
Cai.Pr. Caines' Practice (USA)
Cai.R. Caines' New York Cases in Error. 1796–1805
Caines' New York Supreme Court Reports. 1803–5
Caines' Term Reports, New York Supreme Court
Cai.T.R. Caines' Term Reports, New York Supreme Court
Cain. Caines' New York Cases in Error. 1796–1805
Caines' New York Supreme Court Reports. 1803–5
Caines' Term Reports, New York Supreme Court
Caines Caines' New York Cases in Error. 1796–1805
Caines' New York Supreme Court Reports. 1803–5
Caines' Term Reports, New York Supreme Court
Caines Cas. Caines' New York Cases in Error. 1796–1805
Caines' New York Supreme Court Reports. 1803–5
Caines' Term Reports, New York Supreme Court
Caines (N.Y.) Caines' New York Cases in Error. 1796–1805
Caines' New York Supreme Court Reports. 1803–5
Caines' Term Reports, New York Supreme Court
Cairns Dec. Cairns' Decisions in the Albert Assurance Arbitration, by Reilly. 1871–5
Cairns, Legal Science Cairns, The Theory of Legal Science. 1941
Cairns, Plato to Hegel Cairns, Legal Philosophy from Plato to Hegel. 1949
cal. calendar
Cal. All India Reporter, Calcutta Series. 1914–
Calcutta
Caldecott's Settlement Cases. 1776–85
Calendars of the Proceedings in Chancery, Record Commission
California
California Supreme Court Reports. 1850–
Calthrop's City of London Cases, King's Bench (80 ER) 1609–18
Indian Law Reports, Calcutta Series. 1876–
Indian Rulings, Calcutta. 1929–47
Cal.2d California Reports, Second Series
Cal.3d California Reports, Third Series
Cal.Adm.Code California Administrative Code
Cal.Adv.Legis.Serv. California Advance Legislative Service
Cal.Agr.Code California Agricultural Code
Cal.App. California Appellate Reports. 1905–
Cal.App.2d California Appellate Reports, Second Series
Cal.App.3d California Appellate Reports, Third Series

Cal.App.Dec. California Appellate Decisions
Cal.App.Supp. California Appellate Reports, Supplement. 1929–
Cal.Ch. Calendar of Proceedings in Chancery tempore Elizabeth. 1377–1600
Cal.Chanc.Warrants Calendar of Chancery Warrants
Cal.Comp.Cases California Compensation Cases
Cal.Dec. California Decisions
Cal.Gen.Laws Ann. Deering's California General Laws Annotated
Cal.I.A.C.C.C. California Industrial Accident Commission Compensation Cases
Cal.I.A.C.Dec. California Industrial Accident Commission Decisions
Cal.Jur. California Jurisprudence
Cal.Jur.2d California Jurisprudence, Second Series
Cal.L.J. Calcutta Law Journal (India) 1905–
California Law Journal. 1862–3
Cal.L.R. Calcutta Law Reports (India) 1877–84
Cal.L.Rev. California Law Review. 1912–
Cal.Law. California Lawyer
Cal.Leg.Adv. Calcutta Legal Adviser (India)
Cal.Leg.Obs. Calcutta Legal Observer (India) 1839–40
Cal.Leg.Rec. California Legal Record, San Francisco. 1878–9
Cal.Legis.Serv. California Legislative Service (West)
Cal.P.Ch. Calendar of Proceedings in Chancery tempore Elizabeth. 1377–1600
Cal.Penal Code California Penal Code
Cal.Prac. Hart's California Practice
Cal.R.C.Dec. California Railroad Commission Decisions
Ca.R.C.Dec.Dig. California Railroad Commission Digest of Decisions
Cal.Real Prop.J. California Real Property Journal
Cal.Rep. California Supreme Court Reports. 1850–
Calthrop's King's Bench Reports (80 ER) 1609–18
Cal.Rptr. California Reporter (West) 1959–
Cal.S.B.J. California State Bar Journal. 1972–
Cal.S.D.A. Calcutta Sudder Dewanny Adawlut Reports (India)
Cal.Ser. Indian Law Reports, Calcutta Series. 1876–
Cal.Sew. Callis on Sewers. 4ed. 1810
Cal.St.B.J. Journal of the State Bar of California
Cal.Stats. Statutes of California
Cal.Sup. California Superior Court Reports
Cal.Unrep. California Unreported Cases. 1855–1910
Cal.Unrep.Cas. California Unreported Cases. 1855–1910
Cal.W.Int'l L.J. California Western International Law Journal
Cal.W.L.Rev. California Western Law Review
Cal.W.N. Calcutta Weekly Notes (India) 1896–
Cal.W.R. Calcutta Weekly Reporter by Sutherland (India) 1864–77
Cal.West.Int'l L.J. California Western International Law Journal
Cal.West.L.Rev. California Western Law Review
Calc. Indian Law Reports, Calcutta Series. 1876–
Calc.L.J. Calcutta Law Journal (India) 1905–
Calc.Ser. Indian Law Reports, Calcutta Series. 1876–
Calc.W.N. Calcutta Weekly Notes (India) 1896–
Calcutt Report Report of the Committee on Privacy and Related Matters (Cm.1102) 1990
Calcutta L.J. Calcutta Law Journal (India) 1905–
Calcutta W.N. Calcutta Weekly Notes (India) 1896–

Cald. Caldecott's Magistrates' and Settlement Cases. 1776–85
Caldwell's Reports (25–36 West Virginia)

Cald.Arb. Caldwell, Arbitration. 2ed. 1825

Cald.J.P. Caldecott's Magistrates' and Settlement Cases. 1776–85

Cald.M.Cas. Caldecott's Magistrates' and Settlement Cases. 1776–85

Cald.Mag.Cas. Caldecott's Magistrates' and Settlement Cases. 1776–85

Cald.Set.Cas. Caldecott's Magistrates' and Settlement Cases. 1776–85

Calif.Hist.Soc'y California Historical Society Quarterly

Calif.L.R.C. California Law Revision Commission

Calif.L.Rev. California Law Review. 1912–

Calif.S.B.J. California State Bar Journal. 1972–

Calif.W.Int'l.L.J. California Western International Law Journal. 1970–

Calif.W.L.Rev. California Western Law Review. 1965–

Calif.West.Int'l.L.J. California Western International Law Journal. 1970–

Calif.West.L.Rev. California Western Law Review

Calif.Western Int.L.J. California Western International Law Journal. 1970–

Calif.Western L.Rev. California Western Law Review. 1965–

Call Call's Virginia Reports (5–10 Va) 1797–1825

Call.Sew. Callis on Sewers. 4ed. 1810

Call.(Va.) Call's Virginia Reports (5–10 Va) 1797–1825

Callis Reading of Robert Callis on the Statute of Sewers. 1622

Calth. Calthrop's City of London Cases, King's Bench (80 ER) 1609–18

Calthr. Calthrop's City of London Cases, King's Bench (80 ER) 1609–18

Calv.Lex. Calvinus Lexicon Juridicum

Calv.Parties Calvert's Parties to Suits in Equity. 2ed. 1847

Calvin. Calvinus Lexicon Juridicum

Calvin.Lex Calvinus Lexicon Juridicum

Calvin.Lex.Jurid. Calvinus Lexicon Juridicum

Calvo Calvo, Le droit international théorique et pratique (Fr.) 5ed. 1896

Cam. Cameron's Privy Council Decisions (Can.) 1832–1929
Cameron's Queen's Bench Reports, Upper Canada. 1844–92
Cameron's Supreme Court Cases (Can.) 1880–1905

Cam.Cas. Cameron's Supreme Court Cases (Can.) 1880–1905

Cam.Duc. Camera Ducata (Duchy Chamber)

Cam.Int.Suc. Cameron, Intestate Succession in Scotland

Cam.Op. Cameron's Opinions, Toronto (Can.)

Cam.Prac. Cameron's Supreme Court Practice (Can.) 1844

Cam.S.C. Cameron's Supreme Court Cases (Can.) 1880–1905

Cam.Scacc. Camera Scaccarii (Exchequer Chamber)

Cam.Stell. Camera Stellata (Star Chamber)

Cam.& N. Cameron & Norwood's North Carolina Conference Reports (1 NC) 1800–4

Cam.& Nor. Cameron & Norwood's North Carolina Conference Reports (1 NC) 1800–4

Camb.Hist.J. Cambridge Historical Journal

Camb.L.J. Cambridge Law Journal. 1921–

Cambr.L.J. Cambridge Law Journal. 1921–

Cambria Cambria County Legal Journal (Pennsylvania)

Cambria Co.L.J. Cambria County Legal Journal (Pennsylvania)

Cambria Co.(Pa.) Cambria County Legal Journal (Pennsylvania)

Cambrian L.R. Cambrian Law Review. 1970–
Cambrian L.Rev. Cambrian Law Review. 1970–
Cambridge L.J. Cambridge Law Journal. 1921–
Camd.Soc. Camden Society
Cameron Cameron's Supreme Court Cases (Can.) 1880–1905
Cameron (Can.) Cameron's Supreme Court Cases (Can.) 1880–1905
Cameron Cas.(Can.) Cameron's Supreme Court Cases (Can.) 1880–1905
Cameron Pr. Cameron's Practice (Can.)
Cameron S.C. Cameron's Supreme Court Cases (Can.) 1880–1905
Camp. Camp's Reports (1 North Dakota)
Campbell's Compendium of Roman Law
Campbell's Legal Gazette Reports (Pennsylvania)
Campbell's Nisi Prius Reports (170–1 ER) 1808–16
Campbell's Reports (27–58 Nebraska)
Campbell's Reports of Taney's Circuit Court Decisions (USA)
Camp.Ch.Jus. Campbell's Lives of the Chief Justices
Camp.Dec. Campbell's Reports of Taney's Circuit Court Decisions (USA)
Camp.Ld.Ch. Campbell's Lives of the Lord Chancellors
Camp.Lives Ld.Ch. Campbell's Lives of the Lord Chancellors
Camp.Merc.L. Campbell, Mercantile Law. 3ed. 1904
Camp.N.P. Campbell's Nisi Prius Reports (170–1 ER) 1808–16
Camp.Neg. Campbell, Negligence. 2ed. 1878
Camp.Rom.L. Campbell's Compendium of Roman Law
Camp.Rom.L.Comp. Campbell's Compendium of Roman Law
Camp.Sale Campbell, Sale of Goods and Commercial Agency. 2ed. 1891
Campb. Campbell's Compendium of Roman Law
Campbell's Legal Gazette Reports (Pennsylvania)
Campbell's Nisi Prius Reports (170–1 ER) 1808–16
Campbell's Reports (27–58 Nebraska)
Campbell's Reports of Taney's Circuit Court Decisions (USA)
Campb.Dec. Campbell's Reports of Taney's Circuit Court Decisions (USA)
Campb.(Pa.) Campbell's Legal Gazette Reports (Pennsylvania)
Campbell Campbell's Compendium of Roman Law
Campbell's Legal Gazette Reports (Pennsylvania)
Campbell's Lives of the Chief Justices
Campbell's Lives of the Lord Chancellors
Campbell's Nisi Prius Reports (170–1 ER) 1808–16
Campbell's Reports (27–58 Nebraska)
Campbell's Reports of Taney's Circuit Court Decisions (USA)
Campbell L.Rev. Campbell Law Review (USA)
Campbell, Lives Campbell, Lives of the Chief Justices
Campbell, Lives of the Lord Chancellors
Can. Canada
Canute
Can.Abr. Canadian Abridgment. 1823–
Can.-Am.L.J. Canadian-American Law Journal (Can.) 1981–
Can.App. Canadian Reports, Appellate Cases
Can.App.Cas. Canadian Appeal Cases
Can.B.A. Canadian Bar Association, Proceedings
Can.B.A.J. Canadian Bar Association Journal. 1970–3
Can.B.J. Canadian Bar Journal. 1958–69
Can.B.R. Canadian Bar Review. 1923–
Can.B.Rev. Canadian Bar Review. 1923–
Can.B.Year Book Canadian Bar Association Year Book

Can.Bank. Canadian Banker and ICB Review
Can.Bank.R. Canadian Bankruptcy Reports. 1920–
Can.Bankr. Canadian Bankruptcy Reports. 1920–
Can.Bankr.Ann. Canadian Bankruptcy Reports Annotated
Can.Bankr.Ann.(N.S.) Canadian Bankruptcy Reports Annotated, New Series
Can.Bar J. Canadian Bar Journal
Can.Bar Rev. Canadian Bar Review. 1923–
Can.Bus.L.J. Canadian Business Law Journal
Can.C.C. Canada Criminal Cases. 1898–
Can.C.L. Canadian Current Law
Can.Chart.Acc. Canadian Chartered Accountant
Can.Com.Cas. Canadian Commercial Law Reports. 1901–3
Can.Com.L.R. Canadian Commercial Law Reports. 1901–3
Can.Com.R. Canadian Commercial Law Reports. 1901–3
Can.Comm.L.Rev. Canadian Communications Law Review
Can.Community L.J. Canadian Community Law Journal
Can.Compet.Policy Rec. Canadian Competition Policy Record. 1979–
Can.Computer L.R. Canadian Computer Law Reporter. 1982–
Can.Corp.Bull. Canadian Corporations Bulletin
Can.Coun.Int.L.Bull. Canadian Council on International Law Bulletin
Can.Counc.Intl.L.Proc. Canadian Council on International Law, Proceedings of the Annual Conference
Can.Cr.Acts Canada Criminal Acts
Can.Cr.Cas. Canadian Criminal Cases. 1898–
Can.Cr.R. Canadian Criminal Reports
Can.Crim. Canadian Criminal Reports
Can.Crim.Cas. Canadian Criminal Cases. 1898–
Can.Crim.Cas.Ann. Canadian Criminal Cases Annotated
Can.Crim.Cas.(N.S.) Canadian Criminal Cases, New Series
Can.Crim.Forum Canadian Criminology Forum. 1977–
Can.Current Tax Canadian Current Tax. 1984–
Can.Environ.L.N. Canadian Environmental Law News. 1972–
Can.Ex.C.R. Canada Exchequer Court Reports. 1875–1922
Can.Ex.R. Canada Exchequer Court Reports. 1875–1922
Can.Exch. Canada Exchequer Court Reports. 1875–1922
Canada Law Reports, Exchequer
Can.Gaz. Canada Gazette
Can.Hum.Rts.Yrbk. Canadian Human Rights Yearbook. 1982–
Can.Human Rights Advocate Canadian Human Rights Advocate. 1984–
Can.Human Rights Y.B. Canadian Human Rights Yearbook. 1982–
Can.J.Afr.Stud. Canadian Journal of African Studies
Can.J.Correct. Canadian Journal of Corrections. 1958–70
Can.J.Correction Canadian Journal of Corrections. 1958–70
Can.J.Crim. Canadian Journal of Criminology and Corrections. 1971–
Can.J.Crim.& Correct. Canadian Journal of Criminology and Corrections. 1971–
Can.J.Criminol. Canadian Journal of Criminology and Corrections. 1971–
Can.J.Ec.Pol.Sc. Canadian Journal of Economics and Political Science
Can.J.Econ. Canadian Journal of Economics and Political Science
Can.J.Fam.L. Canadian Journal of Family Law. 1979–
Can.J.Ins.L. Canadian Journal of Insurance Law. 1982–
Can.J.L.Juris. Canadian Journal of Law and Jurisprudence

Can.J.Pol.Sc. Canadian Journal of Political Science
Can.J.Women & L. Canadian Journal of Women and the Law
Can.L.J. Canada Law Journal, Toronto. 1855–1922
Lower Canada Law Journal, Quebec. 1865–8
Can.L.J.(N.S.) Canada Law Journal, New Series. 1865–1922
Can.L.R. Canada Law Reports. 1923–
Can.L.Rev. Canadian Law Review. 1901–7
Can.L.S. Canadian Legal Studies
Can.L.T. Canadian Law Times. 1881–1922
Can.L.T.Occ.N. Canadian Law Times, Occasional Notes. 1881–1909
Can.Lab. Canadian Labour
Can.Law. Canadian Lawyer. 1976–
Can.Leg.N. Canada Legal News
Can.Leg.Stud. Canadian Legal Studies. 1964–
Can.Legal Aid Bull. Canadian Legal Aid Bulletin
Can.Mun.J. Canadian Municipal Journal. 1891–2
Can.P.R. Canadian Patent Reporter
Can.Par.Rev. Canadian Parliamentary Review
Can.Persp. Canadian Perspectives on International Law and Organisation
Can.Pol.C. Canadian Police Chief
Can.Pub.Admin. Canadian Public Administration
Can.Publ.Policy Canadian Public Policy
Can.R.A.C. Canadian Reports, Appeal Cases
Can.R.App.Cas. Canadian Reports, Appeal Cases
Can.R.Cas. Canadian Railway and Transport Cases. 1902–
Can.Rev.Stat. Revised Statutes of Canada
Can.Ry.Cas. Canadian Railway and Transport Cases. 1902–
Can.Ry.& T.Cas. Canadian Railway and Transport Cases. 1902–
Can.S.C. Canada Supreme Court
Canada Supreme Court Reports. 1876–1922
Can.S.C.R. Canada Supreme Court Reports. 1876–1922
Can.S.C.Rep. Canada Supreme Court Reports. 1876–1922
Can.S.Ct. Canada Law Reports, Supreme Court. 1923–
Canada Supreme Court Reports. 1876–1922
Can.Soc.Forens.Sci.J. Journal of the Canadian Society of Forensic Science
Can.Stat. Statutes of Canada
Can.Sup.Ct. Canada Supreme Court Reports. 1876–1922
Can.T.C. Canada Tax Cases. 1917–
Can.T.S. Canada Treaty Series
Can.Tax App.Bd. Canada Tax Appeal Board Cases
Can.Tax Cas. Canada Tax Cases. 1917–
Can.Tax J. Canadian Tax Journal. 1953–
Can.Tax News Canadian Tax News
Can.Taxation Canadian Taxation: a Journal of Tax Policy
Can.Terr. Territories Law Reports (Can.) 1885–1907
Can.-U.S.L.J. The Canada-United States Law Journal. 1976–
Can.Y.B.I.L. Canadian Yearbook of International Law. 1963–
Can.Y.B.Int'l L. Canadian Yearbook of International Law. 1963–
CanYIL Canadian Yearbook of International Law. 1963–
Can.Yb.Int'l L. Canadian Yearbook of International Law. 1963–
Can.Yearb.Int.L. Canadian Yearbook of International Law. 1963–
Can.Yearbook Int.L. Canadian Yearbook of International Law. 1963–
Canada Commerce Canadian Department of Industry, Trade and Commerce
Canada L.T. Canadian Law Times. 1881–1922
Canal Zone Canal Zone Supreme

Court Reports

Canal Zone Sup.Ct. Canal Zone Supreme Court Reports

Candy Printed Judgments of Sind by Candy and Birdwood (India)

Candy M.C. Candy, Mayor's Court Practice. 1879

Cane & L. Cane & Leigh's Crown Cases Reserved

Caney Novation L.R. Caney, A Treatise on the Law relating to Novation including Delegation, Compromise and Res Judicata (S.Afr.)

Cant.L.R. Canterbury Law Review (N.Z.) 1980–

Canta.L.R. Canterbury Law Review (N.Z.) 1980–

Cantab. Cantabrigiensis (Lat.) of Cambridge

Canterbury L.Rev. Canterbury Law Review

Cantwell Cantwell's Cases on Tolls and Customs (Ire.)

Cantuar. Cantuaria (Lat.) Canterbury
Cantuariensis (Lat.) of Canterbury (signature of the Archbishop of Canterbury)

Cap. Capital
Capitolo (It.) chapter
Chapter

Cap.L. The Capital Letter (N.Z.) 1978–

Cap.U.L.Rev. Capital University Law Review (USA)

Cape Cape Province (S.Afr.)

Cape L.J. Cape Law Journal (S.Afr.) 1884–1900

Cape Law J. Cape Law Journal (S.Afr.) 1884–1900

Cape P.D. South African Law Reports, Cape Provincial Division. 1910–46

Cape P.Div. South African Law Reports, Cape Provincial Division Reports.1910–46

Cape S.A. Cape of Good Hope (or Cape Province), South Africa

Cape S.C.R. Supreme Court Reports, Cape Colony (S.Afr.) 1880–1910

Cape T.R. Cape Times Reports, Supreme Court, Cape of Good Hope (S.Afr.)

Capital U.L.Rev. Capital University Law Review. 1972–

capv. capoverso (It.) paragraph

Car. Carolina
Carolus (Lat.) King Charles

Car.Cr.L. Carrington, Criminal Law. 3ed. 1828

Car.H.& A. Carrow, Hamerton & Allen's Sessions Cases. 1844–51

Car.L.J. Carolina Law Journal. 1830–1

Car.L.Rep. Carolina Law Repository, North Carolina (4 NC) 1813–16

Car.Law Repos. Carolina Law Repository, North Carolina (4 NC) 1813–16

Car.O.& B. Carrow, Oliver & Bevan's Railway and Canal Cases. 1835–54

Car.& K. Carrington & Kirwan's Nisi Prius Reports (174–5 ER) 1843–50

Car.& Kir. Carrington & Kirwan's Nisi Prius Reports (174–5 ER) 1843–50

Car.& M. Carrington & Marshman's Nisi Prius Reports (174 ER) 1840–2

Car.& Mar. Carrington & Marshman's Nisi Prius Reports (174 ER) 1840–2

Car.& O. Carrow & Oliver's Railway and Canal Cases. 1835–54

Car.& Ol. Carrow & Oliver's Railway and Canal Cases. 1835–54

Car.& P. Carrington & Payne's Nisi Prius Reports (171–3 ER) 1823–41

Cardozo Arts & Ent.L.J. Cardozo Arts and Entertainment Law Journal (USA)

Cardozo, Growth B.N. Cardozo, The Growth of the Law (USA) 1924

Cardozo, Judicial Process B.N. Cardozo, Nature of the Judicial Process (USA) 1921

Cardozo L.Rev. Cardozo Law Review (USA)

Cardozo Stud.L.& Lit. Cardozo Studies in Law and Literature (USA)

Carey Manitoba Reports, by Carey (Can.) 1875

Carey M.R. Manitoba Reports, by Carey (Can.) 1875

Carib.L.J. Caribbean Law Journal (Jamaica) 1952–3
Carl. Carleton's New Brunswick Reports. 1895–1902
Carlisle Report The Parole System in England and Wales: Report of the Review Committee (Home Office) 1988
Carp. Carpenter's Reports (52–3 California)
Carpmael's Patent Cases. 1602–1842
Carp.P.C. Carpmael's Patent Cases. 1602–1842
Carp.Pat.Cas. Carpmael's Patent Cases. 1602–1842
Carpenter Carpenter's Reports (52–3 California)
Carr. Carriers
Carr.Cas. Carrau's Summary Cases, Bengal (India) 1834–52
Carr.Ham.& Al. Carrow, Hamerton & Allen's Sessions Cases. 1844–51
Carr.& K. Carrington & Kirwan's Nisi Prius Reports (174–5 ER) 1843–50
Carr.& M. Carrington & Marshman's Nisi Prius Reports (174 ER) 1840–2
Carrau Carrau's Summary Cases, Bengal (India) 1834–52
Carsh. Carshaltown's Court Rolls
Cart. Carter's Common Pleas Reports (124 ER) 1664–76
Carter's Reports (1–2 Indiana)
Carthew's King's Bench Reports (90 ER) 1686–1701
Cartwright's Cases on the British North America Act (Can.) 1868–96
Cart.B.N.A. Cartwright's Cases on the British North America Act (Can.) 1868–96
Cart.Cas.(Can.) Cartwright's Cases on the British North America Act (Can.) 1868–96
Cart.de For. Carta De Foresta (Charter of the Forest)
Cart.Sax. Cartularium Saxonicum, ed. by Birch
Cartel Cartel: Review of Monopoly, Developments and Consumer Protection
Carter Carter's Common Pleas Reports (124 ER) 1664–76
Carter's Reports (1–2 Indiana)
Carth. Carthew's King's Bench Reports (90 ER) 1686–1701
Cartm. Cartmell's Trade Mark Cases. 1876–92
Cartw.C.C. Cartwright's Cases on the British North America Act (Can.) 1868–96
Cartwr.Cas. Cartwright's Cases on the British North America Act (Can.) 1868–96
Carv.Carr. Carver, Carriage of Goods by Sea
Carver Carver, Carriage of Goods by Sea
Cary Cary's Chancery Reports (21 ER) 1557–1604
Cary Lit. Cary's Commentary on Littleton's Tenures
Cary Part. Cary, Partnership. 1827
Cas. Casey's Reports (25–36 Pennsylvania State)
Cas.App. Cases of Appeal to House of Lords
Cas.Arg.& Dec. Cases Argued and Decreed in Chancery (22 ER) 1660–97
Cas.B.R. Cases in Banco Regis tempore William III, 12 Modern Reports (88 ER) 1690–1702
Cas.B.R.Holt Cases and Resolutions of Settlements
Cas.B.R.t.W.III Cases in Banco Regis tempore William III, 12 Modern Reports (88 ER) 1690–1702
Cas.C.L. Leach's Crown Cases (168 ER) 1730–1815
Cas.C.R. Cases tempore William III, 12 Modern Reports (88 ER) 1690–1702
Cas.Ch. Cases in Chancery (22 ER) 1660–97
Cases in Chancery (9 Modern Reports) (88 ER) 1722–55
Select Cases in Chancery. 1724–33
Cas.Com. Arrêt de la section commerciale de la Cour de Cassation (Fr.) Decision of the commercial section of the Cour de Cassation

Cas.Eq. Cases in Equity, Gilbert's Reports (93 ER) 1713–14
Cas.Eq.Abr. Cases in Equity, Abridged (21–2 ER) 1667–1744
Cas.F.T. Cases in Equity tempore Talbot, Forrester's Reports (25 ER) 1733–8
Cas.H.L. Cases in the House of Lords
Cas.in C. Cases in Chancery (22 ER) 1660–97
Select Cases in Chancery. 1724–33
Cas.in Ch. Cases in Chancery (22 ER) 1660–97
Cas.K.B. Cases in King's Bench (8 Modern Reports) 1723–7
Cas.K.B.t.H. Cases tempore Hardwicke (W. Kelynge's King's Bench Reports) (25 ER) 1730–5
Cas.K.B.t.Hard. Cases tempore Hardwicke (W. Kelynge's King's Bench Reports) (25 ER) 1730–5
Cas.L.& Eq. Cases in Law and Equity (10 Modern Reports) (88 ER) 1720–33
(Gilbert's) Cases in Law and Equity (93 ER) 1713–14
Cas.Op. Burton's Cases with Opinions of Eminent Counsel. 1700–95
Cas.P. Cases in Parliament
Cas.Parl. Cases in Parliament
Cas.Pr. Cases of Practice, King's Bench. 1603–1774
Cas.Pr.C.P. Cases of Practice, Common Pleas. 1702–27
Cas.Pr.K.B. Cases of Practice, King's Bench. 1603–1774
Cas.Pra.C.P. Cases of Practice, Common Pleas. 1702–27
Cas.Pra.K.B. Cases of Practice, King's Bench. 1603–1774
Cas.Prac.C.P. Cases of Practice, Common Pleas. 1702–27
Cas.Prac.K.B. Cases of Practice, King's Bench. 1603–1774
Cas.Proc. Cassell, Procedure in the Courts of Canada
Cas.R. Casey's Reports (25–36 Pennsylvania State)
Cas.S.C.(Cape G.H.) Cases in the Supreme Court, Cape of Good Hope
Cas.S.M. Cases of Settlement, King's Bench. 1713–15
Cas.Self Def. Horrigan & Thompson's Cases on Self Defence
Cas.Sett. Cases of Settlement and Removals. 1710–42
Cas.Six Cir. Cases on the Six Circuits (Ire.) 1841–43
Cas.t.Ch.2 Cases in Chancery tempore Charles II. 1681–98
Cas.t.F. Cases in Chancery tempore Finch (23 ER) 1673–81
Cas.t.Finch Cases in Chancery tempore Finch (23 ER) 1673–81
Cas.t.Geo.I Cases in Chancery tempore George I (8–9 Modern Reports) 1721–6
Cas.t.H. Cases tempore Hardwicke, King's Bench (95 ER) 1733–38
Cases tempore Holt, King's Bench (Holt's Reports) (88 ER) 1702–10
West's Chancery Reports tempore Hardwicke (25 ER) 1736–9
Cas.t.Hard. Cases tempore Hardwicke, Lee's King's Bench Reports (95 ER) 1733–38
Cas.t.Hardw. Cases tempore Hardwicke, Lee's King's Bench Reports (95 ER) 1733–38
West's Chancery Reports tempore Hardwicke (25 ER) 1736–9
Cas.t.Holt Cases tempore Holt, King's Bench (Holt's Reports) (88 ER) 1702–10
Cas.t.K. Select Cases tempore King, Chancery (25 ER) 1724–33
Moseley's Chancery Reports tempore King (25 ER) 1726–30
Cas.t.King Select Cases tempore King, Chancery (25 ER) 1724–33
Moseley's Chancery Reports tempore King (25 ER) 1726–30
Cas.t.Lee Ecclesiastical Cases tempore Lee. 1752–8
Cas.t.Mac. Cases in Law and Equity (10 Modern Reports) (88 ER) 1710–25
Cas.t.Maccl. Cases in Law and Equity (10 Modern Reports) (88 ER) 1710–25

Cas.t.Nap. Drury's Irish Chancery Reports tempore Napier. 1858–9
Cas.t.North Eden's Chancery Reports tempore Northington (28 ER) 1757–66
Cas.t.Plunk. Lloyd & Goold's Chancery Reports tempore Plunkett (Ire.) 1834–9
Cas.t.Q.A. Cases tempore Queen Anne (11 Modern Reports) (88 ER) 1702–30
Cas.t.Q.Anne Cases tempore Queen Anne (11 Modern Reports) (88 ER) 1702–30
Cas.t.Sugd. Drury's Chancery Reports tempore Sugden (Ire.) 1841–4
Cas.t.Tal. Cases in Equity tempore Talbot (25 ER) 1733–38
Cas.t.Talb. Cases in Equity tempore Talbot (25 ER) 1733–38
Cas.t.Wm.III Cases tempore William III (12 Modern Reports) (88 ER) 1690–1732
Cas.Tak.& Adj. Cases Taken and Adjudged (first edition of Reports in Chancery)
Cas.Tax Canada Tax Cases Annotated
Cas.temp.F. Cases tempore Finch, Chancery (23 ER) 1673–81
Cas.temp.H. Cases tempore Hardwicke, King's Bench (95 ER) 1733–38
Cas.temp.Hardw. Cases tempore Hardwicke, King's Bench (95 ER) 1733–38
Cas.temp.Lee Ecclesiastical Cases tempore Lee. 1752–8
Cas.temp.Talb. Cases in Equity tempore Talbot (25 ER) 1733–38
Cas.w.Op. Burton's Cases with Opinions of Eminent Counsel. 1700–95
Cas.Wm.I Bigelow's Cases from William I to Richard I. 1066–1195
Cas.W.Res.J.Int.L. Case Western Reserve Journal of International Law (USA) 1968–
Cas.W.Res.L.Rev. Case Western Reserve Law Review (USA) 1967–
Cas.& Op. Burton's Cases with Opinions of Eminent Counsel. 1700–95
Case W.Res.J.Intl.L. Case Western Reserve Journal of International Law (USA) 1968–
Case West.Res.J.Int'l L. Case Western Reserve Journal of International Law (USA) 1968–
Case West.Res.L.Rev. Case Western Reserve Law Review (USA) 1967–
Case & Com. Case and Comment (USA) 1894–
Cases in Ch. Cases in Chancery (22 ER) 1660–97
Select Cases in Chancery. 1724–33
Casey Casey's Reports (25–36 Pennsylvania State)
Cass. Arrêt de la Cour de Cassation (Fr.) Decision of the Cour de Cassation
Cassatie (Neth.) Appeal to the High Court of Justice
Corte di Cassazione (It.) Supreme Court of Appeal
Cour de Cassation (Fr.) Supreme Court of Appeal
Sentenza della Corte Suprema di Cassazione (It.) Decision or judgment of the Supreme Court of Appeals
Cass.ass.plen. Cour de Cassation, Assemblée plenière (Fr.)
Cass.ch.réun. Cour de Cassation, Chambres réunies (Fr.)
Cass.civ. Arrêt de la chambre civile de la Cour de Cassation (Fr.) Decision of the Cour de Cassation, Civil Division
Cassation chambre civile (Fr.)
Sentenza della sezione civile della Corte di Cassazione (It.) Decision of the Court of Appeals, Civil Division
Cass.civ.1re. Cour de Cassation, Première section civile (Fr.)
Cass.civ.2e. Cour de Cassation, Deuxième section civile (Fr.)
Cass.civ.3e. Cour de Cassation, Troisième section civile (Fr.)
Cass.civ.com. Cour de Cassation, Commerciale (Fr.) 1948–
Cass.civ.soc. Cour de Cassation, Sociale (Fr.) 1948–
Cass.com. Cour de Cassation, Commerciale (Fr.) to 1948

Cass.crim. Arrêt de la chambre criminielle de la Cour de Cassation (Fr.) Decision of the Cour de Cassation, Criminal Division
Cass.Dig. Cassel's Digest (Can.)
Cass.L.G.B. Casson's Local Government Board Decisions. 1902–16
Cass.pen. Sentenza della sezine penale della Corte di Cassazione (It.) Decisions of the Court of Appeal, Criminal Division
Cass.Prac. Cassel's Practice Cases (Can.) 1899
Cass.req. Arrêt de la Chambre des requêtes de la Cour de Cassation (Fr.) Decision of the Cour de Cassation, Chamber of Requests
Cass.S.C. Cassel's Supreme Court Decisions
Cass.Sez.Un. The Full Court of Cassation (It.)
Cass.soc. Arrêt de la section sociale de la Cour de Cassation (Fr.) Decision of the social security and labour division of the Cour de Cassation
Cass.Sup.C.Prac. Cassel's Supreme Court Practice
Cast.Rat. Castle, Rating. 4ed. 1903
Casw.Cop. Caswall, Copyholds. 3ed. 1841
cat. catalogue
catalogued
cataloguing
cataloguer
Catellani E.L. Catellani, Il diritto internazionale privato e i suoi recenti progressi (It.) 1895 and 1902
Cates Cates' Reports (109–127 Tennessee Reports)
Cath. Catholic
Cath.Law The Catholic Lawyer (USA) 1955–
Cath.U.A.L.R. Catholic University of America Law Review. 1950–75
Cath.U.L.R. Catholic University Law Review (USA) 1975–
Cath.U.L.Rev. Catholic University Law Review (USA) 1975–
Catholic Law. The Catholic Lawyer (USA) 1955–
Catholic U.A.L.R. Catholic University of America Law Review. 1950–75
Catholic U.L.R. Catholic University Law Review (USA) 1975–
Catholic Univ.L.Rev. Catholic University Law Review (USA) 1975–
Cavaglieri Cavaglieri, Lezioni di diritto internazionale (general part, 1925)
Caveat Caveat (Law Society of New South Wales) 1982–
Caveat (Victoria University Law Faculty Club) 1973–
Cawl. Cawley's Laws against Recusants
Cay.Abr. Cay's Abridgment of the English Statutes
Cb.L.R. Columbia Law Review. 1901–
cc. codice civile (It.) civil code
ccl. contratto collettivo di lavoro (It.)
Cd. Command Papers, 3rd Series (Cd.1–9239) 1900–18
Ce. Compagnie (Fr.) Company
Cel.Tr. Burke's Celebrated Trials
Cent. Central
Central Reporter (Pennsylvania)
Cent.Crim.C.Cas. Central Criminal Court Cases, Sessions Papers. 1834–1913
Cent.Crim.C.R. Central Criminal Court Reports
Cent.Dig. Century Edition of the American Digest System (West)
Cent.L.J. Central Law Journal (St Louis, Missouri) 1874–1927
Century Law Journal (USA)
Cent.L.Mo. Central Law Monthly (USA) 1880–3
Cent.Law J. Central Law Journal (St Louis, Missouri) 1874–1927
Cent.Prov.L.R. Central Provinces Law Reports (India)
Cent.R.(Pa.) Central Reporter (Pennsylvania)
Cent.Rep. Central Reporter (Pennsylvania)
Centr.Cr.Ct.R. Central Criminal Court Reports

cert. certificate
certified
certify
certiorari
cert.den. certiorari denied
cert.dis. certiorari dismissed
cert.dismissed certiorari dismissed
cert.granted certiorari granted
cet.par. ceteris paribus (Lat.) other things being equal
Ceyl.Cr.App.R. Ceylon Criminal Appeal Reports. 1914–15
Ceyl.L.J. Ceylon Law Journal. 1936–
Ceyl.L.R. Ceylon Law Reports. 1892–3
Ceyl.L.Rec. Ceylon Law Recorder. 1919–
Ceyl.L.Rev. Ceylon Law Review. 1899–1912
Ceyl.L.W. Ceylon Law Weekly. 1931–
Ceyl.Lab.L.J. Ceylon Labour Law Journal. 1962–
Ceyl.Leg.Misc. Ceylon Legal Miscellany
Ceylon J.Hist.& Soc.Stud. Ceylon Journal of Historical and Social Studies (Sri L.)
Ceylon L.R. Ceylon Law Reports. 1892–3
Ceylon Law Review. 1899–1912
Ceylon Law Rec. Ceylon Law Recorder. 1919–
Ceylon N.L.R. New Law Reports (Sri L.) 1874–
cf. confer (Lat.) compare
cfr. confronta (It.)
ch. chiffre (Switz.)
Ch. Chalmer's Colonial Opinions
Chancellor's Court
Chancery Court or Division
Chapter
China
Church
Court of Chancery
Law Reports, Chancery. 1891–
Ch.App. Chambre d'Appel
Court of Appeal in Chancery
Law Reports, Chancery Appeals. 1865–75
Ch.App.Cas. Law Reports, Chancery Appeal Cases. 1865–75
Ch.B.Ex. Chief Baron of the Exchequer
Ch.Bills Chitty, Bills of Exchange. 11ed. 1878
Ch.Black Chitty's Blackstone
Chase's Blackstone
Ch.Ca. Cases in Chancery (22 ER) 1660–97
Ch.Cas. Cases in Chancery (22 ER) 1660–97
Select Cases in Chancery. 1724–33
Ch.Cas.Ch. Choyce Cases in Chancery (21 ER) 1557–1606
Ch.Cas.in Ch. Choyce Cases in Chancery (21 ER) 1557–1606
Ch.Ch. Upper Canada Chancery Chambers Reports (Ontario) 1857–72
Ch.Cham. Upper Canada Chancery Chambers Reports (Ontario) 1857–72
Ch.Chamb. Upper Canada Chancery Chambers Reports (Ontario) 1857–72
Ch.Chamb.(Can.) Upper Canada Chancery Chambers Reports (Ontario) 1857–72
Ch.Col.Opp. Chalmers' Colonial Opinions
Ch.Cr.L. Chitty's Criminal Law. 2ed. 1828
Ch.Ct. Chancery Court
Ch.D. Law Reports, Chancery Division. 1876–90
Ch.Dig. Chaney's Digest, Michigan Reports
Ch.Div. Chancery Division
Ch.Div'l.Ct. Chancery Divisional Court
Ch.Is. Channel Islands
Ch.Is.Rolls Rolls of the Assizes in Channel Islands
Ch.J. Chief Justice
Ch.Kent Rev. Chicago Kent Review (USA)
Ch.L. University of Chicago Law Review. 1933–
Ch.L.R. University of Chicago Law Review. 1933–
Ch.Pl. Chitty on Pleading. 7ed. 1844
Ch.Prec. Precedents in Chancery. 1689–1723

Ch.R. Chitty's King's Bench Reports (22–3 ER) 1770–1822
Irish Chancery Reports
Reports in Chancery (21 ER) 1615–1712
Upper Canada Chambers Reports (Ont.) 1846–52

Ch.R.M. Charlton's Reports (Georgia Reports) 1811–37

Ch.Rep. Reports in Chancery (21 ER) 1615–1712
Irish Chancery Reports

Ch.Rep.Ir. Irish Chancery Reports

Ch.Repts. Reports in Chancery (21 ER) 1615–1712
Irish Chancery Reports

Ch.réun. Arrêt de la Cour de Cassation toutes chambres réunies (Fr.) Decision of the full court of the Cour de Cassation

Ch.Rob. Christopher Robinson's Admiralty Reports (165 ER) 1799–1808

Ch.Sent. Chancery Sentinel, Saratoga, New York

Ch.Sent.(N.Y.) Chancery Sentinel, Saratoga, New York

Ch.T.U.P. T.U.P. Charlton's Georgia Reports

Ch.& Cl.Cas. Cripps' Church and Clergy Cases. 1847–50

Ch.& P. Chambers & Pretty, Cases on the Finance Act. 1910

Cha. Charles

Cha.App. Law Reports, Chancery Appeal Cases. 1865–75

Cha.L.& T. Chambers, Landlord and Tenant. 1823

Cha.Pr. Chapman, Practice of the Court of King's Bench. 2ed. 1831

Chal.Op. Chalmers' Opinions on Constitutional Law. 1669–1809

Challis Challis on Real Property. 3ed. 1911

Chalmers Chalmers on Bills of Exchange
Chalmers' Sale of Goods

Cham. Upper Canada Chambers Reports (Ont.) 1846–52

Cham.Com. Chambers, Commons and Open Spaces. 1877

Cham.Leas. Chambers, Leases. 1819

Cham.Rat. Chambers, Rates and Rating. 2ed. 1889

Cham.Rep. Upper Canada Chambers Reports. 1846–52

Chamb. Chamberlain
Upper Canada Chambers Reports (Ont.) 1846–52

Chamb.Dig.P.H.C. Chambers' Digest of Public Health Cases

Chamb.R. Upper Canada Chancery Chambers Reports (Ont.) 1857–72

Chamb.Rep. Upper Canada Chambers Reports (Ont.) 1846–52

Chamber Upper Canada Chambers Reports (Ont.) 1846–52

Champ. Champion's Cases under the Wine and Beer Houses Act. 1885

Chan. Chancellor
Chancery
Chaney's Reports (37–58 Michigan)

Chan.Cas. Cases in Chancery (22 ER) 1660–97

Chan.Chamb. Upper Canada Chancery Chambers Reports (Ont.) 1857–72

Chan.Ct. Chancery Court

Chan.Rep. Reports in Chancery (21 ER) 1615–1710

Chan.Rep.C. Reports in Chancery (21 ER) 1615–1710

Chanc. Chancellor
Chancery

Chanc.Ex. Chancellor of the Exchequer

Chanc.Pow. Chance on Powers. 1831 supp. 1841

Chand. Chandler's Reports (20, 38–44 New Hampshire)
Chandler's Reports (Wisconsin) 1849–52

Chand.Cr.T. Chandler's American Criminal Trials

Chand.Crim.Tr. Chandler's American Criminal Trials

Chand.(NH) Chandler's Reports (20, 38–44 New Hampshire)

Chand.(Wis.) Chandler's Reports (Wisconsin) 1849–52

Chandl. Chandler's Reports (20, 38–44 New Hampshire)

Chandler's Reports (Wisconsin) 1849–52
Chaney Chaney's Reports (37–58 Michigan)
Chaney (Mich.) Chaney's Reports (37–58 Michigan)
Chap. Chaplain
Chapter
Chap.& Sh. Chappell & Shoard, Copyright. 1863
Char.Acctnt.Aust. Chartered Accountant in Australia. 1930–
Char.Cham.Cas. Charley's Chamber Cases. 1875–6
Char.Merc. Charta Mercatoria
Char.Pr.Cas. Charley's Practice Cases. 1875–81
Charl.Cha.Cas. Charley's Chamber Cases. 1875–6
Charl.Cham.Ca Charley's Chamber Cases. 1875–6
Charl.Pr.Cas. Charley's Practice Cases. 1875–81
Charl.R.M. R.M. Charlton's Georgia Reports
Charl.T.U.P. T.U.P. Charlton's Georgia Reports
Charley Ch.Cas. Charley's Chamber Cases. 1875–6
Charley Pr.Cas. Charley's Practice Cases. 1875–81
Charlt. R.M. Charlton's Georgia Reports
T.U.P. Charlton's Georgia Reports
Charlt.R.M. R.M. Charlton's Georgia Reports
Charlt.T.U.P. T.U.P. Charlton's Georgia Reports
Chart. Rotulus Chartarum (The Charter Roll)
Chart.Foresta Charta de Foresta
Chart.Inst.Insur.J. Chartered Insurance Institute Journal
Charter I. Charterparty International
Chartered Acc. Chartered Accountant in Australia. 1930–
Chas. Charles
Chase Chase's United States Circuit Court Decisions
Chase Dec. Chase's United States Circuit Court Decisions
Chase Steph.Dig.Ev. Chase on Stephens' Digest of Evidence
Chase Tr. Chase's Trial (Impeachment) by the United States Senate
Ches.Ca. Report of the Chesapeake Case, New Brunswick
Cheshire Cheshire & North, Private International Law
Chest. Chester County, Pennsylvania
Chest.Co.(Pa.) Chester County Reports (Pennsylvania)
Chest.Co.Rep. Chester County Reports (Pennsylvania)
Chetty Sudder Dewanny Adawlut Cases, Madras (India)
Chev. Cheves' South Carolina Law Reports (25 SCL) 1839–1940
Chev.Ch. Cheves' South Carolina Equity Reports (15 SCEq) 1839–1940
Chev.Eq. Cheves' South Carolina Equity Reports (15 SCEq) 1839–1940
Chevalier, Repertoire U. Chevalier, Repertoire des sources historiques du moyen-age (Fr.) 2ed. 1907
Cheves Cheves' South Carolina Law Reports (25 SCL) 1839–1940
Cheves Eq.(SC) Cheves' South Carolina Equity Reports (15 SCEq) 1839–1940
Cheves L.(SC) Cheves' South Carolina Law Reports (25 SCL) 1839–1940
Chi. Chicago
Chi.B.A.Rec. Chicago Bar Association Record. 1910–32
Chi.B.Rec. Chicago Bar Record. 1934–
Chi-Kent Chicago-Kent Review or Law Review
Chi-Kent L.Rev. Chicago-Kent Law Review. 1938–
Chi-Kent Rev. Chicago-Kent Review. 1923–38
Chi.L.B. Chicago Law Bulletin
Chi.L.J. Chicago Law Journal. 1876–7, 1880–1907
Chi.L.R. Chicago Law Record

Chi.Leg.N. Chicago Legal News. 1868–1925
Chic.-Kent L.Rev. Chicago-Kent Law Review (USA) 1938–
Chic.L.B. Chicago Law Bulletin
Chic.L.J. Chicago Law Journal. 1876–7, 1880–1907
Chic.L.R. Chicago Law Record
Chic.L.T. Chicago Law Times. 1886–9
Chic.Leg.N. Chicago Legal News. 1868–1925
Chicago B.Rec. Chicago Bar Record (USA) 1934–
Chicago L.B. Chicago Law Bulletin
Chicago L.J. Chicago Law Journal. 1876–7, 1880–1907
Chicago L.Rec. Chicago Law Record
Chicago L.Record Chicago Law Record
Chicago L.T. Chicago Law Times. 1886–9
Chicago Leg.News Chicago Legal News. 1868–1925
Child.Ct. Children's Court
Child Wel. Child Welfare (Can.)
Children's Leg.Rights J. Children's Legal Rights Journal (USA)
Chin.Law & Gov. Chinese Law and Government (USA) 1968–
China Bus.Rev. The China Business Review
China J. China Journal, Hong Kong
China L.Rep. China Law Reporter
China Law Rev. China Law Review, Shanghai (China) 1922–37, 1940–
China Q. China Quarterly (UK)
Chinese L.& Govt. Chinese Law and Government
Chinese Soc'y Int'l L.Annals The Annals of the Chinese Society of International Law (Taipei, Taiwan)
Chinese Yb.Int'l L.& Aff. Chinese Yearbook of International Law and Affairs (Taiwan)
Chip. Chipman's New Brunswick Reports (Can.) 1825–38
Chipman's Reports (Vermont) 1789–1824
Chip.D. D. Chipman's Vermont Reports. 1789–1824
Chip.Ms. Chipman's Manuscript Reports, New Brunswick (Can.)
Chip.N. N. Chipman's Vermont Reports. 1789–91
Chip.(Vt.) Chipman's Reports (Vermont) 1789–1824
Chip.W. Chipman's New Brunswick Reports (Can.) 1825–38
Chit. Chitty's Bail Court Reports. 1770–1822
Chitty's King's Bench Practice Reports. 1819–20
Chit.Arch.Pr. Chitty's edition of Archbold's Practice
Chit.Archb.Pr. Chitty's edition of Archbold's Practice
Chit.B.C. Chitty's Bail Court Reports. 1770–1822
Chit.Bills Chitty on Bills of Exchange. 11ed. 1878
Chit.Bl. Chitty's edition of Blackstone's Commentaries
Chit.Bl.Comm. Chitty's edition of Blackstone's Commentaries
Chit.Burn's J. Chitty's edition of Burn's Justice
Chit.Com.L. Chitty on Commercial Law. 1824
Chit.Con. Chitty on Contracts
Chit.Cont. Chitty on Contracts
Chit.Cr.L. Chitty's Criminal Law. 2ed. 1878
Chit.Cr.Law Chitty's Criminal Law. 2ed. 1878
Chit.Crim.Law Chitty's Criminal Law. 2ed. 1878
Chit.Des. Chitty on the Law of Descents. 1875
Chit.F. Chitty's King's Bench Forms
Chit.Gen.Pr. Chitty's General Practice
Chit.Med.Jur. Chitty on Medical Jurisprudence. 1834
Chit.Nat. Chitty, Law of Nations. 1812
Chit.Pl. Chitty on Pleading. 7ed. 1844
Chit.Pr. Chitty's General Practice
Chit.Prec. Chitty's Precedent in Pleading. 3ed. 1867–8

Chit.Prer. Chitty's Prerogatives of the Crown. 1820
Chit.R. Chitty's Bail Court Reports. 1770–1822
Chit.St. Chitty's Statutes of Practical Utility. 1235–1948
Chit.Stat. Chitty's Statutes of Practical Utility. 1235–1948
Chit.& H.Bills Chitty & Hulme on Bills of Exchange
Chitt. Chitty's Bail Court Reports. 1770–1822
Chitt.& Pat. Chitty & Patel's Supreme Court Appeals (India)
Chitty Chitty on Contracts
Chitty's Bail Court Reports. 1770–1822
Chitty B.C. Chitty's Bail Court Reports. 1770–1822
Chitty Bl.Comm. Chitty's edition of Blackstone's Commentaries
Chitty Com.Law Chitty on Commercial Law. 1824
Chitty Contracts Chitty on Contracts
Chitty Eq.Ind. Chitty's Equity Index. 4ed. 1833–9
Chitty's L.J. Chitty's Law Journal. 1950–
chm. chairman
chmn. chairman
Cho.Ca.Ca. Choyce's Cases in Chancery (21 ER) 1557–1606
Cho.Ca.Ch. Choyce's Cases in Chancery (21 ER) 1557–1606
Chowles & Webster Chowles & Webster's South African Law of Trade Marks, Company Names and Trading Styles
Choyce Cas. Choyce's Cases in Chancery (21 ER) 1557–1606
Choyce Cas.Ch. Choyce's Cases in Chancery (21 ER) 1557–1606
Chr. Chronique (Fr.)
Chr.Rep. Chamber Reports, Upper Canada. 1846–52
Chr.Rob. Christopher Robinson's Admiralty Reports (165 ER) 1799–1808
chron. chronicle
chronological
chronologically
chronology
Chron.Div.Cts. Chronicles of the Divorce Courts
Chron.Jur. Chronica Juridicalia
Chron.Reg. Chronological Register (appended to the Historical Register) 1700–
chs. chapters
Chulalongkorn L.Rev. Chulalongkorn Law Review (Thailand)
Church.& Br.Sh. Churchill & Bruce, Office and Duties of Sheriff 2ed. 1882
Chute Eq. Chute, Equity under the Judicature Act. 1874
Chy.Ch. Upper Canada Chancery Chambers Reports (Ont.) 1857–72
Chy.Chrs. Upper Canada Chancery Chambers Reports (Ont.) 1857–72
Ci.L.R. University of Cincinnati Law Review. 1927–42, 1948–
Cia. Compagnia (It.) Company
Cie. Compagnie (Fr.) Company
Cin. Cincinnati
Cin.L.Bull. Cincinnati Weekly Law Bulletin. 1876–9
Cin.L.Rev. University of Cincinnati Law Review. 1927–42, 1948–
Cin.Law Bul. Cincinnati Weekly Law Bulletin. 1876–9
Weekly Cincinnati Law Bulletin. 1879–83
Cin.Law Rev. University of Cincinnati Law Review. 1927–42, 1948–
Cin.Mun.Dec. Cincinnati Municipal Decisions
Cin.R. Cincinnati Superior Court Reports (Ohio)
Cin.S.C.R. Cincinnati Superior Court Reports (Ohio)
Cin.S.C.Rep. Cincinnati Superior Court Reports (Ohio)
Cin.Sup.Ct.Rep. Cincinnati Superior Court Reports (Ohio)
Cin.Super.Ct.Rep'r. Cincinnati Superior Court Reports (Ohio)
Cin.Super.(Ohio) Cincinnati Superior Court Reports (Ohio)

Cinc.L.Bul. Cincinnati Weekly Law Bulletin. 1876–9
Weekly Cincinnati Law Bulletin. 1879–83
Cir. Circuit
Circuit Court
Cir.Ct. Circuit Court
Cir.Ct.App. Circuit Court of Appeal
Cir.Ct.Dec. Circuit Court Decisions
Cir.Ct.Dec.(Ohio) Circuit Court Decisions (Ohio)
Cir.Ct.R. Circuit Court Reports
Cir.Ct.Rule Circuit Court Rule
Cir.Od.N.W.P. Circular Orders, Northwestern Provinces (India)
circ. circa, circiter, circum (Lat.) about
circulaire (Fr.)
circular
Circolari Esteri Ministero degli Affari Esteri, Raccolta delle Circolari e Istruzioni Ministeriali (It.) 1887–1918
Circolari riservate Esteri Ministero degli Affari Esteri, Raccolta delle Circolari e Istruzioni (It.) 1887–1918
cit. citation
citato (It.)
cited
citing
citizen
opera gia citata nel capitolo (It.)
Cit. Citator and Indian Law Journal (India) 1908–14
City Ct. City Court
City Ct.R. City Court Reports (New York)
City Ct.R.Supp. City Court Reports, Supplement (New York)
City Ct.Rep. City Court Reports (New York)
City Ct.Rep.Supp. City Court Reports, Supplement (New York)
City Ct.Supp.(NY) City Court Reports, Supplement (New York)
City H.Rec. New York, City Hall Recorder. 1816–22, 1823
City H.Rep. City Hall Reporter (Lomas, New York)
City Hall Rec. New York, City Hall Recorder. 1816–22, 1823
City Hall Rec.(NY) New York, City Hall Recorder. 1816–22, 1823
City Hall Rep. City Hall Reporter (Lomas, New York)
City Hall Rep.(NY) City Hall Reporter (Lomas, New York)
City Rec. New York, City Record
City Rec.(NY) New York, City Record
civ. civil
civilian
Civ. Arrêt de la Chambre civile de la Cour de Cassation (Fr.) Decision of the Cour de Cassation, civil division
Civil
Civil Appeals
Tribunal civil (Belg.) Civil court
Civ.App. Court of Civil Appeals
Civ.Code Civil Code
Civ.Code Prac. Civil Code of Practice
Civ.Ct. Civil Court
Civ.Ct.Rec. Civil Court of Record
Civ.Lib.Dock. Civil Liberties Docket (USA) 1955–69
Civ.Lib.Rev. Civil Liberties Review (USA) 1973–
Civ.Lib.Rptr. Civil Liberties Reporter (USA) 1950–
Civ.Pr. Civil Procedure Reports, New York
Civ.Pr.Rep. Civil Procedure Reports, New York
Civ.Prac. Civil Practice Law and Rules
Civ.Prac.(NY) New York Civil Practice
Civ.Pro. Civil Procedure Reports (New York) 1881–1907
Civ.Pro.R. Civil Procedure Reports (New York) 1881–1907
Civ.Pro.R.(N.S.) Civil Procedure Reports, New Series (New York) 1908–13
Civ.Proc. Civil Procedure
Civ.Proc.(NY) New York Civil Procedure
Civ.Proc.R. Civil Procedure Reports (New York) 1881–1907
Civ.Proc.R.(N.S.) Civil Procedure Reports, New Series (New York) 1908–13

Civ.Proc.Rep. Civil Procedure Reports (New York) 1881–1907
Civ.Proc.Rep.N.S. Civil Procedure Reports, New Series (New York) 1908–13
Civ.Rights Civil Rights
Civ.Serv. Civil Service
Civ.& Cr.L.S. Civil and Criminal Law Series (India)
Civ.& Military L.J. Civil and Military Law Journal (India)
Civil Just.Q. Civil Justice Quarterly
Cl. Clark
Clarke
Clause
Clearing
Constitutional legislation (It.)
Rotulus Clausarum (Close Roll)
Cl.App. Clark's Appeal Cases, House of Lords
Cl.Ass. Clerk's Assistant
Cl.Can.Ins. Clarke's Canada Insolvent Acts
Cl.Ch. Clarke's New York Chancery Reports. 1839–41
Cl.Ct. Claims Court Reporter (USA)
Cl.Home Clerk Home, Session Cases (Scot.) 1735–44
Cl.R. Clarke's New York Chancery Reports. 1839–41
Cl.& F. Clark & Finnelly's House of Lords Cases (6–8 ER) 1831–46
Cl.& Fin. Clark & Finnelly's House of Lords Cases (6–8 ER) 1831–46
Cl.& H. Clarke & Hall's Contested Election Cases (USA) 1789–1834
Cl.& Sc.Dr.Cas. Clark & Scully's Drainage Cases (Ontario) 1891–1900
Clancy Husb.& W. Clancy's Treatise of the Rights, Duties, and Liabilities of Husband and Wife. 3ed. 1827
Clar.Parl.Chr. Clarendon's Parliamentary Chronicle
Clark Clark's House of Lords Appeal Cases
Clark's Reports (58 Alabama)
Pennsylvania Law Journal Reports, edited by Clark
Supreme Court Judgments, by Clark (Jamaica) 1917–32
Clark (Ala.) Clark's Reports (58 Alabama)
Clark App. Clark's Appeal Cases, House of Lords
Clark Col.Law Clark, Colonial Law. 1834
Clark.Dig. Clark's Digest, House of Lords Reports. 1814–66, 1868
Clark (Jam.) Supreme Court Judgments, by Clark (Jamaica) 1917–32
Clark (Pa.) Clark's Pennsylvania Law Journal Reports
Clark & F. Clark & Finnelly's House of Lords Reports (6–8 ER) 1831–46
Clark & F.(N.S.) Clark & Finnelly's House of Lords Reports, New Series (9–11 ER) 1847–66
Clark & Fin. Clark & Finnelly's House of Lords Reports (6–8 ER) 1831–46
Clark & Fin.(N.S.) Clark & Finnelly's House of Lords Reports, New Series (9–11 ER) 1847–66
Clarke Clarke's Iowa Reports (1–8 Iowa)
Clarke's Michigan Reports (19–22 Michigan)
Clarke's New York Chancery Reports. 1839–41
Clarke's Notes of Cases (Bengal)
Clarke's Pennsylvania Reports. 1842–52
Clarke Ch. Clarke's New York Chancery Reports. 1839–41
Clarke Ch.(NY) Clarke's New York Chancery Reports. 1839–41
Clarke (Ia.) Clarke's Iowa Reports (1–8 Ia.)
Clarke (Mich.) Clarke's Michigan Reports (19–22 Mich.)
Clarke Not. Clarke's Notes of Cases, in his 'Rules and Orders', Bengal (India)
Clarke (Pa.) Clarke's Pennsylvania Reports. 1842–52
Clarke R.& O. Clarke's Notes of Cases, in his 'Rules and Orders', Bengal (India)
Clarke & H.Elec.Cas. Clarke & Hall's Contested Election Cases (USA) 1789–1834

Clarke & S.Dr.Cas. Clarke & Scully's Drainage Cases (Can.) 1891–1900
Clark's Code Clark's Annotated Code of Civil Procedure (North Carolina)
Clark's Summary Clark's Summary of American Law
Clay. Clayton's Reports and Pleas of Assizes at York. 1631–50
Clay's Dig. Clay's Digest of the Laws of Alabama
Clayt. Clayton's Reports, York Assizes. 1631–50
Clayton Clayton's Reports, York Assizes. 1631–50
Clearinghouse Rev. Clearinghouse Review (USA) 1967–
Cleary R.C. Cleary's Registration Cases (Ire.) 1886–7
Cleary Reg.Cas. Cleary's Registration Cases (Ire.) 1886–7
Clem. Clemens Reports (57–59 Kansas)
Clerk Home Clerk Home's Decisions, Court of Session (Scot.) 1735–44
Clerke Pr. Clerk's (or Clarke's) Praxis Curiae Admiralitatis Angliae
Clerke Prax. Clerk's (or Clarke's) Praxis Curiae Admiralitatis Angliae
Clev. Cleveland
Clev.B.Assn.J. Cleveland Bar Association Journal. 1927–33, 1936–
Clev.B.J. Cleveland Bar Journal. 1934–6
Clev.Bar Ass'n.J. Cleveland Bar Association Journal. 1927–33, 1936–
Clev.L.Rec. Cleveland Law Record (Ohio)
Clev.L.Reg. Cleveland Law Register (Ohio)
Clev.L.Rep. Cleveland Law Reporter (Ohio) 1878–9
Clev.–Mar. Cleveland–Marshall
Clev.–Mar.L.Rev. Cleveland–Marshall Law Review. 1951–69
Clev.St.L.Rev. Cleveland State Law Review
Clev.State L.Rev. Cleveland State Law Review
Cleve.L.R.(Ohio) Cleveland Law Reporter (Ohio) 1878–9
Cleve.L.Rec. Cleveland Law Record (Ohio)
Cleve.L.Rec.(Ohio) Cleveland Law Record (Ohio)
Cleve.L.Reg. Cleveland Law Register (Ohio)
Cleve.L.Reg.(Ohio) Cleveland Law Register (Ohio)
Cleve.L.Rep. Cleveland Law Reporter (Ohio) 1878–9
Cleve.Law R. Cleveland Law Reporter (Ohio) 1878–9
Cleve.Law Rec. Cleveland Law Record (Ohio)
Cleve.Law Reg. Cleveland Law Register (Ohio)
Cleve.Law Rep. Cleveland Law Reporter (Ohio) 1878–9
Clif. Clifford, United States Circuit Court Reports
Clif.El. Clifford's Southwark Election Cases. 1796–7
Clif.El.Cas. Clifford's Southwark Election Cases. 1796–7
Clif.South.El. Clifford's Southwark Election Cases. 1796–7
Clif.& R. Clifford & Richard's Locus Standi Reports. 1873–84
Clif.& Rich. Clifford & Richard's Locus Standi Reports. 1873–84
Clif.& Rick. Clifford & Richard's Locus Standi Reports. 1873–84
Clif.& St. Clifford & Stephen's Locus Standi Reports. 1867–72
Clif.& Steph. Clifford & Stephen's Locus Standi Reports. 1867–72
Cliff. Clifford's Southwark Election Cases. 1796–7
Clifford's United States Circuit Court Reports
Cliff.El.Cas. Clifford's Southwark Election Cases. 1796–7
Cliff.& Rich. Clifford & Richard's Locus Standi Reports. 1873–84
Cliff.& Rick. Clifford & Richard's Locus Standi Reports. 1873–84
Cliff.& Steph. Clifford & Stephen's Locus Standi Reports. 1867–72

Clift Clift's Book of Declarations. 1719
Clin.Dig. Clinton's Digest (New York)
Clk. Clerk
Clk's Mag. Clerk's Magazine
Clerk's Magazine (Rhode Island, USA)
Clerk's Magazine (Upper Canada)
clms. claims
Clow L.C.Torts Clow, Leading Cases on Torts
cls. claims
clauses
Clunet Journal du droit international (Fr.) 1874–1945
Cm. Command Papers, 6th series (Cm.1–) 1986–
Cmcl.Law Assoc.Bull. Commercial Law Association Bulletin (Aus.) 1968–83
Cmd. Command Papers, 4th series (Cmd.1–9889) 1919–56
cml. commercial
Cmnd. Command Papers, 5th series (Cmnd.1–9927) 1956–86
cn codice della navigazione (It.) Navigation Code. 1942
cnav. codice della navigazione (It.) Navigation Code. 1942
Co. Coke's Institutes
Coke's King's Bench Reports (76–7 ER) 1572–1616
Colorado
Colorado Reports
Company
County
Co.A. Colorado Court of Appeals Reports
Cook's Vice-Admiralty Reports (Can.) 1873–84
Co.Cop. Coke's Compleat Copyholder. 5ed. 1673
Co.Ct. County Court
Co.Ct.Cas. County Court Cases
Co.Ct.Ch. County Courts Chronicle. 1847–1920
Co.Ct.Chr. County Courts Chronicle. 1847–1920
Co.Ct.I.L.T. Irish Law Times, County Court Reports
Co.Ct.R. County Courts Reports. 1860–1920
Co.Ct.Rep. County Courts Reports. 1860–1920
Pennsylvania County Court Reports
Co.Ct.Rep.(Pa.) Pennsylvania County Court Reports
Co.Cts. Coke's Courts (Fourth Institute)
County Courts
Co.Cts.Chr. County Courts Chronicle. 1847–1920
Co.Ent. Coke's Entries. 1614
Co.G. Coke's Reports and Cases of Practice in Common Pleas (125 ER) 1706–47
Co.Inst. Coke's Institutes
Co.L.Dig. Company Lawyer Digest
Co.L.J. Cochin Law Journal (India) 1934–48
Colonial Law Journal (N.Z.) 1865–75
Co.Law. Company Lawyer. 1980–
Co.Law.Dig. Company Lawyer Digest
Co.Lit. Coke on Littleton (First Institute)
Co.Litt. Coke on Littleton (First Institute)
Co.M.C. Coke's Magna Charta (Second Institute)
Co.on Courts Coke's Courts (Fourth Institute)
Co.P.C. Coke's Pleas of the Crown (Third Institute)
Co.Pl. Coke's Pleadings
Co.R. Code Reporter (New York) 1848–53
Co.R.N.S. Code Reporter, New Series (New York) 1850–3
Co.R.(N.Y.) Code Reporter (New York)
Co.Rep. Code Reporter (New York) 1848–53
Coke's King's Bench Reports (76–7 ER) 1572–1616
Co-Tr. Co-trustee
Co.& Al. Cooke & Alcock's King's Bench Reports (Ire.) 1833–4
Co.& Sec.L.J. Company and Securities Law Journal (Aus.) 1982–
Coastal Zone Managem.J. Coastal Zone Management Journal (USA)

Cob.St.Tr. Cobbett's State Trials. 1163–1820

Cobb Cobb's Digest of Statute Law, Georgia (USA) 1851
Cobb's Reports (121 Alabama)
Cobb's Reports (4–20 Georgia)

Cobb Dig. Cobb's Digest of Statute Law (Georgia) 1851

Cobb.Parl.Hist. Cobbett's Parliamentary History

Cobb.St.Tr. Cobbett's State Trials. 1163–1820

Cobbey Ann.St. Cobbey's Annotated Nebraska Statutes (USA)

Cobbey Repl. Cobbey's Practical Treatise on the Law of Replevin

Coch. Cochran's Nova Scotia Reports (Can.) 1859

Coch.Ch.Ct. Chief Court of Cochin, Select Decisions (India)

Coch.Ind. Cochin, India

Coch.N.Sc. Cochran's Nova Scotia Reports (Can.) 1859

Cochin Cochin Law Reports (India) 1909–48

Cochin L.J. Cochin Law Journal (India) 1934–48

Cochin L.R. Cochin Law Reports (India) 1909–48

Cochr. Cochran's Nova Scotia Reports (Can.) 1859
Cochran's Reports (3–10 North Dakota)

Cochran Cochran's Nova Scotia Reports (Can.) 1859
Cochran's Reports (3–10 North Dakota)

Cock.Tich.Ca. Cockburn's Charge in the Tichborne Case

Cock.& R. Cockburn & Rowe's Election Cases. 1833

Cock.& Rowe Cockburn & Rowe's Election Cases. 1833

Cockb.& R. Cockburn & Rowe's Election Cases. 1833

Cockb.& Rowe Cockburn & Rowe's Election Cases. 1833

Cocke Cocke's Reports (16–18 Alabama)
Cocke's Reports (14–15 Florida)

Cod. Codex Justinianus
Codification
Gibson's Codex Ecclesiastia. 1715
Gibson's Codex Juris Civilis

Cod.Dip. Codex Diplomaticus (ed. Kemble)

Cod.Jur. Codex Juris Civilis (Gibson)

Cod.Jur.Civ. Codex Juris Civilis (Gibson)

Cod.St. Codified Statutes

Cod.Theodos. Codex Theodosianus (Code of Theodosius)

Code The New Zealand Code of Civil Procedure of the High Court

Code Civ. Code civil (Fr.) civil code

Code Civ.Pro. Code of civil procedure

Code Civ.Proc. Code of civil procedure

Code Com.B. Code de commerce belge (Belgian commercial code)

Code Cr.Pro. Code of criminal procedure

Code Cr.Proc. Code of criminal procedure

Code Crim.Proc. Code of criminal procedure

Code de com. Code de commerce (Belg. & Fr.) commercial code

Code d'Instr.Crim. Code d'instruction criminelle (Fr.) code of criminal procedure

Code Fed.Reg. Code of Federal Regulations

Code for. Code forestier (Fr.) Forestry code

Code Gen.Laws Code of general laws

Code I. Code d'instruction criminelle (Fr.) code of criminal procedure

Code La. Civil Code of Louisiana

Code M. Code municipal (Québec)

Code N. Code Napoléon (Fr.) civil code

Code Nap. Code Napoléon (Fr.) civil code

Code P. Code pénal (Fr.) criminal code

Code P.C. Code de procédure civile (Fr.) code of civil procedure

Code Prac. Code of practice

Code Pro. Code of procedure

Code R.N.S. Code Reporter, New Series (New York) 1850–3

Code R.N.S.(N.Y.) Code Reporter, New Series (New York) 1850–3
Code R.(N.Y.) Code Reporter (New York) 1848–53
Code Rep. Code Reporter (New York) 1848–53
Code Rep.N.S. Code Reporter, New Series (New York) 1850–3
Code Supp. Supplement to the Code
Code Theod. Codex Theodosianus (Code of Theodosius)
Code Theodos. Codex Theodosianus (Code of Theodosius)
Codes Fr. Les codes françaises (Fr.) French codes
Coe Ch.Pr. Coe, Practice of the Judges' Chambers. 1876
Cof. Coffey's California Probate Decisions
Cof.Dig. Cofer's Kentucky Digest
Cof.Prob.Dec.(Cal.) Coffey's California Probate Decisions
Coff.Prob. Coffey's California Probate Decisions
Coffey's Prob.Dec. Coffey's California Probate Decisions
Cogh.Epit. Coghlan's Epitome of Hindu Law Cases (India)
Cohen Adm.Law Cohen, Admiralty Jurisdiction, Law and Practice (USA)
Coke Coke's King's Bench Reports (76–7 ER) 1572–1616
Coke Inst. Coke's Institutes
Coke Lit. Coke on Littleton
Col. Coldwell's Reports (41–7 Tennessee)
Coleman's Reports (99, 101, 106, 110–129 Alabama)
Colonial
Colorado Reports
Columbia
Column
Coluna (Port.) column
Col.App. Colorado Appeals Reports
Col.C.C. Collyer's Chancery Cases tempore Bruce, V.-C. (63 ER) 1844–6
Col.Cas. Coleman's Cases of Practice (New York) 1791–1800
Col.Cas.(N.Y.) Coleman's Cases of Practice (New York) 1791–1800
Col.Hum.R.L.Rev. Columbia Human Rights Law Review (USA) 1971–
Col.J.Environ.L. Columbia Journal of Environmental Law (USA) 1974–
Col.J.L.& Soc.Probl. Columbia Journal of Law and Social Problems (USA) 1965–
Col.J.Trans.L. Columbia Journal of Transnational Law (USA) 1964–
Col.J.Transnat'l L. Columbia Journal of Transnational Law (USA) 1964–
Col.J.World Bus. Columbia Journal of World Business (USA)
Col.Journ.trans.law Columbia Journal of Transnational Law (USA) 1964–
Col.Journ.W.Bus. Columbia Journal of World Business (USA)
Col.Jurid. Collectanea Juridica
Col.L.J. Colonial Law Journal (N.Z.) 1865, 1874–75
Col.L.J.N.Z. Colonial Law Journal (N.Z.) 1865–75
Col.L.R. Columbia Law Review (USA) 1901–
Col.L.Rep. Colorado Law Reporter. 1880–4
Col.L.Rev. Columbia Law Review. 1901–
Col.Law Rev. Columbia Law Review. 1901–
Col.N.P. Colorado Nisi Prius Decisions
Col.Part. Collyer, Law of Partnership. 2ed. 1840
Col.& C.Cas. Coleman & Caines' Cases (New York) 1794–1805
Col.& Cai. Coleman & Caines' Cases (New York) 1794–1805
Col.& Cai.Cas. Coleman & Caines' Cases (New York) 1794–1805
Col.& Caines Cas.(N.Y.) Coleman & Caines' Cases (New York) 1794–1805
Cold. Coldwell's Tennessee Supreme Court Reports (41–7 Tenn.) 1860–70
Colds.Pr. Coldstream's Court of Session Procedure (Scot.)
Coldw. Coldwell's Tennessee Supreme Court Reports (41–7 Tenn.) 1860–70
Cole. Cole's Iowa Reports

Coleman's Reports (99, 101, 106, 110–129 Alabama)

Cole.Cas. Coleman's Cases of Practice (New York) 1791–1800

Cole.Cas.Pr. Coleman's Cases of Practice (New York) 1791–1800

Cole Cond. Cole, Particulars and Conditions of Sale. 1879

Cole Cr.Inf. Cole, Criminal Informations. 1843

Cole Ejec. Cole, Ejectment. 1857

Cole.& Cai.Cas. Coleman & Caines' Cases (New York) 1794–1805

Colem.Cas. Coleman's Cases of Practice (New York) 1791–1800

Colem.& C.Cas. Coleman & Caines' Cases (New York) 1794–1805

Coll. Collection
Collector
Colles' Cases in Parliament (1 ER) 1697–1713
Collyer's Chancery Cases tempore Bruce, V.-C. (63 ER) 1844–5

Coll.Bank. Collier, Law of Bankruptcy
Collins, History, Law and Practice of Banking. 1882

Coll.C.C. Collyer's Chancery Cases tempore Bruce, V.-C. (63 ER) 1844–5

Coll.C.R. Collyer's Chancery Cases tempore Bruce, V.-C. (63 ER) 1844–5

Coll.Caus.Cél. Collection des Causes Célèbres, Paris (Fr.)

Coll.Contr. Collier, Law of Contribution. 1875

Coll.Jurid. Collectanea Juridica

Coll.L.D.et O. Collections des Lois, Décrets et Ordonnances (Fr.)
Collection of laws, decrees and ordinances

Coll.N.C. Collyer's Chancery Cases tempore Bruce, V.-C. (63 ER) 1844–5

Coll.of Dec. Collection of Decisions of the European Commission of Human Rights

Coll.P.C. Colles' Cases in Parliament (1 ER) 1697–1713

Coll.& E.Bank. Collier & Eaton's Bankruptcy Reports (USA)

Colles Colles' Cases in Parliament (1 ER) 1697–1713

Colles P.C. Colles' Cases in Parliament (1 ER) 1697–1713

Colliard C.-A. Colliard & A. Manin, Droit international et histoire diplomatique (Fr.) 1970–75

Collier Bank. Collier & Eaton's Bankruptcy Reports (USA)

Collier & E.Am.Bankr. Collier & Eaton's Bankruptcy Reports (USA)

Colly. Collyer's Chancery Reports tempore Bruce, V.-C. (63 ER) 1844–5

Colly.Ch.Cas. Collyer's Chancery Reports tempore Bruce V.-C. (63 ER) 1844–5

Colly.Part. Collyer, Partnership. 2ed. 1840

Colly Partn. Collyer, Partnership. 2ed. 1840

Colo. Colorado
Colorado Supreme Court Reports. 1864–

Colo.App. Colorado Court of Appeals Reports. 1891–1905, 1912–15

Colo.B.A. Colorado Bar Association
Colorado Bar Association Report

Colo.Dec. Colorado Decisions

Colo.L.R. Colorado Law Reporter. 1880–4

Colo.Law. The Colorado Lawyer

Colo.Law Rep. Colorado Law Reporter. 1880–4

Colo.N.P.Dec. Colorado Nisi Prius Decisions. 1900–2

Colo.Rev.Stat. Colorado Revised Statutes

Colo.Sess.Laws Session Laws of Colorado

Colo.St.B.A. Colorado State Bar Association
Colorado State Bar Association Report

Colom. Colombia

Colombo L.J. Colombo Law Journal (Sri L.)

Colombo L.Rev. Colombo Law Review (Sri L.) 1969–

Colombos A Treatise on the Law of Prize. 3ed. 1940
Colq. Colquit's Reports, 1 Modern Reports (86 ER) 1669–70
Colq.Civ.Law Colquhoun, Roman Civil Law
Colquit Colquit's Reports, 1 Modern Reports (86 ER) 1669–70
cols. columns
Colt. Coltman's Registration Cases. 1879–85
Colt.(Reg.Ca.) Coltman's Registration Cases. 1879–85
Colt.Reg.Cas. Coltman's Registration Cases. 1879–85
Coltm. Coltman's Registration Cases. 1879–85
Colum. Columbia
Colum.Bus.L.Rev. Columbia Business Law Review (USA)
Colum.Hum.Rts.L.Rev. Columbia Human Rights Law Review (USA) 1971–
Colum.Human Rights L.Rev. Columbia Human Rights Law Review (USA) 1971–
Colum.J.Environ.L. Columbia Journal of Environmental Law. 1974–
Colum.J.Envtl.L. Columbia Journal of Environmental Law. 1974–
Colum.J.L.& Soc.Prob. Columbia Journal of Law and Social Problems. 1965–
Colum.J.Transnat'l Law Columbia Journal of Transnational Law. 1964–
Colum.Jr. Columbia Jurist. 1885–7
Colum.Jur. Columbia Jurist. 1885–7
Colum.L.R. Columbia Law Review (USA) 1901–
Colum.L.Rev. Columbia Law Review (USA) 1901–
Colum.L.T. Columbia Law Times. 1887–93
Colum.Soc'y Int'l.L.Bull. Columbia Society of International Law Bulletin. 1961–3
Colum.Survey Human Rights L. Columbia Survey of Human Rights Law. 1967–71
Colum.–VLA J.L.& Arts Columbia–VLA Journal of Law and the Arts (USA)
Columb.J.Trans.L. Columbia Journal of Transnational Law (USA) 1964–
Columb.L.R. Columbia Law Review (USA) 1901–
Columbia L.R. Columbia Law Review (USA) 1901–
Colvil Colvil's Manuscript Decisions, Court of Session (Scot.)
Coly.Guar. De Colyar on Guarantees
Com. Blackstone's Commentaries
Comberbach's King's Bench Reports (90 ER) 1685–99
Comment
Commerce
Commercial
Commission
Commissioner
Committee
Common
Commonwealth
Communication(s)
Comstock Reports (1–4 New York Court of Appeals)
Comyn's Reports, King's Bench (92 ER) 1695–1741
La section commerciale de la Cour de Cassation (Fr.) Commercial section of the Cour de Cassation
U.S. Commerce Court Opinions
Com.Affrs. Community Affairs
Com.B. Common Bench Reports (Manning, Granger & Scott) (135–9 ER) 1845–56
Com.B.N.S. Common Bench Reports, New Series (140–4 ER) 1857–66
Com.Cas. Commercial Cases. 1896–1941
Company Cases (India)
Com.Cas.S.C.C. Commercial Cases, Small Cause Court, Bengal (India) 1851–60
Com.Con. Comyn, Law of Contracts. 2ed. 1824
Com.D. Commercial Division

Com.Dig. Comyn's Digest of the Laws of England. 5ed. 1882
Com.G.S. Commissioners of the Great Seal
Com.Jour. House of Commons Journal
Com.Jud.J. Commonwealth Judicial Journal
Com.L. Commercial Law (Can.)
Com.L.A. Commercial Law Annual. 1871–4
Com.L.J. Commercial Law Journal (India) 1947–
Commercial Law Journal (USA) 1930–
Com.L.L. Commonwealth Law Librarian. 1992–
Com.L.League J. Commercial Law League Journal. 1923–30
Com.L.Q. Commercial Law Quarterly (Aus.) 1987–
Com.L.R. Commercial Law Reporter (S.Afr.) 1948–58
Commercial Law Reports. 1903–5
Common Law Reports. 1853–5
Com.Law Commercial Law
Communications and the Law. 1980–
Com.Law Ann. Commercial Law Annual. 1871–4
Com.Law R. Commercial Law Reporter (S.Afr.) 1948–58
Common Law Reports. 1853–5
Com.Law Rep. Commercial Law Reporter (S.Afr.) 1948–58
Common Law Reports. 1853–5
Com.on Con. Comyn's Law on Contracts. 2ed 1824
Com.P.Div. Law Reports, Common Pleas Division
Com.P.Reptr. Common Pleas Reporter (Scranton, Pennsylvania) 1879–87
Com.Pl. Law Reports, Common Pleas
Com.Pl.Div. Law Reports, Common Pleas Division
Com.Pl.R.(Pa.) Common Pleas Reporter (Scranton, Pennsylvania) 1879–87
Com.Pl.Reptr. Common Pleas Reporter (Scranton, Pennsylvania) 1879–87
Com.Rep. Comyn's King's Bench Reports (92 ER) 1695–1741
Com.Serj. Common Serjeant
Com.& Law Communications and the Law. 1980–
Com.& Leg.Rep. Commercial and Legal Reporter
Com.& Mun.L.Rep. Commercial and Municipal Law Reporter (S.Afr.) 1959–
Comb. Comberbach's King's Bench Reports (94 ER) 1685–99
comd. commanded
com'l commercial
comm. commentary
commerce
commercial
commission
committee
Comm. Blackstone's Commentaries
Commentaries
Commercial Court
Commonwealth
Tribunal de commerce (Belg.)
commercial court
Comm.A.R. Commonwealth Arbitration Reports (Aus.) 1905–
Comm.Ct. Commerce Court (USA)
Comm.Fut.L.Rep. Commodity Futures Law Reporter (CCH) (USA)
Comm.Journ. House of Commons Journal
Comm.gouv. Commissiare du gouvernement (Fr.)
Comm.Jud.J. Commonwealth Judicial Journal. 1973–
Comm.L.Assoc.Aust.Bull. Commercial Law Association of Australia Bulletin. 1983–6
Comm.L.Assoc.Bull. Commercial Law Association Bulletin (Aus.) 1968–83
Comm.L.B. Commonwealth Law Bulletin. 1974–
CommLL Commonwealth Law Librarian. 1992–
Comm.L.Q. Commercial Law Quarterly (Aus.) 1987–
Comm.L.R. Commercial Law Reporter (S.Afr.) 1948–58
Commercial Law Reports (Can.)

Commonwealth Law Reports (Aus.) 1903–
Commonwealth Law Review (Aus.) 1903–9

Comm.Law Bull. Commonwealth Law Bulletin. 1975–

Comm.Leases Commercial Leases

Comm.Market L.Rev. Common Market Law Review. 1963–

Comm.Mkt.L.R. Common Market Law Reports. 1962–

Comm.Mkt.L.Rev. Common Market Law Review. 1963–

Comm.Mkt.Rep. Common Market Reporter (CCH)

Comm.Rec. Commonwealth Record (Aus.) 1976–87

Comm.rif.fam. Commentario alla riforma del diritto di famiglia (It.) 1977

Comm.Scialoja e Branca Commentario del codice civile a cura di Scialoja e Branca (It.)

Comm.Sec. Commonwealth Secretariat

Comm.& L. Communications and the Law (USA)

commd. commissioned

commer. commerce
commercial

Commiss. Commission

Commission Franco–Mexicaine La Réparation des Dommages causes aux Ētrangers par des Mouvements Révolutionnaires, Juriprudence de la Commission Franco–Mexicaine des Réclamations (Fr.) 1924–32

comml. commercial

Commn. Commission

Common L.Lawyer The Common Law Lawyer (USA)

Common.L.Rev. Commonwealth Law Review (Aus.)

Commons, Capitalism J.R. Commons, Legal Foundations of Capitalism. 1924

Commonwealth L.Bull. Commonwealth Law Bulletin. 1974–

Commr. Commissioner

Commrs. Commissioners

Commu.L.B. Communications Law Bulletin (Aus.) 1981–

Commun.& Law Communications and the Law. 1980–

Communicaz.Ist.Dir.Intern.Milano Communicazioni e Studi, Istituto de Diritto Internazionale e Straniero della Universita di Milano (It.)

Communita Intern. La Communita Internazionale (It.)

Commw.Arb. Commonwealth Arbitration
Reports (Aus.) 1905–

Commw.Ct. Commonwealth Court

Commw.Jud.J. Commonwealth Judicial Journal. 1973–

Commw.L.B. Commonwealth Law Bulletin. 1974–

Commw.L.R. Commonwealth Law Reports (Aus.) 1903–

Commw.Sec. Commonwealth Secretariat

comp. Company
comparative
compare
compensation
compilation
compile
compiled
compiler
composer
computer

Comp. Acct. Company Accountant

Comp.Armed Forces Compendium of Law of Armed Forces (USA)

Comp.Cas. Company Cases (India) 1930–

Comp.Ct. Compensation Court (N.Z.)

Comp.Dec. Decisions of the Comptroller of the Treasury (USA)

Comp.Gen. Comptroller General
Decisions of the Comptroller General (USA) 1921–

Comp.Gen.Op. Comptroller General's Opinions

Comp.Jur.Rev. Comparative Juridical Review (USA) 1964–

Comp.Jurid.Rev. Comparative Juridical Review (USA) 1964–

Comp.L.Ser. U.S. Bureau of Foreign and Domestic Commerce, Comparative Law Series
Comp.L.Yb. Comparative Law Yearbook (Neth.)
Comp.L.Yrbk.Intl.Bus. Comparative Law Yearbook of International Business (Neth.)
Comp.L.& P. Computer Law and Practice. 1984–
Comp.Lab.L. Comparative Labor Law (USA) 1976–
Comp.Lab.L.J. Comparative Labor Law Journal
Comp.Lab.Law Comparative Labor Law (USA) 1976–
Comp.Law Computer Law (Can.) 1983–
Comp.Law E.C. Competition Law in the European Communities
Comp.Laws Compiled Laws
Comp.Lawy. Company Lawyer. 1980–
Comp.Pol.Stud. Comparative Political Studies (USA)
Comp.Politics Comparative Politics (USA)
Comp.Rev. Compensation Review (USA) 1925–32
Comp.St. Compiled Statutes
Comp.Stat. Compiled Statutes
Comp.& Int'l.L.J.S.Afr. Comparative and International Law Journal of Southern Africa. 1968–
Comp.& L. Computers and Law (Aus.) 1983–
Comp.& Law Computers and Law. 1975–
Company & Sec.L.J. Company and Securities Law Journal (USA)
Comptr.Treas.Dec. Comptroller of the Treasury's Decisions
Comput.& Law Computers and Law. 1975–
Computer L.J. The Computer Law Journal (USA)
Computer & R. Computer und Recht (Ger.)
Com'r. Commissioner
Comr.of Bkg.and Ins. Commissioner of Banking and Insurance
Coms. Comstock's Reports (1–4 New York Court of Appeals)
Comst. Comstock's Reports (1–4 New York Court of Appeals)
Comun.internaz. Comunita internazionale (It.) 1946–
Com'w'th. Commonwealth
Comyn Comyn's King's Bench Reports (92 ER) 1695–1741
Comyn's Dig. Comyn's Digest of the Law of England. 5ed. 1882
con. conjunx (Lat.) consort
contra (Lat.) in opposition to
Con. Conover's Reports (16–153 Wisconsin)
Connoly's New York Criminal Reports
Continuation of Rolle's Reports (2 Rolle)
Con.B.J. Connecticut Bar Journal. 1927–
Con.Cus. Conroy's Custodian Reports (Ire.) 1652–1788
Con.L.R. Connecticut Law Review. 1968–
Construction Law Reports
Con.L.Rev. Connecticut Law Review. 1968–
Con.St. Consolidated Statutes
Con.Sur. Connoly's Surrogate Reports (New York)
Con.& L. Connor & Lawson's Irish Chancery Reports. 1841–3
Con.& Law. Connor & Lawson's Irish Chancery Reports. 1841–3
Con.& Sim. Connor & Simonton's South Carolina Equity Digest
Concil.Cts.Rev. Conciliation Courts Review (Can.)
cond. condensed
Cond.Ch.R. Condensed Chancery Reports
Cond.Ecc.R. Condensed Ecclesiastical Reports
Cond.Eccl. Condensed Ecclesiastical Reports
Cond.Ex.R. Condensed Exchequer Reports

Cond.Exch.R. Condensed Exchequer Reports
Cond.Rep.U.S. Peters' Condensed United States Reports
Condem. Condemnation
Condit.Sale–Chat.Mort.Rep. Conditional Sale – Chattel Mortgage Reporter (CCH) (USA)
Conf. Conference
Conference Reports by Cameron & Norwood, North Carolina (1 NC) 1800–4
Confirmation
Confirming
Conf.Chart. Confirmatio Chartarum
Conf.Comm.Uniformity Legis. Conference of Commissioners on Uniformity of Legislation in Canada
Conf.DIP Fondo della Conferenza di diritto internazionale privato di Roma (It.)
Conf.Rept. Conference Reports by Cameron & Norwood, North Carolina (1 NC) 1800–4
Conference (NC) Conference Reports by Cameron & Norwood, North Carolina (1 NC) 1800–4
Confl. Tribunal des Conflits (Fr.)
Conflict Resolution Journal of Conflict Resolution
Cong. Congress
Congressional
Cong.Deb. Congressional Debates (USA)
Cong.Dig. Congdon's Digest (Can.)
Congressional Digest (USA) 1922–
Cong.El.Cas. Congressional Election Cases (USA)
Cong.Gl. Congressional Globe (USA)
Cong.Rec. Congressional Record, Washington (USA)
Congl. Congregational
Congressional
Conk.Adm. Conkling's Admiralty Jurisdiction
Conn. Connecticut
Connecticut Reports. 1814–
Connoly's Surrogate Reports (New York)
Conn.App.Proc. Maltbie's Appellate Procedure (Connecticut)
Conn.B.J. Connecticut Bar Journal. 1927–
Conn.Cir. Connecticut Circuit Court Reports. 1961–
Conn.Cir.Ct. Connecticut Circuit Court Reports. 1961–
Conn.Comp.Com. Connecticut Compensation Commissioners, Compendium of Awards
Conn.Comp.Dec. Connecticut Workmen's Compensation Decisions
Conn.Dec. Connecticut Decisions
Conn.Gen.Stat. General Statutes of Connecticut
Conn.Gen.Stat.Ann. Connecticut General Statutes Annotated (West)
Conn.J.Int'l L. Connecticut Journal of International Law (USA)
Conn.L.J. Connecticut Law Journal (USA)
Conn.L.Rev. Connecticut Law Review. 1968–
Conn.Legis.Serv. Connecticut Legislative Service (West)
Conn.P.U.C. Connecticut Public Utilities Commission
Conn.Prob.L.J. The Connecticut Probate Law Journal
Conn.Pub.Acts Connecticut Public Acts
Conn.S. Connecticut Supplement. 1935–
Conn.Supp. Connecticut Supplement. 1935–
Conn.Surr. Connoly's New York Surrogate Reports
Connoly Connoly's New York Surrogate Reports
Connor & L. Connor & Lawson's Chancery Reports (Ire.) 1841–3
Conover Conover's Reports (16–153 Wisconsin Reports)
Conr. Conroy's Custodian Reports (Ire.) 1652–1788
cons. conseiller (Fr.) councillor, judge
considérant (Fr.) whereas, in view of
Cons. Conseil (Fr.) Council
Conservator

Consolidated
Constable
Constitution
Constitutional
Consul
Consultant
Consulting
Cons.const. Conseil constitutionnel (Fr.) Constitutional Council
Cons.Cred.Guide Consumer Credit Guide (CCH) (USA)
Cons.d'Et. Conseil d'État
Cons.fed. Conseil fédéral (Switz.)
Cons.L.Today Construction Law Today
Consumer Law Today. 1978–
Cons.Law Constructional Law
Cons.Ord.in Ch. Consolidated General Orders in Chancery
Cons.& Mar.Law Consumer and Marketing Law
Consist. Haggard's Consistorial Reports (161 ER) 1789–1821
Consist.Rep. Haggard's Consistorial Reports (161 ER) 1789–1821
consol. consolidated
consolidation
Consol.Ord. Consolidated General Orders in Chancery
Consp. Conspiracy
Const. Bott's Poor Laws by Const. 1560–1833
Constitution(al)
Harper's Constitutional Reports (South Carolina)
Mills' Constitutional Reports (South Carolina)
Treadway's Constitutional Reports (South Carolina)
Const.Amend. Amendment to Constitution
Const.Commentary Constitutional Commentary
Const.Hist. Hallam's Constitutional History of England
Const.L.J. Construction Law Journal. 1984–
Const.N.S. Constitutional Reports, New Series (South Carolina)
Const.Oth. Constitutiones Othoni (found at the end of Lyndewood's Provinciale)
Const.R.S.C. Constitutional Reports (South Carolina)
Const.Ref. Constitutional Reform
Const.Rep. Constitutional Reports (South Carolina)
Const.Rev. Constitutional Review (London) 1909–
Constitutional Review (Washington) 1917–29
Const.S.C. Constitutional Reports (South Carolina)
Const.S.C.N.S. Constitutional Reports, New Series by Mills (South Carolina)
Const.U.S. Constitution of the United States
Const.U.S.Amend. Amendment to the Constitution of the United States
Const.& Parliam.Inf. Constitutional and Parliamentary Information (Switz.)
constl. constitutional
constn. constitution
Constr. Construction
Constr.L.J. Construction Law Journal
Consuet.Feud. Consuetudines Feudorum; or, the Book of Feuds
Consv. Conservatorship
cont. containing
contents
continent
continental
continue
continued
contra
Cont. Archivo del Consiglio del Contenzioso Diplomatico (It.)
Contract(s)
Control(s)
cont.bon.mor. contra bones mores (Lat.) contrary to good manners
Cont.Cas.Fed. Contract Cases, Federal (USA)
Cont.El. Controverted Elections Judgments
Cont.Elect.Cas. Contested Election Cases (USA) 1789–1834

Cont.L.Rev. Contemporary Law Review (India) 1912–16
Contemp. Contemporary
Contemporary Review
conv. convention
conversion
conveyancing
Conv. Conveyancer. 1915–36
Conveyancer and Property Lawyer. 1936–
conv.curr. convertible currency
Conv.Est. Convention of the Estates of Scotland
Conv.F.J. European Community Convention on the Jurisdiction of the Courts and Enforcement of Judgments in Civil and Commercial Matters, 27 Sept. 1968
Conv.(N.S.) Conveyancer and Property Lawyer (New Series) 1936–
Conv.Rev. Conveyancing Review (Scot.) 1957–63
Conv.Y.B. Conveyancers' Year Book. 1940–551
Conv.& Prop.Law.(n.s.) Conveyancer and Property Lawyer (New Series) 1936–
Convey. Conveyancer. 1915–36
Convey.N.S. Conveyancer and Property Lawyer (New Series) 1936–
Coo.Agr.T. Cooke, Agricultural Tenancies. 3ed. 1882
Coo.Bankr. Cooke, Bankrupt Law. 8ed. 1823
Coo.Cop. Cooke, Enfranchisement of Copyholds. 2ed. 1853
Coo.& Al. Cooke & Alcock's King's Bench Reports (Ire.) 1833–4
Coo.& H.Tr. Cooke & Harwood's Charitable Trusts Acts
Cook Adm. Cooke's Admiralty Cases (Quebec)
Cook's Vice Admiralty Reports (Can.) 1873–84
Cook Corp. Cook on Corporations
Cook V.Adm. Cook's Vice Admiralty Reports (Nova Scotia) 1873–84
Cook Vice-Adm. Cook's Vice Admiralty Reports (Nova Scotia) 1873–84
Cooke Cooke's Act Book of the Ecclesiastical Court of Whalley
Cooke's Practice Cases, Common Pleas (125 ER) 1706–41
Cooke's Reports (3 Tennessee) 1811–14
Cooke B.L. Cooke, Bankrupt Law. 8ed. 1823
Cooke C.P. Cooke's Common Pleas Reports (125 ER) 1706–41
Cooke Incl.Acts Cooke's Inclosure Acts. 4ed. 1864
Cooke Ins. Cooke on Life Insurance
Cooke Pr.Cas. Cooke's Practice Cases, Common Pleas (125 ER) 1706–41
Cooke Pr.Reg. Cooke's Practice Register of the Common Pleas
Cooke (Tenn.) Cooke's Tennessee Reports (3 Tenn.) 1811–14
Cooke & A. Cooke & Alcock's King's Bench Reports (Ire.) 1833–4
Cooke & Al. Cooke & Alcock's King's Bench Reports (Ire.) 1833–4
Cooke & Alc. Cooke & Alcock's King's Bench Reports (Ire.) 1833–4
Cooke & H.Ch.Tr. Cooke & Harwood's Charitable Trust Acts
Cook's Pen.Code Cook's Penal Code (New York)
Cool.Black. Cooley's edition of Blackstone's Commentaries
Cool.Con.Law Cooley's Constitutional Law (USA)
Cool.Con.Lim. Cooley's Constitutional Limitations (USA)
Cooley Cooley's Reports (5–12 Michigan)
Cooley Bl.Comm. Cooley's edition of Blackstone's Commentaries
Cooley L.Rev. Cooley Law Review (USA)
Cooley Tax. Cooley on Taxation
Co-op. Co-operative
Coop. Cooper's Chancery Practice Cases (47 ER) 1837–8
Cooper's Chancery Reports tempore Brougham (47 ER) 1833–4

Cooper's Chancery Reports tempore Cottenham (47 ER) 1846–8
Cooper's Chancery Reports tempore Eldon (35 ER) 1815
Cooper's Florida Reports (21–24 Florida)
Cooper's Tennessee Chancery Reports. 1837–9
Upper Canada Chancery Chamber Reports. 1857–72

Coop.C.C. Cooper's Chancery Cases tempore Cottenham (47 ER) 1846–8
Upper Canada Chancery Chamber Reports. 1857–72

Coop.C.& P.R. Cooper's Chancery and Practice Reporter, Upper Canada. 1857–72

Coop.C.P. C.P. Cooper's Cases tempore Cottenham (47 ER) 1846–8

Coop.Ch. Cooper's Chancery Reports (35 ER) 1815
Cooper's Tennessee Chancery Reports. 1837–9

Coop.Ch.Pr. Cooper's Chancery Practice Reports (47 ER) 1837–8

Co-op.Dig. Co-operative Digest, United States Reports

Coop.Eq.Pl. Cooper's Equity Pleading

Coop.G. G. Cooper's Chancery Reports tempore Eldon (35 ER) 1815

Coop.Inst. Cooper's Institutes of Justinian

Coop.P.C. Cooper's Practice Cases (47 ER) 1837–8

Coop.Pr.C. Cooper's Practice Cases (47 ER) 1837–8

Coop.Pr.Cas. Cooper's Practice Cases (47 ER) 1837–8

Coop.Rec. Cooper's Public Records of Great Britain

Coop.Sel.Ca. Cooper's Select Chancery Cases tempore Eldon (35 ER) 1815

Coop.Sel.E.C. Cooper's Select Early Cases (Scot.)

Coop.t.Br. Cooper's Chancery Cases tempore Brougham (47 ER) 1833–4

Coop.t.Brough. Cooper's Chancery Cases tempore Brougham (47 ER) 1833–4

Coop.t.Brougham Cooper's Chancery Cases tempore Brougham (47 ER) 1833–4

Coop.t.Cott. Cooper's Chancery Reports tempore Cottenham (47 ER) 1846–8

Coop.t.Eld. Cooper's Chancery Reports tempore Eldon (35 ER) 1815

Coop.temp.Brough. Cooper's Chancery Cases tempore Brougham (47 ER) 1833–4

Coop.temp.Brougham Cooper's Chancery Cases tempore Brougham (47 ER) 1833–4

Coop.temp.Cott. Cooper's Chancery Reports tempore Cottenham (47 ER) 1846–8

Coop.temp.Cottenham Cooper's Chancery Reports tempore Cottenham (47 ER) 1846–8

Coop.temp.Eldon Cooper's Chancery Reports tempore Eldon (35 ER) 1815

Coop.Ten.Chy. Cooper's Tennessee Chancery Reports. 1837–9

Coop.Tenn.Ch. Cooper's Tennessee Chancery Reports. 1837–9

Cooper Cooper's Chancery Practice Cases (47 ER) 1837–8
Cooper's Chancery Reports tempore Brougham (47 ER) 1833–4
Cooper's Chancery Reports tempore Cottenham (47 ER) 1846–8
Cooper's Chancery Reports tempore Eldon (35 ER) 1815
Cooper's Florida Reports (21–24 Florida)
Cooper's Tennessee Chancery Reports. 1837–9
Upper Canada Chancery Chamber Reports. 1857–72

Cooper Just.Inst. Cooper's Institutes of Justinian

Cooper Pr.Cas. Cooper's Chancery Practice Cases (47 ER) 1837–8

Cooper t.Brougham Cooper's Chancery Reports tempore Brougham (47 ER) 1833–4

Cooper t.Cott. Cooper's Chancery Reports tempore Cottenham (47 ER) 1846–8
Cooper t.Eldon Cooper's Chancery Reports tempore Eldon (35 ER) 1815
Coote Coote on Mortgages. 9ed. 1927
Coote Pro.Pr. Coote, Practice of the Court of Probate. 9ed. 1883
Cop.Cop. Copinger, Copyright.
Cope Cope's California Reports (63–72 Calif.)
Copp L.L. Copp, Public Land Laws
Copp Land Copp, Land Office Decisions
Copp Min.Dec. Copp's United States Mining Decisions
Copy.Dec. Copyright Decisions (USA) 1909–
Copy.Rep. Copyright Reporter (Aus.) 1983–
Copy.Soc.Aust.News. Copyright Society of Australia Newsletter. 1981–83
Copy.Soc.Bull. Bulletin of the Copyright Society of the U.S.A.
Copyright Copyright: Monthly Review of the United International Bureau for the Protection of Intellectual Property (Switz.)
Copyright Bull. Copyright Bulletin (Fr.) UNESCO Copyright Bulletin
Copyright L.Symp. Copyright Law Symposium
cor. corpus
correction
corrective
Cor. Cornell Law Review. 1967–
Coryton's High Court Reports, Bengal (India) 1864–15
Cor.Cas. American and English Corporation Cases. 1883–94
Cor.Jud. Correspondances Judiciaires (Can.) 1906
Cor.L.Q. Cornell Law Quarterly. 1915–67
Cor.Soc.Cas. Coroner's Society Cases
Corb.& D. Corbett & Daniell's Election Cases. 1819
Corb.& Dan. Corbett & Daniell's Election Cases. 1819
Cord.Sol. Cordery, Solicitors
Corn.Deeds Cornish, Purchase Deeds. 2ed. 1855
Cornell Int.L.J. Cornell International Law Journal (USA) 1968–
Cornell Int'l L.Forum Cornell International Law Forum (USA)
Cornell Int'l L.J. Cornell International Law Journal (USA) 1968–
Cornell L.Q. Cornell Law Quarterly. 1915–67
Cornell L.Rev. Cornell Law Review. 1967–
Cornh. Cornhill Magazine
Cornish Purch.Deeds Cornish, Purchase Deeds. 2ed. 1855
Coroll. Corollary
Corp. Corporate
Corporation
Pennsylvania Corporation Reporter
Corp.Brief Corporate Briefing
Corp.C. Corporations Code
Corp.Guide Corporation Guide (P–H) (USA)
Corp.J. Corporation Journal. 1915–
Corp.Jur. Corpis Juris
Corp.Jur.Can. Corpis Juris Canonici
Corp.Jur.Canon. Corpus Juris Canonici
Corp.Jur.Civ. Corpus Juris Civilis
Corp.Jur.Germ. Corpus Juris Germanici
Corp.L.Guide Corporation Law Guide (CCH) (USA)
CorpLaw Journal of Comparative Corporate Law and Securities Regulation (Neth.) 1978–
Corp.Prac.Com. Corporate Practice Commentator (USA) 1959–
Corp.Prac.Rev. Corporate Practice Review (USA) 1928–32
Corp.Pract.Comment. Corporate Practice Commentator (USA) 1959–
Corp.Reorg.& Am.Bank.Rev. Corporate Reorganization and American Bankruptcy Review. 1937–47
Corp.Rep.(Pa.) Pennsylvania Corporation Reporter
Corp.Tr. Corporate Trustee

Corp.& Ass'ns. Corporations and Associations
corr. correspond
correspondence
correspondent
corresponding
Corr. Tribunal correctionnel (Belg.) Court of first instance in penal matters
correc. correction
Correspondances Jud. Correspondances Judiciaires (Can.) 1906
Corte Cost. Constitutional Court (It.)
Corvin.El. Corvinus Elementa Juris Civilis
Cory. Coryton's High Court Reports, Bengal (India) 1864–5
Cory, Reports Reports of Cases by Thomas Cory. 1657
Coryton Coryton's High Court Reports, Bengal (India) 1864–5
Cosm. Cosmetic
Cost. Costituzione della Repubblica (It.)
Cost Acc'g.Stand.Guide Cost Accounting Standards Guide (CCH) (USA)
Cot.Abr. Cotton's Abridgement of the Records
Cott.Mss. Cottonian Manuscripts (British Museum)
Cou. Couper's Justiciary Reports (Scot.) 1868–85
Coul.& F.Wat. Coulston & Forbes on Waters. 6ed. 1952
couns. counsel
Couns.Mag. Counsellor's Magazine. 1796–8
Count.Cts.Ch. County Courts Chronicle. 1847–1920
Count.Cts.Chron. County Courts Chronicle. 1847–1920
County Co.Cas. County Council Cases (Scot.)
County Ct. County Court
County Cts.Chron. County Courts Chronicle. 1847–1920
County Cts.Rep. County Courts Reports. 1860–1919
County Cts.& Bankr.Cas. County Courts and Bankruptcy Cases
County J.Ct. County Judge's Court
County R. County Reports
Coup. Couper's Justiciary Reports (Scot.) 1868–85
Coup.Just. Couper's Justiciary Reports (Scot.) 1868–85
Couper Couper's Justiciary Reports (Scot.) 1868–85
Cour.& Macl. Courtenay & Maclean's Scotch Appeals (6 & 7 Wilson & Shaw)
Cours La Haye Recueil des cours de l'Academie internationale de La Haye
Court Bott's Poor Laws by Court
Court Cl. Court of Claims Reports (USA)
Court J.& Dist.Ct.Rec. Court Journal and District Court Record
Court Sess.Ca. Court of Session Cases (Scot.)
Court.& Macl. Courtenay & Maclean's Scotch Appeals (6 & 7 Wilson & Shaw)
Cout. Coutlee's Unreported Cases (Can.) 1875–1907
Cout.Dig. Coutlee's Digest, Supreme Court (Can.)
Cout.S.C. Coutlee's Unreported Cases (Can.) 1875–1907
Coutlee Coutlee's Unreported Cases (Can.) 1875–1907
Coutlee Unrep. Coutlee's Unreported Cases (Can.) 1875–1907
Cov.Conv.Ev. Coventry, Conveyancers' Evidence. 1832
Cov.Mort. Coventry, Mortgage Precedents. 1827
Cov.Rec. Coventry, Common Recoveries. 1820
Cov.& H.Dig. Coventry & Hughes, Digest of the Common Law Reports
Cow. Cowen's New York Reports. 1823–9
Cowper's King's Bench Reports (98 ER) 1774–8
Cow.Cr. Cowen's Criminal Reports (New York)
Cow.Cr.Dig. Cowen's Criminal Digest

Cow.Cr.R. Cowen's Criminal Reports (New York)
Cow.Cr.Rep. Cowen's Criminal Reports (New York)
Cow.Crim(N.Y.) Cowen's Criminal Reports (New York)
Cow.Dic. Cowell's Law Dictionary
Cow.Dig. Cowell's East India Digest
Cow.Int. Cowell's Interpreter of the Law
Cow.L.R. Cowan, Land Rights in Scotland
Cow.N.Y. Cowen's New York Reports. 1823–9
Cowell Cowell's Interpretation of the Law
Cowell's Law Dictionary
Cowp. Cowper's King's Bench Reports (98 ER) 1774–8
Cowp.Cas. Cowper's Cases (Reports in Chancery, vol.3)
Cowper, Reports H. Cowper, Reports of Cases in the Court of King's Bench. 2ed. 1800
Cox Cox's Chancery Reports (29–30 ER) 1783–96
Cox's Criminal Cases. 1843–1945
Cox's Reports (25–7 Arkansas)
Cox Adv. Cox, Advocate. 1852
Cox Am.T.Cas. Cox's American Trademark Cases
Cox Am.T.M.Cas. Cox's American Trademark Cases
Cox Anc.L. Cox, Law and Science of Ancient Lights. 2ed. 1871
Cox C.C. Cox's County Court Cases. 1860–1919
Cox's Criminal Cases. 1843–1945
Cox's Crown Cases
Cox C.L.Pr. Cox, Common Law Practice
Cox Ch. Cox's Chancery Reports (29–30 ER) 1783–96
Cox Ch.Cas. Cox's Chancery Reports (29–30 ER) 1783–96
Cox Ch.Pr. Cox, Chancery Practice
Cox Cr.Ca. Cox's Criminal Cases. 1843–1945
Cox Cr.Cas. Cox's Criminal Cases. 1843–1945
Cox Cr.Dig. Cox, Criminal Digest
Cox Crim.Cas. Cox's Criminal Cases. 1843–1945
Cox Cty.Ct.Cas. Cox's County Court Cases. 1860–1919
Cox Elect. Cox, Registration and Elections. 14ed. 1885
Cox Eq. Cox's Equity Cases. 1745–97
Cox Eq.Cas. Cox's Equity Cases. 1745–97
Cox Inst. Cox, Institutions of the English Government
Cox J.S.Cas. Cox's Joint Stock Cases. 1864–72
Cox Jt.Stk. Cox's Joint Stock Cases. 1864–72
Cox M.C. Cox's Magistrates' Cases. 1859–1920
Cox M.& H. Cox, Macrae & Hertslet's County Court Reports. 1847–57
Cox Mag.Cas. Cox's Magistrates' Cases. 1859–1920
Cox Man.Tr.M. Cox, Manual of Trade-Mark Cases (USA)
Cox,Mc.& H. Cox, Macrae & Hertslet's County Court Reports. 1847–57
Cox,McC.& H. Cox, Macrae & Hertslet's County Court Reports. 1847–57
Cox P.W. Cox's edition of Peere Williams' Reports
Cox Pun. Cox, Principles of Punishment. 1877
Cox Tr.M. Cox, Manual of Trade-Mark Cases (USA)
Cox Tr.M.Cas. Cox, Manual of Trade-Mark Cases (USA)
Cox & Atk. Cox & Atkinson's Registration Appeal Cases. 1843–6
Cox & M'C. Cox, Macrae & Hertslet's County Court Cases. 1847–57
Cox & S.Cr.L. Cox & Saunders, Criminal Law Consolidation Acts. 3ed. 1870
Coxe Coxe's New Jersey Law Reports (1 NJL)
Coxe Bract. Coxe's translation of

Guterbach's Bracton
Coy. Company
cp. compare
criminal code (It.) 1930
cpc. code of criminal procedure (It.) 1940
cpp. code of criminal procedure (It.) 1930
Cr. Craig, Jus Feudale (Scot.) 5ed. 1934
Cranch's United States Circuit Court Reports
Cranch's United States Supreme Court Reports (5–13 US) 1801–15
Created
Credit
Creditor
Criminal
Crown
Cr.Act. Criminal Act
Cr.App. Criminal Appeals
Cr.App.R. Criminal Appeal Reports. 1908–
Cr.App.R.(S.) Criminal Appeal Reports (Sentencing) 1979–
Cr.App.Rep. Criminal Appeal Reports. 1908–
Cr.C.C. Cranch's United States Circuit Court Reports
Cr.Cas.Res. Crown Cases Reserved
Cr.Cir.Comp. Crown Circuit Companion (Ire.)
Cr.Code Criminal Code
Cr.Code Prac. Criminal Code of Practice
Cr.J.F. Craig, Jus Feudale (Scot.) 5ed. 1934
Cr.Just. Criminal Justice (USA) 1973–
Cr.L. The Criminal Lawyer (India) 1928–30
Cr.L.J. Criminal Law Journal (India) 1904–
Cr.L.Mag. Criminal Law Magazine (New Jersey) 1880–96
Cr.L.R. Criminal Law Reporter (India) 1911–23
Criminal Law Reporter (Texas) 1886
Cr.Law Mag. Criminal Law Magazine (New Jersey) 1880–96
Cr.Law Rec. Criminal Law Recorder
Cr.Law Rep. Criminal Law Reporter (India) 1911–23
Criminal Law Reporter (Texas) 1886
Cr.M.& R. Crompton, Meeson & Roscoe's Exchequer Reports (149–50 ER) 1834–5
Cr.P. Criminal Procedure
Cr.Pat.Dec. Cranch's Decisions on Patent Appeals (USA)
Cr.Prac. Criminal Practice
Cr.Proc. Criminal Procedure
Cr.R. The Criminal Reports (India)
Cr.Rep. Criminal Reports (Can.) 1946–
Cr.Rg. Criminal Rulings, Bombay (India)
Cr.S.& P. Craigie, Stewart & Paton's Scottish Appeal Cases. 1726–1821
Cr.St. Criminal Statutes
Cr.& Dix Crawford & Dix's Abridged Cases (Ire.) 1837–8
Crawford & Dix's Circuit Court Cases (Ire.) 1839–46
Cr.& Dix Ab.Ca. Crawford & Dix's Abridged Cases (Ire.) 1837–8
Cr.& Dix Ab.Cas. Crawford & Dix's Abridged Cases (Ire.) 1837–8
Cr.& Dix C.C. Crawford & Dix's Circuit Court Cases (Ire.) 1839–46
Cr.& J. Crompton & Jervis' Exchequer Reports (148–9 ER) 1830–2
Cr.& M. Crompton & Meeson's Exchequer Reports (149 ER) 1832–4
Cr.& Ph. Craig & Phillips' Chancery Reports (41 ER) 1840–1
Cr.& St. Craigie, Stewart & Paton's Appeal Cases (Scot.) 1726–1821
Cra. Cranch's United States Circuit Court Reports
Cranch's United States Supreme Court Reports (5–13 US) 1801–15
Cra.C.C. Cranch's United States Circuit Court Reports
Crab. Crabbe's United States District Court Reports
Crabb C.L. Crabb on the Common Law
Crabb Conv. Crabb, Treatise on Conveyancing. 5ed. 1859
Crabb Eng. Crabb, English Synonyms
Crabb Eng.L. Crabb, History of English Law. 2ed. 1840

Crabb Eng.Law Crabb, History of English Law. 2ed. 1840
Crabb Hist.Eng.Law Crabb, History of English Law. 2ed. 1840
Crabb R.P. Crabb, Real Property. 1846
Crabb Real Prop. Crabb, Real Property. 1846
Crabbe Crabbe's United States District Court Reports
Craig.S.& P. Craigie, Stewart & Paton's Appeal Cases (Scot.) 1726–1821
Craig.St.& Pat. Craigie, Stewart & Paton's Appeal Cases (Scot.) 1726–1821
Craig & P. Craig & Phillips' Chancery Reports (41 ER) 1840–1
Craig & Ph. Craig & Phillips' Chancery Reports (41 ER) 1840–1
Craig.& St. Craigie, Stewart & Paton's Appeal Cases (Scot.) 1726–1821
Craik C.C. Craik's Causes Célèbres
Cranch Cranch's District of Columbia Reports (1–5 DC) 1801–40
Cranch's United States Supreme Court Reports (5–13 US) 1801–15
Cranch C.C. Cranch's Circuit Reports (USA)
District of Columbia Reports (1–5 DC) 1801–40
Cranch D.C. Cranch's District of Columbia Reports (1–5 DC) 1801–40
Cranch Pat.Dec. Cranch's Decisions, Patent Appeals (USA)
Cranch (US) Cranch's United States Supreme Court Reports (5–13 US) 1801–15
Crane Crane's Reports (22–9 Montana)
Crane.C.C. Cranenburgh's Criminal Cases (India) 1864–76
cras. on the morrow (return)
cras.Anim. on the morrow of All Souls (return)
Craw. Crawford's Reports (53–69, 71–101 Arkansas Reports)
Craw.(Ark.) Crawford's Reports (53–69, 71–101 Arkansas Reports)
Craw.Co.Leg.J.(Pa.) Crawford County Legal Journal (Pennsylvania)
Craw.& D. Crawford & Dix's Circuit Court Cases (Ire.) 1839–46
Craw.& D.Ab.Cas. Crawford & Dix's Abridged Cases (Ire.) 1837–8
Craw.& D.Abr.Cas. Crawford & Dix's Abridged Cases (Ire.) 1837–8
Craw.& D.C.C.(Ir.) Crawford & Dix's Circuit Court Cases (Ire.) 1839–46
Craw.& D.(Ir.) Crawford & Dix's Abridged Cases (Ire.) 1837–8
Craw.& Dix Crawford & Dix's Circuit Court Cases (Ire.) 1839–46
Crawf.& D. Crawford & Dix's Circuit Court Cases (Ire.) 1839–46
Crawf.& D.Abr.Cas. Crawford & Dix's Abridged Cases (Ire.) 1837–8
Creas.Col.Const. Creasy's Colonial Constitutions
Creas.Eng.Cons. Creasy's Rise and Progress of the English Constitution. 17ed. 1907
Creas.Int.L. Creasy, International Law. 1876
Creasy Creasy's Ceylon Reports. 1859–70
Creighton L.Rev. Creighton Law Review. 1968
Cremer, Reports Reports of Cases by Charles Cremer of Gray's Inn (GI MSS. 33–35) 1650–76
Cress. Cresswell's Insolvency Cases. 1827–9
Cress.Ins.Ca. Cresswell's Insolvency Cases. 1827–9
Cress.Ins.Cas. Cresswell's Insolvency Cases. 1827–9
Cress.Insolv.Cas. Cresswell's Insolvency Cases. 1827–9
Crim. Arrêt de la chambre criminelle de la Cour de Cassation (Fr.) Decision of the criminal division of the Cour de Cassation
Criminal
Criminologie (Can.)
Crim.App. Court of Criminal Appeals
Criminal Appeal Reports. 1908–
Crim.App.R. Criminal Appeal Reports. 1908–

crim.con. criminal conspiracy
criminal conversation
criminal conversion

Crim.Inj.Comp.Bd. Criminal Injuries Compensation Board

Crim.Just. Criminal Justice (USA) 1973–

Crim.Just.J. Criminal Justice Journal (USA)

Crim.L.Bull. Criminal Law Bulletin (USA) 1965–

Crim.L.J. Criminal Law Journal (Aus.) 1977–

Crim.L.J.I. Criminal Law Journal of India. 1904–

Crim.L.J.Ind. Criminal Law Journal of India. 1904–

Crim.L.J.(Sydney) Criminal Law Journal (Aus.) 1977–

Crim.L.Mag. Criminal Law Magazine and Reporter (New Jersey) 1880–96

Crim.L.Q. Criminal Law Quarterly (Can.) 1958–
Criminal Law Quarterly (USA) 1962–3

Crim.L.R. Criminal Law Review. 1954–

Crim.L.R.C. Criminal Law Revision Committee

Crim.L.Rec. Criminal Law Recorder. 1804–9,1815

Crim.L.Rep. Criminal Law Reporter (BNA) (USA)
Criminal Law Reporter (CCH) (USA)
Criminal Law Reporter (India) 1911–23

Crim.L.Rev. Criminal Law Review. 1954–

Crim.L.Rptr. Criminal Law Reporter (BNA) (USA)
Criminal Law Reporter (CCH) (USA)
Criminal Law Reporter (India) 1911–23

Crim.Law Criminal Law

Crim.Law. Criminal Lawyer

Crim.Law Rev.Cttee. Criminal Law Revision Committee

Crim.Pro. Criminal Procedure

Crim.Proc. Criminal Procedure

Crim.R.(Can.) Criminal Reports (Can.) 1946–

Crim.Rec. Criminal Recorder. 1804–9,1815
Criminal Recorder, New York (1 Wheeler's N.Y. Criminal Reports)
Criminal Recorder, Philadelphia

Crim.Rep.(N.S.) Criminal Reports, New Series

Crim.& Delin. Crime and Delinquency (USA) 1961–

Crime & Delin'cy Crime and Delinquency (USA) 1961–

Crime & Just. Crime et/and Justice (Can.)

Crime & Soc.Just. Crime and Social Justice

Criminal L.Q. Criminal Law Quarterly (Can.) 1958–

Criminol. Criminologica (USA) 1963–70
Criminologie (Can.) 1975–
Criminologist. 1967–
Criminology (USA) 1971–

Cripp Ch.Cas. Cripps' Church and Clergy Cases. 1847–50

Cripp Ch.L. Cripps, Law Relating to Church and Clergy. 8ed. 1937

Cripp Comp. Cripps, Compulsory Acquisition of Land. 11ed. 1962

Cripps Cripps' Church and Clergy Cases. 1847–50

Cripps Cas. Cripps' Church and Clergy Cases. 1847–50

Cripps Ch.Cas. Cripps' Church and Clergy Cases. 1847–50

Cripps Church Cas. Cripps' Church and Clergy Cases. 1847–50

Crispi Eredità e Gabinetto Crispi (It.)

crit. criticized in
criticizing

Critch. Critchfield's Reports (5–21 Ohio State)

Critch(Ohio St.) Critchfield's Reports (5–21 Ohio State)

Cro. Croke's King's Bench Reports (72 ER) 1582–1641
Keilway's King's Bench Reports (72 ER) 1496–1531

Cro.Car. Croke's King's Bench Reports tempore Charles I (3 Cro.) (79 ER) 1625–41

Cro.Cas. Croke's King's Bench Reports tempore Charles I (3 Cro.) (79 ER) 1625–41

Cro.Eliz. Croke's King's Bench Reports tempore Elizabeth (1 Cro.) (78 ER) 1582–1603

Cro.Jac. Croke's King's Bench Reports tempore James I (2 Cro.) (79 ER) 1603–25

Crockford Crockford's Maritime Law Reports. 1860–71

Croke Croke's King's Bench Reports tempore Charles I (3 Cro.) (79 ER) 1625–41
Croke's King's Bench Reports tempore Elizabeth (1 Cro.) (78 ER) 1582–1603
Croke's King's Bench Reports tempore James I (2 Cro.) (79 ER) 1603–25
Keilway's King's Bench Reports (72 ER) 1496–1531

Crom. Crompton, Office of Justice of the Peace. 1637

Cromp. Crompton's Star Chamber Cases. 1881

Cromp.Cts. Crompton's Jurisdiction of Courts

Cromp.Exch.R. Crompton's Exchequer Reports

Cromp.J.C. Crompton's Jurisdiction of Courts

Cromp.Jur. Crompton's Jurisdiction of Courts

Cromp.Just. Crompton's Office of Justice of the Peace. 1637

Cromp.M.& R. Crompton, Meeson & Roscoe's Exchequer Reports (149–50 ER) 1834–5

Cromp.R.& C.Pr. Crompton's Rules and Cases of Practice

Cromp.& F. Fitzherbert's Justice, enlarged by Crompton

Cromp.& J. Crompton & Jervis' Exchequer Reports (148–9 ER) 1830–2

Cromp.& Jer. Crompton & Jervis' Exchequer Reports (148–9 ER) 1830–2

Cromp.& Jerv. Crompton & Jervis' Exchequer Reports (148–9 ER) 1830–2

Cromp.& M. Crompton & Meeson's Exchequer Reports (149 ER) 1832–4

Cromp.& Mees. Crompton & Meeson's Exchequer Reports (149 ER) 1832–4

Crompt. Crompton's Star Chamber Cases. 1881

Cros.Wills Crosley, Wills. 1828

Cross Lien Cross, Lien and Stoppage in Transitu. 1840

Crosw.Pat.Ca. Croswell's Collection of Patent Cases (USA) 1888

Crosw.Pat.Cas. Croswell's Collection of Patent Cases (USA) 1888

Crounse Crounse's Reports (3 Nebraska Reports)

Crow. Crowther's Reports (Sri L.) 1863

Crown L.C. Crown Land Cases, New South Wales (Aus.)

Crown's Newsl. Crown's Newsletter (Ontario, Can.) 1981–

Crowth. Crowther's Ceylon Reports (Sri L.) 1863

Crowther Crowther's Ceylon Reports (Sri L.) 1863

Crowther Report Report of the Committee on Consumer Credit (Cmnd.4596) 1971

Cru. Cruise's Digest of the Law of Real Property. 4ed. 1835

Cru.Dig. Cruise's Digest of the Law of Real Property. 4ed. 1835

Cru.Dign. Cruise on Dignities

Cru.Fin. Cruise's Fines and Recoveries

Cru.Us. Cruise on Uses

Cruchaga Cruchaga-Tocornal, Nociones de Derecho internacional. 3ed. 1923–25

Cruise Dig. Cruise's Digest of the Law of Real Property. 4ed. 1835

Crump Ins. Crump on Marine Insurance. 1875

Crump Jud.Pr. Crump, Practice under the Judicature Acts

Crump S.& Pl. Crump, Sale and Pledge

Crumrine Crumrine's Reports (116–146 Pennsylvania)

cs. communis (Lat.) common

Csl. Counsel

Cst. Constitution fédérale (Switz.)

Il Consiglio di Stato (It.)
Cst.fed. Constitution fédérale (Switz.)
Ct. Connecticut
Connecticut Reports
Count
Court
Ct.App. Court of Appeals
Ct.App.N.Z. Court of Appeals Reports (NZ) 1867–77
Ct.Arb. Court of Arbitration (N.Z.)
Ct.Cl. United States Court of Claims Reports. 1856–
Ct.Cl.Act Court of Claims Act
Ct.Cl.N.Y. Court of Claims Reports (New York)
Ct.Cls. Court of Claims (USA)
Ct.Com.Pl. Court of Common Pleas
Ct.Com.Pleas Court of Common Pleas
Ct.Crim.App. Court of Criminal Appeal
Ct.Cust.App. Court of Customs Appeals Reports (USA) 1919–29
Ct.Cust.& Pat.App. Court of Customs and Patent Appeals (USA)
Ct.Err.&.App. Court of Errors and Appeals
Ct.Errors & App. Court of Errors and Appeals
Ct.Gen.Sess. Court of General Sessions
Ct.J. Circuit Judge
Ct.Just. Court of Justiciary
Ct./O. Court Order
Ct.of App. Court of Appeal
Ct.of Cls. United States Court of Claims
Ct.of Com.Pleas Court of Common Pleas
Ct.of Er.and Appeals Court of Errors and Appeals
Ct.of Sess. Court of Session (Scot.)
Session Cases (Scot.)
Ct.of Sp.App. Court of Special Appeals
Ct.Reg. The Court and City Register. 1749–1807
Ct.Rep.N.Z. Court of Appeals Reports (NZ)
Ct.Rev. Court of Review
Ct.Spec.Sess. Court of Special Sessions
Ct.Sess.Cas. Court of Session Cases (Scot.)
Ctf. Certificate
Cth. Commonwealth
Cts.Martial App.Ct. Courts-Martial Appeal Court
Cts.& Jud.Proc. Courts and Judicial Proceedings
Cty. County
Cty.Ct. County Court
Cty.Ct.Chron. County Courts Chronicle. 1847–1920
Cty.Ct.R. County Courts Reports. 1860–1920
Cu.Ct. Customs Court Reports
Cudd.Copyh. Cuddon, Copyhold Acts. 1865
cuj. cujus (Lat.) of which
cujusl. cujuslibet (Lat.) of any
cum. cumulative
cum.div. with dividend
Cum.L.Rev. Cumberland Law Review (USA) 1975–
Cum.P.P. Cumulative Pocket Parts
Cum.-Sam. Cumberland-Samford Law Review (USA) 1970–4
Cum.Supp. Cumulative Supplement
Cum.& Dun.Rem.Tr. Cummins & Dunphy's Remarkable Trials
Cumb. Cumberland Law Journal (Pennsylvania)
Cumb.L.Rev. Cumberland Law Review (USA)
Cumberland L.J.(Pa.) Cumberland Law Journal (Pennsylvania)
Cumberland L.Rev. Cumberland Law Review (USA) formerly Cumberland-Samford Law Review
Cumberland-Samford Cumberland-Samford Law Review (USA)
Cummins Cummins' Reports (Idaho) 1866–7
Cun. Cunningham's King's Bench Reports (94 ER) 1734–6
Cun.Bill.Exch. Cunningham's Law of Notes and Bills of Exchange
Cun.Dict. Cunningham's Law Dictionary
Cunn. Cunningham's King's Bench Reports (94 ER) 1734–6

Cunningham Cunningham's King's Bench Reports (94 ER) 1734–6
cur. current
Cur. Curia
Curtis' United States Circuit Court Reports
Cur.Com. Current Comment and Legal Miscellany (USA) 1889–91
Cur.Dec. Curtis' Decisions, United States Supreme Court Reports
Cur.I.C. Current Indian Cases. 1912–15
Cur.Ind.Cas. Current Indian Cases. 1912–15
Cur.L.R. Current Law Reports (Sri L.) 1909–10
Cur.Leg.Bibliog. Current Legal Bibliography (USA) 1961–
Cur.Leg.Prob. Current Legal Problems. 1948–
Cur.Leg.Thought Current Legal Thought (USA) 1935–48
Cur.Ov.Ca. Curwen, Overruled Cases (Ohio)
Cur.Prop.L. Current Property Law. 1952–3
Cur.Reg.R. Curia Regis Rolls
Curr.L.P. Current Legal Problems. 1948–
Curr.L.Pr. Current Legal Problems. 1948–
Curr.L.T. Current Legal Thought (USA) 1935–48
Curr.L.& S.P. Current Law and Social Problems (Can.)
Current Bibl.Afr.Aff. Current Bibliography in African Affairs
Current Ct.Dec. Current Court Decisions
Current L. Current Law. 1948–
Current L.R. Current Law Reports (Sri L.) 1909–10
Current L.Y.B. Current Law Yearbook. 1948–
Current L.& Soc.Probl. Current Law and Social Problems (Can.)
Current Leg.Bibliog. Current Legal Bibliography (USA) 1961–
Current Leg.Prob. Current Legal Problems. 1948–
Current Prop.L. Current Property Law. 1952–3
Current Review Law Book Company's Industrial Arbitration Service, Current Review (Aus.) 1950–81
Curry Curry's Reports (6–19 Louisiana)
Curt. Curteis' Ecclesiastical Reports (163 ER) 1834–44
Curtis' Circuit Court Reports (USA)
Curtis' Edition, U.S. Supreme Court Reports
Curt.Adm.Dig. Curtis' Admiralty Digest
Curt.C.C. Curtis' United States Circuit Court Reports
Curt.Cop. Curtis, Copyright. 1847
Curt.Dec. Curtis' United States Supreme Court Reports
Curt.Dig. Curtis' Digest (USA)
Curt.Ecc. Curteis' Ecclesiastical Reports (163 ER) 1834–44
Curt.Eccl. Curteis' Ecclesiastical Reports (163 ER) 1834–44
Curt.Pat. Curtis on Patents
Curtis Curtis' Circuit Court Reports (USA)
Curtis' Edition, United States Supreme Court Reports
Curw. Curwen's Overruled Cases (Ohio)
Curwen's Statutes of Ohio
Curw.L.O. Curwen's Laws of Ohio
Curw.Ov.Cas. Curwen's Overruled Cases (Ohio)
Curw.R.S. Curwen's Revised Statutes of Ohio
Cush. Cushing's Massachusetts Supreme Judicial Court Reports (55–6 Massachusetts Reports) 1848–53
Cushman's Mississippi Reports (23–9 Mississippi)
Cush.Elec.Cas. Cushing's Election Cases in Massachusetts
Cush.Leg.Ass. Cushing's Law and Practice of Legislative Assemblies
Cush.Man. Cushing's Manual of Parliamentary Law
Cush.(Mass.) Cushing's Massachusetts Reports (55–6 Massachusetts) 1848–53

Cushing Cushing's Massachusetts Reports (55–6 Massachusetts) 1848–53
Cushm. Cushman's Reports (23–9 Mississippi)
Cust. Custody
Cust.A. United States Customs Appeals
Cust.App. United States Customs Appeals
Cust.B.& Dec. Customs Bulletin and Decisions (USA) 1967–
Cust.Ct. Custom Court Reports (USA) 1938–
Cust.Rep. Custer's Ecclesiastical Reports
Cust.& Pat.App.(Cust.) Customs and Patent Appeals Reports (Customs) (USA)
Cust.& Pat.App.(Pat.) Customs and Patent Appeals Reports (Patents) (USA)
Cut. Indian Law Reports, Orissa. 1950–
Cut.L.T. Cuttack Law Times (Orissa, India) 1935–
Cut.Pat.Cas. Cutler's Reports of Patent and Trademark Cases. 1884–
Cutler Reports of Patent and Trademark Cases. 1884–
Cutt.L.T. Cuttack Law Times (Orissa, India) 1835–
C'wealth Commonwealth
Cwlth. Commonwealth
Cwlth.Record Commonwealth Record (Aus.) 1976–
Cwth. Commonwealth
Cy. Connoly's Surrogate's Court Reports (New York)
Cyc.Ann. Cyclopedia of Law and Procedure, Annotations (USA)
Cyc.Law & Proc. Cyclopedia of Law and Procedure (USA)
Cyprus L.R. Cyprus Law Reports. 1883–

D

d. daily
daughter
day
dead
deceased
decree
décret (Fr.) decree
decreto (It.) decree
degree
delete
died
distinguished

D. Court of Divorce and Matrimonial Causes
Dallas' Pennsylvania Reports. 1754–1809
Dallas' United States Supreme Court Reports (1–4 US) 1790–1800
Dalloz
Decree
Delaware Supreme Court Reports. 1832–
Democrat
Denied
Denio's Supreme Court Reports (New York)
Denison's Crown Cases (169 ER) 1844–52
Deus (Lat.) God
Deutschland
Dicta
Dictionary
Dictum
Digest (Justinian's)
Dismissed
Disney's Ohio Superior Court Reports
District Court (USA)
Doctor
Dominus (Lat.) Lord
Douanes (Fr.) Customs
Doubted
Duchess
Duke
Dunlop, Bell & Murray's Reports, Session Cases, Second Series (Scot.) 1838–62
Durban & Coast Local Division (S.Afr.)
Dutch
Duxbury's Reports of the High Court of the South African Republic. 1895
Dyer's King's Bench Reports, ed. Valiant (73 ER) 1513–82
Recueil Dalloz (Fr.) 1945–

d/a days after acceptance
documents against acceptance

D.A. Defence Act
Deputy Advocate
Development Application
District Attorney
Doctor of Arts
Recueil analytique Dalloz (Fr.) 1941–44

D/A Documents against acceptance

D.A.B. Dictionary of American Biography

DAC Development Assistance Committee (OECD)

D.A.D. Deputy Assistant Director

D.A.E. Dictionary of American English

DAGAS Dangerous Goods Advisory Service

D.A.J.A.G. Deputy Assistant Judge Advocate General

DALBA Dallas Bar Association

D.A.L.C. Danquah, Akan Laws and Customs (Ghana)

d.a.p. documents against payment

DAP Application for writ of error

dismissed by agreement of parties
D.A.P.M. Deputy Assistant Provost Marshall
d.a.s. delivered alongside ship
D.Abr. D'Anvers' General Abridgement of the Common Law. 2ed. 1725–37
D.ad. Droit administratif (Fr.) 1962–
D'Agu.Œuv. D'Aguesseau, Œuvres
D.Alaska United States District Court for the District of Alaska
D'An. D'Anvers' General Abridgement of the Common Law. 2ed. 1725–37
D'Anv.Abr. D'Anvers' General Abridgement of the Common Law. 2ed. 1725–37
D.Ariz. United States District Court for the District of Arizona
DB Der Betrieb (Ger.) 1948–
D.B. Day Book
Dock Brief
Domesday Book
d.b.a. de bonis asportatis (Lat.) of goods carried away; trespass
doing business as
d.b.e. de bene esse (Lat.) provisionally or conditionally
D.B.J. Duke Bar Journal (USA) 1951–8
d.b.n. de bonis non (Lat.) of goods not administered
D.B.& M. Dunlop, Bell & Murray's Court of Session Cases (Scot.) 1838–62
d.c. double column
d.C. dopo Cristo (It.) After Christ i.e. A.D.
D.C. Death Certificate
Deputy Chief
Deputy Commissioner
Deputy Counsel
Deviation Clause
Diplomatic Corps
District Commissioner
District Court
District of Columbia
District of Columbia Supreme Court Reports. 1801–92
Divisional Court
Recueil critique Dalloz (Fr.) 1941–44
United States District Court
D/C Deviation Clause
D.C.2d Pennsylvania District and County Reports, Second Series
D.C.A. Decisions de la Cour d'Appel (Québec, Can.) 1881–4
Development Credit Agreement
Divisional Court of Appeal
Dorion's Queen's Bench Reports (Can.) 1880–6
D.C.A.L. Danquah, Cases in Akan Law (Ghana)
D.C.App. District of Columbia Appeals Reports
D.C.B. Decimal Currency Board
DCBA The Bar Association of the District of Columbia
D.C.B.J. District of Columbia Bar Journal
D.C.C. Diocesan Consistory Court
D.C.C.E. District of Columbia Code Encyclopedia
D.C.Cir. District of Columbia Court of Appeals Cases
D.C.Cir.R. District of Columbia Circuit Court Rules
D.C.Code District of Columbia Code
D.C.Code Ann. District of Columbia Code Annotated
D.C.Code Encycl. West's District of Columbia Code Encyclopedia
D.C.Code Legis.& Admin.Serv. West's District of Columbia Code Legislative and Administrative Service
D.C.Dist.Col. United States District Court for the District of Columbia
D.C.F. Daniell, Chancery Forms. 7ed. 1932
D.C.H. Reports of the United States District Court of Hawaii
D.C.J. District Court Judge
D.C.L. Doctor of Civil Law
Doctor of Comparative Law
D.C.L.R. District Court Law Reports (Hong Kong) 1953–
D.C.L.R.(Can.) Dominion Companies Law Reports (Can.) 1949–
D.C.Lab.S. Dominion of Canada Labour Service (CCH)

D.C.Mun.App. Municipal Court of Appeals, District of Columbia
D.C.O. Duchy of Cornwall Office
D.C.P. Daniell, Chancery Practice. 8ed. 1914
D.C.R. District Court Reports (N.S.W., Aus.) 1963–76
District Court Reports (N.Z.) 1980–
D.C.R.(N.S.W.) District Court Reports (N.S.W., Aus.) 1963–76
D.C.S. Deputy Clerk of Sessions
Documenti Diplomatici (Serie confidenziale, a stampe) (It.) 1870
DCSI Diritto Communitario e degli Scambi Internazionali (It.)
D.C.T. Deputy Commissioner of Taxation (Aus.)
D.Ch. Delaware Chancery Reports
D.Chip. D. Chipman's Vermont Supreme Court Reports. 1789–1824
D.Chip.(Vt.) D. Chipman's Vermont Supreme Court Reports. 1789–1824
D.Chipm. D. Chipman's Vermont Supreme Court Reports. 1789–1824
D.Chr. Recueil Dalloz, section Chronique (Fr.) 1945–
D.Cn.L. Doctor of Canon Law
D-Col. Double-Column
D.Colo. District Court for District of Colorado (USA)
D.Com.L. Doctor of Commercial Law
D.Conn. District Court for District of Connecticut (USA)
D.Ct. District Court (USA)
Divisional Court
D.Ct.'21–5 Selected Judgments of the Divisional Courts (Ghana) 1921–5
D.Ct.'26–9 Selected Judgments of the Divisional Courts (Ghana) 1926–9
D.Ct.'29–31 Selected Judgments of the Divisional Courts (Ghana) 1929–31
d.d. days after date (Bills of Exchange)
delivered at dock
dono dedit (Lat.) gave as a gift
D.D. Delikt en Delinkwent (Neth.)
Developer's Digest: Newsletter of the N.S.W. Division of the Urban Development Institute (Aus.) 1971–
Divinitatis Doctor (Lat.) Doctor of Divinity
DDA Dividend Disbursing Agent
D.D.A. Dangerous Drugs Act
D.D.C. Dewey Decimal Classification
District Court, District of Columbia
Docteur en droit canonique (Fr.) Doctor of Canon Law
D.D.D. dat, dicat, dedicat (Lat.) He gives, devotes and dedicates
dono, dedit dedicavit (Lat.) He gave and consecrated as a gift
D.D.G. Deputy Director-General
DDI Ministero degli Affari Esteri, I documenti Diplomatici Italiani (It.) 1952
d.d.in d. de die in diem (Lat.) from day to day
D.D.R. Deutsche Demokratische Republik (Ger.) German Democratic Republic (E. Germany)
D–D R–Z Deutsch–Deutsche Rechts–Zeitschrift (Ger.)
D.D.& Shpg. Dock Dues and Shipping
D.Dec. Dix, School Law Decisions, New York
D.Del. District Court for District of Delaware (USA)
d.e. deckle edge
D.E. Dail Eireann (Ire.) House of Representatives
Department of Employment
Department of Energy
DEA Drug Enforcement Administration (USA)
DEG Deutsche Entwicklungsgesellschaft
D.E.L.D. Dismissal and Employment Law Digest (Can.) 1986–
D.E.P. Department of Employment and Productivity
D.E.R.V. Diesel-Engined Road Vehicle
D.E.S. Department of Education and Science
D.En. Department of Energy
D.en D. Docteur en Droit (Fr.) Doctor of Law
D.es S.L.J. Dar es Salaam Law Journal. 1963–71

D.es S.U.L.J. Dar es Salaam University Law Journal. 1971–
d.f. dead freight
D.F. Dean of Faculty
Defender of the Faith
D.F.C. De Facto Cases (CCH) (Aus.) 1985–
Development Finance Corporation (N.Z.)
DFI Departement fédéral de l'Intérieur (Switz.)
DFJP Departement fédéral de Justice et Police (Switz.)
D.F.& J. De Gex, Fisher & Jones' Chancery Reports (45 ER) 1860–62
D.F.& J.B. De Gex, Fisher & Jones' Bankruptcy Reports. 1859–61
Dfall. Il diritto fallimentare (It.)
Dfam. Il diritto di famiglia (It.)
d.g. decreto governatoriale (It.) governor's decree
D.G. De Gex's Bankruptcy Reports. 1844–8
Déclaration de Guerre (Fr.) Declaration of war
Dei gratia (Lat.) by the Grace of God
Deo Gratias (Lat.) Thanks be to God
Director General
DGCL Delaware General Corporation Law
D.G.F.& J. De Gex, Fisher & Jones' Chancery Reports (45 ER) 1860–62
D.G.F.& J.B. De Gex, Fisher & Jones' Bankruptcy Reports. 1859–61
D.G.J.& S. De Gex, Jones & Smith's Chancery Reports (46 ER) 1862–66
D.G.J.& S.B. De Gex, Jones & Smith's Bankruptcy Reports. 1862–5
D.G.M.& G. De Gex, Macnaghten & Gordon's Chancery Reports (42–4 ER) 1851–7
D.G.M.& G.B. De Gex, Macnaghten & Gordon's Bankruptcy Reports. 1851–7
DGVDO 19 Durchführungsgesetz zur Verordnung Nr. 19 (Ger.) Implementation of the Regulation 19 Act
D.G.& J. De Gex & Jones' Chancery Reports (44–5 ER) 1857–9
D.G.& J.B. De Gex & Jones' Bankruptcy Reports. 1857–9
D.Guam District Court for District of Guam (USA)
d.h. das heisst (Ger.) that is to say
D.H. Department of Health
Recueil hebdomadaire Dalloz (Fr.) 1924–40
D.H.L. House of Lords Appeals, Dunlop's Court of Session Cases (Scot.)
D.H.S.S. Department of Health and Social Security
D.Hawaii District Court for District of Hawaii (USA)
D.hebd. Recueil hebdomadaire Dalloz (Fr.)
d.i. das ist (Ger.) that is
D.I. Decisions Information (Canada Labour Relations Board)
Department of Industry
Diritto Internazionale (It.)
DIA Defense Intelligence Agency (USA)
DIEL Advisory Committee on Telecommunications for Disabled and Elderly People
DIH Deutsche Industrie – und Handelstag (Ger.)
D.I.P. Document Image Processing
Droit international privé (Fr.) Private international law
DIS Schriftenreihe des Deutschen Instituts für Schiedsgerichtswesen (Ger.) 1986
DITAC Department of Industry, Technology and Commerce (Aus.)
D.J. Denver Law Journal (Colorado) 1966–
District Judge
Recueil Dalloz, Section Jurisprudence (Fr.) 1945–
D.J.A.G. Deputy Judge Advocate General
DJC Application for writ of error dismissed, judgment correct
DJJ District Judges

DJZ Deutsche Juristenzeitung (Ger.) 1896–1936

D.J.& S. De Gex, Jones & Smith's Chancery Reports (46 ER) 1862–66

D.J.& S.B. De Gex, Jones & Smith's Bankruptcy Reports. 1862–65

D.Jurisp.gen. Répertoire Dalloz de jurisprudence générale (Fr.) encyclopedia

DK Denmark

D.K.S. Deputy Keeper of the Signet

D.Kan. District Court for District of Kansas (USA)

DL Danske Lov (Den.) laws in force

D.L. Décret-loi (Fr.) decree-law
decreto legge (It.) decree-law
Doctor of Law
Recueil Dalloz, section Législation (Fr.) 1945–

D.L.J. University of Detroit Law Journal (Michigan) 1931–66

D.L.N. Daily Legal News

D.L.R. Dickinson Law Review (Pennsylvania) 1908–
Directors Law Reporter (Aus.) 1973–
Dominion Law Reporter (India) 1947–
Dominion Law Reports (Can.) 1912–55, 1956–68, 1969–84, 1984–
Driving Licences Regulations

D.L.R.(2d) Dominion Law Reports, 2nd Series (Can.) 1956–68

D.L.R.(3d) Dominion Law Reports, 3rd Series (Can.) 1969–84

D.L.R.(4th) Dominion Law Reports, 4th Series (Can.) 1984–

D.L.R.(Can.) Dominion Law Reports (Can.) 1912–

D.Lg. Decreto Legislativo (It.) legislative decree

D.Lgt. Decreto Luogoteneziale

D.M. Davison & Merivale's King's Bench Reports (64 RR) 1843–44
decreto ministeriale (It.) ministerial decree

DMF Decree of the Minister of Foreign Trade
Departement militaire fédéral (Switz.)

D.M.& G. De Gex, Macnaghten & Gordon's Chancery Reports (42–4 ER) 1851–7

D.M.& G.B. De Gex, Macnaghten & Gordon's Bankruptcy Reports. 1851–7

D.Mass. District Court for District of Massachusetts (USA)

D.Md. District Court for District of Maryland (USA)

D.Me. District Court for District of Maine (USA)

D.Minn. District Court for District of Minnesota (USA)

D.Mont. District Court for District of Montana (USA)

D.N. Dominus noster (Lat.) Our Lord

DNA Deoxyribonucleic acid

D.N.B. Dictionary of National Biography

D.N.D. District Court for the District of North Dakota (USA)

D.N.E.E. Deltion Nafticou Epimelitiriou Ellados (Bulletin of the Greek Chamber of Shipping)

D.N.H. District Court for the District of New Hampshire (USA)

D.N.J. District Court for the District of New Jersey (USA)

D.N.M. District Court for the District of New Mexico (USA)

D.N.P.P. Dominus noster papa pontifex (Lat.) Our Lord the Pope

D.N.S. Dow, New Series (Dow & Clark's House of Lords Cases) (6 ER) 1827–32
Dowling's Bail Court Reports, New Series (63–5 RR) 1841–2

D.Nev. District Court for the District of Nevada (USA)

DNotZ Deutsche Notar-Zeitschrift (Ger.)

D.O. Dissenting Opinion

DOA Dead on arrival at hospital

DOB date of birth

D.O.C. Department of Conservation (N.Z.)

D.O.E. Department of the Environment

D.O.I. Department of Industry

D.O.J. Department of Justice

D.O.P.I.E. Department of Primary Industry and Energy (Aus.)
DOR Revue de Droit Maritime Comparé (Fr.)
D.O.R.A. Defence of the Realm Act
D.O.T. Department of Trade
Department of Transport
DOTAC Department of Transport and Communications (Aus.)
DOV Die Öffentliche Verwaltung (Ger.)
D.of L. Duchy of Lancaster
D.Or. District Court for the District of Oregon (USA)
D.P. Dalloz périodique
Data procesing
Deposited Plan
Deputy President
Discussion Paper
Domus Procerum (Lat.) the House of Lords
D/P Documents against payment
D.P.B. Dampier Paper Book, in Lincoln's Inn Library
Domestic Purposes Benefit (N.Z.)
D.P.C. Dowling's Practice (Bail Court) Cases (36–61 RR) 1830–41
DPCI Droit et Pratique du Commerce International
DPF Departement politique fédéral (Switz.)
D.P.L.R. De Paul Law Review (USA)
D.P.P. Director of Public Prosecutions
DPR Presidential Decree (It.)
United States District Court, Puerto Rico
DPR ra The Presidential Decree on Administrative Review (It.) 1971
D.P.S.A. Deputy Public Service Arbitrator (Aus.)
DR Dacca Reports (India)
De-Rating Appeals. 1930–
Deutsches Recht (Ger.) German Law. 1931–45
Drake Law Review (Iowa) 1951–
D.R. Deputy Remembrancer
District Registry
DRA Dependent relative allowance
D.R.A. De-Rating Appeals. 1930–
D.R.A.(B.B.& S.) Decisions in Review and Appeal Cases (Basutoland, Bechuanaland and Swaziland) 1935–38
D.R.I. District Court for the District of Rhode Island (USA)
D.R.P. Deutsches Reichspatent (German patent)
D.R.S. Dominion Report Service (Can.)
D.R.S.G. Democratic Republic of the Sudan Gazette
D.Rep. Ohio Decisions Reprint
D.Repr. Ohio Decisions Reprint
DRiZ Deutsche Richterzeitung (Ger.) 1909–35, 1950–
D.S. Dalloz-Sirey
d.s.b. debitum sine brevi (Lat.) debit without writ
DSB Department of State Bulletin (USA)
Drug Supervisory Board (UN)
D.S.C. District Court for the District of South Carolina (USA)
D.S.D. District Court for the District of South Dakota (USA)
D.S.L.P. Diary of Social Legislation and Policy (Aus.) 1980–
d.s.p. decessit sine prole (Lat.) died without issue
d.s.p.l. decessit sine prole legitima (Lat.) died without legitimate issue
d.s.p.m. decessit sine prole mascula (Lat.) died without male issue
d.s.p.m.s. decessit sine prole mascula superstite (Lat.) died without surviving male issue
d.s.p.s. decessit sine prole superstite (Lat.) died without surviving issue
d.s.p.v. decessit sine prole virile (Lat.) died without male issue
D.Sc.L. Doctor of Science of Laws
D.Somm. Recueil Dalloz, section Sommaires (Fr.) 1945–
DStZ Deutsche Steuer-Zeitung (Ger.) 1912–45, 1947–
D.T.B.C. Lower Canada Reports (Decisions des Tribunaux du Bas-Canada) 1850–67

D.T.C. Dominion Tax Cases (Can.) 1920–
D.T.I. Department of Trade and Industry
D.T.S. Droit de Tirage Spécial (Fr.)
DTp Department of Transport
D.U.L.J. Dublin University Law Journal (Ire.) 1971–
D.U.L.R. Dublin University Law Review (Ire.) 1969–70
Duquesne University Law Review (USA) 1963/4–1967/8
D.Utah District Court for the District of Utah (USA)
DV Government Law Gazette (Bulgaria)
D VBl Deutsches Verwaltungsblatt (Ger.)
D.V.I. District Court for the District of the Virgin Islands (USA)
D.V.L.C. Driver and Vehicle Licensing Centre
d.v.n. devisavit vel non (Lat.) issue of fact as to whether a will in question was made by the testator
DVO Durchführungsverordnung (Ger.) executive decree
d.v.p. decessit vita patris (Lat.) died during his father's life
D.Vt. District Court for the District of Vermont (USA)
DWB dismissed for want of bond
D.W.I. died without issue
driving while intoxicated
DWP dismissed for want of prosecution
DWT Dead weight ton
DX Document Exchange
D.& A. Dear & Anderson's Session Cases (Scot.) 1829–32
D.& B. Dearsly & Bell's Crown Cases Reserved (169 ER) 1856–8
Devereux & Battle's North Carolina Law Reports (18–20 NC) 1834–9
Devereux & Battle's North Carolina Equity Reports (21–2 NC) 1834–9
D.& B.C.C. Dearsly & Bell's Crown Cases Reserved (169 ER) 1856–8
D.& B.Pr.Pr. Dodd & Brook, Probate Practice. 1865
D.& C. Deacon & Chitty's Bankruptcy Reports. 1832–5
Dean and Chapter
District and County Reports, Pennsylvania
Dow & Clark's House of Lords Appeals (6 ER) 1827–32
D.& C.2d District and County Reports, Second Series, Pennsylvania
D.& C.C. District and County Reports, Pennsylvania
D.& C.(Pa.) District and County Reports, Pennsylvania
D.& Ch. Deacon & Chitty's Bankruptcy Reports. 1832–5
D.& Chit. Deacon & Chitty's Bankruptcy Reports. 1832–5
D.& Cl. Dow & Clark's House of Lords Appeals (6 ER) 1827–32
D.& D. drunk and disorderly
D.& E. Durnford & East's Term Reports, King's Bench (99–101 ER) 1785–1800
D.& F.'11–16 Divisional and Full Court Judgments (Ghana) 1911–16
D.& G. Diprose & Gammon's Reports of Law affecting Friendly Societies. 1801–97
D.& J. De Gex & Jones' Chancery Reports (44–5 ER) 1857–59
D.& J.B. De Gex & Jones' Bankruptcy Reports. 1857–59
D.& L. Dowling & Lowndes' Bail Court Reports (67–82 RR) 1843–9
D.& M. Davison & Merivale's Queen's Bench Reports (64 RR) 1843–4
D.& Mer. Davison & Merivale's Queen's Bench Reports (64 RR) 1843–4
D.& P. Dearsly & Pearce's Crown Cases Reserved (169 ER) 1852–6
Denison & Pearce's Crown Cases Reserved (169 ER) 1844–52
Development and Planning
D.& R. Dowling & Ryland's King's Bench Reports (24–30 RR) 1821–7
D.& R.M.C. Dowling & Ryland's Magistrates' Cases. 1822–7

D.& R.Mag.Cas. Dowling & Ryland's Magistrates' Cases. 1822–7
D.& R.N.P. Dowling & Ryland's Nisi Prius Cases (171 ER) 1822–3
D.& R.N.P.C. Dowling & Ryland's Nisi Prius Cases (171 ER) 1822–3
D.& S. De Gex & Smale's Chancery Reports (63–4 ER) 1846–52
Deane & Swabey's Ecclesiastical Reports (164 ER) 1855–7
Drewry & Smale's Chancery Reports tempore Kindersley (62 ER) 1860–5
D.& Sm. De Gex & Smale's Chancery Reports (63–4 ER) 1846–52
Drewry & Smale's Chancery Reports tempore Kindersley (62 ER) 1860–5
D.& Sw. Deane & Swabey's Ecclesiastical Reports (164 ER) 1855–7
D.& W. Drury & Walsh's Chancery Reports (Ire.) 1837–40
Drury & Warren's Chancery Reports (Ire.) 1841–3
D.& Wal. Drury & Walsh's Chancery Reports (Ire.) 1837–40
D.& War. Drury & Warren's Chancery Reports (Ire.) 1841–3
Da. Dakota
Dakota Territory Reports
Danish
Da.& Bos. Darby & Bosanquet, Statutes of Limitation. 2ed. 1893
Dacca All India Reporter, Dacca Series. 1949–50
Pakistan Law Reports, Dacca Series. 1951–
Dady. Dadyburjor's Supreme Court Appeals (India) 1899–1927
Dahm G. Dahm, Volkerrecht (Ger.) 1958–61
Dai.Reg. New York Daily Register. 1872–89
Daily L.N. Daily Legal News (Pennsylvania)
Daily L.R. Daily Legal Record (Pennsylvania)
Daily Leg.News (Pa.) Daily Legal News (Pennsylvania)
Daily Leg.Rec.(Pa.) Daily Legal Record (Pennsylvania)
Daily Trans. New York Daily Transcript. 1859–72
Dak. Dakota
Dakota Territory Reports
Dak.L.Rev. Dakota Law Review. 1927–32
Dak.Law Rev. Dakota Law Review. 1927–32
Dal. Benloe & Dalison's Common Pleas Reports (123 ER) 1486–1580
Dalison's Common Pleas Reports (123 ER) 1486–1580
Dallas' Pennsylvania Reports. 1754–1809
Dallas' United States Reports (1–4 US) 1790–1800
Dalrymple's Session Cases (Scot.)
Daly's Reports (New York)
Dal.C.P. Dalison's Common Pleas Reports (123 ER) 1486–1580
Dal.in Keil. Dalison's Reports in Keilway. 1533–64
Dale Dale's Ecclesiastical Reports. 1868–71
Dale's Reports (2–4 Oklahoma)
Dale Ecc. Dale's Ecclesiastical Reports. 1868–71
Dale Leg.Rit. Dale's Legal Ritual (Ecclesiastical Reports) 1868–71
Dale Par.Ch. Dale, Law of the Parish Church. 5ed. 1975
Dalhousie L.J. Dalhousie Law Journal (Can.) 1973–
Dalison Dalison's Common Pleas Reports (123 ER) 1486–1580
Dall. Dallam's Texas Supreme Court Decisions
Dallas, Laws of Pennsylvania
Dallas' Pennsylvania Reports. 1754–1809
Dallas' Styles of Writs (Scot.)
Dallas' United States Supreme Court Reports (1–4 US) 1790–1800
Dall.Coop. Dallas, Report of Cooper's Opinions on the Sentence of a Foreign Court of Admiralty

Dall.Dec. Dallam's Texas Supreme Court Decisions
Dall.Dig. Dallam's Digest and Opinions (Texas)
Dall.Laws Dallas' Laws (Pennsylvania)
Dall.S.C. Dallas' United States Supreme Court Reports (1–4 US) 1790–1800
Dall.Sty. Dallas, Styles of Writs (Scot.)
Dall.(Tex.) Dallam's Texas Supreme Court Decisions
Dallam Dig.(Tex.) Dallam's Digest and Opinions (Texas)
Dallas Dallas' Pennsylvania Reports. 1754–1809
Dallas' United States Supreme Court Reports (1–4 US) 1790–1800
Dalloz Dic. Dalloz, Dictionnaire de droit (Fr.)
Dalloz Enc. Dalloz, Encyclopedie Juridique (Fr.)
Dalr. Dalrymple's Decisions, Court of Session (Scot.) 1698–1718
Dalrymple of Hailes' Session Cases (Scot.)
Dalrymple of Stair's Decisions, Court of Session (Scot.)
Dalr.Dec. Dalrymplè's Decisions, Court of Session (Scot.) 1698–1718
Dalr.Feud.Prop. Dalrymple, Feudal Property
Dalrymple Dalrymple's Decisions, Court of Session (Scot.) 1698–1718
Dalrymple of Hailes' Session Cases (Scot.)
Dalrymple of Stair's Decisions, Court of Session (Scot.)
Dalt. Dalton's Justices of the Peace. Latest edition 1756
Daly Daly's New York Common Pleas Reports
Daly (NY) Daly's New York Common Pleas Reports
Dampier MSS Dampier's Paper Book, Lincon's Inn Library
Dan. Dana's Kentucky Reports (31–39 Ky.) 1833–40
Daniell's Exchequer in Equity Reports (159 ER) 1817–23
Daniel's Compendium Compensation Cases
Danish
Danner's Reports (42 Alabama)
Dan.Ch. Daniell's Chancery Practice. 8ed. 1914
Dan.Ch.Pr. Daniell's Chancery Practice. 8ed. 1914
Dan.Exch. Daniell's Exchequer and Equity Reports (159 ER) 1817–23
Dan.Forms Daniell, Forms and Precedents in Chancery. 7ed. 1932
Dan.Neg.Ins. Daniell, Negotiable Instruments
Dan.Ord. Danish Ordinances
Dan.T.M. Daniel, Trade Marks. 1876
Dan.& L. Danson & Lloyd's Mercantile Cases (34 RR) 1828–9
Dan.& Ll. Danson & Lloyd's Mercantile Cases (34 RR) 1828–9
Dana Dana's Kentucky Supreme Court Reports (31–9 Ky.) 1833–40
Dana Wh. Dana's Edition of Wheaton's International Law
Dane Abr. Dane's Abridgement of American Law
Daniel Neg.Inst. Daniel's Negotiable Instruments
Daniell Ch.Pl.& Prac. Daniell's Chancery Pleading and Practice. 8ed. 1914
Daniell Ch.Pr. Daniell's Chancery Pleading and Practice. 8ed. 1914
Daniell Ch.Prac. Daniell's Chancery Pleading and Practice. 8ed. 1914
Dann Dann's Reports (1 Arizona)
Dann's Reports (22 California)
Danner's Reports (42 Alabama)
Danner Danner's Reports (42 Alabama)
Danquah Cases in Gold Coast Law (Ghana)
Dans.& L. Danson & Lloyd's Mercantile Cases (34 RR) 1828–9
Dans.& Ll. Danson & Lloyd's Mercantile Cases (34 RR) 1828–9
Dans.& Lld. Danson & Lloyd's Mercantile Cases (34 RR) 1828–9

Danv. D'Anvers' General Abridgement of the Common Law. 2ed. 1725–37

Danv.Abr. D'Anvers, General Abridgment of the Common Law. 2ed. 1725–37

Darl.Pr.Ct.Sess. Darling, Practice of the Court of Session (Scot.)

Dart Dart on Vendors and Purchasers. 8ed. 1929

Dart.Col.Ca. Dartmouth College Case

Dart Vend. Dart on Vendors and Purchasers. 8ed. 1929

Das. Common Law Reports by Dasent (vol.3)
Dasent's Bankruptcy and Insolvency Reports. 1853–55

Dasent Acts of Privy Council, ed. Dasent
Dasent's Bankruptcy and Insolvency Reports. 1853–55

Dass.Dig. Dassler's Kansas Digest

Dass.Ed. Dassler's Edition, Kansas Reports

Dass.Ed.(Kan.) Dassler's Edition, Kansas Reports

Dass.Stat. Dassler's Kansas Statutes

Dauph. Dauphin County Reporter (Pennsylvania)

Dauph.Co.Rep. Dauphin County Reporter (Pennsylvania)

Dav. Davies' King's Bench and Exchequer Reports (Ire.) (80 ER) 1604–12
Davies' Patent Cases. 1785–1816
Davies' United States District Court Reports
Davis' Reports (Abridgement of Sir Edward Coke's Reports)
Davis' Reports (2 Hawaii)
Davis' United States Supreme Court Reports (108–176 US)

Dav.Coke Davis' Abridgement of Coke's Reports

Dav.Conv. Davidson's Conveyancing

Dav.Dig. Davis' Indiana Digest

Dav.Ir. Davys' or Davies' King's Bench Reports (Ire.) (80 ER) 1604–12

Dav.Ir.K.B. Davys' or Davies' King's Bench Reports (Ire.) (80 ER) 1604–12

Dav.Land Ct.Cas. Davis' Land Court Decisions. 1898–1908

Dav.P.C. Davies' Patent Cases. 1785–1816

Dav.Pat.Cas. Davies' Patent Cases. 1785–1816

Dav.Prec.Conv. Davidson's Precedents in Conveyancing

Dav.Rep. Davies' King's Bench Reports (Ire.) (80 ER) 1604–12

Dav.(U.S.) Davies' District Court Reports (USA)

Dav.& M. Davison & Merivale's Queen's Bench Reports (64 RR) 1843–44

Dav.& Mer. Davison & Merivale's Queen's Bench Reports (64 RR) 1843–44

David–Hazard, Droit Soviètique R. David & J.N. Hazard, Les Systèmes de Droit Contemporains: Le Droit Soviètique (Fr.) 1954

David & Brierley R. David & J.E.C. Brierley, Major Legal Systems in the World Today

Davidson Davidson's Reports (92–111 North Carolina)

Davies Davies' (or Davis' or Davys') Irish King's Bench Reports (80 ER) 1604–12
Davies' Patent Cases. 1785–1816
Davies' United States District Court Reports

Davies (Ir.) Davies' Irish King's Bench Reports (80 ER) 1604–12

Davies (U.S.) Davies' United States District Court Reports

Davis Davies' (or Davis' or Davys') Irish King's Bench Reports (80 ER) 1604–12
Davis' Hawaiian Reports (2 Hawaii)
Davis' United States Supreme Court Reports (108–176 US)

Davis Admin.Law Davis's Administrative Law Treatise

Davis Bldg.Soc. Davis' Law of Building Societies. 5ed 1931

Davis Cr.Law Davis' Criminal Law. 1861

Davis(J.C.B.) Davis' United States Supreme Court Reports (108–176 US)

Davis L.Ct.Cas. Davis' Land Court Decisions. 1898–1908

Davis Land Ct.Dec.(Mass.) Davis' Land Court Decisions. 1898–1908

Davis Rep. Davis' Hawaiian Reports (Sandwich Islands) (2 Hawaii)

Davy Davies' Irish King's Bench Reports (80 ER) 1604–12

Davy's Davies' Irish King's Bench Reports (80 ER) 1604–12

Dawson's Code Dawson's Code of Civil Procedure, Colorado

Day Day's Connecticut Reports. 1802–13
Day's Election Cases. 1892–93

Day (Conn.) Day's Connecticut Reports. 1802–13

Day Elect.Cas. Day's Election Cases. 1892–93

Dayt.Term.Rep. Dayton Term Reports (Dayton, Ohio)

Dayton Dayton (Laning) Reports (Ohio)
Dayton Superior and Common Pleas Reports (Ohio)
University of Dayton Intramural Law Review

Dayton (Ohio) Dayton Ohio Reports

Dayton Term.Rep. Dayton Term Reports (Dayton, Ohio)

dbk. drawback

Dbn. Durban

dct. document

De Delaware

De B.Mar.Int.L. De Burgh's Maritime International Laws. 1868

De Bow Com. De Bow's Commercial Review (USA)

De.Ch. Delaware Chancery Reports

De Col. De Colyar's County Court Cases. 1867–82

De Coly. De Colyar's County Court Cases. 1867–82

de d.in d. de die in diem (Lat.) from day to day

De G. De Gex's Bankruptcy Reports. 1844–8

De G.Bankr. De Gex's Bankruptcy Reports. 1844–8

De G.F.& J. De Gex, Fisher & Jones' Chancery Reports (45 ER) 1860–62

De G.F.& J.By. De Gex, Fisher & Jones' Bankruptcy Appeals. 1859–61

De G.J.& S. De Gex, Jones & Smith's Chancery Reports (46 ER) 1862–6

De G.J.& S.By. De Gex, Jones & Smith's Bankruptcy Appeals. 1862–65

De G.J.& Sm. De Gex, Jones & Smith's Chancery Reports (46 ER) 1862–6

De G.M.& G. De Gex, Macnaghten & Gordon's Bankruptcy Reports. 1851–7
De Gex, Macnaghten & Gordon's Chancery Reports (42–4 ER) 1851–7

De G.M.& G.By. De Gex, Macnaghten & Gordon's Bankruptcy Reports. 1851–7

De G.& J. De Gex & Jones' Chancery Reports (44–5 ER) 1857–9

De G.& J.B. De Gex & Jones' Bankruptcy Appeals. 1857–9

De G.& J.By. De Gex & Jones' Bankruptcy Appeals. 1857–9

De G.& S. De Gex & Smales' Chancery Reports (63–4 ER) 1846–52

De G.& Sm. De Gex & Smales' Chancery Reports (63–4 ER) 1846–52

De Gex De Gex's Bankruptcy Reports. 1844–8

De Gex, F.& J. De Gex, Fisher & Jones' Chancery Reports (45 ER) 1860–62

De Gex, J.& S. De Gex, Jones & Smith's Chancery Reports (46 ER) 1862–6

De Gex, M.& G. De Gex, Macnaghten & Gordon's Chancery Reports (42–4 ER) 1851–7

De Gex, M.& G.B. De Gex, Macnaghten & Gordon's Bankruptcy Reports. 1851–7

De Hart Mil.Law De Hart on Military Law

De Kock A. de Kock, Industrial Law of South Africa

De Krets. De Kretser's Matara Appeals (Sri Lanka)
De Lolme Eng.Const. De Lolme on the English Constitution. 1838
De M. De Mello's Extradition Cases (Malaya) 1877–1913
De Orat. Cicero, De Oratore
De P. De Paul Law Review (USA) 1951–
De Paul Bus.L.J. De Paul Business Law Journal (USA)
De Paul L.Rev. De Paul Law Review (USA) 1951–
De Rebus De Rebus Procuratoriis (S.Afr.) 1968–
De Vos W. de Vos, Verrykingsaanspreeklikheid in die Suid-Afrikaans Reg (S.Afr.)
De Wet & Swanepoel J.C. de Wet & H.L. Swanepoel, Strafreg (S.Afr.)
De Wet & Yeats J.C. de Wet & J.P. Yeats, Die Suid-Afrikaans Kontraktereg en Handelsreg (S.Afr.)
De Witt De Witt's Reports (24–42 Ohio State)
Dea. Deady, United States Circuit and District Court Reports
Dea.& Ch. Deacon & Chitty's Bankruptcy Reports. 1832–5
Dea.& Chit. Deacon & Chitty's Bankruptcy Reports. 1832–5
Dea.& Sw. Deane & Swabey's Ecclesiastical Reports (164 ER) 1855–57
Deac. Deacon's Bankruptcy Reports. 1835–40
Deac.Bank.Pr. Deacon, Bankruptcy Law and Practice. 3ed. 1864
Deac.Cr.Law Deacon, Criminal Law of England
Deac.Dig. Deacon, Digest of the Criminal Law
Deac.& C. Deacon & Chitty's Bankruptcy Reports. 1832–5
Deac.& Ch. Deacon & Chitty's Bankruptcy Reports. 1832–5
Deac.& Chit. Deacon & Chitty's Bankruptcy Reports. 1832–5
Deacon Bankr.Cas. Deacon's Bankruptcy Reports. 1835–40
Deacon & C.Bankr.Cas. Deacon & Chitty's Bankruptcy Reports. 1832–5
Dead.Or.Laws Deady & Lane's Oregon General Laws
Deady Deady's Circuit and District Court Reports (USA)
Deane Deane & Swabey's Ecclesiastical Reports (164 ER) 1855–7
Deane & Swabey's Probate and Divorce Reports
Deane's Blockade Cases
Deane's Reports (24–26 Vermont)
Deane Ecc.Rep. Deane & Swabey's Eccelesiastical Reports (164 ER) 1855–7
Deane Ecc.Rep.B. Deane & Swabey's Ecclesiastical Reports (164 ER) 1855–7
Deane & S.Eccl. Deane & Swabey's Ecclesiastical Reports (164 ER) 1855–57
Deane & S.Eccl.Rep. Deane & Swabey's Ecclesiastical Reports (164 ER) 1855–57
Deane & Sw. Deane & Swabey's Ecclesiastical Reports (164 ER) 1855–7
Dears. Dearsley's Crown Cases Reserved (169 ER) 1852–56
Dears.C.C. Dearsley's Crown Cases Reserved (169 ER) 1852–56
Dears.& B. Dearsley & Bell's Crown Cases Reserved (169 ER) 1856–58
Dears.& B.C.C. Dearsley & Bell's Crown Cases Reserved (169 ER) 1856–58
Dears.& B.Crown Cas. Dearsley and Bell's Crown Cases Reserved (169 ER) 1856–58
Dearsl.Cr.Pr. Dearsley, Criminal Process. 1853
Deas & A. Deas & Anderson's Decisions (Scot.) 1829–33
Deas & And. Deas & Anderson's Decisions (Scot.) 1829–33
Deb. Debenture
debit
Debt.& Cred. Debtor and Creditor
dec. deceased
decimal
declaration
declination
decoration

dec. decidé (-ée) (Fr) deceased
Dec. Decanus (Dean)
December
Decision
Dec.Ch. Decisions from the Chair (Parliamentary)
Dec.Com.Pat. Decisions of the Commissioner of Patents (USA) 1869–
Dec.Dig. American Digest System, Decennial Edition
Dec.Fed.Mar.Comm'n. Decisions of the Federal Maritime Commission (USA). 1947–
Dec.O. Ohio Decisions
Dec.Rep. Ohio Decisions, Reprint
Dec.S.D.A. Bengal Sudder Dewanny Adawlut Decisions (India) 1845–62
Dec.t.H.& M. Admiralty Decisions tempore Hay & Marriott. 1776–9
Dec.U.S.Compt.Gen. Decisions of U.S. Comptroller General. 1921–
Dec.U.S.Mar.Comm'n. Decisions of the U.S. Maritime Commission. 1919–47
Dec.W.C.C. New Zealand Workers' Compensation Cases. 1901–40
Decalogue J. Decalogue Journal (USA) 1950–
decd. deceased
Decen.Dig. American Digest, Decennial Edition
Decision Decision Law Journal (Philippines)
Decision L.J. Decision Law Journal (Philippines)
Decln. Declaration
Decr. Décret
Decs. Decisions
Ded. Dedicated
Dedication
Def. Defence
Defendant
Defined
Definition
Defunctus (Lat.) deceased
Def.Couns.J. Defense Counsel Journal (USA)
Defense L.J. Defense Law Journal (USA) 1957–
deg. degree
Del. Delane's Decisions, Election Revision Cases 1832–35
Delaware
Delaware County Reports, Pennsylvania
Delaware Supreme Court Reports. 1832–
Delegate
Delhi
Del.C.Ann. Delaware Code Annotated
Del.Cas. Delaware Cases. 1792–1830
Del.Ch. Delaware Chancery Reports. 1814–1868
Del.Civ.Dec. Delhi Civil Decisions (India)
Del.Co.L.J.(Pa.) Delaware County Law Journal (Pennsylvania)
Del.Co.(Pa.) Delaware County Reports (Pennsylvania)
Del.Co.R. Delaware County Reports (Pennsylvania)
Del.Code Delaware Code
Del.Code.Ann. Delaware Code Annotated
Del.County Delaware County Reports (Pennsylvania)
Del.Cr.Cas. Delaware Criminal Cases
Del.El.Cas. Delane's Decisions, Election Revision Cases. 1832–5
Del.L.R. Delhi Law Review. 1972–
Del.Laws Laws of Delaware
Del.Order Delegation Order
Del.Term R. Delaware Term Reports
Delane Delane's Decisions, Election Revision Cases. 1832–5
Delaume G.R. Delaume, Les conflits de lois à la veille du Code civil (Fr.) 1947
G.R. Delaume, Legal Aspects of International Lending and Economic Development Financing. 1967
Delaware J.Corp.L. Delaware Journal of Corporate Law (USA)
dele. deleatur (Lat.) omit
Delehanty New York Miscellaneous Reports
Delhi L.R. Delhi Law Review (India) 1972–

Delhi L.Rev. Delhi Law Review (India) 1972–

Dell. Dellam's Texas Opinions. 1840–44

delv. delivered

Dem. Demarest's Surrogate Reports (New York)

Dem.(N.Y.) Demarest's Surrogate Reports (New York)

Dem.Sur. Demarest's Surrogate Reports (New York)

Demol.C.N. Demolobe's Code Napoléon

Den. Denied
Denio's New York Supreme Court Reports. 1845–8
Denis' Reports (32–46 Louisiana)
Denison & Pearce's Crown Cases Reserved (169 ER) 1844–52
Denmark
Denver

den.app. denying appeal

Den.B.A.Rec. Denver Bar Association Record. 1923–8

Den.C.C. Denison & Pearce's Crown Cases Reserved (169 ER) 1844–52

Den.J.I.L.P. Denver Journal of International Law and Policy. 1971–

Den.L.C.J. Denver Law Center Journal. 1963–5

Den.L.J. Denver Law Journal (USA) 1966–

Den.L.N. Denver Legal News. 1887–9

den.rearg. denying reargument

den.reh. denying rehearing

den.writ of error denying writ of error

Den.& P. Denison & Pearce's Crown Cases Reserved (169 ER) 1844–52

Den.& P.C.C. Denison & Pearce's Crown Cases Reserved (169 ER) 1844–52

Den.& Sc.Pr. Denison & Scott's House of Lords Appeal Practice

Denio Denio's New York Supreme Court Reports

Denis Denis' Reports (32–46 Louisiana)

Denison Cr.Cas. Denison & Pearce's Crown Cases Reserved (169 ER) 1844–52

Denning L.J. Denning Law Journal

Denom. Denomination

Dens. Denslow's Notes (1–3 Michigan Reports)

Denv.U.L.Rev. Denver University Law Review (USA)

Denver L.J. Denver Law Journal (USA) 1966–

Denver L.N. Denver Legal Notes. 1887–9

Dep. Department
Deposit(s)
Depositary
Deputy

DePaul Bus.L.J. DePaul Business Law Journal (USA)

DePaul L.Rev. DePaul Law Review (USA)

Dept. Department

Dept.Dec. Departmental Decisions. 1905–

Dept.of State Bull. Department of State Bulletin (USA)

Dept.R. State Department Reports (New York)

Dept.R.Un. New York State Department Reports, Unofficial

Dept.State Bull. Department of State Bulletin (USA)

Des. Desaussure's South Carolina Equity Reports (1–4 SCEq) 1784–1816

Desai Handbook of Criminal Cases (India)

Desaus. Desaussure's South Carolina Equity Reports (1–4 SCEq) 1784–1816

Desaus.Eq. Desaussure's South Carolina Equity Reports (1–4 SCEq) 1784–1816

Descr. Description

desid. desideratum (Lat.) wanted

desig. designate

Dest.Cal.Dig. Desty's California Digest

Dest.Sh.& Adm. Desty, Shipping and Admiralty

Det. Detachable
Detached
Detective
Detroit

Det.B.J. Detroit Bar Journal
Det.C.L.R. Detroit College of Law Review (USA) 1975–
Det.C.L.Rev. Detroit College of Law Review (USA) 1975–
Det.Coll.L.R. Detroit College of Law Review. 1975–
Det.Con. Detective Constable
Det.Insp. Detective Inspector
Det.L.J. Detroit Law Journal. 1898–1917
Det.L.Rev. Detroit Law Review. 1931–48
Det.Law. Detroit Lawyer (Detroit Bar Association) 1931–
Det.Leg.N. Detroit Legal News. 1894–1916
Det.Sgt. Detective Sergeant
Detroit Coll.L. Detroit College of Law
Detroit L.J. Detroit Law Journal. 1898–1917
Detroit L.Rev. Detroit Law Review. 1931–48
Deut. Book of Deuteronomy
Dev. Development
Devereux's North Carolina Equity Reports (16–17 NC) 1826–34
Devereux's North Carolina Law Reports (12–15 NC) 1826–34
Devereux's Reports, United States Court of Claims
DeVilliers Reports, Orange Free State (S.Afr.)
Dev.C.C. Devereux's Court of Claims Reports (USA)
Dev.Ct.Cl. Devereux's Court of Claims Reports (USA)
Dev.Eq. Devereux's North Carolina Equity Reports (16–17 NC) 1826–34
DevG Devisengesetz (Ger.) Law on Exchange Control
Dev.L. Devereux's North Carolina Law Reports (12–15 NC) 1826–34
Dev.& B. Devereux & Battle's North Carolina Equity Reports (21–2 NC) 1834–9
Devereux & Battle's North Carolina Law Reports (18–20 NC) 1834–9
Dev.& B.Eq. Devereux & Battle's North Carolina Equity Reports (21–2 NC) 1834–9
Dev.& B.L. Devereux & Battle's North Carolina Law Reports (18–20 NC) 1834–9
Dev.& Bat. Devereux & Battle's North Carolina Law Reports (18–20 NC) 1834–9
Dev.& Bat.Eq. Devereux & Battle's North Carolina Equity Reports (21–22 NC) 1834–9
Dew. Dewey's Court of Appeals Reports (Kansas)
Dewey's Supreme Court Reports (60–70 Kansas)
dft. defendant
draft
di Decisions Information (Canada Labour Relations Board)
Di. Dyer's Reports, King's Bench (73 ER) 1513–82
Di Gov. Diario do Governo (Port.)
Dial.de Scacc. Dialogus de Scaccario
Diario da Republica Portuguese legislative series
Dic. Dicta (Denver Bar Association) 1928–62
Dic.Dom. Dicey on Domicil. 1879
Dic.Par. Dicey on Parties to an Action. 1870
Dice Dice's Reports (71–91 Indiana)
Dicey Confl.Laws Dicey on Conflict of Laws
Dicey Const. Dicey, Introductory to the Study of the Constitution. 10ed. 1959
Dicey Dom. Dicey, Law of Domicil. 1879
Dicey & Morris Dicey on Conflict of Laws
Dick. Dickens' Chancery Reports (21 ER) 1599–1798
Dickinson's Reports (46–58 New Jersey Equity)
Dick.Ch. Dickens' Chancery Reports (21 ER) 1599–1798
Dick.Ev. Dickson, Law of Evidence in Scotland

Dick.J.Int'l L. Dickinson Journal of International Law (USA)
Dick.L.R. Dickinson Law Review (USA) 1908–
Dick.L.Rev. Dickinson Law Review (USA) 1908–
Dick.(NJ) Dickinson's New Jersey Equity Reports (46–58 NJEq)
Dickens Dickens' Chancery Reports (21 ER) 1599–1798
Dickinson L.Rev. Dickinson Law Review (USA) 1908–
Dict. Dictionary
Dict.C.F. Dictionnaire des Codes Français
Dict.de Jur. Dictionnaire de Jurisprudence
Dict.Dr.Com. Dictionnaire de Droit Commercial
Dict.Droit Civil Dictionnaire de Droit Civil
Dict.Not. Dictionnaire du Notariat
Dicta Dicta of Denver Bar Association. 1928–62
Dictionnaire terminologie Dictionnaire de la terminologie du droit international (Fr.) 1960
Dig. Digest
Digest (Lahore, India) 1901–6
Dig.Crim.Proc. Stephen, Digest of Criminal Procedure. 9ed. 1950
Dig.Fla. Thompson's Digest of Laws (Florida)
Dig.Ops.J.A.G. Digest of the Opinions of the Judge Advocate General (USA)
Dig.R.Pr. Digby, Introduction to the History of Real Property. 5ed. 1897
Dig.St. English's Digest of the Statutes (Arkansas)
Digest Digest of Justinian
Dil. Dillon's United States Circuit Court Reports
Dill. Dillon's United States Circuit Court Reports
Dill.Laws Eng.& Am. Dillon's Laws and Jurisprudence of England and America
Dillon Dillon's United States Circuit Court Reports
Dip.Crim. Diploma of Criminology
Dip.J. Diploma of Jurisprudence
Dip.L. Diploma of Law
Dip.L.(B.A.B.) Diploma of Law (Barristers' Admission Board) (Aus.)
Dip.L.S. Diploma of Legal Studies
Dip.L.(S.A.B.) Diploma of Law (Solicitors' Admission Board) (Aus.)
Dir. Directive
Director
Dir.aer. Diritto aereo (It.) 1962–
Dir.aereo Diritto aereo (It.) 1962–
Dir.aut. Diritto d'autore (It.) 1930–
Dir.autore Diritto d'autore (It.) 1930–
Dir.Com.e degli Scambi Int. Diritto Comunitario e degli Scambi Internazional (It.)
Dir.Comun.& Scambi Intern. Diritto Comunitario e degli Scambi Internazional (It.)
Dir.e Giur. Diritto e Giurisprudenza (It.)
Dir.eccles. Diritto ecclesiastico (It.) 1890–
Dir.Fall. Il diritto fallimentare e delle societa commerciale (It.)
Dir.giur. Diritto e giurisprudenza (It.) 1886–
Dir.Inform. Diritto dell'Informazione e dell'Informatica (It.)
Dir.int. Diritto internazionale (It.) 1937–
Dir.L.R. Directors Law Reporter (Aus.) 1973–
Dir.lav. Diritto del lavoro (It.) 1927–
Dir.mar. Diritto marittimo (It.) 1899–
Dir.maritt. Diritto marittimo (It.) 1899–
Dir.R. Diario da Republica (Port.)
Dir.Sc.Int. Diritto negli scambi internazionale (It.) 1963–
Dir.scambi intern. Diritto negli scambi internazionale (It.) 1963–
Dir.& Giur. Diritto e Giurisprudenza (It.)
Dirl. Dirleton's Decisions, Court of Session (Scot.) 1665–77
Dirl.Dec. Dirleton's Decisions, Court of Session (Scot.) 1665–77
Dis. Disney's Ohio Superior Court Reports

dis.op. dissenting opinion
disappr. disapproved
disapproving
Disc. Discount
Discovered
dism.app. dismissing appeal
Disn. Disney's Ohio Superior Court Reports
Disn.Gam. Disney, Gaming. 1806
disp.att. disposizioni per l'attuazione del codice civile e disposizioni transitorie emanate (It.)
disp.prel. disposizioni sulla legge in generale (preliminari al codice civile) (It.)
diss. dissertation
dissolved/divorced
Diss.ad.Flet. Selden's Dissertatio ad Fletam
Diss.op. Dissenting opinion
Dist. Distinguished
Distinguishing
District
Dist.C. District Court
Dist.Col. District of Columbia
Dist.Col.App. District of Columbia Court of Appeals
Dist.Ct. District Court
Dist.Ct.App. District Court of Appeals (USA)
Dist.Haw. District of Hawaii
Dist.Rep. District Reports
Distr. Distribution
Distributive
Distr.Col.B.A.J. District of Columbia Bar Association Journal
Distr.Fed. Districto Federal (Brazil)
Distrib. Distribute
Distributing
Distributor
District Court L.R. District Court Law Reports (Hong Kong) 1953–
Div. divide
dividend
divinity
division
divorce
Div.C. Division Court (Can.)
Div.Ct. Divisional Court
Selected Judgments of the Divisional Courts of the Gold Coast Colony (Ghana)
Div.de Just. Division de Justice du Departement fédéral de Justice de Police (Switz.)
Div.des A.E. Division des Affaires étrangères du Departement politique fédéral (Switz.)
Div.& Mat.Ct. Divorce and Matrimonial Causes Court
divde. dividende (Fr.) dividend
Dix Dec. Dix's School Decisions, New York
Dix.Farm Dixon on the Law of the Farm. 6ed. 1904
Dix.Part. Dixon, Partnership. 1866
Dix.Pr. Dixon, Probate and Administration Law and Practice. 3ed 1912
Dk.L.R. Dickinson Law Review (USA) 1908–
Dkt. Docket (and the barrister) (Can.) 1889–98
The Docket (USA) 1942–4
West Publishing Co.'s Docket. 1909–41
dl. decreto leigislativo (It.)
Dn.L.J. Denver Law Journal. 1966–
do. ditto (the same)
Doc. Doctor
Document
Doc.fr. Documentation français
Doc.Jur. Documentacion Juridica (Sp.)
Doc.parl. Documents parlementaires (Belg.) official periodical of parliamentary proceedings
Docket Docket (and the barrister) (Can.) 1889–98
The Docket (USA) 1942–4
West Publishing Co.'s Docket. 1909–41
Doct.Plac. Doctrina Placitandi
Dod. Dod's Parliamentary Companion. Annual
Dodson's Admiralty Reports (165 ER) 1811–22
Dod.Adm. Dodson's Admiralty Reports (165 ER) 1811–22

Dods. Dodson's Admiralty Reports (165 ER) 1811–22
Dom. domestic
Dom. Dominion
Dom.Boc. Domesday Book
Dom.Book Domesday Book
Dom.Civ.Law Domat's Civil Law
Dom.L.R. Dominion Law Reports (Can.) 1912–
Dom.Proc. Domus Procerum (Lat.) House of Lords
Dom.Rel. Domestic Relations
Dom.Rel.Ct. Domestic Relations Court (USA)
Domat Civ.Law Domat's Civil Law
Domat Dr.Pub. Domat's Droit Public
Domei Japanese Confederation of Labour
Domes. Domesday Book
Domst. Domsagostadga (Swed.) Instructions for the District Courts
Don.Tr. Donovan, Modern Jury Trials
Donaker Donaker's Reports (154 Indiana)
Donaldson Report Report of the Commercial Court Committee on Arbitration (Cmnd. 7284) 1978
Donn. Donnell's Irish Land Cases. 1871–76
Donnelly's Chancery Reports (47 ER) 1836–37
Donn.Eq. Donnelly's Chancery Reports (47 ER) 1836–37
Donn.Ir.Land Cas. Donnell's Irish Land Cases. 1871–76
Donnelly Donnelly's Chancery Reports (47 ER) 1836–37
Donovan Report Report of the Royal Commission on Trade Unions and Employers' Associations (Cmnd. 3623) 1968
Dor. Dorion's Queen's Bench Reports, Quebec (Can.) 1880–6
Dor.Bank. Doria, Law and Practice in Bankruptcy. 2ed. 1873
Dor.Md.Laws Dorsey's Maryland Laws
Dor.Q.B. Dorion's Quebec Queen's Bench Reports (Can.) 1880–6
Dorion Dorion's Quebec Queen's Bench Reports (Can.) 1880–6
Dorion (Can.) Dorion's Quebec Queen's Bench Reports (Can.) 1880–6
Dorion Q.B. Dorion's Quebec Queen's Bench Reports (Can.) 1880–6
Doshisha L.J. Doshisha Law Journal, International edition (Japan)
Doug. Douglas' Election Cases. 1774–76
Douglas' King's Bench Reports (99 ER) 1778–85
Douglas' Michigan Supreme Court Reports. 1843–7
Doug.El.Ca. Douglas' Election Cases. 1774–76
Doug.El.Cas. Douglas' Election Cases. 1774–76
Doug.K.B. Douglas' King's Bench Reports (99 ER) 1778–85
Doug.(Mich.) Douglas' Michigan Supreme Court Reports. 1843–7
Dougl.El.Cas. Douglas' Election Cases. 1774–76
Dougl.K.B. Douglas' King's Bench Reports (99 ER) 1778–85
Dougl.(Mich.) Douglas' Michigan Supreme Court Reports. 1843–7
Dow. Dowager
Dow's House of Lords Cases (3 ER) 1812–13
Dowling's Practice Cases (36–61 RR) 1830–41
Dow.Inc. Dowell, Income Tax Acts. 9ed. 1934
Dow N.S. Dow & Clark's House of Lords Appeals (6 ER) 1827–32
Dowling's New Series Bail Court Reports (63–5 RR) 1841–3
Dow P.C. Dow's House of Lords Cases (3 ER) 1812–13
Dowling's Practice Cases (36–61 RR) 1830–41
Dow.P.R. Dowling's Practice Cases (36–61 RR) 1830–41
Dow.St. Dowell, Stamp Duties. 1873
Dow & C. Dow & Clark's House of Lords Cases (6 ER) 1827–32

Dow & Cl. Dow & Clark's House of Lords Cases (6 ER) 1827–32

Dow.& L. Dowling & Lowndes' Bail Court Reports (67–82 RR) 1843–9

Dow.& Ry. Dowling & Ryland's King's Bench Reports (24–30 RR) 1821–7
Dowling & Ryland's Nisi Prius Cases (171 ER) 1822–3

Dow.& Ry.K.B. Dowling & Ryland's King's Bench Reports (24–30 RR) 1821–7
Dowling & Ryland's Nisi Prius Cases (171 ER) 1822–3

Dow.& Ry.M.C. Dowling & Ryland's Magistrates' Cases. 1822–7

Dow.& Ry.N.P. Dowling & Ryland's Nisi Prius Cases (171 ER) 1822–3

Dowl. Dowling's Bail Court (Practice) Cases (36–61 RR) 1830–41

Dowl.N.S. Dowling's Bail Court Reports, New Series (63–5 RR) 1841–3

Dowl.P.C. Dowling's Bail Court (Practice) Cases (36–61 RR) 1830–41

Dowl.P.C.(N.S.) Dowling's Practice Cases, New Series (63–5 RR) 1841–3

Dowl.P.R. Dowling's Practice Cases (36–61 RR) 1830–41

Dowl.Pr. Dowling's Practice Cases (36–61 RR) 1830–41

Dowl.Pr.C.N.S. Dowling's Practice Cases, New Series (63–5 RR) 1841–3

Dowl.Pr.Cas. Dowling's Practice Cases (36–61 RR) 1830–41

Dowl.& L. Dowling & Lowndes' Bail Court Reports (67–82 RR) 1843–9

Dowl.& Lownd. Dowling & Lowndes' Bail Court Reports (67–82 RR) 1843–9

Dowl.& R. Dowling & Ryland's King's Bench Reports (24–30 RR) 1821–7

Dowl.& R.Mag.Cas. Dowling & Ryland's Magistrates' Cases. 1822–7

Dowl.& R.N.P. Dowling & Ryland's Nisi Prius Cases (171 ER) 1822–3

Dowl.& Ryl. Dowling & Ryland's King's Bench Reports (24–30 RR) 1821–7

Dowl.& Ryl.M.C. Dowling & Ryland's Magistrates' Cases. 1822–7

Dowl.& Ryl.N.P. Dowling & Ryland's Nisi Prius Cases (171 ER) 1822–3

Down.& Lud. Downton & Luder's Election Cases

Dowrick, Justice F.E. Dowrick, Justice According to the English Common Lawyers. 1961

Dr. Debtor
Doctor
Drawer
Drewry's Vice Chancellor's Reports tempore Kindersley (61–2 ER) 1852–9
Drury's Irish Chancery Reports tempore Napier. 1858–9
Drury's Irish Chancery Reports tempore Sugden. 1843–4

Dr.ad. Droit administratif (Fr.) administrative law

Dr.Bulgare Droit Bulgare (Bulgaria)

Dr.com. Droit commercial (Fr.) commercial law

Dr.europ. Droit européen (Fr.) european law. 1958–63

Dr.fin. Droit financier (Fr.)

Dr.Informat. Droit de l'Informatique et des Télécoms (Belg.)

Dr.L.R. Drake Law Review (USA) 1951–

Dr.Marit.Fr. Droit Maritime Français (Fr.)

Dr.Polon.Contemp. Droit Polonais Contemporain (Poland)

Dr.R.t.Nap. Drury's Irish Chancery Reports tempore Napier. 1858–9

Dr.R.t.Sug. Drury's Irish Chancery Reports tempore Sugden. 1843–4

Dr.Soc. Droit social (Fr.) 1938–

Dr.t.Nap. Drury's Irish Chancery Reports tempore Napier. 1858–9

Dr.t.Sug. Drury's Irish Chancery Reports tempore Sugden. 1843–4

Dr.trav. Droit du travail: revue mensuelle (Fr.) 1950–

Dr.& Nap. Drury's Irish Chancery Reports tempore Napier. 1858–9

Dr.& Prat.Comm.Intern. Droit et Pratique du Commerce International

(Fr.) International Trade Law and Practice

Dr.& Sm. Drewry & Smale's Vice Chancellor's Reports tempore Kindersley (62 ER) 1860–5

Dr.& Soc. Droit et Societé: Revue Internationale de Théorie de Droit et de Sociologie Juridique (Fr.)

Dr.& Sug. Drury's Irish Chancery Reports tempore Sugden. 1843–4

Dr.& Wal. Drury & Walsh's Irish Chancery Reports. 1837–40

Dr.& War. Drury & Warren's Irish Chancery Reports. 1841–3

Dra. Draper's Upper Canada King's Bench Reports. 1829–31

Drake Att. Drake on Attachment

Drake L.Rev. Drake Law Review (USA) 1951–

Draper Draper's Upper Canada King's Bench Reports. 1829–31

Draper (Can.) Draper's Upper Canada King's Bench Reports. 1829–31

Draper (Ont.) Draper's Upper Canada King's Bench Reports. 1829–31

Drew. Drewry's Chancery Reports tempore Kindersley (61–2 ER) 1852–9
Drew's Reports (13 Florida)

Drew.Ch.F. Drewry, Chancery Forms. 1876

Drew.Eq.Pl. Drewry, Equity Pleading. 1858

Drew.Inj. Drewry, Injunctions. 1841

Drew.Pat. Drewry, Patent Law Amendment Act. 1838

Drew.Tr.M. Drewry, Trade Marks. 1878

Drew.& S. Drewry & Smale's Chancery Reports (62 ER) 1860–5

Drew.& Sm. Drewry & Smale's Chancery Reports (62 ER) 1860–5

Drink. Drinkwater's Common Pleas Reports (60 RR) 1840–1

Drinkw. Drinkwater's Common Pleas Reports (60 RR) 1840–1

Drinkwater Drinkwater's Common Pleas Reports (60 RR) 1840–1

Droit C.C. Droit Civil Canadien

Droit et Justice Droit et Justice: Laurentian University Review (Can.)

Droit pol.cont. Droit polonais contemporain (Poland)

Droits et Liberté Droits et liberté: bulletin de la commission de droits de la personne du Québec (Can.) 1977–

Droits Rev.Fr. Droits: Revue Française de Théorie Juridique (Fr.)

Drone Cop. Drone on Copyrights. 1879

Dru. Drury's Irish Chancery Reports tempore Sugden. 1843–4

Dru.t.Nap. Drury's Irish Chancery Reports tempore Napier. 1858–9

Dru.t.Sug. Drury's Irish Chancery Reports tempore Sugden. 1843–4

Dru.t.Sugden Drury's Irish Chancery Reports tempore Sugden. 1843–4

Dru.& Nap. Drury's Irish Chancery Reports tempore Napier. 1858–9

Dru.& Sug. Drury's Irish Chancery Reports tempore Sugden. 1843–4

Dru.& Wal. Drury & Walsh's Irish Chancery Reports. 1837–40

Dru.& War. Drury & Warren's Irish Chancery Reports. 1841–3

Drug Abuse L.R. Drug Abuse Law Review (USA) 1971–

Drury Drury's Irish Chancery Reports tempore Napier. 1858–9
Drury's Irish Chancery Reports tempore Sugden. 1843–4

Drury (Ir.) Drury's Irish Chancery Reports tempore Napier. 1858–9
Drury's Irish Chancery Reports tempore Sugden. 1843–4

Drury t.Nap. Drury's Irish Chancery Reports tempore Napier. 1858–9

Drury t.Sug. Drury's Irish Chancery Reports tempore Sugden. 1843–4

Drury & Wal. Drury & Walsh's Irish Chancery Reports. 1837–40

Drury & War. Drury & Warren's Irish Chancery Reports. 1841–3

Ds. Departementsserien (Swed.) Series of reports published by the ministries

Dss. Duchess

Dt.Justiz Deutsche Justiz: Amtliches Blatt der deutschen Rechtsflege (Ger.)

Dt.Recht Deutsches Recht: Zentralorgan des Nationalsozialistischen Rechtswahrerbundes (Ger.)
Du.L.J. Duke Law Journal (USA) 1959–
Dubl. Dublin
Dublin U.L.J. Dublin University Law Journal. 1976–
Dublin U.L.Rev. Dublin University Law Review. 1969–70
Dud. Dudley's Georgia Reports. 1830–5
Dudley's South Carolina Law Reports (23 SCL) 1837–8
Dud.Ch. Dudley's South Carolina Equity Reports (13 SCEq) 1837–8
Dud.Eq. Dudley's South Carolina Equity Reports (13 SCEq) 1837–8
Dud.Eq.(S.C.) Dudley's South Carolina Equity Reports (13 SCEq) 1837–8
Dud.(Ga.) Dudley's Georgia Reports. 1830–5
Dud.L. Dudley's South Carolina Law Reports (23 SCL) 1837–8
Dud.L.(S.C.) Dudley's South Carolina Law Reports (23 SCL) 1837–8
Dud.Law Dudley's South Carolina Law Reports (23 SCL) 1837–8
Dud.(S.C.) Dudley's South Carolina Law Reports (23 SCL) 1837–8
Dudl. Dudley's Georgia Reports. 1830–5
Dudley's South Carolina Equity Reports (13 SCEq) 1837–8
Dudley's South Carolina Law Reports (23 SCL) 1837–8
Dudley (Ga.) Dudley's Georgia Reports. 1830–5
Duer Duer's New York Superior Court Reports
Duer Mar.Ins. Duer on Marine Insurance
Duer (NY) Duer's New York Superior Court Reports
Duff Duff, Feudal Conveyancing (Scot.)
Dufresne Dufresne's Glossary
Dug.Orig. Dugdale's Origines Juridicales
Dugd. Dugdale, History, or Antiquity of the Inns of Court
Dugdale, Origines Juridicales
Dugd.Orig.Jur. Dugdale, Origines Juridicales
Duguit, Droit Objectif L. Duguit, L'État, le Droit Objectif et la Loi Positive (Fr.) 1901
Duguit, Droit Privé L. Duguit, Les Transformations Générales du Droit Privé depuis le Code Napoléon (Fr.) 1912
Duguit, Droit Public L. Duguit, Les Transformations Générales du Droit Public (Fr.) 1913
Duke Duke, Law of Charitable Uses. 1676
Duke B.A.J. Duke Bar Association Journal (USA) 1933–41/2
Duke B.A.Jo. Duke Bar Association Journal (USA) 1933–41/2
Duke B.J. Duke University Bar Journal (USA) 1951–8
Duke Ch.Us. Duke, Law of Charitable Uses. 1676
Duke L.J. Duke Law Journal (USA) 1959–
Dulck. Dulcken's Eastern District Reports, Cape Colony (S.Afr.)
Dumont J. De Dumont, Corps Universel Diplomatique de Droit des Gens (Fr.) 1726–31
Dun. Duncan
Dunlap
Dunlop
Dun.& Cum. Dunphy & Cummins' Remarkable Trials
Dunc.Eccl.L. Duncan's Parochial Ecclesiastical Law (Scot.)
Dunc.Ent.Cas. Duncan's Entail Cases (Scot.)
Dunc.Mer.Cas. Duncan's Mercantile Cases (Scot.) 1885–6
Dunc.Merc.Cas. Duncan's Mercantile Cases (Scot.) 1885–6
Dunc.N.P. Duncombe's Nisi Prius
Dund.L.C. Dundee Law Chronicle. 1853–8
Dunelm. Dunelmensis (Lat.) of Durham (signature of Bishop of Durham)

Dunl. Dunlop, Bell & Murray's Reports, Second Series Session Cases (Scot.) 1838–62
Dunl.Abr. Dunlap's Abridgement of Coke's Reports
Dunl.Adm.Pr. Dunlap's Admiralty Practice
Dunl.B.& M. Dunlop, Bell & Murray's Reports, Second Series Session Cases (Scot.) 1838–62
Dunl.(Ct.of Sess.) Dunlop, Bell & Murray's Reports, Second Series Session Cases (Scot.) 1838–62
Dunlop Dunlop, Bell & Murray's Reports, Second Series Session Cases (Scot.) 1838–62
Dunn. Dunning's King's Bench Reports. 1753–4
Dunning Dunning's King's Bench Reports. 1753–4
Dup.Jur. Duponceau, Jurisdiction of United States Courts
Duq. Duquesne Law Review (Pennsylvania) 1968/9–
Duq.L.Rev. Duquesne Law Review (Pennsylvania) 1968/9–
Duquesne U.L.Rev. Duquesne University Law Review. 1963/4–1967/8
Dur. Durham
Durand.Spec.Jur. Durandi Speculum Juris
Durf. Durfee's Reports (2 Rhode Island)
Durie Durie's Decisions, Court of Session (Scot.) 1621–42
Durn.& E. Durnford & East's Term Reports, King's Bench (99–101 ER) 1785–1800
Durzh.Pravo Durzhava i Pravo (Bulgaria)
Dut. Dutch
Dutch. Dutcher's Reports (25–29 New Jersey Law Reports)
Duv. Duvall's Kentucky Reports (62–63 Ky)
Duvall's Supreme Court Reports (Can.)
Duv.(Can.) Duvall's Supreme Court Reports (Can.)
Duvall Duvall's Supreme Court Reports (Can.)
Dux. Duxbury's High Court Reports, South African Republic. 1895
Dw.Stat. Dwarris on Statutes. 2ed. 1848
Dwar. Dwarris on Statutes. 2ed. 1848
Dwar.St. Dwarris on Statutes. 2ed. 1848
Dwight Dwight's Charitable Uses
Dy. Dyer's King's Bench Reports (73 ER) 1513–82
Dyer Dyer's King's Bench Reports (73 ER) 1513–82
Dym.Death Dut. Dymond, Death Duties

E

e. eodem (Lat.) in the same place or title
explained

E. Cases in the Eastern District's Local Division of the Supreme Court (S.Afr.) 1910–46
Earl
Earle, A Handbook to the Land Charters and Other Saxonic Documents
East
East's Term Reports, King's Bench (102–4 ER) 1880–12
Easter Term
Eastern
Ecclesiastical
Edward
Eminence
England
English
Entscheidung (Ger.) decision, judgment
Entwurf (Ger.) Draft
Equity
Exchequer
Explained
Second Class Ship on Lloyd's Register

E159 Public Record Office, memoranda rolls of the King's Remembrancer of the Exchequer

E368 Public Record Office, memoranda rolls of the Lord Treasurer's Remembrancer of the Exchequer

E371 Public Record Office, originalia of the Lord Treasurer's Remembrancer of the Exchequer

E.A. Eastern Africa Law Reports. 1957–
Efetion Athinon (Court of Appeal of Athens)
Europ Archiv

EABC European/ASEAN Business Council

EAC East African Community
European Agency for Co-operation

E.A.C.A. Law Reports of the Court of Appeals for Eastern Africa. 1934–56

EADB East African Development Bank

E.A.E.C. Treaty setting up the European Atomic Energy Community

E.A.G.G.F. European Agricultural Guidance and Guarantee Fund

E.A.H.C. East African High Commission

E.A.J.Criminol. East African Journal of Criminology. 1977–

E.A.L.J. East African Law Journal. 1965–

E.A.L.R. East Africa Protectorate Law Reports. 1897–1921
Eastern Africa Law Review. 1968–

E.A.L.Rev. Eastern Africa Law Review. 1968–

E.A.M.A. African States associated with the E.E.C.

E.A.P.L.R. East Africa Protectorate Law Reports. 1897–1921

E.A.Prot.L.R. East Africa Protectorate Law Reports. 1897–1921

E.A.T. Employment Appeals Tribunal

E.Afr.L.R. East Africa Protectorate Law Reports. 1897–1921
Eastern Africa Law Review. 1968–

E.African L.J. East African Law Journal. 1965–

E.B. Encyclopaedia Britannica

E.B.L.R. European Business Law Review

E.B.L.Rev. European Business Law Review

E.B.U. European Broadcasting Union
E.B.U.Rev. EBU Review (Belg.)
E.B.& E. Ellis, Blackburn & Ellis' Queen's Bench Reports (120 ER) 1858
E.B.& S. Ellis, Best & Smith's Queen's Bench Reports (121–2 ER) 1861–9
E.C. Ecclesiastical Commissioner
Election Cases
Employment Commission
English Chancery Reports (American Reprint)
Established Church
European Communities
Ontario Election Cases (Can.) 1884–1900
ECA Economic Commission for Africa (UN)
Exceptional circumstances allowance
ECAFE Economic Commission for Asia and the Far East (UN)
E.C.Bull. Bulletin of the European Communities
E.C.C. European Cultural Convention. 1954
E.C.C.J. European Communities Court of Justice
E.C.C.P. European Committee on Crime Problems
ECDC Economic Co-operation among Developing Countries (UNCTAD)
ECE Economic Commission for Europe
Export Council for Europe
ECER Rules of Procedure of the Economic Commission for Europe
ECG Export Credit Guarantee
E.C.G.D. Export Credits Guarantee Department
E.C.H.R. European Convention on Human Rights
ECICA European Convention on International Commercial Arbitration. 1961
ECICP European Convention on the International Classification of Patents for Inventions. 1954
ECITO European Central Inland Transport Organisation
E.C.J. Court of Justice of the European Communities
ECJR European Court of Justice Reporter. 1982–
ECLA Economic Commission for Latin America (UN)
E.C.L.R. European Competition Law Review. 1980–
E.C.M. European Common Market
E.C.M.T. European Conference of Ministers of Transport
E.C.O. Entry Clearance Officer (Immigration)
ECOSOC United Nations Economic and Social Council
ECOWAS Economic Community of West African States
ECPSD European Convention for the Peaceful Settlement of Disputes. 1957
E.C.R. Canada Exchequer Court Reports. 1875–1922
European Court Reports. 1954–
ECS European Company Statute
E.C.S.C. European Coal and Steel Community
ECSIM European Centre for Study and Information on Multinational Enterprises
ECSM European Convention on Social and Medical Assistance. 1953
ECU European Currency Unit
ECWA Economic Commission for Western Asia (UN)
E.D. Eastern District Court Reports, Cape of Good Hope (S.Afr.) 1880–1909
Entertainment Duty
Estate Duty(ies)
Études et documents (du Conseil d'État) (Fr.) 1947–
EDA Economic Development Administration
Exclusive dealing agreement
E.D.Ark. District Court for the Eastern and Western Districts of Arkansas (USA)
E.D.C. Eastern District Court Reports, Cape of Good Hope (S.Afr.) 1880–1909
European Defence Community
European Documentation Centre

E.D.C.E. Études et documents du Conseil d'État (Fr.) 1947–
E.D.Cal. District Court for the Eastern District of California (USA)
E.D.D. English Dialect Dictionary
E.D.F. European Development Fund
EDI Electronic data interchange
EDIA Electronic Data Interchange Association
EDICA Electronic Data Interchange Council of Australia
E.D.I.T. Estate Duties Investment Trust
E.D.Ill. District Court for the Eastern District of Illinois (USA)
E.D.Ky. District Court for the Eastern District of Kentucky (USA)
E.D.L. Eastern District Local Division Cases of the Supreme Court (S.Afr.) 1910–46
E.D.La. District Court for the Eastern District of Louisiana (USA)
E.D.Mich. District Court for the Eastern District of Michigan (USA)
E.D.Mo. District Court for the Eastern District of Missouri (USA)
E.D.N.C. District Court for the Eastern District of North Carolina (USA)
E.D.N.Y. District Court for the Eastern District of New York (USA)
E.D.Okla. District Court for the Eastern District of Oklahoma (USA)
E.D.P. Electronic Data Processing
E.D.Pa. District Court for the Eastern District of Pennsylvania (USA)
E.D.R. Roscoe, Eastern District Reports, Cape of Good Hope (S.Afr.)
E.D.S. E.D. Smith's New York Common Pleas Reports
E.D.Smith E.D. Smith's New York Common Pleas Reports
E.D.Smith (N.Y.) E.D. Smith's New York Common Pleas Reports
E.D.Tenn. District Court for the Eastern District of Tennessee (USA)
E.D.Tex. District Court for the Eastern District of Texas (USA)
E.D.Va. District Court for the Eastern District of Virginia (USA)
E.D.Wash. District Court for the Eastern District of Washington (USA)
E.D.Wis. District Court for the Eastern District of Wisconsin (USA)
E.E. Early English
English Exchequer Reports (American Reprint)
Equity Exchequer
errors excepted
E.E.B.L. East European Business Law
E.E.C. European Economic Community (Common Market)
E.E.C.Prot.P.I. Protocol on Privileges and Immunities of the European Economic Community
E.E.D. Epitheorisis Emporikou Dkeou (Gr.)
E.E.G. Europese economische gemeenschap (Neth.) European Economic Community
E.E.L.R. European Environmental Law Review
E.E.N. Efimeris Ellinon Nomikou (Journal of Greek Lawyers)
EEOC Equal Employment Opportunity Commission (USA)
EEOC Compl.Man. Equal Employment Opportunity Commission Compliance Manual (CCH) (USA)
E.E.R. English Ecclesiastical Reports (American Reprint)
European Economic Review
EERA East Europe Research and Analysis
E.E.T.S. Early English Text Society
E.E.& M.P. Envoy Extraordinary and Minister Plenipotentiary
E.Emp.D. Epitheorisis Emporikou Dikeou (Commercial Law Review) (Gr.)
E.Eng. Early English
EExt European Convention on Extradition. 1957
EFG Entscheidungen der Finanzgerichte (Ger.) Reports of the Fiscal Courts. 1953–
EFT Electronic funds tranfer
E.F.T.A. European Free Trade Association

e.g. exempli gratia (Lat.) for example
ejusdem generis (Lat.) of a like kind
EG Einführungsgesetz (Switz.)
E.G. Estates Gazette. 1858–
EGBGB Einführungsgesetz zum Bürgerlichen Gesetzbuch (German implementation Act to the Civil Code)
EG.BGB. Deutsches Recht: Zentralorgan des nationalsozialistischen Rechtswahrerbundes (Ger.)
E.G.C.S. Estates Gazette Case Summaries
E.G.D. Estates Gazette Digest of Cases. 1902–
E.G.D.C. Estates Gazette Digest of Cases. 1902–
EGG Bundesgesetz über die Erhaltung des bauerlichen Grundbesitzes (Switz.) 1951
E.G.L. Encyclopedia of Georgia Law
E.G.L.R. Estates Gazette Law Reports. 1985–
EGM Extraordinary General Meeting
e.G.m.b.H. eingetragene Gesellschaft mit beschränkter Haftung (Ger.) registered company with limited liability
EHG Bundesgesetz betreffend die Haftpflicht der Eisenbahn– und Dampfschiff–fahrtsunternehmungen und der Post (Switz.) 1905
E.H.R.R. European Human Rights Reports. 1979–
EHS Eibun horeisha (Japan) Publishers of laws and ordinances in English
E.I. East India
East Indian
East Indies
Executive Instruments (Ghana) 1960–
EIA European Information Association
EIB Environment Information Bulletin
European Investment Bank
E.I.C. East India Company
Energy Industries Council
European Information Centre
E.I.C.S. East India Civil Service
EIG Bundesgesetz betreffend die elektrischen Schwach– und Starkstromanlagen (Switz.) 1902
E.I.L. Essays on International Law. From the Columbia Law Review. 1965
E.I.P.R. European Intellectual Property Review. 1978–
EIRENE European Information Researchers Network
E.I.R.R. European Industrial Relations Review. 1974–
EIS Environmental Impact Statement
Executive information systems
Export Intelligence Service
E.India Co. East India Company
E.J.I.L. European Journal of International Law
E.L.B. Environment Law Brief
Environmental Law Bulletin (Victoria, Aus.)
Export Licensing Branch (BOTB)
E.L.C.Acts Expiring Laws Continuance Acts
E.L.D. European Law Digest
ELDO Convention for the Establishment of a European Organization for the Development and Construction of Space Vehicle Launchers. 1962
ELF Environmental Law Foundation
E.L.J. Ecclesiastical Law Journal
E.L.M. Environmental Law Monthly
E.L.N. Environmental Law Newsletter (N.S.W., Aus.) 1981–
E.L.R. Eastern Law Reporter (Can.) 1906–14
Election Law Reports (India) 1951–
Environmental Law Reporter of New South Wales (Aus.) 1981–
European Law Review. 1975/6–
E.L.Rev. European Law Review. 1975/6–
E.L.T. Eagle, Law of Tithes. 2ed. 1836
E.L.& Eq. English Law and Equity Reports (American Reprint)
E.L.& P.D. European Life and Pensions Digest
E.M. Earl Marshall
European Mergers
European Movement

E.M.A. European Monetary Agreement
EMCF European Monetary Co-operation Fund
EMPT Uniform International Passenger Tariff
EMRS Export Marketing Research Scheme (BOTB)
EMS European Monetary System
EMU Economic and Monetary Union
E.Min.L.Inst. Eastern Mineral Law Institute (USA)
E.N.D. Epitheorisis Naftiliakou Dikeou (Shipping Law Review) (Gr.)
E.N.E.A. European Nuclear Energy Agency
E.N.L.N. Eastern Nigeria Legal Notice. 1961–
E.N.L.R. Eastern Nigeria Law Reports. 1956–60
Eastern Region of Nigeria Law Reports
ENP Exceptional needs payment
e.o. ex officio (Lat.) by virtue of office
E.O. Executive Officer
Presidential Executive Order (USA)
E.O.C. Equal Opportunities Commission
Equal Opportunity Cases (CCH) (Aus.) 1984–
EONR Convention for the Establishment of a European Organization for Nuclear Research. 1953
e.o.o.e. erreur ou omission exceptée (Fr.) error or omission excepted
E.O.R. Equal Opportunities Review
E.O.T. Equal Opportunity Tribunal
E.P. Estate Planning
European Parliament
E.P.A. Emergency Powers Act 1940
E.P.C. East's Pleas of the Crown. 1803
Roscoe's English Prize Cases. 1745–1859
EP(C)A Employment Protection (Consolidation) Act
E.P.D. Employment Practices Decisions (USA) 1971–
Excess Profits Duty
E.P.D.A. Emergency Powers Defence Act
EPF European Policy Forum
E.P.L.J. Environmental and Planning Law Journal (Aus.) 1984–
EPO European Patent Office
E.P.T. Excess Profits Tax
EPTV European Agreement on the Protection of TV Broadcasts. 1960
E.P.U. European Payments Union
E.R. East's Term Reports, King's Bench (102–4 ER) 1800–12
Eastern Region
Edwardus Rex (King Edward)
Election Reports (Ontario) 1884–1900
Elizabeth Regina (Queen Elizabeth)
English Reports (1–176 ER) 1210–1865
E.R.A. English Reports Annotated. 1866–9, 1900
E.R.C. English Ruling Cases, ed. Campbell. 1894–1908
Environmental Reporter Cases (BNA) (USA)
ERDA Energy Research and Development Administration
E.R.et I. Edwardus Rex et Imperator (Lat.) Edward, King and Emperor
E.R.L.R. Eastern Region of Nigeria Law Reports. 1956–
ERM Exchange Rate Mechanism
E.R.N.L.R. Eastern Region of Nigeria Law Reports. 1956–
E.R.O. European Regional Organisation of the International Confederation of Free Trade Unions
E.R.P.N. Eastern Region Public Notice (Nigeria) 1951–3
E.R.T.A. European Road Transport Agreement
e.s. eldest son
ES European Social Charter. 1961
ESA European Space Agency
E.S.B. English Speaking Board
E.S.C. Economic and Social Committee (EEC)
Economic and Social Council (UN)
ESCAP Economic and Social Commission for Asia and the Pacific (UN)

E.S.C.O.R. Official Records of the Economic and Social Council
E.S.D. Epitheorisis Synkinoniakou Dikeou (Transport Law Review) (Gr.)
ESER Einheitliches System elektronischer Rechentechnik
ESRO Convention for the Establishment of a European Space Research Organization. 1962
European Space Research Organisation
EST Electronic share transfer
ESV Experimental Safety Vehicle
E.School L.Rev. Eastern School Law Review (USA)
EStG Einkommensteuergesetz (Ger.) Income tax law
E.T. Easter Term
English Text
English Translation
Entertainment Tax
Estates Times
E.T.C. an electronic tag used for tax cases on CT Online (Can.)
E.T.L. European Transport Law
E.T.Legal Supp. Estates Times Legal Supplement
E.T.Q. Estates and Trusts Quarterly (Can.) 1973–
E.T.R. Estates and Trusts Reports (Can.) 1977–
E.T.S. Electronic Trading Systems
European Treaty Series of Agreements and Conventions of the Council of Europe
EUA European Unit of Account (EEC)
EURATOM European Atomic Energy Community
EURCO Unite Composite Europeenne
E.U.W. European Union of Women
E.V.D. Economische Voorlichtings Dienst (Neth.) Economic Information Service
EVSt Einfuhr-und Vorratsstelle (German Import Control Body)
E.W. Benelux-Verdrag houdende eenvormige wet betreffende het internationaal privaatrecht (Neth.)
England and Wales
EWC Expected week of confinement
E.W.C. European Works Council (of the Societaas Europea)
EWG Europäische Wirtschaftsgemeinschaft (German abbreviation of the EEC)
EXIMBANK Export-Import Bank (USA)
EXPORTIT Information Technology Export Organisation
EXWC Agreement on the Exchange of War Cripples between Member Countries of the Council of Europe with a view to Medical Treatment. 1955
E.& A. Spinks' Ecclesiastical and Admiralty Reports (164 ER) 1853–55
Grant's Error and Appeal Reports, Ontario (Can.) 1846–66
E.& A.R. Grant's Error and Appeal Reports, Ontario (Can.) 1846–66
E.& A.U.C. Grant's Error and Appeal Reports, Ontario (Can.) 1846–66
E.& B. Ellis & Blackburn's Queen's Bench Reports (118–120 ER) 1852–58
E.& E. Ellis & Ellis' Queen's Bench Reports (120–1 ER) 1858–61
English and Empire Digest
E.& E.D. English and Empire Digest
E.& E.Dig. English and Empire Digest
E.& I. English and Irish Appeals
E.& I.App. Law Reports, English and Irish Appeals House of Lords. 1866–75
E.& L. Education and the Law
E.& O.E. Errors and omissions excepted
E.& T.Q. Estates and Trusts Quarterly (Can.) 1977–
E.& W. England and Wales
E.& Y. Eagle & Younge's Tithe Cases. 1204–1825
Ea. East's Notes of Cases (Bengal, India) 1785–1821
East's Term Reports, King's Bench (102–4 ER) 1800–12
Eag.T. Eagle, Law of Tithes. 2ed. 1836
Eag.& Y. Eagle & Younge's Tithe Cases. 1204–1825
Eag.& Yo. Eagle & Younge's Tithe Cases. 1204–1825

Earn. Earnshaw's Gold Coast Judgments (Ghana) 1909–10
Earnshaw Earnshaw's Gold Coast Judgments (Ghana) 1909–10
Earth L.J. Earth Law Journal (Neth.) 1975–
Earw. Earwalker's Manchester Court Leet Records
East East's Term Reports, King's Bench (102–4 ER) 1801–12
East's Notes of Cases in Morley's East Indian Digest (Bengal, India) 1785–1821
Eastern Reporter
East Af. East Africa Court of Appeals Reports
East Afr.J.Criminol. East African Journal of Criminology. 1977–
East Afr.L.J. East African Law Journal (Kenya) 1965–
East.Afr.L.R. Eastern Africa Law Review (Tanzania) 1968–
East.Afr.L.Rev. Eastern Africa Law Review (Tanzania) 1968–
East.D.C. Eastern District Court Reports (S.Afr.)
East.D.L. Eastern Districts, Local Division, South African Law Reports
East Europ.Q. East European Quarterly
East.J.Int.L. Eastern Journal of International Law (India) 1969–
East.L.R. Eastern Law Reporter (Can.)
East N.of C. East's Notes of Cases (Bengal, India) 1785–1821
East P.C. East's Pleas of the Crown. 1803
East Pak. East Pakistan
East Pl.Cr. East's Pleas of the Crown. 1803
East Punjab All India Reporter, East Punjab. 1948–50
East.Rep. Eastern Reporter
East.T. Easter Term
Eastern J.Int.L. Eastern Journal of International Law (India) 1969–
Ebersole Ebersole's Reports (59–80 Iowa)
Ebersole (Ia.) Ebersole's Reports (59–80 Iowa)
Ebor. Eboracum (Lat.) York
Eboracensis (Lat.) of York. Signature of the Archbishop of York
Ec. Ecclesiastical
Ec.& Mar. Notes of Cases in the Ecclesiastical and Maritime Courts. 1841–50
Ecc. Ecclesiastical
Ecc.L.J. Ecclesiastical Law Journal (USA)
Ecc.& Ad. Spink's Ecclesiastical and Admiralty Reports (164 ER) 1853–55
Eccl. Ecclesiastical
Eccl.R. Ecclesiastical Reports
Eccl.Stat. Ecclesiastical Statutes
Eccl.& Ad. Spink's Ecclesiastical and Admiralty Reports (164 ER) 1853–5
Eccl.& Adm. Spink's Ecclesiastical and Admiralty Reports (164 ER) 1853–5
Ecl.Mag. Eclectic Magazine
Ecl.Rev. Eclectic Review
Ecology L.Q. Ecology Law Quarterly (USA) 1971–
Econ. Economic (s)
Economy
Econ.Bull.for Europe Economic Bulletin for Europe
Econ.Cont. Economic Controls (CCH) (USA)
Econ.Rev. Economic Review
Ed. Eden's Chancery Reports (28 ER) 1757–66
Edgar's Decisions, Court of Session (Scot.) 1724–5
Edinburgh
Edited
Edition
Editor
Edward
Ed.Ass. Eddis, Administration of Assets. 1880
Ed.Bro. Eden's Chancery Reports (28 ER) 1757–66
Ed.C.R. Edwards' New York Chancery Reports
Ed.Ch. Edwards' New York Chancery Reports

Ed.Comment Editorial Comment
Éd.et Ord. Édits et Ordonnances (Lower Canada)
Ed.Gaz. Edinburgh Gazette
Ed.Inj. Eden, Injunctions. 1821
Ed.L.J. Edinburgh Law Journal. 1831–7
Ed.Law Education and the Law
Ed.Rev. Edinburgh Review
Eden Eden's Chancery Reports (28 ER) 1757–66
Eden Bankr. Eden's Bankrupt Law. 3ed. 1832
Eden Pen.Law Eden's Principles of Penal Law
Edg. Edgar
Edgar's Decisions, Court of Session (Scot.) 1724–25
Edg.C. Canons enacted under King Edgar
Edict Edicts of Justinian
Edicta Edicts of Justinian
Edinb.Gaz. Edinburgh Gazette
Edinb.L.J. Edinburgh Law Journal. 1831–7
Edit. Edited
Edition
Editor
Edm. Edmund
Edm.Sel.Ca. Edmonds' New York Select Cases
Edm.Sel.Cas. Edmonds' New York Select Cases
Edm.Sel.Cas.(NY) Edmonds' New York Select Cases
Edmonds'St.at Large Edmonds' Statutes at Large (New York)
Eds. Editions
Editors
Educ. Educated
Education
Educational
Edw. Edward
Edwards' Admiralty Reports (165 ER) 1808–12
Edwards' Chester Palatine Courts
Edwards' New York Chancery Reports. 1831–50
Edwards' Reports (2–3 Missouri)
Edw.Abr. Edwards' Abridgement of Prerogative Court Cases. 1846
Edw.Adm. Edwards' Admiralty Reports (165 ER) 1808–12
Edw.Adm.Jur. Edwards, Admiralty Jurisdiction. 1847
Edw.Bailm. Edwards on the Law of Bailments
Edw.Bills & N. Edwards on Bills and Notes
Edw.Ch. Edwards' New York Chancery Reports. 1831–50
Edw.Ch.(N.Y.) Edwards' New York Chancery Reports. 1831–50
Edw.Conf. Edward the Confessor
Edw.Fac. Edwards, Factors and Brokers
Edw.Lead.Dec. Edwards' Leading Decisions in Admiralty (Edwards' Admiralty Reports) (165 ER) 1808–12
Edw.Mo. Edwards' Reports (2–3 Missouri)
Edw.P.C. Edwards' Prize Cases (Admiralty Reports) (165 ER) 1808–12
Edw.Pr.Cas. Edwards' Prize Cases (Admiralty Reports) (165 ER) 1808–12
Edw.Pr.Ct.Cas. Edwards' Abridgement of Prerogative Court Cases. 1846
Edw.Rec. Edwards on Receivers in Equity
Edw.(Tho.) Edwards' Admiralty Reports (165 ER) 1808–12
Eff. Effective
Efird Efird's Reports (45–56 South Carolina)
Ég.Contemp. L'Égypte contemporaine (Egypt)
Eg.Ext. Egan, Extradition. 1846
L'Égale L'Égale: a Journal of Women and the Law (Can.)
Egan Bills Egan, Bills of Sale. 4ed. 1882
EheG Ehegesetz (Ger.) Marriage Law
Ehrenzweig A.A. Ehrenzweig, Private International Law: a Comparative Treatise on American International Conflicts Law, Including the Law of Admiralty. 1967
Ehrlich, Sociology E. Ehrlich,

Fundamental Principles of the Sociology of Law. 1936

Eil.Wom. Eiloart, Laws relating to Women. 1878

Einspr. Einspruch (Ger.) objection, opposition, caveat

Eir. Lambert's Eirenarcha

ejusd. ejusdem (Lat.) of the same

El. Elchies' Decisions, Court of Session (Scot.) 1733–54

El.B.& E. Ellis, Blackburn & Ellis' Queen's Bench Reports (120 ER) 1858

El.B.& El. Ellis, Blackburn & Ellis' Queen's Bench Reports (120 ER) 1858

El.B.& S. Ellis, Best & Smith's Queen's Bench Reports (121–2 ER) 1861–9

El.Bl.& El. Ellis, Blackburn & Ellis' Queen's Bench Reports (120 ER) 1858

El.Cas. Election Cases (Ontario)
New York Election Cases (Armstrong's)

El.Cas.(NY) New York Election Cases (Armstrong's)

El.Dict. Elchies' Dictionary of Decisions, Court of Session (Scot.)

El.Dig. Eller's Minnesota Digest

El.& B. Ellis & Blackburn's Queen's Bench Reports (118–120 ER) 1851–58

El.& Bl. Ellis & Blackburn's Queen's Bench Reports (118–120 ER) 1851–58

El.& El. Ellis & Ellis' Queen's Bench Reports (120–1 ER) 1858–61

Elch. Elchies' Decisions, Court of Session (Scot.) 1733–54

Elchies Elchies' Decisions, Court of Session (Scot.) 1733–54

Elchies' Dict. Elchies' Dictionary of Decisions, Court of Session (Scot.) 1733–54

eld. elder
eldest

Elec. Election
Electric
Electricity
Electronic

Elec.C. Elections Code

Elec.L.R. Election Law Reports (India) 1951–

Elect.Cas.N.Y. New York Election Cases (Armstrong's)

Elect.Rep. Election Reports (Ontario)

Eliz. Queen Elizabeth

Ell.B.& Ell. Ellis, Blackburn & Ellis' Queen's Bench Reports (120 ER) 1858

Ell.B.& S. Ellis, Best & Smith's Queen's Bench Reports (121–2 ER) 1861–9

Ell.Bl.& Ell. Ellis, Blackburn & Ellis' Queen's Bench Reports (120 ER) 1858

Ell.D.& Cr. Ellis, Debtor and Creditor. 1822

Ell.Dig. Eller's Minnesota Digest

Ell.& Bl. Ellis & Blackburn's Queen's Bench Reports (118–120 ER) 1851–8

Ell.& Ell. Ellis & Ellis' Queen's Bench Reports (120–1 ER) 1858–61

Elliott Supp. Elliott's Supplement to the Indiana Revised Statutes

Ellis & Bl. Ellis & Blackburn's Queen's Bench Reports (118–120 ER) 1851–8

Elm.Dig. Elmer's Digest of Laws (New Jersey)

Elm.Dilap. Elmes on (Ecclesiastical Civil) Dilapidation. 3ed. 1829

Elmer Lun. Elmer's Practice in Lunacy. 7ed. 1892

Elph. Elphinstone, Norton & Clark, Interpretation of Deeds. 1885

Elph.Conv. Elphinstone's Introduction to Conveyancing. 7ed. 1918

Elph.Interp.Deeds Elphinstone's Rules for Interpretation of Deeds. 1885

Els.Lothr.JZ. Juristische Zeitschrift fur Elsass-Lothringen (Ger.)

Els.W.Bl. Elsley's edition of Wm. Blackstone's King's Bench Reports

Elton Com. Elton on Commons and Waste Lands. 1868

Elton Copyh. Elton on Copyholds. 2ed. 1893

Elw.Mal. Elwell on Malpractice and Medical Jurisprudence

Elw.Med.Jur. Elwell on Malpractice and Medical Jurisprudence

Elz. Elzevir

Em.App. Emergency Court of Appeals (USA)

Em.Ct.App. Emergency Court of Appeals (USA)
Em.L.J. Emory Law Journal (USA) 1974–
Emer. Emeritus
Emer.Ct.App. Emergency Court of Appeals (USA)
Emer.Ins. Emerigon on Insurance. 1850
Emer.Mar.Lo. Emerigon on Maritime Loans
Emerig.Tr.des Ass. Emerigon, Traité des Assurances
Emory Int'l L.Rev. Emory International Law Review (USA)
Emory L.J. Emory Law Journal (USA) 1974–
Emp. Emperor
Empire
Empress
Empl.Comp.App.Bd. Decisions of the Employees' Compensation Appeals Board (USA) 1947–
Empl.Prac.Dec. Employment Practices Decisions (CCH) (USA)
Empl.Prac.Guide Employment Practices Guide (CCH) (USA)
Empl.Rel.L.J. Employee Relations Law Journal (USA) 1975–
Empl'rs.Liab. Employer's Liability
En.Users Rep. Energy Users Report (CCH) (USA)
Enc.Amer. Encyclopedia Americana
Enc.Brit. Encyclopaedia Britannica
Enc.Dir. Enciclopedia del diritto (It.)
Enc.Forms Encyclopedia of Forms and Precedents
Enc.jur.D. Encyclopédie juridique Dalloz (Fr.) 1951–
Enc.Law American and English Encyclopedia of Law
Enc.Pl.& Pr. Encyclopedia of Pleading and Practice
Enc.Pl.& Prac. Encyclopedia of Pleading and Practice
Enc.U.S.Sup.Ct.Rep. Encyclopedia of United States Supreme Court Reports
Ency. Encyclopaedia
Ency.Brit. Encyclopaedia Britannica
Ency.Forms Encyclopedia of Forms and Precedents
Ency.L.& P. American and English Encyclopedia of Law and Practice
Ency.Law American and English Encyclopedia of Law and Practice
Ency.of Forms Encyclopedia of Forms and Precedents
Ency.U.S.Sup.Ct. Encyclopedia of United States Supreme Court Reports
End.Interp.Stat. Endlich's Commentaries on the Interpretation of Statutes
Enf'd Enforced
Eng. England
English
English Reports (American reprint by N.C. Moak)
English's Reports (6–13 Arkansas)
Eng.Ad. English Admiralty
English Admiralty Reports (American Reprint)
Eng.Adm.R. English Admiralty Reports (American Reprint)
Eng.C.C. English Crown Cases (American Reprint)
Eng.C.L. English Common Law Reports (American Reprint)
Eng.Ch. English Chancery Reports (American Reprint)
Eng.Cr.Cas. English Crown Cases (American Reprint)
Eng.Com.L.R. English Common Law Reports (American Reprint)
Eng.Ecc.R. English Ecclesiastical Reports (American Reprint)
Eng.Eccl. English Ecclesiastical Reports (American Reprint)
Eng.Exch. English Exchequer Reports (American Reprint)
Eng.Judg. Scotch Court of Session Cases decided by English Judges. 1655–61
Eng.L.& Eq. English Law and Equity Reports (American Reprint)
Eng.L.& Eq.R. English Law and Equity Reports (American Reprint)

Eng.Pr.Cas. Roscoe's Prize Cases. 1745–1858
Eng.R.R.Ca. Railway and Canal Cases. 1835–54
Eng.R.& C.Cas. Railway and Canal Cases. 1835–54
Eng.Rep. English Reports Full Reprint. 1210–1865
English Reports (Moak's American Reprint)
English's Reports (6–13 Arkansas)
Eng.Rep.Anno. English Reports Annotated. 1866–9, 1900
Eng.Rep.R. English Reports (Full Reprint) 1210–1865
Eng.Rep.Re. English Reports (Full Reprint) 1210–1865
Eng.Ru.Ca. English Ruling Cases, ed. by Campbell. 1894–1908
Eng.Rul.Cas. English Ruling Cases, ed. by Campbell. 1894–1908
Eng.& Emp. English and Empire Digest
Eng.& Ir.App. Law Reports, English and Irish Appeal Cases. 1866–75
Engl. England
English English's Reports (6–13 Arkansas)
Eng'r. Engineer
Engineering
Ent. Coke's Entries
Rastell's Entries
Ent.L.R. Entertainment Law Review
Ent.Sta.Hall Entered at Stationers' Hall
Entsch. Entscheidung (Ger.) decision, judgment
Entsch.kgl.Ob.Trib. Entscheidungen des königlichen geheimen Obertribunals (Prussia) 1837–79
Entw. Entwurf (Ger.) draft
Env.Aff. Environmental Affairs (USA)
Env.Extr. Envoy Extraordinary
Env.L. Environmental Law (USA) 1970–
Env.L.Rev. Environment Law Review (USA) 1970–
Env.L.Rptr. Environmental Law Reporter
Env.Law Environmental Law
Env.Risk Environmental Risk
Envir.Conserv. Environmental Conservation
Envir.L.Rep. Environment Law Reporter
Envir.Rep. Environment Reporter (BNA) (USA)
Environm.& Behav. Environment and Behavior (USA)
Environm.L. Environmental Law (USA)
Environm.Policy & L. Environmental Policy and Law (USA)
Envt'l Environmental
Envtl.L. Environmental Law (USA)
Envtl.& Plan.L. Environmental and Planning Law Journal (USA)
Eph.iur.can. Ephemorides iuris canonici (It.) 1945–
Ephem.Hellenon Nom. Ephemeris Hellenon Nomikon (Gr.)
Epiph. Epiphany
Episc. Episcopal
Epith.Empor.Dik. Epitheorisis tou Emporikou Dikaiou (Gr.)
Epith.Kypr.Dik. Epitheorese Kypriakou Dikaiou (Cyprus Law Review)
Eq. Eqitable
Equity
Equity Cases. 1866–75
Equity Court or Division
Eq.Ab. Abridgment of Cases in Equity (21–2 ER) 1667–1744
Eq.Ca.Abr. Abridgment of Cases in Equity (21–2 ER) 1667–1744
Eq.Cas. Equity Cases, 9 Modern Reports (88 ER) 1722–55
Eq.Cas.Abr. Abridgment of Cases in Equity (21–2 ER) 1667–1744
Eq.Cas.Mod. Equity Cases, 9 Modern Reports (88 ER) 1722–55
Eq.Draft. Van Heythuysen's Equity Draftsman, edited by Hughes
Eq.Judg. A'Beckett's Reserved Judgments, New South Wales (Aus.) 1845
Eq.R. Common Law and Equity Reports. 1853–55
Gilbert's Equity Reports (25 ER) 1705–27

Harper's South Carolina Equity Reports. 1824

Eq.Rep. Common Law and Equity Reports. 1853–55
Gilbert's Equity Reports (25 ER) 1705–27
Harper's South Carolina Equity Reports. 1824

Equip. Equipment

Equity Rep. Common Law and Equity Reports. 1853–55
Gilbert's Equity Reports (25 ER) 1705–27
Harper's South Carolina Equity Reports. 1824

Erck Erck's Ecclesiastical Register. 1608–1825

Erg. Ergänzung (Ger.) Amendment, supplement

Erie Co.L.J.(Pa.) Erie County Law Journal (Pennsylvania)

Erl. Erlass (Ger.) decree, edict, order

Erler Festgabe Wirtschaft und Atomenergie im internationalen Recht

Err.& App. Grant's Error and Appeals Reports (Ontario) 1846–66

erron. erroneous
erroneously

Ersk. Erskine's Institutes of the Law of Scotland. 8ed. 1871
Erskine's Principles of the Law of Scotland

Ersk.Dec. Erskine's United States Circuit Court Decisions (35 Georgia)

Ersk.Inst. Erskine's Institutes of the Law of Scotland. 8ed. 1871

Ersk.Prin. Erskine's Principles of the Law of Scotland

Erskine I. Erskine's Institutes of the Law of Scotland. 8ed. 1871

Erskine Inst. Erskine's Institutes of the Law of Scotland. 8ed. 1871

esp. especially

Esp. Espinasse's Nisi Prius Reports (170 ER) 1793–1807

Esp.Act Espinasse, Actions on Statutes

Esp.Bank. Espinasse, Law of Bankrupts. 1825

Esp.Dig. Espinasse's Digest of the Law of Actions at Nisi Prius. 4ed. 1812

Esp.Ev. Espinasse, Evidence. 2ed. 1825

Esp.N.P. Espinasse's Nisi Prius Reports (170 ER) 1793–1807

Esq. Esquire

est. established

Est. Estate(s)

Est.Gaz. Estates Gazette. 1858–

Est.Gaz.Dig. Estates Gazette Digest of Land and Property Cases. 1902–

Est.Powers & Trusts Estates, Powers and Trusts

Est.Prac. Estee's Code Pleading, Practice and Forms

Est.Prac.Pl. Estee's Code Pleading, Practice and Forms

Est.& Trusts Estates and Trusts

Estab. Established
Establishment

Estates Gaz. Estates Gazette. 1858–

Estee Estee's District Court of Hawaii Reports

Estee (Hawaii) Estee's District Court of Hawaii Reports

Estoppel Estoppel: Otago University Law Students' Association (N.Z.) 1975

Estud.Der. Estudios de Derecho (Colombia)

Estudios Trelles L. Legaz Lacambra & L. Garcia Arias (eds.), Estudios de derecho internacional: Homenaje al Profesor Barcia Trelles. 1958

et al. et alia (Lat.) and other things
et alibi (Lat.) and elsewhere
et alii (Lat.) and others

et s. et suivants (Fr.) and following (sections, paragraphs, etc.)

et seq. et sequens, et sequentes or sequentia (Lat.) and the following
et sequitur (Lat.) and as follows

et ux. et uxor (Lat.) and wife

Ét.& Doc.Cons d'État Études et Documents, Conseil d'État (Fr.)

etc. et cetera (Lat.) and the rest

Études Georges Scelle La technique et les principes du droit public: études en honneur de Georges Scelle. 1950

Études Int. Études Internationales (Can.)
EuGRZ Europäische Grundrechte Zeitschrift (Ger.)
EuR. Europarecht (Ger.) 1966–
Euer Euer Doctrina Placitandi
Eun. Wynne's Eunomus
euphem. euphemism
Eur. Europe
European
Eur.Access European Access
EurArch Europa Archiv
Eur.Ass.Arb. European Assurance Arbitration. 1872–75
Eur.C.J. European Court of Justice
Eur.Comm.on Human Rights European Commission on Human Rights
Eur.Commiss.H.R. European Commission on Human Rights
Eur.Conslt.Ass.Deb. Council of Europe, Debates of the Consultative Assembly
Eur.Ct.H.R. European Court of Human Rights
Eur.Intell.Prop.R. European Intellectual Property Review. 1978–
Eur.L.Rev. European Law Review
EurOJ Official Journal of the European Communities
Eur.Parl.Deb. Debates of the European Parliamentary Assembly
Eur.Parl.Doc. European Parliament Working Documents
EurR Europa-Recht (Ger.)
Eur.T.L. European Transport Law (Belg.) 1966–
Eur.T.S. European Treaty Series (Council of Europe)
Eur.Tax. European Taxation (Neth.) 1961–
EurTrL European Transport Law (Belg.) 1966–
EurY European Yearbook/Annuaire Europeen
Euratom European Atomic Energy Community
Euro.Compet.L.Rev. European Competition Law Review
Euro.J.Intl.L. European Journal of International Law
Euro.L.Rev. European Law Review
Euro.Tax. European Taxation (Neth.)
Euro.Transp.L. European Transport Law (Belg.) 1966–
Eurocontrol European Organization for the Safety of Air Navigation
Europ.Bus. European Business
Europ.Compet.L.Rev. European Competition Law Review
Europ.Intell.Prop.Rev. European Intellectual Property Review. 1978–
Europ.J.Pol.Res. European Journal of Political Research (Neth.)
Europ.L.Rev. European Law Review
Europ.Stud.Rev. European Studies Review
Europ.T.S. European Treaty Series
Europ.Transp.L. European Transport Law (Belg.) 1966–
Europ.Yb.in L.& Sociology European Yearbook in Law and Sociology (Neth.)
European Ct.J. European Court of Justice
European Y.B. European Year Book
Ev. Evidence
Ev.Tr. Evans' Trials
Evans Evans' King's Bench Reports. 1756–88
Evans' Reports, Washington Territory
Lord Mansfield's Decisions. 1799–1814
Everybody's L.M. Everybody's Law Magazine (USA) 1928
Evid. Evidence
Ewell Bl. Ewell's edition of Blackstone
Ewell Cas.Inf. Ewell's Leading Cases on Infancy, etc.
Ewell Fix. Ewell, Law of Fixtures.
Ewell L.C. Ewell's Leading Cases on Infancy, etc.
ex. ex (Lat.) without
example
exchange
executive
executor
extract
Ex. Court of Exchequer
Exchequer

Exchequer Reports (154–6 ER) 1847–56
Law Reports, Exchequer. 1865–75
Ex.C.R. Canada Exchequer Court Reports. 1875–1922
Canada Law Reports (Exchequer Court) 1923–
Ex.D. Law Reports, Exchequer Division. 1875–80
ex.div. without dividend
Ex.Div. Law Reports, Exchequer Division. 1875–80
ExFC Agreement between the Government of the UK and the Government of the FRG on the Extradition of Fugitive Criminals. 1960
ex.gr. exempli gratia (Lat.) for example
ex lib. ex libris (Lat.) from the library of
ex off. ex officio (Lat.) by virtue of office
ex p. ex parte (Lat.) on one side only
ex rel. ex relatione (Lat.) on the relation of
Ex.Sess. Extra Sessions
Exam. The Examiner (L'Observateur) (Quebec, Can.) 1861
Examiner The Examiner (L'Observateur) (Quebec, Can.) 1861
Exc. Excellency
Exch. Exchange
Exchequer
Exchequer Reports (Welsby, Hurlstone & Gordon) (154–6 ER) 1847–56
Law Reports, Exchequer. 1865–75
Exch.C. Canada Law Reports, Exchequer Court. 1923–
Exch.C.R. Exchequer Court Reports (Can.) 1875–1922
Canada Law Reports, Exchequer Court. 1923–
Exch.Can. Exchequer Court Reports (Can.) 1875–1922
Canada Law Reports, Exchequer Court. 1923–
Exch.Cas. Exchequer Cases (Scot.) 1840–56
Exch.Ct.(Can.) Canada Law Reports, Exchequer Court. 1923–
Exch.Div. Law Reports, Exchequer Division. 1875–80
Exch.Rep. Exchequer Reports (Welsby, Hurlstone & Gordon) (154–6 ER) 1847–56
Exch.Rep.W.H.& G. Exchequer Reports (Welsby, Hurlstone & Gordon) (154–6 ER) 1847–56
excl. excluded
Exec. Execution
Executive
Executor
Exec.Order Presidential Executive Order (USA)
execx. executrix
Eximbank Export-Import Bank (USA)
Exon. Exoniensis (Lat.) of Exeter, signature of the Bishop of Exeter
exor. executor
exor/s. executors
exp. ex parte (Lat.) on one side only
expenses
expired
explained
expression
expropriation
expld. explained
ExprL Lag om expropriation (Swed.) Expropriation Law. 1917
exr. executor
exrx. executrix
ext. except
extended
extension
external
extract
Ext.Affairs External Affairs: Monthly Bulletin of the Department of External Affairs (Can.)
extd. extended
extl. external
extn. extension
Extra.Sess. Extraordinary Session
exx. executrix
Eyre Eyre's King's Bench Reports tempore William III
Eyre MS Eyre, Manuscript Notes of Cases, King's Bench

F

f. female
folio
followed
footnote

F. Faculty Decisions, Court of Session (Scot.)
Federal Reporter (USA) 1880–1924
Finance
Folge (Ger.) series
Foord, Supreme Court Reports, Cape Colony (S.Afr.) 1880–
Forum
France
Fraser, Session Cases, 5th Series (Scot.) 1898–1906
French

F.2d. Federal Reporter, Second Series (USA) 1924–

F.A. Factory Act
Faculty of Advocates

f.a.a. free of all average

FAA Federal Arbitration Act (USA)

FAIT Families Against Intimidation and Terror (N. Ireland)

FAME Financial Analysis Made Easy (CD-ROM)

FAO Food and Agriculture Organisation (UN)

f.a.s. free alongside ship

F.A.Z. Frankfurter Allgemeine Zeitung

F.Abr. Fitzherbert's Abridgment. 1516

F.B. Föräldrabalk (Swed.) Code on parents and children. 1949
Full Bench

F.B.A. Federal Bar Association (USA)
Fellow of the British Academy

f.b.c. Fallen building clause

F.B.C. Fonblanque's Bankruptcy Reports. 1849–52

f.b.c.w. fallen building clause waiver

F.B.I. Federal Bureau of Investigation
Federation of British Industries
Full Bench Decisions (India)

F.B.J. Federal Bar Journal (USA) 1944/5–

FBL Lag om fastighetsbildning i stad (Swed.) Law on the development of land in municipalities. 1917

F.B.R. Full Bench Rulings, Bengal (India)

F.B.R.N.W.P. Full Bench Rulings, Northwest Provinces (Pak.) 1874

f.c. fidei commissum (Lat.) bequeathed in trust

F.C. All India Reporter, Federal Court. 1947–50
British Guiana Full Court Reports (Official Gazette) 1899–
Canada Law Reports, Federal Court
European Fisheries Convention. 1964
Faculty of Advocates, Collection of Decisions (Scot.) 1738–1841
Federal Cases (USA) 1789–1880
Federal Court
Finance Confidential
Full Court
Full Court Judgments (Ghana) 1919–29

F.C.'20–1 Full Court Judgments (Ghana) 1920–1

F.C.'22 Full Court Judgments (Ghana) 1922

F.C.'23–25 Full Court Judgments (Ghana) 1923–5

F.C.'26–29 Full Court Judgments (Ghana) 1926–9

F.C.A. Federal Code Annotated (USA)
Federal Court of Australia

F.C.C. Federal Communications Commission (USA)
Federal Communications Commission Reports (USA) 1934–
Foreign Compensation Commission

F.C.(C.C.)'19 Full Court Judgments at Cape Coast (Ghana) 1919

FCF Foreign Controlled Firm (Japan)

F.C.Feb.'19 Full Court Judgments (Ghana) 1919

FCI Finance Corporation for Industry

F.C.J. Federal Chief Justice (Nigeria)
Federal Court Judgments (unreported decisions available on QL) (Can.) 1986–

F.C.L. Sarbah, Fanti Customary Law (Ghana)

F.C.N.Treaties Treaties of Friendship, Commerce and Navigation

F.C.O. Foreign & Commonwealth Office

F.C.O.I.T. Flight Crew Officers Industrial Tribunal (Aus.)

F.C.R. Family Court Reporter. 1987–
Fearne on Contingent Remainders. 10ed. 1844
Federal Court Reporter (Aus.) 1982–
Federal Court Reports (Aus.) 1984–
Federal Court Reports (India) 1937–50
Federal Court Reports (Pak.) 1950–
Federal Court Rules (Aus.)

F.C.R.Inf.Bull. Federal Court Reporter Information Bulletin (Aus.) 1982–

F.C.S.C. Foreign Claims Settlement Commission (USA)

F.C.T. Federal Capital Territory

f.c.& s. free from capture and seizure

f'cap foolscap

F.Carr.Cas. Federal Carriers Cases (CCH) 1936–

F.Cas. Federal Cases. 1789–1880

F.Comm. Full Commission

F.(Ct.of Sess.) Fraser's Session Cases (Scot.) 1898–1906

F.Ct.Sess. Fraser's Session Cases (Scot.) 1898–1906

f/d free docks

F.D. Family Division
Fidei Defensor (Lat.) Defender of the Faith

F.D.Cosm.L.Rep. Food, Drug, Cosmetic Law Reporter (CCH) (USA)

F.Dict. Kames & Woodhouslee's (Folio) Dictionary, Court of Session Cases (Scot.) 1540–1796

F.E.C.B. Foreign Exchange Control Board

FECL Foreign Exchange Control Law (Japan)

F.E.L.R. Far Eastern Law Review (Philippines) 1953–

F.E.P. Fair Employment Practice Cases (USA)

F.E.U.L.Q. Far Eastern University Law Quarterly (Philippines)

F.E.U.L.Rev. Far Eastern Law Review (Philippines) 1953–

ff. and following pages

FF Feuille fédérale de la Conféderation Suisse (Switz.) legislative series

FG Finanzgericht (Ger.) Tax Court

f.g.a. free of general average

F.G.C.M. Field General Court Martial

F.(H.L.) Fraser's Session Cases, 5th Series (Scot.) 1898–1906

f.i. for instance

F.I. Il Foro italiano (It.)

F.I.Arb.A. Fellow of the Institute of Arbitrators Australia

FIC Foreign Investment Council (Japan)

F.I.C.Q. Federation of Insurance Counsel Quarterly (USA)

FIL Foreign Investment Law (Japan)

F.I.L.E. Fellow of the Institute of Legal Executives

FIN.E.F.T.A. Finland-European Free Trade Association Treaty

F.I.R.B. Foreign Investment Review Board (Aus.)

FIS Family Income Supplement

f.i.t. free of income tax

F.J. Federal Justice (Nigeria)

F.(J.C.) Fraser, Court of Session Cases (Scot.) 1898–1906

F.JJ. Federal Justices (Nigeria)
F.J.R. Factories Journal Reports (India)
F.J.S. Fiches juridiques suisses (Switz.)
F.K.H.P. Chung-hua Jen-min Kung-ho-kuo Fa-kuei Hui-pien (China) Collection of laws and regulations
F.L.A. Fellow of the Library Association
F.L.A.G. Family Law Action Group (Aus.)
Feminist Legal Action Group (Aus.)
F.L.B. Family Law Bulletin (N.Z.) 1985–
F.L.C. Australian Family Law Cases (in Australian Family Law and Practice) (CCH) 1976–
Family Law Council (Aus.)
F.L.C.W.P. Family Law Council Working Papers (Aus.)
F.L.D. Family Law Digest (Can.) 1984–
F.L.H.P. Fa ling hui pen (China)
F.L.J. Federal Law Journal (India) 1944–9
Federal Law Journal (USA) 1939
Fortnightly Law Journal (Can.) 1931–
F.L.J.(Can.) Fortnightly Law Journal (Can.) 1931–
F.L.J.Ind. Federal Law Journal of India. 1937–43
F.L.N. Family Law Notes (in New Zealand Family Law Reports) 1981–
F.L.P. Florida Law and Practice
F.L.R. Family Law Reports. 1980–
Family Law Reports (Aus.) 1976–
Family Law Review (Can.) 1978–
Federal Law Reports (Aus.) 1956–
Federal Law Reports (India)
Federal Law Review (Aus.) 1964–
Fiji Law Reports. 1875–1959
University of Florida Law Review. 1948–
F.L.R.A.C. Family Law Reform Act Cases (Ontario, Can.) 1980–
F.L.R.R. Family Law Reform Reporter (Ontario, Can.) 1978–
F.L.Rev. Federal Law Review (Aus.) 1964–
F.L.T. Family Law Today
F.M.B. Federal Maritime Board (USA)
F.M.I. Financial Management Initiative
Fonds Monétaire International
F.M.S. Federated Malay States
F.M.S.L.R. Federated Malay States Reports. 1899–1941
F.M.S.R. Federated Malay States Reports. 1899–1941
F.Mac.N. MacNaghten, Hindu Law (India)
F.Moore King's Bench Reports (72 ER) 1512–1621
F.N.B. Fitzherbert's Natura Brevium
F.N.C.B. First National City Bank
F.N.D. Finnemore's Notes and Digest of Natal Cases (S.Afr.) 1860–67
FNV Federatie van Nederlandse Vakverenigingen (Neth.) Federation of Dutch Trade Unions
f.o.b. free on board
f.o.c. free of charge
f.o.d. free of damage
FOI Freedom of information
FOI Handbook Freedom of Information Handbook, Victoria (Aus.) 1985–
FoI Review Freedom of Information Review (Aus.) 1986–
F.O.R. Foreign Office Reports
F.of M. Federation of Malaya
F.P. Federal Parliament
Field Punishment
f.p.a. free of particular average
FPAdR Fundamental Principles of Legislation of the USSR and Union Republics on Administrative Responsibility
F.P.C. Federal Power Commission Reports (USA) 1931–
FPCivL Fundamental Principles of Civil Legislation of the USSR and Union Republics
FPCivPL Fundamental Principles of Civil Procedure Legislation of the USSR and Union Republics
FPCorL Fundamental Principles of Correctional-Labour Legislation of the USSR and Union Republics

FPCrimL Fundamental Principles of Criminal Legislation of the USSR and Union Republics
FPCrimP Fundamental Principles of Criminal Procedure Legislation of the USSR and Union Republics
FPFL Fundamental Principles of Legislation of the USSR and Union Republics on Forestry
F.P.I. Federal Publications Inc.
FPL Fundamental Principles of Legislation of the USSR and Union Republics
FPLCOrg Fundamental Principles of Legislation of the USSR and Union Republics on Court Organisation
FPLL Fundamental Principles of Land Legislation of the USSR and Union Republics
FPLabL Fundamental Principles of the USSR and Union Republics on Labour Legislation
FPML Fundamental Principles of Legislation of the USSR and Union Republics on Minerals
FPMarL Fundamental Principles of Legislation of the USSR and Union Republics on Marriage and the Family
FPPubEd Fundamental Principles of Legislation of the USSR and Union Republics on Public Education
FPPubH Fundamental Principles of Legislation of the USSR and Union Republics on Public Health
F.P.R. Federal Procurement Regulations
Fisheries Pollution Reports (Can.) 1976–
FPWL Fundamental Principles of Water Legislation of the USSR and Union Republics
F.pad. Il Foro padano (It.)
f.r. folio recto (Lat.) right hand page
F.R. Federal Register (USA) 1936–
Federal Reporter (USA) 1880–
Federal Republic
Fordham Law Review (New York) 1914–
Foreign Relations
FRA Federal Railroad Administration (USA)
Federal Reports Act (USA)
F.R.B. Federal Reserve Bulletin (USA)
F.R.C.P. Federal Rules of Civil Procedure (USA)
F.R.D. Federal Rules Decisions (USA) 1938–
FRF Foreign Related Firm (Japan)
FRG Family Rights Group
F.R.N.Z. Family Reports of New Zealand. 1983–
F.R.R. Financial Regulation Report
FRU Free Representation Unit
F.R.& N. Federation of Rhodesia and Nyasaland
F.S. Fabian Society
Federal Supplement (USA) 1932–
Friendly Society
F.S.A. Federal Statutes Annotated
Florida Statutes Annotated
Friendly Societies Act
FSB Federation of Small Businesses
F.S.C. Selected Judgments, Federal Supreme Court (Nigeria) 1956–61
F.S.C.(Nig.) Judgments of the Federal Supreme Court (Nigeria) 1956–61
F.S.L.L. Financial Services Law Letter
F.S.P.R. Fleet Street Reports of Patent Cases. 1963–
F.S.R. Fleet Street Reports of Patent Cases. 1963–
F.Supp. Federal Supplement (USA) 1932–
F/T Foreign Trade
F.T. Financial Times
Förvaltningsrättslig tidskrift (Swed.) administrative law periodical. 1938–
FTA Free Trade Agreement
FTAC Foreign Trade Arbitration Commission
F.T.C. Fair Trade Commission (Japan)
Federal Trade Commission Decisions (USA) 1915–
Foreign Trade Corporation
F.T.L.R. Financial Times Law Reports
FTO Foreign Trade Organization

FTR Australian Federal Tax Reporter (CCH) 1969–
F.T.R. Federal Trial Reports (Can.) 1986–
F.Tr. 'Fusion Treaty' setting up a single Commission of the European Communities, 8 April 1965
f.v. folio verso (Lat.) left hand page, on the back of the page
F.W.A. Factories and Workshops Act
Family Welfare Association
F.W.I. Federation of West Indies
FX Foreign Exchange
F.& C.C. Fire and Casualty Cases (CCH)
f.& d. freight and demurrage
F.& F. Foster & Finlason's Nisi Prius Reports (175–6 ER) 1858–67
F.& Fitz. Falconer & Fitzherbert's Election Cases. 1835–38
F.& J.Bank. De Gex, Fisher & Jones' Bankruptcy Reports. 1859–61
F.& S. Fox & Smith's Irish King's Bench Reports. 1822–24
Fox & Smith's Registration Cases. 1886–1895
F.& W.Pr. Frend & Ware, Precedents of Instruments – Transfer of Land to Railway Companies. 2ed. 1866
Fac. Faculty of Advocates, Collection of Decisions, Court of Session (Scot.) 1738–1841
Fac.Coll. Faculty of Advocates, Collection of Decisions, Court of Session (Scot.) 1738–1841
Fac.Dec. Faculty of Advocates, Collection of Decisions, Court of Session (Scot.) 1738–1841
Fac.L.Rev. Faculty of Law Review, Toronto University (Can.) 1956–
Fac.of L.R. Faculty of Law Review, Toronto University (Can.) 1956–
Face/Justice Face à la Justice (Can.)
Facs. Facsimile
Facsimile Transmission
Fair Empl.Prac.Cas. Fair Employment Practices Cases (USA)
Fairf. Fairfield's Reports (10–12 Maine)
Fairf.(Me.) Fairfield's Reports (10–12 Maine)
Falc. Falconer's Decisions, Court of Session (Scot.) 1744–1751
Falc.Co.Cts. Falconer's Reports, County Court Cases. 1870
Falc.& F. Falconer & Fitzherbert's Election Cases. 1835–8
Falc.& Fitz. Falconer & Fitzherbert's Election Cases. 1835–8
Falk.Is. Falkland Islands
Fam. Family
Fam.Adv. Family Advocate (USA) 1978–
Fam.Cas.Cir.Ev. Famous Cases of Circumstantial Evidence, by Phillips
Fam.Ct. Family Court
Fam.I.S. Family Impact Seminar (Aus.)
Fam.L.N. Family Law Notes (Aus.) 1975–
Family Law Notes (in Federal Law Reports) (Aus.) 1976–9
Fam.L.Q. Family Law Quarterly (USA) 1967–
Fam.L.R. Family Law Reports (Aus.) 1976–
Fam.L.Rep. Family Law Reporter (BNA) (USA)
Family Law Reports. 1980–
Family Law Reports (Aus.) 1976–
Fam.L.Rev. Family Law Review (Can.)
Fam.Law Family Law. 1971–
FamRZ Zeitschrift für das gesamte Familienrecht (Ger.) 1954–
Family Adv. Family Advocate (USA) 1978–
Family L. Family Law. 1971–
Family L.Q. Family Law Quarterly (USA) 1967–
Far. Farresley's Cases in Holt's King's Bench Reports
Farresley's Reports (7 Modern Reports) (87 ER) 1733–45
Far East.L.R. Far Eastern Law Review (Philippines) 1953–
Far East.Rev. Far Eastern Review
Far Eastern Q. Far Eastern Quarterly
Farm T.B. Farm Tax Brief

Farm T.& F. Farm Tax and Finance
Farr. Farresley's Reports (7 Modern Reports) (87 ER) 1733–45
Farrand Committee Conveyancing Committee (Julian T. Farrand, chairman) (Lord Chancellor's Department) 1st Report: non-solicitor conveyances: competence and consumer protection. 1984. 2nd Report: conveyancing simplifications. 1985
Farrant Digest of Manx Cases. 1925–47
Farresley Farresley's Reports (7 Modern Reports) (87 ER) 1733–45
Farwell Farwell on Powers. 3ed. 1916
fasc. fascicule (Fr.) fascicolo (It.) part of, or number of, a periodical or book
Fauchille Traité de droit international public (Fr.) Vol. 1: Peace. 1922–26. Vol. 2: War. 1921.
Faulks' Report Lord Chancellor's Office Report of the Committee on Defamation (Cmnd. 5909) 1975
Faust Faust's Compiled Laws (South Carolina)
Fawc. Fawcett, Court of Referees. 1866
Fawc.Ref. Fawcett, Court of Referees. 1866
Fawcett Fawcett on Landlord and Tenant. 3ed. 1905
Fax Facsimile transmission
Faxue Lun Ts'ung Faxue Lun Ts'ung: National Taiwan University Law Journal
Faxue Pinglun Faxue Pinglun: Legal Science Review (China)
Faxue Yanjiu Faxue Yanjiu: Studies in Law (China)
Fay.L.J. Fayette Legal Journal (Pennsylvania)
fcp foolscap
Fdn. Foundation
Fear.Rem. Fearne on Contingent Remainders. 10ed. 1844
fec. fecit (Lat.) he/she made it
Fed. Federal
Federal Reporter (USA)
The Federalist, by Hamilton
Fed.2d Federal Reporter, Second Series
Fed.Anti-Tr.Cas. Federal Anti-Trust Cases, Decrees and Judgments. 1890–1918
Fed.Anti-Tr.Dec. Federal Anti-Trust Decisions. 1890–1931
Fed.B.A.J. Federal Bar Association Journal (USA) 1931–1943/4
Fed.B.A.Jo. Federal Bar Association Journal (USA) 1931–43/4
Fed.B.J. Federal Bar Journal (USA) 1944/5–
Fed.B.N. Federal Bar News (USA) 1952–
Fed.B.News & J. Federal Bar News and Journal (USA)
Fed.Banking L.Rep. Federal Banking Law Reporter (CCH) (USA)
Fed.Bar J. Federal Bar Journal (USA) 1944/5–
Fed.Ca. Federal Cases (USA) 1789–1880
Fed.Carr.Cas. Federal Carrier Cases (CCH) (USA) 1936–
Fed.Carr.Rep. Federal Carriers Reporter (CCH) (USA)
Fed.Cas. Federal Cases (USA) 1789–1880
Fed.Cas.No. Federal Case Number
Fed.Comm.B.J. Federal Communications Bar Journal (USA) 1937–
Fed.Comm.L.J. Federal Communications Law Journal (USA)
Fed.Cncl.Aust. Federal Council of Australasia
Fed.Ct. Federal Court of Australia
Indian Rulings, Federal Court. 1938–47
Fed.Est.& Gift Tax Rep. Federal Estate and Gift Tax Reporter (CCH) (USA)
Fed.Ex.Tax Rep. Federal Excise Tax Reporter (CCH) (USA)
Fed.Juror Federal Juror (USA) 1929–
Fed.L.J. Federal Law Journal (India) 1944–9
Federal Law Journal (USA) 1939
Fed.L.J.Ind. Federal Law Journal of India. 1937–43
Fed.L.Q. Federal Law Quarterly. 1918

Fed.L.R. Federal Law Reports (Aus.) 1956–
Federal Law Review (Aus.) 1964–
Fed.L.Rep. Federal Law Reports
Fed.L.Rev. Federal Law Review (Aus.) 1964–
Fed.Nigeria Federation of Nigeria
Fed.Prob. Federal Probation (Washington, D.C.) 1938–
Fed.Prob.N.L. Federal Probation Newsletter (USA) 1937
Fed.R. Federal Reporter (USA) 1880–
Fed.R.Civ.P. Federal Rules of Civil Procedure
Fed.R.D. Federal Rules Decisions (USA) 1941–
Fed.R.Evid. Federal Rules of Evidence
Fed.Reg. Federal Register (USA) 1936–
Fed.Rep. Federal Reporter (USA) 1880–
Fed.Res.Bull. Federal Reserve Bulletin (USA) 1915–
Fed.Rules Civ.Proc. Federal Rules of Civil Procedure
Fed.Rules Cr.Proc. Federal Rules of Criminal Procedure
Fed.Rules Dec. Federal Rules Decisions (USA) 1941–
Fed.Rules Serv. Federal Rules Service
Fed.Rules Serv.2d Federal Rules Service, Second Series
Fed.Sec.L.Rep. Federal Securities Law Reporter (CCH) (USA)
Fed.Stat.Ann. Federal Statutes Annotated
Fed.Sup. Federal Supplement (USA) 1932–
Fed.Supp. Federal Supplement (USA) 1932–
Fed.Taxes Federal Taxes (P–H) (USA)
Fed.Taxes Est.& Gift Federal Taxes: Estate and Gift Taxes (P–H) (USA)
Fed.Taxes Excise Federal Taxes: Excise Taxes (P–H) (USA)
Fed.Tr.Rep. Federal Trade Reporter (USA)
Fed'n Federation
Fed'n Ins.Counsel.Q. Federation of Insurance Counsel Quarterly (USA) 1950–
Fed'n Ins.& Corp.Couns.Q. Federation of Insurance and Corporate Counsel Quarterly (USA)
Fent. Fenton's Important Judgments in the Compensation Court and Native Land Court (N.Z.) 1866–79
Fent.Imp.Judg. Fenton's Important Judgments (N.Z.) 1866–79
Fent.N.Z. Fenton's Important Judgments (N.Z.) 1866–79
Fent.(New Zealand) Fenton's Important Judgments (N.Z.) 1866–79
Fenton Fenton's Important Judgments (N.Z.) 1866–79
Ferard Fixt. Amos & Ferard on Fixtures
Ferg. Ferguson of Kilerran's Session Cases (Scot.) 1738–52
Ferguson's Consistorial Decisions (Scot.) 1811–17
Fergusson's Scotch Railway Cases
Ferg.Cons. Ferguson's Consistorial Decisions (Scot.) 1811–17
Ferg.M.& D. Ferguson's Divorce Decisions by Consistorial Courts (Scot.)
Ferg.Ry.Cas. Fergusson's Railway Cases (Scot.)
Ferguson Ferguson's Consistorial Decisions (Scot.) 1811–17
Ferguson of Kilerran's Session Cases (Scot.) 1738–52
Ferreira J.C. Ferreira, Strafprosesreg in die Landdroshof (S.Afr.)
Ferrière Ferrière's Dictionnaire de Droit et de Pratique
Fess.Pat. Fessenden on Patents
Fett.Carr. Fetter's Treatise on Carriers of Passengers
Feud. Feudal
Feud.Lib. The Book of Feuds (Liber Feudorum)
Feversham Cttee. Committee on Human Artificial Insemination. Report (Cmnd. 1105) 1960
fi.fa. fieri facias (Lat.) that you cause to be done
Fid.Def. Fidei Defensor (Lat.) Defender of the Faith

Fid.L.Chron. Fiduciary Law Chronicle (USA) 1929–32
Fiduciary Fiduciary Review (Pennsylvania) 1933–9
Field Corp. Field on Corporations
Fiji L.R. Fiji Law Reports. 1875–1959
Fin. Finance
Financial
Finch's Reports, Chancery (23 ER) 1673–81
Finland
Finlay's Irish Digest. 1769–71
Fin.C. Financial Code
Fin.Dig. Finlay's Irish Digest. 1769–71
Fin.H. Finch's Chancery Reports (23 ER) 1673–81
Fin.L.R. Financial Law Reports
Fin.PR T. Finch's Precedents in Chancery (24 ER) 1689–1723
Fin.Pr. T. Finch's Precedents in Chancery (24 ER) 1689–1723
Fin.Prec. T. Finch's Precedents in Chancery (24 ER) 1689–1723
Fin.T. Finch's Precedents in Chancery (24 ER) 1689–1723
Fin.& Dul. Finnemore & Dulcken's Natal Law Reports (S.Afr.) 1873–9
Finch Finch's Precedents in Chancery (24 ER) 1689–1723
Chancery Reports tempore Finch (23 ER) 1673–81
Finch Cas.Cont. Finch's Cases on Contract. 1886
Finch Cas.Contr. Finch's Cases on Contract. 1886
Finch Nomot. Finch's Nomotechnia. 1613
Finch Prec. Finch's Precedents in Chancery (24 ER) 1689–1723
Finer Cttee. Committee on One-Parent Families. Report (Cmnd. 5629) 1974
Finl.Dig. Finlay's Irish Digest. 1769–71
Finl.L.C. Finlason's Leading Cases on Pleading. 1847
Finl.Rep. Finlason's Report of the Gurney Case
Finl.Ten. Finlason, History of the Law of Tenures of Land. 1870
Fire & Casualty Cas. Fire and Casualty Cases (CCH) (USA) 1939–
First Bk.Judg. First Book of Judgments. 1655
First Book Judg. First Book of Judgments. 1655
First Pt.Edw.III Part II of the Year Books
First Pt.H.VI Part VII of the Year Books
Fish. Fisher's U.S. Patent Cases. 1848–73
Fisher's U.S. Prize Cases
Fish.C.L.Dig. Fisher's Common Law Digest
Fish.Cas. Fisher's Cases, United States District Courts
Fish.Crim.Dig. Fisher's Digest of English Criminal Law
Fish.Dig. Fisher's English Common Law Digest
Fish.Mortg. Fisher on Mortgages. 9ed. 1977
Fish.Pat. Fisher's United States Patent Cases. 1848–73
Fish.Pat.Cas. Fisher's United States Patent Cases. 1848–73
Fish.Pat.Rep. Fisher's United States Patent Reports. 1821–50
Fish.Pr.Cas. Fisher's United States Prize Cases
Fish.Prize Fisher's United States Prize Cases
Fish.Prize Cas. Fisher's United States Prize Cases
Fish & G.C. Fish and Game Code (California)
Fish.& L.Mort. Fisher & Lightwood, Mortgages
Fisher Fisher & Lightwood on Mortgages
Fisher's Patent Cases (USA) 1848–73
Fisher's Patent Reports (USA) 1821–50
Fisher's Prize Cases (USA)
Fisher Pat.Cas.(F.) Fisher's Patent Cases (USA) 1848–73
Fisher Pr.Cas.(F.) Fisher's Prize Cases (USA)

Fisher Pr.Cas.(Pa.) Fisher's Pennsylvania Prize Cases

Fisher & Lightwood Fisher & Lightwood on Mortgages

Fisk Anal. Fisk, Analysis of Coke on Littleton. 1824

Fisk Report Public access to environmental information: report of an interdepartmental working party on public access to information held by pollution control authorities (DOE) 1986

Fitz.Abridg. Fitzherbert's Abridgement. 1516

Fitz.-G. Fitzgibbon's King's Bench Reports (94 ER) 1727–31

Fitz.L.G.Dec. Fitzgibbon, Irish Local Government Decisions

Fitz.Land R. Fitzgibbon's Land Reports (Ire.) 1895–1920

Fitz.Nat.Brev. Fitzherbert's Natura Brevium. 1534

Fitzg. Fitzgibbon's King's Bench Reports (94 ER) 1727–31
Fitzgibbon's Land Reports (Ire.) 1895–1920
Fitzgibbon's Registration Appeals (Ire.) 1894

Fitzg.L.G.Dec. Fitzgibbon's Irish Local Government Decisions

Fitzg.Land R. Fitzgibbon's Irish Land Reports. 1895–1920

Fitzg.Reg.Ca. Fitzgibbon's Irish Registration Appeals. 1894

Fitzh.Abr. Fitzherbert's Abridgement. 1516

Fitzh.N.B. Fitzherbert's Natura Brevium. 1534

Fitzh.N.Br. Fitzherbert's Natura Brevium. 1534

Fitzh.Nat.Brev. Fitzherbert's Natura Brevium. 1534

Fixt. Fixtures

Fl. Fleta, seu Commentarius Juris Anglicani. 1647
Florida

Fl.L.R. University of Florida Law Review. 1948–

Fl.S. Florida Supplement. 1952–

Fl.& K. Flanagan & Kelly's Irish Rolls Court Reports. 1840–42

Fla. Florida
Florida Supreme Court Reports. 1846–1948

Fla.B.J. Florida Bar Journal. 1953–

Fla.Dig. Thompson's Digest of Laws (Florida)

Fla.Jur. Florida Jurisprudence

Fla.Just. Florida Justice. 1938–9

Fla.L.J. Florida Law Journal. 1934–53

Fla.L.Rev. University of Florida Law Review. 1948–

Fla.Laws Laws of Florida

Fla.R.C. Railroad Commission for the State of Florida

Fla.S.B.A.Jo. Florida State Bar Association Law Journal. 1927–34

Fla.S.B.A.L.J. Florida State Bar Association Law Journal. 1927–34

Fla.Sess.Law Serv. Florida Session Law Service (West)

Fla.Stat. Florida Statutes

Fla.Stat.Ann. Florida Statutes Annotated

Fla.Stat.Anno. Florida Statutes Annotated

Fla.State L.J. Florida State Law Journal

Fla.State Univ.L.Rev. Florida State University Law Review

Fla.Supp. Florida Supplement. 1952–

Flan.& K. Flanagan & Kelly's Irish Rolls Court Reports. 1840–42

Flan.& Ke. Flanagan & Kelly's Irish Rolls Court Reports. 1840–42

Flan.& Kel. Flanagan & Kelly's Irish Rolls Court Reports. 1840–42

Fland.Ch.J. Flanders' Lives of the Chief Justices of the United States

Flax.Reg. Flaxman, Registration of Births and Deaths. 1875

Fleta Fleta, seu Commentarius Juris Anglicani. 1647

Fleury Hist. Fleury's History of the Origin of French Laws. 1724

Flint.R.Pr. Flintoff, Real Property. 1839–40

Flip. Flippin's Circuit Court Reports (USA)
Flipp.(F.) Flippin's Circuit Court Reports (USA)
Flood El.Eq. Flood, Equitable Doctrine of Election. 1880
Flood Lib. Flood, Slander and Libel. 1880
Flor. Florida
Florida Reports. 1846–1948
Florida Florida Reports. 1846–1948
Florida B.J. Florida Bar Journal. 1953–
Flournoy-Hudson Flournoy & Hudson, A Collection of Nationality Laws. 1929
Fluckiger, Geschichte F. Fluckiger, Geschichte des Naturrechts (Ger.) 1954
fo. folio
Fo.L.R. Fordham Law Review (USA) 1914–18, 1934–
Foelix Dr.Int. Foelix, Droit International Privé
Fogg Fogg's Reports (32–35 New Hampshire)
Fol. Foley's Poor Law Cases. 1556–1730
folio
Fol.Dic. Kames & Woodhouselee's Folio Dictionary, Court of Session (Scot.) 1540–1796
Fol.Dict. Kames & Woodhouselee's Folio Dictionary, Court of Session (Scot.) 1540–1796
Fol.P.L.C. Foley's Poor Law Cases. 1556–1730
Fol.P.L.Cas. Foley's Poor Law Cases. 1556–1730
Folk.Pl. Folkard, Loans and Pledges. 2ed. 1876
foll. followed in
following
fols. folios
Fon.B.C. Fonblanque's Bankruptcy Reports. 1849–52
Fonb.Eq. Fonblanque's Equity. 5ed. 1820
Fonbl. Fonblanque's Bankruptcy Reports. 1849–52
Fonblanque's Equity. 5ed. 1820
Fonblanque's Medical Jurisprudence
Fonbl.Eq. Fonblanque's Equity. 5ed. 1820
Fonbl.Med.Jur. Fonblanque's Medical Jurisprudence
Fonbl.N.R. Fonblanque's New Reports in Bankruptcy. 1849–52
Fonbl.R. Fonblanque's Cases (or New Reports) in Bankruptcy. 1849–52
Fonbl.R.& Wr. Fonblanque, Rights and Wrongs. 1860
Fontes Fontes Iuris Gentium
Food Drug Cos.L.Rep. Food, Drug and Cosmetic Law Reporter (CCH) (USA)
Food Drug Cosm.L.J. Food, Drug, Cosmetic Law Journal (CCH) 1950–
Food Drug Cosm.L.Q. Food, Drug, Cosmetic Law Quarterly. 1946–9
Food L.M. Food Law Monthly
Food & Agric. Food and Agriculture: International Law Journal (F.A.O.) (It.) 1947
Food & Drugs I.B. Food and Drugs Industry Bulletin
Foord Foord's Supreme Court Reports, Cape Colony (S.Afr.) 1880
For. Foreign
Forensic
Forrest's Exchequer Reports (145 ER) 1800–1801
Forrester's Chancery Reports (cases tempore Talbot) (25 ER) 1733–38
Fortescue, de Laudibus Legum Angliae. 1616
For.Aff. Foreign Affairs. 1919–31
Foreign Affairs (USA) 1922–
For.Cas.& Op. Forsyth's Cases and Opinions on Constitutional Law. 1704–1856
For.de Laud. Fortescue, de Laudibus Legum Angliae. 1616
For.Exch.Bull. Foreign Exchange Bulletin (Association of American Law Schools)
For.Pla. Brown's Formulae Bene Placitandi
For.Pr. Foran, Code of Civil Procedure of Quebec
For.Q. Foreign Quarterly Review

For.Rev. Forum Review
For.Tax L.S.-W.Bull. Foreign Tax Law Semi-Weekly Bulletin (USA) 1953–
For.Tax L.W.Bull. Foreign Tax Law Weekly Bulletin (USA) 1950–3
Forb. Forbes' Cases in St Andrews Bishops Court
Forbes' Decisions in the Court of Session (Scot.) 1705–13
Forb.Inst. Forbes' Institutes of the Law of Scotland
Forbes Forbes' Decisions in the Court of Session (Scot.) 1705–13
Ford.L.Rev. Fordham Law Review (USA) 1914–18, 1934–
Ford Oa. Ford, Oaths. 8ed. 1903
Ford.Urban L.J. Fordham Urban Law Journal (USA) 1972–
Fordham Corp.Inst. Proceedings of the Fordham Corporate Law Institute (USA)
Fordham Int'l L.Forum Fordham International Law Forum (USA)
Fordham Int'l L.J. Fordham International Law Journal
Fordham L.Rev. Fordham Law Review (USA) 1914–18, 1934–
Fordham Urb.L.J. Fordham Urban Law Journal (USA) 1972–
Foreign L.Ser. Foreign Law Series (Fr.)
Forester Forrester's Cases tempore Talbot (25 ER) 1733–8
Form. Forman's Reports (1 Scammon, 2 Illinois)
Form.Pla. Brown, Formulae Bene Placitandi
Forman Forman's Reports (1 Scammon, 2 Illinois)
Foro It. Foro Italiano (It.) 1876–
Foro Ital. Foro Italiano (It.) 1876–
Foro Ital.Rep. Foro Italiano, Repertorio (It.)
Foro Nap. Foro Napoletano (It.) 1951–
Foro Pad. Foro Padano (It.)
Foro Pen. Foro Penale (Naples, It.) 1946–
Foro Penale (Rome, It.) 1891–1901
Forr. Forrest's Exchequer Reports (145 ER) 1800–1801
Forrester's Chancery Cases tempore Talbot (25 ER) 1733–38
Forrest Forrest's Exchequer Reports (145 ER) 1800–1801
Forrester Forrester's Chancery Cases tempore Talbot (25 ER) 1733–38
Fors.Cas.& Op. Forsyth's Cases and Opinions on Constitutional Law. 1704–1856
Fort. Fortescue's King's Bench Reports (92 ER) 1695–1738
Fortnightly
Fort.de Laud. Fortescue, de Laudibus Legum Angliae. 1616
Fort.L.J. Fortnightly Law Journal (Can.) 1931–48
Fortes. Fortescue's King's Bench Reports (92 ER) 1695–1738
Fortes.de Laud. Fortescue, de Laudibus Legum Angliae. 1616
Fortes.Rep. Fortescue's King's Bench Reports (92 ER) 1695–1738
Fortesc. Fortescue's King's Bench Reports (92 ER) 1695–1738
Fortesc.de L.L.Angl. Fortescue, de Laudibus Legum Angliae. 1616
Fortescue Fortescue's King's Bench Reports (92 ER) 1695–1738
Fortn.L.J. Fortnightly Law Journal (Can.) 1931–48
Fortnightly L.J. Fortnightly Law Journal (Can.) 1931–48
Forum The Forum (American Bar Association) 1965–
Forum: Bench & Bar Review (USA) 1874–5
Forum Law Review (USA) 1874
Forum of the Dickinson School of Law (USA) 1897–1908
Forum (A.B.A.) The Forum (American Bar Association) 1965–
Forum (L) Forum Law Review (USA) 1874
Forum L.R. Forum Law Review (USA) 1874
Forum (N.Y.) Forum Review (USA)

Forum Rev. Forum Law Review (USA) 1874
Forvaltnings Tids Forvaltningsrattslig Tidskrift (Swed.)
Foss.Judg. Foss's Judges of England. 1066–1864
Fost. Foster's Crown Cases (168 ER) 1743–61
Foster's Legal Chronicle Reports (Pennsylvania)
Foster's New Hampshire Reports (21–31 N.H.)
Foster's Reports (5, 6 & 8 Hawaii)
Fost.C.L. Foster's Crown Law or Crown Cases (168 ER) 1743–61
Fost.Cr.Law Foster's Crown Law or Crown Cases (168 ER) 1743–61
Fost.Crown Law Foster's Crown Law or Crown Cases (168 ER) 1743–61
Fost.El.Jur. Foster, Elements of Jurisprudence. 1853
Fost.(Haw.) Foster's Hawaiian Reports (5, 6 & 8 Hawaii)
Fost.(N.H.) Foster's New Hampshire Reports (21–31 N.H.)
Fost.Sci.Fa. Foster on the Writ of Scire Facias. 1851
Fost.& F. Foster & Finlason's Nisi Prius Reports (175–6 ER) 1856–67
Fost.& Fin. Foster & Finlason's Nisi Prius Reports (175–6 ER) 1856–67
Foster Foster's Crown Cases (168 ER) 1743–61
Foster's Legal Chronicle Reports (Pennsylvania)
Foster's New Hampshire Reports (21–31 N.H.)
Foster (Pa.) Foster's Legal Chronicle Reports (Pennsylvania)
Fount. Fountainhall's Decisions, Court of Session (Scot.) 1678–1712
Fount.Dec. Fountainhall's Decisions, Court of Session (Scot.) 1678–1712
Fowl.Col. Fowler, Collieries and Colliers. 4ed. 1884
Fowl.L.Cas. Fowler's Leading Cases on Collieries
Fox Fox's Circuit and District Court Decisions (USA)
Fox's Patent, Trade Mark, Design and Copyright Cases (Can.) 1940–
Fox's Registration Cases. 1866–95
Fox P.C. Fox's Patent, Trade Mark, Design and Copyright Cases (Can.) 1940–
Fox Pat.Cas. Fox's Patent, Trade Mark, Design and Copyright Cases (Can.) 1940–
Fox Reg.Ca. Fox's Registration Cases. 1866–95
Fox & S. Fox & Smith's Irish King's Bench Reports. 1822–4
Fox & Smith's Registration Cases. 1886–95
Fox & S.Ir. Fox & Smith's Irish King's Bench Reports. 1822–4
Fox & S.Reg. Fox & Smith's Registration Cases. 1886–95
Fox & Sm. Fox & Smith's Irish King's Bench Reports. 1822–4
Fox & Smith's Registration Cases. 1886–95
Fox & Sm.R.C. Fox & Smith's Registration Cases. 1886–95
Fpad. Il Foro padano (It.)
Fr. Fragment or Excerpt
France
Freeman's Chancery Reports (22 ER) 1660–1706
Freeman's King's Bench Reports (89 ER) 1670–1704
French
Fr.Ch. Freeman's Chancery Reports (22 ER) 1660–1706
Freeman's Mississippi Chancery Reports. 1839–43
Fr.Chy. Freeman's Chancery Reports (22 ER) 1660–1706
Freeman's Mississippi Chancery Reports. 1839–43
Fr.E.C. Fraser's Election Cases. 1776–7
Fr.Jud. France Judiciaire (Fr.) 1876–1910
Fr.& W.Prec. Frend & Ware, Precedents of Instruments relating to

the Transfer of Land to Railway Companies. 2ed. 1866

Fra. Francis' Maxims of Equity. 4ed. 1746

Frac. Fractional

Fran.Char. Francis, Law of Charities. 2ed. 1855

Fran.Eng.Law Francillon, Lectures on English Law. 1860–1

Fran.Max. Francis' Maxims of Equity. 4ed. 1746

Franc.Judg. Francillon's County Court Judgments. 1850–2

France France's Reports (3–11 Colorado)

France (Colo.) France's Reports (3–11 Colorado)

France Jud. France Judiciaire (Fr.) 1876–1910

Francis Max. Francis' Maxims of Equity. 4ed. 1746

Franks' Cttee. Committee on Administrative Tribunals and Enquiries. Report (Cmnd. 218) 1957
Home Office Departmental Committee on Section 2 of the Official Secrets Act, 1911. Report (Cmnd. 5104) 1972

Fras. Fraser's Election Cases. 1776–7

Fras.Dom.Rel. Fraser on Personal and Domestic Relations (Scot.)

Fras.Elec.Cas. Fraser's Election Cases. 1776–7

Fras.Par.& Ch. Fraser, Parent and Child (Scot.)

Fraser Fraser's Court of Session Cases, 5th Series. 1898–1906
Fraser's Election Cases. 1776–7
Fraser's Husband and Wife (Scot.) 1876–78

Fraser (Scot.) Fraser's Court of Session Cases, 5th Series. 1898–1906

Fraz. Frazer's Admiralty Cases (Scot.)

Fraz.Adm. Frazer's Admiralty Cases (Scot.)

Fred.Code Frederician Code (or Code Frederic), Prussia

Free. Freeman's Chancery Reports (22 ER) 1660–1706
Freeman's King's Bench Reports (89 ER) 1670–1704
Freeman's Reports (31–96 Illinois)

Free.C.C. Freeman's Chancery Reports (22 ER) 1660–1706

Free.Ch. Freeman's Chancery Reports (22 ER) 1660–1706
Freeman's Missisippi Chancery Reports. 1839–43

Free.K.B. Freeman's King's Bench Reports (89 ER) 1670–1704

Free Speech Y.B. Free Speech Yearbook (USA)

Freem.C.C. Freeman's Chancery Reports (22 ER) 1660–1706

Freem.Ch. Freeman's Chancery Reports (22 ER) 1660–1706

Freem.Ch.(Miss.) Freeman's Mississippi Chancery Reports. 1839–43

Freem.Eng.Const. Freeman, Growth of the English Constitution. 3ed. 1876

Freem.(Ill.) Freeman's Reports (31–96 Illinois)

Freem.Judgm. Freeman on Judgments

Freem.K.B. Freeman's King's Bench and Common Pleas Reports (89 ER) 1670–1704

Freem.(Miss.) Freeman's Mississippi Chancery Reports. 1839–43

French French's Reports (6 New Hampshire)

French (N.H.) French's Reports (6 New Hampshire)

Freund P.A. Freund, The Supreme Court of the United States: Its Business, Purposes and Performance. 1961

Frewen Judgments of the Court of Criminal Appeal (Ire.) 1924–

Fries Tr. Trial of John Fries (Treason)

FrirgL Lag om fri rättegång (Swed.) law on free legal proceedings. 1919

Frith. United States Opinions of Attorneys-General

Fry Fry on Specific Performance of Contracts

Fry Lun. Fry on Lunacy. 4ed. 1914

Fry Sp.Per. Fry on Specific Performance of Contracts
Full B.R. Bengal Full Bench Rulings (North-Western Provinces) (India)
Full S. Full Session
Fuller Fuller's Reports (59–105 Michigan)
Fuller (Mich.) Fuller's Reports (59–105 Michigan)
Fult. Fulton's Supreme Court Reports, Bengal (India) 1842–4
Fulton Fulton's Supreme Court Reports, Bengal (India) 1842–4
Fulton Cttee. Treasury. Committee on the Civil Service 1966–8. Report (Cmnd. 3638) 1968
Fw Faillissementswet (Neth.)

G

G. Gale's Exchequer Reports. 1835–6
Georgia
Gericht (Ger.) Court
German
Geschichte (Ger.)
Gesetz (Ger.) Law
Gift Tax
Government
Granted
Gregorowski's Reports of the High Court of the Orange Free State (S.Afr.) 1883–7
Grondwet (Neth.) Constitution
Guernsey
King George
Reports of the High Court of Griqualand (S.Afr.) 1882–1910

G.A. Decisions of General Appraisers (USA)
General Assembly (House of Representatives) (N.Z.)
General Assembly (UN)
Governmental Affairs
Grands arrêts (de la jurisprudence civile) (Fr.)

G.A.B. Gewestelijk Arbeidsbureau (Neth.) Regional Labourmarket Agency

GAC General Administration Council (China)

G.A.O.R. General Assembly Official Record (UN)

G.A.Resol. General Assembly Resolution (UN)

GATT General Agreement on Tariffs and Trade

GATT/CP General Agreement on Tariffs and Trade, Contracting Parties

G.A.W. Guaranteed Annual Wage

GB Giftermålsbalk (Swed.) Marriage Code. 1920
Grundbuch (Ger.) Land Register

G.B. Great Britain

GBA Grundbuchamt (Ger.) Land Registry

GBE Government business enterprise (Aus.)

G.B.J. Georgia Bar Journal. 1938–64

GBV Verordnung betreffend das Grundbuch (Switz.) 1910

GBl Gesetzblatt (Ger.) Gazette

G.C. General Code

GC I First Geneva Convention for the Amelioration of the Condition of the Wounded and Sick in Armed Forces in the Field. 1949

GC II Second Geneva Convention for the Amelioration of the Condition of the Wounded, Sick and Shipwrecked Members of Armed Forces at Sea. 1949

GC III Third Geneva Convention relative to the Treatment of Prisoners of War. 1949

GC IV Fourth Geneva Convention relative to the Protection of Civilian Persons in Time of War. 1949

GCC Geneva Convention on the Continental Shelf. 1958

G.C.D.C. Gold Coast Divisional Court Reports, Selected Judgments (Ghana) 1921–5, 1926–9, 1929–31

G.C.Div.C. Selected Judgments of the Gold Coast Divisional Court (Ghana) 1921–5, 1926–9, 1929–31

G.C.Div.Ct. Selected Judgments of the

Gold Coast Divisional Court (Ghana) 1921–5, 1926–9, 1929–31
GCF Geneva Convention on the Fishing and Preservation of Living Resources. 1958
G.C.F.C. Gold Coast Full Court Selected Judgments (Ghana) 1920–1, 1922, 1923–5, 1926–9
G.C.Full Ct. Gold Coast Full Court Selected Judgments (Ghana) 1920–1, 1922, 1923–5, 1926–9
GCHS Geneva Convention on the High Seas. 1958
GCTS Geneva Convention on the Territorial Sea and Contigious Zone. 1958
G.civ. Giustizia civile (It.)
G.comm. Giurisprudenza commerciale (It.)
G.Coop. G. Cooper's Chancery Reports (35 ER) 1815
G.Cooper G. Cooper's Chancery Reports (35 ER) 1815
G.cost. Giurisprudenza costituzionale (It.)
G.D. Grandes décisions (de la jurisprudence administrative) (Fr.)
G.D.C. General Dental Council
GDP Gross Domestic Product
G.del F. Gaceta del Foro (Argentina)
G.du P. Gazette du Palais (Fr.)
GEISAR Group of Experts on International Accounting and Reporting Standards
GESP General Exports Services Branch
GG Government Gazette
Governor General
Grundgesetz (Ger.) Basic Law of the Federal Republic
G.Gr. G. Green's Reports (Iowa) 1847–54
G.Greene(Iowa) G. Green's Reports (Iowa) 1847–54
G.I. Giurisprudenza italiana (It.)
Gray's Inn
GIA General International Agreement
G.I.O. Government Insurance Office (N.S.W., Aus.)
G.J. British Guiana General Jurisdiction (Official Gazette) 1899–
Gill & Johnson's Reports (Maryland)
G.J.W. Great Jurists of the World, by Sir John MacDonnel & Edward Manson. 1913
G KES USSR State Committee on Foreign Economic Relations
G.L. General Laws
G.L.C. Greater London Council
G.L.D. Cases in the Griqualand West Local Division of the Supreme Court (S.Afr.) 1910–46
G.L.J. Guernsey Law Journal
G.L.R. Gazette Law Reports (N.Z.) 1898–1953
Georgia Law Review. 1966–
Ghana Law Reports. 1959–
Gujarat Law Reporter (India) 1960–
G.L.R.(N.Z.) Gazette Law Reports (N.Z.) 1898–1953
G.L.& J. Gazette of Law and Journalism (Aus.) 1986–
GM General Meeting of Shareholders
GmbH Gesellschaft mit beschränkter Haftung (Ger.) limited liability company
GmbHG Gesetz betreffend der Gesellschaft mit beschränkter Haftung (Ger.) law governing limited liability companies
G.M.Dud. Dudley's Reports (Georgia) 1830–33
G.M.Dudl. Dudley's Reports (Georgia) 1830–33
G.M.J. Gabinete do Ministro da Justica (Port.)
G.mer. Giurisprudenza di merito (It.)
G.N. Gazette Notice (Ghana)
G.N.P. Gross national product
G.O. General Orders, Court of Chancery (Ontario)
GOSSIP Government Open Systems Inter-connection Procurement Policy (Aus.)
GPO General Post Office
Government Printing Office (USA)
GRBPL The Gravitas Review of

Business and Property Law (Nigeria) 1988–

GREAT Government and Related Employees Appeal Tribunal (New South Wales, Aus.)

G.R.O. General Register Office

G.R.O.B.D.M. General Register Office for Births, Deaths and Marriages

GRT Gross register ton

GRUR Gewerblicher Rechtsschutz und Urheberrecht (Ger.) 1896–1941, 1948–

GRUR Int. Gewerblicher Rechtsschutz und Urheberrecht – internationaler Teil. 1967–

GS Gesetzsammlung (Ger.) Collection of Statutes, Gazette

G.S.B. Georgia State Bar Journal. 1964–

G.S.M. General Synod Measure

G.S.P. Generalised System of Preferences for Developing Countries

G.S.R. Gongwer's State Reports (Ohio)

G.S.T. Goods and Services Tax (N.Z.)

G.S.T.P. Generalised System of Tariff and Preferences (U.N.)

GT Gift Tax Ruling (USA)

G.T.D. General Terms (Conditions of Delivery)

G.T.G.D. General Terms of Goods Delivery

GU Gazzetta ufficiale dello Stato (It.)

GUCE Gazzetta ufficiale delle Comunita Europee (It.) Official Journal of the European Community

G.U.R.I. Gazzetta Ufficiale della Repubblica Italiana (Italian legislative series)

G.W. Cases in the Griqualand West Local Division of the Supreme Court (S.Afr.) 1910–46
George Washington Law Review. 1932–

GWB Gesetz gegen Wettbewerbsbeschränkungen (Ger.) Law against restraint of competition

G.W.D. Cases in the Griqualand West Division of the Supreme Court (S.Afr.) 1910–46

G.W.L. Cases in the Griqualand West Local Division of the Supreme Court (S.Afr.) 1910–46

G.W.L.D. Cases in the Griqualand West Local Division of the Supreme Court (S.Afr.) 1910–46

G.W.L.R. George Washington Law Review. 1932–

G.W.R. Griqualand High Court Reports (S.Afr.) 1882–1910

G.Wash.L.R. George Washington Law Review (USA) 1932–

GYIL German Yearbook of International Law

G.& D. Gale & Davison's Queen's Bench Reports (55–62 RR) 1841–3

G.& E.I. Gilbert and Ellice Islands

G.& G. Goldsmith & Guthrie's Reports (36–67 Missouri Appeals)
Gyandoh & Griffiths, Sourcebook of the Constitutional Law of Ghana

G.& G.(Mo.) Goldsmith & Guthrie's Reports (36–67 Missouri Appeals)

G.& H. Gavin & Hord's Indiana Statutes

G.& J. Gill & Johnson's Maryland Court of Appeals Reports. 1829–42
Glyn & Jameson's Bankruptcy Reports. 1819–28

G.& R. Geldert & Russell's Nova Scotia Reports (Can.) 1895–1910

G.& T. Gin and tonic
Gould & Tucker's Notes on Revised Statutes of the United States

G.& Wh.Eas. Gale & Whatley, Easements (afterwards Gale alone).

Ga. Georgia
Georgia Supreme Court Reports. 1846–

Ga.App. Georgia Appeals Reports. 1807–

Ga.B.A. Georgia Bar Association

Ga.B.J. Georgia Bar Journal. 1938–64

Ga.Bus.Law. Georgia Business Lawyer

Ga.Code Code of Georgia

Ga.Code Ann. Code of Georgia Annotated

Ga.Dec. Georgia Decisions

GaJICL Georgia Journal of

International and Comparative Law. 1970–

Ga.J.Int'l.& Comp.L. Georgia Journal of International and Comparative Law. 1970–

Ga.L. Georgia Law Review. 1966–
Georgia Lawyer. 1930–2
Georgia Session Laws

Ga.L.J. Georgia Law Journal. 1884

Ga.L.Rep. Georgia Law Reporter. 1885–6

Ga.L.Rev. Georgia Law Review. 1966–

Ga.Laws Georgia Laws

Ga.Lawyer Georgia Lawyer. 1930–2

Ga.P.S.C. Georgia Public Service Commission Reports

Ga.Prac. Stand's Georgia Practice

Ga.St.B.J. Georgia State Bar Journal. 1964–

Ga.Supp. Lester's Supplement to Georgia Reports (33 Ga.)

Gab. Archivio di Gabinetto, della Segreteria Generale e del Sottosegretariato agli Esteri (It.)

Gabb.Cr.Law Gabbett, Criminal Law

Gabb.Stat.L. Gabbett, Abridgment of Statute Law. 1812–18

Gac.del foro Gaceta del foro: jurisprudencia, legislacion, doctrina· (Argentina)

Gaii. Gaius' Institutes (Gaii Institutionum Commentarii)

Gaius Gaius' Institutes (Gaii Institutionum Commentarii)

Gaius Inst. Gaius' Institutes

Gal. Gallison's Circuit Court Reports (USA)

Gal.& Dav. Gale & Davison's Queen's Bench Reports (55–62 RR) 1841–3

Galb. Galbraith's Reports (9–11 Florida)

Galb.& M. Galbraith & Meek's Reports (12 Florida)

Galb.& M.(Fla.) Galbraith & Meek's Reports (12 Florida)

Galbraith Galbraith's Reports (9–11 Florida)

Gale Gale's Exchequer Reports. 1835–6
Gale's New Forest Decisions
Gale on Easements

Gale Eas. Gale on Easements

Gale & D. Gale & Davison's Queen's Bench Reports (55–62 RR) 1841–3

Gale & Dav. Gale & Davison's Queen's Bench Reports (55–62 RR) 1841–3

Gale & Wh.Eas. Gale & Whatley (afterwards Gale) on Easements

Gale's St. Gale's Statutes (Illinois)

Gall. Gallison's Circuit Court Reports (USA)

Gall.Cr.Cas. Gallick's Reports (French Criminal Cases)

Gallison Gallison's Circuit Court Reports (USA)

Gamb.& Bart. Gamble & Barlow's Irish Equity Digest

Gamboa Gamboa's Introduction to Philippine Law

Ganatra Ganatra's Criminal Cases (India)

Gane Eastern District Court Reports, Cape Colony (S.Afr.)

Gantts Dig. Gantt's Digest of Arkansas Statutes

Gard.Ev. Garde, Evidence. 1830

Gard.N.Y.Rep. Gardenier's New York Reporter

Gard.N.Y.Rept. Gardenier's New York Reporter

Gard.N.Y.Reptr. Gardenier's New York Reporter

Garden. Gardenhire's Reports (14–15 Missouri)

Gardenhire Gardenhire's Reports (14–15 Missouri)

Gardn.P.C. Gardner Peerage Case, reported by Le Marchant

Garner, Developments Garner, Recent Developments in International Law. 1925

Garo F.J. Garo, Derecho Comercial (Argentina) 1956

Gaspar Gaspar's Small Causes Court Reports (Bengal, India) 1850–60

Gav.& H.Rev.St. Gavin & Hord's Revised Statutes (India)

Gay.(La.) Gayarre's Reports (25–28 Louisiana Annual)

Gay Rights Digest on Gay Rights: Human/Civil Rights Legislation (Can.)

Gayarre Gayarre's Reports (25–28 Louisiana Annual)

Gaz. New Zealand Gazette. 1853–
Weekly Law Gazette, Cincinnati. 1858–60

Gaz.Bank. Gazette of Bankruptcy. 1861–63

Gaz.Bank.Dig. Gazzam, Digest of Bankruptcy Decisions

Gaz.Jur.S.Paulo Gazeta Juridca: revista mensal de legislacao, doutrina e jurisprudencia do Estado de Sao Paulo (Brazil)

Gaz.L.R. Gazette Law Reports (N.Z.) 1898–1953

Gaz.L.R.(N.Z.) Gazette Law Reports (N.Z.) 1898–1953

Gaz.L.& J. Gazette of Law and Journalism (Aus.) 1986–

Gaz.of Bank. Gazette of Bankruptcy. 1861–63

Gaz.Pal. La Gazette du Palais (Fr.) 1881–

Gaz.Trib. Gazette des Tribunaux (Fr.)

Gaz.Trib.Mixtes Gazette des Tribunaux Mixtes d'Égypte

Gaz.Zan.E.A. Gazette for Zanzibar and East Africa. 1892–1922

Gaz.& B.C.Rep. Gazette and Bankruptcy Court Reporter, New York

Gazette The Law Society of Upper Canada Gazette. 1966–
The Law Society's Gazette. 1903–

Gazz.Uff. Gazzeta Ufficiale (It.) Official Gazette

Gbl. Gesetzblatt (Ger.)

gdn. guardian

GebrMG Gebrauchsmustergesetz (Ger.) Industrial Designs Act

ged. gedaagde (Neth.) defendant

Geh. Gehalt (Ger.) contents
Geheimrat (Ger.) Privy Councillor

Geld.& M. Geldart & Maddock's Chancery Reports (6 Maddock's Reports)

Geld.& O. Novia Scotia Reports by Geldert & Oxley (Can.) 1866–75

Geld.& Ox. Novia Scotia Reports by Geldert & Oxley (Can.) 1866–75

Geld.& R. Geldert & Russell's Novia Scotia Reports (Can.) 1895–1910

Geldart Geldart & Maddock's Chancery Reports (6 Maddock's Reports)

Geller's Zentralblatt Zentralblatt für die Juristische Praxis, begrundet von Dr. L. Geller (Austria)

Gemma Gemma, Appunti di diritto internazionale (It.) 1923

Gen. General

Gen.Abr.Cas.Eq. General Abridgment of Cases in Equity (Equity Cases Abridged) 1677–1744

Gen.Ass.Res. General Assembly Resolution (UN)

Gen.Assem. General Assembly

Gen.Ass'ns. General Associations

Gen.Bus. General Business

Gen.Dig. General Digest

Gen.Dig.N.S. General Digest, New Series

Gen.Dig.U.S. General Digest of the United States

Gen.Laws General Laws

Gen.Ord. General Orders, Ontario Court of Chancery

Gen.Ord.Ch. General Orders of the High Court of Chancery

Gen.Prov. General Provisions

Gen.Sess. General Sessions

Gen.St. General Statutes

Gen.Stat.Ann. General Statutes Annotated

Gen.T. General Term

Gen.View Cr.L. Stephen, General View of the Criminal Law. 2ed. 1890

Genet Genet, Traité de diplomatie et de droit diplomatique (Fr.) 1931–32

Geny Festschrift E. Lambert (ed.), Recueil d'Études sur les Sources de Droit en l'Honneur de Francois Geny. 1934

Geo. George
Georgetown
Georgetown Law Journal (D.C.) 1912–17/18, 1919/20–
Georgia
Georgia Reports
King George
Geo.Coop. George Cooper's Chancery Cases tempore Eldon (35 ER) 1792–1815
Geo.Dec. Georgia Decisions
Geo.Dig. George's Mississippi Digest
Geo.Immigr.L.J. Georgetown Immigration Law Journal (USA)
Geo.L.J. Georgetown Law Journal. 1912–17/18, 1919/20–
Georgia Law Journal. 1884
Geo.L.Rev. Georgia Law Review (USA) 1966–
Geo.Lib. George, Libel. 1812
Geo.Mason U.L.Rev. George Mason University Law Review (USA)
Geo.Rev. Georgia Law Review. 1966–
Geo.Wash.J.Int'l L.& Econ. The George Washington Journal of International Law and Economics (USA)
Geo.Wash.L.Rev. George Washington Law Review. 1932–
geopp. geopposserde (Neth.) defendant
George George's Reports (30–39 Mississippi)
Georget.L.J. Georgetown Law Journal. 1912–17/18, 1919/20–
Georgia B.J. Georgia Bar Journal. 1938–64
Georgia J.Int.Comp.L. Georgia Journal of International and Comparative Law. 1970–
Georgia L.Rev. Georgia Law Review. 1966–
Georgia St.B.J. Georgia State Bar Journal. 1964–
Ger. Germany
gereq. gerequireerde (Neth.) defendant
Germ.Yrbk.Intl.L. German Yearbook of International Law
Ges. Gesellschaft (Ger.) Association or Company
Gesetz (Ger.) law, statute
GewArch. Gewerbearchiv (Ger.) law reports
GewO Gewerbeordnung (Ger.) Trade regulation law
GfV Guterfernverkehr (Ger.) carriage of goods
Ghana C.C. Ghana Current Cases. 1965–71
Ghana L.R.C. Ghana Law Reform Commission
Gib. Gibbons' Surrogate Court Reports (New York)
Gibraltar
Gib.Cod. Gibson's Codex Juris Ecclesiastici Anglicani
Gib.Dec. Durie's Decisions, Court of Session (Scot.) 1621–42
Gib.Dil. Gibbons, Dilapidations and Nuisances. 2ed. 1849
Gib.Fix. Gibbons, Law of Fixtures. 1836
Gib.L.N. Gibson's Law Notes. 1882–4
Gibb.Sur. Gibbons' Surrogate Court Reports (New York)
Gibb.Surr. Gibbons' Surrogate Court Reports (New York)
Gibbons Gibbons' Surrogate Court Reports (New York)
Gibbons (N.Y.) Gibbons' Surogate Court Reports (New York)
Gibbs Gibbs' Reports (2–4 Michigan)
Gibbs'Jud.Chr. Gibbs' Judicial Chronicle
Gibs.Code Gibson's Codex Juris Ecclesiastici Anglicani
Gibs.L.N. Gibson's Law Notes. 1882–4
Gibson Durie's Decisions, Court of Session (Scot.) 1621–42
Gif. Giffard's Chancery Reports (65–6 ER) 1857–65
Giff. Giffard's Chancery Reports (65–6 ER) 1857–65
Giff.& H. Giffard & Hemming's Chancery Reports (65–6 ER) 1857–65
Giffard Giffard's Chancery Reports (65–6 ER) 1857–65
Gil. Gilbert's Cases in Law and Equity (93 ER) 1713–14

Gilbert's Chancery Reports (25 ER) 1705–26
Gilfillan's Reports (1–20 Minnesota)
Gilman's Reports (6–10 Illinois)
Gilmer's Reports (21 Virginia) 1820–21

Gil.(Minn.) Gilfillan's Reports (1–20 Minnesota)

Gil.& Fal. Gilmour & Falconer's Decisions, Session Cases (Scot.) 1661–6

Gilb. Gilbert's Cases in Law and Equity (93 ER) 1713–14
Gilbert's Chancery Reports (25 ER) 1705–26

Gilb.Cas. Gilbert's Cases in Law and Equity (93 ER) 1713–14

Gilb.Cas.L.& Eq. Gilbert's Cases in Law and Equity (93 ER) 1713–14

Gilb.Ch. Gilbert's Chancery Reports (25 ER) 1705–26

Gilb.Com.Pl. Gilbert's Common Pleas (Cases in Law and Equity) (93 ER) 1713–14

Gilb.Eq. Gilbert's Equity or Chancery Reports (25 ER) 1705–26

Gilb.Eq.Rep. Gilbert's Equity or Chancery Reports (25 ER) 1705–26

Gilb.Ev. Gilbert, Law of Evidence

Gilb.Exch. Gilbert's Exchequer Reports (25 ER) 1705–26

Gilb.For.Rom. Gilbert's Forum Romanum (History and Practice of Chancery)

Gilb.Forum Rom. Gilbert's Forum Romanum (History and Practice of Chancery)

Gilb.Hist.P.C. Gilbert, History of Common Pleas

Gilb.K.B. Gilbert's Cases in Law and Equity (93 ER) 1713–14

Gilb.P.C. Gilbert's Common Pleas (Cases in Law and Equity) (93 ER) 1713–14

Gilb.Rents Gilbert's Treatise on Rents

Gilb.Rep. Gilbert's Equity or Chancery Reports (25 ER) 1705–26

Gilb.Repl. Gilbert on Replevin

Gilb.Ten. Gilbert on Tenures

Gilb.Uses Gilbert on Uses and Trusts

Gilchr. Gilchrist's Local Government Cases

Gild. Gildersleeve's Supreme Court Reports (New Mexico) 1883–9

Gildersleeve Gildersleeve's Supreme Court Reports (New Mexico) 1883–9

Gildr. Gildersleeve's Supreme Court Reports (New Mexico) 1883–9

Gilfillan Gilfillan's Reports (1–20 Minnesota)

Gill Gill's Maryland Court of Appeals Reports. 1843–51

Gill (Md.) Gill's Maryland Court of Appeals Reports. 1843–51

Gill Pol.Rep. Gill's Police Court Reports (Boston, Massachusetts)

Gill & J. Gill & Johnson's Reports (Maryland) 1829–42

Gill & J.(Md.) Gill & Johnson's Reports (Maryland) 1829–42

Gill & Johns. Gill & Johnson's Reports (Maryland) 1829–42

Gilm. Gilman's Illinois Supreme Court Reports (6–10 Ill.) 1845–9
Gilmer's Reports (21 Virginia) 1820–1
Gilmour & Falconer's Decisions, Court of Session (Scot.) 1661–66

Gilm.Dig. Gilman's Digest of Decisions (Illinois and Indiana)

Gilm.(Ill.) Gilman's Illinois Supreme Court Reports (6–10 Ill.) 1845–9

Gilm.& F. Gilmour & Falconer's Decisions, Court of Session (Scot.) 1661–66

Gilm.& Fal. Gilmour & Falconer's Decisions, Court of Session (Scot.) 1661–66

Gilm.& Falc. Gilmour & Falconer's Decisions, Court of Session (Scot.) 1661–66

Gilman Gilman's Illinois Supreme Court Reports (6–10 Ill.) 1845–9

Gilmer Gilmer's Reports (21 Virginia) 1820–1

Gilmer (Va.) Gilmer's Reports (21 Virginia) 1820–1

Gilp. Gilpin's District Court Reports (USA)

Gilp.Opin. Gilpin, Opinions of the United States Attorneys-General

Ginsberg, 20th Century M. Ginsberg (ed.), Law and Opinion in England in the 20th Century. 1959

Giur.comp.civ. Giurisprudenza comparata di diritto civile (It.) 1938–

Giur.Comp.DIP Giurisprudenza comparata di diritto internazionale privato (It.) 1932–

Giur.comp.dir.civ. Giurisprudenza comparata di diritto civile (It.) 1938–

Giur.comp.dir.iter.priv. Giurisprudenza comparata di diritto internazionale privato (It.) 1932–

Giur.cost. Giurisprudenza costituzionale (It.) 1956–

Giur.Costituz Giurisprudenza costituzionale (It.) 1956–

Giur.It. Giurisprudenza italiana (It.)

Giur.ital. Giurisprudenza italiana (It.)

Giur.lig. Giurisprudenza ligure (It.)

Giur.tosc. Giurisprudenza toscana (It.)

Gius.civ. Giustizia civile (It.)

Giust.pen. Giustizia penale e la procedera penale italiana (It.) 1895–

Giust.soc. Giustizia sociale (It.) 1960–

Gl. Gleaver's Reports (Jamaica)

Gl.& J. Glyn & Jameson's Bankruptcy Reports. 1819–28

Glan.El.Cas. Glanville's Election Cases. 1623–24

Glanv. Glanville, De Legibus et Consuetudinibus Angliae. 1554

Glanv.El.Cas. Glanville's Election Cases. 1623–24

Glas. Glascock's Reports in all the Courts of Ireland. 1831–32

Glasc. Glascock's Reports in all the Courts of Ireland. 1831–32

Glascock Glascock's Reports in all the Courts of Ireland. 1831–32

Glendale L.Rev. Glendale Law Review (USA)

Glenn Glenn's Reports (16–18 Louisiana Annual)

Gloag & Henderson Gloag & Henderson, Introduction to the Law of Scotland

Glov.Mun.Cor. Glover's Minicipal Corporations. 1835

Glyn & J. Glyn & Jameson's Bankruptcy Reports. 1819–28

Glyn & Jam. Glyn & Jameson's Bankrupcty Reports. 1819–28

GmbH Gesellschaft mit beschränkter Haftung (Ger.) limited liability company

GmbHG Gesetz betreffend der Gesellschaft mit beschränkter Haftung (Ger.) law governing limited liability company

Gnomon Kritische Zeitschrift für dic gesamte klassische Altertumswissenschaft (Ger.)

Go. Goebel's Probate Court Cases (Ohio)

Godb. Godbolt's King's Bench Reports (78 ER) 1574–1638

Godd.Ease Goddard on Easements

Godef.Trust Godefroi, Law of Trusts and Trustees. 5ed. 1927

Godo. Godolphin on Admiralty Jurisdiction. 2ed. 1685
Godolphin's Orphan's Legacy. 1701
Godolphin's Repertorium Canonicum (Abridgment of the Ecclesiastical Laws) 3ed. 1687

Godolph.Adm.Jur. Godolphin, Admiralty Jurisdiction. 2ed. 1685

Godolph.Leg. Godolphin's Orphan's Legacy. 1701

Godolph.Rep.Can. Godolphin's Repertorium Canonicum. 3ed. 1687

Gods.Pat. Godson, Patents. 2ed. 1840

Godson Godson's Mining Commissioners' Cases (Ontario) 1910–7

Goeb. Goebel's Probate Court Cases (Ohio)

Goebel(Ohio) Goebel's Probate Court Cases (Ohio)

Gold. Goldesborough's or Gouldesborough's King's Bench Reports (75 ER) 1586–1601

Gold.& G. Goldsmith & Guthrie's Reports (36–7 Missouri Appeals)

Golden Gate L.Rev. Golden Gate Law Review (USA) 1971–5
Golden Gate U.L.Rev. Golden Gate University Law Review (USA) 1975–
Goldes. Goldesborough's or Gouldesborough's King's Bench Reports (75 ER) 1586–1601
Golds.Eq. Goldsmith, Doctrine and Practice of Equity. 6ed. 1871
Golt.Arch. Goltdammer's Archiv fur Strafrecht (Ger.)
Gonzaga L.Rev. Gonzaga Law Review (USA) 1966–
Good.Pat. Goodeve's Abstract of Patent Cases. 1785–1883
Good.& Wood. Goodeve & Woodman's Full Bench Rulings, Bengal (India)
Goodeve Goodeve on Real Property. 5ed. 1906
Gord.Tr. Gordon, Treason Trials
Gordon Gordon's Reports (24–26 Colorado and 10–13 Colorado Appeals)
Gore-B.Comp. Gore-Browne on Companies
Gosf. Gosford's Manuscript Reports, Court of Session (Scot.) 1668–1677
Gottschall Gottschall's Dayton Superior Court Reports (Ohio)
Gould. Gouldsborough's King's Bench Reports (75 ER) 1586–1601
Gould Pl. Gould, Principles of Pleading in Civil Actions
Gould Sten.Rep. Gould's Stenographic Reporter, Monographic Series (Albany, New York)
Gould & T. Gould & Tucker's Notes on Revised Statutes of the United States
Gould's Dig. Gould's Digest of Laws (Arkansas)
Gouldsb. Gouldsborough's King's Bench Reports (75 ER) 1586–1601
Gour. Gourick's Patent Digest. 1889–91
Gov. Governor
Gov.Gen. Governor General
Govr. Governor
Govt. Government
Gov't.Cont.Rep. Government Contract Reports (CCH) (USA)
Govt.Pub.Rev. Government Publications Review. 1974–
Govt.Pubns.Rev. Government Publications Review. 1974–
govtl. governmental
Gow Gow's Nisi Prius Cases (171 ER) 1818–20
Gow N.P. Gow's Nisi Prius Cases (171 ER) 1818–20
Gow Part. Gow on Partnership. 4ed. 1840
Gr. Grant's Chancery Chamber Reports, Upper Canada. 1850–65
Grant's Pennsylvania Cases. 1814–63
Grant's Reports (Jamaica) 1774–87
Grant's Upper Canada Chancery Reports. 1849–82
Greece
Greek
Green's New Jersey Equity Reports (2–4, 16–27 N.J. Eq.)
Green's New Jersey Law Reports (13–15 N.J. Law)
Greenleaf's Reports (1–9 Maine)
Gr.Brice Green's edition of Brice on Ultra Vires
Gr.Brit. Great Britain
Gr.Ct.Cass. Great Court of Cassation (Japan)
Gr.Eq. Green's New Jersey Equity Reports (2–4, 16–27 N.J. Eq.)
Gresley's Equity Evidence
Gr.Ev. Greenleaf on Evidence
GrV Grundvertrag (Ger.) 1972
Gra. Graham's Reports (98–107 Georgia)
Gra.& Wat.N.T. Graham & Waterman on New Trials
Granger Granger's Reports (22–23 Ohio)
Grant Elchies' Decisions, Court of Session (Scot.) 1733–54
Grant's Chancery Chamber Reports, Upper Canada. 1850–65
Grant's Pennsylvania Cases. 1814–63
Grant's Reports (Jamaica) 1774–87
Grant's Upper Canada Chancery Reports (Ontario) 1849–82

Grant Bank. Grant on Bankers and Banking. 7ed. 1923
Grant Cas. Grant's Pennsylvania Cases. 1814–63
Grant Cas.(Pa.) Grant's Pennsylvania Cases. 1814–63
Grant Ch. Grant's Upper Canada Chancery Reports (Ontario) 1849–82
Grant Ch.(Can.) Grant's Upper Canada Chancery Reports (Ontario) 1849–82
Grant Corp. Grant on Corporations. 1850
Grant E.& A. Grant's Error and Appeal Reports (Ontario) 1846–66
Grant Err.& App. Grant's Error and Appeal Reports (Ontario) 1846–66
Grant Jamaica Grant's Jamaica Reports. 1774–81
Grant Pa. Grant's Pennsylvania Cases. 1814–63
Grant (Pa.) Grant's Pennsylvania Cases. 1814–63
Grant U.C. Grant's Upper Canada Chancery Reports. 1849–82
Grant's R. Grant's Reports (Jamaica) 1774–87
Grap.Just. Grapel, Translation of the Institutes of Justinian
Grat. Grattan's Virginia Supreme Court Reports (42–74 Va.) 1844–80
Gratt. Grattan's Virginia Supreme Court Reports (42–74 Va.) 1844–80
Gratt.(Va.) Grattan's Virginia Supreme Court Reports (42–74 Va.) 1844–80
Grav.de Jur.Nat.Gent. Gravina, De Jure Naturale Gentium, etc.
Graves Proceedings in King's Council. 1392–93
Gravin. Gravina, Originum Juris Civilis
Gray Gray's Massachusetts Supreme Judicial Court Reports (67–82 Mass.) 1854–60
Gray's Reports (112–22 North Carolina)
Gray Att.Pr. Gray, Country Attorney's Practice. 9ed. 1869
Gray (Mass.) Gray's Massachusetts Supreme Judicial Court Reports (67–82 Mass.) 1854–60
Gray Perpetuities Gray's Rule Against Perpetuities. 4ed. 1942
Greav.Cr.L. Greaves, Criminal Consolidation. 2ed. 1862
Greaves Judgments of the Windward Islands Court of Appeal. 1866–1904
Green Green's Irish Land Cases. 1898–9
Green's New Jersey Chancery Reports (2–4 N.J. Eq.)
Green's New Jersey Equity Reports (16–27 N.J. Eq.)
Green's New Jersey Law Reports (13–15 N.J. Law)
Green's Reports (1 Oklahoma)
Green's Reports (11–17 Rhode Island)
Greenleaf's Reports (1–9 Maine)
Green Bri. Green's Edition of Brice's Ultra Vires
Green C.E. Green's New Jersey Equity Reports (16–27 N.J. Eq.)
Green (C.E.) Green's New Jersey Equity Reports (16–27 N.J. Eq.)
Green Ch. H.W. Green's New Jersey Chancery Reports (2–4 N.J. Eq.)
Green.Conv. Greenwood, Manual of Conveyancing. 9ed. 1897
Green Cr. Green's Criminal Cases (Scot.) 1820
Green Cr.Cas. Green's Criminal Cases (Scot.) 1820
Green Cr.L.Rep. Green's Criminal Law Reports (Scot.)
Green L. J.S. Green's New Jersey Law Reports (13–15 N.J. Law)
Green (N.J.) C.E. Green's New Jersey Equity Reports (16–27 N.J. Eq.)
H.W. Green's New Jersey Equity (or Chancery) Reports (2–4 N.J. Eq.)
J.S. Green's New Jersey Law Reports (13–15 N.J. Law)
Green.Ov.Cas. Greenleaf's Overruled Cases
Green R.I. Green's Reports (11–17 Rhode Island)
Green (R.I.) Green's Reports (11–17 Rhode Island)

Green Sc.Cr.Cas. Green's Criminal Cases (Scot.) 1820
Green Sc.Tr. Green's Scottish Trials for Treason
Greene Greene's Iowa Reports. 1847–54 Greene's New York Reports (7 N.Y. Ann. Cas.)
Greene G.(Iowa) G. Greene's Iowa Reports. 1847–54
Greenl. Greenleaf's Reports (1–9 Maine)
Greenl.Cr. Greenleaf's Edition of Cruise's Digest of Real Property
Greenl.Ev. Greenleaf on Evidence
Greenl.Ov.Cas. Greenleaf's Overruled Cases
Green's Brice Green's Edition of Brice's Ultra Vires
Greer Greer's Irish Land Cases. 1872–1903
Greg. Gregorowski's Reports of the High Court of the Orange Free State (S.Afr.) 1883–7
Gregorowski Gregorowski's Reports of the High Court of the Orange Free State (S.Afr.) 1883–7
Grein.Pr. Greiner, Louisiana Practice
Gren. Grenier's Ceylon Reports (Sri L.) 1872–4
Grenier Grenier's Ceylon Reports (Sri L.) 1872–4
Gres.Eq.Ev. Gresley's Equity Evidence. 2ed. 1847
Gretton Oxford Quarter Sessions Records
Grey Deb. Grey, House of Commons Debates
Grif.L.Reg. Griffith's Law Register (New Jersey)
Grif.P.C. Griffin's Patent Cases. 1866–87
Grif.P.L.C. Griffith's London Poor Law Cases. 1821–31
Grif.P.L.Cas. Griffith's London Poor Law Cases. 1821–31
Grif.P.R.C. Griffith's Poor Rate Cases
Grif.P.R.Cas. Griffith's Poor Rate Cases
Grif.Pat.C. Griffin's Patent Cases. 1866–87
Griff.Pat.Cas. Griffin's Patent Cases. 1866–87
Griffin P.C. Griffin's Patent Cases. 1866–87
Griffin Pat.Cas. Griffin's Patent Cases. 1866–87
Griffith Griffith's Reports (1–5 Indiana Appeals and 117–132 Indiana)
Grisw. Griswold's Reports (14–19 Ohio)
Griswold Griswold's Reports (14–19 Ohio)
Gro. Gross' Select Cases concerning the Law Merchant. 1239–1633 (Selden Society) 1908–32
Grotius
Gro.B.P. Grotius, De Jure Belli ac Pacis
Gro.de J.B. Grotius, De Jure Belli ac Pacis
Gro.Dr. Grotius, Le Droit de la Guerre
Gro.P.C. Grotius, De Jure Praedae Commmentarius
Gross St. Gross' Illinois Compiled Statutes
Grot.de J.B. Grotius, De Jure Belli ac Pacis
Grot.Soc'y Transactions of the Grotius Society
Grotius-Ann.Int. Grotius Annuaire International
Grotius Annuaire Grotius Annuaire International
Gruchot's Beitrage Beitrage zur Erläuterung des deutschen Rechts, begrundet von Dr. J.A. Gruchot
Grunhut's Z. Zeitschrift für das Privat- und Öffentliche Recht der Gegenwart, herausgegeben von Dr. C.S. Grunhut (Austria)
Gt.L.J. Georgetown Law Journal. 1912–1917/8, 1919/20–
Gtd. Guaranteed
Gu. Guam
Guam Civ.Code Guam Civil Code
Guam Code Civ.Pro. Guam Code of Civil Procedure
Guam Gov't Code Guam Government Code
Guam Prob.Code Guam Probate Code

Guar. Guarantee
Gude Pr. Gude, Practice of the Crown Side of the Court of King's Bench. 1828
Guern.Eq.Jur. Guernsey, Key to Equity Jurisprudence
Guild Law. Guild Lawyer (New York) 1938–42
Guild Lawyer (Washington) 1945–50
Guild Prac. Guild Practitioner (USA) 1965–
Guild Q. National Lawyers' Guild Quarterly (USA)
Guj.Ind. Gujerat, India
Guj.L.Rep. Gujerat Law Reporter (India) 1960–
Guj.L.T. Gujerat Law Times (India) 1964–
Gul. William
Gul.Mar. William and Mary
Gunby Gunby's District Court Reports (Louisiana) 1885
Gunby (La.) Gunby's District Court Reports (Louisiana) 1885
Gundry Gundry's Manuscripts in Lincoln's Inn Library
Gunton's Mag. Gunton's Magazine of Practical Economics and Political Science
Gut.Brac. Guterbock's Bracton
Guth.Pr. Guthrie, Principles of the Laws of England. 1843
Guth.Sh.Cas. Guthrie's Sheriff Court Cases (Scot.) 1861–85
Guth.Sher.Cas. Guthrie's Sheriff Court Cases (Scot.) 1861–85
Guthrie Guthrie's Reports (33–83 Missouri Appeals)
Guthrie's Sheriff Court Cases (Scot.) 1861–85
Gutzwiller, Histoire M. Gutzwiller, Le developpement historique du droit international privé. 1929
Gutzwiller,IPR M. Gutzwiller, Internationalprivatrecht (Ger.) 1930
Guy For.Med. Guy, Forensic Medicine. 7ed. 1895
Gwil. Gwillim's Tithe Cases. 1224–1824
Gwil.Ti.Cas. Gwillim's Tithe Cases. 1224–1824
Gwill. Gwillim's Tithe Cases. 1224–1824
Gwill.Bac.Abr. Gwillim's edition of Bacon's Abridgment
Gwill.T.Cas. Gwillim's Tithe Cases. 1224–1824
Gwill.Ti.Cas. Gwillim's Tithe Cases. 1224–1824

H

h. harmonized
husband

H. Handy's Reports (Ohio)
Hare's Chancery Reports (66–8 ER) 1841–53
Hawaii Reports
Heft (Ger.) number, part
Hertzog's High Court Reports (S.Afr.) 1893
Hill's New York Reports. 1841–44
Hic (Lat.) here, in the same paragraph
Hilary Term
House Bill (USA)
Howard's Supreme Court Reports (42–65 U.S.)
King Henry

H.A. High Authority of the European Coal and Steel Community
Highways Acts
Hoc anno (Lat.) this year

H.A.L.L. Health and Law Letter

HAO Arbetsordning för rikets hovrätter (Swed.) Instructions for the Courts of Appeals. 1947

HAS Hospital Advisory Service

H.B. H. Blackstone's Common Pleas Reports (126 ER) 1788–96
Handelsbalk (Swed.) Commercial code. 1734
House Bill (USA)

H.B.M. His (or Her) Britannic Majesty

H.B.R. Hansell's Bankruptcy Reports. 1915–17

H.Bl. H. Blackstone's Common Pleas Reports (126 ER) 1788–96

H.Black. H. Blackstone's Common Pleas Reports (126 ER) 1788–96

H.C. Habeas Corpus
Hague Convention
High Commission(er)
High Court
Highway Code
House of Commons
Housing Centre
Reports of the High Court of Griqualand (S.Afr.) 1882–1910

H.C.A. High Court of Australia

H.C.B. House of Commons Bill

H.C.G. Reports of the High Court of Griqualand (S.Afr.) 1882–1910

H.C.J. High Court of Justice
High Court of Justiciary (Scot.)
Journals of the House of Commons

H.C.Jour. House of Commons Journal

HCM Decree of the Council of Ministers (Romania)

H.C.of A. High Court of Australia

H.C.R. High Court Reports (India) 1910–13

H.C.R.N.W.F. High Court Reports, North West Frontier

H.C.R.N.W.P. High Court Reports, North West Provinces (Pak.) 1869–75

H.C.Res. House of Representatives Concurrent Resolution (USA)

H.C.S. Higher Civil Servant (Japan)
Home Civil Service

H.C.T. High Comission Territories

H.C.T.L.R. High Commission Territories Reports (Basutoland,

Bechuanaland and Swaziland) 1926–
H.C.Wkly.Inf.Bull. House of Commons Weekly Information Bulletin. 1978–
H.Cr. Houston's Criminal Reports (Delaware)
H.Ct. High Court
H.D. Hogsta Domstol (Swed.) Supreme Court
H.Doc. House of Representatives Document (USA)
H.E.C. Hodgin's Reports of Election Petitions (Ontario) 1871–9
H.E.L. History of English Law edited by W. Holdsworth
H.E.O. Higher Executive Officer
HGB Handelsgesetzbuch (Ger.) Commercial Code
H.H. Hayward & Hazelton's Reports
H.H.C.L. Hale, History of the Common Law. 6ed. 1820
H.H.L. Court of Session Cases, House of Lords (Scot.)
H.H.P.C. Hale, History of Pleas of the Crown
H.I.A. Housing Improvement Association
H.I.H. His (or Her) Imperial Highness
HILJ Harvard International Law Journal
H.I.Rep. Hawaiian Islands Reports
H.K. Handelskammer (Ger.) Chamber of Commerce
Hong Kong
House of Keys
H.K.L.J. Hong Kong Law Journal. 1971–
H.K.L.R. Hong Kong Law Reports. 1905–
H.K.Law Reports Hong Kong Law Reports. 1905–
HKTAG Hong Kong Trade Advisory Group (BOTB)
H.L. Clark's House of Lords Cases (9–11 ER) 1847–66
The Health Law (It.) 1934
House of Lords
Law Reports, House of Lords, English and Irish Appeals. 1866–75
H.L.C. Clark's House of Lords Cases (9–11 ER) 1847–66
H.L.Cas. Clark's House of Lords Cases (9–11 ER) 1847–66
H.L.G. Housing and Local Government
H.L.J. Hastings Law Journal (USA) 1949–
Hindu Law Journal (India) 1918–25
Journals of the House of Lords
H.L.Jour. House of Lords Journal
H.L.R. Harvard Law Review. 1887–
Housing Law Reports. 1967–
Houston Law Review. 1963–
H.L.R.O. House of Lords Record Office
H.L.R.S. Homosexual Law Reform Society
H.L.Rep. Clark's House of Lords Cases (9–11 ER) 1847–66
HLS Harvard Law School
H.L.Sc.App.Cas. Law Reports, House of Lords, Scotch and Divorce Appeal Cases. 1866–75
H.L.Wkly.Inf.Bull. House of Lords Weekly Information Bulletin. 1978–
h.M. herrschende Meinung (Ger.) prevailing opinion
H.M. His (Her) Majesty
House Magazine (for Senators and Members of the House of Representatives) (Aus.) 1982–
H.M.C. Royal Commission on Historical Manuscripts
H.M.G. His (Her) Majesty's Government
H.M.S.O. Her Majesty's Stationery Office
H.N.J.V. Handelingen der Nederlandse Juristenvereniging (Neth.)
H.O. Home Office
H.of C. House of Commons
H.of K. House of Keys
H.of L. House of Lords
H.of R. House of Representatives (USA)
H.P. All India Reporter, Himachal Pradesh. 1949–
Hire Purchase
Houses of Parliament
H.P.C. The Hague Peace Conferences,

by A. Pearce Higgins. 1909
Hale's Pleas of the Crown
Haute Parties Contractantes
Hawkin's Pleas of the Crown

H.P.D.T. Handicapped Persons Discrimination Tribunal (South Australia)

H.Pr. Howard's Practice Reports, New Series (New York)

H.Q. Headquarters

H.R. Hoge Raad (Neth.) High Court of Justice
Hojesteret (Den.) Supreme Court
House of Representatives Bill (USA)
House Roll
Human Rights Convention (Council of Europe)

H.R.C. Human Rights Commission

H.R.Comm. Commission on Human Rights (Council of Europe)

H.R.Conv. Human Rights Convention (Council of Europe)

H.R.Court Court of Human Rights (Council of Europe)

H.R.L.J. Human Rights Law Journal (Ger.)

HRR Höchstrichterliche Rechtsprechung (Ger.)

H.R.Rep. House of Representatives Report (USA)

HRegV Verordnung über das Handelsregister (Switz.) 1937

H.Rept. House of Representatives Report (USA)

H.Res. House of Representatives Resolution (USA)

H.S. Hansard Society
Home Secretary

H.S.C. Health Service Commissioner

H.S.E. Health and Safety Executive

H.S.I. Halsbury's Statutory Instruments

H.S.I.B. Health and Safety Information Bulletin

H.T. Hilary Term
Hoc titulo (Lat.) in or under this title

H.U.L. Houston Law Review (Texas) 1963–

H.V. Hoc verbum (Lat.) at this word

HVG Gesetz zur Anderung d. Handelsgesetzbuchs (Ger.) Law on commercial agency

H.W.Gr. H.W.Green's New Jersey Equity Reports (2–4 N.J.Eq.)

HZA Hauptzollamt (Ger.) Head Custom Office

H.& B. Hudson & Brooke's Irish King's Bench Reports. 1827–31

H.& C. Hurlston & Coltman's Exchequer Reports (158–9 ER) 1862–66

H.& D. Hill & Denio's New York Reports. 1842–4

H.& E. Hlothhere and Eadric

H.& G. Harris & Gill's Maryland Court of Appeals Reports. 1826–29
Hurlstone & Gordon's Exchequer Reports (156 ER) 1854–6

H.& H. Harrison & Hodgin's Upper Canada Municipal Reports. 1945–51
Horn & Hurlstone's Exchequer Reports (51 RR) 1838–39

H.& J. Harris & Johnson's Maryland Court of Appeals Reports. 1800–26
Hayes & Jones' Exchequer Reports (Ire.) 1832–34

H.& J.Ir. Hayes & Jones' Exchequer Reports (Ire.) 1832–34

H.& M. Hay & Marriott's Admiralty Reports (165 ER) 1776–79
Hemming & Miller's Chancery Reports (71 ER) 1862–65
Hening & Munford's Reports (11–14 Virginia) 1806–10

H.& M.Ch. Hemming & Miller's Chancery Reports (71 ER) 1862–65

H.& M.(Va.) Hening & Munford's Reports (11–14 Virginia) 1806–10

H.& McH. Harris & MacHenry's Maryland Court of Appeals Reports. 1785–99

H.& N. Hurlstone & Norman's Exchequer Reports (156–8 ER) 1856–62

H.& P. Hopwood & Philbrick's Registration Cases. 1863–67

H.& R. Harrison & Rutherford's Common Pleas Reports. 1865–66

H.& R.Bank. Hazlitt & Roche's

Bankruptcy Reports
H.& S. Harris & Simrall's Reports (49–52 Mississippi)
H.& S.M. Health and Safety Monitor
H.& T. Hall & Twell's Chancery Reports (47 ER) 1849–50
H.& Tw. Hall & Twell's Chancery Reports (47 ER) 1849–50
H.& W. Harrison & Wollaston's King's Bench Reports (47 RR) 1835–36
Hazzard & Warburton's Prince Edward Island Reports
Hurlstone & Walmsley's Exchequer Reports (58 RR) 1840–41
Ha. Haggard
Hall
Hare's Chancery Reports (66–8 ER) 1841–53
Hawaii
Ha.App. Appendix to Hare's Chancery Reports (68 ER) 1852–3
Ha.& Tw. Hall & Twell's Chancery Reports (47 ER) 1849–50
Hab.Corp. Habeas Corpus
Habil.–Schr. Habilitationsschrift (Ger.)
Hackworth, Digest G.H. Hackworth, A Digest of International Law. 1940–44
Had. Haddington's Court of Session Reports (Scot.) 1592–1624
Hadley's Reports (45–48 New Hampshire)
Hadd. Haddington's Court of Session Reports (Scot.) 1592–1624
Haddington Haddington's Court of Session Reports (Scot.) 1592–1624
Hadl. Hadley's Reports (45–48 New Hampshire)
Hadl.Rom.Law Hadley's Introduction to the Roman Law
Hadley Hadley's Reports (45–48 New Hampshire)
Hag. Hagan's Reports (1–2 Utah)
Hagans' Reports (1–5 West Virginia)
Haggard's Admiralty Reports (166 ER) 1822–38
Hag.Adm. Haggard's Admiralty Reports (166 ER) 1822–38
Hag.Con. Haggard's Consistorial Reports (161 ER) 1789–1821
Hag.Ecc. Haggard's Ecclesiastical Reports (162 ER) 1827–33
Hagan Hagan's Reports (1–2 Utah)
Hagans Hagans' Reports (1–5 West Virginia)
Hagg.Adm. Haggard's Admiralty Reports (166 ER) 1822–38
Hagg.Con. Haggard's Consistorial Reports (161 ER) 1789–1821
Hagg.Cons. Haggard's Consistorial Reports (161 ER) 1789–1821
Hagg.Consist. Haggard's Consistorial Reports (161 ER) 1789–1821
Hagg.Ecc. Haggard's Ecclesiastical Reports (162 ER) 1827–33
Hagg.Eccl. Haggard's Ecclesiastical Reports (162 ER) 1827–33
Hagn.& M. Hagner & Miller's Reports (2 Maryland Chancery)
Hagn.& Mill. Hagner & Miller's Reports (2 Maryland Chancery)
Hague Ct.Rep. Hague Court Reports
Hague Recueil Recueil des Cours de l'Académie de Droit International (Neth.)
Hague Yrbk.Int.L. Hague Yearbook of International Law (Neth.)
Hailes Hailes' Decisions of the Court of Session (Scot.) 1766–91
Hailes' Ann. Hailes, Annals of Scotland
Hailes Dec. Hailes' Decisions of the Court of Session (Scot.) 1766–91
Hal.Anal. Hale, Analysis of the Law. 6ed. 1820
Hal.Int.Law Halleck's International Law
Hal.Law Halsted's Reports (6–12 New Jersey Law)
Halc. Halcomb's Mining Cases. 1826
Halc.Min.Cas. Halcomb's Mining Cases
Haldane S.S.L.B. Haldane Society of Socialist Lawyers Bulletin
Hale Hale's History of the Common Law. 6ed. 1820
Hale's Precedents in Ecclesiastical Criminal Cases. 1475–1640
Hale's Reports (33–37 California)

Hale Anal. Hale's Analysis of the Law. 6ed. 1820
Hale C.L. Hale's History of the Common Law. 6ed. 1820
Hale Com.Law Hale's History of the Common Law. 6ed. 1820
Hale Cr.Prec. Hale's Precedents in Ecclesiastical Criminal Cases. 1475–1640
Hale De Jure Mar. Hale's De Jure Maris
Hale De Port.Mar. Hale's De Portibus Maris
Hale Ecc. Hale's Ecclesiastical Reports. 1583–1736
Hale Jur.H.L. Hale, Jurisdiction of the House of Lords. 1796
Hale P.C. Hale's Pleas of the Crown
Hale Parl. Hale, History of Parliament. 2ed. 1745
Hale Prec. Hale's Precedents in Ecclesiastical Criminal Cases. 1475–1640
Hale Sum. Hale, Summary of the Pleas of the Crown
Halk. Halkerston's Compendium of Scotch Faculty Decisions
Halkerston's Digest of the Scotch Marriage Law
Halkerston's Latin Maxims
Halk.Comp. Halkerston's Compendium of Scotch Faculty Decisions
Halk.Lat.Max. Halkerston's Latin Maxims
Halk.Max. Halkerston's Latin Maxims
Halk.Tech.Terms Halkerston's Technical Terms of the Law
Hall. Decisions of the Water Court (S.Afr.) 1913–36
Hall, Treatise on International Law
Hall's New York Superior Court Reports
Hall's Reports (56–57 New Hampshire)
Hallett's Reports (1–2 Colorado)
Hall A.L.J. Hall's American Law Journal. 1808–17
Hall Am.L.J. Hall's American Law Journal. 1808–17
Hall.(Col.) Hallett's Reports (1–2 Colorado)
Hall.Const.Hist. Hallam's Constitutional History of England
Hall Int.Law Hall on International Law. 8ed. 1924
Halleck's International Law. 4ed. 1908
Hall Jour.Jur. Journal of Jurisprudence (Hall's) (USA) 1821
Hall L.J. Hall's American Law Journal. 1808–17
Hall.Law of W. Halleck's Law of War
Hall N.H. Hall's Reports (56–57 New Hampshire)
Hall(N.Y.) Hall's New York Superior Court Reports
Hall Neut. Hall, Rights and Duties of Neutrals. 1874
Hall Profits à Prendre Hall, Treatise on the Law Relating to Profits à Prendre, etc. 1871
Hall, Readings J. Hall, Readings in Jurisprudence. 1938
Hall Shores Hall, Rights in Sea Shores
Hall & T. Hall & Twell's Chancery Reports (47 ER) 1849–50
Hall & Tw. Hall & Twell's Chancery Reports (47 ER) 1849–50
Hallam Hallam's Constitutional History of England
Halleck Int.Law Halleck's International Law. 4ed. 1908
Hallett Hallett's Reports (1–2 Colorado)
Hallif.C.L. Hallifax, Analysis of the Civil Law
Hallifax Anal. Hallifax, Analysis of the Civil Law
Hall's Am.L.J. Hall's American Law Journal. 1808–17
Hall's J.Jur. Journal of Jurisprudence (Hall's) (USA) 1821
Hals. Halsted's Reports (6–12 New Jersey Law Reports)
Hals.Ch. Halsted's New Jersey Equity Reports (5–8 N.J. Eq.) 1845–53
Hals.Eq. Halsted's New Jersey Equity Reports (5–8 N.J. Eq.) 1845–53
Hals.Laws Halsbury's Laws of England (4ed. current)

Hals.Stats. Halsbury's Statutes of England (4ed. current)

Halsbury Halsbury's Laws of England (4ed. current)
Halsbury's Statutes of England (4ed. current)

Halsbury L.Eng. Halsbury's Laws of England (4ed. current)

Halsbury's Laws Halsbury's Laws of England (4ed. current)

Halsbury's S.I.s Halsbury's Statutory Instruments

Halsbury's Statutes Halsbury's Statutes of England (4ed. current)

Halst. Halsted's New Jersey Equity Reports (5–8 N.J. Eq.) 1845–53
Halsted's New Jersey Law Reports (6–12 N.J. Law)

Halst.Ch. Halsted's New Jersey Equity Reports (5–8 N.J. Eq.) 1845–53

Ham. Haddington's Reports, Court of Session (Scot.) 1592–1624
Hammond's India and Burma Election Cases. 1920–8
Hammond's Reports (1–9 Ohio)

Ham.A.& O. Hamerton, Allen & Otter's Magistrates' Cases

Ham.Cust. Hamel's Laws of the Customs. 3ed. 1881

Ham.Mar.Laws Hammick, Marriage Laws. 2ed. 1887

Ham.N.P. Hammond's Nisi Prius. 1816

Ham.Parties Hammond on Parties to Actions. 1817

Ham.Pl. Hammond, Principles of Pleading. 1819

Ham.& J. Hammond & Jackson's Reports (45 Georgia)

Hamilton Haddington's Reports, Court of Session (Scot.) 1592–1624
Hamilton's American Negligence Cases
Hamilton on Company Law. 3ed. 1910

Hamlin Hamlin's Reports (81–99 Maine)

Hamline J.Pub.L.& Pol'y Hamline Journal of Law and Public Policy (USA)

Hamline L.Rev. Hamline Law Review (USA)

Hammond Hammond's Reports (36–44 Georgia)
Hammond's Reports (1–9 Ohio)

Hammond & Jackson Hammond & Jackson's Reports (45 Georgia)

Hamp.Tr. Hampson, Trustees. 2ed. 1830

Hamps.Co.Cas. Hampshire County Court Reports

Han. Handy's Ohio Reports (12 Ohio Decisions)
Hannay's New Brunswick Reports (12–13 NB) (Can.) 1867–71
Hansard's Book of Entries. 1685
Hanson's Bankruptcy Cases. 1915–17

Han.Deb. Hansard, Parliamentary Debates

Han.(N.B.) Hannay's New Brunswick Reports (12–13 NB) (Can.) 1867–71

Hand. Hand's Reports (40–45 New York)
Handelingen (Neth.) parliamentary records
Handy's Ohio Reports (12 Ohio Decisions)

Handai Hog Handai hogaku (Japan) Osaka Law Review

Handb.Mag. Handbook for Magistrates. 1853–55

Handler, Anti-Trust M. Handler, Anti-Trust in Perspective: the Complementary Roles of Rule and Discretion (USA) 1957

Handy Handy's Reports (12 Ohio Decisions)

Handy (Ohio) Handy's Reports (12 Ohio Decisions)

Hanf. Hanford's Entries. 1685

Hanm. Lord Kenyon's Notes, King's Bench, ed. by Hanmer (96 ER) 1753–9

Hanmer Lord Kenyon's Notes, King's Bench, ed. by Hanmer (96 ER) 1753–9

Hann. Hannay's New Brunswick Reports (12–13 NB) (Can.) 1867–71

Hans.Deb. Hansard, Parliamentary Debates

Hans.Parl.Deb. Hansard, Parliamentary Debates

HansRGZ Hanseatische Rechts-und Gerichts-Zeitschrift (Ger.)
HansRZ Hanseatische Rechts-Zeitschrift (Ger.)
Hansard Hansard, Parliamentary Debates
Hansb. Hansbrough's Reports (76–90 Virginia)
Har. Harrington's Chancery Reports (Michigan) 1836–42
Harrington's Delaware Reports (1–5 Del.) 1832–55
Harris' Pennsylvania Reports (13–24 Pa. State)
Harrison's Reports (15–17, 23–29 Indiana)
Harrison's Reports (16–19 New Jersey Law Reports)
Har.App. Hare's Chancery Reports, Appendix to vol. 10
Har.Del. Harrington's Reports (1–5 Delaware) 1832–55
Har.L.R. Harvard Law Review. 1887–
Har.St.Tr. Hargrave's State Trials. 4ed. 1776–81
Har.& Gil. Harris & Gill's Maryland Appeal Reports. 1826–9
Har.& Gill Harris & Gill's Maryland Appeal Reports. 1826–9
Har.& J. Harris & Johnson's Maryland Appeal Reports. 1800–26
Har.& J.(Md.) Harris & Johnson's Maryland Appeal Reports. 1800–26
Har.& John. Harris & Johnson's Maryland Appeal Reports. 1800–26
Har.& McH. Harris & McHenry's Maryland Appeal Reports. 1785–99
Har.& Nav. Harbors and Navigation (USA)
Har.& Ruth. Harrison & Rutherford's Common Pleas Reports. 1865–66
Har.& W. Harrison & Wollaston's King's Bench Reports (47 RR) 1835–36
Har.& Woll. Harrison & Wollaston's King's Bench Reports (47 RR) 1835–36
Harari, Negligence A. Harari, The Place of Negligence in the Law of Torts. 1962
Harb.& Nav.C. Harbors and Navigation Code (California)
Harc. Harcase's Decisions, Court of Session (Scot.) 1681–91
Hard. Hardin's Reports (3 Kentucky) 1805–08
Hardres' Exchequer Reports (145 ER) 1655–69
W. Kelynge's Chancery Reports tempore Hardwicke (25 ER) 1730–34
Hardes. Hardesty's Reports (Delaware Term)
Hardin Hardin's Kentucky Reports (3 Ky.) 1805–8
Hardin (Ky.) Hardin's Kentucky Reports (3 Ky.) 1805–8
Hardr. Hardres' Exchequer Reports (145 ER) 1655–69
Hardres Hardres' Exchequer Reports (145 ER) 1655–69
Kelynge's Chancery Reports (25 ER) 1730–4
Hardw. Cases tempore Hardwicke by Lee (95 ER) 1733–38
Cases tempore Hardwicke by Ridgeway
Kelynge's Chancery Reports (25 ER) 1730–4
Hardw.Cas.Temp. Cases tempore Hardwicke by Lee (95 ER) 1733–8
Cases tempore Hardwicke by Ridgeway
Hardw.N.B. Hardwicke, Note Books
Hardwicke, Cases temp. Cases tempore Hardwicke by Lee (95 ER) 1733–8
Hare Hare's Chancery Reports (66–8 ER) 1841–53
Hare(App.) Hare's Reports (Appendix to vol. 10) 1852–3
Hare Const.Law Hare's American Constitutional Law
Hare & W. Hare & Wallace's American Leading Cases
Hare & Wal.L.C. Hare & Wallace's American Leading Cases
Harg. Hargrave's State Trials. 1407–1776
Hargrove's Reports (68–76 North Carolina)
Harg.Co.Litt. Hargrave's Notes to Coke upon Littleton

Harg.Coll.Jur. Hargrave, Collectanea Juridica. 1791–2
Harg.Law Tracts Hargrave's Law Tracts (Collectanea Juridica) 1791–2
Harg.St.Tr. Hargrave's State Trials. 1407–1776
Harg.State Tr. Hargrave's State Trials. 1407–1776
Harg.& B.Co.Litt. Hargrave & Butler's Edition of Coke upon Littleton
Hargrove Hargrove's Reports (68–75 North Carolina)
Hari Rao Income Tax Cases (India) 1919–25
Harland Manchester Court Leet Records. 1552–1602 (Chetham Society) 1864–5
Harm. Harman's Upper Canada Common Pleas Reports. 1850–82
Harmon's Reports (13–15 California)
Harman Harman's Upper Canada Common Pleas Reports. 1850–82
Harman Cttee. Committee on the Law Relating to Rights of Light (Cmnd. 473) 1957–8
Harp. Harper's South Carolina Equity Reports (5 SCEq.) 1824
Harper's South Carolina Law Reports (16 SCL) 1823–30
Harp.Con.Cas. Harper's Conspiracy Cases (Maryland)
Harp.Eq. Harper's South Carolina Equity Reports (5 SCEq.) 1824
Harp.Eq.(S.C.) Harper's South Carolina Equity Reports (5 SCEq.) 1824
Harp.L. Harper's South Carolina Law Reports (16 SCL) 1823–30
Harp.L.(S.C.) Harper's South Carolina Law Reports (16 SCL) 1823–30
Harper Harper's Conspiracy Cases (Maryland)
Harper's South Carolina Equity Reports (5 SCEq.) 1824
Harper's South Carolina Law Reports (16 SCL) 1823–30
Harr. Harrington's Chancery Reports (Michigan) 1836–42
Harrington's Delaware Reports (1–5 Del.) 1832–55
Harris' Reports (13–24 Pennsylvania)
Harrison's Reports (15–17, 23–29 Indiana)
Harrison's Reports (16–19 New Jersey Law Reports)
Harr.Adv. Harris, Hints on Advocacy. 18ed. 1943
Harr.Ch. Harrington's Chancery Reports (Michigan) 1836–42
Harrison, Chancery Practice. 9ed. 1908
Harr.Ch.(Mich.) Harrington's Chancery Reports (Michigan) 1836–42
Harr.Con.La.R. Harrison's Condensed Louisiana Reports
Harr.Cr.L. Harris, Principles of the Criminal Law. 22ed. 1973
Harr.(Del.) Harrington's Delaware Reports (1–5 Del.) 1832–55
Harr.Dig. Harris' Georgia Digest
Harrison's Digest of English Common Law Reports
Harr.(Ga.) Harris' Georgia Digest
Harr.(Mich.) Harrington's Chancery Reports (Michigan) 1836–42
Harr.N.J. Harrison's Reports (16–19 New Jersey Law Reports)
Harr.& G. Harris & Gill's Maryland Reports. 1826–9
Harr.& H. Harrison & Hodgins' Upper Canada Municipal Reports. 1845–51
Harr.& Hodg. Harrison & Hodgins' Upper Canada Municipal Reports. 1845–51
Harr.& J. Harris & Johnson's Maryland Reports. 1800–26
Harr.& J.(Md.) Harris & Johnson's Maryland Reports. 1800–26
Harr.& M'H. Harris & M'Henry's Maryland Court of Appeals Reports. 1785–99
Harr.& McH. Harris & McHenry's Maryland Court of Appeals Reports. 1785–99
Harr.& McH.(Md.) Harris & MacHenry's Court of Appeals Reports. 1785–99

Harr.& R. Harrison & Rutherford's Common Pleas Reports. 1865–6

Harr.& Ruth. Harrison & Rutherford's Common Pleas Reports. 1865–6

Harr.& Sim. Harris & Simrall's Reports (49–52 Mississippi)

Harr.& W. Harrison & Wollaston's King's Bench Reports (47 RR) 1835–6

Harr.& Woll. Harrison & Wollaston's King's Bench Reports (47 RR) 1835–6

Harring. Harrington's Delaware Reports (1–5 Del.) 1832–55
Harrington's Michigan Chancery Reports. 1836–42

Harrington Harrington's Delaware Reports (1–5 Del.) 1832–55
Harrington's Michigan Chancery Reports. 1836–42

Harris Harris' Reports (13–24 Pennsylvania)

Harris Dig. Harris' Georgia Digest

Harris & G. Harris & Gill's Reports (Maryland) 1826–9

Harris & S. Harris & Simrall's Reports (49–52 Mississippi)

Harris & Sim. Harris & Simrall's Reports (49–52 Mississippi)

Harris & Simrall Harris & Simrall's Reports (49–52 Mississippi)

Harrison Harrison's Reports (15–17, 23–29 Indiana)
Harrison's Reports (16–19 New Jersey Law Reports)

Harrison Ch. Harrison's Chancery Practice. 9ed. 1908

Harrison Dig. Harrison's Digest of English Common Law Reports

Harrison, Jurisprudence F. Harrison, Jurisprudence and the Conflict of Laws. 1878–79, 1919 ed.

Hart. Hartley's Digest of Laws (Texas)
Hartley's Reports (4–10 Texas)

Hart.Dig. Hartley's Digest of Laws (Texas)

Hart, Law H.L.A. Hart, The Concept of Law. 1961

Hart.& H. Hartley & Hartley's Reports (11–21 Texas)

Hartley Hartley's Reports (4–10 Texas)

Hartley & Hartley Hartley & Hartley's Reports (11–21 Texas)

Harv. Harvard

Harv.Bus.Rev. Harvard Business Review

Harv.Bus.World Harvard Business World

Harv.C.R.–C.L.Law Rev. Harvard Civil Rights – Civil Liberties Law Review. 1966–

Harv.Civ.Lib.L.Rev. Harvard Civil Liberties Law Review. 1966–

Harv.Ed.Rev. Harvard Education Review

Harv.Env.L.Rev. Harvard Environmental Law Review

Harv.I.L.J. Harvard International Law Journal. 1967–

Harv.Int'l.L.Club Bull. Harvard International Law Club Bulletin. 1959–62

Harv.Int'l.L.Club J. Harvard International Law Club Journal. 1962–66

Harv.Int'l.L.J. Harvard International Law Journal. 1967–

Harv.J.L.& Publ.Pol. Harvard Journal of Law and Public Policy

Harv.J.L.& Tech. Harvard Journal of Law and Technology

Harv.J.Legis. Harvard Journal on Legislation. 1964–

Harv.J.on Legis. Harvard Journal on Legislation. 1964–

Harv.L.Lib.Inf.Bull. Harvard Law Library Information Bulletin. 1947–

Harv.L.Rev. Harvard Law Review. 1887–

Harv.L.S.Bull. Harvard Law School Bulletin. 1948–

Harv.L.S.Rec. Harvard Law School Record. 1946–

Harv.Women's L.J. Harvard Women's Law Journal

Harvard I.L.J. Harvard International Law Journal. 1967–

Harvard on Treaties Harvard Law School, Research in International Law,

Draft Code on the Law of Treaties. 1935

Harvard Research Research in International Law, Harvard Law School

Hasb. Hasbrouck's Reports (Idaho)

Hask. Haskell's Reports for U.S. Courts in Maine (Fox's Decisions)

Hast. Hastings' Reports (69, 70 Maine)

Hast.Const.L.Q. Hastings Constitutional Law Quarterly (USA) 1974–

Hast.L.J. Hastings Law Journal (USA) 1949–

Hast.Tr. Trial of Warren Hastings

Hastings Comm.& Ent.L.J. Hastings Communications and Entertainment Law Journal

Hastings Const.L.Q. Hastings Constitutional Law Quarterly

Hastings Int'l & Comp.L.Rev. Hastings International and Comparative Law Review (USA)

Hastings L.J. Hastings Law Journal (USA) 1949–

Hatcher's Kan.Dig. Hatcher's Kansas Digest

Hats. Hatsell's Parliamentary Precedents. 1290–1818

Hats.Pr. Hatsell's Parliamentary Precedents. 1290–1818

Hats.Prec. Hatsell's Parliamentary Precedents. 1290–1818

Hav. Haviland's Prince Edward Island Chancery Reports, by Peters (Can.) 1850–72

Hav.Ch.Rep. Haviland's Prince Edward Island Chancery Reports, by Peters (Can.) 1850–72

Hav.P.E.I. Haviland's Prince Edward Island Chancery Reports, by Peters (Can.) 1850–72

Havana (ITO) Charter Havana Charter for an International Trade Organization. 1948

Havana Reports United Nations Conference on Trade and Employment, Reports of Committees and Principal Subcommittees. 1948

Havil. Haviland's Prince Edward Island Chancery Reports, by Peters (Can.) 1850–72

Haw. Hawarde's Star Chamber Cases. 1593–1609
Hawaii Supreme Court Reports. 1847–
Hawkins' Pleas of the Crown. 8ed. 1824
Hawkins' Reports (19–24 Louisiana Annual)
Hawley's Reports (10–20 Nevada)

Haw.B.J. Hawaii Bar Journal

Haw.Cr.Rep. Hawley's American Criminal Reports

Haw.Rev.Stat. Hawaii Revised Statutes

Haw.Sess.Laws Session Laws of Hawaii

Haw.W.C. Hawes' Will Cases

Hawaii Hawaii (Sandwich Islands) Reports

Hawaii B.J. Hawaii Bar Journal. 1959–

Hawaii B.N. Hawaii Bar News. 1961–2

Hawaii Dist. District Courts of Hawaii

Hawaii Rep. Hawaii Supreme Court Reports. 1847–

Hawaii Rev.Stat. Hawaii Revised Statutes

Hawaiian Rep. Hawaii (Sandwich Islands) Reports

Hawarde Hawarde's Star Chamber Cases. 1593–1609

Hawarde St.Ch. Hawarde's Star Chamber Cases. 1593–1609

Hawes Jur. Hawes on Jurisdiction of Courts

Hawk. Hawkins' Pleas of the Crown. 8ed. 1824

Hawk.Abr. Hawkins, Abridgment of Coke upon Littleton

Hawk.Co.Litt. Hawkins, Abridgment of Coke upon Littleton

Hawk.Coke Abr. Hawkins, Abridgment of Coke upon Littleton

Hawk.P.C. Hawkins' Pleas of the Crown. 8ed. 1824

Hawk.Pl.Cr. Hawkins' Pleas of the Crown. 8ed. 1824

Hawk.Wills Hawkins' Construction of Wills. 3ed. 1925

Hawkins Hawkins' Reports (19–24 Louisiana Annual)
Hawks Hawks' North Carolina Reports (8–11 NC) 1820–6
Hawks(N.C.) Hawks' North Carolina Reports (8–11 NC) 1820–6
Hawl. Hawley's Reports (10–20 Nevada)
Hawl.Cr.R. Hawley's American Criminal Reports
Hawley Hawley's American Criminal Reports
Hawley's Reports (10–20 Nevada)
Hay. Hay's High Court Appeals Reports (Bengal, India) 1862–63
Hay's Poor Law Decisions (Scot.) 1711–1859
Hayes' Irish Exchequer Reports. 1830–32
Haywood's North Carolina Reports (2–3 NC) 1789–1806
Haywood's Tennesssee Reports (4–6 Tenn.) 1816–18
Hay.Acc. Hay's Decisions on Accidents and Negligence (Scot.) 1860
Hay (Calc.) Hay's High Court Appeals Reports (Bengal, India) 1862–3
Hay Dec. Hay's Decisions on Accidents and Negligence (Scot.) 1860
Hay.Eq. Haynes, Outlines of Equity. 5ed. 1880
Hay.Exch. Hayes' Irish Exchequer Reports. 1830–32
Hay P.L. Hay's Poor Law Decisions (Scot.) 1711–1859
Hay.& Haz. Hayward & Hazelton, District of Columbia Circuit Court Reports. 1840–63
Hay.& J. Hayes & Jones' Exchequer Reports (Ire.) 1832–34
Hay.& Jo. Hayes & Jones' Exchequer Reports (Ire.) 1832–34
Hay & M. Hay & Marriott's Admiralty Decisions Reports (165 ER) 1776–79
Hay & Mar. Hay & Marriott's Admiralty Decisions Reports (165 ER) 1776–79
Hay & Marr. Hay & Marriott's Admiralty Decisions Reports (165 ER) 1776–79
Hayes Hayes' Irish Exchequer Reports. 1830–32
Hayes Conv. Hayes' Introduction to Conveyancing. 5ed. 1840
Hayes Exch. Hayes' Irish Exchequer Reports. 1830–32
Hayes Exch.(Ir.) Hayes' Irish Exchequer Reports. 1830–32
Hayes & J. Hayes & Jones' Irish Exchequer Reports. 1832–34
Hayes & J.Wills Hayes & Jarman, Concise Forms of Wills. 18ed. 1952
Hayes & Jo. Hayes & Jones' Irish Exchequer Reports. 1832–34
Hayes & Jon. Hayes & Jones' Irish Exchequer Reports. 1832–34
Hayn.Ch.Pr. Haynes' Chancery Practice. 1879
Hayn.Eq. Haynes' Outlines of Equity. 5ed. 1880
Hayn.Lead.Cas. Haynes' Students' Leading Cases. 2ed. 1884
Hayw. Haywood's North Carolina Reports (2–3 NC) 1789–1806
Haywood's Tennessee Reports (4–6 Tenn.) 1816–18
Hayw.L.R. Hayward's Law Register, Boston
Hayw.N.C. Haywood's North Carolina Reports (2–3 NC) 1789–1806
Hayw.Tenn. Haywood's Tennessee Reports (4–6 Tenn.) 1816–18
Hayw.(Tenn.) Haywood's Tennessee Reports (4–6 Tenn.) 1816–18
Hayw.& H. Hayward & Hazelton's District of Columbia Reports. 1840–63
Hayward & Hazelton's United States Circuit Court Reports
Haz.P.Reg. Hazard's Pennsylvania Register
Haz.Pa.Reg. Hazard's Pennsylvania Register
Haz.Reg. Hazard's Pennsylvania Register
Haz.U.S.Reg. Hazard's United States Register
hdbk. handbook

HdlVertrG Gesetz zur Anderung des Handelsgesetzbuchs (Ger.) Law on commercial agency
Hdqrs. Headquarters
Head Head's Tennessee Supreme Court Reports (38–40 Tenn.) 1858–59
Head(Tenn.) Head's Tennessee Supreme Court Reports (38–40 Tenn.) 1858–59
Headnote Headnote (Otago University Law Students' Association) (N.Z.) 1979–81
Health L.Can. Health Law in Canada. 1979–
Health & S.C. Health and Safety Code (California)
Hearnshaw Southampton Court Leet Records. 1550–1624
Hearsay Hearsay: Legal Aid Practice Notes and Information Bulletin of the Legal Aid Commission of Western Australia. 1980–
Heath Heath's Reports (36–40 Maine)
Heath Max. Heath's Maxims and Rules of Pleading. 1694
Heck.Cas. Hecker's Cases on Warranty
Hedges Hedges' Reports (2–6 Montana)
Heffter Heffter, Das europäische Völkerrecht der Gegenwart (Ger.) 8ed. 1888
Heilborn, System Heilborn, Das System des Volkerrechts entwickelt aus den völkerrechtlichen Begriffen (Ger.) 1896
Heilbron Cttee. Home Office Advisory Group on the Law of Rape. Report (Cmnd. 6352) 1975
Hein. Heineccius, System of Universal Law. 1763
Hein.de Naut. Heineccius, Scriptorum de Jure Nautico et Maritimo Fasciculus. 1740
Heinecc.Elem. Heineccius, Elementa Juris Civilis (Elements of the Civil Law)
Heisk. Heiskell's Tennessee Supreme Court Reports (48–59 Tenn.) 1870–74
Heisk.(Tenn.) Heiskell's Tennessee Supreme Court Reports (48–59 Tenn.) 1870–74
Helm Helm's Reports (2–9 Nevada)
Hem. Hempstead's United States Circuit Court Reports
Hem.& M. Hemming & Miller's Chancery Reports (71 ER) 1862–65
Hem.& Mill. Hemming & Miller's Chancery Reports (71 ER) 1862–65
Heming. Hemingway's Reports (53–65 Mississippi)
Heming.(Miss.) Hemingway's Reports (53–65 Mississippi)
Hemmant Hemmant's Select Cases in the Exchequer Chamber (Selden Society, vol. 51) 1377–1460
Hemp. Hempstead's United States Circuit Court Reports
Hempst. Hempstead's United States Circuit Court Reports
Hen. King Henry
Hen.Bl. Henry Blackstone's Common Pleas Reports (126 ER) 1788–96
Hen.La.Dig. Hennen, Louisiana Digest
Hen.Man.Cas. Henry's Manumission Cases. 1817
Hen.St. Hening's Virginia Statutes
Hen.& M. Hening & Munford's Virginia Supreme Court Reports (11–14 Va.) 1806–10
Hen.& Mun. Hening & Munford's Virginia Supreme Court Reports (11–14 Va.) 1806–10
Hennepin Law. Hennepin Lawyer (USA) 1933–
Henry Judg. Henry, Judgment in Odwin v. Forbes
Hepb. Hepburn's Reports (3–4 California)
Hepburn's Reports (13 Pennsylvania)
Her. Herne's Law of Charitable Uses. 2ed. 1663
Her.Char.U. Herne's Law of Charitable Uses. 2ed. 1663
Her.Chat. Herman on Chattel Mortgages
Her.Est. Herman's Law of Estoppel
Her.Ex. Herman's Law of Executors
Her.Jur. Heron, Jurisprudence. 1860
Herbert, Inns of Court W. Herbert, Antiquities of the Inns of Court and Chancery. 1804

Herm. Hermand's Consistorial Decisions (Scot.) 1684–1777
Hermand Hermand's Consistorial Decisions (Scot.) 1684–1777
Hertslet Hertslet, Collection of Treaties and Conventions between Great Britain and Other Powers, so far as they relate to Commerce and Navigation
Hertzog Hertzog's Cases in the Transvaal High Court (S.Afr.) 1893
Het. Hetley's Common Pleas Reports (124 ER) 1627–31
Hetl. Hetley's Common Pleas Reports (124 ER) 1627–31
Heyw.Ca. Heywood's Table of Cases (Georgia)
Heyw.Co.Ct. Heywood, County Courts Practice. 4ed. 1876
Heywood & Massey Heywood & Massey, Court of Protection Practice
HgI Hague Convention on the Peaceful Settlement of International Disputes. 1907
Hi. Hawaii
Hawaii Supreme Court Reports
Hindi
Hibb. Hibbard's Reports (67 New Hampshire)
Hibbard's Reports (20 Opinions of Attorneys-General) (USA)
Hicks Leg.Research Hicks, Materials and Methods of Legal Research (USA) 1923
Hig.Pat.Dig. Higgins' Digest of Patent Cases. 2ed. 1890
Hig.Waterc. Higgins, Pollution and Obstruction of Water-courses. 1877
Higgins Higgins' Tennessee Civil Appeal Reports
Higgins & Colombos Higgins & Colombos, The International Law of the Sea. 2ed. 1951
High. Highway
High Ct. High Court
High Court Reports North West Provinces (Pak.) 1869–75
Reports of the High Court of Griqualand (S.Afr.) 1882–1910
High Ex.Rem. High, Extraordinary Legal Remedies (USA)
High Inj. High, Injunctions (USA)
High Rec. High, Law of Receivers (USA)
High Tech.L.J. High Technology Law Journal (USA)
Highlights Highlights of Current Legislation and Activities in Mid-Europe
Hight Hight's Reports (57–58 Iowa)
Hikakuho Kenkyu Hikakuho Kenkyu (Japan) Comparative Law Journal
Hil. Hilary Term
Hil.Elem.Law Hilliard's Elements of Law
Hil.T. Hilary Term
Hil.Torts Hilliard on the Law of Torts (USA)
Hill Hill's New York Supreme Court Reports. 1841–44
Hill's South Carolina Equity Reports (10–11 SCEq.) 1833–7
Hill's South Carolina Law Reports (19–21 SCL) 1833–7
Hill.Abr. Hilliard, Abridgment of Real Property Law
Hill.Am.Jur. Hilliard, American Jurisprudence
Hill.Am.Law Hilliard, American Law
Hill Ch. Hill's South Carolina Equity Reports (10–11 SCEq.) 1833–7
Hill.Cont. Hilliard on Contracts
Hill.Elem.Law Hilliard's Elements of Law
Hill Eq. Hill's South Carolina Equity Reports (10–11 SCEq.) 1833–7
Hill Eq.(S.C.) Hill's South Carolina Equity Reports (10–11 SCEq.) 1833–7
Hill Law Hill's South Carolina Law Reports (19–21 SCL) 1833–7
Hill.Mortg. Hilliard, Law of Mortgages
Hill N.Y. Hill's New York Supreme Court Reports. 1841–4
Hill.New Trials Hilliard on New Trials
Hill.Real Prop. Hilliard on Real Property

Hill S.C. Hill's South Carolina Equity Reports (10–11 SCEq.) 1833–7
Hill's South Carolina Law Reports (19–21 SCL) 1833–7

Hill & D. Hill & Denio's Reports (New York) 1842–44

Hill & D.Supp. Hill & Denio's Reports, Lalor's Supplement (New York) 1842–44

Hill & Den. Hill & Denio's Reports (New York) 1842–44

Hill & Den.Supp. Hill & Denio's Reports, Lalor's Supplement (New York) 1842–44

Hill & Redman Hill & Redman's Law of Landlord and Tenant

Hill's 'Ann.Codes & Laws Hill's Annotated Codes and General Laws (Oregon)

Hill's Ann.St.& Codes Hill's Annotated General Statutes and Codes (Washington)

Hill's Code Hill's Annotated Codes and General Laws (Oregeon)
Hill's Annotated General Statutes and Codes (Washington)

Hillyer Hillyer's Reports (20–22 California)

Hilt. Hilton's New York Common Pleas Reports

Hilt.(NY) Hilton's New York Common Pleas Reports

Him.Pra. All India Reporter, Himachal Pradesh. 1949–

Hind.L.J. Hindu Law Journal (India) 1918–25

Hind.L.Q. Hindu Law Quarterly (India) 1930–36

Hindc Ch.Pr. Hinde, Modern Practice of the High Court of Chancery. 1786

Hindu L.J. Hindu Law Journal (India)

Hines Hines' Reports (83–96 Kentucky)

Hispanic Am.Hist.Rev. Hispanic-American Historical Review

Hist. Historical
History

Hist.Pol.Econ. History of Political Economy

Hist.Pol.Thought History of Political Thought

Historia Historia Zeitschrift für alte Geschichte (Ger.)

Hitch.Pr.& Proc. Hitch's Practice and Procedure in the Probate Court of Massachusetts

Hitotsubashi J.L.& Pol. Hitotsubashi Journal of Law and Politics (Japan)

Hitt.Cod. Hittell's California Code

Hittell's Laws Hittell's General Laws (California)

Ho.L.Cas. Clark's House of Lords Cases (9–11 ER) 1847–66

Ho.Lords.C. Clark's House of Lords Cases (9–11 ER) 1847–66

Ho.Lords.Cas. Clark's House of Lords Cases (9–11 ER) 1847–66

Ho.of Dels. House of Delegates

Ho.of Reps. House of Representatives

Hob. Hobart's Common Pleas Reports (80 ER) 1613–25
Hobart's King's Bench Reports (80 ER) 1603–25

Hob.R. Hobart's Common Pleas Reports (80 ER) 1613–25
Hobart's King's Bench Reports (80 ER) 1603–25

Hobart Hobart's Common Pleas Reports (80 ER) 1613–25
Hobart's King's Bench Reports (80 ER) 1603–25

Hod. Hodges' Common Pleas Reports (42–3 RR) 1835–7

Hodg. Hodges' Common Pleas Reports (42–3 RR) 1835–7
Hodgin's Election Petitions (Ontario) 1871–9

Hodg.Can.Elec.Cas. Hodgin's Election Petitions (Ontario) 1871–9

Hodg.El. Hodgin's Election Petitions (Ontario) 1871–9

Hodg.El.Cas. Hodgin's Election Petitions (Ontario) 1871–9

Hodg.El.Cas.(Ont.) Hodgin's Election Petitions (Ontario) 1871–9

Hodg.Ont.Elect. Hodgin's Election Petitions (Ontario) 1871–9

Hodges Hodges' Common Pleas Reports (42–3 RR) 1835–7

Hodgson Report Civil Justice Review: Report of the Review Body on Civil Justice (Lord Chancellor's Department) (Cm. 394) 1988

Hof. Gerechtshof (Neth.) District Court of Appeal

Hoff. Hoffman's Land Cases, United States District Court
Hoffman's New York Chancery Reports. 1838–40

Hoff.Cha. Hoffman's New York Chancery Reports. 1838–40

Hoff.Dec. Hoffman's Decisions, United States District Court

Hoff.L.C. Hoffman's Land Cases, United States District Court

Hoff.L.Cas. Hoffman's Land Cases, United States District Court

Hoff.Land Hoffman's Land Cases, United States District Court

Hoff.Lead.Cas. Hoffman's Leading Cases

Hoff.Mast.Ch. Hoffman's Master in Chancery

Hoff.N.Y. Hoffman's New York Chancery Reports. 1838–40

Hoff.Op. Hoffman's Opinions, United States District Court

Hoffm. Hoffman's New York Chancery Reports. 1838–40
Hoffman's Land Cases, United States District Court

Hoffm.Ch.(N.Y.) Hoffman's New York Chancery Reports. 1838–40

Hoffm.Dec.(F.) Hoffman's Decisions, United States District Court

Hoffm.Land Cas.(F.) Hoffman's Land Cases, United States District Court

Hoffm.Ops.(F.) Hoffman's Opinions, United States District Court

Hofstra L.Rev. Hofstra Law Review. 1973–

Hofstra Prop.L.J. Hofstra Property Law Journal (USA)

Hog. Harcase's Decisions (Hog of Harcase), Court of Session (Scot.) 1681–91
Hogan's Irish Rolls Court Reports tempore M'Mahon. 1816–34

Hog.Kyokai Zasshi Hogaku Kyokai zasshi (Japan) Journal of the Jurisprudence Association

Hog.Ronso Hogaku ronso (Japan) Kyoto Law Review

Hog.Shimpo Hogaku shimpo (Japan) The Chuo Law Review

Hog.St.Tr. Hogan's State Trials (Pennsylvania)

Hogan Hogan's Irish Rolls Court Reports tempore M'Mahon. 1816–34

Hogue Hogue's Reports (1–4 Florida)

Holc.Eq.Jur. Holcombe, Equity Jurisdiction

Holc.L.Cas. Holcombe, Leading Cases of Commercial Law

Hold.L.R. Holdsworth Law Review

Holdsw.Hist.E.L. Holdsworth's History of English Law

Holl. Holland
Hollinshead's Reports (1 Minnesota)

Holl.Jur. Holland's Elements of Jurisprudence. 12ed. 1924

Holl.Just. Holland, Institutes of Justinian

Holland, Lectures Holland, Lectures on International Law. 1933

Holland, Studies Holland, Studies in International Law. 1898

Holliday Report Report of the independent review of radioactive waste in the Northeast Atlantic (F.G.T. Holliday, chairman) (DOE & MAFF) 1984

Hollinshead Hollinshead's Reports (1 Minnesota)

Holm. Holmes' Reports (15–17 Oregon)
Holmes' United States Circuit Court Reports

Holm.Com.Law Holmes, Common Law. 1881

Holt Holt's Equity Reports (71 ER) 1845
Holt's Judgments in Ashby v. White and Re Patey et al. 1704–5

Holt's King's Bench Reports (90 ER) 1688–1711
Holt's Nisi Prius Reports (171 ER) 1815–17

Holt Adm. Holt's Admiralty Cases, Rule of the Road. 1863–67

Holt Adm.Ca. Holt's Admiralty Cases, Rule of the Road. 1863–67

Holt Adm.Cas. Holt's Admiralty Cases, Rule of the Road. 1863–67

Holt Eq. Holt's Equity Reports (71 ER) 1845

Holt K.B. Holt's King's Bench Reports (90 ER) 1688–1711

Holt N.P. F. Holt's Nisi Prius Reports (171 ER) 1815–17

Holt R.of R. Holt's Admiralty Cases, Rule of the Road. 1863–67

Holt Shipp. Holt on Shipping. 2ed. 1824

Holtz.Enc. Holtzendorff Encyclopadie der Rechtswissenschaft (Ger.) Encyclopedia of Jurisprudence

Holtzendorff Holtzendorff, Handbuch des Völkerrechts (Ger.) 1885–89

Home Home's Decisions, Court of Session (Scot.) 1735–44

Home (Cl.) Home's Decisions, Court of Session (Scot.) 1735–44

Home (Clk.) Home's Decisions, Court of Session (Scot.) 1735–44

Home Ct.of Sess. Home's Decisions, Court of Session (Scot.) 1735–44

Home H.Dec. Home's Decisions, Court of Session (Scot.) 1735–44

Hon. Honorary
Honourable

Hon.Magist. Honorary Magistrate (Aus.) 1904–

Hond. Honduras

Hong Kong L.J. Hong Kong Law Journal. 1971–

Hong Kong L.R. Hong Kong Law Reports. 1905–

Hong Kong U.L.Jo. Hong Kong University Law Journal. 1926–27

Hooker Hooker's Reports (25–62 Connecticut)

Hoon. Hoonahan's Sind Reports (India)

Hoonahan Hoonahan's Sind Reports (India)

Hop.Maj.Pr. Hope, Major Practicks (Scot.)

Hop.Min. Hope, Minor Practicks (Scot.)

Hop.& C. Hopwood & Coltman's Registration Cases. 1868–78

Hop.& Colt. Hopwood & Coltman's Registration Cases. 1868–78

Hop.& Ph. Hopwood & Philbrick's Registration Cases. 1863–67

Hop.& Phil. Hopwood & Philbrick's Registration Cases. 1863–67

Hope Hope's Manuscript Decisions, Court of Session (Scot.) 1610–32

Hope Dec. Hope's Manuscript Decisions, Court of Session (Scot.) 1610–32

Hopk.Adm. Hopkinson's Pennsylvania Admiralty Judgments. 1779–89

Hopk.Adm.Dec. Admiralty Decisions of Hopkinson in Gilpin's U.S. District Court Reports

Hopk.Av. Hopkins, Average. 4ed. 1884

Hopk.Ch. Hopkins' New York Chancery Reports. 1823–26

Hopk.Judg. Hopkinson's Pennsylvania Admiralty Judgments. 1779–89

Hopw.& C. Hopwood & Coltman's Registration Cases. 1868–78

Hopw.& Colt. Hopwood & Coltman's Registration Cases. 1868–78

Hopw.& P. Hopwood & Philbrick's Registration Cases. 1863–67

Hopw.& Phil. Hopwood & Philbrick's Registration Cases. 1863–67

Hor.& Th.Cas. Horrigan & Thompson's Cases on Self Defence

Horitsu J. Horitsu jiho (Japan) Law Journal

Horn & H. Horn & Hurlstone's Exchequer Reports (51 RR) 1838–39

Horne M.J. Horne's Mirrour of Justices

Horne Mir. Horne's Mirrour of Justices

Horner Horner's Reports (11–28 South Dakota)

Horner's Ann.St. Horner's Annotated Revised Statutes (Indiana)

Horner's Rev.St. Horner's Annotated Revised Statutes (Indiana)
Horr.& Th. Horrigan & Thompson's Cases on Self Defence
Horw.Y.B. Horwood's Year Books of Edward I
Hosea Hosea's Reports (Ohio)
Hoskins Hoskins' Reports (2 North Dakota)
Hoso J. Hoso jiho (Japan) Lawyers Association Journal
Hosp. Hospital
Hou. Houston's Delaware Reports (6–14 Del.) 1855–93
Hou.L.R. Houston Law Review. 1963–
Hough V.Adm. Reports of Cases in Vice-Admiralty of the Province of New York. 1715–88
Houghton Houghton's Reports (97 Alabama)
Houghton Cttee. Home Office Departmental Committee on the Adoption of Children. Report (Cmnd. 5107) 1972
Hous. Housing
Houston's Delaware Reports (6–14 Del.) 1855–93
Hous.J.Int'l L. Houston Journal of International Law (USA)
Hous.L.Rev. Houston Law Review (USA)
Hous.Life Ass. Houseman, Life Assurance
Hous.Pr. Housman, Precedents in Conveyancing. 1861
Hous.& Dev.Rep. Housing and Development Reporter (BNA) (USA)
House Mag. House Magazine: for Senators and Members of the House of Representatives (Aus.) 1982–
House of L. House of Lords Cases (9–11 ER) 1847–66
Houst. Houston's Delaware Reports (6–14 Del.) 1855–93
Houst.Cr. Houston's Criminal Cases (Delaware) 1856–79
Houst.Cr.Cas. Houston's Criminal Cases (Delaware) 1856–79
Houst.L.Rev. Houston Law Review. 1963–
Houston Houston's Delaware Supreme Court Reports (6–14 Del.) 1855–93
Hov. Hovenden on Frauds. 1825
Hovenden's Supplement to Vesey, Junior's Chancery Reports (34 ER) 1789–1817
Hov.Sup. Hovenden's Supplement to Vesey, Junior's Chancery Reports (34 ER) 1789–1817
Hov.Supp. Hovenden's Supplement to Vesey, Junior's Chancery Reports (34 ER) 1789–1817
How. Howard's New York Practice Reports. 1844–86
Howard's Reports (2–8 Mississippi) 1834–43
Howard's Supreme Court Reports (42–65 US) 1843–60
Howell's Reports (22–26 Nevada)
How.A.Cas. Howard's Appeal Cases (New York) 1847–8
How.Ann.St. Howell's Annotated Statutes (Michigan)
How.App. Howard's Appeal Cases (New York) 1847–8
How.C. Howard's Chancery Practice (Ire.) 1775
How.Cas. Howard's New York Court of Appeals Cases. 1847–8
Howard's Popery Cases (Ire.) 1720–73
How.Ch. Howard's Chancery Practice (Ire.) 1775
How.Ch.P. Howard's Chancery Practice (Ire.) 1775
How.Ch.Pr. Howard's Chancery Practice (Ire.) 1775
How.Cr.Tr. Howison's Criminal Trials (Virginia) 1850–1
How.E.E. Howard's Equity Exchequer Reports (Ire.)
How.Eq.Exch. Howard's Equity Exchequer Reports (Ire.)
How.J. Howard Journal. 1921–64
How.J.Pen. Howard Journal of Penology and Crime Prevention. 1964–
How.L.J. Howard Law Journal. 1955–

How.L.Rev. Howard Law Review

How.N.P.(Mich.) Howell, Nisi Prius Reports (Michigan)

How.N.S. Howard's New York Practice Reports, New Series

How.Po.Ca. Howard's Popery Cases (Ire.) 1720–73

How.Po.Cas. Howard's Popery Cases (Ire.) 1720–73

How.Pr. Howard's New York Practice Reports. 1844–86

How.Pr.N.S. Howard's New York Practice Reports, New Series

How.Prac.(N.S.) Howard's New York Practice Reports, New Series

How.Prac.(N.Y.) Howard's New York Practice Reports. 1844–86

How.Prob.Pr. Howell, Probate Practice (Ontario, Can.)

How.S.C. Howard's United States Supreme Court Reports (42–65 US) 1843–60

How.St. Howell's Annotated Statutes (Michigan)

How.St.Tr. Howell's State Trials. 1163–1820

How.State Tr. Howell's State Trials. 1163–1820

How.U.S. Howard's United States Supreme Court Reports (42–65 US) 1843–60

How.& Beat. Howell & Beatty's Reports (22 Nevada)

How.& H.St. Howard & Hutchinson's Statutes (Mississippi)

How.& Nor. Howell & Norcross' Reports (23–24 Nevada)

Howard Howard's Mississippi Supreme Court Reports (2–8 Mississippi) 1834–43

Howard J.Criminol. Howard Journal of Penology and Crime Prevention (now Howard Journal of Criminal Justice) 1964–

Howard Journal Howard Journal. 1921–64
Howard Journal of Criminal Justice
Howard Journal of Penology and Crime Prevention. 1964–

Howard L.J. Howard Law Journal

Howard S.C. Howard's Supreme Court Reports (42–65 US) 1843–60

Howell N.P. Howell's Nisi Prius Reports (Michigan) 1868–84

Howell St.Tr. Howell's State Trials. 1163–1820

Hrgw Handelsregisterwet (Neth.) Trade Register Act

Hu. Hughes' Kentucky Reports (1 Ky.) 1785–1801
Hughes' United States Circuit Court Reports

Hub. Hobart's Common Pleas Reports (80 ER) 1613–25
Hobart's King's Bench Reports (80 ER) 1603–25

Hub.Leg.Direc. Hubbell's Legal Directory (USA)

Hub.Prael.J.C. Huber, Praelectiones Juris Civilis

Hubb. Hubbard's Reports (45–51 Maine)

Hubb.Succ. Hubback's Evidence of Succession. 1844

Hubbard Hubbard's Reports (45–51 Maine)

Hud.& B. Hudson & Brooke's Irish King's Bench Reports. 1827–31

Hud.& Br. Hudson & Brooke's Irish King's Bench Reports. 1827–31

Hud.& Bro. Hudson & Brooke's Irish King's Bench Reports. 1827–31

Hudson Hudson on Building Contracts

Hudson, Cases M.O. Hudson, Cases and Other Materials on International Law. 3ed. 1951

Hudson, Int.Leg. M.O. Hudson, International Legislation: a Collection of the Texts of Multipartite International Instruments of General Interest (USA) 1919–45

Hudson, Legislation M.O. Hudson, International Legislation (USA) 1919–45

Hudson, Permanent M.O. Hudson, The Permanent Court of International Justice, 1920–42 (USA) 1943

Hudson's B.C. Hudson on Building Contracts

Hugh. Hughes' Circuit Court Reports (USA)
Hughes' Reports (1 Kentucky) 1785–1801

Hugh.Abr. Hughes' Abridgment. 1663–65

Hugh.Conv. Hughes, Precedents in Conveyancing. 2ed. 1855–7

Hugh.Ent. Hughes' Entries. 1659

Hughes Hughes' Circuit Court Reports (USA)
Hughes' Kentucky Supreme Court Reports (1 Ky.) 1785–1801

Hughes Fed.Prac. Hughes' Federal Practice

Hughes Report Review of child care law: report to ministers of an interdepartmental working party (DHSS) 1985

Hull C.A. Hull Claims Analysis

Hult.Conv. Hulton, Convictions. 1835

Hum. Humphreys' Tennessee Supreme Court Reports (20–30 Tenn.) 1839–51

Hum.Rts.Q. Human Rights Quarterly (USA)

Human Rights Q. Human Rights Quarterly (USA)

Human Rights Rev. Human Rights Review. 1976–

Human Rts. Human Rights (USA) 1971–
Human Rights: Newsletter of the Human Rights Commission (Aus.) 1982–

Human Rts.J. Human Rights Journal. 1968–

Human Rts.Rev. Human Rights Review. 1976–

Hume Hume's Decisions, Court of Session (Scot.) 1781–1822

Hume.Com. Hume, Commentaries on Crimes (Scot.)

Humph. Humphrey's Tennessee Reports (20–30 Tenn.) 1839–51

Humph.Dist.Reg. Humphreys, District Registry Practice and Procedure

Humph.Prec. Humphry, Common Precedents in Conveyancing. 2ed. 1882

Hun. Hun's New York Appellate Division Reports
Hun's New York Supreme Court Reports

Hung.L.Rev. Hungarian Law Review. 1961–

Hunt. Hunt's Annuity Cases. 1776–96
Hunter's Torrens Cases (Can., Aust., NZ) 1865–93

Hunt Ann.Cas. Hunt's Annuity Cases. 1776–96

Hunt Bound. Hunt's Law of Boundaries and Fences. 6ed. 1912

Hunt Cas. Hunt's Annuity Cases. 1776–96

Hunt.Eq. Hunter's Suit in Equity

Hunt Fr.Conv. Hunt, Fraudulent Conveyances. 2ed. 1897

Hunt.L.& T. Hunter, Landlord and Tenant (Scot.)

Hunt.Torrens Hunter's Torrens Cases (Can., Aus., NZ) 1865–93

Hunter Rom.Law Hunter on Roman Law

Hunter Suit Eq. Hunter's Suit in Equity

Hunt's A.C. Hunt's Annuity Cases. 1776–96

Hurd Rev.St. Hurd's Revised Statutes (Illinois)

Hurd St. Hurd's Illinois Statutes

Hurl.Bonds Hurlstone on Bonds. 1835

Hurl.Colt. Hurlstone & Coltman's Exchequer Reports (158–159 ER) 1862–6

Hurl.& C. Hurlstone & Coltman's Exchequer Reports (158–159 ER) 1862–6

Hurl.& Colt. Hurlstone & Coltman's Exchequer Reports (158–159 ER) 1862–6

Hurl.& G. Hurlstone & Gordon's Exchequer Reports (156 ER) 1854–6

Hurl.& Gord. Hurlstone & Gordon's Exchequer Reports (156 ER) 1854–6

Hurl.& N. Hurlstone & Norman's Exchequer Reports (156–8 ER) 1856–62

Hurl.& Nor. Hurlstone & Norman's Exchequer Reports (156–8 ER) 1856–62

Hurl.& W. Hurlstone & Walmsley's Exchequer Reports (58 RR) 1840–1

Hurl.& Walm. Hurlstone & Walmsley's Exchequer Reports (58 RR) 1840–1

Hurlst.& C. Hurlstone & Coltman's Exchequer Reports (158–9 ER) 1862–6

Hurlst.& G. Hurlstone & Gordon's Exchequer Reports (156 ER) 1854–6

Hurlst.& N. Hurlstone & Norman's Exchequer Reports (156–8 ER) 1856–62

Hurlst.& W. Hurlstone & Walmsley's Exchequer Reports (58 RR) 1840–1

Hut. Hutton's Common Pleas Reports (123 ER) 1612–39

Hut.Ct.Req. Hutton's Court of Requests. 4ed. 1840

Hutch. Hutcheson's Reports (81–84 Alabama)

Hutch.Car. Hutchinson on Carriers

Hutch.Code Hutchinson's Code (Mississippi)

Hutt. Hutton's Common Pleas Reports (123 ER) 1612–39

Hutt.Ct.Req. Hutton's Court of Requests. 4ed. 1840

Hutton Hutton's Common Pleas Reports (123 ER) 1612–39

Hux.Judg. Huxley's Second Book of Judgments. 1675

Hy. All India Reporter, Hyderabad. 1950–7

Hy.Bl. Henry Blackstone's Common Pleas Reports (126 ER) 1788–96

Hyd. All India Reporter, Hyderabad. 1950–7

Hyde Hyde's High Court Reports (Bengal, India) 1862–4
Hyde's International Law, chiefly as interpreted and applied by the United States. 2ed. 1945
Hyde's Notes of Cases, Supreme Court (Bengal, India) 1791–1861

Hyde Cttee. Home Office Committee on the Feasibility of an Experiment in the Tape recording of Police Interrogation. Report (Cmnd. 6630) 1976

Hyderabad Indian Law Reports, Hyderbad Series. 1953–

I

I. Idaho
Illinois
Imperator (Emperor)
Imperatrix (Empress)
Income Tax
Independent
Indiana
Institutes of Justinian
Iowa
Ireland
Irish
Isle(s)
Island(s)
Italian

i.A. im Auftrage (Ger.) by order of

I.A. Indian Affairs
Law Reports, Indian Appeals. 1872–75

IAC Industrial Accident Commission Decisions (USA)
Intercantonal Arbitration Convention (Switz.)

I.A.C. Immigration Appeal Cases (Can.) 1972–
Industrial Assurance Commissioner
Inflation Accounting Committee

IACAC Inter-American Commercial Arbitration Commission

I-ACHR Inter-American Commission on Human Rights

IADB InterAmerican Development Bank

I.A.D.L. International Association of Democratic Lawyers

I.A.E.A. International Atomic Energy Agency (UN)

IAI Interatom-Instrument

I.A.I.C. International Association of Insurance Counsel

I.A.L.A. International African Law Association

I.A.L.L. International Association of Law Libraries

I.A.L.L.Bull. Bulletin of the International Association of Law Libraries. 1960–72

I.A.L.S. Institute of Advanced Legal Studies (London University)
International Association of Legal Science

IALS Bull. Institute of Advanced Legal Studies Bulletin

IAPIP International Association for the Protection of Industrial Property

I.A.R.I. International Agricultural Research Institute

I.A.S. Industrial Arbitration Service (Aus.) 1950–81

I.A.Sup.Vol. Law Reports, Indian Appeals, Supplementary Volume

IATA International Air Transport Association

IATA A.G.M. IATA Annual General Meeting Reports and Proceedings (Can.) 1972–

IATA Bull. IATA Bulletin (Can.) 1945–71

I.Arb. Institute of Arbitrators

I.B. Industrial Board

I.B.A. Independent Broadcasting Authority
International Bar Association

I.B.A.C. Information Bulletin of Australian Criminology. Old Series 1974–82, New Series 1984–

I.B.A.Report International Bar Association, Report of the Conference

I.B.C. International Broadcasting Convention
I.B.C.A. Interior Board of Contract Appeals (in Decisions of the United States Department of the Interior)
IBCC International Bureau of Chambers of Commerce
IBEC International Bank for Economic Co-operation
I.B.F.D. International Bureau of Fiscal Documentation
I.B.F.L. International Banking and Financial Law
I.B.F.L.B. International Banking and Fianancial Law Bulletin. 1985–
I.B.J. Illinois Bar Journal. 1931–
I.B.L. International Banking Law. 1982–
International Business Lawyer. 1973–
I.B.R.D. International Bank for Reconstruction and Development (World Bank)
I.B.R.D. G.C. General Conditions Applicable to Loan and Guarantee Agreements
I.Bull. Interights Bulletin
I.C. Indian Cases. 1909–47
Industrial Arbitration Cases (Western Australia)
Industrial Court
Interstate Commerce Reports (USA)
I.C.A. Indian Council of Arbitration
Institute of Chartered Accountants
International Commodity Agreement
International Co-operative Alliance
International Court of Arbitration
Iowa Code Annotated
I.C.A.Arb.Q. Indian Council of Arbitration Quarterly
I.C.A.C. Independent Commission Against Corruption (New South Wales, Aus.)
Interstate Corporate Affairs Commission 1974–81 (Aus.)
ICAN International Commission for Air Navigation
ICAO International Civil Aviation Organisation (UN)
ICAO Bull. Bulletin of the International Civil Aviation Organisation (Can.) 1946–
ICC Agreement providing for the provisional application of the Draft International Customs Conventions on Touring, on Commercial Road Vehicles and on the International Transportation of Goods by Road. 1949
I.C.C. Indian Claims Commission (USA)
International Chamber of Commerce
Interstate Commerce Commission (USA)
ICCA Draft International Convention (Customs) on Touring. 1949
ICCB Draft International Convention (Customs) on the Transport of Goods by Road. 1949
ICCC International Convention for the Suppression of Counterfeiting Currency. 1929
I.C.C.L.R. International Company and Commercial Law Review
ICCPR International Covenant on Civil and Political Rights
I.C.C.Pract.J. Interstate Commerce Commission Practitioners' Journal. 1933–
I.C.C.Practitioners'J. Interstate Commerce Commission Practitioners' Journal. 1933–
I.C.C.Rep. Interstate Commerce Commission Reports (USA) 1931–
I.C.C.Valuation Rep. Interstate Commerce Commission, Valuation Reports (USA) 1929–
ICEF International Children's Emergency Fund (UN)
I.C.E.M. Inter-governmental Committee for European Migration
ICEREPAT Paris Union Committee for International Co-operation in Information Retrieval Among Patent Offices
I.C.F.C. Industrial and Commercial Finance Corporation

I.C.F.T.U. International Confederation of Free Trade Unions

ICITO Interim Commission for International Trade Organisation (UN)

I.C.J. International Commission of Jurists
International Court of Justice

I.C.J.Pleadings International Court of Justice, Pleadings, Oral Arguments, Documents

I.C.J.R. International Court of Justice Law Reports. 1947–

I.C.J.Reports International Court of Justice Law Reports. 1947–

I.C.J.Rev. Review of the International Commission of Jurists. 1968–

I.C.J.Y.B. International Court of Justice Yearbook

I.C.L. International Corporate Law

I.C.L.A. International Computer Law Adviser (USA) 1986–

I.C.L.Q. International and Comparative Law Quarterly. 1952–

I.C.L.R. International Construction Law Review. 1983–
Irish Common Law Reports, 2nd Series. 1850–66

I.C.L.R.Can. Index to Current Legal Research in Canada. 1972–

I.C.M.P. International Conference on Marine Pollution

ICO International Coffee Organisation

ICOD International Centre for Ocean Development

ICPCP Statutes of the International Centre for the Study of the Preservation and Restoration of Cultural Property. 1956

I.C.R. Industrial Cases Reports. 1975–
Industrial Court Reports
Irish Chancery Reports, 2nd Series. 1850–66
Irish Circuit Reports. 1841–43

ICRC International Committee of the Red Cross

I.C.R.V. Inns of Court Rifle Volunteers

I.C.Rep. Interstate Commerce Commission Reports (USA) 1931–

I.C.S. International Chamber of Shipping

ICSAB International Civil Service Advisory Board

ICSC International Civil Service Commission

I.C.S.I.D. International Centre for the Settlement of Investment Disputes

ICTB International Customs Tariff Bureau

ICVA International Council of Voluntary Agencies

I.Ch.R. Irish Chancery Reports, 2nd Series. 1850–66

I.D. Interior Department Decisions (USA)

I.D.A. International Development Association

I.D.A. G.C. General Conditions Applicable to Development Credit Agreements

I.D.I. Institut de Droit International (Institute of International Law)

I.D.I.Annuaire Annuaire de l'Institut de Droit International

I.D.R.C. International Development Research Centre

IDS Brief IDS Brief, Employment Law and Practice

IDS P.S.B. IDS Pensions Service Bulletin

IDX Interbank Data Exchange

i.e. id est (Lat.) that is

I.E.A. International Energy Agency (OECD)

I.E.A.J. Internacia Esperanto-Associo de Juristoj (International Esperanto Association of Jurists)

IECL International Encyclopedia of Comparative Law

I.E.L. International Economic Law

I.E.R. Irish Equity Reports, 1st Series. 1838–50

I.Eq.R. Irish Equity Reports, 1st Series. 1838–50

I.F.A. International Fiscal Association

I.F.C. International Finance Corporation

I.F.C.L. International Faculty of Comparative Law
I.F.L.P. Index to Foreign Legal Periodicals. 1960–
I.F.L.Rev. International Financial Law Review. 1982–
I.F.L.S. International Federation of Law Students
IFR Imported Food Regulations
I.F.S. Institute of Family Studies (Aus.)
I.F.S.Newsl. Institute of Family Studies Newsletter (Aus.) 1980–
I.F.S.W.P. Institute of Family Studies Working Papers (Aus.) 1981–
I.F.T.U. International Federation of Trade Unions
I.F.W.L. International Federation of Women Lawyers
I.G.C.C. Inter-Governmental Copyright Committee
IGWG Inter-Governmental Working Group
IGO International Governmental Organisation
I.H.A. Issuing Houses Association
IHK Internationale Handelskammer (Ger.)
I.I.A.C. Industrial Injuries Advisory Council
I.I.B. Industrial Information Bulletin (Aus.)
Institut international des brevets (International Patent Institute)
International Investment Bank
IIC International Institute of Communications
International Review of Industrial Property and Copyright Law (Ger.) 1970–
I.I.C. Indian Investment Centre
I.I.I.A. International Investment Insurance Agency
I.I.L.P. Index to Indian Legal Periodicals. 1963–
I.I.P. Industrial and Intellectual Property in Australia. 1961–
I.I.R. Institute for International Research
I.I.S.L. International Institute of Space Law
IITOPS International Institute for Transportation and Ocean Policy Studies
I.Inf.Sc. Institute of Information Scientists
I.J. Indian Jurist, Old Series
Instituto Jurídico da Faculdade de Direito da Universidade de Coimbra (Port.)
Irish Jurist. 1849–66, 1935–
I.J.A. Institute of Judicial Administration
I.J.C. Irvine's Justiciary Cases (Scot.) 1852–67
I.J.Cas. Irvine's Justiciary Cases (Scot.) 1852–67
I.J.E.C.L. International Journal of Estuarine and Coastal Law
I.J.I. International Juridical Institute
I.J.I.L. Indian Journal of International Law. 1960–
I.J.L.I. International Journal of Legal Information
I.J.L.L. International Journal of Law Libraries (now International Journal of Legal Information) 1973–
I.J.L.F. International Journal of Law and the Family. 1987–
I.J.N.S. Irish Jurist, New Series. 1935–
I.J.O. International Juridical Organisation for Developing Countries
I.J.P.A. Indian Journal of Public Administration. 1955–
I.J.R.L. International Journal of Refugee Law
I.J.S.L. International Journal for the Semiotics of Law
I.L. Fitzgibbon's Irish Land Reports. 1895–1920
I.L.A. International Law Association
I.L.A.A. International Legal Aid Association
I.L.A.Report International Law Association, Report of the Conference
I.L.B. Insurance Law Bulletin (Aus.) 1985–

I.L.C. International Law Commission (United Nations)
I.L.E. Institute of Legal Executives
I.L.E.A. Inner London Education Authority
I.L.J. Indiana Law Journal. 1925–
Industrial Law Journal
Insurance Law Journal (Aus.) 1988–
I.L.M. International Legal Materials (USA) 1962–
I.L.N. International Lawyers' Newsletter (Neth.) 1979–
i.l.o. in lieu of
I.L.O. International Labour Office
International Labour Organisation
ILOC International Labour Organisation Convention Number
Irrevocable Letter of Credit
I.L.P. Illinois Law and Practice
Index to Legal Periodicals. 1908–
International Legal Practitioner (USA) 1976–
I.L.P.L. Index to Legal Periodical Literature (USA) 1887–1937
I.L.Q. Indian Law Quarterly. 1914–17
International Law Quarterly. 1947–51
I.L.Q.R. Indian Law Quarterly Review. 1956–
I.L.R. Indian Law Reports. 1876–
Indian Law Review. 1947–54, 1957
Industrial Law Review. 1946–60
Insurance Law Reporter (Can.) 1934–
International Law Reports. 1950–
Iowa Law Review. 1925–
Irish Law Reports, 1st Series. 1838–50
I.L.R.All. Indian Law Reports, Allahabad Series. 1876–
I.L.R.And. Indian Law Reports, Andhra. 1959–
I.L.R.Assam Indian Law Reports, Assam. 1949–
I.L.R.Bom. Indian Law Reports, Bombay Series. 1876–
I.L.R.C. Indian Law Reports, Calcutta Series. 1876–
I.L.R.Cal. Indian Law Reports, Calcutta Series. 1876–
I.L.R.Calc. Indian Law Reports, Calcutta Series. 1876–
I.L.R.Cut. Indian Law Reports, Orissa. 1950–
I.L.R.Hyderabad Indian Law Reports, Hyderabad. 1953–
I.L.R.Kar. Indian Law Reports, Karachi Series. 1939–47
I.L.R.Ker. Indian Law Reports, Kerala. 1950–
I.L.R.Lah. Indian Law Reports, Lahore Series. 1920–47
I.L.R.Luck. Indian Law Reports, Lucknow Series. 1926–49
I.L.R.M. Irish Law Reports Monthly. 1981–
I.L.R.Mad. Indian Law Reports, Madras Series. 1876–
I.L.R.Madhya Bharat Indian Law Reports, Madhya Bharat. 1952–
I.L.R.Mysore Indian Law Reports, Mysore. 1953–
I.L.R.Nag. Indian Law Reports, Nagpur Series. 1904–
I.L.R.Or. Indian Law Reports, Orissa. 1950–
I.L.R.P. Indian Law Reports, Patna. 1922–
I.L.R.Pat. Indian Law Reports, Patna. 1922–
I.L.R.Patiala Indian Law Reports, Patiala. 1953–
I.L.R.Pun. Indian Law Reports, Punjab. 1949–
I.L.R.R. Industrial and Labor Relations Review (USA) 1946–
I.L.R.Rajasthan Indian Law Reports, Rajasthan. 1952–
I.L.R.Ran. Indian Law Reports, Rangoon.
I.L.R.Trav.-Cochin Indian Law Reports, Kerala. 1950–
I.L.S. Incorporated Law Society
I.L.T. Irish Law Times (Dublin) 1867–
I.L.T.Jo. Irish Law Times Journal. 1867–
I.L.T.R. Irish Law Times Reports (Ire.) 1867–

I.L.T.& S.J. Irish Law Times and Solicitors' Journal. 1867–
I.L.& P. Insolvency Law and Practice. 1985–
I.M. Industrial Magistrate
I.M.C.O. Inter-Governmental Maritime Consultative Organisation (UN)
I.M.D.G. International Maritime Dangerous Goods (Code)
I.M.F. International Monetary Fund (UN)
I.M.L. International Media Law
IMO International Maritime Organisation
International Meteorological Organisation (UN)
I.M.T. International Military Tribunal
I.M.T.A. Institute of Municipal Treasurers and Accountants
INDIS Industrial Information System (UNIDO)
I.N.G.O. International Non-Governmental Organisation
INMARSAT International Maritime Satellite Organisation
INS Information Network Service
INSA International Shipowners' Association
INTELSAT International Telecommunications Satellite Consortium
INTERPOL International Criminal Police Organisation
INTUG International Telecommunication User Group
I.O. India Office
Individual Opinion
I.O.C.U. International Office of Consumers' Unions
IOE International Organisation of Employers
I.O.M. Isle of Man
I.o.W. Isle of Wight
I.of M. Isle of Man
I.P. Industrial Property (World Intellectual Property Organisation) 1962–
Intellectual Property (Aus.) 1988–
I.P.A. Institute of Public Affairs (Aus.)
I.P.A.A. Insolvency Practitioners Association of Australia
I.P.A.Rev. Institute of Public Affairs Review (Aus.)
I.P.A.A. International Prisoners' Aid Association
I.P.A.L. Index to Periodical Articles Related to Law (USA) 1958–
I.P.B. Intellectual Property in Business
I.P.B.Rev. Intellectual Property in Business
I.P.B.Rev.Brief Intellectual Property in Business, Briefing
I.P.C. International Classification of Patents for Invention (Council of Europe Convention)
International Publishing Corporation
I.P.C.S. Institution of Professional Civil Servants
I.P.F. Intellectual Property Forum (Aus.) 1985–
I.P.H.E. Institution of Public Health Engineers
I.P.I. Institute of Patentees and Inventors
International Press Institute
I.P.J. Intellectual Property Journal (Can.) 1985–
I.P.L. International Pension Lawyer
I.P.L.A. Institute of Public Loss Assessors
I.P.M.S. Institution of Professionals, Managers and Scientists
IPNS Izvestiia na Presidiuma na Narodnoto Subranie (Bulgaria) Bulletin of the Presidium of the National Assembly
I.P.News Intellectual Property Newsletter
I.P.P. In Propria Persona (Lat.) in person
I.P.P.C. International Penal and Penitentiary Commission (UN)
I.P.P.F. International Penal and Penitentiary Foundation
International Planned Parenthood Federation

IPR Internationales Privatrecht (Ger.) private international law
I.P.R. Institute of Public Relations
Intellectual Property Reports (Aus.) 1982–
Investerings Premie Regeling (Neth.) Investment Premium Regulation
I.P.R.A. International Public Relations Association
IPRspr. Die deutsche Rechtsprechung auf dem Gebiete des internationalen Privatrechts (Ger.)
I.P.U. Inter-Parliamentary Union
I.R. Indian Rulings. 1929–47
Industrial Relations
Industrial Reports (Aus.) 1982–
Inland Revenue
Internal Revenue Decisions (U.S. Treasury Department)
International Relations
Irish Reports. 1894–
Law Reports, Ireland (4th series) 1878–93
South Australian Industrial Reports. 1916–
I.R.All. Indian Rulings, Allahabad Series. 1929–47
I.R.B. Industrial Relations Bureau (Aus.)
Internal Revenue Bulletin (USA)
I.R.Bom. Indian Rulings, Bombay Series. 1929–47
I.R.C. Industrial Relations Commission (Victoria, Aus.)
Inland Revenue Commissioners
Internal Revenue Code (USA) 1954
International Red Cross
I.R.C.L. Irish Reports Common Law Series (3rd series) 1866–78
I.R.C.T.L. International Review of Computers, Technology and the Law (Aus.) 1985–6
I.R.Cal. Indian Rulings, Calcutta Series. 1929–47
I.R.Comrs. Inland Revenue Commissioners
I.R.D. Inland Revenue Department (N.Z.)
I.R.Eq. Irish Reports, Equity (3rd series) 1866–78
I.R.Fed.Ct. Indian Rulings, Federal Court. 1938–47
I.R.Jour. Indian Rulings, Journal Section
I.R.L.I.B. Industrial Relations Legal Information Bulletin
I.R.L.R. Industrial Relations Law Reports
I.R.Lah. Indian Rulings, Lahore Series. 1929–47
I.R.Mad. Indian Rulings, Madras Series. 1929–47
I.R.Nag. Indian Rulings, Nagpur Series. 1929–47
I.R.O. International Refugee Organization
I.R.Oudh Indian Rulings, Oudh Series. 1929–47
I.R.P.C. Indian Rulings, Privy Council. 1929–47
I.R.Pat. Indian Rulings, Patna Series. 1929–47
I.R.Pesh. Indian Rulings, Peshawar Series. 1933–47
I.R.Peshawar Indian Rulings, Peshawar Series. 1933–47
I.R.Pr.C. Indian Rulings, Privy Council. 1929–47
I.R.R. Inland Revenue Regulation Act 1890
Internal Revenue Record (New York)
I.R.R.C. Industrial Relations Research Centre (Aus.)
I.R.R.& L. Irish Reports, Registry Appeals in the Court of Exchequer Chambers and Appeals in the Court for Land Cases Reserved. 1868–76
I.R.Ran. Indian Rulings, Rangoon Series
I.R.Rep. Reports of the Inland Revenue Commissioners
I.R.Sind. Indian Rulings, Sind Series. 1929–47
I.R.U. Convention establishing the International Relief Union. 1927
Industrial Rehabilitation Unit
International Recruitment Unit (ODA)
International Road Transport Union

I.S.A.L.P.A. Incorporated Society of Auctioneers and Landed Property Agents
ISBA Indiana State Bar Association
ISBN International Standard Book Number
I.S.C. Insurance and Superannuation Commission (Aus.)
Inter-State Commission (Aus.)
ISD International subscriber dialling
ISDN Integrated services digital network
I.S.F. International Shipping Federation
I.S.L.L. International Survey of Legal Decisions on Labour Law. 1925–38
ISNT Informal Single Negotiating Text
ISO International Standards Organisation
I.S.S.J. International Social Science Journal. 1949–
ISSN International Standard Serial Number
I.T. Income Tax
Inner Temple
I.T.A. Independent Television Authority
I.T.C. Srinivasan's Reports of Income Tax Cases (India) 1886–
I.T.D.A. Income Tax Decisions of Australasia. 1928
I.T.G. Australian Income Tax Guide (CCH) 1969–
ITI International Transit of Goods (Customs Convention)
I.T.J. Indian Tax Journal
I.T.L.J. Income Tax Law Journal (India) 1932–40
I.T.O. International Trade Organisation (UN)
I.T.R. Income Tax Relief
Income Tax Reports (India) 1933–
Indian Tax Reports
Industrial Tribunal Reports
International Tax Report. 1972–
International Tax Review
Irish Term Reports (Ridgeway, Lapp & Schoales) 1793–5
I.T.Rulings Income Tax Rulings (Aus.)
ITS International Trade Secretariats
I.T.U. International Telecommunication Union (UN)
I.U.C. Inter-University Council for Higher Education Overseas
I.U.E.F. International University Exchange Fund
I.U.L.A. International Union of Local Authorities
IUOTO International Union of Official Travel Organisations
I.U.W. Industrial Union of Workers (N.Z.)
i.v. in verbo (Lat.) under the word
I.V.S. International Voluntary Service
IW Invaliditeitswet (Neth.) Disability Act
I.W.C. International Whaling Commission
IWI Interimwet Invaliditeitsrentetrekkers (Neth.) Interim Act on the Beneficiaries of Disability Pensions
I.W.S. Industrial Welfare Society
I.Y.L.C.T. International Yearbook of Law, Computers and Technology
IZRspr. Die deutsche Rechtsprechung auf dem Gebiete des interzonalen Rechts (Ger.) 1945–53
I.& C.L.Q. International & Comparative Law Quarterly. 1952–
I.& N.Dec. Immigration & Nationality Decisions (USA) 1940–
I.& N.L.& P. Immigration & Nationality Law and Practice
I.& N.S. Immigration & Naturalisation Service (USA)
I.& R.L.I. Insurance and Reinsurance Law International (Neth.) 1982–
Ia. Iowa
Iowa Reports
Ia.B.Rev. Iowa Bar Review. 1934–40
Ia.Bar Rev. Iowa Bar Review. 1934–40
Ia.L.Bull. Iowa Law Bulletin. 1915–25
Ia.L.R. Iowa Law Review. 1925–
Ia.L.Rev. Iowa Law Review. 1925–
ib. ibidem (Lat.) in the same place
ibid. ibidem (Lat.) in the same place
Ictus. Iuriconsultus (Counsellor-at-law)

id. idem (Lat.) the same
Id. Idaho
Idaho Reports. 1866–
Id.L.J. Idaho Law Journal. 1931–3
Id.L.R. Idaho Law Review. 1964–
Ida. Idaho Reports (USA) 1866–
Idaho Idaho Supreme Court Reports. 1866–
Idaho L.J. Idaho Law Journal. 1931–3
Idaho L.Rev. Idaho Law Review. 1964–
Idaho Sess.Laws Session Laws, Idaho
Idd.T.R. Idding's Term Reports (Dayton, Ohio)
Iddings T.R.D. Idding's Term Reports (Dayton, Ohio)
Idea Idea: the Journal of Law and Technology (USA) 1976–
Idea: the Patent, Trademark and Copyright Journal of Research and Education (USA) 1965–75
Ilex. Institute of Legal Executives
Ill. Illinois
Illinois Supreme Courts. 1819–
Ill.2d. Illinois Reports, Second Series
Ill.A. Illinois Appellate Court Reports. 1877–
Ill.A.2d. Illinois Appellate Court Reports, Second Series
Ill.A.3d. Illinois Appellate Court Reports, Third Series
Ill.Ann.Stat. Smith-Hurd's Illinois Annotated Statutes
Ill.App. Illinois Appellate Court Reports. 1877–
Ill.App.2d. Illinois Appellate Court Reports, Second Series
Ill.App.3d. Illinois Appellate Court Reports, Third Series
Ill.B.A.Bull. Illinois State Bar Association Quarterly Bulletin. 1912–31
Ill.B.J. Illinois Bar Journal. 1931–
Ill.C.C. Illinois Commerce Commission Opinions & Orders
Ill.Cir.Ct. Illinois Circuit Court Reports
Ill.Cont.Legal Ed. Illinois Continuing Legal Education. 1963–
Ill.Ct.Cl. Illinois Court of Claims Reports. 1899–
Ill.L.B. Illinois Law Bulletin. 1917–18
Ill.L.F. Illinois Law Forum
Ill.L.Q. Illinois Law Quarterly. 1917–24
Ill.L.Rec. Illinois Law Record. 1880
Ill.L.Rev. Illinois Law Review. 1906–52
Ill.Laws Laws of Illinois
Ill.Leg.N. Illustrated Legal News (India) 1935
Ill.Legis.Serv. Illinois Legislative Service (West)
Ill.Rev.Stat. Illinois Revised Statutes
Ill.S.B.A. Illinois State Bar Association Reports
Ill.S.B.A.Q.B. Illinois State Bar Association Quarterly Bulletin. 1912–31
Ill.W.C.C. Illinois Workmen's Compensation Cases
imm. immediately (of a writ returnable sine dilate)
Imm.A.R. Immigration Appeal Reports
Imm.L.R.(2d) Immigration Law Reporter, Second Series. 1985–
Imm.& Nat.L.& P. Immigration and Nationality Law and Practice
Immig.B.Bull. Immigration Bar Bulletin. 1947–
Immig.& Naturalization Serv.Mo.Rev. Immigration and Naturalization Service Monthly Review (USA)
Immigr.Brief. Immigration Briefings (USA)
imp. implement(ed)
imprimatur (Lat.) let it be printed
imprimé (Fr.) printed
imprimeur (Fr.) printer
Imp. Imperial
Imperator (Lat.) Emperor
Imperatrix (Lat.) Empress
Imp.Man. Impey, Law and Practice of Mandamus. 1826
Imp.Pl. Impey, Modern Pleader. 2ed. 1814
Imp.Sh. Impey, Office of Sheriff. 6ed. 1835
impt. important
improvement
In.A. Indiana Appellate Court Reports. 1890–1971

Indiana Court of Appeals Reports. 1972–
In.L.F. Indiana Legal Forum. 1967–71
In.L.J. Indiana Law Journal. 1898–9, 1925–
In.L.R. Indiana Law Review. 1972–
in loc. in loco (Lat.) in place of
in loc.cit. in loco citato (Lat.) in the place cited
in pr. in principio (Lat.) in the beginning
In re In reference to
inc. included
includes
including
income
Inc. Income
Incorporated
Inc.Tax Cas. Reports of Tax Cases. 1875–
Inc.Tax L.J. Income Tax Law Journal (India) 1933–
Inc.Tax R. Income Tax Reports (India) 1933–
incho. inchoate
Incl. Included
Includes
Including
incorp. incorporated
Ind. Independent
Index
India
Indiana
Indiana Supreme Court Reports. 1848–
Industrial
Industry
Ind.A.Dig. Indian Affairs Office, Digest of Decisions (USA)
Ind.Acts Indiana Acts
Ind.Adv. Indian Advocate (Bombay) 1961–
Indian Advocate (Lahore) 1937–
Ind.Advocate Indian Advocate (New Delhi)
Ind.App. Indiana Appellate Court Reports. 1890–1971
Indiana Court of Appeals Reports. 1972–
Law Reports, Indian Appeals. 1872–1875
Ind.App.Supp. Law Reports, Indian Appeals Supplementary Volume. 1872–73
Ind.Awards Industrial Arbitration Awards (N.Z.) 1894–
Ind.C.Aw. Industrial Court Awards. 1919–
Ind.Can.L.P.Lit. Index to Canadian Legal Periodical Literature. 1961–
Ind.Cas. Indian Cases (India) 1909–47
Ind.Code Indiana Code
Ind.Code Ann. Burn's Indiana Statutes Annotated Code Edition
Ind.Com.Law Indermaur & Thwaites, Principles of the Common Law. 12ed. 1914
Ind.Comm. Industrial Commission
Ind.Court Aw. Industrial Court Awards. 1919–
Ind.Ct. Judgments, etc. of the Industrial Court of New Zealand. 1976–8
Ind.Ct.Awards Industrial Court Awards. 1919–
Ind.Dig. All India Reporter, Indian Digest. 1946–52
Ind.Div. Inderwick, Divorce & Matrimonial Causes Acts. 1862
Ind.Ind.L.P. Index to Indian Legal Periodicals. 1963–
Ind.J.Comp.L. Indian Journal of Comparative Law
Ind.J.Industr.Rel. Indian Journal of Industrial Relations
Ind.J.Int.L. Indian Journal of International Law. 1960–
Ind.J.Pol.Sci. Indian Journal of Political Science
Ind.J.Pub.Admin. Indian Journal of Public Administration. 1955–
Ind.Jur. Indian Jurist (Calcutta) 1862–3, 1866–7
Indian Jurist (Madras) 1877–83, 1884–93
Ind.Jur.N.S. Indian Jurist, New Series (Calcutta) 1866–7
Indian Jurist, New Series (Madras) 1884–93

Ind.Jur.O.S. Indian Jurist, Old Series (Calcutta) 1862–3
Indian Jurist, Old Series (Madras) 1877–83

Ind.Jur.Pr. Indermaur, Practice of the Supreme Court of Judicature. 12ed. 1919

Ind.L.C.Com.Law Indermaur, Leading Cases in Common Law. 10ed. 1921

Ind.L.C.Eq. Indermaur, Leading Cases in Conveyancing and Equity. 10ed. 1913

Ind.L.H. Indian Law Herald. 1905

Ind.L.J. Indian Law Journal. 1957–
Indiana Law Journal. 1925–
Industrial Law Journal. 1972–

Ind.L.Mag. Indian Law Magazine (Bombay) 1878
Indian Law Magazine (Calcutta) 1895

Ind.L.Q. Indian Law Quarterly. 1914–17

Ind.L.R. Indian Law Reports. 1876–
Indian Law Review. 1947–54, 1957
Indiana Law Reporter. 1881
Indiana Law Review. 1972–
Indiana Legal Register. 1871–2
Industrial Law Review. 1946–60

Ind.L.R.All. Indian Law Reports, Allahabad Series. 1876–

Ind.L.R.Alla. Indian Law Reports, Allahabad Series. 1876–

Ind.L.R.And. Indian Law Reports, Andhra Series. 1959–

Ind.L.R.Assam Indian Law Reports, Assam Series. 1949–

Ind.L.R.Bomb. Indian Law Reports, Bombay Series. 1876–

Ind.L.R.Calc. Indian Law Reports, Calcutta Series. 1876–

Ind.L.R.Hyderabad Indian Law Reports, Hyderabad Series. 1953–

Ind.L.R.Kar. Indian Law Reports, Karachi Series. 1939–47

Ind.L.R.Ker. Indian Law Reports, Kerala Series. 1950–

Ind.L.R.Lah. Indian Law Reports, Lahore Series. 1920–47

Ind.L.R.Luck. Indian Law Reports, Lucknow Series. 1926–49

Ind.L.R.Mad. Indian Law Reports, Madras Series. 1876–

Ind.L.R.Madhya Bharat Indian Law Reports, Madhya Bharat Series. 1952–

Ind.L.R.Mysore Indian Law Reports, Mysore Series. 1953–

Ind.L.R.Or. Indian Law Reports, Orissa Series. 1950–

Ind.L.R.Pat. Indian Law Reports, Patna Series. 1922–

Ind.L.R.Patiala Indian Law Reports, Patiala Series. 1953–

Ind.L.R.Pun. Indian Law Reports, Punjab Series. 1949–

Ind.L.R.Rajasthan Indian Law Reports, Rajasthan Series. 1952–

Ind.L.R.Ran. Indian Law Reports, Rangoon Series.

Ind.L.Reg. Indiana Legal Register. 1871–2

Ind.L.Rep. Indian Law Reports. 1876–
Indiana Law Reporter. 1881

Ind.L.Rev. Indian Law Review. 1947–
Industrial Law Review. 1946–60

Ind.L.S. Indiana Law Student. 1896

Ind.L.T. Indian Law Times. 1906–28

Ind.Law Bull. Industrial Law Bulletin (N.Z.) 1981–

Ind.Leg.Per. Index to Legal Periodicals. 1908–

Ind.Leg.F. Indiana Legal Forum

Ind.Op. Individual Opinion

Ind.Prop. Industrial Property. 1962–

Ind.Prop.Q. Industrial Property Quarterly. 1956–61

Ind.Rel. Industrial Relations (P–H) (USA)
Industrial Relations – Relations industrielles (Can.)

Ind.Rel.L.J. Industrial Relations Law Journal (USA) 1976–

Ind.Relations Industrial Relations

Ind.Rep. Indiana Reports. 1848–

Ind.S.B.A. Indiana State Bar Association

Ind.Socio-Leg.J. Indian Socio-Legal Journal

Ind.Sol. Independent Solicitor

Ind.Stb. Staatsblad van Nederlands-Indië (Statute Book of the Netherlands Indies)

Ind.Stbl. Staatsblad van Nederlands-Indië (Statute Book of the Netherlands Indies)

Ind.Super. Wilson's Indiana Superior Court Reports. 1871–4

Ind.T. Indian Territory (USA)

Ind.T.Ann.St. Indian Territory Annotated Statutes (USA)

Ind.Terr. Indian Territory (USA)

Ind.Trib. Industrial Tribunal

Ind.Trib.R. Industrial Tribunal Reports. 1966–78

IndTvhR Indisch Tijdschrift van het Recht (Neth.)

Ind.Wills Inderwick, Wills. 1866

Ind.Y.B.I.A. Indian Year Book of International Affairs. 1952–

Ind.Yb.Int'l Aff. Indian Yearbook of International Affairs. 1952–

Ind.& Int.Prop.Aus. Industrial and Intellectual Property in Australia. 1961–

Ind.& L.R.Rev. Industrial and Labor Relations Review (USA) 1947–

Ind.& L.Rel.Rev. Industrial and Labor Relations Review (USA) 1947–

Ind.& Lab.Rel.Forum Industrial and Labor Relations Forum (USA)

Ind.& Lab.Rel.Rev. Industrial and Labor Relations Review (USA) 1947–

Indem. Indemnity

India Cen.Acts Central Acts (India)

India Code Civ.P. Code of Civil Procedure (India)

India Code Crim.P. Code of Criminal Procedure (India)

India Crim.L.J.R. Criminal Law Journal Reports (India) 1904–

India Gen.R.& O. General Rules and Orders (India)

India L.C. Law Commission of India

India Pen.Code Penal Code (India)

India S.Ct. Supreme Court Reports (India)

India Subs.Leg. Subsidiary Legislation (India)

Indian App. Law Reports, Privy Council, Indian Appeals. 1873–75

Indian Cas. Indian Cases. 1909–47

Indian Econ.Journ. Indian Economic Journal

Indian J.I.L. Indian Journal of International Law. 1960–

Indian J.Int.Law Indian Journal of International Law. 1960–

Indian J.Int'l.L. Indian Journal of International Law. 1960–

Indian J.Pub.Admin. Indian Journal of Public Administration. 1955–

Indian L.J. Indian Law Journal. 1957–

Indian L.R. Indian Law Reports. 1876–

Indian L.Rev. Indian Law Review. 1947–54, 1957

Indian Lab.J. Indian Labour Journal

Indian Rul. Indian Rulings

Indian Terr. Indian Territory Reports (USA)

Indian Y.B.I.A. Indian Yearbook of International Affairs

Indian Yrbk.Intl.Aff. Indian Yearbook of International Affairs

Indiana L.J. Indiana Law Journal (USA) 1925–

Indiana L.Rev. Indiana Law Review (USA)

Inductive Approach G. Schwarzenberger, The Inductive Approach to International Law. 1965

Indus.L.J. Industrial Law Journal. 1972–

Indus.Prop. Industrial Property: Monthly Review of the World Intellectual Property Organization (Switz.)

Indus.Rel.L.J. Industrial Relations Law Journal (USA) 1976–

Indust. Industrial
Industry

Indust.Bull. Industrial Bulletin (USA) 1922–

Indust.C.Aw. Industrial Court Awards. 1919–

Indust.Ct.Aw. Industrial Court Awards. 1919–

Indust.L.J. Industrial Law Journal. 1972–

Indust.L.Rev. Industrial Law Review. 1946–60

Indust.L.Soc. Industrial Law Society

Indust.L.Soc.Bull. Bulletin of the Industrial Law Society. 1968–72

Indust.Law Rev. Industrial Law Review. 1946–60

Indust.Prop. Industrial Property. 1962–

Indust.Prop.Q. Industrial Property Quarterly. 1956–61

Indust.Prop'y Yb. Industrial Property Yearbook

Indust.Rel.L.J. Industrial Relations Law Journal (USA) 1976–

Indust.Trib.Rep. Industrial Tribunal Reports. 1966–78

Indust.& L.Rel.Rev. Industrial and Labor Relations Review. 1947–

Industr.Prop'y Industrial Property: Monthly Review of the International Bureau for the Protection of Intellectual Property (Switz.)

Industr.Prop'y Q. Industrial Property Quarterly (Switz.) 1956–61

Industrl.Rel. Industrial Relations: a Journal of Economy and Society (USA)

InfL Lag om införsel i avlöning, pension eller livränta (Swed.) Law on garnishment of wage, pension and annuity payments. 1917

Inform.Jur. Informacion Juridica (Port.)

Ing.Comp. Ingram, Compensation for Interest in Lands. 2ed. 1869

Ing.cons. Ingénieur-Conseil (Belg.) 1911–35
Revue de droit intellectuel, l'ingénieur-conseil. 1935–

Ing.Ves. Vesey, Junior's Chancery Reports, ed. by Ingraham. 1789–1817

Ingleby Cttee. Home Office. Committee on Children and Young Persons. Report (Cmnd. 1191) 1960

Inher. Inheritance

inl. inleiding (Neth.) introduction

Inn.Eas. Innes, Easements. 8ed. 1911

Inn.Sc.Leg.Ant. Innes, Scotch Legal Antiquities

Innes Innes' Registration of Title (Mal.) 1907–13

Inq.Chanc.Misc. Public Record Office, Chancery, Miscellaneous Inquisitions (C.145)

Ins. Insolvency
Insurance

Ins.C. Insurance Code (USA)

Ins.Counsel J. Insurance Counsel Journal (USA) 1934–

Ins.Int. Insurance International

Ins.L.J. Insurance Law Journal (USA) 1939–

Ins.L.M. Insurance Law Monthly

Ins.L.R. Insurance Law Reporter (Can.) 1934–41

Ins.L.Rep. Insurance Law Reporter (CCH) (USA)

Ins.L.& P. Insolvency Law and Practice
Insurance Law & Practice

Ins.Law J. Insurance Law Journal (USA) 1939–

Ins.Rep. Insurance Reporter (Pennsylvania) (USA)

Insolv. Insolvency

Insolv.Int. Insolvency Intelligence

Inst. Coke's Institutes
Institute
Institution
Justinian's Institutes

Inst.Com.Com. Interstate Commerce Commission Reports (USA)

Inst.Enreg. Instruction de la Direction générale de l'Enregistrement (Fr.)

Inst.Epil. Epilogue to Coke's Institutes

Inst.Jur.Angl. Institutions Juris Anglicani by Cowell

Inst.of Fam.Studies Institute of Family Studies (Aus.)

Inst.on Est.Plan. Institute on Estate Planning (University of Miami)

Inst.on Fed.Tax'n Institute on Federal Taxation

Inst.on Min.L. Institute on Mineral Law (Louisiana State University)

Inst.on Oil & Gas L.& Tax'n Institute on Oil and Gas Law and Taxation (Southwestern Legal Foundation)

Inst.on Plan.Zoning & Eminent Domain Institute on Planning, Zoning and Eminent Domain (Southwestern Legal Foundation)

Inst.on Sec.Reg. Institute on Securities Regulation (Practising Law Institute)

Inst.Proem. Proeme (Introduction) to Coke's Institutes

Inst.v.Arbeidsr.Bull. Instituut voor Arbeidsrecht Bulletin (Belg.)

Institutes Justinian's Institutes

Instn. Institution

instr. instruction

Instr.Cler. Instructor Clericalis. 1693

Insur.Counsel J. Insurance Counsel Journal (USA) 1934–

Insur.L.J. Insurance Law Journal (USA) 1939–

Insur.L.Rep. Insurance Law Reporter (CCH) (USA)
Insurance Law Reporter (Can.) 1934–41

Insur.L.& P. Insurance Law and Practice

Int. Intelligence
Interest
International
Introduction

Int.-Am.Econ.Aff. Inter-American Economic Affairs

Int.-Am.L.Rev. Inter-American Law Review

Int.Arb.J. International Arbitration Journal (USA) 1945

Int.Bank.L. International Banking Lawyer. 1982–

Int.Bar J. International Bar Journal. 1970–

Int.Bull.Indust.Prop. International Bulletin of Industrial Property (USA) 1947–53

Int.Bull.Res.E.Eur. International Bulletin for Research on Law in Eastern Europe (Ger.) 1972–

Int.Bus.Lawy. International Business Lawyer. 1973–

Int.Cas. Rowe's Interesting Cases (England and Ireland) 1798–1823

Int.Case Rowe's Interesting Cases (England and Ireland) 1798–1823

Int.Com.Rep. Interstate Commerce Commission Reports (USA)

Int.Comp.L.Q. International and Comparative Law Quarterly. 1952–

Int.Comp.Law Quart. International and Comparative Law Quarterly. 1952–

Int.Conc. International Conciliation (USA) 1907–72

Int.Concil. International Conciliation (USA) 1907–72

Int.Dig. International Digest (USA) 1930–2

Int.Enc.Comp.Law International Encyclopedia of Comparative Law

Int.Entcycl.Comp.L. International Encyclopedia of Comparative Law

Int.Gesell.Urheber.R. Internationale Gesellschaft für Urheberrecht E.V. (Austria)

Int.J. International Journal (Can.)

Int.J.Comp.L.L.I.R. International Journal of Comparative Labour Law & Industrial Relations

Int.J.Criminol. International Journal of Criminology and Penology. 1973–

Int.J.Law Libs. International Journal of Law Libraries (now International Journal of Legal Information) 1973–

Int.J.Law & Fam. International Journal of Law and the Family

Int.J.Leg.Inf. International Journal of Legal Information

Int.J.Soc.L. International Journal of the Sociology of Law. 1973–

Int.J.Sociol.Law International Journal of the Sociology of Law. 1973–

Int.Jo.Ethics International Journal of Ethics

Int.Jurid.Assn.Bull. International Juridical Association Bulletin (USA) 1932–42

Int.L. The International Lawyer (USA) 1966/7–

Int.L.Bull. International Law Bulletin (USA) 1963

Int.L.N. International Law Notes. 1916–19

Int.L.Notes International Law Notes. 1916–19

Int.L.Q. International Law Quarterly. 1947–51

Int.Lab.Rev. International Labour Review (I.L.O.) 1921–

Int.Law The International Lawyer (USA) 1966/7–

Int.Law Tr. International Law Tracts

Int.Lawyer The International Lawyer (USA) 1966/7–

Int.Med.Law International Medical Law

Int.Org. International Organization (USA) 1937–

Int.Parl.Un.Bull. Inter-Parliamentary Union Bulletin (Switz.)

Int.Parl.Un.Inf.S. Inter-Parliamentary Union Constitutional and Parliamentary Information, New Series (Switz.)

Int.Phil.Q. International Philosophical Quarterly

Int.R.& Diplom. Internationales Recht und Diplomatie (Ger.)

Int.Rel. International Relations

Int.Rev.Code Internal Revenue Code (USA)

Int.Rev.Crim.Pol. International Review of Criminal Policy (U.N.) 1952–

Int.Rev.Law & Econ. International Review of Law and Economics

Int.Rev.Rec. Internal Revenue Record (New York)

Int.Trade L.J. International Trade Law Journal (USA) 1975–

Int.& Comp. International and Comparative Law Quarterly. 1952–

Int.& Comp.L.Q. International and Comparative Law Quarterly. 1952–

Integ.Latinoam. Integracion Latinoamericana: Revista Mensual del INTAL (Argentina)

Intellect.Prop'y L.Rev. Intellectual Property Law Review

Inter.Am. Inter-American Quarterly. 1939–41

Inter-Am.L.Rev. Inter-American Law Review. 1959–66

Inter.Bank.Law International Banking Law. 1982–

Interior Dec. Decisions of the Department of the Interior (USA) 1881–

Interjection Interjection: Newsletter of the New South Wales Society for Labour Lawyers (Aus.) 1984–

Internat. International

Internat.Comp.L.Q. International and Comparative Law Quarterly. 1952–

Internat.L.N. International Law Notes. 1916–19

Internat.L.Q. International Law Quarterly. 1947–51

Interp. Interpretation

Interparl.Bull. Interparliamentary Bulletin (Switz.)

Inters.Com.Com. Interstate Commerce Commission (USA)

Interstate Com.R. Interstate Commerce Commission Reports (USA)

Intertax Intertax, European Tax Review (Neth.)

Intl. International

Int'l Adm.Sci.Q. International Administrative Science Quarterly (USA)

Int'l Aff. International Affairs. 1922–

Int'l Affairs International Affairs. 1922–

Int'l Arb.J. International Arbitration Journal (USA) 1945

Int'l Assoc.L.Lib.Bull. International Association of Law Libraries Bulletin

Int'l Atomic Energy Agency Bull. International Atomic Energy Agency Bulletin

Int'l B.A.Bull. International Bar Association Bulletin (USA)

Int'l Bar J. International Bar Journal

Int'l Bull.Research E.Eur. International Bulletin for Research on Law in Eastern Europe (Ger.) 1972–

Int'l Bus.Lawyer International Business Lawyer. 1973–
Int'l Com.Jurists Rev. International Commission of Jurists: The Review (Switz.)
Int'l Conciliation International Conciliation Documents (USA) 1907–72
Int'l Constr.L.Rev. International Construction Law Review
Int'l Contr. The International Contract: Law and Finance Review (Switz.)
Int'l Dig. International Digest (USA) 1930–2
Int'l Econ.& Soc.Hist.Rev. International Economic and Social History Review
Int'l Encyc.Comp.L. International Encyclopedia of Comparative Law (Ger.)
Int'l Fin.L.Rev. International Financial Law Review
Int'l J. International Journal (Can.) 1946–
Int'l J.Comp.& Appl.Crim.Just. International Journal of Comparative and Applied Criminal Justice (USA)
Int'l J.Crimin.& Penol. International Journal of Criminology and Penology. 1973–
Int'l J.Envir.Stud. International Journal of Environmental Studies
Int'l J.L.Lib. International Journal of Law Libraries
Int'l J.L.& Psychiatry International Journal of Law and Psychiatry (USA)
Int'l J.Leg.Info. International Journal of Legal Information
Int'l J.Mid.East Stud. International Journal of Middle East Studies (USA)
Int'l J.of Publ.Admin. International Journal of Public Administration
Int'l J.Offend.Ther. International Journal of Offender Theory (USA)
Int'l J.Pol. International Journal of Politics
Int'l J.Soc.L. International Journal of the Sociology of Law. 1973–
Int'l J.Sociol.L. International Journal of the Sociology of Law. 1973–
Int'l L.Ass'n.Bull. Bulletin of the International Law Association. 1936–8
Int'l L.Assoc.Rep. International Law Association, Report of Conference
Int'l L.N. International Law Notes. 1916–19
Int'l L.Q. International Law Quarterly. 1947–51
Int'l L.Rep. International Law Reports
Int'l Lab.Off.Leg.S. International Labour Office, Legislative Series (Switz.)
Int'l Lab.Rep International Labour Reports
Int'l Lab.Rev. International Labour Review (I.L.O.) 1921–
Int'l Law. The International Lawyer (USA) 1966/7–
Int'l Lawy. The International Lawyer (USA) 1966/7–
Int'l Leg.Materials International Legal Materials: Current Documents
Int'l Leg.Practitioner International Legal Practitioner
Int'l Legal Prac. International Legal Practitioner
Int'l Organiz. International Organization (USA) 1937–
Int'l Philos.Q. International Philosophical Quarterly
Int'l Publ.Fin. International Public Finance
Int'l Rev.Adm.Sci. International Review of Administrative Sciences (Belg.)
Int'l Rev.Agr. International Review of Agriculture
Int'l Rev.Ind.Prop.& C'right L. International Review of Industrial Property and Copyright Law (Ger.) 1970–
Int'l Rev./Indus.Prop.& Copy.L. International Review of Industrial Property and Copyright Law (Ger.) 1970–
Int'l Rev.L.& Econ. International Review of Law and Economics

Int'l Soc.Sci.Bull. International Social Science Bulletin (UNESCO)
Int'l Soc.Sci.J. International Social Science Journal (UNESCO)
Int'l Soc.Sec.Rev. International Social Security Review (Switz.)
Int'l Soc'y Barristers International Society of Barristers Quarterly
Int'l Stud.Q. International Studies Quarterly
Int'l Tax J. International Tax Journal
Int'l Tax & Bus.Law. International Tax and Business Lawyer
Int'l Trade L.J. International Trade Law and Journal (USA) 1975–
Int'l Trade L.& Prac. International Trade Law and Practice
Int'l & Comp.L.Q. International and Comparative Law Quarterly. 1952–
Int'le Gesellsch.f.Urheberr.Jahrb. Internationale Gesellschaft für Urheberrecht, Jahrbuch (Austria)
Intra. Intramural
Intra.L.Rev.(N.Y.U.) Intramural Law Review, New York University. 1945–68
Intra.L.Rev.(St.L.U.) Intramural Law Review, St Louis University. 1949
Intra.L.Rev.(U.C.L.A.) Intramural Law Review, University of California at Los Angeles
Introd. Introduction
Inv. Investment
Invoice
Inv.Man. Investment Management
Inv.Reg.Cas. Notes of Decisions of the Appeal Court of Registration at Inverness (Scot.) 1835–53
Iowa Iowa Supreme Court Reports. 1855–
Iowa Acts Acts and Joint Resolutions of the State of Iowa
Iowa B.Rev. Iowa Bar Review. 1934–40
Iowa Bar Rev. Iowa Bar Review. 1934–40
Iowa Code Ann. Iowa Code Annotated
Iowa L.B. Iowa Law Bulletin. 1915–25
Iowa L.Bull. Iowa Law Bulletin. 1915–25
Iowa L.Rev. Iowa Law Review. 1925–
Iowa Legis.Serv. Iowa Legislative Service (West)
Iowa S.B.A. Iowa State Bar Association
Iowa St.B.A.News Bull. Iowa State Bar Association News Bulletin. 1940–
Iowa St.B.A.Q. Iowa State Bar Association Quarterly. 1929–32
Iowa Univ.L.Bull. Iowa University Law Bulletin. 1891–1901
Iowa W.C.S. Iowa Workmen's Compensation Commission Reports
Iqbal Rev. Iqbal Review (Pakistan)
Ir. Iredell's North Carolina Law Reports (23–35 NC) 1840–52
Iredell's North Carolina Equity Reports (36–43 NC) 1840–52
Ireland
Irish
Ir.C.L. Irish Common Law Reports (2nd Series) 1850–66
Irish Common Law Reports. 1866–78
Ir.Ch. Irish Chancery Reports (2nd Series) 1850–66
Ir.Ch.Rep. Irish Chancery Reports. 1850–66
Ir.Cir. Irish Circuit Reports. 1841–3
Ir.Cir.Cas. Crawford & Dix's Abridged Circuit Cases (Ire.) 1837–8
Ir.Cir.Rep. Irish Circuit Reports. 1841–3
Ir.Circ.Cas. Crawford & Dix's Abridged Circuit Cases (Ire.) 1837–8
Ir.Circ.Rep. Irish Circuit Reports. 1841–3
Ir.Com.L.Rep. Irish Common Law Reports (2nd Series) 1850–66
Irish Common Law Reports. 1866–78
Ir.Com.Law Rep. Irish Common Law Reports (2nd Series) 1850–66
Irish Common Law Reports. 1866–78
Ir.Eccl. Milward's Ecclesiastical Reports (Ire.) 1819–43
Ir.Eq. Irish Equity Chancery Reports (1st Series) 1838–50
Ir.Eq.Rep. Irish Equity Chancery Reports (1st Series) 1838–50
Ir.Jur. Irish Jurist. 1849–67
Irish Jurist. 1935–

Ir.Jur.N.S. Irish Jurist (New Series) 1856–67
Irish Jurist (New Series) 1966–
Ir.Jur.Rep. Irish Jurist Reports. 1935–
Ir.Jur.(Rep.) Irish Jurist Reports. 1935–
Ir.Jurist The Irish Jurist
Ir.L. Irish Law Reports (1st Series) 1838–50
Ir.L.J. Irish Law Journal. 1895–1902
Ir.L.(N.S.) Irish Common Law Reports. 1866–78
Ir.L.R. Irish Law Reports (1st Series) 1838–50
Irish Law Reports (4th Series) 1878–93
Ir.L.Rec. Irish Law Recorder (1st Series) 1827–31
Ir.L.Rec.N.S. Irish Law Recorder, New Series. 1833–38
Ir.L.T. Irish Law Times and Solicitor's Journal. 1867–
Ir.L.T.J. Irish Law Times and Solicitor's Journal. 1867–
Ir.L.T.Journal Irish Law Times and Solicitor's Journal. 1867–
Ir.L.T.R. Irish Law Times Reports. 1867–
Ir.L.T.Rep. Irish Law Times Reports. 1867–
Ir.L.& Eq. Irish Law and Equity Reports (1st Series) 1838–50
Ir.Law Rec. Irish Law Recorder (1st Series) 1827–31
Ir.Law Rec.N.S. Irish Law Recorder (New Series) 1833–8
Ir.Law Rep. Irish Law Reports (1st Series) 1838–50
Ir.Law Rep.N.S. Irish Common Law Reports. 1866–78
Ir.Law T. Irish Law Times and Solicitor's Journal. 1867–
Ir.Law & Ch. Irish Chancery Reports (2nd Series) 1850–66
Ir.Law & Eq. Irish Equity Reports (1st Series) 1838–50
Ir.Pat.Off. Irish Patent Office
Ir.Pet.S.J. Irish Petty Sessions Journal. 1893–9, 1899–1901 (New Series)
Ir.R. Irish Reports. 1894–
Ir.R.C.L. Irish Common Law Reports (2nd Series) 1850–66, (3rd Series) 1866–78
Ir.R.Ch. Irish Chancery Reports (2nd Series) 1850–66
Ir.R.Eq. Irish Equity Reports (1st Series) 1838–50
Ir.R.Reg.App. Irish Reports, Registration Appeals. 1868–76
Ir.R.Reg.& L. Irish Reports, Registry and Land Cases. 1868–76
Ir.Rep.C.L. Irish Common Law Reports (2nd Series) 1850–66, (3rd Series) 1866–78
Ir.Rep.Ch. Irish Chancery Reports (2nd Series) 1850–66
Ir.Rep.Eq. Irish Equity Reports (1st Series) 1838–50
Ir.Rep.N.S. Irish Common Law Reports (2nd Series) 1850–66
Ir.Rep.V.R. Irish Reports, Verbatim Reprint
Ir.St.Tr. Irish State Trials (Ridgeway's) 1867
Ir.Stat. Irish Statutes
Ir.T.R. Irish Term Reports (Ridgeway, Lapp & Schoales) 1793–5
Ir.Term Rep. Irish Term Reports (Ridgeway, Lapp & Schoales) 1793–5
Ir.W.C.C. Irish Workmen's Compensation Cases. 1934–8
Ir.W.L.R. Irish Weekly Law Reports. 1895–1902
Ire. Ireland
Ired. Iredell's North Carolina Equity Reports (36–43 NCEq) 1840–52
Ired.Dig. Iredell, North Carolina Digest
Ired.Eq. Iredell's North Carolina Equity Reports (36–43 NCEq) 1840–52
Ired.Eq.(N.C.) Iredell's North Carolina Equity Reports (36–43 NCEq) 1840–52
Ired.L. Iredell's North Carolina Law Reports (23–35 NCL) 1840–52
Ired.L.(N.C.) Iredell's North Carolina Law Reports (23–35 NCL) 1840–52
Irish Jur. Irish Jurist. 1849–67
Irish Jurist. 1935–

Irish L.T. Irish Law Times and Solicitor's Journal. 1867–
Irr.N. Tasmanian Irregular Notes (Aus.)
irreg. irregular
Irv. Irvine's High Court and Circuit Courts of Justiciary Reports (Scot.) 1851–68
Irv.Civ.Law Irving's Civil Law
Irv.Just. Irvine's High Court and Circuit Courts of Justiciary Reports (Scot.) 1851–68
Irvine Just.Cas. Irvine's High Court and Circuit Courts of Justiciary Reports (Scot.) 1851–68
Irwin's Code Clark, Cobb & Irwin's Georgia Code
Is. Islands
Isles
Islam.& Comp.L.Q. Islamic and Comparative Law Quarterly (India)
Islam & Mod.Age Islam and the Modern Age (India)
Islam & Mod.World Islam and the Modern World (Bangladesh)
Islamic Q. Islamic Quarterly
Islamic Stud. Islamic Studies (Pakistan)
Islamic & Comp.L.Q. Islamic and Comparative Law Quarterly (India)
Israel L.Rev. Israel Law Review. 1966–
Israel Stud.Criminol. Israel Studies in Criminology
Israel Yrbk.Hum.Rts. Israel Yearbook of Human Rights
Iss. Issue
Issues L.& Med. Issues in Law and Medicine
Issues & Stud. Issues and Studies
It. Italian
Italy
Ital. Italian
Italy
Ital.Aff. Italian Affairs
ItalYIL Italian Yearbook of International Law
Ital.Yrbk.Intl.L. Italian Yearbook of International Law
Iura Iura: Rivista Internazionale di Diritto Romano e Antico (It.)
Iust. Iustitia (It.) 1948–
Iustitia (USA) 1973–
Iv.Ersk. Ivory, Notes on Erskine's Institutes

J

J. Jahrbuch (Ger.) Yearbook
Johnson's New York Reports
Journal
Judge
Justice
Justiciary
Justiciary Cases (Scot.)
Justinian's Institutes
Juta's Supreme Court Cases (Cape, S.Afr.) 1880–1910
Lower Canada Jurist (Quebec) 1848–91
Scottish Jurist. 1829–73

J.A. Judge Advocate
Judge or Justice of Appeal
Jurisprudencia Argentina

J.A.A. Journal of African Administration. 1949–61

J.A.A.M.L. Journal of American Academy of Matrimonial Lawyers. 1970–

J.A.F. Judge Advocate of the Fleet

J.A.G. Judge Advocate General

JAG Bull. JAG Bulletin (USA) 1959–64

JAG Dig.Op. Judge Advocate General Digest of Opinions

JAGJ JAG Journal (USA)

JAG L.Rev. United States Air Force Judge Advocate General Law Review. 1965–73

JAIL Japanese Annual of International Law

J.A.J. Judge Advocate Journal (USA) 1944–5, 1949–

J.A.L. Journal of African Law. 1957–

JALC Journal of Air Law and Commerce (USA) 1930–

J.A.L.T. Journal of the Association of Law Teachers. 1967–70

J.A.Med.L.S. Journal of the Auckland Medico-Legal Society (N.Z.) 1971–

J.A.S.S.A. Journal of the Securities Institute of Australia. 1962–

J.Account. Journal of Accountancy

J.Admin.Overseas Journal of Administration Overseas. 1966–

J.Adv. Judge Advocate

J.Afr.Admin. Journal of African Administration

J.Afr.Hist. Journal of African History

J.Afr.L. Journal of African Law. 1957–

J.Afr.Stud. Journal of African Studies (USA)

J.Agric.Tax'n & L. Journal of Agricultural Taxation and Law (USA)

J.Air L. Journal of Air Law and Commerce (USA) 1930–

J.Air L.& Com. Journal of Air Law and Commerce (USA) 1930–

L.Am.Acad.Matrimonial Law. Journal of the American Academy of Matrimonial Lawyers

J.Am.Bankers' Assn. Journal of American Bankers' Association

J.Am.J.Soc. Journal of the American Judicature Society. 1917–66

J.Am.Jud.Soc. Journal of the American Judicature Society. 1917–66

J.Am.Soc.C.L.U. Journal of the American Society of Chartered Life Underwriters

J.As. Judicial Assessor (Ghana)

J.Asian Stud. Journal of Asian Studies (USA)

J.Ass'n.L.Teachers Journal of the Association of Law Teachers. 1967–70

J.Assoc.L.Teachers Journal of the Association of Law Teachers. 1967–70

JB Jordabalk (Swed.) Real Property Code. 1734

J.B. Jurum Baccalaureus (Lat.) Bachelor of Laws
Justiciar's Bench (Ire.)

J.B.A.D.C. Journal of the Bar Association of the District of Columbia. 1934–

J.B.A.Dist.Colum. Journal of the Bar Association of the District of Columbia. 1934–

J.B.A.Kan. Journal of the Kansas Bar Association. 1932–

J.B.C. Journal of the State Bar of California. 1943–71

J.B.I.I.A. Journal of the British Institute for International Affairs

J.B.K. Journal of the Kansas Bar Association. 1932–

J.B.L. Journal of Business Law. 1957–

J.B.Moore J.B. Moore's Common Pleas Reports

J.Beverley Hills B.A. Journal of the Beverley Hills Bar Association. 1967–

J.Bl. Juristische Blätter (Austria)
Justizblatt (Ger.) Ministry of Justice Gazette

J.Bridg. Sir John Bridgman's Common Pleas Reports (123 ER) 1613–21

J.Bridgm. Sir John Bridgman's Common Pleas Reports (123 ER) 1613–21

J.Brit.Stud. Journal of British Studies (USA)

J.Broadcast. Journal of Broadcasting (USA)

J.Bus.L. Journal of Business Law. 1957–

J.C. Johnson's Cases or Reports (New York)
Judicial Committee (of the Privy Council)
Justiciary Cases (Scot.) 1917–
Juvenile Court

J.C.A. Jurisclasseur administratif (Fr.)

JCAA Japanese Commercial Arbitration Association

J.C.B. Kansas Judicial Council Bulletin
Juris Canonici Baccalaureus (Bachelor of Canon Law)
Juris Civilis Baccalaureus (Bachelor of Civil Law)
Jurisprudence commerciale de Bruxelles (Belg.) periodical collection of reports

J.C.Br. Jurisprudence commerciale de Bruxelles (Belg.) periodical collection of reports

J.C.C. Joint Consultative Document

J.C.C.C. Joint Customs Consultative Committee

J.C.Comm. Jurisclasseur commercial (Fr.)

J.C.D. Juris Canonici Doctor (Doctor of Canon Law)
Juris Civilis Doctor (Doctor of Civil Law)

J.C.D.C. Jurisclasseur de droit comparé (Fr.)

J.C.D.I. Jurisclasseur de droit international (Fr.)

JCED Japan Committee for Economic Development

J.C.J. Journal of Criminal Justice (Aus.) 1973–

J.C.L. Journal of Child Law
Journal of Comparative Legislation and International Law. 1896–1951
Journal of Contract Law (Aus.) 1988–
Journal of Criminal Law. 1937–
Juris Canonici Lector
Juris Canonici Licentiatus (Licentiate in Canon Law)
Juris Civilis Licentiatus (Licentiate in Civil Law)

J.C.L.& I.L. Journal of Comparative Legislation and International Law. 1896–1951

J.C.M.S. Juris-Classeur Périodique (La Semaine Juridique) (Fr.)

J.C.P. Journal of Consumer Policy (Neth.) 1978–
Juris-Classeur Périodique (La Semaine Juridique) (Fr.)
Justice of the Common Pleas

J.C.P.(C.I.) Juris-Classeur Périodique (La Semaine Juridique) Édition Commerce et Industrie

J.C.R. Johnson's Chancery Reports (New York) 1814–23
Judicial Council Reports

J.C.Rettie Rettie, Crawford & Melville's Court of Session Cases, 4th series (Scot.) 1873–98

J.C.& U.L. The Journal of College and University Law (USA)

J.Can.B.A. Journal of the Canadian Bar Association. 1970–3

J.Can.B.Ass'n. Journal of the Canadian Bar Association. 1970–3

J.Cent.Europ.Aff. Journal of Central European Affairs (USA)

J.Ceylon Law Journal of Ceylon Law (Sri L.) 1970–

J.Ch. Johnson's New York Chancery Reports. 1814–23

J.Ch.L. Journal of Child Law

J.Chin.L. Journal of Chinese Law (USA)

J.Chinese Philos. Journal of Chinese Philosophy (Neth.)

J.Christ.Jurispr. Journal of Christian Jurisprudence (USA)

J.Church & State Journal of Church and State (USA)

J.Cin.B.A. Journal of the Cincinnati Bar Association. 1973–

J.Coll.& Univ.L. Journal of College and University Law (USA) 1973–

J.Com.Mar.St. Journal of Common Market Studies. 1962–

J.Comm. Journal of Communication (USA)

J.Common Market Stud. Journal of Common Market Studies. 1962–

J.Commun. Journal of Communication (USA)

J.Comp.Corp.L. Journal of Comparative Corporate Law and Securities Regulation (Neth.) 1978–

J.Comp.L. Journal of Comparative Legislation and International Law. 1896–1951

J.Comp.Leg. Journal of Comparative Legislation and International Law. 1896–1951

J.Comp.Leg.& Int.Law Journal of Comparative Legislation and International Law. 1896–1951

J.Conat.Law Journal of Conational Law (USA) 1920–2

J.Confl.Resolution Journal of Conflict Resolution (USA)

J.Const.& Parliam.Stud. Journal of Constitutional and Parliamentary Studies (Switz.)

J.Cont.L. Journal of Contract Law

J.Contemp.Health L.& Pol'y The Journal of Contemporary Health Law and Policy (USA)

J.Contemp.L. Journal of Contemporary Law (USA) 1974–

J.Contemp.Legal Issues Journal of Contemporary Legal Issues (USA)

J.Copr.Soc'y Journal of the Copyright Society of the U.S.A.

J.Copyright Soc'y U.S.A. Journal of the Copyright Society of the U.S.A.

J.Corp.Disclosure & Confid. Journal of Corporate Disclosure and Confidentiality (USA)

J.Corp.L. Journal of Corporation Law (USA) 1975–

J.Corp.Tax. Journal of Corporate Taxation (USA)

J.Corpn.L. Journal of Corporation Law (USA) 1975–

J.Crim.Just. Journal of Criminal Justice (USA) 1973–

J.Crim.L. Journal of Criminal Law. 1937–

J.Crim.L.C.& P.S. Journal of Criminal Law, Criminology and Police Science (USA) 1951–72

J.Crim.L.Crimin.& Pol.Sc. Journal of Criminal Law, Criminology and Police Science (USA) 1951–72

J.Crim.L.& Criminology Journal of Criminal Law and Criminology (USA) 1941–51, 1973–

J.Crim.Law Journal of American Institute of Criminal Law and

Criminology (Chicago) 1910–41
Journal of Criminal Law. 1937–

J.Crim.Sci. Journal of Criminal Science. 1948, 1950

J.D. Juris Doctor (Doctor of Jurisprudence)

J.D.I. Joint Declaration of Intent (EEC)
Journal du droit international (Fr.) 1915–

J.D.I.P. Journal du droit international privé (Fr.) 1874–1914

JDL Lag om delning av jord på landet (Swed.) Law on the development of rural land. 1926

J.D.R. Juta's Daily Reporter (Cape, S.Afr.) 1915–26

J.d.T. Journal des Tribunaux: I. Droit fédéral (Switz.)

J.Denning L.S. Journal of the Denning Law Society (Tanzania) 1963–9

J.Dev.Planning Journal of Development Planning (USA)

J.Dev.Stud. Journal of Development Studies

J.Developing Areas Journal of Developing Areas (USA)

J.Disp.Resol. Journal of Dispute Resolution (USA)

J.Divorce Journal of Divorce (USA)

J.du Droit Int'l Journal du Droit International (Clunet) (Fr.)

JERC Japanese Economic Research Centre

J.E.R.L. Journal of Energy and Natural Resources Law. 1983–

J.Ec.Hist. The Journal of Economic History (USA)

J.Econ.Hist. The Journal of Economic History (USA)

J.Econ.& Soc.Hist.Orient Journal of Economic and Social History of the Orient (Neth.)

J.Energy L.& Pol'y Journal of Energy Law and Policy (USA)

J.Energy & Nat.Resources L. Journal of Energy and Natural Resources Law (USA)

J.Env.L. Journal of Environmental Law

J.Envtl.L.& Litig. Journal of Environmental Law and Litigation (USA)

J.Ethiopian L. Journal of Ethiopian Law (Ethiopia)

J.Ethiopian Stud. Journal of Ethiopian Studies (Ethiopia)

J.Europ.Econ.Hist. Journal of European Economic History (It.)

J.Europ.Integr. Journal of European Integration (Can.)

J.Europ.Stud. Journal of European Studies (USA)

JFEA Japanese Federation of Employers' Associations

J.f.I.R. Jahrbuch für Internationales Recht

J.Fam.L. Journal of Family Law (USA) 1961–

J.Finance Journal of Finance (USA)

J.For.Med. Journal of Forensic Medicine (S.Afr.) 1953–71

J.For.Sci. Journal of Forensic Sciences (USA) 1956–

J.For.Sci.Soc'y. Journal of the Forensic Science Society. 1960–

J.Forestry Journal of Forestry (USA)

J.H. Journal, House of Representatives (USA)

J.H.Univ.Studies Johns Hopkins University Studies (USA)

J.Health Pol. Journal of Health Politics, Policy and Law (USA) 1975–

J.Hellenic Stud. Journal of Hellenic Studies (USA)

J.Hist.Phil. Journal of the History of Philosophy (USA)

J.Homosexuality Journal of Homosexuality (USA)

J.I.A. Journal of International Affairs
Journal of International Arbitration

JIAOR Jahrbuch für internationales und ausländisches öffentliches Recht (Ger.)

J.I.B.L. Journal of International Banking Law. 1986–

J.I.C.J. Journal of the International Commission of Jurists. 1957–68

J.I.F.D.L. Journal of International Franchising and Distribution Law. 1986–

J.I.L.I. Journal of the Indian Law Institute. 1958–

J.I.L.T.A. Journal of the Indian Law Teachers Association. 1958–

J.I.R. Jahrbuch für Internationales Recht
Journal of Industrial Relations (Aus.) 1959–

J.I.S.E.L. Journal of the Irish Society for European Law

J.I.S.L.L. Journal of the Irish Society for Labour Law

J.Ind.L.Inst. Journal of the Indian Law Institute. 1958–

J.Indian L.Inst. Journal of the Indian Law Institute. 1958–

J.Inst.of Arbitrators Journal of the Institute of Arbitrators (USA)

J.Inst.of Bankers Journal of the Institute of Bankers

J.Interdiscip.Hist. Journal of Interdisciplinary History (USA)

J.Int'l Arb. Journal of International Arbitration (USA)

J.Int'l Comm.Jurists Journal of the International Commission of Jurists (Neth.)

J.Int'l.L.& Econ. Journal of International Law and Economics (USA) 1970–

J.Irish Soc'y Europ.L. Journal of the Irish Society of European Law (Ir.)

J.Islam & Comp.L. Journal of Islamic and Comparative Law (Nig.) 1968–

JJ Judges
Justices

J.J. Jersey Judgments. Judgments of the Royal Court and of the Court of Appeal
Junior Judge

JJ.A. Justices of Appeal

J.J.Mar. J.J. Marshall's Kentucky Supreme Court Reports (24–30 Ky.) 1829–32

J.J.Marsh. J.J. Marshall's Kentucky Supreme Court Reports (24–30 Ky.) 1829–32

J.J.Marsh(Ky.) J.J. Marshall's Kentucky Supreme Court Reports (24–30 Ky.) 1829–32

JJ.S.C. Justices of the Supreme Court

J.Jap.Stud. Journal of Japanese Studies (USA)

J.Jur. Journal of Jurisprudence (USA) 1821
Journal of Jurisprudence and Scottish Law Magazine

J.Jur.Papyrol. Journal of Juristic Papyrology (Poland)

J.Juv.L. Journal of Juvenile Law (USA)

JK Justitiekansler (Swed.) Attorney General

J.K.B. Justice of the King's Bench

J.Kan.B.A. Journal of the Kansas Bar Association. 1932–

J.Kel. Sir John Kelyng's Crown Cases (84 ER) 1662–1707

J.Kelyng Sir John Kelyng's Crown Cases (84 ER) 1662–1707

J.L. Jurisprudence de la Cour d'Appel de Liège (Belg.) periodical collection of reports

J.L.H. Journal of Legal History

J.L.I.S. Journal of Law and Information Science (Aus.) 1981–

J.L.R. Jamaica Law Reports. 1933–
Johore Law Reports (Mal.) 1915–40

J.L.S. Journal of the Law Society of Scotland. 1956–

J.L.S.S. Journal of the Law Society of Scotland. 1956–

J.L.S.Scotland Journal of the Law Society of Scotland. 1956–

J.L.Soc.Pol. Journal of Law and Social Policy (Can.)

J.L.Soc.Scotland Journal of the Law Society of Scotland. 1956–

J.L.Soc'y. Journal of the Law Society of Scotland. 1956–

J.L.& Com. Journal of Law and Commerce (Hong Kong) 1928–9

J.L.& Com.Soc. Journal of the Law and Commerce Society (Hong Kong) 1936–7

J.L.& Econ. Journal of Law and Economics (USA) 1958–
J.L.& Econ.Dev. Journal of Law and Economic Development (USA) 1968–70
J.L.& Econ.Develop. Journal of Law and Economic Development (USA) 1968–70
J.L.& Educ. Journal of Law and Education (USA) 1972–
J.L.& Health Journal of Law and Health (USA)
J.L.& Inf.Sc. Journal of Law and Information Science (Aus.) 1981–
J.L.& Pol. The Journal of Law and Politics
J.L.& Relig. Journal of Law and Religion (USA)
J.L.& Soc. Journal of Law and Society
J.L.& Soc.Pol'y Journal of Law and Social Policy (USA)
J.Land Use & Envtl.L. Journal of Land Use and Environmental Law (USA)
J.Lat.Am.Stud. Journal of Latin American Studies (USA)
J.Law Reform Journal of Law Reform (Michigan, USA) 1968–70
J.Law Soc.Sc. Journal of the Law Society of Scotland. 1956–
J.Law Soc'y Scotland Journal of the Law Society of Scotland. 1956–
J.Law & Econ. Journal of Law and Economics (USA) 1958–
J.Law & Econ.Dev. Journal of Law and Economic Development (USA) 1968–70
J.Law & Politics Journal of Law and Politics (Japan)
J.Law & Soc. Journal of Law and Society
J.Leg.Ed. Journal of Legal Education (USA) 1948–
J.Leg.Hist. Journal of Legal History. 1980–
J.Leg.Med. Journal of Legal Medicine (USA) 1973–
J.Leg.Pluralism Journal of Legal Pluralism and Unofficial Law (USA)
J.Leg.Prof. Journal of the Legal Profession (USA)
J.Leg.Stud. Journal of Legal Studies (USA) 1972
J.Legal Educ. Journal of Legal Education (USA) 1948–
J.Legal Hist. Journal of Legal History. 1980–
J.Legal Med. Journal of Legal Medicine (USA) 1973–
J.Legal Stud. Journal of Legal Studies (USA) 1972
J.Legal Studies Journal of Legal Studies (USA) 1972
J.Legisl.(Notre Dame) Journal of Legislation (Notre Dame) (USA)
J.Lib.Hist. Journal of Library History (USA)
J.Lib.Stud. Journal of Libertarian Studies (USA)
J.Loc.Admin.Overseas Journal of Local Administration Overseas
JM Justizminister(-ium) (Ger.) Minister (Ministry) of Justice
J.M. Master of Jurisprudence
J.M.A.S. Journal of Modern African Studies
J.M.J. John Marshall Journal of Practice and Procedure (USA) 1967–
J.M.L.P. Journal of Media Law and Practice. 1980–
J.M.L.& P. Journal of Media Law and Practice. 1980–
J.M.V.L. Journal of Motor Vehicle Law (Can.) 1989–
J.Mal.& Comp.L. Journal of Malaysian and Comparative Law. 1974–
J.Mar.L.& Com. Journal of Maritime Law and Commerce (USA) 1969–
J.Mar.Law & Com. Journal of Maritime Law and Commerce (USA) 1969–
J.Maritime L.& Comm. Journal of Maritime Law and Commerce (USA) 1969–
J.Marr.& Fam. Journal of Marital and Family Law (Can.)
J.Marriage & the Fam. Journal of Marriage and the Family (USA)
J.Marshall J. John Marshall Journal of

Practice and Procedure (USA)
J.Marshall L.Rev. John Marshall Law Review (USA)
J.Media L.& Practice Journal of Media Law and Practice
J.Mediev.& Renaissance Stud. Journal of Medieval and Renaissance Studies (USA)
J.Mediev.Hist. Journal of Medieval History (Neth.)
J.Min.L.& Pol'y Journal of Mineral Law and Policy (USA)
J.Mo.B. Journal of the Missouri Bar. 1945–
J.Mo.Bar Journal of the Missouri Bar. 1945–
J.Mod.Afr.Stud. Journal of Modern African Studies
J.Mod.Hist. Journal of Modern History (USA)
J.N.A.Referees Bank. Journal of the National Association of Referees in Bankruptcy (USA) 1926–65
J.N.C.Referees Bank. Journal of the National Conference of Referees in Bankruptcy (USA) 1966–70
J.Nat.Assoc.Admin.L.Judges Journal of the National Association of Administrative Law Judges (USA)
J.Near East Stud. Journal of Near East Studies (USA)
J.Northeast Asian Stud. Journal of Northeast Asian Studies (USA)
JO Justitieombudsmannens ambetsberattelse (Swed.) The Parliamentary Report of the Civil Ombudsman. 1810–
Riksdagens justitieombudsman (Swed.) Civil Ombudsman
J.O. Journal Officiel (Fr.) Official gazette. 1869–
Journal Officiel des Communautés Européenes (Official Journal of the European Communities)
JOB Judicial Officers' Bulletin (N.S.W., Aus.) 1988–
J.O.C.E. Journal Officiel des Communautés Européenes (Official Journal of the European Communities)
J.O.Comm.Eur. Journal Officiel des Communautés Européenes (Official Journal of the European Communities)
J.O.Deb.Parl. Journal Officiel, Débats Parlementaires
J.O.R.F. Journal Officiel de la République Française (French Official Gazette)
J.Occ.Health Safety Aust. Journal of Occupational Health and Safety in Australia. 1985–
J.of Afr.Admin. Journal of African Administration
J.of Air L.& Commerce Journal of Air Law and Commerce (USA) 1930–
J.of B.L. Journal of Business Law. 1957–
J.of I.C.J. Journal of the International Commission of Jurists
J.of Inst.of Arbitrators Journal of the Institute of Arbitrators (USA)
J.of Inst.of Bankers Journal of the Institute of Bankers
J.of Law & Politics Journal of Law and Politics (Japan)
J.of Publ.L. Journal of Public Law (USA) 1952–73
J.of the B.A.of Kansas Journal of the Bar Association of the State of Kansas. 1932–
J.P. Journal of Politics
Justice de paix (Belg.) Justice of the Peace
Justice of the Peace
Justice of the Peace and Local Government Review. 1837–
Justice of the Peace (Weekly Notes of Cases)
J.P.A. Jurisprudence du Port d'Anvers (Belg.) 1856–
J.P.C. Judge of the Prize Court
J.P.Ct. Justice of the Peace's Court
J.P.E.L. Journal of Planning and Environment Law. 1973–
J.P.J. Justice of the Peace and Local Government Review. 1837–
J.P.Jo. Justice of the Peace and Local Government Review. 1837–

J.P.L. Journal of Planning Law. 1948–53
Journal of Planning and Property Law. 1954–72
Journal of Planning and Environment Law. 1973–
Journal of Public Law (USA) 1952–73

J.P.L.E. Journal of Professional Legal Education (Aus.) 1983–

J.P.N. Justice of the Peace Journal

J.P.(N.S.W.) Justice of the Peace (New South Wales) 1914–33

J.P.O.S. Journal of the Patent Office Society (USA) 1918–

J.P.P.L. Journal of Planning and Property Law. 1954–72

J.P.R. Justice of the Peace and Local Government Review Reports. 1837–

J.P.Sm. J.P. Smith's King's Bench Reports (7–8 RR) 1803–6

J.P.Smith J.P. Smith's King's Bench Reports (7–8 RR) 1803–6

J.P.(W.A.) Justice of the Peace (Western Australia) 1957–

J.Pakistan Hist.Soc'y Journal of the Pakistan Historical Society

J.Palestine Stud. Journal of Palestine Studies (Lebanon)

J.Pat.Off.Socy. Journal of the Patent Office Society (USA) 1964–

J.Pat.& Trademark Off.Soc'y Journal of the Patent and Trademark Office Society (USA)

J.Peace Res. Journal of Peace Research (Norway) 1964–

J.Philos. Journal of Philosophy (USA)

J.Philos.of Ideas Journal of Philosophy of Ideas (USA)

J.Pl.L. Journal of Planning Law. 1948–53

J.Plan.& Environ.L. Journal of Planning and Environment Law. 1973–

J.Plan.& Prop.L. Journal of Planning and Property Law. 1954–72

J.Pol. Journal of Politics (USA)

J.Pol.Econ. Journal of Political Economy (USA)

J.Prod.Liab. Journal of Products Liability. 1977–

J.Prop.Fin. Journal of Property Finance

J.Psych.& Law Journal of Psychiatry and Law (USA) 1973–

J.Psychological Medicine Journal of Psychological Medicine and Medical Jurisprudence

J.Pub.L. Journal of Public Law (USA) 1952–73

J.Q.B. Justice of the Queen's Bench

JR Juristische Rundschau (Ger.) 1925–35, 1947

J.R. Jacobus Rex (King James)
Johnson's Reports (New York)
Judges' Rules
Juridical Review (Scot.) 1889–
Jurist Reports (N.Z.) 1873–5
Juristische Rundschau (Ger.)

J.R.(N.S.) Jurist Reports, New Series (N.Z.) 1875–9

J.R.N.S.C.A. Jurist Reports, New Series, Court of Appeal (N.Z.) 1875–9

J.R.N.S.M.L. Jurist Reports, New Series, Mining Law Cases (N.Z.) 1875–9

J.R.N.S.S.C. Jurist Reports, New Series, Supreme Court (N.Z.) 1875–9

J.R.S. Journal of Roman Studies

J.Radio L. Journal of Radio Law (USA) 1931–2

J.Real Est.Tax'n The Journal of Real Estate Taxation (USA)

J.Res.Crime & Del. Journal of Research in Crime and Delinquency (USA)

J.Rom.Stud. Journal of Roman Studies

J.Roy.Asiatic Soc'y Journal of the Royal Asiatic Society

J.S. Jones & Spencer's Superior Court Reports, New York (36–61 NY Sup)
Jury Sittings (Faculty Cases) (Scot.)

J.S.A.L. Journal of South African Law. 1976–

J.S.A.M.E.S. Journal of South Asian and Middle Eastern Studies

J.S.Asian & M.E.Stud. Journal of South Asian and Middle Eastern Studies

J.S.C. Justice of the Supreme Court
Judgments of the Supreme Court of Cyprus

J.S.C.C. Journal des sociétés civiles et commerciales (Fr.) 1880–
J.S.Com.Ind.L. Journal of the Society of Commercial and Industrial Law. 1923–
J.S.D. Doctor of Juridical Science Doctor of Juristic Science
J.S.Gr. J.S. Green's New Jersey Law Reports (13–15 NJL)
J.S.Gr.(N.J.) J.S. Green's New Jersey Law Reports (13–15 NJL)
J.S.M. Master of the Science of Law
J.S.P.T.L. Journal of the Society of Public Teachers of Law. 1924–38, 1947–
J.S.W.L. Journal of Social Welfare Law
J.Scott. Common Bench Reports. 1834–40
J.Scott,N.S. Common Bench Reports. 1840–5
J.Semitic Stud. Journal of Semitic Studies (USA)
J.Shaw John Shaw's Justiciary Reports (Scot.) 1848–52
J.Shaw Just. John Shaw's Justiciary Reports (Scot.) 1848–52
J.Soc.Issues Journal of Social Issues (USA)
J.Soc.Pub.T.L. Journal of the Society of Public Teachers of Law. 1924–38, 1947–
J.Soc.Pub.Teach.Law Journal of the Society of Public Teachers of Law. 1924–38, 1947–
J.Soc.Pub.Teach.Law N.S. Journal of the Society of Public Teachers of Law (New Series) 1947–
J.Soc.Sci. Journal of Social Science (USA)
J.Soc.Wel. & Fam.L. Journal of Social Welfare and Family Law
J.Soc.Welfare L. Journal of Social Welfare Law
J.Soc'y of Publ.Teachers L. Journal of the Society of Public Teachers of Law
J.Southern Afr.Aff. Journal of Southern African Affairs
J.Space L. Journal of Space Law (USA) 1973–
J.St.Bar Calif. Journal of the State Bar of California. 1943–71
J.Sup.Ct.Hist. Journal of Supreme Court History (USA)
JT Juridisk Tidsskrift (Den.) 1820–40
J.T. Journal des tribunaux (Belg.) 1881
J.T.C. Journal des tribunaux de commerce (Fr.) 1852–
J.T.R.S. Joint tenant with right of survivorship
J.Tax. Journal of Taxation (USA) 1954–
J.Taxation Journal of Taxation (USA) 1954–
J.Transn.L. Journal of Transnational Law
J.Tribun. Journal des Tribunaux (Belg.)
JU Juridisk ugeskrift (Den.) 1839–68
J.U.B. Justice of the Upper Bench
J.U.D. Juris Utriusque Doctor (Doctor of Civil and Canon Law)
J.U.L. Journal of Urban Law (Michigan) 1966–76
J.Urban Journal of Urban Law (Michigan) 1966–76
JV Jahrbuch des Völkerrechts Joint Venture
JW Juristische Wochenschrift (Ger.) 1872–1939
JWG Jugendwohlfahrtsgesetz (Ger.) Youth welfare law
JWP Joint Working Party
J.W.T.L. Journal of World Trade Law. 1967–
J.World Tr.L. Journal of World Trade Law. 1967–
J.World Trade L. Journal of World Trade Law. 1967–
J.Y.B.I.L. Jewish Yearbook of International Law
JZ Juristen-Zeitung (Ger.) 1951–
J.& C. Jones & Cary's Irish Exchequer Reports. 1838–9
J.& H. Johnson & Hemming's Vice Chancellor's Reports (70 ER) 1860–62
J.& K. All India Reporter, Jammu and Kashmir. 1951–
J.& L. Jones & La Touche's Irish Chancery Reports. 1844–6

J.& La T. Jones & La Touche's Irish Chancery Reports. 1844–6

J.& Lat. Jones & La Touche's Irish Chancery Reports. 1844–6

J.& S. Jebb & Symes' Irish Queen's Bench Reports. 1838–41
Jones & Spencer's Reports (33–61 New York Superior)
Judah & Swan's Reports (Jamaica) 1839

J.& S.Jam. Judah & Swan's Reports (Jamaica) 1839

J.& V. Jones & Varick, Laws of New York

J.& W. Jacob & Walker's Chancery Reports (37 ER) 1819–21

Ja. James

Jac. Jacobus (King James)
Jacob's Chancery Reports (37 ER) 1821–2
Jacob's Law Dictionary

Jac.Fish.Dig. Jacob's American edition of Fisher's English Digest

Jac.L.Dict. Jacob's Law Dictionary. 16ed. 1835

Jac.Law.Dict. Jacob's Law Dictionary. 16ed. 1835

Jac.Sea Laws Jacobsen's Laws of the Sea. 1818

Jac.& W. Jacob & Walker's Chancery Reports (37 ER) 1819–21

Jac.& Walk. Jacob & Walker's Chancery Reports (37 ER) 1819–21

Jack Pl. Jackson, Pleadings. 1933

Jack Report Banking Services: law and practice – Review Committee on Banking Services Law (Cm.622) 1989

Jack.Tex.App. Jackson's Texas Reports (1–20 Texas Appeals)

Jackson Jackson's Reports (46–58 Georgia)
Jackson's Reports (1–20 Texas Appeals)

Jackson & Lumpkin Jackson & Lumpkin's Reports (59–64 Georgia)

Jacob Jacob's Chancery Reports (37 ER) 1821–2
Jacob's Law Dictionary. 16ed. 1835

Jahrb.DR. Jahrbuch des Deutschen Rechts

Jahrb.FG. Jahrbuch für Entscheidungen in Angelegenheiten der freiwilligen Gerichtsbarkeit und des Grundbuchrechts (Ger.)

Jahrb.f.internat.Recht Jahrbuch für internationales Recht (Ger.9

Jahrb.f.Ostrecht Jahrbuch für Ostrecht (Ger.)

Jahrb.H.E. Jahrbuch höchstrichtterlicher Entscheidungen (Ger.)

Jahrb.Int.Recht Jahrbuch für Internationales Rechts (Ger.)

Jahrbuch f.Afrikan.Rech. Jahrbuch für Afrikanisches Recht (Ger.)

Jaipur L.J. Jaipur Law Journal (India) 1961–

Jam. Jamaica

Jam.L.J. Jamaica Law Journal. 1970–7

Jam.St. Jamaica Statutes

Jamaica L.R.C. Jamaica Law Reform Committee

James Novia Scotia Reports, by James (2 N.Sc.) 1853–5

James (N.Sc.) Novia Scotia Reports, by James (2 N.Sc.) 1853–5

James Op. James, Opinions, Charges, etc. 1820

James Salv. James, Salvage. 1867

James Sel.Cases James's Select Cases and Reports (Nova Scotia) 1853–5

James Sh. James, Merchant Shipping. 1866

James.& Mont. Jameson & Montague's Bankruptcy Reports. 1821–8

Jan.Angl. Jani Anglorum facies Nova. 1680

Janssen Festschrift E. Kraenzlin & H.E.A. Muller (eds.) Der Schutz des privaten Eigentums im Ausland: Festschrift für Hermann Janssen. 1958

Jap.AIL Japanese Annual of International Law

Jap.Ann. Japanese Annual of International Law

Jap.Ann.Int'l L. Japanese Annual of International Law

Jap.Ann.of Law & Pol. Japan Annual of Law and Politics (Japan)
Jap.Sci.Rev. Japan Science Review (Japan)
Japan.Ann.Intl.L. Japanese Annual of International Law
Japan Q. Japan Quarterly
Jar.Chy.Pr. Jarman's Chancery Practice. 3ed. 1864
Jar.Cr.Tr. Jardine's Criminal Trials
Jar.Wills Jarman on Wills. 8ed. 1851
Jas. James
Jay.W. Jaywardine's Appeal Cases (Sri L.)
Jb. Jahrbuch (Ger.) Yearbook
Jb.afrik.R. Jahrbuch für afrikanisches Recht (Ger.)
Jb.d.öffentl.Rechts N.F. Jahrbuch des öffentliches Rechts, Neue Folge (Ger.)
JbIntR Jahrbuch für internationales und ausländisches öffentliches Recht (Ger.) 1948–
JbOffR Jahrbuch des öffentliches Rechts der Gegenwart (Ger.) Yearbook on matters of temporary public law. 1907–14, 1920–39, 1951–
Jb.offent.R. Jahrbuch des öffentliches Recht der Gegenwart (Ger.) Yearbook on matters of temporary public law. 1907–14, 1920–39, 1951–
JbOstR Jahrbuch für Ostrecht (Ger.)
Jctus. Jurisconsultus
JdT Journal des Tribunaux (Switz.)
Jebb Jebb's Crown Cases Reserved (Ire.) 1822–40
Jebb C.C. Jebb's Crown Cases Reserved (Ire.) 1822–40
Jebb Cr.& Pr.Cas Jebb's Irish Crown and Presentment Cases
Jebb & B. Jebb & Burke's Queen's Bench Reports (Ire.) 1841–2
Jebb & S. Jebb & Symes' Queen's Bench Reports (Ire.) 1838–41
Jebb & Sym. Jebb & Symes' Queen's Bench Reports (Ire.) 1838–41
Jeff. Jefferson's Reports (Virginia General Court)
Jeff.Man. Jefferson's Manual of Parliamentary Law
Jeff.(Va.) Jefferson's Reports (Virginia General Court)
Jenck.Bills Jencken, Bills of Exchange. 1880
Jenck.Neg.S. Jencken, Negotiable Securities. 1880
Jenk. Jenkins' Exchequer Reports (145 ER) 1220–1623
Jenk.Cent. Jenkins' Exchequer Reports (145 ER) 1220–1623
Jenk.& Formoy Jenkinson & Formoy's Select Cases in the Exchequer of Pleas (Selden Society) 1236–1300
Jenkins Jenkins' Exchequer Reports (145 ER) 1220–1623
Jenkins Cttee. Company Law Committee. Report (Cmnd. 1749) 1962 Leasehold Committee. Report (Cmd. 7982) 1950
Jenks Jenks' Reports (58 New Hampshire)
Jenn. Jennison's Reports (14–18 Michigan)
Jenn.Sug.A. Jennett, Sugden's Acts
Jer.Dig. Jeremy's Digest. 1817–23, 1838–49
Jer.Undang-Undang Jernal Undang-Undang: Journal of Malaysian and Comparative Law (Malaysia)
Jeremy Eq. Jeremy's Equity Jurisdiction. 1828
Jeremy Eq.Jur. Jeremy's Equity Jurisdiction. 1828
Jernal Undang-Undang Jernal Undang-Undang: Journal of Malaysian and Comparative Law (Malaysia)
Jerv.Cor. Jervis, Coroners
Jes. Analysis and Digest of the Decisions of Sir George Jessell
Jessup The Law of Territorial Waters and Maritime Jurisdiction (USA) 1927
Jewish J.Social. Jewish Journal of Sociology
Jewish L.Annual Jewish Law Annual (Neth.)

Jewish Q.Rev. Jewish Quarterly Review (USA)
Jewish Soc.Stud. Jewish Social Studies (USA)
Jherings Jahrb. Jherings Jahrbücher für die Dogmatik des burgerlichen Rechts (Ger.)
Jick.Est. Jickling, Legal and Equitable Estates. 1829
Jnl. Journal
Jnl.of Bus.L. Journal of Business Law. 1957–
Jnl.of Indust.Rel. Journal of Industrial Relations (Aus.) 1959–
Jnls. Journals
Jo. T. Jones' Exchequer Reports (Ire.) 1834–8
Jo.Ex.Ir. T. Jones' Exchequer Reports (Ire.) 1834–8
Jo.Ex.Pro.W. Jones' Exchequer Proceedings concerning Wales. 1839
Jo.Jur. Journal of Jurisprudence (USA)
Jo.Radio Law Journal of Radio Law (USA) 1931–2
Jo.T. T. Jones' King's Bench Reports (84 ER) 1667–85
Jo.& Car. Jones & Carey's Exchequer Reports (Ire.) 1838–9
Jo.& La T. Jones & La Touche's Chancery Reports (Ire.) 1844–6
Jo.& Lat. Jones & La Touche's Chancery Reports (Ire.) 1844–6
Jog.Kozlony Jogtudomanyi kozlony (Hungary)
Joh. Feast of St John the Baptist (24 June)
John. Johnson's Chancery Reports (70 ER) 1859
Johnson's Chancery Reports (Maryland)
Johnson's New York Reports. 1806–23
Johnson's Reports of Chase's Circuit Court Decisions (USA)
John.Am.Not. John's American Notaries
John.Eng.Ch. Johnson's Chancery Reports (70 ER) 1859
John.Mar.J.Prac.& Proc. John Marshall Journal of Practice and Procedure (USA) 1967–
John Marsh.L.J. John Marshall Law Journal (USA) 1930–49
John Marsh.L.Q. John Marshall Law Quarterly (USA) 1935–43
John Marsh.L.Rev. John Marshall Law Review
John Marshall J. John Marshall Journal of Practice and Procedure (USA) 1967–
John Marshall L.Q. John Marshall Law Quarterly (USA) 1935–43
John.& H. Johnson & Hemming's Chancery Reports (70 ER) 1859–62
Johns. Johnson's Chancery Reports (70 ER) 1859
Johnson's Chancery Reports (Maryland)
Johnson's Chancery Reports (New York) 1814–23
Johnson's Reports of Chase's Circuit Court Decisions (USA)
Johns.Bills Johnson, Bills of Exchange. 2ed. 1839
Johns.Cas. Johnson's Cases (New York) 1799–1803
Johns.Cas.(N.Y.) Johnson's Cases (New York) 1799–1803
Johns.Ch. Johnson's Chancery Reports (70 ER) 1859
Johnson's Chancery Reports (Maryland)
Johnson's Chancery Reports (New York) 1814–23
Johns.Ch.Cas. Johnson's Chancery Reports (New York) 1814–23
Johns.Ch.(N.Y.) Johnson's Chancery Reports (New York) 1814–23
Johns.Ct.Err. Johnson's Reports, Court of Errors (New York) 1806–23
Johns.Dec. Johnson's Maryland Chancery Decisions or Reports
Johns.Eng.Ch. Johnson's Chancery Reports (70 ER) 1859
Johns.H.R.V. Johnson's Chancery Reports (70 ER) 1859

Johns.(N.Y.) Johnson's Chancery Reports (New York) 1814–23
Johnson's Supreme Court Reports (New York) 1806–23

Johns.N.Z. Johnston's New Zealand Reports, Court of Appeal. 1867–77

Johns.Rep. Johnson's Chancery Reports (New York) 1814–23
Johnson's Supreme Court Reports (New York) 1806–23

Johns.Tr. Johnson's Impeachment Trial

Johns.U.S. Johnson's Reports of Chases's United States Circuit Court Decisions

Johns.(V.C.) Johnson's Chancery Reports (70 ER) 1859

Johns.& H. Johnson & Hemming's Chancery Reports (70 ER) 1860–2

Johns.& Hem. Johnson & Hemming's Chancery Reports (70 ER) 1860–2

Johnson Johnson's Chancery Reports (70 ER) 1859
Johnson's Chancery Reports (Maryland)
Johnson's Chancery Reports (New York) 1814–23
Johnson's Supreme Court Reports (New York) 1806–23

Johnst.(N.Z.) Johnston's Court of Appeal Reports (N.Z.) 1867–77

Jon. Jones' Exchequer Reports (Ire.) 1834–8
T. Jones' King's Bench and Common Pleas Reports (84 ER) 1667–85
W. Jones' King's Bench and Common Pleas Reports (82 ER) 1620–41

Jon.Ex. Jones' Exchequer Reports (Ire.) 1834–8

Jon.Exch. Jones' Exchequer Reports (Ire.) 1834–8

Jon.Ir.Exch. Jones' Exchequer Reports (Ire.) 1834–8

Jon.& Car. Jones & Carey's Exchequer Reports (Ire.) 1838–9

Jon.& L. Jones & La Touche's Chancery Reports (Ire.) 1844–6

Jon.& La T. Jones & La Touche's Chancery Reports (Ire.) 1844–6

Jones Jones' Alabama Reports (43–8, 52–7, 61–2 Alabama)
Jones' Exchequer Reports (Ire.) 1834–8
Jones' Missouri Reports (22–30 Missouri)
Jones' North Carolina Equity Reports (54–9 NC) 1853–62
Jones' North Carolina Law Reports (46–53 NC) 1853–62
Jones' Pennsylvania Reports (11–12 Pa.)
Jones' Upper Canada Common Pleas Reports. 1850–82

Jones(1) Sir William Jones' King's Bench Reports (82 ER) 1620–41

Jones(2) Sir Thomas Jones' King's Bench Reports (84 ER) 1676–85

Jones B. Jones' Law of Bailments. 4ed. 1833–4

Jones B.& W.(Mo.) Jones, Barclay & Whittelsey's Reports (31 Missouri)

Jones Bailm. Jones' Law of Bailments. 4ed. 1833–4

Jones, Barclay & Whittelsey Jones, Barclay & Whittelsey's Reports (31 Missouri)

Jones Ch.Mort. Jones on Chattel Mortgages

Jones Cttee. Committee on County Courts and Magistrates' Courts in Northern Ireland. Report (Cmnd. 5824) 1974

Jones Eq. Jones' North Carolina Equity Reports (54–9 NNC) 1853–62

Jones Exch. T. Jones' Exchequer Reports (Ire.) 1834–8

Jones French Bar Jones's History of the French Bar

Jones Ir. Jones' Exchequer Reports (Ire.) 1834–8

Jones L. Jones' North Carolina Law Reports (46–53 NC) 1853–62

Jones Lib. Jones, Libel. 1812

Jones N.C. Jones' North Carolina Law Reports (46–53 NC) 1853–62

Jones (Pa.) Jones' Pennsylvania Reports (11–12 Pa.)

Jones T. Sir Thomas Jones' King's Bench Reports (84 ER) 1667–85
Jones U.C. Jones' Upper Canada Common Pleas Reports. 1850–82
Jones W. Sir William Jones' King's Bench Reports (82 ER) 1620–41
Jones & C. Jones & Carey's Exchequer Reports (Ire.) 1838–9
Jones & L. Jones & La Touche's Chancery Reports (Ire.) 1844–6
Jones & L.(Ir.) Jones & La Touche's Chancery Reports (Ire.) 1844–6
Jones & La T. Jones & La Touche's Chancery Reports (Ire.) 1844–6
Jones & McM. Jones & McMurtrie's Pennsylvania Supreme Court Reports
Jones & McM.(Pa.) Jones & McMurtrie's Pennsylvania Supreme Court Reports
Jones & S. Jones & Spencer's New York Reports (33–61 N.Y. Superior)
Jones & Sp. Jones & Spencer's New York Reports (33–61 N.Y. Superior)
Jones & Spen. Jones & Spencer's New York Reports (33–61 N.Y. Superior)
Jones & V.Laws Jones & Varick's Laws (New York)
Jos. Joseph's Reports (21 Nevada)
Jos.& Bev. Joseph & Beven's Digest of Decisions (Sri L.)
Jour.Am.Jud.Soc. Journal of the American Judicature Society. 1917–66
Jour.Comp.Leg. Journal of Comparative Legislation and International Law. 1918–51
Jour.Conat.Law Journal of Conational Law
Jour.Crim.L. Journal of Criminal Law and Criminology (USA) 1941–51, 1973–
Jour.dr.int. Journal de droit international
Jour.Jur. Hall's Journal of Jurisprudence (USA) 1821
Jour.Jur.Sc. Journal of Jurisprudence and Scottish Law Magazine. 1857–91
Jour.Juris. Hall's Journal of Jurisprudence (USA) 1821
Jour.Law Journal of Law (USA) 1830–1
Jour.of Juristic Papyrology Journal of Juristic Papyrology (Poland)
Jour.of the Warburg & Courtauld Inst. Journal of the Warburg & Courtauld Institute
Jour.Ps.Med. Journal of Psychological Medicine and Medical Jurisprudence (USA) 1867–72
Jour.Soc.Legis.Comp. Journées de la Société de Législation Comparé (Fr.)
Journ.agrées. Revue de Jurisprudence commerciale. Journal des agrées (Fr.)
Journ.bus.law Journal of Business Law
Journ.Comp.Leg. Journal of Comparative Legislation and International Law. 1918–51
Journ.cont.bus. Journal of Contemporary Business
Journ.Dr.intern. Journal du Droit international (Clunet) (Fr.)
Journ.Enreg. Journal de l'Enregistrement (Fr.)
Journ.Faill. Journal des faillites et liquidations judiciaires
Journ.int.bus.stud. Journal of International Business Studies
Journ.int.law and econ. Journal of International Law and Economics
Journ.of Polit.econ. Journal of Political Economics
Journ.res.and educ. Journal of Research and Education, Patent, Trade Mark and Copyright
Journ.Soc. Journal des societés (Fr.)
Journ.Trib.com. Journal des Tribunaux de commerce (Fr.)
Journ.World trade law Journal of World Trade Law
Jow.Dict. Jowitt, Dictionary of English Law
Joy Acc. Joy, Evidence of Accomplices. 1836
Joy Chal. Joy, Peremptory Challenge of Jurors. 1844
Joy Conf. Joy, Admissibility of Confessions. 1842
Joy Ev. Joy, Evidence of Accomplices. 1836

Joyce Prac.Inj. Joyce, Law and Practice of Injunctions. 1872
Joyce Prin.Inj. Joyce, Doctrines and Principles of Injunctions. 1877
Jp. Jurisprudence (Belg.) Case law
Jt. Joint
Jt.Com. Joint Committee
Ju.D. Juris Doctor (Doctor of Law)
JuS Juristische Schulung (Ger.)
Ju.St.Karlsruhe Schr. Juristische Studiengesellschaft Karlsruhe Schriftenreihe (Ger.)
Jud. Book of Judgments
Judicature
Judicial
Judiciary
Sir R. Phillimore's Ecclesiastical Judgments. 1867–75
Jud.Chr. Judicial Chronicle
Jud.Coun.N.Y. Judicial Council, New York, Annual Reports
Jud.G.C.C. Judgments, Gold Coast Colony (Ghana)
Jud.Q.R. Judicature Quarterly Review. 1896
Jud.Rep. Judicial Repository (New York)
Jud.Repos. Judicial Repository (New York)
Jud.& Sw. Judah & Swan's Reports (Jamaica) 1839
Judd Judd's Reports (4 Hawaii)
Judg.U.B. First Book of Judgments (Judgments of the Upper Bench) 1655
Judge Advo.J. The Judge Advocate Journal (USA) 1944–5, 1949–
Judge's J. Judge's Journal (USA) 1971–
Judicature Judicature: Journal of the American Judicature Society. 1966–
Jugo.Rev.Krim.Prav. Jugoslovenska Revija za Kriminologiju Krivicno Pravo (Yugoslavia)
Jugo.Rev.Med.Prav. Jugoslovenska Revija za Medunarodno Pravo (Yugoslavia)
Jur. Juridical
Jurisprudence
Jurist. 1937–67
The Jurist. 1887–91
The Jurist (Washington DC) 1941–
The Jurist or Quarterly Journal of Jurisprudence and Legislation. 1827–33
Jurist Reports. 1837–54
Juristen (Den.) 1919–73
Jur.adm.fasc. Jurisprudence des autorités administratives, fascicule
Jur.Blatter Juristische Blätter
Jur.Comp.Brux. Jurisprudence commerciale de Bruxelles
Jur.D. Juris Doctor (Doctor of Law)
Jur.F. Juristische Fakultät
Jur.Liège Jurisprudence de la Cour d'Appel de Liège (Belg.) periodical collection of reports
Jur.N.S. Jurist Reports, New Series. 1855–67
Jur.(N.S.) Jurist Reports, New Series. 1855–67
Jur.N.Y. The Jurist or Law and Equity Reporter (New York)
Jur.Rev. Juridical Review (Scot.) 1889–
Jur.(Sc.) The Scottish Jurist (Edinburgh) 1829–73
Jur.Soc.P. Juridical Society Papers (Scot.) 1858–74
Jur.St. Juridical Styles (Scot.)
JurW. Juristische Wochenschrift (Ger.) 1872–1939
Jura Jura: rivista internazionale di diritto romano et antico (It.) 1950–
Jura Falconis Jura Falconis: Juridisch Wetenschappelijk Studentenijdschrift (Belg.)
Jurid.Rev. Juridical Review (Scot.) 1889–
Jurid.Socy.Pap. Juridical Society Papers
Jurid.Tids. Juridisk Tidskift vid Stockholms (Swed.)
Juridical R. Juridical Review (Scot.) 1889–
Jurimetrics Jurimetrics Journal (USA) 1966–
Jurimetrics J. Jurimetrics Journal (USA) 1966–
Juris. Jurisprudence
jurisd. jurisdiction

Jurispr. The Jurisprudent (Boston) 1830–1

Jurisprudentie Jurisprudentie van het Hof van Justitie (Neth.) Official series of reports of Judgments of the European Court

Juristen (Denmark) Juristen/Danmarks Jurist og Okonomforbund

Jurisuto Jurisuto (The Jurist) (Japan)

Jus. Jus: Rivista di Scienze Giuridiche (It.) 1950–
Justice

Jus.Int. Institutes of Justinian

Jus.Riv.Sci.Giur. Jus: Rivista di Scienze Giuridiche (It.) 1950–

Just. Justice
Justices' Law Reporter (Pennsylvania) 1902–18
Justiciary

Just.Cas. Justiciary Cases

Just Cause Just Cause: a Journal of Law and People with Disabilities (Can.) 1982–

Just.Children Newsl. Justice for Children Newsletter (Can.)

Just.Ct. Justice Court

Just.Dig. Digest of Justinian

Just.Inst. Institutes of Justinian

Just.L.R. Justices' Law Reporter (Pennsylvania) 1902–18

Just.P. Justice of Peace and Local Government Review. 1837–

Just.Peace Justice of Peace and Local Government Review. 1837–

Just.Port. Justica Portuguesa

Just.Syst.J. The Justice System Journal (USA)

Justice British Section of the International Commission of Jurists
Justice: la magazine du Ministère la Justice de Québec (Can.)

Justice Rep. The Justice Reporter (USA)

Justice's L.R.(Pa.) Justice's Law Reporter (Pennsylvania) 1902–18

Justn. Justinian (Aus.) 1979–

Juta Juta's Daily Reporter (S.Afr.) 1915–26
Juta's Prize Cases (S.Afr.)
Juta's Supreme Court Reports, Cape of Good Hope (S.Afr.) 1880–1910

Juv. Juvenile

Juv.Ct. Juvenile Court

Juv.Ct.J.J. Juvenile Court Judges Journal (USA) 1949–72

Juv.Just. Juvenile Justice (USA) 1972–

Juv.Justice Juvenile Justice (USA) 1972–

Juv.& Dom.Rel.Ct. Juvenile and Domestic Relations Court

Juv.& Fam.Court J. Juvenile and Family Court Justice

K

K. Kammer (Ger.) Chamber, division
Kemble, Codex Diplomaticus Ævi Saxonici
Kenyon's Notes of Cases, King's Bench (96 ER) 1753–9
Keyes' Court of Appeals Reports (40–3 New York)
King
Kotze's High Court Reports, Transvaal (S.Afr.) 1877–81
Wetboek van Koophandel (Neth.) commercial code

KA Kammarrattens arsbok (Swed.) The annual Fiscal Court reporter. 1925–

K.B. King's Bench
Kommanditbolaget (Ger.) Limited partnership
Koninkijk Besluit (Neth.) Royal Decree
Law Reports King's Bench. 1901–52

KB 27 Public Record Office, Plea Rolls of the Court of King's Bench

KBA Kansas Bar Association

K.B.B. Kentucky Bench and Bar. 1975–

K.B.C. King's Bench Court

K.B.D. King's Bench Division

K.B.Div'l.Ct. King's Bench Divisional Court

K.B.J. Kentucky Bar Journal. 1971–4
Kentucky State Bar Journal. 1936–71

K.B.U.C. Upper Canada King's Bench Reports

KBr Kungl. brev (Swed.) Royal letter – decree

K.C. King's Counsel

K.C.L.J. Kings College Law Journal

K.C.R. Kansas City Law Review. 1932–8
Reports tempore King (25 ER) 1724–33
The University of Kansas City Law Review. 1938–63
The University of Missouri at Kansas City Law Review. 1964–8

KCirk Kungl. cirkular (Swed.) Royal circular – decree

KF Kungl. forordning (Swed.) Royal statute – law

K.F. Gold Coast Judgments and the Masai Cases, by King-Farlow (Ghana) 1915–17

KFC Kentucky Fried Chicken

KG Bundesgesetz über Kartelle und ahnliche Organisationen (Switz.) 1962
Kammergericht (Ger.) Appeal Court, Berlin
Kommanditgesellschaft (Ger.) Limited partnership

K.Ga.A. Kommanditgesellschaft auf Aktien (Ger.) Limited partnership on share basis

K.H.C.D. Kenya High Court Digest

KH.HC. Khartoum High Court

K.I.R. Knight's Industrial Reports. 1966–75

KK Kungl. kungorelse (Swed.) Royal regulation – decree

K.K. Kabushiki kaisha (Japan) Stock corporation

KKM Ministry of Foreign Trade (Hungary)

KL Konkurslag (Swed.) Bankruptcy Law. 1921

K.L.G.R. Knight's Local Government Reports. 1903–

K.L.J. Kentucky Law Journal. 1912–

K.L.R. Kathiawar Law Reports (India) Kenya Law Reports. 1919–

K.L.T. Kerala Law Times (India) 1948–

KM:t Kungl. Majestat (Swed.) the King in Council or the Cabinet

KO Konkursordnung (Ger.) Bankruptcy Konsumentombudsman (Swed.) Consumer Ombudsman

KPDR Korean People's Democratic Republic (North Korea)

KS Kungl. stadga (Swed.) Royal regulation – decree

K.S. King's Sergeant

K.S.C. Kenny, A Selection of Cases Illustrative of the English Criminal Law. 1901

KUVG Bundesgesetz über die Kranken- und Unfallversicherung (Switz.) 1911

KVO Kraftverkehrsordnung für den Guterfernverkehr mit Kraftfahrzeugen (Ger.) Regulation of carriage of goods by motor vehicles

KWG Reichsgesetz über das Kreditwesen (Ger.) Law on credit operations

K.W.I.C. Keyword in context

K.& B. Kotze & Barber's High Court Reports (Transvaal, S.Afr.) 1855–88

K.& B.Dig. Kerford & Box, Victorian Digest

K.& E.Conv. Key & Elphinstone, Conveyancing. 15ed. 1953–4

K.& F.N.S.W. Knox & Fitzharding's New South Wales Reports. 1878–9

K.& G. Keane & Grant's Registration Appeal Cases. 1854–62

K.& G.R.C. Keane & Grant's Registration Appeal Cases. 1854–62

K.& Gr. Keane & Grant's Registration Appeal Cases. 1854–62

K.& J. Kay & Johnson's Vice Chancellors' Reports (69–70 ER) 1854–8

K.& O. Knapp & Ombler's Election Cases. 1834–5

K.& R. Kent & Radcliffe's Law of New York, Revision of 1801

K.& W. Kames & Woodhouselee's Dictionary of Decisions (Scot.) 1540–1796

K.& W.Dic. Kames & Woodhouselee's Dictionary of Decisions (Scot.) 1540–1796

Ka.A. Kansas Appeal Reports

Kahn Contract E. Kahn, Contract and Mercantile Law (S.Afr.)

Kahn Domicile E. Kahn, The South African Law of Domicile of Natural Persons

Kakyu minshu Kakyu saibansho minji saiban reishu (Japan) Lower court civil case reports

Kam. Kames & Woodhouselee's Dictionary of Decisions (Scot.) 1540–1796 Kames' Remarkable Decisions, Court of Session (Scot.) 1716–52

Kam.Eluc. Kames, Elucidations of the Laws of Scotland

Kam.Eq. Kames, Principles of Equity

Kam.L.Tr. Kames, Historical Law Tracts (Scot.)

Kam.Rem. Kames' Remarkable Decisions, Court of Session (Scot.) 1716–52

Kam.Sel. Kames' Select Decisions (Scot.) 1752–68

Kam.Sel.Dec. Kames' Select Decisions (Scot.) 1752–68

Kames Kames & Woodhouselee's Dictionary of Decisions (Scot.) 1540–1796 Kames' Remarkable Decisions, Court of Session (Scot.) 1716–52 Kames' Select Decisions (Scot.) 1752–68

Kames Dec. Kames & Woodhouselee's Dictionary of Decisions, Court of Session (Scot.) 1540–1796

Kames Dict.Dec. Kames & Woodhouselee's Dictionary of Decisions, Court of Session (Scot.) 1540–1796

Kames Elucid. Kames' Elucidations of the Laws of Scotland
Kames Eq. Kames' Principles of Equity (Scot.)
Kames Sel.Dec. Kames' Select Decisions (Scot.) 1752–68
Kan. Kansas
Kansas Supreme Court Reports. 1862–
Kan.App. Kansas Appeals Reports
Kan.B.Ass'n.J. Kansas Bar Association Journal
Kan.C.L.Rep. Kansas City Law Reporter. 1888
Kan.City L.Rev. Kansas City Law Review. 1932–8
Kan.Civ.Pro.Stat.Ann. Kansas Code of Civil Procedure
Kan.Crim.Code & Code of Crim.Proc. Kansas Criminal Code and Code of Criminal Procedure
Kan.Dig. Hatcher's Kansas Digest
Kan.Jud.Council Bul. Kansas Judicial Council Bulletin
Kan.L.J. Kansas Law Journal. 1885–7
Kan.Law Kansas Lawyer. 1895–1911
Kan.Sess.Laws Session Laws of Kansas
Kan.St.L.J. Kansas State Law Journal
Kan.Stat. Kansas Statutes
Kan.Stat.Ann. Kansas Statutes Annotated
Kan.U.C.C.Ann.(Vernon) Vernon's Kansas Statutes Annotated, Uniform Commercial Code
Kan.U.Lawy. Kansas University Lawyer. 1895–6
Kan.Univ.Lawy. Kansas University Lawyer. 1895–6
Kans. Kansas Supreme Court Reports. 1862–
Kans.App. Kansas Appeals Reports
Kans.B.A. Kansas City Bar Journal
Kans.S.B.A. Kansas State Bar Association
Kansai Univ.Rev.L.& Pol. Kansai University Review of Law and Politics (Japan)
Kansas City L.Rev. Kansas City Law Review
Kansas L.J. Kansas Law Journal. 1885–7
Kansas Law. Kansas Lawyer
Kar. Indian Law Reports, Karachi Series. 1939–47
Pakistan Law Reports, Karachi Series. 1947–53
Kar.L.J. Karachi Law Journal. 1964–
Kaser M. Kaser, Roman Private Law (S.Afr.)
Kashmir L.J. Kashmir Law Journal. 1929
Kashmir Law Journal. 1962–
Katch.Pr.Law Katchenovsky, Prize Law. 2ed. 1867
Kauf.Mack. Kaufmann's Edition of Mackeldey's Civil Law
Kay Kay's Vice Chancellors' Reports (69 ER) 1853–4
Kay Ship. Kay, Shipmasters and Seamen. 2ed. 1894
Kay & J. Kay & Johnson's Vice Chancellors' Reports (69–70 ER) 1854–8
Kay & John. Kay & Johnson's Vice Chancellors' Reports (69–70 ER) 1854–8
Kay & Johns. Kay & Johnson's Vice Chancellors' Reports (69–70 ER) 1854–8
Ke. Keen's Rolls Court Reports (48 ER) 1836–8
Keane & G.R.C. Keane & Grant's Registration Appeal Cases. 1854–62
Keane & Gr. Keane & Grant's Registration Appeal Cases. 1854–62
Keat.Fam.Sett. Keatinge, Family Settlements. 1810
Keb. Keble's King's Bench Reports (83–4 ER) 1661–79
Kebl. Keble's King's Bench Reports (83–4 ER) 1661–79
Keble Keble's King's Bench Reports ((83–4 ER) 1661–79
Keen Keen's Rolls Court Reports (48 ER) 1836–8
Keen Ch. Keen's Rolls Court Reports (48 ER) 1836–8

Keesing's Keesing's Contemporary Archives: Weekly Diary of World Events
Keidanren Keizai Dantai Rengokai (Japan) Federation of Economic Organisations
Keiho Zasshi Keiho Zasshi (Journal of Criminal Law) (Japan)
Keil Keilwey's King's Bench Reports (72 ER) 1496–1578
Keilw. Keilwey's King's Bench Reports (72 ER) 1496–1578
Keilwey Keilwey's King's Bench Reports (72 ER) 1496–1578
Keio L.Rev. Keio Law Review (Japan)
Keishu Saiko saibansho keiji hanreishu (Japan) Supreme Court Criminal Case Report
Keith Ch.Pa. Registrar's Book, Keith's Court of Chancery (Pennsylvania)
Keith Committee Committee on Enforcement Powers of the Revenue Departments. Vols.1 & 2 (Cmnd. 8822) 1983; vol.3 (Cmnd. 9120) 1984; vol.4 (Cmnd. 9440) 1985
Kel. Sir John Kelyng's Crown Cases (84 ER) 1662–9
Kel.(1) Sir John Kelyng's Crown Cases (84 ER) 1662–9
Kel.(2) Wm. Kelynge's Chancery Reports (25 ER) 1730–4
Kel.An. Kelly, Life Annuities. 1835
Kel.C.C. Sir John Kelyng's Crown Cases (84 ER) 1662–9
Kel.Draft Kelly's Draftsman
Kel.Ga. Kelly's Reports (1–3 Georgia)
Kel.J. Sir John Kelyng's Crown Cases (84 ER) 1662–9
Kel.Sc.Fac. Kelly, Scire Facias. 2ed. 1849
Kel.Us. Kelly, Usury. 1835
Kel.W. Wm. Kelynge's Chancery Reports tempore Hardwicke (25 ER) 1730–4
Kelh. Kelham's Norman French Law Dictionary
Kellen Kellen's Massachusetts Reports (146–55 Mass.)
Kelly Kelly's Reports (1–3 Georgia)
Kelly & Cobb Kelly & Cobb's Reports (4–5 Georgia)
Kelyng J. Sir John Kelyng's Crown Cases (84 ER) 1662–9
Kelynge W. Wm. Kelynge's Chancery Reports (25 ER) 1730–4
Ken. Kenyon's King's Bench Reports (96 ER) 1753–9
Ken.Dec. Sneed's Kentucky Decisions (2 Ky.)
Ken.L.Re. Kentucky Law Reporter. 1880–1908
Ken.Opin. Kentucky Opinions. 1864–86
Kenan Kenan's Reports (76–91 North Carolina)
Kenn.Ch. Kennedy, Chancery Practice. 2ed. 1852–3
Kennett Kennett's Glossary
Kennett upon Impropriations
Kennett Gloss. Kennett's Glossary
Kent Kent's Commentaries on American Law
Kent Com. Kent's Commentaries on American Law
Kent & R.St. Kent & Radcliff's Law of New York, Revision of 1801
Kentucky L.J. Kentucky Law Journal
Keny. Kenyon's Notes of King's Bench Cases (96 ER) 1753–9
Keny.Ch. Chancery Cases (2 Ky.) 1753–4
Kenya L.R. Kenya Law Reports. 1922–
Ker. Indian Law Reports, Kerala Series. 1950–
Ker.Ind. Kerala, India
Ker.L.T. Kerala Law Times (India) 1928–
Kerala All India Reporter, Kerala. 1957–
Kern. Kern's Reports (100–116 Indiana)
Kernan's Reports (11–14 New York)
Kerr Kerr's New Brunswick Reports (3–5 NB) 1840–8
Kerr's Reports (18–22 Indiana)
Kerr's Reports (27–29 New York Civil Procedure)
Kerr Act. Kerr, Actions at Law. 3ed. 1861

Kerr Black. Kerr's Blackstone. 12ed. 1895
Kerr Disc. Kerr, Discovery. 1870
Kerr F.& M. Kerr, Fraud and Mistake. 7ed. 1952
Kerr Inj. Kerr on Injunctions. 6ed. 1927
Kerr (N.B.) Kerr's New Brunswick Reports (3–5 NB) 1840–8
Kerr Rec. Kerr, Law and Practice as to Receivers
Kerse Kerse's (Hope) Manuscript Decisions, Court of Session (Scot.) 1610–32
Key. Keyes' New York Court of Appeals Reports (40–3 NY)
Key & Elph.Conv. Key & Elphinstone, Conveyancing. 15ed. 1953–4
Keyes Keyes' New York Court of Appeals Reports (40–3 NY)
Keyl. Keilwey's King's Bench Reports (72 ER) 1496–1578
Keylway Keilwey's King's Bench Reports (72 ER) 1496–1578
Keys.St.Ex. Keyser, Stock Exchange. 1850
Kg. Kantongerecht (Neth.)
Khaipur, Pak. Khaipur, Pakistan
Kilb. Kilburn's Magistrates' Cases
Kilbrandon Report Committee on Children and Young Persons. Report (Cmnd. 2306) (Scot.) 1964
Royal Commission on the Constitution. Report (Cmnd. 5460) 1973
Kilk. Kilkerran's Court of Session Decisions (Scot.) 1738–52
Kilkerran Kilkerran's Court of Session Decisions (Scot.) 1738–52
King King's Reports (5–6 Louisiana Annual)
Select Cases in Chancery, tempore King (25 ER) 1724–33
King Cas.temp. Select Cases in Chancery, tempore King (25 ER) 1724–33
King Dig. King, Tennessee Digest
King-Farlow Gold Coast Judgments and the Masai Case by King-Farlow (Ghana) 1915–17
King's Con.Cs. King's Conflicting Cases (Texas) 1840–1911
King's Conf.Ca. King's Conflicting Cases (Texas) 1840–1911
Kingston L.R. Kingston Law Review. 1968–
Kingston L.Rev. Kingston Law Review. 1968–
Kir. Kirby's Reports and Supplement (Connecticut) 1785–9
Kirb. Kirby's Reports and Supplement (Connecticut) 1785–9
Kirby Kirby's Reports and Supplement (Connecticut) 1785–9
Kit. Kitchin's Retourna Brevium. 4ed. 1592
Kitchin on Jurisdictions of Courts-Leet, Courts-Baron, etc. 5ed. 1675
Kit.Ct. Kitchin on Jurisdictions of Courts-Leet, Courts-Baron, etc. 5ed. 1675
Kit.Jur. Kitchin on Jurisdictions of Courts-Leet, Courts-Baron, etc. 5ed. 1675
Kit.Rd.Trans. Kitchin, Road Transport Law
Kitch.Cts. Kitchin on Jurisdictions of Courts-Leet, Courts-Baron, etc. 5ed. 1675
Kitchen Griqualand West Reports, Cape Colony (S.Afr.)
Kl. Kläger (Ger.) plaintiff
Kn. Knapp's Privy Council Appeal Cases (12 ER) 1829–36
Knox's Supreme Court Report, New South Wales (Aus.) 1877
Kn.A.C. Knapp's Privy Council Appeal Cases (12 ER) 1829–36
Kn.L.G.R. Knight's Local Government Reports. 1903–
Kn.N.S.W. Knox's Supreme Court Reports, New South Wales (Aus.) 1877
Kn.P.C. Knapp's Privy Council Appeal Cases (12 ER) 1829–36
Kn.& Moo. Knapp's Privy Council Appeal Cases Vol. 3 (12 ER) 1829–36

Kn.& O. Knapp & Ombler's Election Cases. 1834–5

Kn.& Omb. Knapp & Ombler's Election Cases. 1834–5

Knapp Knapp's Privy Council Appeal Cases (12 ER) 1829–36

Knapp P.C.C. Knapp's Privy Council Appeal Cases (12 ER) 1829–36

Knapp & O. Knapp & Ombler's Election Cases. 1834–5

Knight's Ind. Knight's Industrial Reports. 1966–75

Knowles Knowles' Reports (3 Rhode Island)

Knox Knox's Supreme Court Reports, New South Wales (Aus.) 1877

Knox (N.S.W.) Knox's Supreme Court Reports, New South Wales (Aus.) 1877

Knox & F. Knox & Fitzharding's Supreme Court Reports, New South Wales (Aus.) 1878–9

Knox & Fitz. Knox & Fitzharding's Supreme Court Reports, New South Wales (Aus.) 1878–9

knt. knight

KoAG Kommanditgesellschaft auf Aktien (Ger.)

Kobe U.L.R. Kobe University Law Review (Japan)

Kobe Univ.L.Rev.Int'l Ed. Kobe University Law Review, International Edition (Japan)

Koch Koch's Ceylon Supreme Court Decisions (Sri L.) 1899

Kok.Gaiko Zasshi Kokusaiho Gaiko Zasshi (Journal of International Law and Diplomacy) (Japan)

Kollewijn R.D.Kollewijn, Geschiedenis van de Nederlandse Wetenschap van het internationaal privaatrecht tot 1880 (Neth.) 1937

Konst.Rat.App. Konstam's Rating Appeals. 1904–8

Konst.& W.Rat.App. Konstam & Ward's Rating Appeals. 1909–12

Korea & World Aff. Korea and World Affairs

Korea J. Korea Journal

Korean J.Comp.L. Korean Journal of Comparative Law

Korm. Governmental Decree (Hungary)

Kosai minshu Koto saibansho minji hanreishu (Japan) High Court civil case reports

Kotze Kotze's Transvaal High Court Reports. 1877–81

Kotze & B. Supreme Court Reports, Transvaal (S.Afr.) 1885–8

Kotze & Barb. Supreme Court Reports, Transvaal (S.Afr.) 1885–8

Kotze & Barber Supreme Court Reports, Transvaal (S.Afr.) 1885–8

Kr.Vjschr. Kritische Vierteljahresschrift für Gesetzbung und Rechtswissenschaft (Ger.)

Kreider Kreider's Reports (1–23 Washington)

Kress Kress's Reports (166–194 Pennsylvania State)
Kress's Reports (2–12 Pennsylvania Superior)

Krummeck Decisions of the Water Courts (S.Afr.) 1913–36

Ks. Kansas Reports

Ks.L.R. University of Kansas Law Review. 1952–

KstG. Körperschaftsteuergesetz (Ger.) Corporation Taxation Act

Kt. Knight

Ktg. Kantongerecht

Kulp Kulp's Luzerne Legal Register Reports (Pennsylvania)

Kungl.Maj:t Kungl. Majestat (Swed.) the King in Council or the Cabinet

Kunz Kunz, Die Anerkennung von Staaten und Regierungen im Volkerrecht. 1928

Kutch All India Reporter, Kutch. 1949–56

Kwansei Gakuin L.Rev. Kwansei Gakuin Law Review (Japan)

Ky. Kentucky Supreme Court Reports. 1879–1951
Kyshe's Reports (Mal.) 1808–90

Ky.Acts Kentucky Acts

Ky.B.J. Kentucky Bar Journal. 1971–4

Ky.(B.Mon.) B. Monroe's Kentucky Reports

Ky.Dec. Sneed's Kentucky Decisions (2 Ky.)

Ky.L.J. Kentucky Law Journal. 1912–

Ky.L.R. Kentucky Law Reporter. 1880–1908

Ky.L.Rep. Kentucky Law Reporter. 1880–1908

Ky.Law Rep. Kentucky Law Reporter. 1880–1908

Ky.Op. Kentucky Court of Appeals Opinions

Ky.Rev.Stat. Kentucky Revised Statutes. 1970

Ky.Rev.Stat.Ann. Baldwin's Kentucky Revised Statutes Annotated

Ky.Rev.Stat.& Rules Serv. Baldwin's Kentucky Revised Statutes and Rules Service

Ky.S.B.A. Kentucky State Bar Association

Ky.S.B.J. Kentucky State Bar Journal. 1936–71

Ky.St.B.J. Kentucky State Bar Journal. 1936–71

Ky.St.Law Morehead and Brown's Digest of Statute Laws (Kentucky)

Ky.W.C.Dec. Kentucky Workmen's Compensation Board Decisions

Kyd Aw. Kyd on Awards

Kyd Bills Kyd on Bills of Exchange

Kyd Corp. Kyd on Corporations

Kyshe Kyshe's Reports (Mal.) 1808–90

L

L. Lansing's Select Cases in Chancery (New York) 1824, 1826
Lansing's Supreme Court Reports (New York) 1869–73
Law
Lawson, Notes of Registration Decisions
Legge (It.) law, act, statute
Liber (Lat.) law
Limited
Loi (Belg. & Fr.) law, act, statute
London
Lord

L.A. Labor Arbitration Reports (USA) 1946–
Law Agent
Lawyers' Reports Annotated
Legal Adviser
Legislative Assembly
Library Association
Licensing Act
Loan Agreement
Local Authority
Los Angeles

L/A Letter of authority

L.A.A.C. Lord Chancellor's Legal Aid Advisory Committee

LAAD Latin American Agri-business Development Corporation

L.A.B. Los Angeles Bar Bulletin. 1925–75

L.A.B.Bull. Los Angeles Bar Bulletin. 1925–75

L.A.B.J. Los Angeles Bar Journal. 1975–

L.A.B.L. Australian Company Secretary's Business Law Manual (CCH) 1987–

L.A.C. Labour Appeal Cases (India) 1951–
Labour Arbitration Cases (Can.)

L.A.C.B. Legal Aid Clearinghouse Bulletin (Aus.) 1981–

L.A.C.C. Land Appeal Court Cases (N.S.W., Aus.) 1890–1921

LACSAB Local Authorities' Conditions of Service Advisory Board

LAES Latin American Economic System

LAFTA Latin American Free Trade Association

L.A.G. Legal Action Group

L.A.G.Bull. Legal Action Group Bulletin. 1972–

LAMA Loi fédérale sur l'assurance en cas de maladie ou d'accidents

L.A.N. Labour Arbitration News (Can.)
Local Area Network

L.A.R. Labor Arbitration Reports (USA) 1946–

LAWLIP Library and Information Plan for Law

L.Arb. Lilly's Abridgment

L.Adv. Lord Advocate

L.All. Leges Allemanni

L.Am.Soc. Law in American Society (USA) 1972–

L.Ap. Louisiana Court of Appeal Reports

LArbG Landesarbeitsgericht (Ger.) Provincial Labour Court of Appeal

l.aut. legge sulla protezione del diritto di autore (It.) 1941

L.B.C. Law Book Company (Aus.)

L.B.C.Newsl. Law Book Company

Newsletter (Aus.) 1979–84
L.B.C.Newsl.N.S. Law Book Company Newsletter, New Series (Aus.) 1985–
L.B.Co's Indust.Arb.Serv. Law Book Company's Industrial Arbitration Service. 1950–81
LBGU London Boroughs Grant Unit
L.B.R. Lower Burma Rulings
L.Bai. Leges Baiarum
L.C. Labor Cases (USA)
Land Court
Law Commission
Law Courts
Leading Cases
Library of Congress (USA)
Loan Contract
Lord Chancellor
Lower Canada
Scottish Land Court Reports. 1913–
L/C Letter of Credit
L.C.A. Law Council of Australia (Canberra)
Leading Cases Annotated
Loi fédérale sur le contrat d'assurance (Switz.)
L.C.A.B.L.S. Law Council of Australia, Business Law Section
L.C.A.B.L.S.Bull. Law Council of Australia, Business Law Section Bulletin. 1982–5
L.C.B. Land and Concessions Bulletin (Ghana) 1960–
Lord Chief Baron
L.C.C. Land Appeal Court Cases (N.S.W., Aus.) 1890–1921
Leach's Crown Cases. 1730–1815
London County Council
L.C.C.C. Lower Canada Civil Code
LCCI London Chamber of Commerce and Industry
L.C.C.(N.S.W.) Land Appeal Court Cases (N.S.W., Aus.) 1890–1921
L.C.C.P. Lower Canada Civil Procedure
L.C.D. Lord Chancellor's Department
Lower Court Decisions
L.C.D.L.S. Lord Chancellor's Department Library Services
L.C.Eq. White & Tudor's Leading Cases in Equity
LCF Law Centres Federation
Lawyers' Christian Fellowship (New South Wales, Aus.)
L.C.G. Lower Courts Gazette (Ontario)
L.C.J. Lord Chief Justice
Lower Canada Jurist (Quebec) 1848–91
L.C.Jur. Lower Canada Jurist (Quebec) 1848–91
L.C.L. Licentiate of Civil Law
L.C.L.J. Lower Canada Law Journal (Quebec) 1865–8
L.C.L.Jo. Lower Canada Law Journal (Quebec) 1865–8
L.C.N. Law Council Newsletter (Aus.) 1964–77
L.C.News Law Centres News
L.C.O. Lord Chancellor's Office
L.C.P. Law and Contemporary Problems (USA) 1933–
L.C.R. Land Compensation Reports (Can.) 1972–
Loi fédérale sur la circulation routière (Switz.)
Lower Canada Reports. 1850–67
L.C.Rep.S.Qu. Lower Canada Reports Seignorial Questions
L.C.W.P. Law Commission Working Paper
L.C.Z. Laws of the Canal Zone
L.C.& M.Gaz. Lower Courts and Municipal Gazette (Can.) 1865–72
L.Chr. Law Chronicle
L.Chr.& J.Jur. Law Chronicle and Journal of Jurisprudence (Scot.)
L.Comment'y. Law Commentary
L.const. loi constitutionnelle (Fr.) constitutional law
l.cost. legge costituzionale (It.) constitutional law
L.Ct. Law Court
L.D.B. Legal Decisions Affecting Bankers. 1879–
LDC Less Developed Countries
L.E. Lawyers' Edition, United States Supreme Court Reports
Lawyers' Europe

L.E.2d. Lawyers' Edition, United States Supreme Court Reports, Second Series
L.E.A. Local Education Authority
L.e.C. Fondo Legazioni e Consolati (It.)
L.E.C. Land and Environment Court (New South Wales, Aus.)
Landed Estates Courts Commission
LEG Bundesgesetz über die Entschuldung landwirtschaftlicher Heimwesen (Switz.) 1940
L.E.N. Land and Environment Notes (Aus.) 1980–
L.E.S. Licensing Executives Society – Australia and New Zealand
L.East.Eur. Law in Eastern Europe (Neth.)
L.Ed. Lawyers' Edition, United States Supreme Court Reports
L.Ed.2d. Lawyers' Edition, United States Supreme Court Reports, Second Series
L.Ed.(U.S.) Lawyers' Edition, United States Supreme Court Reports
L.Ex. Legal Executive
L.F. Law French
loi fédérale (Switz.)
LFG Bundesgesetz über die Luftfahrt (Switz.) 1948
l.fall. regio decreto sulla disciplina generale del fallimento e delle altre procedure concursuali (It.) 1942
L.Fr. Law French
LG Landgericht (Ger.) Regional Court
L.G. Law Glossary
L.G.A.T.R.(N.S.W.) Local Government Appeals Tribunal Reports (N.S.W., Aus.) 1972–80
L.G.B. Local Government Board
Local Government Bulletin (Aus.)
Local Government Bulletin (Ghana) 1960–
L.G.C. Local Government Chronicle. 1855–
Lord Great Chamberlain
LGDJ Librairie générale de droit et de jurisprudence
L.G.R. Knight's Local Government Reports. 1903–
Local Government Reports (N.S.W., Aus.) 1911–56
Local Government Review. 1971–
L.G.R.A. Local Government Reports of Australia. 1956–
L.G.R.(N.S.W.) Local Government Reports (N.S.W., Aus.) 1911–56
L.G.Rep.Aus. Local Government Reports of Australia. 1956–
L.G.Rev. Local Government Review. 1971–
L.G.& L. Local Government and Law
L.Guard. Law Guardian. 1965–73
L.Guild R. Law Guild Review
L/H Leasehold
L.H.C. Lord High Chancellor
L.I. Legal Intelligencer (Philadelphia) 1843–
Legislative Instrument (Ghana) 1960–
Lincoln's Inn
L.I.C. Law in Context (La Trobe University) (Aus.) 1983–
LIFO Last in – First out (Accounting principle)
L.I.J. Law Institute Journal (Victoria, Aus.) 1927–
L.I.L. Lincoln's Inn Library
L.I.N. Law Institute News (Victoria, Aus.) 1986–
LIP Library and Information Plan
L.I.R. Legal Information Resources Limited
L.I.S. Legal Information Service (N.Z.)
LISC Library and Information Services Council
LIV Legislative indexing vocabulary
LIX Legal Information Exchange
L.in Trans.Q. Law in Transition Quarterly (USA) 1964–7
L.Inst.J. Law Institute Journal (Aus.) 1927–
L.Inst.J.Vict. Law Institute Journal (Aus.) 1927–
L.Int. Law Intelligencer
L.Intell. Legal Intelligencer (Philadelphia) 1843–
L.J. British Guiana Limited Jurisdiction (Official Gazette)

1899–1955
Hall's American Law Journal. 1808–17
House of Lords Journal
Law Journal. 1866–1965
Law Judge
Library Journal
Lord Justice
Lower Canada Law Journal (Quebec) 1865–8
New York Law Journal. 1888–
Ohio State Law Journal. 1935–41, 1948–

L.J.Adm. Law Journal Reports, Admiralty, New Series. 1865–75

L.J.Adm.N.S. Law Journal Reports, Admiralty, New Series. 1865–75

L.J.App. Law Journal Reports, Appeals

L.J.Bank. Law Journal Reports, Bankruptcy, New Series. 1832–80

L.J.Bank.N.S. Law Journal Reports, Bankruptcy, New Series. 1832–80

L.J.Bankr. Law Journal Reports, Bankruptcy, New Series. 1832–80

L.J.Bankr.N.S. Law Journal Reports, Bankruptcy, New Series. 1832–80

L.J.Bcy. Law Journal Reports, Bankruptcy, New Series. 1832–80

L.J.C. Law Journal Reports, New Series, Common Pleas. 1831–75
London Juvenile Court

L.J.C.C. Law Journal, County Courts Reporter. 1912–33

L.J.C.C.A. Law Journal, County Court Appeals. 1935

L.J.C.C.R. Law Journal County Courts Reporter. 1912–33

L.J.C.P. Law Journal Reports, New Series, Common Pleas. 1831–75

L.J.C.P.D. Law Journal Reports, Common Pleas Decisions, New Series. 1831–75

L.J.C.P.N.S. Law Journal Reports, Common Pleas Decisions, New Series. 1831–75

L.J.C.P.(O.S.) Law Journal Common Pleas, Old Series. 1822–31

L.J.Ch. Law Journal Reports, Chancery, New Series. 1831–46

L.J.Ch.N.S. Law Journal Reports, Chancery, New Series. 1831–46

L.J.Ch.(O.S.) Law Journal Reports, Chancery, Old Series. 1822–31

L.J.D.& M. Law Journal Reports, Divorce and Matrimonial, New Series

L.J.Ecc. Law Journal Reports, Ecclesiastical Cases, New Series. 1866–75

L.J.Eccl. Law Journal Reports, Ecclesiastical Cases, New Series. 1866–75

L.J.Eq. Law Journal Reports, Chancery, New Series. 1831–1946

L.J.Ex. Law Journal Reports, Exchequer, New Series. 1831–75

L.J.Ex.D. Law Journal Reports, Exchequer, New Series. 1831–75

L.J.Ex.Eq. Law Journal Reports, Exchequer in Equity. 1835–41

L.J.Exch. Law Journal Reports, Exchequer, New Series. 1831–75

L.J.Exch.N.S. Law Journal Reports, Exchequer, New Series. 1831–75

L.J.Exch.(O.S.) Law Journal Reports, Exchequer, Old Series. 1822–31

L.J.H.L. Law Journal Reports, House of Lords, New Series. 1831–1949

L.J.I.F.S. Law Journal, Irish Free State. 1931–2

L.J.Ir. Law Journal, Irish. 1933–4

L.JJ. Lords Justices

L.J.K.B. Law Journal Reports, King's Bench, New Series. 1831–1946

L.J.K.B.(N.S.) Law Journal Reports, King's Bench, New Series. 1831–1946

L.J.L.C. Law Journal (Lower Canada) 1865–8

L.J.M.C. Law Journal Reports, Magistrates' Cases, New Series. 1831–96

L.J.M.C.O.S. Law Journal Reports, Magistrates' Cases, Old Series. 1822–31

L.J.M.Cas. Law Journal Reports, Magistrates' Cases, New Series. 1831–96

L.J.M.P.A. Law Journal Reports, Matrimonial, Probate and Admiralty

L.J.M.& W. Morgan & Williams' Law Journal. 1803–4
L.J.Mag. Law Journal Reports, Magistrates' Cases, New Series. 1831–96
L.J.Mag.Cas. Law Journal Reports, Magistrates' Cases. 1822–31
L.J.Mag.Cas.N.S. Law Journal Reports, Magistrates' Cases, New Series. 1831–96
L.J.(Malta) Law Journal, Valetta (Malta)
L.J.Mat. Law Journal, Matrimonial
L.J.Mat.Cas. Law Journal, Divorce and Matrimonial, New Series
L.J.N.C. Law Journal, Notes of Cases. 1866–92
L.J.N.C.C.A. Law Journal Newspaper, County Court Appeals
L.J.N.C.C.R. Law Journal Newspaper, County Court Reports. 1934–47
L.J.N.S. Law Journal Reports, New Series. 1832–1949
L.J.News. Law Journal Newspaper. 1866–1965
L.J.Newsp. Law Journal Newspaper. 1866–1965
L.J.O.S. Law Journal Reports, Old Series. 1822–31
L.J.(O.S.) Law Journal Reports, Old Series. 1822–31
L.J.O.S.C.P. Law Journal Reports, Old Series, Common Pleas. 1822–31
L.J.O.S.Ch. Law Journal Reports, Old Series, Chancery. 1822–33
L.J.O.S.Ex. Law Journal Reports, Old Series, Exchequer. 1830–31
L.J.O.S.K.B. Law Journal Reports, Old Series, King's Bench. 1822–31
L.J.O.S.M.C. Law Journal Reports, Old Series, Magistrates' Cases. 1826–31
L.J.of the Marut Bunnag Int'l L.Office Law Journal of the Marut Bunnag International Law Office (Thailand)
L.J.P. Law Journal Reports, New Series, Privy Council. 1865–1946 Law Journal Reports, New Series, Probate, Divorce, Admiralty. 1875–1946
L.J.P.C. Law Journal Reports, New Series, Privy Council. 1865–1946
L.J.P.C.N.S. Law Journal Reports, New Series, Privy Council. 1865–1946
L.J.P.D.& A. Law Journal Reports, New Series, Probate, Divorce and Admiralty. 1875–1946
L.J.P.D.& Adm. Law Journal Reports, New Series, Probate, Divorce and Admiralty. 1875–1946
L.J.P.M.& A. Law Journal Reports, New Series, Probate, Matrimonial and Admiralty. 1860–5
L.J.P.& M. Law Journal Reports, New Series, Probate and Matrimonial. 1858–9, 1866–75
L.J.Prob. Law Journal Reports, New Series, Probate and Matrimonial. 1858–9, 1866–75
L.J.Prob.N.S. Law Journal Reports, New Series, Probate and Matrimonial. 1858–9, 1866–75
L.J.Prob.& Mat. Law Journal Reports, New Series, Probate and Matrimonial. 1858–9, 1866–75
L.J.Q.B. Law Journal Reports, New Series, Queen's Bench. 1831–1946
L.J.Q.B.D. Law Journal Reports, New Series, Queen's Bench. 1831–1946
L.J.Q.B.D.N.S. Law Journal Reports, New Series, Queen's Bench. 1831–1946
L.J.Q.B.N.S. Law Journal Reports, New Series, Queen's Bench. 1831–1946
L.J.R. Law Journal Reports. 1947–9
L.J.Rep. Law Journal Reports. 1947–9
L.J.Rep.N.S. Law Journal Reports, New Series. 1831–1946
L.J.Rep.O.S. Law Journal Reports, Old Series. 1822–31
L.J.Sm. Smith's Law Journal. 1804–6
L.J.U.C. Law Journal of Upper Canada. 1855–64
L.Japan:Ann. Law in Japan: an Annual
L.Jo. Law Journal Newspaper. 1866–1965
L.Jo.N.C. Law Journal, Notes of Cases. 1866–92

LK Leipziger Kommentar. Strafgesetzbuch (Ger.)
Lord Keeper of the Great Seal

LKartB Landeskartellbehörde (Ger.) Provincial Cartel Authority

LL. Legum (Lat.) Laws

L.L. La Ley: Revista Juridica Argentina
Law Latin
Law List

LL.Aluredi Laws of Alfred

LL.Athelst. Laws of Athelstan

LL.B. Legum Baccalaureus (Lat.) Bachelor of Laws

L.L.B. Lawyers' Law Books. 2ed. 1985

L.L.B.R. Licensing Law and Business Report (USA)

LLC Law Library of Congress

LL.C.M. Master of Comparative Laws

LL.Canuti R. Laws of King Canute

LL.D. Legum Doctor (Lat.) Doctor of Laws

LL.Edw.Conf. Laws of Edward the Confessor

LL.Hen.I Laws of Henry I

L.L.J. Labor Law Journal (USA) 1949–
Labour Law Journal (India) 1949–
Lahore Law Journal (India) 1919–
Law Library Journal (USA) 1936–

LL.L. Licentiate of Laws

LL.M. Legum Magister (Lat.) Master of Laws

LL.Malcolm,R.Scot. Laws of Malcolm, King of Scotland

L.L.N. Labour Law News (Can.) 1975–

L.L.R. High Court of Lagos Law Reports (Nigeria) 1956–
Leader Law Reports (S.Afr.) 1909–10
Liberian Law Reports

L.L.S. Land Laws Service (Aus.) 1938–

L.L.T. Lahore Law Times (India) 1922–

LL.Wm.Conq. Laws of William the Conqueror

LL.Wm.Noth. Laws of William the Bastard

L.Lat. Law Latin

L.Lib. Law Librarian. 1970–
Law Library

L.Lib.J. Law Library Journal (USA) 1936–

L.Libn. Law Librarian: British & Irish Association of Law Librarians. 1970–

LM Lindenmaier-Möhring, Nachschlagewerk des Bundesgerichtshofes (Ger.) Collection of Decisions of the Federal Supreme Court, together with Comments

L.M. Law Magazine. 1828–1915

L.M.C.L.Q. Lloyd's Maritime and Commercial Law Quarterly. 1974–

L.M.C.S. Legal Management Consultancy Services (Sydney, Aus.)

L.M.C.S.Newsletter Legal Management Consultancy Services' Law Practice Management Newsletter (Aus.) 1987–

L.M.D. Legal Monthly Digest (Aus.) 1947–6

L.M.E.L.R. Land Management and Environmental Law Report

L.M.L.N Lloyd's Maritime Law Newsletter

L.M.Q. Legal Medical Quarterly (Can.) 1977–

L.M.T.P.I. Legal Member of the Town Planning Institute

L.M.& L.R. Law Magazine and Law Review. 1828–1915

L.M.& P. Lowndes, Maxwell & Pollock's Bail Court and Practice Reports (86 RR) 1850–1

L.Mag. Law Magazine. 1828–1915

L.Mag.& L.R. Law Magazine and Law Review. 1828–1915

L.Mag.& Rev. Law Magazine and Law Review. 1828–1915

L.Med.Q. Legal Medical Quarterly (Can.)

L.N. Law Notes. 1885–
Law Notes (Northport, New York) 1897–1946
Law Notes, American Bar Association Section of General Practice (USA) 1964–
League of Nations
Legal News (Can.) 1878–97
Legal Notification (Ghana)
Liber Niger, or the Black Book

L.N.T.S. League of Nations Treaty Series
L.Notes Law Notes. 1885–
L.Notes (N.Y.) Law Notes (Northport, New York) 1897–1946
LO Landsorganisationen (Swed.) The Confederation of Trade Unions
L.O. Law Observer (India) 1872
Lay Observer
Legal Observer (USA) 1830–56
Legal Opinion (USA) 1870–3
L.O.A. Life Offices' Association
L.O.M.J. Law Office Management Journal (Can.) 1989–
L.o.N. League of Nations
L.o.N.O.J. League of Nations, Official Journal
L.O.R. C.O. Reports of the Law Officers of the Crown – made at the request of and to the Colonial Office
L.O.R. F.O. Reports of the Law Officers of the Crown – made at the request of and to the Foreign Office
LP Decisions of the Lands Tribunal (restrictive covenants) 1950–
Loi fédérale sur la poursuite pour dettes et la faillite (Switz.) 1889
L.P.B. Laurence's Paper Book in Lincoln's Inn Library
L.P.C. Lords of the Privy Council
Lower Provinces Code (India)
L.P.R. Lilly's Practical Register. 1745
L.P.U. Legal Practices Update (Aus.) 1987–
L.Q. International and Comparative Law Quarterly. 1952–
L.Q.R. Law Quarterly Review. 1885–
L.Q.Rev. Law Quarterly Review. 1885–
LQUT Queensland Unit and Group Titles Law and Practice (CCH) (Aus.) 1980–
L.R. Alabama Law Review. 1948–
Land Registry
Law Record (India) 1911–12
Law Recorder (Ire.) 1827–38
Law Register (USA) 1880–1909
Law Reporter. 1821–2
Law Reports. 1865–
Law Review. 1844–56
Loan Regulations
Louisiana Reports
New Zealand Law Reports. 1883–
Ohio Law Reporter. 1934–
L.R.A. Lawyers' Reports Annotated
L.R.A.C. Law Reports, Appeal Cases. 1891–
LRAL Labour Relations Adjustment Law (Japan) Rodo kankei choseiho
L.R.A.N.S. Lawyers' Reports Annotated, New Series
L.R.A.& E. Law Reports, Admiralty and Ecclesiastical Cases. 1865–75
L.R.Adm.& Ecc. Law Reports, Admiralty and Ecclesiastical Cases. 1865–75
L.R.Adm.& Eccl. Law Reports, Admiralty and Ecclesiastical Cases. 1865–75
L.R.App. Law Reports, Appeal Cases. 1875–90
L.R.App.Cas. Law Reports, Appeal Cases. 1875–90
L.R.B.G. Law Reports of British Guiana. 1890–1955
Reports of the Supreme Court (British Guiana) 1914–60
L.R.Burm. Law Reports (Burma) 1948–
L.R.Burma Law Reports (Burma) 1948–
L.R.C. Law Reform Commission
Law Reform Committee
Law Reports of the Commonwealth. 1985–
Law Revision Committee
L.R.C.A. Law Reports, Court of Appeals (N.Z.) 1883–7
L.R.C.C. Law Reports, Crown Cases Reserved. 1865–75
L.R.C.C.R. Law Reports, Crown Cases Reserved. 1865–75
L.R.C.Canada Law Reform Commission of Canada
L.R.C.Comm. Law Reports of the Commonwealth, Commercial Law Reports. 1985–
L.R.C.Const.& Admin. Law Reports of the Commonwealth, Constitutional

and Administrative Law Reports. 1985–

L.R.C.Crim. Law Reports of the Commonwealth, Criminal Law Reports. 1985–

L.R.C.P. Law Reports, Common Pleas. 1865–75

L.R.C.P.D. Law Reports, Common Pleas Division. 1875–80

L.R.C.P.Div. Law Reports, Common Pleas Division. 1875–80

L.R.Ch. Law Reports, Chancery Division. 1891–

L.R.Ch.App. Law Reports, Chancery Appeal Cases. 1865–75

L.R.Ch.D. Law Reports, Chancery Division. 1875–90

L.R.Cr.Cas.Res. Law Reports, Crown Cases Reserved. 1865–75

L.R.Dig. Law Reports Digest

L.R.E.A. East Africa Protectorate Law Reports. 1897–1921

L.R.E.& I.App. Law Reports, English and Irish Appeals. 1866–75

L.R.Eng.& Ir.App. Law Reports, English and Irish Appeals. 1866–75

L.R.Eq. Law Reports, Equity Cases. 1865–75

L.R.Ex. Law Reports, Exchequer. 1865–75

L.R.Ex.Cas. Law Reports, Exchequer. 1865–75

L.R.Ex.D. Law Reports, Exchequer Division. 1875–80

L.R.Ex.Div. Law Reports, Exchequer Division. 1875–80

L.R.Exch. Law Reports, Exchequer. 1865–75

L.R.Exch.D. Law Reports, Exchequer Division. 1875–80

L.R.Exch.Div. Law Reports, Exchequer Division. 1875–80

L.R.F. Legal Research Foundation (N.Z.)

L.R.H.L. Law Reports, English & Irish Appeals. 1866–75

L.R.H.L.Sc. Law Reports, House of Lords, Scotch & Divorce Appeal Cases. 1866–75

L.R.H.L.Sc.App.Cas. Law Reports, House of Lords, Scotch & Divorce Appeal Cases. 1866–75

L.R.I.A. Law Reports, Indian Appeals. 1872–5

L.R.Ind.App. Law Reports, Indian Appeals. 1872–5

L.R.Ind.App.Supp. Law Reports, Indian Appeals Supplement. 1872–3

L.R.Indian App. Law Reports, Indian Appeals. 1872–5

L.R.Ir. Law Reports, Ireland. 1878–93

L.R.K. Kenya Law Reports. 1897–1956

L.R.K.B. Law Reports, King's Bench. 1891–

Quebec Official Reports, King's Bench (Can.) 1942–

L.R.Mad. Indian Law Reports, Madras Series. 1876–

L.R.N.S. Irish Law Recorder, New Series. 1833–8

L.R.(N.S.W.) Law Reports, New South Wales (Aus.) 1880–1900

L.R.(N.S.W.)B.& P. Law Reports, Bankruptcy & Probate (N.S.W., Aus.) 1880–1900

L.R.(N.S.W.)D. Law Reports, Divorce (N.S.W., Aus.) 1880–1900

L.R.(N.S.W.)Eq. Law Reports, Equity (N.S.W., Aus.) 1880–1900

L.R.(N.S.W.)Vice-Adm. Law Reports, Vice-Admiralty (N.S.W., Aus.) 1880–1900

L.R.N.Z. Law Reports (N.Z.) 1883–

L.R.P. Law Reports, Probate. 1891–1971

L.R.P.C. Law Reports, Privy Council. 1865–75

L.R.P.D. Law Reports, Probate Division. 1875–90

L.R.P.Div. Law Reports, Probate, Divorce & Admiralty Division. 1865–75

L.R.P.& D. Law Reports, Probate & Divorce Cases. 1865–75

L.R.Prob.Div. Law Reports, Probate, Divorce & Admiralty Division. 1865–75

L.R.Q.B. Law Reports, Queen's Bench. 1865–75, 1891–
Quebec Official Reports, Queen's Bench (Can.) 1942–
L.R.Q.B.D. Law Reports, Queen's Bench Division. 1875–90
L.R.Q.B.Div. Law Reports, Queen's Bench Division. 1875–90
L.R.R. Labor Relations Reporter (USA) 1937–46
L.R.R.M. Labor Relations Reference Manual (USA) 1935–
L.R.R.P. Law Reports, Restrictive Practices Cases. 1958–72
L.R.R.P.C. Law Reports, Restrictive Practices Cases. 1958–72
L.R.S. London Record Society
L.R.S.A. Law Reports (South Australia) 1865–92, 1899–1920
L.R.S.C. Law Reports, Supreme Court (N.Z.) 1883–7
L.R.S.L. Law Reports, Sierra Leone Series
L.R.S.& D.App. Law Reports, Scotch & Divorce Appeals. 1866–75
L.R.Sc.App. Law Reports, Scotch Appeals. 1866–75
L.R.Sc.Div.App. Law Reports, Scotch & Divorce Appeals. 1866–75
L.R.Sc.& D. Law Reports, Scotch & Divorce Appeals. 1866–75
L.R.Sc.& D.App. Law Reports, Scotch & Divorce Appeals. 1866–75
L.R.Sc.& Div. Law Reports, Scotch & Divorce Appeals. 1866–75
L.R.Stat. Law Reports, Statutes. 1866–
L.Rec. Law Recorder (Ire.)
L.Rec.N.S. Law Recorder, New Series (Ire.) 1833–8
L.Rec.O.S. Law Recorder, 1st Series (Ire.) 1827–31
L.Reg. Law Register
L.Rep. Law Reporter
L.Rep.Mont. Law Reporter (Montréal) 1853–4
L.Repos. Law Repository
L.Rev. Law Review. 1844–56
Law Review (Philippines)
Law Review (USA) 1866
L.Rev.U.Detroit Law Review, University of Detroit. 1916–31
L.Rev.& Quart.J. Law Review and Quarterly Journal of British and Foreign Jurisprudence. 1844–56
L.S. Legal Studies
Locus sigilli (the place of the seal)
Locus standi
LSB Legal Services Bulletin (Aus.) 1974–
Louisiana State Bar
L.S.B.(S.A.) Law Society Bulletin, South Australia. 1979–
l.s.c. loco supra citato (Lat.) in the place before cited
L.S.D.R.S.G. Legislative Supplement to the Democratic Republic of the Sudan Gazette
LSEC Australian Company Secretary's Practice Manual (CCH) 1978–
L.S.G. Law Society's Gazette. 1903–
L.S.Gaz. Law Society's Gazette. 1903–
L.S.J. Law Society Journal, New South Wales (Aus.) 1963–
LSJS Law Society Judgment Scheme (South Australia)
L.S.Judg.Sch. Law Society Judgment Scheme (South Australia)
LSL Labour Standards Law (Japan) Rodo kijunho
LSPP Step-by-Step Precedents and Procedures – Companies, Trusts, Superannuation Funds (CCH) (Aus.) 1980
L.S.R. Locus Standi Reports. 1936–60
L.Sea. Law of the Sea (USA) 1966–
L.Soc.Gaz. Law Society's Gazette. 1903–
L.Soc.J. Law Society Journal (USA) 1929–49
L.Soc'y Gaz. Law Society's Gazette. 1903–
L.Soc'y Gazette (Upper Canada) Law Society Gazette (Law Society of Upper Canada)
L.Soc'y J. Law Society Journal (USA) 1929–49
l.st.civ. regio decreto legge sull'orinamento dello stato civile (It.)

L.Stu.Mag. Law Students' Magazine. 1844–54

L.Stu.Mag.N.S. Law Students' Magazine, New Series. 1949–54

L.Stu.Mag.O.S. Law Students' Magazine, Old Series. 1844–48

L.Stud.H. Law Student's Helper (USA)

L.T. Law Times Newspaper. 1843–
Law Times Reports. 1859–1947
Law Times (Scranton, Pennsylvania) 1873–85

L.T.B. Law Times Bankruptcy Reports (USA)

L.T.C. Land Transfer Committee

L.(T.C.) Tax Cases Leaflets. 1938–

L.T.J. Law Technology Journal
Law Times. 1843–

L.T.Jo. Law Times. 1843–

L.T.Jour. Law Times. 1843–

L.T.N.S. Law Times, New Series (Pennsylvania) 1879–85
Law Times Reports, New Series. 1859–1947

L.T.Newsp. Law Times. 1843–

L.T.O. Land Titles Office (Aus.)

L.T.O.S. Law Times, Old Series (Pennsylvania) 1873–8
Law Times Reports, Old Series. 1843–59

L.T.Q. Law Teachers Quarterly (Can.)

L.T.R. Law Times Reports. 1859–1947

L.T.R.A. Lands Tribunal Rating Appeals. 1950–

L.T.R.N.S. Law Times Reports, New Series. 1859–1947

L.T.Rep. Law Times Reports, New Series. 1859–1947

L.T.Rep.N.S. Law Times Reports, New Series. 1859–1947

L.T.Rulings Land Tax Rulings (in New South Wales Revenue Rulings) (Aus.) 1986–

L.T.T. Land title trust

L.Teach. Law Teacher. 1971–

L.Teacher Law Teacher. 1971–

L.Th. La Thémis (Québec) 1879–83

L.Trans.Q. Law in Transition Quarterly (USA) 1964–7

LUL Labour Union Law (Japan) Rodo kumiaiho

LUSL Loyola University School of Law (USA)

LV Ministero degli Affari Esteri, Libro Verde (It.)

L.V.App.Ct. Lands Valuation Appeal Court (Scot.)

LVC Decisions of the Lands Tribunal (Rating) 1950–

LVCB Land and Valuation Case Book (N.Z.)

L.V.Ct. Land Valuation Court (N.Z.)

L.V.R. Land and Valuation Court Reports (N.S.W., Aus.) 1922–70

L.V.R.(N.S.W.) Land and Valuation Court Reports (N.S.W., Aus.) 1922–70

L.V.Rep. Lehigh Valley Law Reporter (Pennsylvania) 1885–7

L.W. Law Weekly, Madras (India) 1914–

L.W.L.R. Land and Water Law Review (USA) 1966–

L.W.R. Land and Water Law Review (USA) 1966–

L.& A. Leembruggen & Asirvatham's Appeal Court Reports (Sri L.)

L.& B. Leadam & Baldwin's Select Cases before the King's Council

L.& B.Prec. Leake & Bullen, Precedents of Pleading (now Bullen, Leake & Jacob)

L.& Bank. Lawyer and Banker (USA)

L.& C. Lefroy & Cassel's Practice Cases (Ontario) 1881–3
Leigh & Cave's Crown Cases Reserved (169 ER) 1861–65

L.& C.C.C. Leigh & Cave's Crown Cases Reserved (169 ER) 1861–5

L.& C.Prob. Law and Contemporary Problems (USA) 1933–

L.& Comm. Law and Communication (USA)

L.& Comp.Tech. Law and Computer Technology (Aus.) 1968–

L.& Contemp.Prob. Law and Contemporary Problems (USA) 1933–

L.& D.Conv. Leigh & Dalzell, Conversion of Property. 1825

L.& E. Law and Equity Reports

L.& E.Rep. Law and Equity Reporter (New York)

L.& G.t.P. Lloyd & Goold's Irish Chancery Cases tempore Plunkett. 1834–9

L.& G.t.Plunk. Lloyd & Goold's Irish Chancery Cases tempore Plunkett. 1834–9

L.& G.t.S. Lloyd & Goold's Irish Chancery Cases tempore Sugden. 1835

L.& G.t.Sug. Lloyd & Goold's Irish Chancery Cases tempore Sugden. 1835

L.& G.temp.Plunk. Lloyd & Goold's Irish Chancery Cases tempore Plunkett. 1834–9

L.& G.temp.Sugd. Lloyd & Goold's Irish Chancery Cases tempore Sugden. 1835

L.& Human Behav. Law and Human Behavior (USA)

L.& J. Law and Justice. 1974–

L.& Just. Law and Justice. 1974–

L.& Legisl.in the German Dem.Rep. Law and Legislation in the German Democratic Republic

L.& LeM. Leigh & Le Marchant, Elections. 4ed. 1885

L.& M. Lowndes & Maxwell's Bail Court Reports. 1852–4

L.& Phil. Law and Philosophy (Neth.)

L.& Pol.Int'l.Bus. Law and Policy in International Business (USA) 1969–

L.& Policy Intl.Bus. Law and Policy in International Business (USA) 1969–

L.& Soc.Order Law and the Social Order (USA) 1969–73

L.& Soc.Rev. Law and Society Review (USA)

L.& T. Longfield & Townsend's Irish Exchequer Reports. 1841–2

L.& W. Lloyd & Welsby's Commercial and Mercantile Cases. 1829–30

L.& Welsb. Lloyd & Welsby's Commercial and Mercantile Cases. 1829–30

La. Lane's Exchequer Reports (145 ER) 1605–11
Louisiana
Louisiana Supreme Court Reports. 1901–

La.A. Louisiana Annual Reports. 1846–1900
Louisiana Court of Appeals Reports. 1924–32

La.Acts Acts of the Louisiana Legislature

La.An. Lawyers' Reports, Annotated (USA)

La.Ann. Louisiana Annual Reports. 1846–1900

La.App. Louisiana Court of Appeals Reports. 1924–32

La.App.(Orleans) Court of Appeals, Parish of Orleans Reports by Teissier. 1903–17

La.B. The Louisiana Bar. 1942–53

La.B.A. Louisiana Bar Association

La.B.A.J. Louisiana Bar Association Journal

La.B.J. Louisiana Bar Journal. 1953–

La.Bar The Louisiana Bar. 1942–53

La.Civ.Code Ann.(West) West's Louisiana Civil Code Annotated

La.Code Civ.Pro.Ann. West's Louisiana Code of Civil Procedure Annotated

La.Code Crim.Pro.Ann. West's Louisiana Code of Criminal Procedure Annotated

La Fontaine H. La Fontaine, Pasicrisie internationale: Histoire documentaire des arbitrages internationaux, 1794–1900

La.L.J. Louisiana Law Journal (New Orleans) 1875–6
Louisiana Law Journal (Schmidt's) (New Orleans) 1841–2

La.L.R. Louisiana Law Review. 1938–

La.L.Rev. Louisiana Law Review. 1938–

La Ley La Ley: Revista Juridica Argentina

La.Rev.Stat.Ann.(West) West's Louisiana Revised Statutes Annotated

La.S.B.A. Louisiana State Bar Association
Louisiana State Bar Association Reports

La.S.U.Q. Louisiana State University Quarterly

La.Sess.Law Serv. Louisiana Session Law Service

La.T.R. Louisiana Term Reports (3–12 Martin's Louisiana Reports) 1813–23

La.T.R.(N.S.) Louisiana Term Reports, New Series (Martin) 1823–30

La Th. La Thémis (Québec, Can.) 1879–83

La Thém.L.C. La Thémis (Québec, Can.) 1879–83

Lab. Labatt's District Court Reports (California) 1857–8
Labour

Lab.A.C. Labour Appeal Cases (India) 1951–

Lab.Arb. Labor Arbitration Reports (USA)

Lab.Arb.Awards Labor Arbitration Awards (CCH) (USA)

Lab.Arb.Serv. Labor Arbitration Service (P–H) (USA)

Lab.Cas. Labor Cases (USA)

Lab.Ind. Labour and Industry (Griffith University, Queensland) (Aus.) 1987–

Lab.L.J. Labor Law Journal (USA) 1949–
Labour Law Journal (India) 1949–

Lab.L.News Labour Law News (Can.)

Lab.L.Rep. Labor Law Reporter (CCH) (USA)

Lab.Law. The Labor Lawyer (USA)

Lab.Rel.Rep. Labor Relations Reporter (USA)

Lab.& Soc'y Labour and Society (Switz.)

Labeo Labeo: rassegna di diritto romano (It.) 1955

Labor C. Labor Code

Labor L.J. Labor Law Journal (USA) 1949–

Labour L.J. Labour Law Journal (India) 1949–

Lac.Jur. Lackawanna Jurist (Pennsylvania) 1888–

Lac.R.R.Dig. Lacey, Digest of Railroad Decisions

Lack.Bar Lackawanna Bar (Pennsylvania) 1878

Lack.Bar R. Lackawanna Bar Reports (Pennsylvania) 1906

Lack.Co.(Pa.) Lackawanna County Reports

Lack.Jur. Lackawanna Jurist (Pennsylvania) 1888–

Lack.L.N. Lackawanna Legal News (Pennsylvania) 1895–1903

Lack.L.R. Lackawanna Legal Record (Pennsylvania) 1878–9

Lack.Leg.N. Lackawanna Legal News (Pennsylvania) 1895–1903

Lack.Leg.Rec. Lackawanna Legal Record (Pennsylvania) 1878–9

Ladd Ladd's Reports (59–64 New Hampshire)

Lagos H.C.R. Lagos High Court Reports

Lagos R. Judgments in the Supreme Court, Lagos (Nigeria) 1884–92

LagsL Lag om lagsokning och betalningsforelaggande (Lagsokningslag) (Swed.) Law on documentary and dunning process

Lah. Indian Law Reports (Lahore) 1920–47
Indian Rulings, Lahore. 1929–47
Pakistan Law Reports, Lahore Series. 1947–55

Lah.Cas. Lahore Cases (India)

Lah.L.J. Lahore Law Journal (India) 1919–30

Lah.L.T. Lahore Law Times (India) 1922–39

Lahore All India Reporter, Lahore. 1914–50

Laine A. Laine, Introduction au droit international privé, contenant une étude historique et critique de la théorie des status (Fr.) 2 vols. 1888, 1892

Lakimies Lakimies (Finland)

Lalor Lalor's Supplement to Hill & Denio's New York Reports . 1842–4

Lalor Supp. Lalor's Supplement to Hill & Denio's New York Reports. 1842–4

Lamar Lamar's Reports (25–40 Florida)

Lamb. Lambard's Archaionomia. 1568
Lambard's Archeion. 1635
Lambard's Eirenarcha. Numerous editions. 1581–1619
Lamb's Reports (103–5 Wisconsin)

Lamb.Arch. Lambard's Archaeionomia. 1568
Lambard's Archeion. 1635

Lamb.Const. Lambard, Duties of Constables, etc. Numerous editions. 1582–1633

Lamb.Eir. Lambard's Eirenarcha. numerous editions. 1581–1619

Lamont, Moral Judgment W.D. Lamont, The Principles of Moral Judgment. 1946

Lanc.Bar Lancaster Bar (Pennsylvania) 1869–83

Lanc.L.Rev. Lancaster Law Review (Pennsylvania) 1883–

Land App.Ct.Cas. Land Appeal Court Cases, N.S.W. (Aus.)

Land Com.Rep. Land Reports by Roche, Dillon & Kehoe (Ire.) 1881–2

Land Comp.Rep. Land Reports by Roche, Dillon & Kehoe (Ire.) 1881–2

Land Dec. Land Decisions (USA)

Land Econ. Land Economics: a Quarterly Journal of Planning, Housing and Public Utilities (USA)

Land.Est.C. Landed Estates Court

Land L.Serv. Law Book Company's Land Laws Service (N.S.W., Aus.) 1938–

Land Trans.Com. Land Transfer Committee

Land & Water L.Rev. Land and Water Law Review (USA) 1966–

Landsberg, Geschichte E. Landsberg, Geschichte der deutschen Rechtswissenschaft (Ger.) 1898–1910

Lane Lane's Exchequer Reports (145 ER) 1605–11

Lang. Language

Lang.Ca.Cont. Langdell's Cases on the Law of Contracts

Lang.Ca.Sales Langdell's Cases on the Law of Sales

Lang.Cont. Langdell's Cases on the Law of Contracts
Langdell's Summary of the Law of Contracts

Lang.Eq.Pl. Langdell's Cases in Equity Pleading
Langdell's Summary of Equity Pleading

Lang.Sales Langdell's Cases on the Law of Sales

Lang.Sum.Cont. Langdell's Summary of the Law of Contracts

Langdon Committee Control Review Committee: Managing the Long-Term Prison System (Home Office) 1984

Lans. Lansing's Supreme Court Reports (New York) 1869–73

Lans.Ch. Lansing's Select Chancery Cases (New York) 1824, 1826

Lap.Dec. Laperrière's Speaker's Decisions (Can.) 1841–72

Lapradelle-Politis A. de Lapradelle & N. Politis, Recueil des arbitrages internationaux

Lasc.H.War. Lascelles, Horse Warranty. 2ed. 1880

Lat. Latch's King's Bench Reports (82 ER) 1625–8

Lat.Am.Rs.Rev. Latin American Research Review

Latch Latch's King's Bench Reports (82 ER) 1625–8

Latey Report Report of the Committee on the Age of Majority (Cmnd. 3342) 1967

Lath. Lathrop's Reports (115–145 Massachusetts)

Lathrop Lathrop's Reports (115–145 Massachusetts)

Latomus Latomus: Revue d'Études Latines (Belg.)

Latt.Pr.C.Pr. Lattey, Privy Council Practice. 1869

Lauder Fountainhall's Decisions, Session Cases (Scot.) 1678–1712

Laun Festschrift G.C. Hemmarck (ed.),

Festschrift zur Ehren Rudolf Launs. 1947

Laur. Laurence's Reports of the High Court of Griqualand (S.Afr.) 1882–1910

Laur.H.C.Ca. Laurence's Reports of the High Court of Griqualand (S.Afr.) 1882–1910

Laur.Prim. Laurence, Primogeniture. 1878

Laura Laura (La Trobe University Legal Studies Students' Association) 1980–

Laurence Laurence's Reports of the High Court of Griqualand (S.Afr.) 1882–1910

Laurent F. Laurent, Le droit civil international. 1881

Law. Alabama Lawyer. 1940–
The Law. 1874–5
The Law (USA) 1889–90
Lawyer (s)
Lawyer (India) 1955–

Law Advert. Law Advertiser. 1823–31

Law Am.Jour. Law Amendment Journal. 1855–8

Law Amdt.J. Law Amendment Journal. 1855–8

Law Bk.Rev.Dig. Law Book Review Digest and Current Legal Bibliography (USA) 1931–2

Law Bul. Law Bulletin (San Francisco, USA) 1870–1
Law Bulletin (Washington) 1928–37

Law Bul.Ia. Law Bulletin, State University of Iowa. 1891–1901

Law Bul.& Br. Law Bulletin and Brief. 1903–6

Law Bull. Law Bulletin (Zambia) 1970–

Law Cas.Wm.I Bigelow's Cases, William I to Richard I. 1066–1195

Law.Ch.P. Lawes, Charterparties. 1813

Law Chr. Law Chronicle. 1811–12
Law Chronicle. 1854–8
Law Chronicle (S.Afr.) 1908–9
Law Chronicle, a Legal Newspaper (Aus.) 1892–9
Law Chronicle, or Journal of Jurisprudence (Scot.) 1829–32

Law Chr.& Auct.Reg. Law Chronicle and Auction Register. 1813–37

Law Chr.& Jour.Jur. Law Chronicle, or Journal of Jurisprudence (Scot.) 1829–32

Law Cl. Law Clerk and Municipal Assistant. 1906–13

Law Cl.Rec. Law Clerk Record. 1910–11

Law Com. Law Commission
Law Commission Report

Law.Con. Lawson on Contracts

Law Cont.Probl. Law and Contemporary Problems (USA) 1933–

Law Council Newsl. Law Council Newsletter (Aus.) 1964–77

Law Dept.Bull. Law Department Bulletin, Union Pacific Railroad Company (USA) 1911–29

Law Dig. Law Digest and Recorder (India) 1896–1901

Law Ecc.Law Law, Ecclesiastical Law. 2ed. 1844

Law.Ed. Lawyers' Edition, United States Supreme Court Reports

Law Ex.J. Law Examination Journal and Law Students' Magazine. 1869–85

Law Ex.Rep. Law Examination Reporter. 1866–69

Law for Bus. Law for Business

Law for Bus.Brief Law for Business Brief

Law Gaz. Law Gazette. 1822–47
Law Gazette. 1890–94
Law Gazette (Aus.) 1930–2

Law Guard. Law Guardian

Law.Guild M. Lawyers' Guild Monthly (USA) 1944–

Law.Guild Rev. Lawyers' Guild Review (USA) 1940–

Law in Cont. Law in Context (La Trobe University) (Aus.) 1983–

Law.in Eur. Lawyers in Europe

Law Inst.J. Law Institute Journal (Aus.) 1927–

Law Int. Law Intelligencer. 1843

Law J. Law Journal. 1866–1965
Law Journal Reports. 1822–31, 1832–1949

Law J.Ch. Law Journal Reports, New Series, Chancery. 1831–1946
Law J.Exch. Law Journal Reports, New Series, Exchequer. 1831–75
Law J.P.D.& A. Law Journal Reports, New Series, Probate, Divorce and Admiralty. 1875–1946
Law J.Q.B. Law Journal Reports, New Series, Queen's Bench. 1831–1946
Law J.R.Q.B. Law Journal Reports, New Series, Queen's Bench. 1831–1946
Law Jour. Law Journal. 1866–1965
Law Journal Reports. 1822–31, 1832–1949
Law Jour.(M.& W.) Morgan & Williams, Law Journal (London) 1803–4
Law Jour.(Smith's) J.P. Smith's Law Journal (London) 1804–6
Law Lat.Dict. Law Latin Dictionary
Law Lib. Law Librarian (British & Irish Association of Law Librarians) 1970–
Law Library. 1892–3
Law Lib.J. Law Library Journal (USA) 1936–
Law Lib.N. Law Library News (USA) 1927–37
Law Libn. Law Librarian
Law Librarian (British & Irish Association of Law Librarians) 1970–
Law Librarian (USA) 1887–90
Law Libr.J. Law Library Journal (USA) 1936–
Law Mag. Law Magazine. 1828–56
Law Magazine. 1987–88
Law Mag.& Law Rev. Law Magazine and Law Review. 1856–61
Law Mag.& R. Law Magazine and Review. 1872–1915
Law Mag.& Rev. Law Magazine and Review. 1872–1915
Law N. Law News, St Louis (USA) 1872–3
Law Notes. 1885–
Law Notes (Northport, New York) 1897–1946
Law Pat.Dig. Law's Digest of United States Patent Cases
Law.Pl. Lawes, Pleading in Assumpsit. 1810
Lawes, Pleading in Civil Actions. 1806
Law Practice Mgmt. Law Practice Management (Can.) 1984–
Law Q.Rev. Law Quarterly Review. 1885–
Law Quar.Rev. Law Quarterly Review. 1885–
Law Rec. Ceylon Law Recorder. 1919–
Irish Law Recorder. 1827–8
Law Recorder (Ire.) 1828–31, 1833–8
Law Rec.(N.S.) Law Recorder, New Series (Ire.) 1833–8
Law Rec.(O.S.) Law Recorder, Old Series (Ire.) 1828–31
Law Ref.Com. Law Reform Committee
Law Ref.Cttee. Law Reform Committee
Law Reg. American Law Register, Philadelphia. 1852–1907
Law Register, Chicago. 1880–1909
Law Reg.Cas. Lawson's Registration Cases (Ire.) 1885–1914
Law Rep. Law Reporter. 1821–2
Law Reporter (Boston, USA) 1838–48
Law Reporter (Ramsey & Morin) (Can.) 1853–4
Law Reports
New Zealand Law Reports. 1883–
Ohio Law Reporter. 1934–
Law Rep.A.& E. Law Reports, Admiralty & Ecclesiastical. 1865–75
Law Rep.App.Cas. Law Reports, Appeal Cases. 1891–
Law Rep.C.C. Law Reports, Crown Cases Reserved. 1865–75
Law Rep.C.P. Law Reports, Common Pleas. 1865–75
Law Rep.C.P.D. Law Reports, Common Pleas Division. 1875–80
Law Rep.Ch. Law Reports, Chancery. 1891–
Law Rep.Ch.App. Law Reports, Chancery Appeal Cases. 1865–75
Law Rep.Ch.D. Law Reports, Chancery Division. 1875–90
Law Rep.Dig. Law Reports Digest

Law Rep.Eq. Law Reports, Equity Cases. 1865–75

Law Rep.Ex. Law Reports, Exchequer. 1865–75

Law Rep.Ex.D. Law Reports, Exchequer Division. 1875–80

Law Rep.H.L. Law Reports, House of Lords, English & Irish Appeal Cases. 1866–75

Law Rep.H.L.Sc. Law Reports, Scotch and Divorce Appeal Cases, House of Lords. 1866–75

Law Rep.Ind.App. Law Reports, Indian Appeals. 1872–5

Law Rep.Ir. Law Reports, Ireland. 1878–93

Law Rep.P. Law Reports, Probate. 1891–

Law Rep.P.C. Law Reports, Privy Council, Appeal Cases. 1865–75

Law Rep.P.& D. Law Reports, Probate & Divorce Cases. 1865–75

Law Rep.Q.B. Law Reports, Queen's Bench. 1865–75, 1891–

Law Rep.Q.B.D. Law Reports, Queen's Bench Division. 1875–90

Law Repos. Carolina Law Repository (USA) 1813–16

Law Repr. Law Reporter (Ramsey & Morin) (Can.) 1853–4

Law Rev. Law Review (Albany, USA) 1866

Law Rev.Com. Law Revision Committee

Law Rev.Cttee. Law Revision Committee

Law Rev.U.Det. Law Review University of Detroit. 1917

Law Rev.& Qu.J. Law Review and Quarterly Journal of British and Foreign Jurisprudence. 1844–56

Law School Rec. Law School Record (Chicago) 1951–

Law School Rev. Law School Review, Toronto University (Can.) 1940–2

Law Ser.Mo.Bull. University of Missouri Bulletin, Law Series. 1913–35

Law Soc.A.C.T.N.L. Law Society of the Australian Capital Territory Newsletter

Law Soc.Bull. Law Society Bulletin (South Australia) 1979–

Law Soc.Gaz. Law Society's Gazette. 1903–
Law Society's Gazette (Regina, Can.) 1929–35

Law Soc.J. Law Society Journal (N.S.W., Aus.) 1963–

Law Soc.Jo. Law Society of Massachusetts Journal. 1929–49

Law Soc.Tas.N.L. Law Society of Tasmania Newsletter (Aus.)

Law Soc'y.Gaz. Law Society's Gazette. 1903–
Law Society's Gazette (Regina, Can.) 1929–35

Law Soc'y.J. Law Society Journal (N.S.W., Aus.) 1963–

Law Stu. Law Student. 1947–9
Law Student (Brooklyn, N.Y.) 1923–43

Law Stu.H. Law Students' Helper (USA) 1893–1915

Law Stud. Law Student. 1947–9
Law Student (Brooklyn, N.Y.) 1923–43

Law Stud.Mag. Law Students' Magazine. 1844–54

Law Stud.Mag.N.S. Law Students' Magazine, New Series. 1849–54

Law T. Law Times Reports. 1843–59, 1859–1947

Law T.N.S. Law Times Reports, New Series. 1859–1947
Law Times, New Series (Pennsylvania) 1879–85

Law T.Rep.N.S. Law Times Reports, New Series. 1859–1947

Law T.Rep.O.S. Law Times Reports, Old Series. 1843–59

Law Teach. Law Teacher. 1971–

Law/Tech. Law/Technology (World Peace through Law Center) 1968–

Law Tr. Law Tracts

Law W. Law Weekly (India) 1914–

Law.& Bank. Lawyer & Banker and Central Law Journal (New Orleans) 1909–34
Lawyers' & Bankers' Quarterly (St Louis) 1903–22

Law.& Banker Lawyer & Banker and Central Law Journal (New Orleans) 1909–34

Law & Bk.Bull. Weekly Law and Bank Bulletin (Ohio) 1858

Law & Comput.Tech. Law and Computer Technology (USA) 1968–

Law & Contemp.Prob. Law and Contemporary Problems (USA) 1933–

Law & Crit. Law and Critique

Law & Eq.Rep. Law and Equity Reporter (New York)

Law & Int.Aff. Law and International Affairs (Bangladesh) 1975–

Law & Just. Law and Justice. 1974–

Law.& L.N. Lawyer and Law Notes (USA) 1946–52

Law & Legis.GDR Law and Legislation in the German Democratic Republic

Law & Lib. Law and Liberty (USA) 1974–

Law.& Mag. Lawyer and Magistrate. 1898–9

Law.& Mag.Mag. The Lawyer's and Magistrate's Magazine. 1790–4

Law & Pol. Law and Policy

Law & Pol.Int.Bus. Law and Policy in International Business (USA) 1969–

Law & Pol'y.Int'l.Bus. Law and Policy in International Business (USA) 1969–

Law & Psych.Rev. Law and Psychology Review (USA) 1975–

Law & Soc.Ord. Law and the Social Order (USA) 1969–73

Law & Soc'y.Rev. Law and Society Review (USA) 1966–

Law & Tax R. Law and Tax Review

Lawasia Law Association for Asia and the Western Pacific
Lawasia: Journal of the Law Association for Asia and the Western Pacific (Aus.) 1966–74

Lawasia C.L.B. Lawasia Commercial Law Bulletin (Aus.) 1980–

Lawasia H.R.B. Lawasia Human Rights Bulletin (Aus.) 1982–

Lawasia (N.S.) Lawasia, New Series (University of Technology, Sydney) (Aus.) 1979–

Lawasia Newsl.N.S. Lawasia Newsletter, New Series (Aus.) 1984–

Lawes,Pl. Lawes, Pleading in Assumpsit. 1810
Lawes, Pleading in Civil Actions. 1806

Lawr. Lawrence High Court Reports, Griqualand (S.Afr.)

Lawrence Lawrence's Reports (20 Ohio)

Lawrence Comp.Dec. Lawrence's First Comptroller's Decisions (USA)

Laws Austl.Cap.Terr. Laws of the Australian Capital Territory. 1911–59

Laws.Reg.Cas. Lawson's Irish Registration Cases. 1885–1914

Lawtalk Lawtalk (New Zealand Law Society) 1974–

Lawy. Lawyer
Lawyer. 1900
Lawyer. 1961–5
Lawyer (Brooklyn, USA) 1938–46
Lawyer (India) 1955–
Lawyer (Nig.) 1965–74

Lawy.Mag. Lawyers' Magazine. 1761–2

Lawy.Med.J. Lawyers' Medical Journal (USA) 1965–

Lawy.Rev. The Lawyers' Review (Seattle, Wash.) 1915–21

Lawy.& L.N. Lawyer and Law Notes (USA) 1946–52

Lawyer & Banker Lawyer and Banker and Central Law Journal (USA) 1909–34

Lawyers' Med.J. Lawyers' Medical Journal (USA) 1965–

Lawyers' Rev. The Lawyers' Review (Seattle, Wash.) 1915–21

Lay Lay's Chancery Reports

Layfield Report Local Government Finance: Report of the Committee of Enquiry (Cmnd. 6453) 1976

Ld.Birk. Lord Birkenhead's Judgments, House of Lords

Ld.Ken. Lord Kenyon's King's Bench Reports (96 ER) 1753–9

Ld.Kenyon Lord Kenyon's King's Bench Reports (96 ER) 1753–9

Ld.Ray. Lord Raymond's King's Bench Reports (91–2 ER) 1694–1732
Ld.Raym. Lord Raymond's King's Bench Reports (91–2 ER) 1694–1732
Le Mar. Le Marchant's Gardner Peerage Case. 1828
Le.& Ca. Leigh & Cave's Crown Cases Reserved (169 ER) 1861–5
Lea Lea's Tennessee Reports (69–84 Tenn.)
Leach Leach's Cases in Crown Law (168 ER) 1730–1815
Leach C.C. Leach's Cases in Crown Law (168 ER) 1730–1815
Leach C.L. Leach's Cases in Crown Law (168 ER) 1730–1815
Leach Cl.Cas. Leach's Club Cases. 2ed. 1879
Leach Cr.Cas. Leach's Cases in Crown Law (168 ER) 1730–1815
Lead. Leader Law Reports (S.Afr.) 1909–10
Lead.Cas.Am. American Leading Cases by Hare & Wallace
Lead.Cas.Eq. Leading Cases in Equity, by White & Tudor
Lead.Cas.in Eq. Leading Cases in Equity, by White & Tudor
Lead.L.R. Leader Law Reports (S.Afr.) 1909–10
Leadam Leadam's Select Cases before King's Council in the Star Chamber (Selden Society)
Leadam Req. Leadam's Select Cases in the Court of Requests (Selden Society)
League of Nations O.J. League of Nations Official Journal
League of Nations O.J.Spec.Supp. League of Nations Official Journal, Special Supplement
League of Nations Off.J. League of Nations Official Journal
Leake Leake, Digest of Property in Land. 2ed. 1909
Leake, Law of Contracts. 8ed. 1931
Leake Cont. Leake, Law of Contracts. 8ed. 1931
Leam.& Spic. Leaming & Spicer's Laws, Grants, Concessions and Original Constitutions (New Jersey)
Learn.& Law Learning and the Law (USA) 1974–
Lebon Recueil des arrêts du Conseil d'État (Fr.) Collection of Decisions of the Conseil d'Etat. 1821–
Lec.El.Dr.Civ.Rom. Leçons Élementaires du Droit Civil Romain
Lec.Elm. Leçons Élementaires du Droit Civil
Lee Lee's Ecclesiastical Judgments (161 ER) 1752–8
Lee's Reports (9–12 California)
Lee Abs. Lee, Abstracts of Title. 1843
Lee Bank. Lee, Law and Practice of Bankruptcy. 3ed. 1887
Lee Dict. Lee, Dictionary of Practice. 2ed. 1825
Lee Eccl. Lee's Ecclesiastical Reports (161 ER) 1752–8
Lee G. Sir George Lee's Ecclesiastical Reports (161 ER) 1752–8
Lee t.Hard. Lee's King's Bench Cases tempore Hardwicke (95 ER) 1733–8
Lee t.Hardw. Lee's King's Bench Cases tempore Hardwicke (95 ER) 1733–8
Lee & H. Lee's King's Bench Cases tempore Hardwicke (95 ER) 1733–8
Leese Leese's Reports (26 Nebraska)
Lef.Cr.L. Lefroy, Irish Criminal Law
Lef.Dec. Lefevre's Parliamentary Decisions by Bourke
Lef.& Cas. Lefroy & Cassel's Practice Cases (Ontario, Can.) 1881–3
Lef.& Cass. Lefroy & Cassel's Practice Cases (Ontario, Can.) 1881–3
Lefroy Lefroy's Railroad and Canal cases
Leg. Legal
Leges (Lat.) Laws
Legislation
Legislative
Legislature
Leg.Adv. Legal Adviser
Leg.Aid Rev. Legal Aid Review (USA) 1903–72
Leg.Alfred Leges Alfredi (Laws of King Alfred)

Leg.Bib. Legal Bibliography (Boston) 1881–1913, 1923–4

Leg.Canut. Leges Canute (Laws of King Canute)

Leg.Chron. Legal Chronicle, Foster's Reports (Pennsylvania) 1873–5

Leg.Chron.Rep. Legal Chronicle, Foster's Reports (Pennsylvania) 1873–5

Leg.Econ. Legal Economics (USA) 1975–

Leg.Edm. Leges Edmundi (Laws of King Edmund)

Leg.Ethel. Leges Ethelredi (Laws of Ethelred)

Leg.Exam. Legal Examiner. 1831–3
Legal Examiner. 1862–8
Legal Examiner (USA) 1850

Leg.Exam.W.R. Legal Examiner Weekly Reporter and Journal of Medical Jurisprudence. 1852

Leg.Exam.& L.C. Legal Examiner and Legal Chronicle. 1833–5

Leg.Exam.& Med.J. Legal Examiner Medical Jurist. 1853

Leg.Exec. Legal Executive. 1963–

Leg.G. Legal Guide. 1838–43

Leg.Gaz. Legal Gazette (Philadelphia, USA) 1869–76
Legal Gazette (Huntington, Tennessee) 1900

Leg.Gaz.Re. Campbell's Legal Gazette Reports (Pennsylvania) 1869–71

Leg.H.I Laws of King Henry the First

Leg.Hist. Legal Historian (USA) 1958–61
Legal History (India) 1975–

Leg.Inf.Bul. Legal Information Bulletin (USA) 1924–32

Leg.Info.Serv. Legal Information Services (Can.)

Leg.Inq. Legal Inquirer. 1869–72

Leg.Int. Legal Intelligencer (Philadelphia) 1843–

Leg.Issues Legal Issues of European Integration (Neth.) 1974–

Leg.Issues Europ.Integr. Legal Issues of European Integration (Neth.) 1974–

Leg.M.Dig. Legal Monthly Digest (Aus.) 1947–

Leg.Med.Q. Legal Medical Quarterly (Can.)

Leg.Misc.& Rev. Legal Miscellany & Review (India) 1915–16

Leg.News Legal News (Montréal, Can.) 1878–
Legal News (Sunbury, Pa., USA) 1888–9
Legal News (Toledo, Ohio) 1894–1902

Leg.Notes Legal Notes on Local Government (New York) 1936–41

Leg.Ob. Legal Observer, or Record of Jurisprudence. 1831–2
Legal Observer and Solicitors' Journal. 1830–56

Leg.Obs. Legal Observer, or Record of Jurisprudence. 1831–2
Legal Observer and Solicitors' Journal. 1830–56

Leg.Oler. Laws of Oleron

Leg.Op. Legal Opinion (Harrisburg, Pennsylvania) 1870–83

Leg.Pract.& Sol.J. Legal Practitioner and Solicitors' Journal. 1846–7, 1849–51

Leg.R.(Tenn.) Legal Reporter (Tennessee) 1877–9

Leg.Rec. Legal Record. 1844–5
Legal Record (Detroit, Michigan) 1933–41

Leg.Rec.Rep. Legal Record Reports (Schuykill) (Pennsylvania) 1879–

Leg.Ref. Legal Reformer. 1819–20

Leg.Rem. Legal Remembrancer (Calcutta, India) 1864
Legal Remembrancer (Mirzapur, India) 1879–82

Leg.Rep. Legal Reporter (Aus.) 1980–
Legal Reporter (Ire.) 1840–3

Leg.Rep.(Ir.) Legal Reporter (Ire.) 1840–3

Leg.Rep.S.L. Legal Reporter, Special Leave Supplement (Aus.)

Leg.Res.J. Legal Research Journal (USA) 1976–

Leg.Rev. Legal Review. 1812–13
The Legal Review (Can.)

Leg.Serv.Bull. Legal Service Bulletin (American Bankers' Association, New York) 1926
Legal Service Bulletin (Monash University, Aus.) 1974–

Leg.Stud.Q. Legislative Studies Quarterly (USA) 1976–

Leg.T.Cas. Legal Tender Cases

Leg.Ult. The Last Law

Leg.W. Legal World (India) 1920–21

Leg.Y.B. Legal Year Book. 1849–51

Leg.& Ins.Rept. Legal and Insurance Reporter (Pennsylvania) 1859–67

Legal Adv. Legal Advertiser. 1881–7
Legal Adviser (Chicago) 1861–1920
Legal Adviser (Denver) 1897–1902

Legal Aid Rev. Legal Aid Review (USA) 1903–72

Legal Bus. Legal Business

Legal Educ.Rev. Legal Education Review

Legal Gaz.(Pa.) Legal Gazette (Pennsylvania) 1869–76

Legal Iss.Europ.Integ. Legal Issues of European Integration (Neth.) 1974–

Legal Reference Services Q. Legal Reference Services Quarterly

Legal Rep. Legal Reporter (Aus.) 1980–

Legal Stud. Legal Studies

Legg. Leggett's Reports, Sind (India)

Legge Legge's Reports (Aus.)
Legge's Supreme Court Cases (N.S.W., Aus.) 1825–62

Leggi e Decreti Raccolta Ufficiale delle Leggi e dei Decreti del Regno d'Italia. 1861

Legis. Legislation
Legislative
Legislature

Legis.Stud.Q. Legislative Studies Quarterly (USA) 1976–

Legul. The Leguleian. 1850–1, 1856–65

Leh.Co.L.J.(Pa.) Lehigh County Law Journal (Pennsylvania)

Leh.V.L.R.(Pa.) Lehigh Valley Law Reporter (Pennsylvania)

Leiden J.Intl.L. Leiden Journal of International Law (Neth.)

Leigh Leigh's Virginia Supreme Court Reports (28–39 Va.) 1829–42
Ley's King's Bench Reports (80 ER) 1608–29

Leigh Abr. Leigh, Abridgment of the Law of Nisi Prius. 1838

Leigh (Va.) Leigh's Virginia Supreme Court Reports (28–39 Va.) 1829–42

Leigh & C. Leigh & Cave's Crown Cases Reserved (169 ER) 1861–5

Leigh & C.C.C. Leigh & Cave's Crown Cases Reserved (169 ER) 1861–5

Leigh & D.Conv. Leigh & Dalzell, Conversion. 1825

Leigh & L.M.Elec. Leigh & Le Marchant, Elections. 4ed. 1885

Leipz.Z. Leipziger Zeitschrift für Deutsches Recht

Leith Black. Leith, Blackstone on Real Property. 2ed. 1880

Lely Railw. Lely, Regulation of Railway Acts. 1873

Lely & F.Elec. Lely & Foulkes, Elections. 3ed. 1887

Lely & F.Jud.Acts Lely & Foulkes, Judicature Acts. 4ed. 1883

Lely & F.Lic.Acts Lely & Foulkes, Licensing Acts. 3ed. 1887

Leo. Leonard's Reports (74 ER) 1540–1615

Leon. Leonard's Reports (74 ER) 1540–1615

Leon.La.Dig. Leonard, Louisiana Digest of United States Cases

Leon.Prec. Leonard, Precedents in County Courts. 1869

Lesotho L.J. Lesotho Law Journal

Lessing, Staadsangehoerigkeit Lessing, Das Recht der Staatsangehoerigkeit und die Aberkennung der Staatsangehoerigkeit zu Straf- und Sicherungszwecken. 1937

Lest.P.L. Lester's Decisions in Public Land Cases

Lest.& But. Lester & Butler's Supplement to Lester's Georgia Reports

Lester Lester's Reports (31–3 Georgia)

Lester Supp. Lester & Butler's Supplement to Lester's Georgia Reports
Lester & B. Lester & Butler's Supplement to Lester's Georgia Reports
Lev. Levinz's King's Bench and Common Pleas Reports (83 ER) 1660–97
Lev.Ent. Levinz's Entries
Lev.J.P. Levinge, Irish Justice of the Peace
Levi Com.L. Levi, International Commercial Law. 2ed. 1863
Levi Merc.L. Levi, Mercantile Law. 1854
Lew. Lewin's Crown Cases Reserved (168 ER) 1822–38
Lewis' Missouri Reports (29–35 Mo. App.)
Lewis' Nevada Reports (1 Nev.)
Lew.App. Lewin, Apportionment. 1869
Lew.C.C. Lewin's Crown Cases Reserved (168 ER) 1822–38
Lew.C.L. Lewis' Criminal Law. 1879
Lew.L.Cas. Lewis' Leading Cases on Public Land Law
Lew.Perp. Lewis, Law of Perpetuities. 1843
Lew.Tr. Lewin, Trusts
Lewin Lewin, Trusts
Lewin C.C. Lewin's Crown Cases Reserved (168 ER) 1822–38
Lewin.Cr.Cas. Lewin's Crown Cases Reserved (168 ER) 1822–38
Lewis Lewis' Kentucky Law Reporter. 1880–1908
Lewis' Missouri Reports (29–35 Missouri Appeals)
Lewis' Nevada Reports (1 Nev.)
Lewis Perp. Lewis, Law of Perpetuities. 1843
Lex Cust. Lex Custumaria
Lex et Scientia Lex et Scientia: Official Organ of the International Academy of Law and Science
Lex Man. Lex Maneriorum
Lex Mer.Am. Lex Mercatoria Americana
Lex–Merc. Lex Mercatorum. 1866–7
Lex Merc.Red. Lex Mercatoria Rediviva, by Beawes
Lex Parl. Lex Parliamentaria
Ley Ley's King's Bench Reports (80 ER) 1608–29
Liab. Liability
Lib. Liber (Lat.) Book
Liberal Party
Librarian
Library
Lib.Ass. Liber Assisarum (Book of Assizes) 1327–77
Lid.de Ant.Leg. Liber de Antiquis Legibus seu Chronica Majorum et Vicecomitum Londoniarum (ed. by T. Stapleton, 1846)
Lib.Ent. Old Book of Entries
Lib.Feud. Liber Feudorum, at the end of the Corpus Juris Civilis
Lib.Int. Liber Intrationum (Old Book of Entries) 1510
Lib.Intr. Liber Intrationum (Old Book of Entries) 1510
Lib.L.J. Liberian Law Journal. 1965–
Lib.L.& Eq. Library of Law and Equity
Lib.Nig. Liber Niger (the Black Book)
Lib.Nig.Scacc. Liber Niger Scaccarii (Black Book of the Exchequer)
Lib.Pl. Liber Placitandi (Book of Pleading)
Lib.Plac. Liber Placitandi (Book of Pleading)
Lib.Quot. Liber Quotidianus contrarotulatoris Garderobae
Lib.Reg. Register Books
Lib.Rub. Liber Rubens (the Red Book)
Liberian L.J. Liberian Law Journal. 1965–
Libertarian Stud. Libertarian Studies
Lieb.Herm. Lieber, Hermeneutics
Lieber Civ.Lib. Lieber, Civil Liberty
Liecht JZ Liechtensteinische Juristenzeitung (Liechtenstein)
Life C. Life Cases, including Health and Accident (CCH Insurance Cases Series) (USA) 1938–

Life Cas. Life Cases, including Health and Accident (CCH Insurance Cases Series) (USA) 1938–
Life & Acc.Ins.R. Bigelow, Life and Accident Insurance Reports
Lil. Lilly's Assize Reports (170 ER) 1688–93
Lil.Abr. Lilly's Abridgment. 2ed. 1735
Lil.Conv. Lilly's Practical Conveyancer. 3ed. 1742
Lil.Reg. Lilly's Practical Register. 2ed. 1735
Lill.Ent. Lilly's Entries. 2ed. 1741
Lilly Lilly's Reports and Pleadings of Cases in Assize (170 ER) 1688–93
Lilly Abr. Lilly's Abridgment or Practical Register. 2ed. 1735
Lilly Assize Lilly's Reports and Pleadings of Cases in Assize (170 ER) 1688–93
Lincoln L.Rev. Lincoln Law Review (Buffalo) 1927–32
Lincoln Law Review (San Francisco) 1965–
Lind.Part. Lindley's Law of Partnership
Lindley Comp. Lindley's Law of Companies. 6ed. 1902
Lindley Part. Lindley's Law of Partnership
Linn Ind. Linn's Index of Pennsylvania Reports
Linn Laws Prov.Pa. Linn on the Laws of the Province of Pennsylvania
Lip.Bib.Lur. Lipenius, Bibliotheca Juridica
Lit. Litigation
Littell's Reports (11–15 Kentucky) 1822–24
Littleton's Common Pleas Reports (124 ER) 1626–32
Littleton's Tenures. Various editions
Lit.Brooke Brooke's New Cases, King's Bench (73 ER) 1515–58
Lit.L. Litigation Letter
Lit.Sel.Ca. Littell's Select Kentucky Cases (16 Ky.) 1795–1821
Lit.& Bl.Dig. Littleton & Blatchley's Insurance Digest
Litig. Litigation
Litt. Littell's Kentucky Supreme Court Reports (11–15 Ky.) 1822–4
Littleton's Common Pleas Reports (124 ER) 1626–32
Litt.Comp.Laws Littell's Statute Law (Kentucky)
Litt.(Ky.) Littell's Kentucky Supreme Court Reports (11–15 Ky.) 1822–4
Litt.Rep. Littleton's Common Pleas Reports (124 ER) 1626–32
Litt.Sel.Cas. Littell's Select Kentucky Cases (16 Ky.) 1795–1821
Litt.Ten. Littleton's Tenures. Various editions
Litt.& S.St.Law Littell & Swigert's Digest of Statute Law (Kentucky)
Littell Littell's Kentucky Supreme Court Reports (11–15 Ky.) 1822–4
Little Brooke Brooke's New Cases (73 ER) 1515–58
Littleton Littleton's Common Pleas Reports (124 ER) 1626–32
liv. livre (Fr.) book
Liv. Livingston, Mayor's Court Reports (New York)
Liv.Ag. Livermore, Principal and Agent
Liv.Cas. Livingston's Cases in Error (New York)
Liv.Jud.Cas. Livingston, Judicial Opinions (New York)
Liv.Jud.Op. Livingston, Judicial Opinions (New York)
Liv.L.Mag. Livingston's Monthly Law Magazine (New York) 1853–6
Liv.L.Reg. Livingston's Law Register (New York)
Liverpool L.R. Liverpool Law Review
Liz.Sc.Exch. Lizar's Exchequer Cases (Scot.) 1840–50
Lizars Lizar's Exchequer Cases (Scot.) 1840–50
Ll.Comp. Lloyd, Compensation for Lands, etc. 6ed. 1895
Ll.Jud.Act Lloyd, Supreme Court of Judicature Acts. 1875
Ll.L.L.R. Lloyd's List Law Reports. 1919–50

Ll.L.Pr.Cas. Lloyd's List Prize Cases. 1914–24

Ll.L.R. Lloyd's List Law Reports. 1919–50

Ll.L.Rep. Lloyd's List Law Reports. 1919–50

Ll.List L.R. Lloyd's List Law Reports. 1919–50

Ll.M.C.L.Q. Lloyd's Maritime and Commercial Law Quarterly

Ll.Mar.L.N. Lloyd's Maritime Law Newsletter. 1979–

Ll.P.C. Lloyd's List Prize Cases

Ll.Pr. Lloyd, Prohibition. 1849

Ll.Pr.Cas. Lloyd's List Prize Cases. 1914–24

Ll.Pr.Cas.N.S. Lloyd's List Prize Cases, Second Series. 1939–53

Ll.R.Pr.Cas. Lloyd's List Prize Cases, Second Series. 1939–53

Ll.Rep. Lloyd's List Law Reports. 1919–50

Ll.Suc. Lloyd, Succession Laws. 1877

Ll.& G.t.P. Lloyd & Goold's Irish Chancery Reports tempore Plunkett. 1834–9

Ll.& G.t.Pl. Lloyd & Goold's Irish Chancery Reports tempore Plunkett. 1834–9

Ll.& G.t.S. Lloyd & Goold's Irish Chancery Reports tempore Sugden. 1835

Ll.& W. Lloyd & Welsby's Commercial and Mercantile Cases. 1829–30

Ll.& Wels. Lloyd & Welsby's Commercial and Mercantile Cases. 1829–30

Lloyd L.R. Lloyd's List Law Reports. 1919–50

Lloyd Pr.Cas. Lloyd's List Prize Cases Reports. 1914–24

Lloyd Pr.Cas.N.S. Lloyd's List Prize Cases Reports, Second Series. 1939–53

Lloyd & Goold (t.Plunkett) Lloyd & Goold's Irish Chancery Reports tempore Plunkett. 1834–9

Lloyd & Goold (t.Sugden) Lloyd & Goold's Irish Chancery Reports tempore Sugden. 1835

Lloyd & W. Lloyd & Welsby's Commercial and Mercantile Cases. 1829–36

Lloyd's List L.R. Lloyd's List Law Reports. 1919–50

Lloyd's Mar.L.N. Lloyd's Maritime Law Newsletter. 1979–

Lloyd's Mar.& Com.L.Q. Lloyd's Maritime and Commercial Law Quarterly

Lloyd's Pr.Cas. Lloyd's List Prize Cases Reports. 1914–24

Lloyd's Rep. Lloyd's List Law Reports. 1951–

Lo.L.R. Loyola Law Review (USA) 1941–

Loc.Acts Local Acts

loc.cit. loco citato (Lat.) the place already cited

Loc.Code Local Code

Loc.Ct.Gaz. Local Courts and Municipal Gazette (Toronto) 1865–72

Loc.Gov. Local Government

Loc.Gov.Rev. Local Government Review. 1971–

Loc.Govt.Chr.& Mag.Rep. Local Government Chronicle and Magisterial Reporter. 1855–

Loc.Govt.Rev. Local Government Review. 1971–

Loc.Laws Local laws

loc primo cit. loco primo citato (Lat.) in the place first cited

Local Gov.Chron. Local Government Chronicle

Local Gov't. Local Government

Local Govt.R.Austl. Local Government Reports of Australia. 1956–

Local Govt.R.(N.S.W.) Local Government Reports, New South Wales (Aus.) 1911–56

Loc.Govt.Rev. Local Government Review

Locc. Loccenius de Jure Maritimo et Navali. 1650

Lock.G.L. Locke, Game Laws. 5ed. 1866

Lock.Rev.Cas. Lockwood's Reversed Cases (New York) 1799–1847

Locus Standi Locus Standi Reports. 1936–60

Lofft Lofft's King's Bench Reports (98 ER) 1772–4

Lofft Append. Lofft's Maxims, appended to Lofft's Reports

Lofft Max. Lofft's Maxims, appended to Lofft's Reports

Lois Rec. Lois Récentes du Canada

Lom.C.H.Rep. Lomas's City Hall Reporter (New York)

Lom.Dig. Lomax's Digest of Real Property

Lom.Ex. Lomax on the Law of Executors

Lond.Jur. Jurist Reports. 1837–54

Lond.Jur.N.S. Jurist Reports, New Series. 1855–67

Lond.L.M. London Law Magazine

London Report Report of the First Session of the Preparatory Committee of the United Nations Conference on Trade and Employment

Long Q. Long Quinto (Year Books Part X) (5 Edward 4) 1465

Long Quinto Long Quinto (Year Books Part X) (5 Edward 4) 1465

Long.& T. Longfield & Townsend's Exchequer Reports (Ire.) 1841–2

Longf.& T. Longfield & Townsend's Exchequer Reports (Ire.) 1841–2

loq. loquitor (Lat.) he or she speaks

Lor.Inst. Lorimer, Institutes of Law. 2ed. 1880

Lor.& Russ. Loring & Russell's Election Cases (Massachusetts) 1853–85

Lords Jour. House of Lords Journal

Lorenz Lorenz's Ceylon Reports (Sri L.) 1856–9

Lorenz App.R. Lorenz's Ceylon Reports (Sri L.) 1856–9

Lorenz Rep. Lorenz's Ceylon Reports (Sri L.) 1856–9

Loring & Russell Loring & Russell's Election Cases (Massachusetts) 1853–85

Los Angeles B.A.B. Los Angeles Bar Association Bulletin

Los Angeles B.Bull. Los Angeles Bar Bulletin. 1925–

Los Angeles L.Rev. Los Angeles Law Review. 1934

Loss & Dam.Rev. Loss and Damage Review (USA) 1917–40

Lou. Louisiana

Lou.L.Jour. Louisiana Law Journal. 1841–2

Lou.L.Rev. Louisiana Law Review. 1938–

Lou.Leg.N. Louisiana Legal News. 1923

Louisiana L.R. Louisiana Law Review

Lov og Rett Lov og Rett: Norsk Juridisk Tidsskrift (Norway)

Love.Arb. Lovesy, Arbitration. 1867

Love.Bank. Lovesy, Bankruptcy Act, 1869. 1870

Lovelock Report Review of the National Association of Citizens Advice Bureaux: Report (Cmnd. 9139) 1984

Low. Lowell's District Court Reports (Massachusetts)

Low.C.Seing. Lower Canada Reports, Seignorial Questions

Low.Can. Lower Canada Reports (Québec) 1850–67

Low.Can.L.J. Lower Canada Law Journal (Québec) 1865–8

Low.Can.R. Lower Canada Reports (Québec) 1850–67

Low.Can.Rep. Lower Canada Reports (Québec) 1850–67

Low.Can.Rep.S.Q. Lower Canada Reports, Seignorial Questions

Low.Pr.Code Lower Provinces Code (India)

Lowell Lowell's District Court Reports (Massachusetts)

Lower Can. Lower Canada Reports (Québec) 1850–67

Lower Can.Jur. Lower Canada Jurist (Québec) 1848–91

Lower Can.S.Q. Lower Canada Reports, Seignorial Questions

Lower Ct.Dec. Ohio Lower Court Decisions

Lown.M.& P. Lowndes, Maxwell & Pollock's Bail Court Reports (86 RR) 1850–1

Lown.& M. Lowndes & Maxwell's Bail Court Reports. 1852–4

Lownd.Av. Lowndes, General Average. 10ed. 1975

Lownd.Leg. Lowndes on Legacies. 1824

Lownd.M.& P. Lowndes, Maxwell & Pollock's Bail Court Reports (86 RR) 1850–1

Lownd.& M. Lowndes & Maxwell's Bail Court Reports. 1852–4

Lowndes, M.& P. Lowndes, Maxwell & Pollock's Bail Court Reports (86 RR) 1850–1

Lowndes & M. Lowndes & Maxwell's Bail Court Reports. 1852–4

Loy. Loyola

Loy.Chi.L.J. Loyola University of Chicago Law Journal. 1970–

Loy.Con.Prot.J. Loyola Consumer Protection Journal (Los Angeles) 1972–

Loy.L.A.Ent.L.J. Loyola Entertainment Law Journal

Loy.L.A.Int'l & Comp.L.J. Loyola of Los Angeles International and Comparative Law Journal

Loy.L.A.L.Rev. Loyola University of Los Angeles Law Review. 1968–

Loy.L.J. Loyola Law Journal (New Orleans) 1920–32

Loy.L.Rev. Loyola Law Review (New Orleans) 1941–

Loy.R. Loyola Law Review (New Orleans) 1941–

Loy.U.Chi.L.J. Loyola University Law Journal (Chicago)

Loyola Dig. Loyola Digest

Loyola L.A.Int'l & Comp.L.J. Loyola of Los Angeles International and Comparative Law Journal

Loyola L.A.L.Rev. Loyola of Los Angeles Law Review

Loyola L.Rev. Loyola Law Review (New Orleans) 1941–

Loyola Los A.L.Rev. Loyola of Los Angeles Law Review

Loyola Los Ang.Int'l & Comp.L.Ann. Loyola of Los Angeles International and Comparative Law Annual

Loyola U.Chi.L.J. Loyola University of Chicago Law Journal. 1970–

Loyola U.L.A.L.Rev. Loyola University of Los Angeles Law Review. 1968–

Loyola U.L.J.(Chicago) Loyola University of Chicago Law Journal. 1970–

Loyola U.L.Rev.(LA) Loyola University of Los Angeles Law Review. 1968–

Loyola Univ.L.Rev. Loyola University of Chicago Law Review

Ltd. Limited

Luc. Lucas' Reports (10 Modern Reports) (88 ER) 1710–25

Lucas Lucas' Reports (10 Modern Reports) (88 ER) 1710–25

Luck. Indian Law Reports, Lucknow Series. 1926–49

Lud.E.C. Luder's Election Cases. 1784–7

Lud.El.Cas. Luder's Election Cases. 1784–7

Ludd. Ludden's Reports (43, 44 Maine)

Ludden Ludden's Reports (43, 44 Maine)

Luder Elec.Cas. Luder's Election Cases. 1784–7

Lum.(P.L.C.) Lumley's Poor Law Cases. 1834–42

Lum.P.L.Cas. Lumley's Poor Law Cases. 1834–42

Lum.Pub.H. Lumley's Public Health Acts

Lumley P.L.C. Lumley's Poor Law Cases. 1834–42

Lumpkin Lumpkin's Reports (59–77 Georgia)

Lush. Lushington's Admiralty Reports (167 ER) 1859–62

Lush.Adm. Lushington's Admiralty Reports (167 ER) 1859–62

Lush Pr. Lush, Practice at Westminster. 3ed. 1865

Lush.Pr.L. Lushington, Prize Law. 1866

Lut.E. Lutwyche's Entries and Reports, Common Pleas (125 ER) 1682–1704

Lut.Elec.Cas. Lutwyche's Election Cases. 1843–53

Lut.Ent. Lutwyche's Entries and Reports, Common Pleas (125 ER) 1682–1704

Lut.R.C. Lutwyche's Registration Cases. 1843–53

Lut.Reg.Cas. Lutwyche's Registration Cases. 1843–53

Lutw. A.J. Lutwyche's Registration Cases. 1843–53
E. Lutwyche's Entries and Reports, Common Pleas (125 ER) 1682–1704

Lutw.E. Lutwyche's Entries and Reports, Common Pleas (125 ER) 1682–1704

Lutw.Reg.Cas. Lutwyche's Registration Cases. 1843–53

Lux. Luxembourg

Luz.L.J. Luzerne Law Journal (Pennsylvania) 1871

Luz.L.Reg.Rep. Luzerne Legal Register Reports (Pennsylvania) 1882–

Luz.L.T.(N.S.) Luzerne Law Times, New Series (Pennsylvania) 1879–85

Luz.Law T. Luzerne Law Times (Pennsylvania) 1873–85

Luz.Leg.Obs. Luzerne Legal Observer (Pennsylvania) 1860–4

Luz.Leg.Reg. Luzerne Legal Register (Pennsylvania) 1872–86

Luz.Leg.Reg.Rep. Luzerne Legal Register Reports (Pennsylvania) 1882–

Luzerne L.J.(Pa.) Luzerne Law Journal (Pennsylvania) 1871

Luzerne Leg.Obs.(Pa.) Luzerne Legal Observer (Pennsylvania) 1860–4

Luzerne Leg.Reg.(Pa.) Luzerne Legal Register (Pennsylvania) 1872–86

Luzerne Leg.Reg.R.(Pa.) Luzerne Legal Register Reports (Pennsylvania) 1882–

Lycoming Lycoming Reporter (Pennsylvania) 1947–

Lycoming R.(Pa.) Lycoming Reporter (Pennsylvania) 1947–

Lynd. Lyndwood, Provinciale seu Constitutiones Angliae. Various eds. from 1483

Lynd.Prov. Lyndwood, Provinciale seu Constitutiones Angliae. Various eds. from 1483

Lyndw.Prov. Lyndwood, Provinciale seu Constitutiones Angliae. Various eds. from 1483

Lyne Wallis' Select Cases ed. by Lyne (Ire.) 1766–91

Lyne(Wall.) Wallis' Select Cases ed. by Lyne (Ire.) 1766–91

M

m. male
married

M. All India Reporter, Madras. 1914–
Indian Law Reports, Madras Series. 1876–
Macpherson's Session Cases, 3rd Series (Scot.) 1862–73
Madras
Magistrate
Maine
Manitoba
Maritime
Marquess
Maryland
Massachusetts
Mémorial: journal officiel du Grand-Duché de Luxembourg. 1832–
Menzies Supreme Court Reports, Cape of Good Hope (S.Afr.) 1828–49
Michaelmas Term
Michigan
Miles' Pennsylvania Reports
Minnesota
Mississippi
Missouri
Modified
Montana
Morison's Dictionary of Decisions (Scot.) 1540–1808
Mortgage
New York Miscellaneous Reports
Ohio Miscellaneous Reports
Queen Mary

M.A. Magistrates' Association
Maritime Administration
Missouri Appeals Reports
Munitions Tribunals Appeals. 1916–20

M.A.C. Magistrates Appeal Cases (Mal.) 1884–93
Maori Appellate Court (N.Z.)
Maritime Arbitration Commission
Motor Accidents Cases (CCH) (Aus.) 1981–

MAE Ministero degli Affari Esteri (It.)

M.A.F. Ministry of Agriculture and Fisheries (N.Z.)

M.A.F.F. Ministry of Agriculture, Fisheries and Food

MAI Archivio del Ministero dell'Africa italiana, gia Ministero delle Colonie (It.)

M.A.L.D. Master of Arts in Law and Diplomacy

M.A.R. Municipal Association Reports, New South Wales (Aus.) 1886–1911

MARC Machine readable catalogue

MARLAW Marine Law Database and Document Delivery Service (International Centre for Ocean Development & University of the West Indies)

MAS Market Advisory Service (BOTB)

MAT Maritime, Aviation and Transport (Insurance)
Mixed Arbitration Tribunal

M.B. All India Reporter, Madhya Bharat. 1950–57
Minute Book (Maori Land Court) (N.Z.)
Modern Business Law
Moniteur Belge (Belg.)
Monthly Bulletin of Decisions of the High Court of Uganda
Morrell's Bankruptcy Reports. 1884–93

M.B.A. Master of Business Administration
MBCA Model Business Corporation Act
m.b.H. mit beschränkter Haftung (Ger.) limited liability
MBIT Masters of the Bench of the Inner Temple. 1883
M.B.J. Michigan State Bar Journal. 1921–
M.B.L.R. Madhya Bharat Law Reports (India) 1952–
MBN J. Chamberlayne (ed.), Magnae Britanniae Notitia. 1710–55
M.Belg. Moniteur Belge (Belg.)
M.Bulletin Mercer Bulletin European Newsletter
M.C. Magistrates' Cases. 1892–1910
Magistrates' Court
Malayan Cases. 1908–58
Marriage Certificate
Matara Cases (Sri L.)
Mayor's Court
M.C.A.C. Marché Commun d'Amérique Centrale
M.C.C. MacGillivray's Copyright Cases. 1901–49
Martins Mining Cases (British Columbia) 1853–1902
Mining Commissioner's Cases (Can.)
Mixed Claims Commission
Moody's Crown Cases Reserved (168–9 ER) 1824–44
Motor Carrier Cases (USA) 1936–
Municipal Corporations Circular. 1878–1929
M.C.Cas. Municipal Corporation Cases Annotated
M.C.D. Magistrates' Court Decisions (N.Z.) 1939–79
M.C.J. Master of Comparative Jurisprudence
Michigan Civil Jurisprudence
M.C.L. Master of Civil Law
Master of Comparative Law
M.C.L.A. Michigan Compiled Laws Annotated
M.C.L.E. Mandatory Continuing Legal Education
M.C.M. Manual for Courts Martial (USA)
Municipal Court of Montreal
M.C.P.Q. Municipal Code of the Province of Quebec
M.C.R. Magistrates' Court Reports (N.Z.) 1905–53
Matrimonial Causes Rules
Montreal Condensed Reports (Quebec, Can.) 1853–4
M.C.R.(N.Z.) Magistrates' Court Reports (N.Z.) 1905–53
M'Cl. M'Cleland's Exchequer Reports (148 ER) 1824
M'Cl.& Y. M'Cleland & Younge's Exchequer Reports (148 ER) 1824–5
M'Cle. M'Cleland's Exchequer Reports (148 ER) 1824
M'Cle.& Yo. M'Cleland & Younge's Exchequer Reports (148 ER) 1824–5
M'Clel. M'Cleland's Exchequer Reports (148 ER) 1824
M'Clel.& Y. M'Cleland & Younge's Exchequer Reports (148 ER) 1824–5
M'Cord.Eq.(S.C.) M'Cord's South Carolina Equity Reports (6–7 SCEq.) 1825–7
M'Cord.L.(S.C.) M'Cord's South Carolina Law Reports (12–15 S.C.) 1821–8
M.Cr.C. Madras Criminal Cases (India) 1924–
M.D. Application for writ of mandamus dismissed for want of jurisdiction
Doctor of Medicine
M.D.Ala. District Court for the Middle District of Alabama (USA)
M.D.C. Metropolitan District Council
M.D.Fla. District Court for the Middle District of Florida (USA)
M.D.Ga. District Court for the Middle District of Georgia (USA)
M.D.La. District Court for the Middle District of Louisiana (USA)
M.D.N.C. District Court for the Middle District of North Carolina (USA)

M.D.Pa. District Court for the Middle District of Pennsylvania (USA)
MDR Monatsschrift für Deutsches Recht (Ger.) 1947–
M.D.Tenn. District Court for the Middle District of Tennessee (USA)
M.D.U. Medical Defence Union
M.D.& D. Montagu, Deacon & DeGex's Bankruptcy Reports. 1840–44
M.D.& DeG. Montagu, Deacon & DeGex's Bankruptcy Reports. 1840–44
M.Dict. Morison's Dictionary of Decisions, Court of Session (Scot.) 1540–1808
M.Direct Mercer Direct European Communication Newsletter
M.E.C. Mercato Comune Europeo (European Common Market)
M.EC News Mercer European Community Newsletter
MEDLARS Medical Literature Analysis and Retrieval System
MEGS Market Entry Guarantee Scheme (BOTB)
MFER Ministry of Foreign Economic Relations (USSR)
MFN Most Favoured Nation
M'F.R. MacFarlane's Jury Trials (Scot.) 1838–9
M.F.Review Mercer Fraser Review
M.F.Update Mercer Fraser Update
M.G. Motion for mandamus granted
M.G.L.A. Massachusetts General Laws Annotated
M.G.P. Application for mandamus granted in part
M.G.& S. Manning, Granger & Scott's Common Bench Reports (135–9 ER) 1845–56
M.H.A. Member of the House of Assembly
M.H.C. Madras High Court Reports (India) 1862–75
M.H.C.R. Madras High Court Reports (India) 1862–75
M.H.K. Member of the House of Keys (Isle of Man)
M.H.L. Macpherson's Session Cases, 3rd Series (Scot.) 1862–73
M.(H.L.) Macpherson's Session Cases, 3rd Series (Scot.) 1862–73
M.H.R. Member of the House of Representatives
M.I. Monumental inscription
Writ of mandamus will issue
M.I.A. Moore's Indian Appeal Cases (18–20 ER) 1836–72
M.I.B. Motor Insurers' Bureau Limited
M.I.C. Metropolitan Industrial Court (Victoria, Aus.)
MICC Malaysian International Chamber of Commerce
MICLE University of Michigan Institute of Continuing Legal Education
MIND National Association for Mental Health
M.I.P. Managing Intellectual Property
MITI Ministry of International Trade and Industry (Japan) Tsusho Sangyosho
M.J. Madras Jurist (India) 1866–76
Manitoba Judgments (unreported decisions available on QL) (Can.) 1986–
Ministry of Justice
M.J.S. Master of Juridical Science
ML Military Laws of the United States Army Annotated
M.L. Master of Law
Medieval Latin
Middle Latin
M.L.A. Member of the Legislative Assembly
M.L.A.A.N.Z. Maritime Law Association of Australia and New Zealand
M.L.A.A.N.Z.J. Maritime Law Association of Australia and New Zealand Journal. 1983–
M.L.A.A.N.Z.Newsl. Maritime Law Association of Australia and New Zealand Newsletter. 1978–82
M.L.A.A.N.Z.Papers Maritime Law Association of Australia and New Zealand Papers. 1979–

M.L.B. Manx Law Bulletin
M.L.C. Member of the Legislative Council
M.L.Dig.& R. Monthly Law Digest and Reporter (Quebec, Can.) 1892–3
M.L.E. Maryland Law Encyclopedia
M.L.J. Madras Law Journal (India) 1891–
Makere Law Journal (Uganda) 1971–
Malayan Law Journal. 1932–
Manitoba Law Journal. 1854–85, 1962–
Memphis Law Journal. 1878–9
Mississippi Law Journal. 1928–
M.L.J.Supp. Malayan Law Journal, Supplement. 1948–
M.L.L. Master of Law Librarianship
M.L.P. Michigan Law and Practice
M.L.Q. Malabar Law Quarterly (India) 1906–7
Manila Law Quarterly (Philippines)
M.L.R. Malayan Law Reports. 1950–4
Manitoba Law Reports (Can.) 1883–
Maryland Law Record. 1878–89
Mauritius Law Reports. 1861–
Minimum Lending Rate
Modern Law Review. 1937–
Montreal Law Reports
M.L.R.C. Manitoba Law Reform Commission
M.L.R.,C.B.R. Montreal Law Reports, Queen's Bench (Québec, Can.) 1884–91
M.L.R.,C.S. Montreal Law Reports, Superior Court (Québec, Can.) 1880–91
M.L.R.,Q.B. Montreal Law Reports, Queen's Bench (Québec, Can.) 1884–91
M.L.R.(Q.B.) Montreal Law Reports, Queen's Bench (Québec, Can.) 1884–91
M.L.R.S.C. Montreal Law Reports, Superior Court (Québec, Can.) 1880–91
M.L.R.(S.C.) Montreal Law Reports, Superior Court (Québec, Can.) 1880–91
M.L.S. Master of Library Science
M.L.T. Madras Law Times (India) 1906–28
M.L.W. Madras Law Weekly (India)
M'Laur. M'Laurin's Justiciary Cases (Scot.) 1774
m.m. med mera (Lat.) and so forth
mutatis mutandis (Lat.) with the necessary changes
M.M. Money Marketing
M.M.C. Martin's Reports of Mining Cases (British Columbia, Can.) 1853–1902
M.M.Cas. Martin's Reports of Mining Cases (British Columbia, Can.) 1853–1902
M.M.R. Mitchell's Maritime Register. 1856–83
M'Mul.Ch.(S.C.) M'Mullan's South Carolina Equity Reports (16 SCEq.) 1840–2
M'Mul.L.S.C. M'Mullan's South Carolina Law Reports (26–7 SCL) 1840–2
MNC Multinational Corporations
MNE Multinational Enterprise
MNTB Moscow Nuclear Test Ban Treaty. 1963
MO Militarorganisation der schweizerischen Eidgenossenschaft (Switz.)
Riksdagens militieombudsman (Swed.) Military Ombudsman
M.O. Motion for mandamus overruled
M.O.D. Ministry of Defence
Ministry of Overseas Development
M.o.T. Ministry of Transport
MOU Memorandum of understanding
M.O.W. Ministry of Works (N.Z.)
M.O.W.D. Ministry of Works and Development (N.Z.)
M.P. All India Reporter, Madhya Pradesh. 1957–
Member of Parliament
M.P.A. Monomeles Protodikion Athinon (One-member First Instance Court of Athens)
M.P.C. Matrimonial Property Act Cases (N.Z.) 1978–82
Moore's Privy Council Cases (12–15 ER) 1836–62
M.P.Ind. Madhya Pradesh, India
M.P.L. Master of Patent Law
M.P.L.R. Municipal and Planning Law Reports (Can.) 1976–

M.P.N.I. Ministry of Pensions and National Insurance

MPP Maternity pay period

M.P.P. Monomeles Protodikion Pireos (One-member First Instance Court of Piraeus)

M.P.R. Maritime Provinces Reports (Nova Scotia, Can.) 1931–68

M.Prospect Mercer Prospect Eastern European Newsletter

M.Q. Massachusetts Law Quarterly. 1915–77

M.r. Meester in de rechten (Neth.) law graduate

M.R. Application for writ of mandamus refused
Manitoba Law Reports (Can.) 1883–
Master of the Rolls
Mauritius Reports (or Decisions) 1861–
Mining Reports (R.S. Morison) (Chicago)
Montana Law Review. 1940–

MRG Minority Rights Group

M.R.P. Application for writ of mandamus refused in part

M.R.S.A. Maine Revised Statutes Annotated

MRT Militairrechtelijk Tijdschrift (Neth.)

M.S.A. Minnesota Statutes Annotated

m.s.c. mandatum sine clausula (Lat.) authority without restriction

MSC Manpower Services Commission

MSCE Manpower Services Commission Employment Services Division

M.S.L.S. Master of Science in Law and Society
Master of Science in Library Service

MS.U.C. Jeremy Bentham's unpublished manuscripts, University College, London

MShC Merchant Shipping Code of the USSR

M.St. More, Notes on Stair's Institutes

M.T. Memorandum of Trade
Michaelmas Term
Middle Temple

MTGU Australian Master Tax Guide Updater. 1984–

MTNs Multilateral Trade Negotiations

MTR Middle Temple Records, ed. by C.H. Hopwood

MT Rulings Miscellaneous Tax Rulings (Aus.)

M.T.& F. Matrimonial Tax and Finance

M.Translantic Mercer Transatlantic

M.U. Malayan Union

M.U.C.C. Michigan Unemployment Compensation Commission

M.U.L.L. Modern Uses of Logic in Law (Yale Law School)

M.U.L.R. Malayan Union Law Reports. 1946–7
Melbourne University Law Review. 1957–

M.U.R. Montana Utilities Reports

MvA Memorie van Antwoord (Neth.)

M.V.R. Motor Vehicle Reports (Aus.) 1984–
Motor Vehicle Reports (Can.) 1979–

MvT Memorie van Toelichting (Neth.)

MVT Ministerstvo vneshnei torgovli (USSR) Ministry of Foreign Trade

M.V.& P. Morton, Vendors and Purchasers. 1837

M.W. Money Week

M.W.D. Ministry of Works and Development (N.Z.)

M.W.N. Madras Weekly Notes (India) 1910–

M.W.N.C.C. Madras Weekly Notes, Criminal Cases (India) 1929–

M.W.N.L.N. Mid-West Nigeria Legal Notice

m.w.Nachw. mit weiteren Nachweisen

M.& A. Montagu & Ayrton's Bankruptcy Reports. 1833–8

M.& Ayr. Montagu & Ayrton's Bankruptcy Reports. 1833–8

M.& B. Montagu & Bligh's Bankruptcy Reports. 1832–3

M.& C. Montagu & Chitty's Bankruptcy Reports. 1838–40
Mylne & Craig's Chancery Reports (140–1 ER) 1835–51

M.& C.L.Ct. Mayor's and City of London Court

M.& Chit.Bankr. Montagu & Chitty's Bankruptcy Reports. 1838–40

M.& G. Macnaghten & Gordon's Chancery Reports (41–2 ER) 1848–51
Maddock & Geldert's Chancery Reports (56 ER) 1815–22
Manning & Granger's Common Pleas Reports (133–5 ER) 1840–4

M.& Gel. Maddock & Geldert's Chancery Reports (56 ER) 1815–22

M.& Gord. Macnaghten & Gordon's Chancery Reports (41–2 ER) 1848–51

M.& H. Murphy & Hurlestone's Exchequer Reports (51 RR) 1836–7

M.& K. Mylne & Keen's Chancery Reports (39–40 ER) 1832–5

M.& M. Montagu & MacArthur's Bankruptcy Reports. 1828–9
Moody & Malkin's Nisi Prius Reports (173 ER) 1826–30

M.& M'A. Montagu & MacArthur's Bankruptcy Reports. 1828–9

M.& McA. Montagu & MacArthur's Bankruptcy Reports. 1828–9

M.& P. Moore & Payne's Common Pleas Reports (29–33 RR) 1827–31

M.& P.Sh. Maude & Pollock, Law of Merchant Shipping. 4ed. 1881

M.& R. Maclean & Robinson's Scotch Appeal Cases (9 ER) 1839
Manning & Ryland's King's Bench Reports (31–4 RR) 1827–30
Manning & Ryland's Magistrates' Cases. 1827–30
Moody & Robinson's Nisi Prius Reports (174 ER) 1830–44

M.& R.M.C. Manning & Ryland's Magistrates' Cases. 1827–30

M.& Rob. Maclean & Robinson's Scotch Appeal Cases (9 ER) 1839
Moody & Robinson's Nisi Prius Reports (174 ER) 1830–44

M.& S. Manning & Scott's Common Bench Reports (135–9 ER) 1845–56
Maule & Selwyn's King's Bench Reports (105 ER) 1813–17
Moore & Scott's Common Pleas Reports (34–8 RR) 1831–4

M.& Sc. Moore & Scott's Common Pleas Reports (34–8 RR) 1831–4

M.& Scott Moore & Scott's Common Pleas Reports (34–8 RR) 1831–4

M.& W. Meeson & Welsby's Exchequer Reports (150–3 ER) 1836–47

M.& W.Cas. Mining and Water Cases Annotated (USA)

M.& W.Law Dic. Mozley & Whiteley, Concise Law Dictionary. 9ed. 1977

M.& Y. Martin & Yerger's Reports (8 Tennessee) 1825–8

M.& Y.R. Martin & Yerger's Reports (8 Tennessee) 1825–8

Ma. Massachusetts Reports

Ma.A. Massachusetts Appeals Court Reports

Maasdorp I Maasdorp's Institutes of South African Law vol. I: The Law of Persons

Maasdorp II Maasdorp's Institutes of South African Law vol. II: The Law of Property

Maasdorp III Maasdorp's Institutes of South African Law vol. III: The Law of Contracts

Mac. Macassey's Reports (N.Z.) 1861–72
Macnaghten's Select Cases in Chancery (25 ER) 1724–33

Mac.C.C. MacGillivray's Copyright Cases. 1901–49

Mac.N.Z. Macassey's New Zealand Reports. 1861–72

Mac.P.C. Macrory's Patent Cases. 1847–60

Mac.Pat.Cas. Macrory's Patent Cases. 1847–60

Mac.R. Macdougall's Reports (Jamaica) 1839

Mac.& G. Macnaghten & Gordon's Chancery Reports. 1848–51

Mac.& H. Macrae & Hertslet's Insolvency Cases. 1847–52

Mac.& R. Maclean & Robinson's Appeal Cases (Scot.) (9 ER) 1839

Mac.& Rob. Maclean & Robinson's Appeal Cases (Scot.) (9 ER) 1839

MacA.Pat.Cas. MacArthur's District of Columbia Patent Cases (USA) 1841–59

Macal. McAllister's Circuit Court Reports (USA)

Macall. McAllister's Circuit Court Reports (USA)

MacAr. MacArthur's District of Columbia Patent Cases (USA) 1841–59
MacArthur's District of Columbia Supreme Court Reports (8–10 D.C.) 1873–9

MacAr.& M. MacArthur & Mackey's District of Columbia Supreme Court Reports (11 D.C.) 1879–80

MacAr.& Mackey MacArthur & Mackey's District of Columbia Supreme Court Reports (11 D.C.) 1879–80

MacArth. MacArthur's District of Columbia Patent Cases (USA) 1841–59
MacArthur's District of Columbia Supreme Court Reports (8–10 D.C.) 1873–9

MacArth.Pat.Cas. MacArthur's District of Columbia Patent Cases (USA) 1841–59

MacArth.& M. MacArthur & Mackey's District of Columbia Supreme Court Reports (11 D.C.) 1879–80

MacArth.& M.(Dist.Col.) MacArthur & Mackey's District of Columbia Supreme Court Reports (11 D.C.) 1879–80

MacArthur MacArthur's District of Columbia Patent Cases (USA) 1841–59
MacArthur's District of Columbia Supreme Court Reports (8–10 D.C.) 1873–9

MacArthur Pat.Cas. MacArthur's District of Columbia Patent Cases (USA) 1841–59

MacArthur & M. MacArthur & Mackey's District of Columbia Supreme Court Reports (11 D.C.) 1879–80

Macas. Macassey's Reports (N.Z.) 1861–72

Macassey Macassey's Reports (N.Z.) 1861–72

Macc.Cas. Maccala's Breach of Promise Cases

MacCarthy MacCarthy's Irish Land Cases (Ire.) 1887–92

Maccl. 10 Modern Cases, tempore Macclesfield (88 ER) 1710–24

Maccl.Tr. Macclesfield's Trial (Impeachment) 1725

Macd. MacDevitt's Irish Land Cases. 1882–4
Macdougall's Reports (Jamaica) 1839

Macd.Cr.L. Macdonald, Scotch Criminal Law

Macd.Jam. Macdougall's Reports (Jamaica) 1839

MacDermott Commission Commission on the Isle of Man Constitution. Report. 1959

MacDev. MacDevitt's Irish Land Cases. 1882–4

MacDonnell Cttee. Home Office Departmental Committee on the Constitution, etc. of the Isle of Man. Report (Cd.5950, 6026) 1911–13

Macf. MacFarlane's Jury Trials (Scot.) 1838–9

MacF. MacFarlane's Jury Trials (Scot.) 1838–9

Macf.Pr. MacFarlane, Practice of the Court of Sessions

Macfar. MacFarlane's Jury Trials (Scot.) 1838–9

MacFarl. MacFarlane's Jury Trials (Scot.) 1838–9

MacFarlane MacFarlane's Jury Trials (Scot.) 1838–9

MacG.C.C. MacGillivray's Copyright Cases. 1901–49

MacG.Cop.Cas. MacGillivray's Copyright Cases. 1901–49

MacGillivray & Parkington MacGillivray & Parkington's Insurance Law

Mach. Machine
Machinery

Mack.Crim. MacKenzie's Criminal Law (Scot.) 4ed. 1699
Mack.Ct.Sess. Mackay, Court of Session Practice
Mack.Inst. Mackenzie's Institutes of the Law of Scotland. 9ed. 1758
Mack.Law of Prop. Mackay, Law of Property. 1882
Mack.Nat. Mackintosh, Law of Nature and Nations. 5ed. 1835
Mack.Obs. Mackenzie's Observations on Acts of Parliament (Scot.) 1675
Mackey Mackey's District of Columbia Reports (6–7 D.C.) 1863–72, (12–20 D.C.) 1880–92
Macl. Maclaurin's Remarkable Cases (Scot.) 1670–1773
McLean's Circuit Court Reports (USA)
Macl.Bank. Macleod, Theory and Practice of Banking
Macl.Rem.Cas. Maclaurin's Remarkable Cases (Scot.) 1670–1773
Macl.Sh. Maclachlan on Merchant Shipping. 7ed. 1932
Macl.& R. Maclean & Robinson's Scotch Appeal Cases (9 ER) 1839
Macl.& Rob. Maclean & Robinson's Scotch Appeal Cases (9 ER) 1839
Maclean & R. Maclean & Robinson's Scotch Appeal Cases (9 ER) 1839
Macn. Macnaghten's Hindu Law Cases (India) 1812–23
Macnaghten's Nizamut Adawlut Cases (Bengal, India) 1805–50
Macnaghten's Select Cases in Chancery tempore King (25 ER) 1724–33
Macnaghten's Select Cases, Sudder Dewanny Adawlut (Bengal, India) 1791– 1858
Macn.Fr. Francis Macnaghten's Bengal Reports
Macn.N.A.Beng. Macnaghten's Nizamut Adawlut Cases (Bengal, India) 1805– 50
Macn.Nul Macnamara, Nullities and Irregularities in Law. 1842
Macn.S.D.A. Macnaghten's Select Cases, Sudder Dewanny Adawlut (Bengal, India) 1791–1858
Macn.Sel.Cas. Macnaghten's Select Cases in Chancery tempore King (25 ER) 1724–33
Macn.& G. Macnaghten & Gordon's Chancery Reports (41–2 ER) 1848–51
Macph. Macpherson's Court of Session Cases, 3rd Series (Scot.) 1862–73
Macph.Jud.Com. Macpherson, Practice of the Judicial Committee of the Privy Council. 2ed. 1873
Macph.L.& B. Macpherson, Lee & Bell's Session Cases (Scot.) 1862–73
Macph.Pr.C. Macpherson's Practice of the Judicial Committee of the Privy Council. 2ed. 1873
Macq. Macqueen's Scotch Appeal Cases. 1851–65
Macq.D. Macqueen's Debates on Life Peerage Questions. 1856–7
Macq.H.L.Cas. Macqueen's Scotch Appeal Cases (House of Lords) 1851–65
Macq.H.& W. Macqueen, Rights and Liabilities of Husband and Wife. 4ed. 1905
Macq.Mar. Macqueen, Marriage, Divorce and Legitimacy. 2ed. 1860
Macq.Sc.App.Cas. Macqueen's Scotch Appeal Cases. 1851–65
Macr. Macrory's Patent Cases. 1847–60
Macr.P.Cas. Macrory's Patent Cases. 1847–60
Macr.Pat.Cas. Macrory's Patent Cases. 1847–60
Macr.& H. Macrae & Hertslet's Insolvency Cases. 1847–52
MacS. MacSweeney, Mines, Quarries and Minerals. 5ed. 1822
Mad. All India Reporter, Madras. 1914–
Indian Law Reports, Madras. 1876–
Indian Rulings, Madras. 1929–47
Maddock's Chancery Reports (56 ER) 1815–22
Maddock's Reports (9–18 Montana)
Madras High Court Reports (India) 1862–75
Mad.Bar. Madox, Baronia Anglia

Mad.Ch.Pr. Maddock, Chancery Practice. 3ed. 1837

Mad.Co. Madras Code (India)

Mad.Exch. Madox, History of the Exchequer

Mad.Form.Angl. Madox's Formulare Anglicanum

Mad.H.C. Madras High Court Reports (India) 1862–75

Mad.Hist.Exch. Madox, History of the Exchequer

Mad.Jur. Madras Jurist (India) 1866–76

Mad.L.J. Madras Law Journal (India) 1891–

Mad.L.Rep. Madras Law Reporter (India) 1876–7

Mad.L.T. Madras Law Times (India) 1906–28

Mad.L.W. Madras Law Weekly (India) 1914–

Mad.Law Rep. Madras Law Reporter (India) 1876–7

Mad.S.D.A.R. Madras Sudder Dewanny Adawlut Reports (India) 1805–62

Mad.Sel.Dec. Madras Select Decrees

Mad.Ser. Indian Law Reports, Madras Series. 1876–

Mad.W.N. Madras Weekly Notes (India) 1910–

Mad.W.N.C.C. Madras Weekly Notes, Criminal Cases (India) 1929–

Mad.& B. Maddox & Bach's Reports (19 Montana)

Mad.& Gel. Maddock & Geldert's Chancery Reports (56 ER) 1821–2

Madd. Maddock's Chancery Reports (56 ER) 1815–22
Maddock's Reports (9–18 Montana)

Madd.Ch. Maddock's Chancery Reports (56 ER) 1815–22

Madd.Ch.Pr. Maddock's Chancery Practice. 3ed. 1837

Madd.& B. Maddox & Bach's Reports (19 Montana)

Madd.& G. Maddock & Geldert's Chancery Reports (56 ER) 1821–2

Madd.& Gel. Maddock & Geldert's Chancery Reports (56 ER) 1821–2

Madh.Pra. All India Reporter, Madhya Pradesh. 1957–

Madhya Bharat Indian Law Reports, Madhya Bharat. 1952–

Madox Madox's Formulare Anglicanum
Madox's History of the Exchequer

Madras L.J. Madras Law Journal. 1891–

Mag. The Magistrate. 1848–9
The Magistrate. 1921–
Magistrate (Sydney, Aus.) 1905–14
Magistrate (W. Aus.) 1916–57
Magistrate & Municipal & Parochial Lawyer. 1848–53
Magruder's Maryland Reports (1, 2 Md.)

Mag.Cas. Bittleston, Wise & Farnell's Magistrates' Cases. 1844–52
Magisterial Cases. 1896–1946
Magistrates' Cases from Law Journal Reports. 1892–1910

Mag.Char. Magna Carta or Charta

Mag.Ct. Magistrates' Court

Mag.Dig. Magrath's South Carolina Digest

Mag.(Md.) Magruder's Maryland Reports (1, 2 Md.)

Mag.Rot. Magnus Rotulus (the Great Roll of the Exchequer)

Mag.& Con. Magistrate and Constable (Pennsylvania) 1895

Mag.& E.Comp. Magnus & Estrin, Companies

Mag.& M.& P.L. Magistrate & Municipal & Parochial Lawyer. 1848–53

Magis.Ct. Magistrate's Court

Magis.& Const.(Pa.) Magistrate and Constable (Pennsylvania) 1895

Magna Rot.Pip. Magnus Rotulus Pipae (Great Roll of the Pipe)

Magruder Magruder's Maryland Reports (1, 2 Md.)

Mah.L.J. Maharashtra Law Journal (India) 1963–

Mah.& D.R.T. Mahaffy & Dodson, Road Traffic
Maharashtra L.J. Maharashtra Law Journal (India) 1963–
Mai. Maine
Maine Reports. 1820–
Mai.Anc.L. Maine's Ancient Law
Mai.Inst. Maine's History of Institutions
Maine Maine Reports. 1820–
Maine, Anc.Law Maine's Ancient Law
Maine, Institutions H. Maine, Early History of Institutions. 1875
Maine L.Rev. Maine Law Review. 1908–20, 1962–
Maine S.B.A. Maine State Bar Association
maint. maintenance
Mait. Maitland's Select Pleas of the Crown, 1220–25. 1888
Mait.Gl. Maitland's Pleas of the Crown for the County of Gloucester. 1884
Maitland Maitland's Manuscript Session Cases (Scot.)
Maitland's Select Pleas of the Crown, 1220–25. 1888
Major Tax Plan. Major Tax Planning (USA)
Mak.L.J. Makerere Law Journal (Uganda) 1971–
Makerere L.J. Makerere Law Journal (Uganda) 1971–
Mal. Malaya
Malayan
Malaysia
Mal.L.J. Malayan Law Journal. 1932–
Mal.L.R. Malaya Law Review (now Singapore Journal of Legal Studies) 1962–
Malaya L.R. Malaya Law Review. 1962–
Malaya L.Rev. Malaya Law Review. 1962–
Malayan L.J. Malayan Law Journal. 1932–
Malaysia R.C. Royal Commission on Non-Muslim Marriage and Divorce Laws (Malaysia)
Mallory Mallory's Chancery Reports (Ire.)
Malone Heiskell's Tennessee Reports ed. by Malone (6,9,10 Tenn.)
Man. Manhattan
Manitoba
Manitoba Law Reports (Can.) 1883–
Manning's Reports (1 Michigan)
Manning's Revision Cases. 1832–5
Manson's Bankruptcy Cases. 1894–1914
Man.B.News Manitoba Bar News (Can.) 1928–
Man.Bar News Manitoba Bar News (Can.) 1928–
Man.Cas. Manumission Cases in New Jersey by Bloomfield
Man.Dec. Manitoba Decisions (Can.) 1975–
Man.Dem. Mansel, Demurrer. 1828
Man.El.Cas. Manning's Revision Cases. 1832–5
Man.Exch.Pr. Manning's Exchequer Practice. 2ed. 1826–7
Man.G.& S. Manning, Granger & Scott's Common Bench Reports (135–9 ER) 1845–56
Man.Gr.& S. Manning, Granger & Scott's Common Bench Reports (135–9 ER) 1845–56
Man.Int.Law Manning, Commentaries on the Law of Nations. 2ed. 1875
Man.L. Managerial Law
Man.L.J. Manitoba Law Journal (Can.) 1884–5, 1962–
Man.L.R. Manitoba Law Reports (Can.) 1883–
Man.L.R.C. Manitoba Law Reform Commission
Man.L.S.Chron. Manchester Law Students' Chronicle. 1901–
Man.L.S.J. Manchester Law Students' Journal. 1926
Manitoba Law School Journal
Man.Law Managerial Law
Man.Lim. Mansel, Limitation. 1839
Man.R. Manitoba Law Reports (Can.) 1883–

Man.R.t.Wood Manitoba Reports tempore Wood (Can.) 1875–83
Man.Rev.Stat. Manitoba Revised Statutes (Can.)
Man.Stat. Manitoba Statutes (Can.)
Man.t.Wood Manitoba Reports tempore Wood (Can.) 1875–83
Man.Unrep.Cas. Manning's Unreported Cases (Louisiana)
Man.Unrep.Cas.(La.) Manning's Unreported Cases (Louisiana)
Man.& G. Manning & Granger's Common Pleas Reports (133–5 ER) 1840–4
Man.& R. Manning & Ryland's King's Bench Reports (31–4 RR) 1827–30
Manning & Ryland's Magistrates' Cases. 1827–30
Man.& Ry. Manning & Ryland's King's Bench Reports (31–4 RR) 1827–30
Manning & Ryland's Magistrates' Cases. 1827–30
Man.& Ry.K.B. Manning & Ryland's King's Bench Reports (31–4 RR) 1827–30
Man.& Ry.M.C. Manning & Ryland's Magistrates' Cases. 1827–30
Man.& Ry.Mag.Cas. Manning & Ryland's Magistrates' Cases. 1827–30
Man.& S. Manning, Granger & Scott's Common Bench Reports (135–9 ER) 1845–56
Man.& Sc. Manning, Granger & Scott's Common Bench Reports (135–9 ER) 1845–56
Manb.Coke Manby's Abridgment of Coke's Reports
Manip. All India Reporter, Manipur. 1957–
Manitoba Armour's Queen's Bench & County Court Reports tempore Wood (Manitoba) 1875–83
Manitoba Law Reports (Can.) 1883–
Manitoba L.(Can.) Manitoba Law Reports (Can.) 1883–
Mann. Manning's Digest of the Nisi Prius Reports
Manning's Revision Cases. 1832–5
Manning's Reports (1 Michigan)
Mann.E.C. Manning's Revision Cases. 1832–5
Mann.G.& S. Manning, Granger & Scott's Common Bench Reports (135–9 ER) 1845–56
Mann.& G. Manning & Granger's Common Pleas Reports (133–5 ER) 1840–4
Mann.& R. Manning & Ryland's King's Bench Reports (31–4 RR) 1827–30
Manning & Ryland's Magistrates' Cases. 1827–30
Manning Manning's Reports (1 Michigan)
Manning's Unreported Cases (Louisiana)
Serviens ad Legem. 1840
Mans. Mansfield's Reports (49–52 Arkansas)
Manson's Bankruptcy and Companies' Winding-Up Cases. 1894–1914
Mansf.Dig. Mansfield's Digest of Statutes (Arkansas)
Manson Manson's Bankruptcy and Companies' Winding-Up Cases. 1894–1914
Manson,Bankr.Cas. Manson's Bankruptcy and Companies' Winding-Up Cases. 1894–1914
Manum.Cas. Bloomfield's Manumission Cases (New Jersey)
Manw. Manwood's Forest Laws. 1592
Mar. March's New Cases, King's Bench (82 ER) 1639–42
Maritime
Marriage
Marshall & Sevestre's Appeals (Bengal, India) 1862–4
Marshall's Ceylon Reports (Sri L.) 1833–6
Marshall's Circuit Court Reports (USA)
Marshall's Reports (8–10 Kentucky) 1817–21, (24–30 Kentucky) 1829–32
Martin's Reports (Louisiana) 1809–30
Martin's Reports (1 North Carolina) 1778–97

Marvel's Delaware Reports (15–16 Del.) 1893–7
Mary
Maryland

Mar.B.J. Maryland Bar Journal. 1968–

Mar.Br. March's Brooke's New Cases (73 ER) 1515–58

Mar.Cas. Crockford & Cox's Maritime Cases. 1860–71

Mar.Conv. Marcy, Epitome of Conveyancing. 1881

Mar.Conv.St. Marcy, Conveyancing Statutes. 5ed. 1893

Mar.L.C. Crockford's Maritime Law Cases, 1st Series. 1860–71

Mar.L.C.N.S. Aspinall's Maritime Law Cases, New Series. 1870–1940

Mar.L.J. Maryland Law Journal & Real Estate Record. 1878–89

Mar.L.R. Maritime Law Cases, 1st Series by Crockford. 1860–71
Maritime Law Cases, New Series by Aspinall. 1870–1940

Mar.L.Rec. Maryland Law Record. 1878–89

Mar.L.Rev. Maryland Law Review. 1936–51, 1953–

Mar.La. Martin's Louisiana Reports

Mar.Leg.Bib. Marvin, Legal Bibliography

mar.lic. marriage licence

Mar.N.C. March's New Cases, King's Bench (82 ER) 1639–42
Martin's Reports (1 North Carolina) 1778–97

Mar.N.R. March's New Cases, King's Bench (82 ER) 1639–42

Mar.N.S. Martin's Louisiana Reports, New Series. 1809–30

Mar.N.& Q. Maritime Notes and Queries. 1873–1900

Mar.Prov. Maritime Provinces Reports (Nova Scotia, Can.) 1929–52

Mar.R. Mitchell's Maritime Register. 1856–83

Mar.Reg. Mitchell's Maritime Register. 1856–83

mar.settl. marriage settlement

March March's New Cases, King's Bench (82 ER) 1639–42
March's Translation of Brooke's New Cases, King's Bench (73 ER) 1515–58

March N.C. March's New Cases, King's Bench (82 ER) 1639–42

March[N.C.] March's Translation of Brooke's New Cases, King's Bench (73 ER) 1515–58

March N.R. March's New Cases, King's Bench (82 ER) 1639–42

Marine Ct.R. McAdam's Marine Court Reporter (New York)

marit. maritime

Marius Marius, Concerning Bills of Exchange. 4ed. 1684

Mark.El. Markby, Elements of Law. 6ed. 1905

Marks & Sayre Marks & Sayre's Reports (108 Alabama)

Marq.L.Rev. Marquette Law Review (USA) 1916–

Marqu.L.R. Marquette Law Review (USA) 1916–

Marquette Bus.Rev. Marquette Business Review (USA)

Marquette L.Rev. Marquette Law Review (USA) 1916–

Marr. Marrack's European Assurance Cases. 1872–4
Marriage
Marriott's Admiralty Reports (165 ER) 1776–9

Marr.Adm. Marriott's Admiralty Reports (165 ER) 1776–9

Marr.Form Marriott, Formulare Instrumentorum (Admiralty Court) 1802

Mars. Mars, Law of Insolvency in South Africa
Marsden's Select Pleas in the Court of Admiralty (Selden Society)

Mars.Adm. Marsden's Select Pleas in the Court of Admiralty (Selden Society)

Mars.Coll. Marsden, Collisions at Sea

Marsh. Marshall & Sevestre's Appeals (Bengal, India) 1862–4

Marshall's Ceylon Reports (Sri L.) 1833–6
Marshall's Circuit Court Decisions (USA)
Marshall's Common Pleas Reports (15, 17 RR) 1813–16
Marshall's Kentucky Reports (8–10 Ky.) 1817–21, (24–30 Ky.) 1829–32
Marshall's Reports (4 Utah)

Marsh.A.K. A.K. Marshall's Kentucky Reports (8–10 Ky.) 1817–21

Marsh.Beng. Marshall & Sevestre's Appeals (Bengal, India) 1862–4

Marsh.C.P. Marshall's Common Pleas Reports (15,17 RR) 1813–16

Marsh.Calc. Marshall & Sevestre's Appeals, Calcutta (Bengal, India) 1862–4

Marsh.Ceylon Marshall's Ceylon Reports (Sri L.) 1833–6

Marsh.Dec. Marshall's Circuit Court Decisions, by Brockenbrough (USA)

Marsh.Ins. Marshall on Insurance. 5ed. 1865

Marsh.(Ky.) Marshall's Kentucky Reports (8–10 Ky.) 1817–21, (24–30 Ky.) 1829–32

Marsh.J.J. J.J. Marshall's Kentucky Reports (24–30 Ky.) 1829–32

Marsh.Op. Marshall's Constitutional Opinions

Marshall Marshall & Sevestre's Appeals (Bengal, India) 1862–4
Marshall's (Judgments) Reports (Sri L.) 1833–6

Marshall's Judgments Marshall's Ceylon Reports (Sri L.) 1833–6

Marshall's Rep. Marshall's Ceylon Reports (Sri L.) 1833–6

Mart. feast of St Martin (Martinmas)

Mart.Ark. Martin's Decisions in Equity (Arkansas) 1895–1900

Mart.Cond.La. Martin's Condensed Louisiana Reports

Mart.Dec. Martin's North Carolina Reports (1 NC) 1778–98

Mart.Ga. Martin's Reports (21–30 Georgia)

Mart.Ind. Martin's Reports (54–70 Indiana)

Mart.La. Martin's Louisiana Term Reports. 1809–30

Mart.M.C. Martin's Mining Cases (Can.)

Mart.N.C. Martin's North Carolina Reports (1 NC) 1778–98

Mart.N.S. Martin's Louisiana Reports, New Series. 1823–30

Mart.N.S.(La.) Martin's Louisiana Reports, New Series. 1823–30

Mart.O.S.(La.) Martin's Louisiana Reports, Old Series. 1809–23

Mart.U.S.C.C. Martin's Circuit Court Reports (USA)

Mart.& Y. Martin & Yerger's Tennessee Reports (8 Ten.) 1825–8

Mart.& Y.(Tenn.) Martin & Yerger's Tennessee Reports (8 Ten.) 1825–8

Mart.& Yer. Martin & Yerger's Tennessee Reports (8 Ten.) 1825–8

Mart.& Yerg. Martin & Yerger's Tennessee Reports (8 Ten.) 1825–8

Martens,N.R. Martens, Nouveau recueil des traités d'alliance. 1817–42

Martens, N.R.G. Martens, Nouveau recueil general de traités. 1843–75

Martens, N.R.G.,2nd ser. Martens, Nouveau recueil general de traités. 1876–1908

Martens, N.R.G.,3rd ser. Martens, Nouveau recueil general de traités. 1909–

Martens, N.S. Martens, Nouveaux supplements au recueil des traités. 1839–42

Martens, R. Martens, Recueil des traités d'alliance. 1791–1801

Martens,Rec. Martens, Recueil des traités d'alliance. 1791–1801

Martin Martin's Reports (21–30 Georgia)
Martin's Reports (54–70 Indiana)
Martin's Reports (Louisiana) 1809–30
Martin's Reports (1 North Carolina) 1778–98

Martin Index Martin's Index to Virginia Reports

Marv. Marvel's Delaware Reports (15–16 Del.) 1893–7

Marv.(Del.) Marvel's Delaware Reports (15–16 Del.) 1893–7

Marvel Marvel's Delaware Reports (15–16 Del.) 1893–7

Mary.L.Rev. Maryland Law Review

Maryland Maryland Reports. 1851–

Mas. Mason, United States Circuit Court Reports
Massachusetts Reports

Mason's Code Mason's United States Code Annotated

Mass. Massachusetts
Massachusetts Supreme Judicial Court Reports. 1804–

Mass.Acts Acts and Resolves of Massachusetts

Mass.Adv.Legis.Serv. Massachusetts Advance Legislative Service (Lawyer's Co-op)

Mass.Adv.Sh. Massachusetts Supreme Judicial Court Advance Sheets

Mass.Ann.Laws Annotated Laws of Massachusetts

Mass.App.Ct. Massachusetts Appeals Court Reports. 1976–

Mass.App.Ct.Adv.Sh. Massachusetts Appeals Court Advance Sheets

Mass.App.Dec. Massachusetts Appellate Decisions. 1941–

Mass.App.Div. Massachusetts Appellate Division Reports. 1936–50

Mass.B.T.A. Massachusetts Board of Tax Appeals

Mass.Elec.Cas. Massachusetts Election Cases

Mass.Gen.Laws Massachusetts General Laws

Mass.Gen.Laws Ann.(West) Massachusetts General Laws Annotated (West Pub. Co.)

Mass.I.A.B. Massachusetts Industrial Accident Board Reports of Cases

Mass.L.Q. Massachusetts Law Quarterly. 1915–77

Mass.L.R. Massachusetts Law Reporter. 1872

Mass.L.Rev. Massachusetts Law Review. 1978–

Mass.St.B.C.& A. Massachusetts State Board of Conciliation & Arbitration Reports

Mass.U.C.C.Op. Massachusetts Unemployment Compensation Commission Opinions

Mass.W.C.C. Massachusetts Workmen's Compensation Cases

Mast. Master's Reports (25–28 Canada Supreme Court)

Mast.El. Masterman, Parliamentary Elections. 1880

Mat. Maturity

Math. Mathieu's Quebec Reports (Can.)

Math.Pres.Ev. Matthews, Presumptive Evidence. 1827

Mats. Matson's Reports (22–24 Connecticut)

Matson Matson's Reports (22–24 Conecticut)

Matth.Exe. Matthews, Executors and Administrators. 2ed. 1839

Matthews Matthews' Reports (75 Virginia)
Matthews' Reports (6–9 West Virginia)

Mau.& Sel. Maule & Selwyn's King's Bench Reports (105 ER) 1813–17

Maude & P. Maude & Pollock's Law of Merchant Shipping. 4ed. 1881

Maug.Att. Maugham, Attorneys, Solicitors and Agents. 1825
Maugham, Statutes relating to Attorneys, etc. 1839

Maug.Cr.L. Maugham, Outlines of Criminal Law. 2ed. 1842

Maug.Jur. Maugham, Outlines of the Jurisdiction. 1838

Maug.Law Maugham, Outlines of Law. 1837

Maugh.Lit.Pr. Maugham, Literary Property. 1828

Maugh.R.P. Maugham, Outlines of Real Property Law. 1842

Maul.& Sel. Maule & Selwyn's King's Bench Reports (105 ER) 1813–17

Maule & S. Maule & Selwyn's King's Bench Reports (105 ER) 1813–17

Maur.Dec. Mauritius Decisions (Reports) 1861–

Max.Dig. Maxwell's Nebraska Digest

Max.Int.Stat. Maxwell's Interpretation of Statutes

Maxw.Cr.Proc. Maxwell's Treatise on Criminal Procedure

Maxwell Irish Land Purchase Cases. 1904–11

Maxwell's Interpretation of Statutes

May.Act Mayhew, Action at Law. 1828

May Fr.Conv. May, Fraudulent Conveyances. 3ed. 1908

May Ins. May on Insurance

May.L.R. Mayurbhani Law Reporter (India)

May.Merg. Mayhew, Merger. 1861

May P.L. May's Parliamentary Practice

May Parl. May's Parliamentary Practice

May Parl.Pr. May's Parliamentary Practice

Mayn. Maynard's Reports. 1273–1326

McA.L.& Ten. McAdam on Landlord and Tenant

McAll. McAllister's Circuit Court Reports (USA)

McAr. MacArthur's District of Columbia Reports (8–10 DC) 1873–9

McArth.& M. MacArthur & Mackey's District of Columbia Reports (11 DC) 1879–80

McBride McBride's Reports (1 Missouri)

McCah. McCahon's Reports (Kansas) 1858–68

McCahon McCahon's Reports (Kansas) 1858–68

McCar. McCarter's New Jersey Equity Reports (14,15 N.J.Eq.)

McCart. McCarter's New Jersey Equity Reports (14,15 N.J.Eq.)

McCarty's Civil Procedure Reports (New York)

McCarter McCarter's New Jersey Equity Reports (14,15 N.J.Eq.)

McCarty McCarty's Civil Procedure Reports (New York)

McCarty Civ.Proc. McCarty's Civil Procedure Reports (New York)

Mccl. 10 Modern Reports, Macclesfield's Cases in Law and Equity. 1710–24

McCl. McClelland's Exchequer Reports (148 ER) 1824

McCl.Dig. McClellan, Florida Digest

McCl.Ia.Co. McClain, Iowa Code

McCl.& Y. McClelland & Younge's Exchequer Reports (148 ER) 1824–5

McClain's Code McClain's Annotated Code and Statutes (Iowa)

McCle.& Yo. McClelland & Younge's Exchequer Reports (148 ER) 1824–5

McClel.Dig. McClellan's Digest of Laws (Florida)

McClell. McClelland's Exchequer Reports (148 ER) 1824

McClell.& Y. McClelland & Younge's Exchequer Reports (148 ER) 1824–5

McCook McCook's Reports (1 Ohio)

McCord McCord's South Carolina Law Reports (12–15 SCL) 1821–8

McCord Ch. McCord's South Carolina Chancery Reports (6–7 SCEq.) 1825–7

McCord Eq. McCord's South Carolina Chancery Reports (6–7 SCEq.) 1825–7

McCorkle McCorkle's Reports (65 North Carolina)

McCr. McCrary's Circuit Court Reports (USA)

McDer.Land L. McDermot, Land Laws (Ire.)

McDevitt McDevitt's Land Commissioner's Reports (Ire.) 1882–4

McDonnell McDonnell's Sierra Leone Reports

McDow.Inst. McDowall, Institutes of the Law of Scotland

McFar. McFarlane's Jury Trials (Scot.) 1838–9

McGill McGill's Manuscript Decisions, Court of Session (Scot.)

McGill L.J. McGill Law Journal (Can.) 1952–

McGl. McGloin's Louisiana Court of Appeal Reports. 1881–84

McGl.Al. McGlashan, Aliment (Scot.)

McGl.Sh. McGlashan, Sheriff Court Practice (Scot.)

McGloin McGloin's Louisiana Court of Appeal Reports. 1881–84

McGrath McGrath's Mandamus Cases (Michigan)

McGregor Report Royal Commission on the Press Report (Cmnd. 6810) 1977

Mch. Michigan Reports. 1847–

McK.E.B.B. McKenna Employee Benefits Bulletin

McK.P.L.B. McKenna Pension Law Bulletin

McL. McLean's Circuit Court Reports (USA)

McL.& R. McLean & Robinson's Scotch Appeal Cases (9 ER) 1839

McLar.Tr. McLaren, Trusts in Scotland

McLar.W. McLaren, Law of Wills (Scot.)

McM.Com.Cas. McMaster's Commercial Cases (USA)

McM.Com.Dec. McMaster's Commercial Cases (USA)

McMul. McMullan's Law Reports, South Carolina (26–27 SCL) 1840–2

McMul.Eq. McMullan's South Carolina Equity Reports (16 SCEq.) 1840–2

McMull.Eq.(S.C.) McMullan's South Carolina Equity Reports (16 SCEq.) 1840–2

McMull.L.(S.C.) McMullan's South Carolina Law Reports (26–27 SCL) 1840–2

McNair, Opinions McNair, International Law Opinions. 1956

McNair, Treaties McNair, The Law of Treaties, British Practice and Opinions. 1938

McPherson McPherson, Lee & Bell's Session Cases, Third Series (Scot.) 1862–73

McQ. McQueen's Scotch Appeal Cases (House of Lords) 1851–65

McVey Dig. McVey's Ohio Digest

McWillie McWillie's Reports (73–6 Mississippi)

Md. Maryland
Maryland Reports. 1851–

Md.A. Maryland Appellate Reports. 1967–

Md.Ann.Code Annotated Code of Maryland

Md.App. Maryland Appellate Reports. 1967–

Md.B.J. Maryland Bar Journal. 1968–

Md.Ch. Johnson's Chancery Reports, Maryland

Md.Code Ann. Annotated Code of Maryland

Md.J.Int'l L.& Trade Maryland Journal of International Law and Trade

Md.L.R. Maryland Law Review. 1936–51, 1953–

Md.L.Rec. Maryland Law Record. 1878–89

Md.L.Rev. Maryland Law Review. 1936–51, 1953–

Md.Laws Laws of Maryland

Md.S.B.A. Maryland State Bar Association
Maryland State Bar Association Reports

Md.W.C.C. Maryland Workmen's Compensation Cases

Mdse. Merchandise

Me. Maine
Maine Supreme Judicial Court Reports. 1820–1965

Me.Acts Acts, Resolves and Constitutional Resolutions of the State of Maine

Me.L. University of Maine Law Review. 1908–20, 1962–

Me.Legis.Serv. Maine Legislative Service

Me.Rev.Stat. Maine Revised Statutes

Me.Rev.Stat.Ann. Maine Revised Statutes Annotated

Means Means' Kansas Reports

Mears Just. Mears' edition of Justinian & Gaius

Mecmuasi Istanbul U.Huk.Fac. Mecmuasi Istanbul Universitesi Hukuk Fakultesi (Turkey)
Med. Mediator
Medical
Medicine
Med.Jur. Medical Jurisprudence
Med.L.J. Medico-Legal Journal. 1933–
Medico-Legal Journal (New York) 1883–1933
Med.L.N. Medico Legal News (New York)
Med.L.R. Medical Law Reports. 1989–
Med.L.& P. Media Law and Practice. 1980–
Med.Leg.Bull. Medico-Legal Bulletin (USA) 1903–9
Med.Leg.J. Medico-Legal Journal. 1933–
Medico-Legal Journal (New York) 1883–1933
Med.Leg.N. Medico Legal News (New York)
Med.Leg.Soc.Trans. Transactions of the Medico-Legal Society. 1902–32
Med.Leg.& Crim.Rev. Medico-Legal and Criminological Review. 1933–46
Med.Sci.Law Medicine, Science and the Law. 1960–
Med.Sci.& L. Medicine, Science and the Law. 1960–
Med.Tr.T.Q. Medical Trial Technique Quarterly (USA) 1954–
Med.Trial Tech.Q. Medical Trial Technique Quarterly (USA) 1954–
Medd. Meddaugh's Reports (13 Michigan)
Meddaugh Meddaugh's Reports (13 Michigan)
Media L.& P. Media Law and Practice. 1980–
Medico-Legal Soc.N.S.W.Proc. Proceedings of the Medico-Legal Society of New South Wales (Aus.) 1960–
Medico-Legal Soc.Vic.Proc. Proceedings of the Medico-Legal Society of Victoria (Aus.) 1931–
Mees.& Ros. Meeson & Roscoe's Exchequer Reports. 1834–6
Mees.& W. Meeson & Welsby's Exchequer Reports (150–3 ER) 1836–47
Mees.& Wels. Meeson & Welsby's Exchequer Reports (150–3 ER) 1836–47
Meg. Megone's Companies Acts Cases. 1888–91
Megarry Megarry, The Rent Acts
Megg.Ass. Meggison, Assets in Equity. 1832
Megone Megone's Companies Acts Cases. 1888–91
Meigs Meigs' Tennessee Supreme Court Reports (19 Tenn.) 1838–9
Meigs Dig. Meigs' Digest of Decisions of the Courts of Tennessee
Meijo L.Rev. Meijo Law Review (Japan)
Melanesian L.J. Melanesian Law Journal (Papua New Guinea) 1970–
Mélanges Mahaim Mélanges offerts à Ernest Mahaim. 1935
Melb. Melbourne
Melb.U.L.Rev. Melbourne University Law Review. 1957–
Melb.Univ.L.R. Melbourne University Law Review. 1957–
Melb.Univ.L.Rev. Melbourne University Law Review. 1957–
Melbourne U.L.R. Melbourne University Law Review. 1957–
Melv.Tr. Melville's Trial (Impeachment)
Mem. Mémorial: journal officiel du Grand-Duché de Luxembourg. 1832–
Memphis
Mem.L.J. Memphis Law Journal (Tennessee) 1878–9
Mem.St.U.L.Rev. Memphis State University Law Review
Memp.L.J. Memphis Law Journal (Tennessee) 1878–9
Memphis L.J. Memphis Law Journal (Tennessee) 1878–9
Memphis St.U.L.Rev. Memphis State University Law Review. 1970–
Men. Menzies' Cape of Good Hope Reports (S.Afr.) 1828–49
Mence Lib. Mence, Law of Libel. 1824

Menken Menken's Reports (30 New York Civil Procedure Reports)
Menz. Menzies' Cape of Good Hope Reports (S.Afr.) 1828–49
Menzies Menzies' Cape of Good Hope Reports (S.Afr.) 1828–49
Mer. Mercer Law Review (Georgia) 1949–
Merivale's Chancery Reports (35–6 ER) 1815–17
Mer.L.J. Mercantile Law Journal (Madras, India) 1911–13
Mercantile Law Journal (New York) 1884
Merc.Cas. Mercantile Cases
Merc.L.J. Mercantile Law Journal (Madras, India) 1911–13
Mercantile Law Journal (New York) 1884
Mercer B.L.Rev. Mercer Beasley Law Review (New Jersey) 1932–6
Mercer Beasley L.Rev. Mercer Beasley Law Review (New Jersey) 1932–6
Mercer L.Rev. Mercer Law Review (Georgia) 1949–
Mercer Law Rev. Mercer Law Review (Georgia) 1949–
Merchand.Rep. Merchandising Reporter (USA) 1982–
Merignhac Merignhac, Traité de droit public international. 3 vols. 1905, 1907, 1912
Meriv. Merivale's Chancery Reports (35–6 ER) 1815–17
Merr.Att. Merrifield, Attorneys. 1830
Mert. Merten's Law of Federal Income Taxation (USA)
Met. Metcalf's Reports (58–61 Kentucky) 1858–63
Metcalf's Reports (42–54 Massachusetts) 1840–7
Metcalf's Reports (3 Rhode Island)
Metropolitan
Metropolitan Police
Metc. Metcalf's Reports (58–61 Kentucky) 1858–63
Metcalf's Reports (42–54 Massachusetts)
Metcalf's Reports (3 Rhode Island)
Metc.Ky. Metcalf's Reports (58–61 Kentucky) 1858–63
Metc.Mass. Metcalf's Reports (42–54 Massachusetts) 1840–7
Meth.Ch.Ca. Report of the Methodist Church Case
Metrop. Metropolis
Metropolitan
Mews Mews' Digest of English Case Law
Mews Dig. Mews' Digest of English Case Law
Mfg. Manufacturing
Mfgr. Manufacturer
Mfr. Manufacturer
mfre. manufacture
Mgmt. Management
mgr. manager
Mi. Michigan
Michigan Reports. 1847–
Mi.L. Michigan Law Review. 1902–
University of Miami Law Review (Florida) 1957–
Miami L.Q. Miami Law Quarterly. 1947–57
Miami L.Rev. University of Miami Law Review (Florida) 1957–
Mich. Michaelmas Term
Michigan
Michigan Supreme Court Reports. 1847–
Mich.Adv. Michigan Reports Advance Sheets
Mich.App. Michigan Court of Appeals Reports
Mich.C.C.R. Michigan Circuit Court Reporter
Mich.Comp.L.Ann. Michigan Compiled Laws Annotated
Mich.Comp.Laws Michigan Compiled Laws
Mich.Comp.Laws Ann. Michigan Compiled Laws Annotated
Mich.Cr.Ct.Rep. Michigan Circuit Court Reporter
Mich.J.Int'l L. Michigan Journal of International Law

Mich.L. Michigan Lawyer. 1875–9
Mich.L.J. Michigan Law Journal. 1892–8
Mich.L.Rev. Michigan Law Review. 1902–
Mich.Lawyer Michigan Lawyer. 1875–9
Mich.Leg.News Michigan Legal News. 1886
Mich.Legis.Serv.(West) Michigan Legislation Service (West Pub. Co.)
Mich.N.P. Brown's Michigan Nisi Prius Reports. 1869–71
Howell's Michigan Nisi Prius Cases. 1868–84
Mich.Pol.Sci.Assn. Michigan Political Science Association
Mich.Pub.Acts Public and Local Acts of the Legislature of the State of Michigan
Mich.S.B.A.Jo. Michigan State Bar Journal. 1921–
Mich.S.B.J. Michigan State Bar Journal. 1921–
Mich.St.B.J. Michigan State Bar Journal. 1921–
Mich.Stat.Ann. Michigan Statutes Annotated
Mich.T. Michaelmas Term
Mich.Vac. Michaelmas Vacation
Mich.W.C.C. Michigan Industrial Accident Board, Workmen's Compensation Cases
Michie's Jur. Michie's Jurisprudence (Virginia & West Virginia)
Middle East J. Middle East Journal
Middle East L.Rev. Middle East Law Review
Middle East Stud. Middle East Studies
Middx.Sit. Sittings for Middlesex at Nisi Prius
Midw.J.Pol.Sc. Midwest Journal of Political Science
Midwest J.Pol. Midwest Journal of Political Science
migr. migrated
Mij. Maatschappij (Neth.) joint stock company
Mil. Miles' Pennsylvania Reports. 1825–41
Military
Miller's Reports (1–5 Louisiana) 1830–3
Miller's Reports (3–18 Maryland) 1850–1
Mill's South Carolina Constitutional Reports. 1817–18
Mill's Surrogate Court Reports (New York) 1899–1917
Mil.L.Rev. Military Law Review (USA) 1958–
Mil.Rep. Militia Reporter (Boston) 1810
Mil.& Vet.C. Military and Veterans Code (California)
Miles Miles' District Court Reports (Pennsylvania) 1825–41
Miles(Pa.) Miles' District Court Reports (Pennsylvania) 1825–41
Milit. Military
Milit.L.R. Military Law Review (USA) 1958–
Military L.J. Military Law Journal (USA)
Military L.Rev. Military Law Review (USA)
Mill. Miller's Reports (1–5 Louisiana) 1830–3
Miller's Reports (3–18 Maryland) 1850–1
Mill's South Carolina Constitutional Reports (8–9 SCL) 1817–18
Mill's Surrogate Court Reports (New York) 1899–1917
Mill.Civ.L. Miller, Civil Law of England. 1825
Mill.Code Miller's Iowa Code
Mill Const. Mill's South Carolina Constitutional Reports (8–9 SCL) 1817–18
Mill Const.(S.C.) Mill's South Carolina Constitutional Reports (8–9 SCL) 1817–18
Mill.Dec. Miller's Circuit Court Decisions (Woolworth) (USA)
Miller's U.S. Supreme Court Decisions
Mill.Eq.M. Miller, Equitable Mortgages. 1844
Mill.La. Miller's Reports (1–5 Louisiana) 1830–3

Mill.Md. Miller's Reports (3–18 Maryland) 1850–1
Mill.Op. Miller's Circuit Court Decisions (Woolworth) (USA)
Mill.& V.Code Milliken & Vertrees' Code (Tennessee)
Miller Miller's Reports (1–5 Louisiana) 1830–3
Miller's Reports (3–18 Maryland) 1850–1
Miller, Lectures W.G. Miller, Lectures on the Philosophy of Law. 1884
Miller's Code Miller's Revised and Annotated Code (Iowa)
Millin Petty Sessions Cases (Ire.) 1875–98
Mills Mills' Surrogate Court Reports (New York) 1899–1917
Mills'Ann.St. Mills' Annotated Statutes (Colorado)
Mills(N.Y.) Mills' Surrogate Court Reports (New York) 1899–1917
Mills'Surr.Ct. Mills' Surrogate Court Reports (New York) 1899–1917
Milw. Milward's Irish Ecclesiastical Reports. 1819–43
Milw.B.A.G. Milwaukee Bar Association Gavel. 1938–
Milw.Ir.Ecc.Rep. Milward's Irish Ecclesiastical Reports. 1819–43
Min. Mineral
Minnesota Supreme Court Reports. 1851–
Minister
Ministry
Minor
Minor's Alabama Reports. 1820–6
Minute
Min.Ev. Minutes of Evidence
Min.H.M.D. National Health Insurance (Ministry of Health Decisions)
Min.Inst. Minor's Institutes of Common and Statute Law
Min.publ. Ministère public
Minn. Minnesota
Minnesota Supreme Court Reports. 1851–
Minn.Ct.Rep. Minnesota Court Reporter
Minn.Gen.Laws Minnesota General Laws
Minn.L.J. Minnesota Law Journal (St. Paul, Minn.) 1893–7
Minn.L.Rev. Minnesota Law Review. 1917–
Minn.S.B.A. Minnesota State Bar Association
Minn.Sess.Law Serv.(West) Minnesota Session Law Service (West Pub. Co.)
Minn.Stat. Minnesota Statutes
Minn.Stat.Ann. Minnesota Statutes Annotated
Minn.Stat.Ann.(West) Minnesota Statutes Annotated (West Pub. Co.)
Minn.W.C.D. Minnesota Workmen's Compensation Decisions
Minor Minor's Alabama Supreme Court Reports. 1820–26
Minor's Institutes of Common and Statute Law
Minor (Ala.) Minor's Alabama Supreme Court Reports. 1820–26
Minor Inst. Minor's Institutes of Common and Statute Law
Minroku Daishin'in minji hanketsuroku (Japan) Great Court of Cassation Civil Case Reports
Minshu Saiko saibansho minji hanreishu (Japan) Supreme Court Civil Case Reports
Mir. Horne's Mirrour of Justices
Mir.Just. Horne's Mirrour of Justices
Mir.Parl. Mirror of Parliament, London
Mireh.Advow. Mirehouse, Advowsons. 1824
Mireh.Ti. Mirehouse, Tithes. 2ed. 1822
Mis. Mississippi
Mississippi Supreme Court Reports. 1850–1966
Missouri
misc. miscellaneous
Misc. Miscellaneous Reports (New York) 1892–
Misc.2d. Miscellaneous Reports, Second Series (New York)
Misc.Dec. Ohio Miscellaneous Decisions (Gottschall) 1865–73

Misc.(N.Y.) Miscellaneous Reports (New York) 1892–
Misc.Pr. Miscellaneous Provisions
Misc.Rep. Miscellaneous Reports (New York) 1892–
Miscel. Miscellaneous Reports (New York) 1892–
Miss. Mississippi
Mississippi Supreme Court Reports. 1850–1966
Missouri
Miss.C.L.Rev. Mississippi College Law Review
Miss.Code Ann. Mississippi Code Annotated
Miss.Dec. Mississippi Decisions
Miss.L.J. Mississippi Law Journal. 1928–
Miss.Law Rev. Mississippi Law Review. 1922–3
Miss.Laws General Laws of Mississippi
Miss.Lawyer Mississippi Lawyer
Miss.S.B.A. Mississippi State Bar Association
Miss.St.Ca. Morris' Mississippi State Cases. 1818–72
Miss.St.Cas. Morris' Mississippi State Cases. 1818–72
Mister Mister's Reports (17–32 Missouri Appeal Reports)
Mit.M.R. Mitchell's Maritime Register. 1856–83
Mitch.B.& N. Mitchell, Bills, Notes, etc. 1829
Mitch.M.R. Mitchell's Maritime Register. 1856–83
Mitch.Mar.Reg. Mitchell's Maritime Register. 1856–83
Mitf.Eq.Pl. Mitford on Equity Pleading. 5ed. 1847
Mitt. Mitteilung (Ger.) report
Mitteilungen (Ger.) bulletin, proceedings
Mkt. Market
Mktg. Marketing
Mktng. Marketing
Mktng.& L. Marketing and the Law: National Information Bulletin (N.S.W., Aus.) 1981–
Mkts. Markets
Mn. Minnesota
Mn.L.R. Minnesota Law Review. 1917–
Mo. Missouri
Missouri Supreme Court Reports. 1821–1956
Modern Reports (86–8 ER) 1669–1755
Moore's Common Pleas Reports (19–29 RR) 1817–27
Moore's Indian Appeal Cases (18–20 ER) 1836–72
Moore's King's Bench Reports (72 ER) 1512–1621
Moore's Privy Council Reports (12–15 ER) 1836–62
Mo.A.R. Missouri Appellate Reporter
Mo.Ann.Stat.(Vernon) Vernon's Annotated Missouri Statutes
Mo.App. Missouri Appeal Reports. 1876–1951
Mo.App.Rep. Missouri Appeal Reports. 1876–1951
Mo.B.A. Missouri Bar Journal
Mo.Bar Missouri Bar. 1879
Mo.Bar J. Missouri Bar Journal. 1930–44
Mo.Dec. Missouri Decisions
Mo.(F.) Sir Francis Moore's King's Bench Reports (72 ER) 1512–1621
Mo.I.A. Moore's Indian Appeals (18–20 ER) 1836–72
Mo.J.B. J.B. Moore's Common Pleas Reports (19–29 RR) 1817–27
Mo.Jur. Monthly Jurist (Bloomington, Ill.) 1877–9
Mo.L. Missouri Law Review. 1936–
Mo.L.Mag. Monthly Law Magazine. 1838–41
Mo.L.Rev. Missouri Law Review. 1936–
Mo.Labor Rev. Monthly Labor Review (USA)
Mo.Law Rep. Monthly Law Reporter (USA) 1838–66
Mo.Laws Laws of Missouri
Mo.Leg.Exam. Monthly Legal Examiner (New York) 1850
Mo.Legis.Serv.(Vernon) Missouri Legislative Service

Mo.P.C. Moore's Privy Council Cases (12–15 ER) 1836–62
Mo.Rev. Monthly Review
Mo.Rev.Stat. Missouri Revised Statutes
Mo.St.Ann. Missouri Statutes Annotated
Mo.St.B.A. Missouri State Bar Association
Mo.W.Jur. Monthly Western Jurist (Bloomington, Ill.) 1874–7
Mo.& P. Moore & Payne's Common Pleas Reports (29–33 RR) 1827–31
Mo.& R. Moody & Robinson's Nisi Prius Reports (174 ER) 1830–44
Mo.& S. Moore & Scott's Common Pleas Reports (34–8 RR) 1831–4
Mo.& Sc. Moore & Scott's Common Pleas Reports (34–8 RR) 1831–4
Moak Moak's English Reports
Moak Eng.Rep. Moak's English Reports
Moak Und. Moak's edition of Underhill on Torts
Mob. Mobley, Contested Election Cases, U.S. House of Representatives. 1882–9
Mobl. Mobley, Contested Election Cases, U.S. House of Representatives. 1882–9
mod. modification
modified
modifying
Mod. Modern
Modern Reports (86–8 ER) 1669–1755
Style's King's Bench Reports. 1646–55
Mod.Am.Law Modern American Law
Mod.Asian Stud. Modern Asian Studies
Mod.Ca.L.& Eq. 8 & 9 Modern Reports (88 ER) 1721–55
Mod.Ca.per.Far. 6 & 7 Modern Reports (87 ER) 1703–45
Mod.Ca.t.Holt 7 Modern Reports, King's Bench (87 ER) 1703–45
Mod.Cas. Modern Cases (6 Modern Reports) (87 ER) 1703–45
Mod.Cas.L.& Eq. Modern Cases at Law and Equity (8–9 Modern Reports) (88 ER) 1721–55
Mod.Cas.per Far. Modern Cases tempore Holt, by Farresley (7 Modern Reports) (87 ER) 1703–45
Mod.Cas.t.Holt Modern Cases tempore Holt (7 Modern Reports) (87 ER) 1703–45
Mod.Ent. Modern Entries
Mod.L.R. Modern Law Review. 1937–
Mod.L.Rev. Modern Law Review. 1937–
Mod.Rep. Modern Reports (86–8 ER) 1669–1755
Style's King's Bench Reports. 1646–55
Modern L.R. Modern Law Review. 1937–
Modern L.Rev. Modern Law Review. 1937–
mod'g. modifying
modif. modified
modification
mods. modifications
Mol. Molloy's Chancery Reports (Ire.) 1827–31
Molloy's De Jure Maritimo et Navali
Moll. Molloy's Chancery Reports (Ire.) 1827–31
Molloy Molloy's De Jure Maritimo et Navali
Moly. Molyneaux's Reports tempore Car. I
Mon. Monaghan's Unreported Cases (Pennsylvania Superior Court) 1888–90
Moniteur Belge (Official Gazette of Belgium)
B. Monroe's Reports (40–57 Kentucky) 1840–57
T.B. Monroe's Reports (17–23 Kentucky) 1824–8
Montana
Montana Supreme Court Reports. 1868–
Monthly
Mon.Angl. Monasticon Anglicanum
Mon.B. Monroe's Reports (40–57 Kentucky) 1840–57
Mon.L.R. Monash University Law Review (Aus.) 1974–
Mon.L.Rev.,Univ.of Detroit Monthly Law Review of University of Detroit. 1916

Mon.Law Mag. Monthly Law Magazine. 1834–41
Mon.Law Rep. Monthly Law Reporter (Boston) 1838–66
Mon.Leg.R.(Pa.) Monroe Legal Reporter (Pennsylvania) 1938–
Mon.Meth. Monahan, Method of the Law. 1878
Mon.T.B. T.B. Monroe's Kentucky Reports (17–23 Ky.) 1824–8
Mon.Trib. Monitore dei tribunali
Mon.W.J. Monthly Western Jurist (USA) 1874–7
Mona. Monaghan's Superior Court Reports (147–165 Pennsylvania) 1888–90
Monag. Monaghan's Superior Court Reports (147–165 Pennsylvania) 1888–90
Monaghan Monaghan's Superior Court Reports (147–165 Pennsylvania) 1888–90
Monaghan(Pa.) Monaghan's Superior Court Reports (147–165 Pennsylvania) 1888–90
Monash L.R. Monash University Law Review (Aus.) 1974–
Monash U.L.R. Monash University Law Review (Aus.) 1974–
Monash U.L.Rev. Monash University Law Review (Aus.) 1974–
Monatsch.für Krim.und Strafr. Monatschrift für Kriminalpsychologie und Strafrechtsreform
Monc.Inn. Moncrieff, Liability of Innkeepers. 1874
Monde Jur. Le Monde Juridique (Can.) 1984–
Monitore Monitore dei Tribunali
Monro Monro's Acta Cancellariae. 1545–1625
Monro A.C. Monro's Acta Cancellariae. 1545–1625
Monroe L.R. Monroe Legal Reporter (Pennsylvania) 1938–
Mont. Montagu's Bankruptcy Reports. 1829–32
Montana
Montana Supreme Court Reports. 1868–
Montriou's Cases of Hindu Law (Bengal, India) 1779–1840
Montriou's Reports, Supreme Court (Bengal, India) 1846
Mont.B.C. Montagu's Bankruptcy Reports. 1829–32
Mont.Bank.Rep. Montagu's Bankruptcy Reports. 1829–32
Mont.Bankr. Montagu's Bankruptcy Reports. 1829–32
Mont.Bk.L. Montagu, Bankrupt Law. 4ed. 1827
Mont.Cas. Montriou's Cases of Hindu Law (Bengal, India) 1779–1840
Mont.Co.L.Rep. Montgomery County Law Reporter (Pennsylvania)
Mont.Comp. Montagu, Composition. 1823
Mont.Cond.Rep. Montreal Condensed Reports (Quebec, Can.) 1853–54
Mont.D.& DeG. Montagu, Deacon & DeGex's Bankruptcy Reports. 1840–44
Mont.Dig. Montagu's Digest of Pleadings in Equity
Mont.Ind. Monthly Index to Reporters
Mont.Inst. Montriou, Institutes of Jurisprudence
Mont.L.R. Montreal Law Reports. 1885–91
Mont.L.R.Q.B. Montreal Law Reports, Queen's Bench
Mont.L.R.S.C. Montreal Law Reports, Superior Court
Mont.L.Rev. Montana Law Review. 1940–
Mont.Laws Laws of Montana
Mont.Leg.News Montreal Legal News. 1878–97
Mont.Rep. Montriou's Reports, Supreme Court (Bengal, India) 1846
Mont.Rev.Code Ann. Montana Revised Code Annotated
Mont.S.O. Montagu, Set-Off. 2ed. 1828
Mont.Sp.L. Montesquieu's Spirit of Laws

Mont.Super. Montreal Law Reports, Superior Court
Mont.& A. Montagu & Ayrton's Bankruptcy Reports. 1833–8
Mont.& Ayr. Montagu & Ayrton's Bankruptcy Reports. 1833–8
Mont.& Ayr.B.L. Montagu & Ayrton on the Bankruptcy Laws. 2ed. 1844
Mont.& Ayr.Bankr. Montagu & Ayrton's Bankruptcy Reports. 1833–8
Mont.& B. Montagu & Bligh's Bankruptcy Reports. 1832–3
Mont.& B.Bankr. Montagu & Bligh's Bankruptcy Reports. 1832–3
Mont.& Bl. Montagu & Bligh's Bankruptcy Reports. 1832–3
Mont.& C. Montagu & Chitty's Bankruptcy Reports. 1838–40
Mont.& C.Bankr. Montagu & Chitty's Bankruptcy Reports. 1838–40
Mont.& Ch. Montagu & Chitty's Bankruptcy Reports. 1838–40
Mont.& Chitt. Montagu & Chitty's Bankruptcy Reports. 1838–40
Mont.& M. Montagu & MacArthur's Bankruptcy Reports. 1828–9
Mont.& M.Bankr. Montagu & MacArthur's Bankruptcy Reports. 1828–9
Mont.& MacA. Montagu & MacArthur's Bankruptcy Reports. 1828–9
Montana L.Rev. Montana Law Review. 1940–
Montesq. Montesquieu, Esprit des Lois – Spirit of the Laws
Montg. Montgomery County Law Reporter (Pennsylvania)
Montg.Co.L.R. Montgomery County Law Reporter (Pennsylvania)
Month.J.L. Monthly Journal of Law (USA) 1881
Month.Jur. Monthly Jurist (Bloomington, Ill.) 1877–9
Month.L.Bull.(N.Y.) Monthly Law Bulletin (New York) 1878–83
Month.L.J. Monthly Journal of Law (Washington) 1881
Month.L.M. Monthly Law Magazine. 1838–41
Month.L.Rep. Monthly Law Reporter (Boston) 1838–66
Monthly Law Reports (Can.)
Month.L.Rev. Monthly Law Review (University of Detroit) 1916
Month.Law Bul. Monthly Law Bulletin (New York) 1878–83
Month.Law Rep. Monthly Law Reporter (Boston) 1838–66
Month.Leg.Ex. Monthly Legal Examiner (New York) 1850
Month.Leg.Exam. Monthly Legal Examiner (New York) 1850
Month.Leg.Exam.(N.Y.) Monthly Legal Examiner (New York) 1850
Month.West.Jur. Monthly Western Jurist (USA) 1874–7
Montr. Montriou's Cases of Hindu Law (Bengal, India) 1779–1840
Montriou's Reports, Supreme Court (Bengal, India) 1846
Montriou's Supplement to Morton's Reports
Montr.Cond.Rep. Montreal Condensed Reports
Montr.Leg.N. Montreal Legal News. 1878–97
Montr.Q.B. Montreal Law Reports, Queen's Bench
Montr.Super. Montreal Law Reports, Superior Court
Montreal L.Q.B.(Can.) Montreal Law Reports, Queen's Bench
Montreal L.R.Q.B. Montreal Law Reports, Queen's Bench
Montreal L.R.S.C. Montreal Law Reports, Superior Court
Montreal L.S.C.(Can.) Montreal Law Reports, Superior Court
Moo. Moody's Crown Cases (168–9 ER) 1824–44
E.F. Moore's Privy Council Cases (12–15 ER) 1836–62
Francis Moore's King's Bench Reports (72 ER) 1512–1621
J.B. Moore's Common Pleas Reports (19–29 RR) 1817–27

Moo.A. Moore's Reports (1 Bosanquet & Puller, p. 471ff.) (126 ER) 1796–7

Moo.C.C. Moody's Crown Cases Reserved (168–9 ER) 1824–44

Moo.C.P. Moore's Common Pleas Reports (19–29 RR) 1817–27

Moo.Cr.C. Moody's Crown Cases Reserved (168–9 ER) 1824–44

Moo.F. Francis Moore's King's Bench Reports (72 ER) 1512–1621

Moo.G.C. Moore, The Gorham Case, Privy Council

Moo.Ind.App. Moore's Indian Appeal Cases, Privy Council (18–20 ER) 1836–72

Moo.J.B. Moore's Common Pleas Reports (19–29 RR) 1817–27

Moo.K.B. Moore's King's Bench Reports (72 ER) 1512–1621

Moo.N.S. E.F. Moore's Privy Council Cases, New Series (15–17 ER) 1862–73

Moo.P.C. Moore's Privy Council Cases (12–15 ER) 1836–62

Moo.P.C.C. Moore's Privy Council Cases (12–15 ER) 1836–62

Moo.P.C.C.N.S. Moore's Privy Council Cases, New Series (15–17 ER) 1862–73

Moo.P.C.(N.S.) Moore's Privy Council Cases, New Series (15–17 ER) 1862–73

Moo.P.Cas.N.S. Moore's Privy Council Cases, New Series (15–17 ER) 1862–73

Moo.Sep.Rep. Moore, Separate Report of Westerton v. Liddell

Moo.Tr. Moore's Divorce Trials

Moo.& M. Moody & Malkin's Nisi Prius Reports (173 ER) 1826–30

Moo.& Mal. Moody & Malkin's Nisi Prius Reports (173 ER) 1826–30

Moo.& P. Moore & Payne's Common Pleas Reports (29–33 RR) 1827–31

Moo.& Pay. Moore & Payne's Common Pleas Reports (29–33 RR) 1827–31

Moo.& R. Moody & Robinson's Nisi Prius Reports (174 ER) 1831–44

Moo.& Rob. Moody & Robinson's Nisi Prius Reports (174 ER) 1831–44

Moo.& S. Moore & Scott's Common Pleas Reports (34–8 RR) 1831–34

Moo.& Sc. Moore & Scott's Common Pleas Reports (34–8 RR) 1831–34

Mood. Moody's Crown Cases Reserved (168–9 ER) 1824–44

Mood.C.C. Moody's Crown Cases Reserved (168–9 ER) 1824–44

Mood.& M. Moody & Malkin's Nisi Prius Reports (173 ER) 1826–30

Mood.& Malk. Moody & Malkin's Nisi Prius Reports (173 ER) 1826–30

Mood.& R. Moody & Robinson's Nisi Prius Reports (174 ER) 1831–44

Mood.& Rob. Moody & Robinson's Nisi Prius Reports (174 ER) 1831–44

Moody Moody's Crown Cases Reserved (168–9 ER) 1824–44

Moody C.C. Moody's Crown Cases Reserved (168–9 ER) 1824–44

Moody Cr.C. Moody's Crown Cases Reserved (168–9 ER) 1824–44

Moody & M. Moody & Malkin's Nisi Prius Reports (173 ER) 1826–30

Moody & R. Moody & Robinson's Nisi Prius Reports (174 ER) 1831–44

Moon Moon's Appeals Reports (6–14 Indiana Appeals)
Moon's Supreme Court Reports (133–144 Indiana)

Moore Moore's Common Pleas Reports (19–29 RR) 1817–27
Moore's King's Bench Reports (72 ER) 1512–1621
Moore's Privy Council Reports (12–15 ER) 1836–62
Moore's Reports (67 Alabama)
Moore's Reports (28–34 Arkansas)
Moore's Reports (22–24 Texas)

Moore A. Moore's Reports (1 Bosanquet & Puller p. 471ff.) (126 ER) 1796–7

Moore Abs. Moore, Abstracts of Title. 6ed. 1925

Moore, Adjudications J.B. Moore, International Adjudications, Ancient and Modern, 1929–36

Moore, Arbitrations J.B. Moore, History and Digest of the International

Arbitrations to which the United States has been a Party. 1898

Moore C.P. Moore's Common Pleas Reports (19–29 RR) 1817–27

Moore, Digest J.B.Moore, A Digest of International Law. 1906

Moore E.I. Moore's East India Appeals. 1836–72

Moore G.C. Moore, The Gorham Case, Privy Council

Moore Ind.App. Moore's Indian Appeal Cases (18–20 ER) 1836–72

Moore K.B. Moore's King's Bench Reports (72 ER) 1512–1621

Moore P.C. Moore's Privy Council Cases (12–15 ER) 1836–62

Moore P.C.C. Moore's Privy Council Cases (12–15 ER) 1836–62

Moore P.C.C.N.S. Moore's Privy Council Cases, New Series (15–17 ER) 1862–73

Moore P.C.N.S. Moore's Privy Council Cases, New Series (15–17 ER) 1862–73

Moore Q.B. Moore's Queen's Bench Reports (72 ER) 1512–1621

Moore & P. Moore & Payne's Common Pleas Reports (29–33 RR) 1827–31

Moore & S. Moore & Scott's Common Pleas Reports (34–8 RR) 1831–4

Moore & W. Moore & Walker's Reports (22–24 Texas)

Moore & Walker Moore & Walker's Reports (22–24 Texas)

Moot Ct.Bull. University of Illinois Moot Court Bulletin. 1902–26

Mor. Morison's Dictionary of Decisions in the Court of Session (Scot.) 1540–1808
Morris's Reports (Jamaica) 1836–44

Mor.Chy.Acts Morgan, Chancery Acts and Orders. 6ed. 1885

Mor.Dic. Morison's Dictionary of Decisions (Scot.) 1540–1808

mor.dict. more dicto (Lat.) in the manner directed

Mor.Dict. Morison's Dictionary of Decisions (Scot.) 1540–1808

Mor.Dig. Morley, Digest of the Indian Reports
Morrison, New Hampshire Digest

Mor.Dil. Morris, Dilapidations. 2ed. 1871

Mor.E.& R.D.Law Morice, English and Roman Dutch Law

Mor.Ia. Morris's Iowa Reports. 1839–46

Mor.Min.Rep. Morrison's Mining Reports (USA) 1749–1906

Mor.Miss. Morris' Reports (43–48 Mississippi)

Mor.St.Cas. Morris' State Cases (Mississippi) 1818–72

Mor.Supp. Morison's Dictionary of Court of Session Decisions, Supplement (Scot.) 1620–1768

Mor.Syn. Morison's Synopsis, Session Cases (Scot.) 1808–16

Mor.Tran. Morrison's Transcript of United States Supreme Court Decisions

Mor.& Carl. Moreau–Lislet & Carleton's Laws of Las Siete Partidas in force in Louisiana

More Lect. More, Lectures on the Law of Scotland

More St. More, Notes on Stair's Institutions of Scotland

Morg.Ch. Morgan, Chancery Acts and Orders. 6ed. 1885

Morg.& W.L.J. Morgan & Williams, Law Journal. 1803–4

Morgan Morgan's Ceylon Digest (Sri L.)

Morgan L.M. Morgan's Legal Miscellany (Sri L.)

Morl.Dig. Morley's East Indian Digest of Supreme Court Cases

Morr. Morrell's Bankruptcy Reports. 1884–93
Morris' Iowa Reports. 1839–46
Morris' Reports (5 California)
Morris' Reports (Jamaica) 1836–44
Morris' Reports (23–26 Oregon)
Morris' Sudder Dewanny Adawlut Reports (Bombay, India) 1847–54

Morr.B.C. Morrell's Bankruptcy Reports. 1884–93

Morr.Bankr.Cas. Morrell's Bankruptcy Reports. 1884–93

Morr.Bomb. Morris' Sudder Dewanny Adawlut Reports (Bombay, India) 1847–54

Morr.Cal. Morris' Reports (5 California)

Morr.Dig. Morrison, Digest of Mining Decisions (USA)
Morrison, New Hampshire Digest

Morr.(Jam.) Morris' Reports (Jamaica) 1836–44

Morr.M.R. Morrison's Mining Reports (USA) 1749–1906

Morr.Min.R. Morrison's Mining Reports (USA) 1749–1906,

Morr.Mines Morrison, Digest of Mining Decisions (USA)

Morr.Miss. Morris' Reports (43–48 Mississippi)

Morr.St.Cas. Morris' State Cases (Mississippi) 1818–72

Morr.Supp. Supplement to Morrison's Dictionary, Court of Session (Scot.) 1620–1768

Morr.Trans. Morrison's Transcript of United States Supreme Court Decisions

Morrell B.C. Morrell's Bankruptcy cases. 1884–93

Morris Morris' Reports (5 California)
Morris' Reports (Iowa) 1839–46
Morris' Reports (Jamaica) 1836–44
Morris' Reports (43–48 Mississippi)
Morris' Reports (23–26 Oregon)
Morris' Sudder Dewanny Adawlut Reports (Bombay, India) 1847–54
Morrissett's Reports (80, 98 Alabama)

Morris R. Morris's Reports (Jamaica) 1836–44

Morris & Har. Morris & Harrington's Sudder Dewanny Adawlut Reports (Bombay, India) 1854–62

Morse Bk. Morse on the Law of Banks and Banking

Morse Exch.Rep. Morse's Exchequer Reports (Can.)

Morse Tr. Morse's Famous Trials

mort. mortgage

Mort.Vend. Morton, Vendors and Purchasers. 1837

Morton Morton's Supreme Court Reports (Bengal, India) 1776–1841

Morton Commission Royal Commission on Marriage and Divorce. Report (Cmd. 9678) 1955–6

Mos. Moseley's Chancery Reports (25 ER) 1726–31

Mos.Cont. Moseley, Contraband of War. 1861

Mos.El.L. Moseley, Elementary Law. 2ed. 1878

Moseley Moseley's Chancery Reports (25 ER) 1726–31

Moult.Ch. Moulton's Chancery Practice (New York)

Moult.Ch.P. Moulton's Chancery Practice (New York)

Mow.St. Mowbray, Styles of Deeds

Moyle Moyle's Criminal Circulars (India)
Moyle's Entries. 1658

Moz.& W. Mozley & Whiteley's Law Dictionary

Mozley & Whiteley Mozley & Whiteley's Law Dictionary

Mq.L. Marquette Law Review (USA) 1916–

Mq.L.R. Marquette Law Review (USA) 1916–

Mqs. Marquess

Mr Meester in de rechten (Neth.) Law graduate

ms. manuscript

Ms. Mississippi

Ms.D. Manuscript Decisions, Commissioner of Patents (USA)
Manuscript Decisions, Comptroller General (USA)

Ms.L.J. Mississippi Law Journal. 1928–

Ms.U.C. Unpublished manuscripts of Jeremy Bentham, University College, London

Msc. New York Miscellaneous Reports. 1892–

Msc.2d. New York Miscellaneous Reports, Second Series

mss. manuscripts
Mt. Montana
Montana Reports (Supreme Court) 1868–
Mt.L.R. Montana Law Review. 1940–
mtg. meeting
mortgage
mtgee. mortgagee
mtgor. mortgagor
mthly. monthly
Mu.Corp.Ca. Municipal Corporation Cases (USA) 1894–1903
Mu.Corp.Cir. Municipal Corporations Circular (USA) 1878–1929
Mu.L.J. Municipal Law Journal (USA) 1936–
Muir.Gai. Muirhead, Institutes of Gaius
Mult.Bus. Multinational Business
Mum.Jam. Mumford's Reports (Jamaica) 1838
Mumf. Mumford's Reports (Jamaica) 1838
Mun. Munford's Virginia Reports (15–20 Va.) 1810–20
Municipal
Municipal Law Reporter (Pennsylvania) 1909–
Municipal Law Reports (Scot.) 1903–13
Municipal Reports (Can.) 1845–51
Munitions Appeal Reports. 1916–20
Mun.App. Munitions Appeal Reports. 1916–20
Mun.App.Rep. Munitions Appeal Reports. 1916–20
Mun.App.Sc. Munitions of War Acts, Scottish Appeal Reports. 1916–20
Mun.Code Municipal Code
Mun.Corp.Cas. Municipal Corporation Cases (USA) 1894–1903
Mun.Ct. Municipal Court
Mun.L.Ct.Dec. Municipal Law Court Decisions
Mun.L.J. Municipal Law Journal (USA) 1936–
Mun.L.R. Municipal Law Reporter (Pennsylvania) 1909–
Municipal Law Reports (Scot.) 1903–13
Mun.Ord.Rev. Municipal Ordinance Review (USA) 1948–
Mun.Rep. Municipal Reports (Can.) 1845–51
Mun.& El.Cas. Municipal and Election Cases (India) 1934–
Mundy Mundy's Abstracts of Star Chamber Proceedings. 1550–58
Munf. Munford's Reports (15–20 Virginia) 1810–20
Munf.(Va.) Munford's Reports (15–20 Virginia) 1810–20
Munic. Municipal
Munic.L.R.(Pa.) Municipal Law Reporter (Pennsylvania) 1909–
Munk.Emp.Liab. Munkman, Employer's Liability at Common Law
Mur. Murphey's North Carolina Reports (5–7 NC) 1804–19
Murray's Ceylon Reports (Sri L.) 1846–7
Murray's Jury Court Cases (Scot.) 1815–30
Murray's New South Wales Reports (Aus.)
Mur.Tab.Cas. Murray, Table of United States Cases
Mur.U.S.Ct. Murray's Proceedings in the United States Courts
Mur.& H. Murphy & Hurlstone's Exchequer Reports (51 RR) 1836–7
Mur.& Hurl. Murphy & Hurlstone's Exchequer Reports (51 RR) 1836–7
Murd.Epit. Murdoch's Epitome (Can.)
Murp.& H. Murphy & Hurlstone's Exchequer Reports (51 RR) 1836–7
Murph. Murphey's North Carolina Reports (5–7 NC) 1804–19
Murph.(N.C.) Murphey's North Carolina Reports (5–7 NC) 1804–19
Murph.& H. Murphy & Hurlstone's Exchequer Reports (51 RR) 1836–7
Murr. Murray's Ceylon Reports (Sri L.) 1846–7
Murray's Jury Court Cases (Scot.) 1815–30
Murray's Laws and Acts of Parliament (Scot.)

Murray's New South Wales Reports (Aus.)

Murr.Over.Cas. Murray's Overruled Cases

Murray Murray's Jury Court Cases (Scot.) 1815–30

Murray (Ceylon) Murray's Ceylon Reports (Sri L.) 1846–7

Murray (Scot.) Murray's Jury Court Cases (Scot.) 1815–30

Mus.Helv. Museum Helveticum: Schweizerische Zeitschrift fur klassisches Altertumswissenschaft (Switz.)

Mut. Mutual
Mutukisna's Ceylon Reports (Sri L.)

Mutukisna Mutukisna's Ceylon Reports (Sri L.)

My. All India Reporter, Mysore. 1950–
Maatschappij (Neth.) Company

My.L.J. Mysore Law Journal (India) 1923–51

My.& C. Mylne & Craig's Chancery Reports (40–1 ER) 1835–41

My.& Cr. Mylne & Craig's Chancery Reports (40–1 ER) 1835–41

My.& K. Mylne & Keen's Chancery Reports (39–40 ER) 1832–5

Myer Dig. Myer's Texas Digest

Myer Fed.Dec. Myer's Federal Decisions (USA)

Myl.& C. Mylne & Craig's Chancery Reports (40–1 ER) 1835–41

Myl.& Cr. Mylne & Craig's Chancery Reports (40–1 ER) 1835–41

Myl.& K. Mylne & Keen's Chancery Reports (39–40 ER) 1832–5

Mylne & K. Mylne & Keen's Chancery Reports (39–40 ER) 1832–5

Myr. Myrick's California Probate Court Reports. 1872–9

Myr.Prob. Myrick's California Probate Court Reports. 1872–9

Myrick (Cal.) Myrick's California Probate Court Reports. 1872–9

Myrick Prob.(Cal.) Myrick's California Probate Court Reports. 1872–9

Mys. All India Reporter, Mysore. 1950–

Mys.Ch.Ct. Mysore Chief Court Reports (India)

Mys.H.C.R. Mysore High Court Reports (India)

Mys.Ind. Mysore, India

Mys.L.J. Mysore Law Journal (India) 1923–51

Mys.L.R. Mysore Law Reports (India) 1878–

Mys.R.(R.) Mysore Reports (Reprint) (India) 1878–1923

Mys.W.N. Mysore Weekly Notes (India) 1891–2

Mysore Indian Law Reports, Mysore Series. 1953–

N

n. footnote
note
number

N. All India Reporter, Nagpur. 1914–57
Name
Nebraska
Nevada
Newfoundland
North
Northern
Northeastern Reporter (USA)
Northern Ireland Law Reports. 1925–
Northwestern Reporter (USA)
Note
South African Law Reports, Natal Province Divsion. 1910–46

N.A. Nizamut Adawlut Reports (India)
Nonacquiescence

N.A.A. National Academy of Arbitrators (USA)

N.A.C. Native Appeal Cases (S.Afr.) 1894–1929
Noise Advisory Council

N.A.C.A.B. National Association of Citizens' Advice Bureaux

N.A.C.(C.) Selected Decisions of the Native Appeal Court (Central Division) (S.Afr.) 1948–51

NACCALJ National Association of Claimants' Compensation Attorneys Law Journal. 1948–

N.A.C.(C.& O.) Reports of the Decisions of the Native Appeal Courts, Cape Province & the Orange Free State (S.Afr.) 1929–

N.A.C.L. North American Commercial Law. 1986–

N.A.C.M. National Association of Credit Management

N.A.C.(N.E.) Decisions of the Native Appeal Court (North Eastern Division) (S.Afr.) 1948–51

N.A.C.(N.& T.) Decisions of the Native Appeal and Divorce Court (Transvaal and Natal) (S.Afr.) 1929–48

N.A.C.R.O. National Association for the Care and Resettlement of Offenders

N.A.C.R.(S.R) Native Appeal Court Reports (Southern Rhodesia) 1928–

N.A.C.(S.) Selected Decisions of the Native Appeal Court (Southern Division) (S.Afr.) 1948–51

N.A.C.(T.& N.) Reports of the Decisions of the Native Appeal Courts, Transvaal and Natal (S.Afr.) 1929–48

N.A.C.& O. Reports of the Decisions of the Native Appeal Courts, Cape Province & the Orange Free State (S.Afr.) 1929–

NAG. Bundesgesetz betreffend die zivilrechtlichen Verhaltnisse der Niedergelassen und Aufenthalter (Switz.)

N.A.I. Nederlands Arbitrage Instituut (Netherlands Arbitration Institute)

N.A.L.G.O. National and Local Government Officers' Association

N.A.L.L. Nigerian Association of Law Librarians

N.A.L.N. Native Authority Legal Notice (N. Nigeria) 1958–

N.A.L.T. Nigerian Association of Law Teachers

N.A.M.L.Dig. National Association of Manufacturers Law Digest (USA)

NAO National Audit Office
NAPF National Association of Pension Funds
N.A.P.N. Native Authority Public Notice (Nigeria) up to 1953
N.A.P.O. National Association of Probation Officers
NASA National Aeronautics and Space Agency (USA)
NASD National Association of Securities Dealers (USA)
NASPyC National Association of Solicitors' Property Centres
N.A.So.Rhod. Southern Rhodesia Native Appeal Court Reports
NAT Nordisk administrativt tidsskrift (Den.) 1924–
North Atlantic Treaty
N.A.T.O. North Atlantic Treaty Organisation
NATOS Agreement to the Status of the NATO National Representatives and International Staff. 1951
NATOSF Agreement between the Parties to the North Atlantic Treaty regarding the Status of their Forces. 1963
N.A.T.& N. Selected Decisions of the Native Appeal Court (Transvaal & Natal) (S.Afr.)
N.A.& D.,C.& O. Native Appeal and Divorce Court Decisions, Cape and Orange Free State (S.Afr.)
N.A.& D.,T.& N. Native Appeal and Divorce Court Decisions, Transvaal and Natal (S.Afr.)
N.Ar.Z. Neue Zeitschrift für Arbeits- und Sozialrecht (Ger.)
N.Atlantic Reg.Bus.L.Rev. North Atlantic Regional Business Law Review
N.B. New Benloe or Bendloe King's Bench Reports (73 ER) 1531–1628
New Brunswick, Canada
New Brunswick Reports (Can.) 1825–1929
N.B.2d. New Brunswick Reports, 2nd Series (Can.)
NBEET National Board for Employment, Education and Training (Aus.)
N.B.Eq. New Brunswick Equity Reports (Can.) 1894–1911
N.B.Eq.Ca. New Brunswick Equity Reports (Can.) 1894–1911
N.B.Eq.R. New Brunswick Equity Reports (Can.) 1894–1911
N.B.Eq.Rep. New Brunswick Equity Reports (Can.) 1894–1911
N.B.J. National Bar Journal (USA) 1941–51
New Brunswick Judgments (unreported decisions available on QL) (Can.) 1986–
Nigerian Bar Journal. 1958–
N.B.L.B. Nebraska Law Bulletin
N.B.L.R. National Banking Law Review (Can.) 1982–
North Borneo Law Reports
N.B.N.R. National Bankruptcy News and Reports (USA) 1898–1901
N.B.N.Rep. National Bankruptcy News and Reports (USA) 1898–1901
N.B.R. National Bankruptcy Register Reports (USA) 1868–82
National Business Review (N.Z.) 1970–
New Brunswick Reports. 1825–1929
N.B.R.2d. New Brunswick Reports, 2nd Series (Can.)
N.B.R.All. Allen's New Brunswick Reports (Can.) 1848–66
N.B.R.Ber. Berton's New Brunswick Reports (Can,) 1835–9
N.B.R.Carl. Carleton's New Brunswick Reports (Can.) 1895–1902
N.B.R.Chip. Chipman's New Brunswick Reports (Can.) 1825–38
N.B.R.Han. Hannay's New Brunswick Reports (Can.) 1867–71
N.B.R.Kerr Kerr's New Brunswick Reports (Can.) 1840–8
N.B.R.P.& B. Pugsley & Burbridge's New Brunswick Reports (Can.) 1878–82
N.B.R.P.& T. Pugsley & Trueman's New Brunswick Reports (Can.) 1882–3
N.B.R.Pug. Pugsley's New Brunswick Reports (Can.) 1876–93

N.B.R.Pugs. Pugsley's New Brunswick Reports (Can.) 1876–93

N.B.R.Tru. Trueman's New Brunswick Reports (Can.) 1876–93

N.B.Rep. New Brunswick Reports (Can.) 1825–1929

N.B.Rev.Stat. New Brunswick Revised Statutes (Can.)

N.B.S. National Bureau of Standards (USA)

N.B.Stat. New Brunswick Statutes (Can.)

N.B.V.Ad. New Brunswick Vice Admiralty Reports

N.Ben. New Benloe's Reports, King's Bench (73 ER) 1531–1628

N.Benl. New Benloe's Reports, King's Bench (73 ER) 1531–1628

N.Bruns. New Brunswick Reports (Can.) 1825–1929

N.C. Bingham's New Cases, Common Pleas (131–3 ER) 1834–40
North Carolina
North Carolina Supreme Court Reports. 1868–
Northern Cape Division (S.Afr.)
Notes of Cases (Ecclesiastical & Maritime) ed. Thornton. 1841–50
Strange's Notes of Cases (Madras, India) 1798–1816

N.C.A. No copies available
North Carolina Court of Appeals Reports. 1968–

NCAIR National Center for Automated Information Retrieval (USA)

NCAJ National Center for Administrative Justice (USA)

N.C.Adv.Legis.Serv. North Carolina Advance Legislative Service

N.C.App. North Carolina Court of Appeals Reports. 1968–

N.C.B. National Children's Bureau
National Coal Board

NCBF North Carolina Bar Foundation

N.C.C. National Consumer Council
Young & Collyer's Chancery Reports (New Chancery Cases) (62–3 ER) 1841–4

N.C.C.A.N.S. Negligence and Compensation Cases Annotated, New Series

NCCD National Council on Crime and Delinquency News (USA) 1960–72

N.C.C.D.L. National College of Criminal Defense Lawyers and Public Defenders (USA)

N.C.C.L. National Council for Civil Liberties

N.C.Cent.L.J. North Carolina Central Law Journal

N.C.Conf. North Carolina Conference Reports. 1800–4

N.C.Conf.Rep. North Carolina Conference Reports. 1800–4

N.C.D. Nemine contra dicente (Lat.) no one dissenting

N.C.Ecc. Notes of Cases in Ecclesiastical and Maritime Courts. 1841–50

N.C.F.A. National Consumers' Finance Association
National Consumers' Finance Association Bulletin

N.C.Gen.Stat. General Statutes of North Carolina

NCHP Nederlandse Centrale voor Hoger Personeel (Dutch Centre of Higher Ranked Personnel)

NCIC National Crime Information Center (USA)

NCJCJ National Council of Juvenile Court Judges (USA)

N.C.J.Int'l L.& Com.Reg. The North Carolina Journal of International Law and Commercial Regulation

NCJJ National College of Juvenile Justice (USA)

N.C.J.of L. North Carolina Journal of Law. 1904–5

N.C.L. National Central Library
North Carolina Law Review. 1922–

NCLE Nebraska Continuing Legal Education Inc.

N.C.L.J. North Carolina Law Journal. 1900–2

N.C.L.Rep. North Carolina Law Repository

N.C.L.Rev. North Carolina Law Review. 1922–
N.C.Law Repos. North Carolina Law Repository
N.C.M. Court-Martial Reports, Navy Cases (USA)
N.C.O.P.F. National Council for One Parent Families
N.C.P.S. Non-contributory Pension Scheme
NCR National Cash Register
N.C.S.A. Newsletter of the Copyright Society of Australia. 1981–3
N.C.S.C. National Companies and Securities Commission (Aus.)
N.C.S.C.Man. National Companies and Securities Commission Manual (Aus.) 1981–
NCSJ National College of the State Judiciary (USA)
N.C.S.S. National Council of Social Science
N.C.Sess.Laws Session Laws of North Carolina
N.C.Str. Strange's Notes of Cases (Madras, India) 1798–1816
N.C.T.Rep. North Carolina Term Reports (4 NC) 1816–18
N.C.Term R. North Carolina Term Reports (4 NC) 1816–18
N.C.Term Rep. North Carolina Term Reports (4 NC) 1816–18
N.C.U.M.C. National Council for the Unmarried Mother and her Child
NCV No commercial value
N.C.V.O. National Council for Voluntary Organisations
NCW Nederlands Christelijk Werkgeversverbond (Netherlands Federation of Christian Employers)
N.Car. North Carolina
N.Car.Central L.J. North Carolina Central Law Journal
N.Cent.School L.Rev. North Central School Law Review (USA)
N.Ch.R. H. Finch's Chancery Reports (23 ER) 1673–81
Nelson's Chancery Reports (21 ER) 1625–93
N.Chip. N. Chipman's Reports (Vermont) 1789–91
N.Chip.(Vt.) N. Chipman's Reports (Vermont) 1789–91
N.Chipm. N. Chipman's Reports (Vermont) 1789–91
N.Cr. New York Criminal Reports
N.Ct. Native Court (Ghana)
n.d. no date
N.D. Nordiske Domme i Sjofartsanliggender (Nordic Shipowners' Association publication, Oslo)
North Dakota
North Dakota Supreme Court Reports. 1890–1953
NDAA National District Attorneys' Association (USA)
N.D.B.B. North Dakota Bar Brief. 1948–50
N.D.Cent.Code North Dakota Century Code
NDI Novissimo Digesto italiano
N.D.L. Notre Dame Lawyer (USA) 1925–
N.D.L.R. North Dakota Law Review. 1951–
N.D.L.Rev. North Dakota Law Review. 1951–
N.D.Sess.Laws Laws of North Dakota
N.E. New Edition
New England
Northeastern Reporter (USA)
N.E.2d. Northeastern Reporter, Second Series
N.E.B. National Enterprise Board
N.E.C. National Exhibition Centre
Notes of Ecclesiastical Cases
N.E.D. New English Dictionary
N.E.D.C. National Economic Development Council
N.E.D.O. National Economic Development Office
N.E.I. Non est inventus (Lat.) he is not found
NEP New Economic Policy (USSR)
NEPB National Environment

Protection Board (Swed.) Statens naturvårdsverk

N.E.R. New England Reporter (Can.)
North Eastern Reporter (USA)

N.E.R.C. National Environment Research Council

N.E.Rep. New England Reporter (Can.)
North Eastern Reporter (USA)

n.e.s. not elsewhere specified (tariffs)

N.Eng.L.Rev. New England Law Review (Can.) 1969–

N.Eng.Rep. New England Reporter (Can.)

n.F. neu Folge (Ger.) new series

N.F. Newfoundland
Newfoundland Law Reports. 1817–1949

N.-F. Norman–French

N.F.C.G. National Federation of Consumer Groups

N.F.H.A. National Federation of Housing Associations

NGOs Non-Governmental Organisations

N.H. New Hampshire
New Hampshire Supreme Court Reports. 1816–

N.H.B.J. New Hampshire Bar Journal

N.H.B.R.C. National House-Builders Registration Council

N.H.C. Native High Court Reports (S.Afr.)
Reports of the Decisions of the Natal Native High Court (S.Afr.)

N.H.J. New Hampshire Bar Journal. 1958–

N.H.L.Rep. New Hampshire Law Reporter. 1897

N.H.Laws Laws of the State of New Hampshire

N.H.R. New Hampshire Reports. 1816–

N.H.Rev.Stat.Ann. New Hampshire Revised Statutes Annotated

N.H.S. National Health Service

N.H.& C. Nicholl, Hare & Carrow's Railway and Canal Cases. 1835–54

N.Hamp.S.B.A. New Hampshire State Bar Association

N.I. Northern Ireland
Northern Ireland Law Reports. 1925–

N.I.A.C. National Insurance Advisory Committee

N.I.A.L.S. Nigerian Institute of Advanced Legal Studies

N.I.C. National Insurance Commissioner
National Insurance Contribution

N.I.C.B. National Industrial Conference Board

N.I.C.R.A. Northern Ireland Civil Rights Association

N.I.C.S. Northern Ireland Court Service

N.I.D.L.R. Office of the Director of Law Reform, Northern Ireland

NIEO New International Economic Order

NIESR National Institute of Economic and Social Research

N.I.J. New Irish Jurist Reports. 1900–5

N.I.J.B. Northern Ireland Judgment Bulletin

N.I.J.R. New Irish Jurist Reports. 1900–5

NILECJ National Institute of Law Enforcement and Criminal Justice (USA)

N.I.L.Q. Northern Ireland Legal Quarterly. 1951–

N.I.L.R. Netherlands International Law Review. 1953–
Northern Ireland Law Reports. 1925–

N.I.L.Rev. Netherlands International Law Review. 1953–

N.I.O.C. National Iranian Oil Company

N.I.R. National Insolvency Review (Can.) 1983–

N.I.R.C. National Industrial Relations Court

NITA National Institute for Trial Advocacy (USA)

N.I.T.M. National Income Tax Magazine (USA) 1923–30

N.Ill.U.L.Rev. Northern Illinois University Law Review

N.Ir. Northern Ireland

N.Ir.L.Q. Northern Ireland Legal Quarterly. 1951–

N.Ir.L.R. Northern Ireland Law Reports. 1925–
N.Ir.Legal Q. Northern Ireland Legal Quarterly. 1951–
NJ Neue Justiz (Ger.) 1947–
Nederlandse Jurisprudentie (Neth.) law reports. 1913–
N.J. New Jersey
New Jersey Supreme Court Reports. 1948–
Newfoundland Judgments (unreported decisions available on QL) (Can.) 1986–
NJA Nyt juridisk archiv (Den.) 1812–20
Nytt Juridiskt Arkiv (Swed.) Annual Supreme Court Reporter. 1874–
NJ(A) Nederlandse Jurisprudentie (Administratiefrechtelijke Beslissingen) (Neth.) law reports. 1913–
NJA II Nytt Juridisk Arkiv, Avd. II (Swed.) The Annual Digest of Legislative Preparatory Materials. 1876–
N.J.B. Nederlands Juristenblad (Neth.) 1926–
NJCLE New Jersey Institute for Continuing Legal Education
NJCM Bulletin Nederlands Juristen Comite voor de Mensenrechten Bulletin
N.J.Eq. New Jersey Equity Reports. 1830–1948
N.J.L. New Jersey Law Reports. 1790–1948
N.J.L.J. New Jersey Law Journal. 1878–
N.J.L.Rev. New Jersey Law Review. 1915, 1916, 1935–6
N.J.Law New Jersey Law Reports. 1790–1948
N.J.Law J. New Jersey Law Journal. 1878–
N.J.Law N. New Jersey Law News. 1935
N.J.Laws Laws of New Jersey
N.J.Lawy. New Jersey Lawyer. 1935–6
N.J.Leg.Rec. New Jersey Legal Record. 1931–2
NJM New Jersey Miscellaneous Reports. 1923–49
N.J.Misc. New Jersey Miscellaneous Reports. 1923–49
NJ(O) Nederlandse Jurisprudentie (Onteigning) (Neth.) 1913–
N.J.Re.Tit.N. New Jersey Realty Title News. 1944
N.J.Rev.Stat. New Jersey Revised Statutes
N.J.S. New Jersey Superior Court Reports. 1948–
N.J.S.A. New Jersey Statutes Annotated
N.J.S.B.A. New Jersey State Bar Association
N.J.S.B.A.Q. New Jersey State Bar Association Quarterly. 1934–7
N.J.S.B.J. New Jersey State Bar Journal
N.J.S.B.T.A.Ops. New Jersey State Board of Tax Appeals, Opinions
N.J.Sess.Law Serv. New Jersey Session Law Service
N.J.St.B.J. New Jersey State Bar Journal
N.J.Stat.Ann.(West) New Jersey Statutes Annotated (West Pub. Co.)
N.J.Super. New Jersey Superior Court Reports. 1948–
NJU Nyt juridisk ugeskrift (Den.) 1869–75
N.J.V. Nederlandse Juristenvereniging (Neth.) Netherlands Lawyers Association
NJW Neue Juristische Wochenschrift (Ger.) 1947–
N.Ky.L.Rev. Northern Kentucky Law Review
N.L. Nelson's Lutwyche's Common Pleas Reports. 1682–1704
N.L.B. Nuclear Law Bulletin (O.E.C.D.) 1968–
N.L.C.D. National Liberation Council Decree (Ghana) 1966–9
NLCPI National Legal Center for the Public Interest (USA)
NLF National Law Foundation (USA)
N.L.G.Q. National Lawyers' Guild Quarterly (USA)

N.L.J. Nagpur Law Journal (India) 1918–
New Law Journal. 1965–
N.L.J.Rep. New Law Journal Reports
N.L.L. National Lending Library
New Library of Law (Harrisburg, Pennsylvania)
New Library of Law and Equity
N.L.Q. Nigeria Lawyers' Quarterly. 1964–
N.L.Q.R. Nigeria Law Quarterly Review. 1946–7
N.L.R. Nagpur Law Reports (India) 1904–36
Natal Law Reports (S.Afr.) 1879–1910
New Law Reports (Sri L.) 1874–
Newfoundland Law Reports (Can.) 1817–1949
Nigeria Law Reports. 1881–1955
Nyasaland Law Reports. 1922–
South African Law Reports, Natal Province Division. 1910–46
N.L.R.B. National Labor Relations Board Decisons and Orders (USA) 1935–
N.L.R.B.Dec. National Labor Relations Board Decisions and Orders (USA) 1935–
N.L.R.(O.S.) Natal Law Reports, Old Series (S.Afr.) 1867–72
N.L.Rev. Northeastern Law Review (USA) 1951–
N.M. New Mexico
New Mexico Supreme Court Reports. 1890–
NMA J. le Neve, Monumenta Anglicana. 1717–19
NMCLE Continuing Legal Education of New Mexico Inc.
N.M.(G.) New Mexico Reports (Gildersleeve) 1852–89
N.M.G.C. National Marriage Guidance Council
N.M.(J.) New Mexico Reports (Johnson) 1883–6, 1887–9
N.M.L. New Mexico Law Review. 1971–
N.M.L.R. New Mexico Law Review. 1971–
Nigerian Monthly Law Reports. 1964–5
N.M.L.Rev. New Mexico Law Review. 1971–
N.M.Laws Laws of New Mexico
N.M.S.B.A. New Mexico State Bar Association
N.M.St.Bar Assn. New Mexico State Bar Association
N.M.Stat.Ann. New Mexico Statutes Annotated
N.Mag.Ca. New Magistrates' Cases
N.Mex.L.Rev. New Mexico Law Review. 1971–
N.N.C.N. Northern Nigeria Cases Notes
N.N.H.C. Natal Native High Court Reports (S.Afr.) 1899–1915
N.N.L.N. Northern Nigeria Legal Notes
N.N.L.R. Northern Nigeria Law Reports. 1962–4
Northern Region Law Reports (Nigeria) 1956–
N.N.P.D. Nabarro Nathanson: The Pension Dimension
NO Näringsfrihetsombudsman (Swed.) Antitrust Commissioner
N.O.H.S.C. National Occupational Health and Safety Commission (Aus.)
NOTO Non-Official Trade Organisation
N.O.V. Non Obstate Veredicto (Lat.) the judgment not withstanding
N.of Cas. Notes of Cases in the Ecclesiastical and Maritime Courts. 1841–50
Strange's Notes of Cases (Madras, India) 1798–1816
N.of Cas.Madras Strange's Notes of Cases (Madras, India) 1798–1816
n.p. not printed
N.P. New Practice
Nisi Prius
Northern Perspectives (Can.)
Notary Public
Nova Placita
Ohio Nisi Prius Reports. 1893–1901

N.P.C. New Practice Cases, Bail Court. 1844–8
New Property Cases
Nisi Prius Cases

N.P.D. South African Law Reports, Natal Province Division. 1910–46

N.P.L.R. Nyasaland Protectorate Law Reports. 1922

N.P.N.S. Ohio Nisi Prius Reports, New Series. 1902–34

N.P.Ohio Ohio Nisi Prius Reports. 1893–1901

NPP National Physical Planning (Swed.) Fysisk riksplanering

N.P.P.A.J. National Probation and Parole Association Journal (USA)

N.P.R. Ohio Nisi Prius Reports. 1893–1901

N.P.& G.T.Rep. Nisi Prius and General Term Reports (Ohio)

N.R. Bosanquet & Puller's New Reports (127 ER) 1804–7
Natal Law Reports (S.Afr.) 1873–1910
National Reporter (Can.) 1974–
New Reports. 1862–5
Northern Region
Northern Rhodesia

N.R.A.B. National Railroad Adjustment Board (USA) 1934–

N.R.B.P. Bosanquet & Puller's New Reports (127 ER) 1804–7

N.R.C.D. National Redemption Council Decree (Ghana) 1972–5

NRCLS National Resource Center for Consumers of Legal Services (USA)

N.R.D. Notes of Recent Decisions (Canada Immigration Board) 1979–

N.R.D.C. National Research Development Corporation

N.R.G. Northern Rhodesia Gazette. 1911–
Nouveau Recueil Général de Traités et autres actes relatifs aux rapports de droit international, by G.F. de Martens

N.R.G.T. Nouveau Recueil Général de Traités et autres actes relatifs aux rapports de droit international, by G.F. de Martens

NRH Nouvelle Revue Historique de droit français et étranger (Fr.) 1877

N.R.L.N. Northern Region Legal Notice (Nigeria) 1954–61

N.R.L.R. Northern Rhodesia Law Reports. 1931–55
Northern Region Law Reports (Nigeria) 1956–

N.R.N.L.R. Northern Region of Nigeria Law Reports. 1956–

N.(R.)N.L.R. Northern Region of Nigeria Law Reports. 1956–

N.R.P.B. National Radiological Protection Board

N.R.T. Net Register Ton

N.S. New Series
New Style
Nova Scotia
Nova Scotia Reports (Can.) 1834–1929

N.S.C. New Session Cases by Carrow, Hamerton & Allen (Scot.) 1844–51

N.S.D. Geldert & Oxley's Nova Scotia Decisions (NSR 7–9) (Can.) 1866–75

N.S.Dec. Geldert & Oxley's Nova Scotia Decisions (NSR 7–9) (Can.) 1866–75

NSGT United Nations, Non Self-Governing Territories

N.S.J. Nova Scotia Judgments (unreported decisions available on QL) (Can.) 1986–

N.S.L.R. Nova Scotia Reports (Can.) 1834–1929

N.S.P.C.C. National Society for the Prevention of Cruelty to Children

N.S.R. Nova Scotia Reports (Can.) 1834–1929

N.S.R.2d. Nova Scotia Reports, Second Series (Can.)

N.S.R.Coch. Cochran's Nova Scotia Reports (NSR 4) (Can.) 1859

N.S.R.G.& O. Geldert & Oxley's Nova Scotia Decisions (NSR 7–9) (Can.) 1866–75

N.S.R.G.& R. Geldert & Russell's Nova Scotia Reports (NSR 28–39) 1895–1907, (NSR 41–60) 1907–29

N.S.R.J. James' Nova Scotia Reports (NSR 2) 1853–5

N.S.R.James James' Nova Scotia Reports (NSR 2) 1853–5

N.S.R.Old. Oldright's Nova Scotia Reports (NSR 5, 6) 1860–6

N.S.R.(Old.) Oldright's Nova Scotia Reports (NSR 5, 6) 1860–6

N.S.R.R.& C. Russell & Chesley's Nova Scotia Reports (NSR 10–12) 1875–9

N.S.R.R.& G. Russell & Geldert's Nova Scotia Reports (NSR 13–27) 1879–95

N.S.R.Thom. Thompson's Nova Scotia Reports (NSR 1) 1834–51, (NSR 3) 1856–9

N.S.R.(Thom.) Thompson's Nova Scotia Reports (NSR 1) 1834–51, (NSR 3) 1856–9

N.S.R.Wall. Wallace's Nova Scotia Reports (NSR 6) 1884–1907

N.S.Rep. Nova Scotia Reports (Can.) 1834–1929

N.S.Rev.Stat. Nova Scotia Revised Statutes (Can.)

N.S.W. New South Wales (Aus.)

N.S.W.A.R. New South Wales Industrial Arbitration Reports. 1902–

N.S.W.Ad. Law Reports, Vice Admiralty (New South Wales, Aus.) 1880–1900

N.S.W.Adm. Law Reports, Vice Admiralty (New South Wales, Aus.) 1880–1900

N.S.W.B. New South Wales Reports, Bankruptcy Cases. 1890–99

N.S.W.Bktcy.Cas. New South Wales Reports, Bankruptcy Cases. 1890–99

N.S.W.C.A.C.Rep. New South Wales Corporate Affairs Commission Report (Aus.) 1972–

N.S.W.C.Eq. Law Reports Equity (N.S.W., Aus.) 1880–1900

N.S.W.C.R.D. New South Wales Court of Review Decisions

N.S.W.Conv.R. New South Wales Conveyancing Reports (in NSW Conveyancing Law and Practice) (CCH) 1980–

N.S.W.Ct.of App. New South Wales Court of Appeal (Aus.)

N.S.W.Eq. Equity Law Reports (N.S.W., Aus.) 1880–1900

N.S.W.Eq.Rep. Equity Law Reports (N.S.W., Aus.) 1880–1900

N.S.W.G.G. New South Wales Government Gazette (Aus.)

N.S.W.I.C. New South Wales Industrial Commission (Aus.)

N.S.W.I.C.Ct.S. New South Wales Industrial Commission in Court Session (Aus.)

N.S.W.I.G. New South Wales Industrial Gazette (Aus.) 1912–

N.S.W.Ind.Arbtn.Cas. New South Wales Industrial Arbitration Reports. 1902–

N.S.W.J.B. New South Wales Judgments Bulletin (Aus.) 1984–

N.S.W.L.R. New South Wales Law Reports (Aus.) 1880–1900, 1971–

N.S.W.L.R.C. New South Wales Law Reform Commission

N.S.W.L.V.R. New South Wales Land Valuation Reports. 1922–70

N.S.W.Land App.Cas. New South Wales Land Appeal Court Cases (Aus.) 1890–1921

N.S.W.Land App.Cts. New South Wales Land Appeal Court Cases (Aus.) 1890–1921

N.S.W.Priv.Com.Papers New South Wales Privacy Committee Papers (Aus.) 1975–

N.S.W.R. New South Wales Reports. 1960–70

N.S.W.Regs.B.& Ords. New South Wales Regulations, By-Laws and Ordinances (Aus.)

N.S.W.S.C.L. New South Wales Society for Computers and the Law (Aus.)

N.S.W.S.C.L.Proc. Proceedings of the New South Wales Society for Computers and the Law (Aus.) 1983–

N.S.W.S.C.R. New South Wales Supreme Court Reports. 1862–76

N.S.W.S.C.R.(Eq.) Supreme Court Reports, Equity (N.S.W., Aus.) 1862–76

N.S.W.S.C.R.(L.) Supreme Court Reports, Law (N.S.W., Aus.) 1862–76
N.S.W.S.C.R.N.S. New South Wales Supreme Court Reports, New Series. 1878–9
N.S.W.S.R. New South Wales State Reports. 1901–70
N.S.W.Soc.for Comp.& Law New South Wales Society for Computers and the Law (Aus.)
N.S.W.St.R. New South Wales State Reports. 1901–70
N.S.W.W.C.R. New South Wales Workers Compensation Reports. 1926–
N.S.W.W.N. New South Wales Weekly Notes (Aus.) 1884–1970
N.Sc.Dec. Geldert & Oxley's Nova Scotia Decisions (NSR 7–9) 1866–75
N.St.Z. Neue Zeitschrift für Strafrecht (Ger.)
N.T.I.R. Nederlands tijdschrift voor international recht (Neth.) Netherlands International Law Review. 1953–
N.T.J. Northern Territory Supreme Court Judgments (Aus.) 1951–76
N.T.L.R.C. Northern Territory Law Review Committee (Aus.)
N.T.R. Northern Territory Reports (Aus.) 1979–
NTRR Nederlands Tidsschrift voor Rechtsfilosofie en Rechtstheorie (Neth.)
N.T.Rep. New Term Reports, Queen's Bench. 1835–41
N.T.Repts. New Term Reports, Queen's Bench. 1835–41
N.Trans.S.Dec. National Transportation Safety Board Decisions (USA) 1967–
N.U. Nations Unies (United Nations) Nebraska Unofficial Reports. 1901–4
N.U.L.R. Northwestern University Law Review (Chicago) 1952–
n.v. naamloze vennootschap (Neth.) limited company
N/V No Value
N.V.I.R. Nederlandse Vereniging voor Internationaal Recht (Neth.)
N.W. North Western Reporter (National Reporter System) (USA) North West Provinces High Court Reports (Pak.) 1869–75
N.W.2d. North Western Reporter, Second Series
N.W.A.F. National Women's Aid Federation
N.W.F.Pak. North West Frontier, Pakistan
N.W.L. Northwestern University Law Review (Chicago) 1952–
N.W.L.Rev. Northwestern University Law Review (Chicago) 1952–
N.W.Law Rev. Northwestern University Law Review (Chicago) 1952–
N.W.P. North West Provinces High Court Reports (Pak.) 1869–75
N.W.P.H.C. North West Provinces High Court Reports (Pak.) 1869–75
N.W.T. North-West Territories, Canada
North-West Territories Reports (Can.) 1887–98
N.W.T.J. North-West Territories Judgments (unreported decisions available on QL) (Can.) 1986–
N.W.T.L.R. North-West Territories Reports (Can.) 1887–98
N.W.T.Ord. North-West Territories Ordinances (Can.)
N.W.T.R. North-West Territories Reports (Can.) 1887–98
N.W.T.Rep. North-West Territories Reports (Can.) 1887–98
N.W.Terr. North-West Territories Supreme Court Reports (Can.) 1887–98
N.W.Terr.(Can.) North-West Territories Reports (Can.) 1887–98
NWU Northwestern University School of Law (Chicago)
N.W.U.L.Rev. Northwestern University Law Review (Chicago) 1952–
NX Naftica Chronica (Marine Annals) (Greece)
N.Y. New York
New York Court of Appeals Reports. 1847–

N.Y.2d. New York Court of Appeals Reports, Second Series
N.Y.Ann.Ca. New York Annotated Cases
N.Y.Ann.Cas. New York Annotated Cases
N.Y.Anno.Dig. New York Annotated Digest
N.Y.Annot.Dig. New York Annotated Digest
N.Y.App.Dec. New York Court of Appeals Decisions. 1847–
New York Appellate Division Decisions. 1896–
N.Y.App.Div. New York Supreme Court Appellate Division Reports. 1896–
NYBCL New York Business Corporation Law
N.Y.C.B.A. New York City Bar Association
N.Y.C.B.A.Bull. Bulletin of the Association of the Bar of the City of New York
N.Y.C.C.H. New York Advance Digest Service (CCH)
N.Y.C.R.R. New York Codes, Rules and Regulations
N.Y.Cas.Err. Caines' New York Cases in Error. 1796–1805
N.Y.Ch.Sent. New York Chancery Sentinel. 1841–7
N.Y.City.Ct. New York City Court
N.Y.City Ct.Rep. New York City Court Reports
N.Y.City Ct.Supp. New York City Court Reports Supplement
N.Y.City H.Rec. New York City Hall Recorder. 1816–22
N.Y.City Hall Rec. New York City Hall Recorder. 1816–22
N.Y.Civ.Pr.Rep. New York Civil Procedure Reports. 1881–1907
N.Y.Civ.Prac.Law & R. New York Civil Practice Law and Rules
N.Y.Civ.Pro. New York Civil Procedure
N.Y.Civ.Pro.R. New York Civil Procedure Reports. 1881–1907
N.Y.Civ.Pro.R.N.S. New York Civil Procedure Reports, New Series. 1908–13
N.Y.Civ.Proc. New York Civil Procedure
N.Y.Civ.Proc.(N.S.) New York Civil Procedure Reports, New Series. 1908–13
N.Y.Civ.Proc.R. New York Civil Procedure Reports. 1881–1907
N.Y.Civ.Proc.R.,N.S. New York Civil Procedure Reports, New Series. 1908–13
N.Y.Code R. New York Code Reporter. 1848–50
N.Y.Code R.N.S. New York Code Reporter, New Series. 1850–2
N.Y.Code Rep. New York Code Reporter. 1848–50
N.Y.Code Rep.N.S. New York Code Reporter, New Series. 1850–2
N.Y.Code Report. New York Code Reporter. 1848–50
N.Y.Code Report.N.S. New York Code Reporter, New Series. 1850–2
N.Y.Code Reptr. New York Code Reporter. 1848–50
N.Y.Code Reptr.N.S. New York Code Reporter, New Series. 1850–2
N.Y.Cond. New York Condensed Reports. 1881–2
N.Y.County B.Bull. New York County Lawyers' Association Bar Bulletin. 1843–
N.Y.County Law.Ass'n.B.Bull. New York County Lawyers' Association Bar Bulletin. 1843–
N.Y.Cr. New York Criminal Reports. 1878–1924
N.Y.Cr.R. New York Criminal Reports. 1878–1924
N.Y.Cr.Rep: New York Criminal Reports. 1878–1924
N.Y.Crim. New York Criminal Reports. 1878–1924
N.Y.Ct.App. New York Court of Appeals
N.Y.D.R. New York Department Reports. 1914–

N.Y.Daily L.Gaz. New York Daily Law Gazette. 1858

N.Y.Daily L.Reg. New York Daily Law Register. 1872–89

N.Y.Daily Tr. New York Daily Transcript (Old Series) 1859–67, (New Series) 1868–72

N.Y.E.T.R. New York Estate Tax Reports (P–H)

N.Y.El.Cas. New York Contested Election Cases (Armstrong) 1777–1871 (Baxter) 1777–1899

N.Y.Elect.Cas. New York Contested Election Cases (Armstrong) 1777–1871, (Baxter) 1777–1899

N.Y.F. New York Law Forum. 1955–76

N.Y.I.L. Netherlands Yearbook of International Law. 1970–

N.Y.Int'l L.Rev. New York International Law Review

N.Y.Jud.Rep. New York Judicial Repository. 1818–19

N.Y.Jur. New York Jurisprudence New York Jurist

N.Y.L. New York University Law Review. 1924–42, 1944–

N.Y.L.C.Ann. New York Leading Cases Annotated. 1912–14

N.Y.L.Cas. New York Leading Cases Annotated. 1912–14

N.Y.L.F. New York Law Forum. 1955–76

N.Y.L.Forum New York Law Forum. 1955–76

N.Y.L.Gaz. New York Law Gazette. 1858

N.Y.L.J. New York Law Journal. 1888–

N.Y.L.Rec. New York Monthly Law Record. 1896–98

N.Y.L.Rev. New York Law Review. 1929, 1940

N.Y.L.S.Rev. New York Law School Review. 1928–30

N.Y.L.S.Stud.L.Rev. New York Law School Student Law Review

N.Y.L.Sch.J.Hum.Rts. New York Law School Journal of Human Rights

N.Y.L.Sch.J.Int'l & Comp.L. New York Law School Journal of International and Comparative Law

N.Y.L.Sch.L.Rev. New York Law School Law Review

N.Y.L.School Rev. New York Law School Law Review

N.Y.Law (Consol.) New York Consolidated Law Services

N.Y.Law Forum New York Law Forum

N.Y.Law Gaz. New York Law Gazette. 1858

N.Y.Law J. New York Law Journal. 1888–

N.Y.Law (McKinney) McKinney's Consolidated Laws of New York

N.Y.Law Rev. New York Law Review. 1929, 1940

N.Y.Laws Laws of New York

N.Y.Leg.N. New York Legal News. 1880–2

N.Y.Leg.Obs. New York Legal Observer (Owen's) 1842–54

N.Y.Leg.Reg. New York Legal Register. 1850

N.Y.Misc. New York Miscellaneous Reports. 1892–

N.Y.Misc.2d. New York Miscellaneous Reports, Second Series

N.Y.Mo.L.Bul. New York Monthly Law Bulletin. 1878–83

N.Y.Mo.L.R. New York Monthly Law Record. 1896–8

N.Y.Mo.L.Rec. New York Monthly Law Record. 1896–8

N.Y.Mo.Law Bul. New York Monthly Law Bulletin. 1878–83

N.Y.Month.L.Bul. New York Monthly Law Bulletin. 1878–83

N.Y.Month.L.R. New York Monthly Law Record. 1896–8

N.Y.Mun.Gaz. New York Municipal Gazette. 1841–6

N.Y.Op.Att.Gen. Sickel's Opinions of the Attorneys-General of New York

n.y.p. not yet published

N.Y.Pr. New York Practice Reports

N.Y.Pr.Rep. New York Practice Reports

N.Y.R.L. New York Revised Laws
N.Y.R.S. New York Revised Statutes
N.Y.Rec. New York Monthly Law Record. 1896–8
N.Y.Reg. New York Daily Register. 1872–89
N.Y.Rep. New York Court of Appeals Reports. 1847–
N.Y.Reptr. New York Reporter (Gardenier's) 1820
N.Y.S. New York State
New York State Reporter. 1886–96
New York Supplement. 1888–1937
N.Y.S.2d. New York Supplement Reporter, Second Series. 1938–
NYSBA New York State Bar Association
N.Y.S.B.A.Bull. New York State Bar Association Bulletin. 1928–61
N.Y.S.B.J. New York State Bar Journal. 1961–
N.Y.S.D.R. New York State Department Reports. 1913–14
N.Y.S.E.Guide New York Stock Exchange Guide (CCH)
N.Y.S.R. New York State Reporter. 1886–96
N.Y.Sen.J. New York Senate Journal
N.Y.Spec.Term R. Howard's Practice Reports. 1844–84, (N.S.) 1884–6
N.Y.Spec.Term Rep. Howard's Practice Reports. 1844–84, (N.S.) 1884–6
N.Y.St. New York State Reporter. 1886–96
N.Y.St.B.A. New York State Bar Association
N.Y.St.B.J. New York State Bar Journal. 1961–
N.Y.St.Bar A.Rep. New York State Bar Association Report
N.Y.St.Dept.Rep. New York State Department Reports. 1913–14
N.Y.St.R. New York State Reporter. 1886–96
N.Y.St.Rep. New York State Reporter. 1886–96
N.Y.State Bar J. New York State Bar Journal. 1961–
N.Y.Sup.Ct. New York Supreme Court Reports. 1873–96
N.Y.Super. New York Superior Court Reports
N.Y.Super.Ct. New York Superior Court Reports
N.Y.Supp. New York Supplement. 1888–1937
N.Y.Supp.2d. New York Supplement, Second Series. 1938–
N.Y.Supr.Ct. New York Supreme Court Reports. 1837–96
N.Y.Suprm.Ct. New York Supreme Court Reports. 1837–96
N.Y.T.R. New York Term Reports (Caines' Reports) 1803–5
N.Y.Tax Cas. New York Tax Cases (CCH) 1903–
N.Y.Trans. New York Transcript Reports. 1858–68
New York Weekly Transcript. 1861
N.Y.Trans.App. New York Transcript Appeal
N.Y.Trans.N.S. New York Transcript Reports, New Series.1868–72
N.Y.Trans.Rep. New York Transcript Reports. 1858–68
NYU New York University
N.Y.U.Conf.on Lab. New York University Conference on Labor
N.Y.U.Intra.L.Rev. New York University Intramural Law Review
N.Y.U.J.I.L.P. New York University Journal of International Law and Politics. 1968–
N.Y.U.J.Int'l.Law & Pol. New York University Journal of International Law and Politics. 1968–
N.Y.U.L.Center Bull. New York University Law Center Bulletin
N.Y.U.L.Q.R. New York University Law Quarterly Review. 1929–47
N.Y.U.L.Q.Rev. New York University Law Quarterly Review. 1929–47
N.Y.U.L.Qu.Rev. New York University Law Quarterly Review. 1929–47
N.Y.U.L.R. New York University Law Review. 1924–42, 1944–

N.Y.U.L.Rev. New York Univerity Law Review. 1924–42, 1944–

N.Y.U.Rev.L.& Soc.Change New York University Review of Law and Social Change. 1971–

N.Y.U.Rev.Law & Soc.C. New York University Review of Law and Social Change. 1971–

N.Y.Unconsol.Laws New York Unconsolidated Laws (McKinney)

N.Y.Week.Dig. New York Weekly Digest. 1876–88

N.Y.Wkly.Dig. New York Weekly Digest. 1876–88

N.Z. New Zealand
New Zealand Law Reports. 1883–

N.Z.A.C.R. New Zealand Accident Compensation Reports. 1981–3

N.Z.A.R. New Zealand Administrative Reports. 1976–

N.Z.App.Rep. New Zealand Appeal Reports

N.Z.B.L.C. New Zealand Business Law Cases (CCH) 1984–

N.Z.B.L.C.(Com.) New Zealand Business Law Cases, Commerce Commission Decisions. 1984–

N.Z.C.A. New Zealand Court of Appeal Reports. 1867–77

N.Z.C.C.L.R.C. New Zealand Contracts and Commercial Law Reform Committee

N.Z.C.L.C. New Zealand Company Law Cases (CCH) 1981–

N.Z.C.L.R.C. New Zealand Criminal Law Reform Committee

N.Z.C.P.R. New Zealand Conveyancing and Property Reports. 1959–82

N.Z.C.T. New Zealand Current Taxation. 1956–

N.Z.Col.L.J. New Zealand Colonial Law Journal. 1865–75

N.Z.Ct.App. New Zealand Court of Appeals

N.Z.Ct.Arb. New Zealand Court of Arbitration

N.Z.D.S.C. New Zealand Duties and Sales Tax Cases (CCH) 1983–4

N.Z.E.L.C. New Zealand Employment Law Cases (CCH) 1986–

N.Z.F.L.R. New Zealand Family Law Reports. 1981–

N.Z.Fam.Rep. New Zealand Family Law Reports. 1981–

N.Z.G.L.R. Gazette Law Reports (New Zealand) 1898–1953

N.Z.Gaz. New Zealand Gazette. 1853–

N.Z.Gaz.L.R. Gazette Law Reports (New Zealand) 1898–1953

N.Z.I.I.R.R. New Zealand Institute of Industrial Relations Research

N.Z.I.P.R. New Zealand Intellectual Property Reports. 1967–

N.Z.Ind.Arb. New Zealand Industrial Arbitration Awards

N.Z.J.I.R. New Zealand Journal of Industrial Relations. 1976–

N.Z.J.P. New Zealand Justice of the Peace. 1876–7

N.Z.J.P.A. New Zealand Journal of Public Administration. 1938–77

N.Z.J.Pub.Admin. New Zealand Journal of Public Administration. 1938–77

N.Z.Jur. Jurist Reports (N.Z.) 1873–5

N.Z.Jur.Mining Law Jurist Reports, New Series, Cases in Mining Law (N.Z.) 1875–9

N.Z.Jur.N.S. Jurist Reports, New Series (N.Z.) 1875–9

N.Z.L.G.R. Local Government Reports (N.Z.) 1935–71

N.Z.L.J. New Zealand Law Journal. 1925–

N.Z.L.J.M.C. New Zealand Law Journal Magistrates' Court Decisions

N.Z.L.R. New Zealand Law Reports. 1883–

N.Z.L.R.C. New Zealand Law Revision Commission

N.Z.L.R.C.A. New Zealand Law Reports, Court of Appeal. 1883–7

N.Z.L.R.F. New Zealand Legal Research Foundation

N.Z.L.R. S.C. New Zealand Law Reports, Supreme Court. 1883–7

N.Z.L.S. New Zealand Law Society

N.Z.Law Soc.N. New Zealand Law Society Newsletter. 1965–

N.Z.Med.J. New Zealand Medical Journal. 1900–

N.Z.P.A.L.R.C. New Zealand Public and Administrative Law Reform Committee

N.Z.P.C.C. New Zealand Privy Council Cases. 1840–1932

N.Z.P.C.Cas. New Zealand Privy Council Cases. 1840–1932

N.Z.P.D. New Zealand Parliamentary Debates. 1854–

N.Z.P.L.E.R.C. New Zealand Property Law and Equity Reform Committee

N.Z.R.L. New Zealand Recent Law. 1966–

N.Z.R.,Regs.& B. Rules, Regulations and By-Laws under New Zealand Statutes

N.Z.Recent L.Rev. New Zealand Recent Law Review

N.Z.Rep. New Zealand Law Reports. 1883–

N.Z.S. New Zealand Standard Specification

N.Z.S.C. New Zealand Supreme Court

N.Z.S.S. New Zealand Standard Specification

N.Z.T.B.R. New Zealand Taxation Board of Review Decisions. 1961–74

N.Z.T.C. New Zealand Tax Cases (CCH) 1973–

N.Z.T.C.P.A. Town and Country Planning Appeals (N.Z.) 1955–71

N.Z.T.G.L.R.C. New Zealand Torts and General Law Reform Committee

N.Z.T.P.A. New Zealand Town Planning Appeals. 1971–

N.Z.T.P.R. New Zealand Tax Planning Report (CCH) 1979–

N.Z.T.S. New Zealand Treaty Series. 1943–

N.Z.U.L.R. New Zealand Universities Law Review. 1963–

N.Z.U.L.Rev. New Zealand Universities Law Review. 1963–

N.Z.Univ.L.R. New Zealand Universities Law Review. 1963–

N.Z.Val. New Zealand Valuer. 1942–86
New Zealand Valuers' Journal. 1987–

N.Z.Val.J. New Zealand Valuers' Journal. 1987–

NZW Neue Zeitschrift für Wehrrecht (Ger.) 1959–

N.Z.W.C.C. New Zealand Workers' Compensation Cases. 1901–40

N.& H. Nott & Hopkins' Reports (8–29 US Court of Claims)
Nott & Huntington's Reports (1–7 US Court of Claims)

N.& Hop. Nott & Hopkins' Reports (8–29 US Court of Claims)

N.& Hunt. Nott & Huntington's Reports (1–7 US Court of Claims)

N.& M. Nevile & Manning's King's Bench Reports (38–43 RR) 1832–6

N.& M.M.C. Nevile & Manning's Magistrate Cases. 1832–6

N.& M.Mag. Nevile & Manning's Magistrate Cases. 1832–6

N.& Macn. Neville & Macnamara's Railway and Canal Cases. 1855–1950

N.& Mc. Nott & McCord's South Carolina Reports (10–11 SCL) 1817–20

N.& McN. Neville & Macnamara's Railway and Canal Cases. 1855–1950

N.& P. Nevile & Perry's King's Bench Reports (44–5 RR) 1836–8

N.& P.M.C. Nevile & Perry's Magistrate Cases. 1836–7

N.& P.Mag. Nevile & Perry's Magistrate Cases. 1836–7

N.& S. Nicholls & Stops' Reports (Tasmania, Aus.) 1897–1904

Nag. All India Reporter, Nagpur. 1914–51
Indian Law Reports, Nagpur. 1904–
Indian Rulings, Nagpur. 1929–47

Nag.L.J. Nagpur Law Journal (India) 1918–

Nag.L.N. Nagpur Law Notes (India) 1938–9

Nag.L.R. Nagpur Law Reports (India) 1904–36

Nag.U.C.L.Mag. Nagpur University College of Law Magazine (India) 1933–4
Nagendra Singh International Conventions of Merchant Shipping (British Shipping Laws, vol.8)
Nap.Pres. Napier, Prescription. 1839
Napt. Napton's Reports (4 Missouri)
Napton Napton's Reports (4 Missouri)
Nar.Conv. Nares, Penal Convictions. 1815
Narr.Mod. Narrationes Modernae, or Style's King's Bench Reports. 1646–55
Nas.Inst.Priv. Nasmith, Institutes of English Public Law. 1873
Nassau L. Nassau Lawyer
Nat. Natal
National
Natural
Nat.(A.B.C.) National (Association du Barreau Canadien – Canadian Bar Association) 1973–
Nat.B.C. National Bank Cases (USA)
Nat.B.J. National Bar Journal (USA) 1941–51
Nat.B.L.Rev. National Banking Law Review (Can.) 1981–
Nat.B.R. National Bankruptcy Register (USA) 1867–82
Nat.Bankr.Law National Bankruptcy Law
Nat.Bankr.N.& R. National Bankruptcy News and Reports (USA) 1898–1901
Nat.Bankr.R. National Bankruptcy Register (USA) 1867–82
Nat.Bar Bull. National Bar Bulletin (USA) 1969–
Nat.Bar J. National Bar Journal (USA) 1941–51
Nat.Brev. Natura Brevium
Nat.(C.B.A.) National (Canadian Bar Association – Association du Barreau Canadien) 1973–
Nat.Civ.Rev. National Civic Review (USA) 1958–
Nat.Corp.Rep. National Corporation Reporter (USA) 1890–
Nat.Creditor/Debtor Rev. National Creditor/Debtor Review (Can.) 1984–
Nat.Gas Law J. The Natural Gas Lawyer's Journal (USA)
Nat.Inc.Tax Mag. National Income Tax Magazine (USA) 1923–30
Nat.Ins.Commiss. National Insurance Commissioner
Nat.Insolvency Rev. National Insolvency Review (Can.) 1982–
Nat.J.Crim.Def. National Journal of Criminal Defense (USA) 1975–
Nat.J.Leg.Ed. National Journal of Legal Education (USA) 1937–40
Nat.L.F. Natural Law Forum (USA) 1956–68
Nat.L.Forum Natural Law Forum (USA) 1956–68
Nat.L.Guild Q. National Lawyers' Guild Quarterly (USA)
Nat.L.J. Natal Law Journal (S.Afr.) 1905–7
Nat.L.M. Natal Law Magazine (S.Afr.) 1908–9
Nat.L.Q. Natal Law Quarterly (S.Afr.) 1902–7
Nat.L.R. Natal Law Reports (S.Afr.) 1873–1910
Nat.L.Rec. National Law Record (USA)
Nat.L.Rep. National Law Reporter (USA) 1857
Nat.L.Rev. National Law Review (USA) 1888
Nat.Law.Guild Q. National Lawyers' Guild Quarterly (USA) 1937–40
Nat.Mun.Rev. National Municipal Review. 1912–58
Nat.Q.Rev. National Quarterly Review (USA)
Nat.R.J. Natural Resources Journal (USA)
Nat.Rept.Syst. National Reporter System (USA)
Nat.Res.Forum Natural Resources Forum (USA)
Nat.Res.J. Natural Resources Journal (USA)
Nat.Res.Lawyer Natural Resources Lawyer (USA)

Nat.Resources J. Natural Resources Journal

Nat.Resources & Env't Natural Resources and Environment

Nat.Taiwan Univ.L.J. National Taiwan University Law Journal (Taiwan)

Nat.Tax J. National Tax Journal (USA) 1948–

Nat.Tax Mag. National Tax Magazine (USA) 1930

Nat.U.L.Rev. Natal University Law Review (S.Afr.) 1972–
National University Law Review (USA) 1921–31

Natal L.J. Natal Law Journal (S.Afr.) 1905–7

Natal L.M. Natal Law Magazine (S.Afr.) 1908–9

Natal L.Q. Natal Law Quarterly (S.Afr.) 1902–7

Natal L.R. Natal Law Reports (S.Afr.) 1873–1910

Natal U.L.Rev. Natal University Law Review (S.Afr.) 1972–

Nathan Nathan, Common Law of South Africa

Natl. National

Nat'l Acad.Arb.Proc.Ann.Meeting National Academy of Arbitrators, Proceedings of the Annual Meeting

Nat'l Black L.J. National Black Law Journal (USA)

Nat'l Civ.Rev. National Civic Review (USA) 1958–

Nat'l Jewish L.Rev. National Jewish Law Review (USA)

Nat'l Legal Mag. National Legal Magazine (USA)

Nat'l Mun.Rev. National Municipal Review (USA) 1912–58

Nat'l Rep.Sys. National Reporter System

Nat'l School L.Reptr. National School Law Reporter (USA)

Nat'l Tax J. National Tax Journal (USA)

Natural L.F. Natural Law Forum (USA) 1956–68

Natural Resources J. Natural Resources Journal (USA) 1961

Natural Resources Lawy. Natural Resources Lawyer (USA) 1968–

Nav. Navigation

Naval L.Rev. Naval Law Review (USA)

Nb. Nebraska

Nb.L. Nebraska Law Review. 1941–

Nb.L.B. Nebraska Law Bulletin. 1922–40

Nb.L.R. Nebraska Law Review. 1941–

Nd. Newfoundland
Newfoundland Law Reports (Can.) 1817–1949

Ne. Nepal

Neale, Anti-Trust A.D. Neale, Anti-Trust Law of the United States. 1960

Near East.Stud. Near Eastern Studies

Neb. Nebraska
Nebraska Supreme Court Reports. 1860–

Neb.L.B. Nebraska Law Bulletin. 1922–40

Neb.L.R. Nebraska Law Review. 1941–

Neb.L.Rev. Nebraska Law Review. 1941–

Neb.Laws Laws of Nebraska

Neb.Leg.N. Nebraska Legal News. 1892–1939

Neb.R.C. Nebraska Railway Commission Reports

Neb.Rev.Stat. Revised Statutes of Nebraska

Neb.S.B.J. Nebraska State Bar Journal. 1952–71

Neb.St.B.J. Nebraska State Bar Journal. 1952–71

Neb.Sup.Ct.J. Nebraska Supreme Court Journal. 1931–44

Neb.(Unof.) Nebraska Unofficial Reports. 1901–4

Neb.Unoff. Nebraska Unofficial Reports. 1901–4

Neb.W.C.C. Nebraska Workmen's Compensation Court Bulletin

Nebr.B.A. Nebraska Bar Association
Nebraska State Bar Journal

Nebr.L.B. Nebraska Law Bulletin
Nebr.L.Rev. Nebraska Law Review
Ned.Stbl. Nederlandsch Staatsblad (Neth.)
NedTIR Nederlands Tijdschrift voor Internationaal Recht (Neth.)
Nedrl.Tijdsch.v.Int'l R. Nederlands Tijdschrift voor International Recht (Neth.)
Need. Needham's Annual Summary of Tax Cases
Neg.C. Negligence Cases (CCH) (USA) 1938–
Neg.Cas. Bloomfield's Manumission (or Negro) Cases (New Jersey) 1775–93
Negligence Cases (CCH) (USA) 1938–
Neg.Inst. Negotiable Instrument
Negl.Cas. Negligence Cases (CCH) (USA) 1938–
Negl.Cas.2d Negligence Cases, Second Series (CCH) (USA)
Negl.& Comp.Cas.Ann. Negligence and Compensation Cases Annotated (USA) 1911–36
Negl.& Comp.Cas.Ann.3d Negligence and Compensation Cases Annotated, Third Series
Negl.& Comp.Cas.Ann.(N.S.) Negligence and Compensation Cases Annotated, New Series
Negro Cas. Bloomfield's Manumission Cases (New Jersey) 1775–93
Nel. Finch's Chancery Reports by Nelson (23 ER) 1673–81
Nelson's Chancery Reports (21 ER) 1625–93
Nel.C.R. Nelson's Chancery Reports (21 ER) 1625–93
Nell Nell's Decisions of the Supreme Court (Sri L.) 1845–55
Nels. H. Finch's Chancery Reports by Nelson (23 ER) 1673–81
Nelson's Chancery Reports (21 ER) 1625–93
Nels.8vo. Nelson's Chancery Reports (21 ER) 1625–93
Nels.Abr. Nelson's Abridgment of the Common Law
Nels.F. Finch's Chancery Reports by Nelson (23 ER) 1673–81
Nels.Fol. Finch's Chancery Reports by Nelson (23 ER) 1673–81
Nels.Fol.Rep. Finch's Chancery Reports by Nelson (23 ER) 1673–81
Nelson H. Finch's Chancery Reports by Nelson (23 ER) 1673–81
Nelson's Chancery Reports (21 ER) 1625–93
Nelson's Rep. H. Finch's Chancery Reports by Nelson (23 ER) 1673–81
Nelson's Chancery Reports (21 ER) 1625–93
nem.con. nemine contradicente (Lat.) nobody contradicting
nem.dis. nemine dissentiente (Lat.) nobody dissenting
Neth. Netherlands
Neth.Intl.L.Rev. Netherlands International Law Review
Neth.Yrbk.Intl.L. Netherlands Yearbook of International Law
Netherl.Int'l L.Rev. Netherlands International Law Review
Netherl.Yb.Int'l L. Netherlands Yearbook of International Law
Netherlands R.I.L. Netherlands Review of International Law
neubearb.Aufl. neubearbeitete Auflage
Nev. Nevada
Nevada Supreme Court Reports. 1865–
Nev.Rev.Stat. Nevada Revised Statutes
Nev.S.B.J. Nevada State Bar Journal. 1936–
Nev.St.Bar J. Nevada State Bar Journal. 1936–
Nev.Stats. Statutes of Nevada
Nev.& M. Nevile & Manning's King's Bench Reports (38–43 RR) 1832–6
Nev.& M.K.B. Nevile & Manning's King's Bench Reports (38–43 RR) 1832–6
Nev.& M.M.C. Nevile & Manning's Magistrates' Cases. 1832–6
Nev.& Mac. Neville & Macnamara's Railway and Canal Cases. 1855–1950

Nev.& Macn. Neville & Macnamara's Railway and Canal Cases. 1855–1950

Nev.& MacN. Neville & Macnamara's Railway and Canal cases. 1855–1950

Nev.& Man. Nevile & Manning's King's Bench Reports (38–43 RR) 1832–6

Nev.& Man.Mag.Cas. Nevile & Manning's Magistrate Cases. 1832–6

Nev.& McN. Neville & Macnamara's Railway and Canal Cases. 1855–1950

Nev.& P. Nevile & Perry's King's Bench Reports (44–5 RR) 1836–8
Nevile & Perry's Magistrates' Cases. 1836–7

Nev.& P.K.B. Nevile & Perry's King's Bench Reports (44–5 RR) 1836–8

Nev.& P.M.C. Nevile & Perry's Magistrates' Cases. 1836–7

Nev.& P.Mag.Cas. Nevile & Perry's Magistrates' Cases. 1836–7

New. Newell's Illinois Appeal Reports (48–90 Illinois)

New Ann.Reg. New Annual Register

New B.Eq.Ca. New Brunswick Equity Cases (Can.)

New B.Eq.Rep. New Brunswick Equity Reports (Can.) 1894–1911

New Benl. New Benloe's Reports, King's Bench (73 ER) 1531–1628

New Br. New Brunswick Reports (Can.) 1825–1929

New Br.Eq.(Can.) New Brunswick Equity Reports (Can.) 1894–1911

New Br.Eq.Cas.(Can.) New Brunswick Equity Cases (Can.)

New Br.R. New Brunswick Reports (Can.) 1825–1929

New Cas. Bingham's New Cases (131–3 ER) 1834–40

New Cas.Eq. New Cases in Equity (8, 9 Modern Reports) (88 ER) 1721–55

New Commun. New Community. 1971–

New Eng. New England
New Englander

New Eng.J.on Crim.& Civ.Confinement New England Journal on Criminal and Civil Confinement (USA)

New Eng.J.Prison New England Journal on Prison Law

New Eng.L.Rev. New England Law Review. 1969–

New England L.Rev. New England Law Review. 1969–

New Hamp.B.J. New Hampshire Bar Journal (USA) 1958–

New Hung.Q. New Hungary Quarterly

New Ir.Jur. New Irish Jurist & Local Government Review. 1900–5

New Jersey L.J. New Jersey Law Journal. 1878–

New Jersey L.Rev. New Jersey Law Review (USA) 1915, 1916, 1935–6

New Jersey Leg.Rec. New Jersey Legal Record. 1931–2

New Jersey S.B.A.Qu. New Jersey State Bar Association Quarterly. 1934–7

New L.J. New Law Journal. 1965–

New Mag.Cas. New Magistrates' Cases (Bittleston, Wise & Parnell) 1844–50

New Mex.B.A. New Mexico State Bar Association

New Mex.L.Rev. New Mexico Law Review

New Mex.Q. New Mexico Quarterly

New Mex.S.B.A. New Mexico State Bar Association

New Mexico L.Rev. New Mexico Law Review. 1971–

New Nat.Brev. New Natura Brevium

New Pr.Cases New Practice Cases. 1844–8

New Pract.Cases New Practice Cases. 1844–8

New Prince.Rev. New Princeton Review (USA)

New Rep. Bosanquet & Puller's New Reports (127 ER) 1804–7
New Reports. 1862–5

New Scholast. New Scholasticism

New Sess.Cas. New Session Cases by Carrow, Hamerton & Allen (Scot.) 1844–51

New So.W.L. New South Wales Law Reports. 1880–1900, 1971–

New So.W.St. New South Wales State Reports. 1901–

New So.W.W.N. New South Wales Weekly Notes. 1884–

New Term Rep. New Term Reports. 1835–41
Term Reports, New Series (East) (102–4 ER) 1801–12

New York City B.A.Bull. Bulletin of the Bar Association of the City of New York. 1920–3

New York Supp. New York Supplement. 1888–1937

New Zeal. New Zealand

New Zeal.Jur.R. New Zealand Jurist Reports. 1873–5

New Zeal.L. New Zealand Law Reports. 1883–

New Zeal.L.J. New Zealand Law Journal. 1925–

New Zeal.L.R. New Zealand Law Reports. 1883–

Newark L.Rev. University of Newark Law Review (USA) 1936–42

Newb. Newberry's United States District Court, Admiralty Reports

Newb.Adm. Newberry's United States District Court, Admiralty Reports

Newberry Adm.(F.) Newberry's United States District Court, Admiralty Reports

Newblyth Newblyth's Manuscript Decisions, Session Cases (Scot.) 1668–77

Newbon Newbon's Private Bills Reports. 1895–99

Newell Newell's Reports (48–90 Illinois Appeal)

Newf. Newfoundland

Newf.L.R. Newfoundland Law Reports (Can.) 1817–1949

Newf.S.Ct. Newfoundland Supreme Court Decisions

Newf.Sel.Cas. Newfoundland Select Cases. 1817–28

Newfld.L.R. Newfoundland Law Reports (Can.) 1817–1949

Newfoundl.L.R. Newfoundland Law Reports (Can.) 1817–1949

Newfoundl.R. Newfoundland Law Reports (Can.) 1817–1949

Newfoundl.Sel.Cas. Newfoundland Select Cases. 1817–28

Newl.Ch.Pr. Newland, Chancery Practice. 3ed. 1830

Newl.Cont. Newland, Contracts. 1806

Newsl.Leg.Act Newsletter on Legislative Activities (Council of Europe) 1972–

Nfld. Newfoundland
Newfoundland Supreme Court Decisions (Can.)

Nfld.L.R. Newfoundland Law Reports (Can.) 1817–1949

Nfld.R. Newfoundland Law Reports (Can.) 1817–1949

Nfld.Rev.Stat. Newfoundland Revised Statutes (Can.)

Nfld.Stat. Newfoundland Statutes (Can.)

Nfld.& P.E.I.R. Newfoundland and Prince Edward Island Reports

Nic.Adult.Bast. Nicolas, Adulterine Bastardy. 1836

Nic.Elec. Nicolson, Elections in Scotland

Nic.H.& C. Nicholl, Hare & Carrow's Railway and Canal Cases. 1835–55

Nic.Ha.C. Nicholl, Hare & Carrow's Railway and Canal Cases. 1835–55

Nich.H.& C. Nicholl, Hare & Carrow's Railway and Canal Cases. 1835–55

Nicholl H.& C. Nicholl, Hare & Carrow's Railway and Canal Cases. 1835–55

Nicholson Nicholson's Manuscript Decisions, Session Cases (Scot.) 1610–32

Nicolas Proceedings and Ordinances of the Privy Council, edited by Sir Harry Nicolas

Niemeyers Z. Zeitschrift für internationales Privat – und Strafrecht (Ger.) 1890–1938

Nig. Nigeria
Nigerian

Nig.Ann.Int'l L. Nigerian Annual of International Law
Nig.B.J. Nigerian Bar Journal. 1958–
Nig.Bar J. Nigerian Bar Journal. 1958–
Nig.J.Contemp.L. Nigerian Journal of Contemporary Law. 1970–
Nig.L.J. Nigerian Law Journal. 1964–
Nig.L.Q. Nigeria Lawyers' Quarterly. 1964–
Nig.L.Q.R. Nigerian Law Quarterly Review. 1946–7
Nig.L.R. Nigeria Law Reports. 1881–
Nig.Lawy.Q. Nigeria Lawyers' Quarterly. 1964–
Nigeria L.R. Nigeria Law Reports. 1881–
Nigerian Bar J. Nigerian Bar Journal. 1958–
Nigerian L.J. Nigerian Law Journal
Nihon U.Comp.L. Nihon University Comparative Law (Japan)
Nil.Reg. Niles' Weekly Register (USA)
Nisbet Nisbet of Dirleton's Session Cases (Scot.) 1665–77
Nissho Nihon Shoko Kaigisho (Japan) Chamber of Commerce
Nix.Dig. Nixon's Digest of Laws (New Jersey)
nn. footnotes
notes
no. number
No.Ca.Ecc.& Mar. Notes of Cases in the Ecclesiastical and Maritime Courts. 1841–50
No.Car.S.B.A. North Carolina State Bar Association
No.Cas.L.J. Notes of Cases, Law Journal. 1866–92
No.East.Rep. Northeastern Reporter (USA)
No.Ire.L.Q. Northern Ireland Legal Quarterly. 1936–
No.N. Novae Narrationes. 1516
No.West Rep. Northwestern Reporter (USA)
Noble Noble's Current Court Decisions (New York) 1908–10
Nok.Mort. Nokes, Mortgages and Receiverships. 3ed. 1951
Nol. Nolan's Magistrates' Cases. 1791–2
Nolan's Poor Laws. 4ed. 1825
Nol.Mag. Nolan's Magistrates' Cases. 1791–2
Nol.P.L. Nolan's Poor Laws. 4ed. 1825
nol.pros. nolle prosequi (Lat.) unwilling to prosecute
Nolan Nolan's Magistrates' Cases. 1791–2
Nolan's Poor Laws. 4ed. 1825
Nomos Nomos: Yearbook of the American Society of Political and Legal Philosophy
non cul. non culpabilis (Lat.) not guilty
non pros. non prosequitur (Lat.) delay or neglect in prosecuting
non seq. non sequitur (Lat.) it does not follow
Nor. Norway
Nor.Fr. Norman French
Nor.Pat. Norman, Letters Patent. 1853
Norc. Norcross' Reports (23–4 Nevada)
Nord.Admin.Tids. Nordisk Administrativt Tidsskrift (Den.)
Nord.Immat.Ratts. Nordiskt Immateriellt Rattsskydd (Swed.)
Nord.J.Intl.L. Nordic Journal of International Law (Den.)
NordTIR Nordisk Tidsskrift for International Ret (Den.)
Nord.Tids.Krim. Nordisk Tidsskrift for Kriminalvidenskab (Den.)
Nordisk T.A. Nordisk Tidsskrift for International Ret, Acta scandinavica juris gentium (Den.)
Nordisk Tidssk. Nordisk Tidsskrift for International Ret (Den.)
Nordisk Tidssk.f.Kriminalvidenskab Nordisk Tidskrift for Kriminalvidenskab (Den.)
Nordisk Tidssk.Int'l R. Nordisk Tidskrift for International Ret (Den.)
Norr. Norris' Reports (82–96 Pennsylvania)
Norris Norris' Reports (82–96 Pennsylvania)

Nort.L.C. Norton's Leading Cases on Inheritance (India)

North. Eden's Chancery Reports tempore Northington (28 ER) 1757–66

North Car.J.Int'l L.& Comm. North Carolina Journal of International Law and Commercial Regulation

North.Co. Northampton County Reporter (Pennsylvania)

North.Co.R.(Pa.) Northampton County Reporter (Pennsylvania)

North.Co.Rep. Northampton County Reporter (Pennsylvania)

North Dakota L.Rev. North Dakota Law Review

North.Ireland L.Q. Northern Ireland Legal Quarterly

North.Ken'y S.L.Rev. Northern Kentucky State Law Review

North.Ky.L.R. Northern Kentucky Law Review. 1976–

North.Ky.St.L.F. Northern Kentucky State Law Forum. 1973–6

North Report Road Traffic Law Review Report (DoT) 1988

North St.L. North, Study of the Laws. 1824

North.U.L.Rev. Northwestern University Law Review (Chicago) 1952–

North & G. North & Guthrie's Reports (68–80 Missouri Appeals)

Northam. Northampton Law Reporter (Pennsylvania)

Northam.L.Rep. Northampton Law Reporter (Pennsylvania)

Northum. Northumberland County Legal News (Pennsylvania) 1888

Northum.Co.Leg.N. Northumberland County Legal News (Pennsylvania)

Northw.L.J. Northwestern Law Journal (USA) 1881

Northw.L.Rev. Northwestern University Law Review (Chicago) 1952–

Northw.Pr. Northwestern Provinces (India)

Northw.Rep. Northwestern Reporter

Northw.U.L.R. Northwestern University Law Review (Chicago) 1952–

Northwest.J.Int'l L.& Bus. Northwestern Journal of International Law and Business

Northwestern U.L.Rev. Northwestern University Law Review (Chicago) 1952–

Norton Norton's Cases on Hindu Law of Inheritance (India) 1870–1

nos. numbers

Not.Cas. Notes of Cases, Ecclesiastical and Maritime (ed. Thornton) 1841–50
Strange's Notes of Cases (Madras, India) 1798–1816

Not.Cas.Ecc.& M. Notes of Cases in the Ecclesiastical and Maritime Courts. 1841–50

Not.Cas.Madras Strange's Notes of Cases (Madras, India) 1798–1816

Not.Dec. Notes of Decisions (Martin's North Carolina Reports) 1778–97

Not.J. Notaries Journal (New York) 1877–83

Not.Op. Wilmot's Notes of Opinions and Judgments. 1757–70

Not.Wet Notariswet (Neth.)

Notc.on Fac. Notcutt, Factories and Workshops. 2ed. 1879

Notes of Cases Notes of Cases in the Ecclesiastical and Maritime Courts. 1841–50
Strange's Notes of Cases (Madras, India) 1798–1816

Notre Dame J.L.Ethics & Pub.Pol'y Notre Dame Journal of Law, Ethics and Public Policy (USA)

Notre Dame J.Leg. Notre Dame Journal of Legislation (USA) 1974–

Notre Dame Law. Notre Dame Lawyer (USA) 1925–

Nott & Hop. Nott & Hopkin's Reports (8–29 U.S. Court of Claims)

Nott & Hunt. Nott & Huntington's Reports (1–7 U.S. Court of Claims)

Nott & M'C.(S.C.) Nott & M'Cord, South Carolina Law Reports (10–11 SCL) 1817–20

Nott & McC. Nott & M'Cord, South Carolina Law Reports (10–11 SCL) 1817–20

Nouv.rev.dr.int.pr. Nouvelle revue de droit international privé (Fr.) 1934–43, 1946–9

Nouv.Revue Nouvelle revue de droit international privé (Fr.) 1934–43, 1946–9

Nov.Sc. Nova Scotia Supreme Court Reports (Can.) 1834–1929

Nov.Sc.Dec. Nova Scotia Decisions (NSR 7–9) (Can.) 1866–75

Nov.Sc.L.R. Nova Scotia Law Reports. 1834–1929

Nov.Sc.P.U.C. Nova Scotia Board of Commissioners of Public Utilities (Can.)

Nova L.J. Nova Law Journal (USA)

Nova L.Rev. Nova Law Review (USA)

Nova Scotia L.R.A.C. Nova Scotia Law Reform Advisory Commission

Noy Noy's King's Bench Reports (74 ER) 1559–1649

Noy Max. Noy's Grounds and Maxims. 1641

Nts. Notes

Nuc.L.Bull. Nuclear Law Bulletin (O.E.C.D.) 1968–

Nuclear L.Bull. Nuclear Law Bulletin (O.E.C.D.) 1968–

Nuova riv.dir.comm. Nuova rivista di diritto commerciale, diritto dell'economia, diritto sociale (It.) 1947–57

Nuovelciv. Le nuove leggi civili commentate (It.)

Nv. Nevada

Nw. Northwestern

Nw.J.Int'l L.& Bus. Northwestern Journal of International Law and Business (USA)

Nw.L. Northwestern University Law Review (Chicago) 1952–

Nw.L.S. Northwestern University Law Review Supplement (Chicago)

Nw.U.L.Rev. Northwestern University Law Review (Chicago) 1952–

Ny. Nyasaland

Ny.L.R. Nyasaland Law Reports. 1922–

Nye Nye's Reports (18–21 Utah)

Nys Nys, Le droit international. 2ed. 1912

O

o. order
overruled
O. Law Opinions
Ohio
Ohio Reports. 1821–52
Oklahoma
Ontario
Ontario Reports
Order (Rules of Court)
Oregon
Oregon Reports
Otto's United States Supreme Court Reports (91–107 U.S.)
South African Law Reports, Orange Free State Provincial Division. 1910–46
O.A. Ohio Appellate Reports. 1913–
Oudh Appeals (India)
O.A.2d. Ohio Appellate Reports, Second Series
O.A.C. Ontario Appeal Cases (Can.) 1983–
OAG Opinions of the Attorneys General (USA)
OAPEC Organisation of Arab Petroleum Exporting Countries
O.A.R. Ohio Appellate Reports. 1913–
Ontario Appeal Reports. 1876–1900
OAS Organization of American States (UN)
OAU Organisation of African Unity
O.App. Ohio Appellate Reports. 1913–
O.App.2d. Ohio Appellate Reports, Second Series
O.B. Official Bulletin
Old Bailey
Old Benloe
Orlando Bridgman
O.B.E. Officer of the Order of the British Empire
OBG Oberstes Bundesgericht (Ger.) Federal Supreme Court
O.B.J. The Journal, Oklahoma State Bar Association. 1930–
OBR Overseas Business Reports
O.B.S. Old Bailey Session Papers. 1715–1834
O.B.S.P. Old Bailey Session Papers. 1715–1834
O.B.& F. Ollivier, Bell & Fitzgerald's Court of Appeal Reports (N.Z.) 1878–80
Ollivier Bell & Fitzgerald's Supreme Court Reports (N.Z.) 1878–80
O.B.& F.(C.A.) Ollivier, Bell & Fitzgerald's Reports, Court of Appeal (N.Z.) 1878–80
O.B.& F.(S.C.) Ollivier, Bell & Fitzgerald's Supreme Court Reports (N.Z.) 1878–80
O.Bar Ohio State Bar Association Reports. 1928–
O.Ben. Old Benloe's Reports Common Pleas (Benloe & Dalison) (123 ER) 1486–1580
O.Benl. Old Benloe's Reports Common Pleas (Benloe & Dalison) (123 ER) 1486–1580
O.Bridg. Carter's Reports tempore Bridgman, Common Pleas (124 ER) 1664–76
Orlando Bridgman's Common Pleas Reports (124 ER) 1660–67
O.Bridgm. Carter's Reports tempore Bridgman, Common Pleas (124 ER) 1664–76

Orlando Bridgman's Common Pleas Reports (124 ER) 1660–67
O'Brien O'Brien's Upper Canada Reports
O.C. Official Circular (Poor Law Board, etc.)
Old Code (Louisiana Code of 1808)
Ope consilio (Lat.) by aid and counsel
Order in Council
Ordres du Conseil (Jersey)
Orphans' Court
Oslo Convention
Ottawa Convention
Oudh Cases (India) 1898–1926
O.C.A. Ohio Court of Appeal Reports. 1915–22
OCAM Common Afro-Malagasy Organisation
OCAS Organisation of Central American States
O.C.C. Ohio Circuit Reports or Decisions. 1901–18
O.C.C.F. Office Commun des Consummateurs de Ferraille
O.C.C.N.S. Ohio Circuit Court Reports, New Series. 1903–18
O.C.D. Office of Child Development (USA)
Ohio Circuit Decisions. 1885–1901
O.C.D.E. Organisation de Cooperation et de Developpement Économiques (OECD)
OCF Ordonnance du Conseil fédéral (Switz.)
O.C.P. Ontario Civil Procedure (unreported decisions available on QL) (Can.) 1986–
O.C.S. Office of Contract Settlement Decisions (USA)
Organe de contrôle des stupéfiants (Drug Supervisory Body)
OCTPC Organisation for the Co-operation of Socialist Countries in the Domain of Tele- and Postal Communications
O.Cr. Oklahoma Criminal Reports. 1908–
O.Cr.C. Oudh Criminal Cases (India)
o.d. onrechtmatige daad (Neth.) tort, tortious act
O.D. Office Decisions (U.S. Internal Revenue Bureau)
Ohio Decisions. 1894–1920
Overdose of narcotics
O.D.A. Overseas Development Administration (Ministry of Overseas Development)
O.D.C.C. Ohio Decisions, Circuit Court. 1901–18
O.D.E.C.A. Organisation of Central American States (Organizacion de Estados Centroamericanos)
ODEPLAN Chilean National Planning Office
ODF Office of Development Finance (U.S. State Department)
ODI Overseas Development Institute
O.D.N.P. Ohio Decisions, Nisi Prius. 1893–1903
O'D.Pr.& Acc. O'Dedy, Principal and Accessory. 1812
O'D.& Br.Eq.Dig. O'Donnell & Brady, Equity Digest (Ire.)
O.Dec.Rep. Ohio Decisions Reprint
O.Dep.Rep. Ohio Department Reports. 1914–64
O.E.C. Office of Export Control
Ontario Election Decisions
O.E.C.D. Organisation for Economic Cooperation and Development
O.E.C.E. Organisation Européenne de Cooperation Économique (Organisation for European Economic Co-operation)
O.E.C.F. Overseas Economic Co-operation Fund (OECD)
O.E.D. Oxford English Dictionary
O.E.E.C. Organisation for European Economic Cooperation
O.F.C. High Court Reports of Orange Free State (S.Afr.) 1879–83
O.F.D. Ohio Federal Decisions. 1809–11
O.F.S. Orange Free State Reports, High Court (S.Afr.) 1879–83
O.F.S.S.A. Orange Free State, South Africa

O.F.T. Office of Fair Trading
OG. Bundesgesetz über die Organisation der Bundesrechtspflege (Switz.) 1943
Obergericht (Switz.)
Serie politica ordinaria e di Gabinetto (It.)
O.G. Official Gazette, U.S. Patent Office
O.G.B.G. Official Gazette Reports (British Guiana) 1899–
OGH Oberster Gerichtshof (Austria)
Oberster Gerichtshof für die Britische Zone (Ger.) Supreme Court of the former British Zone of Occupation
O.G.L.T.R. Oil & Gas Law and Taxation Review. 1982–
O.G.Pat.Off. Official Gazette, U.S. Patent Office
O.H. Outer House of Court of Session (Scot.)
O/H Overzuche Handels maatschappij (Neth.) foreign trade company
OHG Offene Handelsgessellschaft (Ger.) unlimited (mercantile) partnership
O.H.L.J. Osgoode Hall Law Journal (Can.) 1958–
OIC Order-in-Council
OIHP Office international d'hygiène publique
O.I.T. Organisation Internationale du Travail
O.in.C. Order in Council
o.J. ohne Jahr (Ger.)
O.J. Loi fédérale d'organisation judiciaire (Switz.)
Official Journal of the European Communities
Ontario Judgments (unreported decisions available on QL) (Can.) 1986–
O.J.Act Ontario Judicature Act
O.J.Eur.Comm. Official Journal of the European Communities
O.J.L.S. Oxford Journal of Legal Studies
O.J.T. On-the-Job Training
OJZ Östereichische Juristen-Zeitung (Austria)
O.Jur. Ohio Jurisprudence. 1928–38
O'Keefe Ord. O'Keefe's Orders in Chancery (Ire.)
O.L. Ohio Laws
O.L.A. Ohio Law Abstract. 1923–
O.L.Abs. Ohio Law Abstract. 1923–
O.L.B. Ohio Law Bulletin. 1876–1921
OLCI Ohio Legal Centre Institute
O.L.D. Ohio Lower Court Decisions. 1894–96
OLG Oberlandesgericht (Austria, Ger.) District Court of Appeal
O.L.J. Ohio Law Journal. 1880–84
Oudh Law Journal (India) 1913–26
O.L.Jour. Ohio Law Journal. 1880–84
Oudh Law Journal (India) 1913–26
O.L.N. Ohio Legal News. 1894–1902
O.L.R. Ohio Law Reporter. 1903–34, 1934–
Ontario Law Reporter
Ontario Law Reports. 1901–30
Oregon Law Review. 1921–
Otago Law Review (N.Z.) 1953–7, 1965–
Oudh Law Reports (India)
O.L.R.B. Ontario Labour Relations Board Monthly Report (Can.)
O.L.R.B.Rep. Ontario Labour Relations Board Reports (Can.) 1974–
O.L.Rep. Ohio Law Reporter. 1903–34, 1934–
O.L.W.C.D. Ontario Lawyers Weekly Consolidated Digest (Can.) 1984–
O.Legal News Ohio Legal News. 1894–1902
O.Lower D. Ohio (Lower) Decisions. 1894–96
O.M.B.R. Ontario Municipal Board Reports (Can.) 1973–
OMPI Organisation Mondiale de la Propriété Intellectuelle (World Intellectual Property Organisation)
O'M.& H. O'Malley & Hardcastle's Election Cases. 1869–1929
O'M.& H.El.Cas. O'Malley & Hardcastle's Election Cases. 1869–1929
O'Mal & H. O'Malley & Hardcastle's Election Cases. 1869–1929

O.Misc. Ohio Miscellaneous Reports. 1965–
O.N.B. Old Natura Brevium
O.N.P. Ohio Nisi Prius Reports. 1893–1901
O.N.P.N.S. Ohio Nisi Prius Reports, New Series. 1902–34
O.N.U. Organisation des Nations Unies (United Nations Organisation)
O.N.U.D.I. Organisation des Nations Unies pour le Developpement Industriel
O.N.U.Intra.L.R. Ohio Northern University Intramural Law Review. 1970–72
O.N.U.L.R. Ohio Northern University Law Review. 1973–
O.O. Ohio Opinions. 1934–
O.O.2d. Ohio Opinions, Second Series
o.O.u.J. ohne Ort und Jahr (Ger.)
O.P. Out of print
OPAC Online Public Access Catalogue
OPAS Programme for Provision of Operational Assistance (UN)
O.P.B. Occupational Pensions Board
OPC ordonnance du Tribunal fédéral concernant la saisie et le réalisation des parts de communautés (Switz.) 1923
O.P.C.S. Office of Population Censuses and Surveys
O.P.D. South African Law Reports, Orange Free State Provincial Division. 1910–46
OPEC Organisation of Petroleum Exporting Countries
OPF Overseas Project Fund (PEP)
OPG Overseas Project Group (PEP)
OPIC Overseas Private Investment Corporation (USA)
O.P.R. Practice Reports (Ontario, Can.) 1850–1900
O.P.S. Official Public Service Reports (New York)
OR Bundesgesetz über das Obligationrecht (Switz.) 1936
O.R. Official Receiver
Official Referee
Official Reports of the South African Republic. 1894–99
Oklahoma Law Review. 1948–
Ontario Reports. 1882–1900, 1931–73
O.R.(2d) Ontario Reports, Second Series (Can.) 1974–
O.R.C. ordonnance (du Conseil fédéral) sur le registre du commerce (Switz.) 1937
Reports of the High Court of the Orange River Colony (S.Afr.) 1903–10
O.R.C.S.A. Orange River Colony, South Africa
O.R.S.A.R. Official Reports, South African Republic. 1894–99
O.S. Ohio State Reports. 1852–
Old Series
Old Style
Ordnance Survey
Out of Stock
Upper Canada Queen's Bench Reports, Old Series. 1831–44
O.S.2d. Ohio State Reports, Second Series
O.S.A. Official Secrets Act
Oklahoma Statutes Annotated
OSAS Overseas Service Aid Scheme (ODA)
OSB Oregon State Bar
OSBA Oregon State Bar Association
OSBABull Ohio State Bar Association Bulletin. 1921–28
O.S.C. Occupational Superannuation Commissioner (Aus.)
O.S.C.Bull. Ontario Securities Commission Bulletin (Can.) 1981–
O.S.C.D. Ohio Supreme Court Decisions, Unreported Cases. 1889–99
O.S.H.D. Occupational Safety and Health Decisions
O.S.I. Open systems interconnection
O.S.L.J. Ohio State Law Journal. 1935–41, 1948–
O.S.Supp. Oklahoma Statutes Supplement
O.S.U. Ohio Supreme Court Decisions, Unreported Cases. 1889–99
O.S.& C.P.Dec. Ohio Superior and Common Pleas Decisions

O.St. Ohio State Reports. 1852–
O.Su. Ohio Supplement
O.Supp. Ohio Supplement
OTAR Overseas Tariffs and Regulations (BOTB)
O.T.C. Overseas Telecommunications System (Aus.)
O.T.P.R. Offshore Tax Planning Review
O.U. Open University
Oxford University
OUP Oxford University Press
O.U.U.I. Decisions given by the Office of the Umpire (Unemployment Insurance) respecting Claims to Out-of-work Donation
O.U.U.I.B.D. Benefit Decisions of the Office of the Umpire
O.U.U.I.D. Office of the Umpire (Unemployment Insurance) Decisions
O.U.U.I.S.D. Office of the Umpire, Selected Decisions
OVG Oberverwaltungsgericht (Ger.) Provincial Administrative Court of Appeal
O.W.C.P. Office of Workman's Compensation Programs (USA)
O.W.N. Ontario Weekly Notes (Can.) 1909–62
Oudh Weekly Notes (India) 1924–
O.W.R. Ontario Weekly Reporter. 1902–14
O.Z.o.R. Österreichische Zeitschrift für öffentliches Recht (Austria)
O.& M. Organisation and Methods
O.& T. Oyer and Terminer
O.& W.Dig. Oldham and White's Digest of Laws (Texas)
ObG Obergericht (Ger.) Court of Appeal
Obiter Obiter (University of Canterbury Law Students' Society) (N.Z.) 1981–
Obs. The Observer
occ. occupation
occurs
Occ.N. Occasional Notes, Canada Law Times
Occ.Newsl. Occasional Newsletter (A.B.A. Committee on Environmental Law) 1973
Occ.Pen. Occupational Pensions
Occ.& Prof. Occupations and Professions
Ocean Dev.& Int.L. Ocean Development and International Law (USA) 1973–
Ocean Man. Ocean Management (Neth.) 1973–
Ocean Yb. Ocean Yearbook (USA)
Oct.Str. Strange's Octavo Select Cases on Evidence. 1698–1732
Odeneal Odeneal's Reports (9–11 Oregon)
Odg.Lib. Odgers, Libel and Slander. 6ed. 1929
Odg.Pl. Odgers, Principles of Pleading. 20ed. 1975
Odgers Odgers on Libel and Slander. 6ed. 1929
Off. Office
Official
Off.Br. Officina Brevium. 1679
Off.Brev. Officina Brevium. 1679
Off.Exec. Wentworth's Office & Duty of Executors. 1641
Off.Gaz. Official Gazette, U.S. Patent Office
Off.Gaz.Pat.Off. Official Gazette, United States Patent Office
Off.J. Official Journal of the League of Nations
Off.Jl.Pat. Official Journal of Patents, Trademarks, Designs and Copyrights (S.Afr.) 1948–60
Off.Rep. Official Reports of the High Court of the South African Republic. 1894–99
OffVerw. Öffentliche Verwaltung (Ger.) 1948–
Offend.Rehab. Offender Rehabilitation (USA) 1976–
Officer Officer's Reports (1–9 Minnesota)
Official J.Ind.Comm.Prop. Official Journal of Industrial and Commercial Property

Ogd. Ogden's Reports (12–15 Louisiana)
Ogden Ogden's Reports (12–15 Louisiana)
Ogs.Med.Jur. Ogston, Medical Jurisprudence. 1878
Oh. Ohio
Oh.A. Ohio Appellate Reports. 1913–
Oh.A.2d. Ohio Appellate Reports, Second Series
Oh.Cir.Ct. Ohio Circuit Court Reports. 1885–1901
Oh.Cir.Ct.N.S. Ohio Circuit Court Reports, New Series. 1903–17
Oh.Cir.Dec. Ohio Circuit Decisions. 1885–1901
Oh.Dec. Ohio Decisions. 1894–1920
Oh.Dec.(Reprint) Ohio Decisions Reprint. 1840–55
Oh.F.Dec. Ohio Federal Decisions. 1809–11
Oh.Jur. Ohio Jurisprudence. 1928–38
Oh.L.Bul. Ohio Law Bulletin. 1876–1921
Oh.L.Ct.D. Ohio Lower Court Decisions. 1894–96
Oh.L.J. Ohio Law Journal. 1880–84
Oh.L.Rep. Ohio Law Reporter. 1903–
Oh.Leg.N. Ohio Legal News. 1894–1902
Oh.Misc. Ohio Miscellaneous Reports. 1965–
Oh.N.P. Ohio Nisi Prius Reports. 1893–1901
Oh.N.P.(N.S.) Ohio Nisi Prius Reports, New Series. 1902–34
Oh.N.U.Intra.L.R. Ohio Northern University Intramural Law Review. 1970–72
Oh.N.U.L.R. Ohio Northern University Law Review. 1973–
Oh.Prob. Ohio Probate. 1885–90
Oh.S.C.D. Ohio Supreme Court Decisions (Unreported Cases) 1889–99
Oh.S.L.J. Ohio State Law Journal. 1935–41,1948–
Oh.S.& C.P. Ohio Superior & Common Pleas Decisions
Oh.St. Ohio State Reports. 1852–
Ohio Ohio Supreme Court Reports. 1821–51
Ohio Abs. Ohio Law Abstract. 1923–
Ohio App. Ohio Appellate Reports. 1913–
Ohio App.2d. Ohio Appellate Reports, Second Series
Ohio B.T.A. Ohio Board of Tax Appeals Reports
Ohio Bar Ohio State Bar Association Reports. 1928–
Ohio C.A. Ohio Courts of Appeals Reports. 1915–22
Ohio C.C. Ohio Circuit Court Reports. 1885–1901
Ohio C.C.Dec. Ohio Circuit Court Decisions. 1910–18
Ohio C.C.N.S. Ohio Circuit Court Reports, New Series. 1903–17
Ohio C.C.R. Ohio Circuit Court Reports. 1885–1901
Ohio C.C.R.N.S. Ohio Circuit Court Reports, New Series. 1903–17
Ohio C.D. Ohio Circuit Decisions. 1885–1901
Ohio C.Dec. Ohio Circuit Decisions. 1885–1901
Ohio C.of R.& T. Ohio Commissioners of Railroads and Telegraphs Reports. 1867–1905
Ohio Cir.Ct. Ohio Circuit Court Decisions. 1901–18
Ohio Cir.Ct.(N.S.) Ohio Circuit Court Reports, New Series. 1903–17
Ohio Cr.Ct.R. Ohio Circuit Court Reports. 1885–1901
Ohio Cir.Ct.R.N.S. Ohio Circuit Court Reports, New Series. 1903–17
Ohio Cir.Dec. Ohio Circuit Decisions. 1885–1901
Ohio Ct.App. Ohio Courts of Appeals Reports. 1915–22
Ohio Dec. Ohio Decisions. 1894–1920
Ohio Dec.N.P. Ohio Decisions Nisi Prius. 1893–1903
Ohio Dec.Reprint Ohio Decisions, Reprint. 1840–55
Ohio Dep't. Ohio Department Reports. 1914–64

Ohio F.Dec. Ohio Federal Decisions. 1809–11
Ohio Fed.Dec. Ohio Federal Decisions. 1809–11
Ohio Gov't. Ohio Government Reports. 1965–
Ohio Jur. Ohio Jurisprudence. 1928–38
Ohio Jur.2d. Ohio Jurisprudence, Second Series
Ohio L.Abs. Ohio Law Abstracts. 1923–
Ohio L.B. Ohio Law Bulletin. 1876 1921
Ohio L.Bull. Ohio Law Bulletin. 1876–1921
Ohio L.J. Ohio Law Journal. 1880–84
Ohio L.R. Ohio Law Reporter. 1903–34
Ohio L.R.& Wk.Bul. Ohio Law Reporter & Weekly Bulletin. 1934–
Ohio L.Rep. Ohio Law Reporter & Weekly Bulletin. 1934–
Ohio Law Abst. Ohio Law Abstract. 1923–
Ohio Law Bull. Ohio Law Bulletin. 1876–1921
Ohio Law J. Ohio Law Journal. 1880–84
Ohio Law R. Ohio Law Reporter. 1903–
Ohio Law Rep. Ohio Law Reporter. 1903–
Ohio Laws State of Ohio, Legislative Acts Passed and Joint Resolutions Adopted
Ohio Leg.N. Ohio Legal News. 1894–1902
Ohio Leg.News Ohio Legal News. 1894–1902
Ohio Legal N. Ohio Legal News. 1894–1902
Ohio Low.Dec. Ohio Lower Decisions. 1894–96
Ohio Lower Dec. Ohio Lower Decisions. 1894–96
Ohio Misc. Ohio Miscellaneous Reports. 1965–
Ohio Misc.Dec. Ohio Miscellaneous Reports. 1965–
Ohio N.P. Ohio Nisi Prius Reports. 1893–1901
Ohio N.P.N.S. Ohio Nisi Prius Reports, New Series. 1902–34
Ohio N.U.L.Rev. Ohio Northern University Law Review
Ohio Northern U.L.Rev. Ohio Northern University Law Review
Ohio Op. Ohio Opinions. 1934–
Ohio Ops. Ohio Opinions. 1934–
Ohio Prob. Ohio Probate Reports by Goebel. 1885–90
Ohio R.Cond. Ohio Reports Condensed. 1821–31
Ohio Rev.Code Ann. Ohio Revised Code Annotated
Ohio S.B.A. Ohio State Bar Association
Ohio S.B.A.Bull. Ohio State Bar Association Bulletin. 1924–28
Ohio S.L.J. Ohio State Law Journal. 1935–41, 1948
Ohio S.U. Ohio Supreme Court Decisions (Unreported Cases) 1889–99
Ohio S.& C.P.Dec. Ohio Superior and Common Pleas Decisions
Ohio St. Ohio State Reports. 1852–
Ohio St.2d. Ohio State Reports, 2nd Series
Ohio St.J.on Disp.Resol. Ohio State Journal on Dispute Resolution
Ohio St.L.J. Ohio State Law Journal
Ohio Sup.& C.P.Dec. Ohio Superior and Common Pleas Decisions
Ohio Supp. Ohio Supplement
Ohio Unrep. Ohio Supreme Court Unreported Cases. 1889–99
Ohio Unrep.Jud.Dec. Pollack's Ohio Unreported Judicial Decisions. 1807–23
Ohio Unrept.Cas. Ohio Supreme Court Decisions (Unreported Cases) 1889–99
Oikeustiede Oikeustiede Jurisprudentia (Finland)
Oil & Gas Oil and Gas Reporter
Oil & Gas L.R. Oil and Gas Law Review (USA) 1939
Oil & Gas Reptr. Oil and Gas Reporter (USA) 1952–
Oil & Gas Tax Q. Oil and Gas Tax Quarterly. 1951–
Ok. Oklahoma

Ok.L.R. Oklahoma Law Review. 1948–
Oke Fish.L. Oke, Fisher Laws. 4ed. 1924
Oke Game L. Oke, Game Laws. 5ed. 1912
Oke Mag.Form. Oke, Magisterial Formulist. 19ed. 1978
Oke Mag.Syn. Oke, Magisterial Synopsis. 14ed. 1893
Oke Turn. Oke, Turnpike Laws. 2ed. 1861
Okl.Cr. Oklahoma Criminal Reports. 1908–
Okl.St.Ann. Oklahoma Statutes Annotated
Okla. Oklahoma
Oklahoma Criminal Reports. 1908–
Oklahoma Supreme Court Reports. 1890–1953
Okla.Ap.Ct.Rep. Oklahoma Appellate Court Reporter
Okla.B.A.J. The Journal, Oklahoma State Bar Association. 1930–
Okla.B.Ass'n.J. The Journal, Oklahoma State Bar Association. 1930–
Okla.City U.L.Rev. Oklahoma City University Law Review
Okla.Cr. Oklahoma Criminal Reports. 1908–
Okla.Crim. Oklahoma Criminal Reports. 1908–
Okla.I.C.R. Oklahoma Industrial Commission Reports
Okla.L.J. Oklahoma Law Journal. 1902–16
Okla.L.Rev. Oklahoma Law Review. 1948–
Okla.Lawy. Oklahoma Lawyer. 1908
Okla.S.B.A. Oklahoma State Bar Association
Oklahoma State Bar Association Journal. 1930–
Okla.S.B.J. Oklahoma State Bar Association Journal. 1930–
Okla.Sess.Law.Serv. Oklahoma Session Law Service (West Pub. Co.)
Okla.Stat. Oklahoma Statutes
Okla.Stat.Ann.(West) Oklahoma Statutes Annotated (West Pub. Co.)
Ol.Horse Oliphant, Law of Horses. 6ed. 1908
Olc. Olcott's District Reports (Admiralty) (U.S.)
Olc.Adm. Olcott's District Reports (Admiralty) (USA)
Olcott Adm.(F.) Olcott's District Court Reports (Admiralty) (USA)
Old. Oldright's Nova Scotia Reports (5,6 N.S.) (Can.) 1860–67
Old Bailey Chr. Old Bailey Chronicle. 1763–86
Old Ben. Benloe's & Dalison's Common Pleas Reports (123 ER) 1486–1580
Old Benloe Benloe's & Dalison's Common Pleas Reports (123 ER) 1486–1580
Old Ent. Rastell, Old Entries
Old Nat.Brev. Old Natura Brevium
Oldr. Oldright's Nova Scotia Reports (5,6 N.S.) (Can.) 1860–67
Oldr.N.S. Oldright's Nova Scotia Reports (5,6 N.S.) (Can.) 1860–67
Oliv.B.& L. Oliver, Beavan & Lefroy Railway & Canal Cases. 1835–54
Oll.B.& F. Olliver, Bell & Fitzgerald's Reports, Court of Appeal (N.Z.) 1878–80
Olliv.B.& F. Olliver, Bell & Fitzgerald's Reports, Court of Appeal (N.Z.) 1878–80
Olms. Olmsted's Privy Council Decisions (Can.) 1867–1954
Olmsted Olmsted's Privy Council Decisions (Can.) 1867–1954
Olwine's L.J.(Pa.) Olwine's Law Journal (Pennsylvania) 1849–50
Om.Mer.Sh. Omond, Merchant Shipping Acts. 1877
Om.Sea Omond, Law of the Sea. 1916
Ombudsman J. The Ombudsman Journal (Can.)
Onsl.N.P. Onslow, Nisi Prius
Onslow Report Royal Commission on Local Government. Report (Cmd. 2506) 1925

Ont. Ontario
Ontario Reports (Can.) 1882–1900
Ont.2d. Ontario Reports, 2nd Series (Can.)
Ont.A. Ontario Appeal Reports. 1876–1900
Ont.App. Ontario Appeal Reports. 1876–1900
Ont.Dig. Digest of Ontario Case Law
Ont.El.Cas. Ontario Election Cases (Can.) 1884–1900
Ont.Elec. Ontario Election Cases (Can.) 1884–1900
Ont.Elec.C. Ontario Election Cases (Can.) 1884–1900
Ont.Elect. Ontario Election Cases (Can.) 1884–1900
Ont.L. Ontario Law Reports. 1901–31
Ont.L.R. Ontario Law Reports (Can.) 1901–31
Ont.L.R.C. Ontario Law Reform Commission
Ont.L.Rep. Ontario Law Reports (Can.) 1901–31
Ont.Lawyers Wkly. Ontario Lawyers Weekly (Can.) 1980–
Ont.P.R. Ontario Practice Reports. 1850–1900
Ont.Pr. Ontario Practice
Ont.Pr.Rep. Ontario Practice Reports. 1850–1900
Ont.R. Ontario Reports (Can.) 1882–1900
Ont.R.& W.N. Ontario Reports and Weekly Notes (Can.)
Ont.Reg. Ontario Regulations (Can.)
Ont.Rev.Stat. Ontario Revised Statutes (Can.)
Ont.Stat. Ontario Statutes (Can.)
Ont.W.N. Ontario Weekly Notes (Can.) 1909–32, 1933–
Ont.W.R. Ontario Weekly Reporter. 1902–14
Ont.Week.N. Ontario Weekly Notes. 1909–32,1933–
Ont.Week.R. Ontario Weekly Reports (Can.) 1902–14
Ont.Wkly.N. Ontario Weekly Notes (Can.) 1909–32, 1933
Ont.Wkly.Rep. Ontario Weekly Reporter (Can.) 1902–14
Ontario Cons.Reg. Ontario Consolidated Regulations (Can.)
Ontario L.R.C. Ontario Law Reform Commission
Onuphr.de Interp.Voc.Eccles. Onuphrius de Interpretatione Vocum Ecclesiae
op. opera (It.) work
Op. Opinion
Op.A.G. Opinions of the Attorneys-General (USA) 1789–
Op.Att.Gen. Opinions of the Attorneys-General (USA) 1789–
Op.Att'y.Gen. Opinions of the Attorneys-General (USA) 1789–
Op.Attys.Gen. Opinions of the Attorneys-General (USA) 1789–
op.cit. opere citato (Lat.) in the work quoted
Op.Let. Opinion letter
Op.N.Y.Atty.Gen. Sickels' Opinions of Attorneys-General of New York
Opp.Int.L. Oppenheim, International Law. vol. 1, 8ed. 1955; vol. 2, 7ed. 1952
Ops. Operations
Opinions
Ops.A.G. Opinions of the Attorneys-General (USA) 1789–
Ops.Atty.Gen. Opinions of the Attorneys–General (USA) 1789–
Or. Oregon
Oregon Supreme Court Reports. 1953–
Orleans
Indian Law Reports, Orissa Series. 1950–
Or.A. Oregon Court of Appeals Reports. 1969–
Or.App. Oregon Court of Appeals Reports. 1969–
Or.Ind. Orissa, India
Or.L.R. Oregon Law Review, 1921–
Or.L.Rev. Oregon Law Review. 1921–
Or.L.S.J. Oregon Law School Journal. 1902–03
Or.Laws Oregon Laws and Resolutions

Or.Laws Adv.Sh. Oregon Laws Advance Sheets

Or.P.S.C. Oregon Public Service Commission Reports

Or.P.U.C.Ops. Oregon Office of Public Utilities Commissioner, Opinions & Decisions

Or.Rev.Stat. Oregon Revised Statutes

Or.S.B.Bull. Oregon State Bar Bulletin. 1935–

Or.T.R. Oregon Tax Reporter. 1962–

Or.T.Rep. Oregon Tax Reporter. 1962–
Orleans Term Reports (1, 2 Martin) (Louisiana) 1809–12

Oracle Oracle (Monash University Law Society) (Aus.)

Ord. Order
Ordinance
Ordonnance

Ord.Austl.Cap.Terr. Ordinances of the Australian Capital Territory

Ord.Con.Jer. Ordres du Conseil Enregistrés à Jersey

Ords.N.Z. Ordinances of the Legislative Council of New Zealand

Ore. Oregon

Ore.L.Rev. Oregon Law Review. 1921–

Ore.Rev.Stat. Oregon Revised Statutes

Oreg.L.R. Oregon Law Review. 1921–

Oreg.L.Rev. Oregon Law Review. 1921–

Oreg.S.B.Bull. Oregon State Bar Bulletin. 1935–

Orestano, Diritto Romano R. Orestano, Introduzione allo Studio Storico del Diritto Romano (It.) 1953

org. organisation

Orient.& Afr.Stud. Oriental and African Studies

Oris. All India Reporter, Orissa. 1949–

Orissa All India Reporter, Orissa. 1949–

Orl.Bridg. Orlando Bridgman's Common Pleas Reports (124 ER) 1660–67

Orl.Bridgman Orlando Bridgman's Common Pleas Reports (124 ER) 1660–67

Orl.T.R. Orleans Term Reports (1, 2 Martin) (Louisiana) 1809–12

Orleans App. Orleans Court of Appeals (Louisiana) 1903–17

Orleans T.R. Orleans Term Reports (1,2 Martin) (Louisiana) 1809–12

Ormond Ormond's Reports (19–107 Alabama)

Orphans'Ct. Orphans' Court (USA)

Ort.Hist. Ortolan, History of the Roman Law

Ort.Inst. Ortolan, Institute de Justinian

Osaka Univ.L.Rev. Osaka University Law Review (Japan)

Osgoode Hall L.J. Osgoode Hall Law Journal (Can.) 1958–

Ost.Eur-R. Osteuropa–Recht (Ger.)

Öst.Z.ö.R. Österreichische Zeitschrift für öffentliches Recht (Austria)

Öst.Zschft.öff.R.N.F. Österreichische Zeitschrift für öffentliches Recht, Neue Folge (Austria)

Österr.Juristen Zeitung Österreichische Juristen Zeitung (Austria)

Österr.Zeitschr.f.öff.Recht Österreichische Zeitschrift für öffentliches Recht und Völkerrecht (Austria)

Osteurop.-R. Osteuropa–Recht (Ger.)

Ot. Otto's United States Supreme Court Reports (91–107 U.S.)

Otago L.R. Otago Law Review (N.Z.) 1965–

Otago L.Rev. Otago Law Review (N.Z.) 1965–

Otago Pol.Gaz. Otago Police Gazette (N.Z.) 1861–64

Ott. Otto's United States Supreme Court Reports (91–107 U.S.)

Ottawa L.R. Ottawa Law Review (Can.) 1966–

Ottawa L.Rev. Ottawa Law Review (Can.) 1966–

Otto Otto's United States Supreme Court Reports (91–107 U.S.)

Oudh All India Reporter, Oudh. 1914–49
Indian Rulings, Oudh. 1929–47

Oudh.C. Oudh Code (India)

Oudh L.J. Oudh Law Journal (India) 1914–26

Oudh.L.R. Oudh Law Reports (India)

Oudh Rev.Sel.Cas. Revised Collection of Selected Cases issued by Chief Commissioner and Financial Commissioner of Oudh

Oudh W.N. Oudh Weekly Notes (India) 1924–48

Oudh Wkly.N. Oudh Weekly Notes (India) 1924–48

Ought. Oughton's Ordo Judiciorum

Oult.Ind. Oulton, Index to Irish Statutes

Oult.Laws Ir. Oulton, Laws of Ireland

Out. Outerbridge's Reports (97, 98 Pennsylvania State)

Outer House Outer House of the Court of Session (Scot.)

overr. overruled in
overruling

Overt. Overton's Tennessee Supreme Court Reports (1–2 Tennessee) 1791–1816

Ow. New South Wales Reports (1–3 NSW) (Aus.)
Owen's King's Bench Reports (74 ER) 1556–1615

Owen Owen's King's Bench & Common Pleas Reports (74 ER) 1556–1615

Ox.J.L.S. Oxford Journal of Legal Studies. 1980–

Oxf.Lawy. Oxford Lawyer. 1958–61

Oxford J.Leg.St. Oxford Journal of Legal Studies

Oxford J.Legal Stud. Oxford Journal of Legal Studies

Oxley Oxley's Railway Cases. 1897–1903
Young's Vice-Admiralty Decisions, ed. Oxley (Nova Scotia) 1865–1880

P

p. page
per (by)
P. All India Reporter, Patna. 1916–
Court of Probate
Indian Law Reports, Patna. 1922–
Law Reports, Probate, Divorce & Admiralty Division. 1891–
Pacific Reporter
Pennsylvania
Peters' Reports (26–41 U.S.) 1828–42
Pickering's Reports (18–41 Massachusetts) 1820–39
President
Pretura (It.)
Prince
Serie politica, detta P (It.)
P.2d. Pacific Reporter, Second Series
P.A. Personal Assistant
Power of Attorney
Press Agent
Press Association
Professional Administrator (Aus.) 1949–
Publishers' Association
P/A Power of Attorney
P.A.B. Planning Appeals Board (Victoria, Aus.)
P.A.B.B. Pay and Benefits Bulletin
P.A.B.R. Planning Appeals Board Reports (Victoria, Aus.) 1983–7
Practice Notes, of the Australian Broadcasting Tribunal (in Durie & Catterns' Broadcasting Law and Practice) 1987–
PABX Private automatic branch exchange
PAC Public access catalogue
P.A.D. Peters' Admiralty Decisions (USA)
Planning Appeal Decisions
PADUD Program of Advanced Professional Development, University of Denver College of Law
PAHO Pan American Health Organization
P.A.I.S. Public Affairs Information Service (USA)
PANS International Civil Aviation Organisation Procedures for Air Navigation Services
P.A.R. Public Administration Review (USA) 1940–
P.A.T. Patents Appeal Tribunal
Pensions Appeal Tribunal
P.A.Y.E. Pay As You Earn
P.B. Parole Board
Pasicrisie Belge (Belg.)
Professional Books Ltd.
PBGI Pension Book of Gray's Inn, ed. by R.J. Fletcher. 1901–10
PBI Pennsylvania Bar Institute
P.C. All India Reporter, Privy Council. 1914–50
British & Colonial Prize Cases. 1914–22
Brottsbalken (Swed.) The Penal Code
Indian Rulings, Privy Council. 1929–47
Law Reports, Privy Council. 1865–75
Parish Council(lor)
Parliamentary Cases
Patent Cases
Penal Code
Pleas of the Crown
Political Code
Practice Cases

Precedents in Chancery
Press Council
Price Control Cases
Privy Council/Privy Councillor
Prize Court
Probate Court
Procédure Civile (Fr.) Civil Procedure

PC 2 Public Record Office, registers of the Privy Council

P.C.'74–'28 Judgments of the Privy Council on Appeal from the Gold Coast (Ghana) 1874–1928

P.C.A. Acts of the Privy Council
Parliamentary Commissioner for Administration
Permanent Court of Arbitration

P.C.Act Probate Court Act

P.C.App. Law Reports, Privy Council Appeals

P.C.C. Palmer's Company Cases
Parochial Church Council
Peters' Circuit Court Reports (USA) 1803–18
Prerogative Court of Canterbury
Privy Council Acts, Colonial Series
Privy Council Cases
Public Record Office, wills registered in the Prerogative Court of York

PCG Convention on the Prevention and Punishment of the Crime of Genocide. 1948

P.C.I. Privy Council Decisions (India)

PCIJ Permanent Court of International Justice
Permanent Court of International Justice Cases

P.C.I.J.Rep. Reports of the Permanent Court of International Justice

PCIJ Series A PCIJ Publications Series A: Judgments and Orders. 1922–30

PCIJ Series A/B PCIJ Publications Series A/B: Judgments, Orders and Advisory Opinions. 1931–40

PCIJ Series B PCIJ Publications Series B: Advisory Opinions. 1922–30

PCIJ Series D PCIJ Publications Series D: Acts and Documents concerning the Organisation of the Court. 1922–40

PCIJ Series E PCIJ Publications Series E: Annual Reports. 1925–39

P.C.Int. Pacific Coast International (USA) 1934–46

P.C.Judg. Privy Council Judgments (India)

P.C.L.B. Practitioners' Child Law Bulletin

P.C.L.J. Pacific Coast Law Journal (USA) 1878–83
Practitioners' Child Law Journal

P.C.L.L.G. Ollennu, Principles of Customary Land Law in Ghana

PCP Convention for the Protection of Cultural Property in the Event of Armed Conflict. 1954

P.C.R. Parker's Criminal Reports (New York) 1823–68
Pennsylvania Corporation Reporter. 1914–39
Pennsylvania County Court Reports. 1885–1921

P.C.Rep. Privy Council Reports

P.C.S. Principal Clerk of Session

P.C.T. Patents Cooperation Treaty (Washington) 1970

PCY Borthwick Institute (York), wills registered in the Prerogative Court of York

P.Cas. British & Colonial Prize Cases (Trehern & Grant) 1914–22

P.Cl.R. Parker's Criminal Reports (New York) 1823–68
Privy Council Reports

P.Coast L.J. Pacific Coast Law Journal (USA) 1878–83

P.Ct. Probate Court

P.D. Law Reports, Probate, Divorce and Admiralty Division. 1875–90
Parliamentary Debates

P.D.A. Probate, Divorce and Admiralty

P.D.Div'l.Ct. Probate, Divorce, and Admiralty Division and Divisional Court

P.Div. Law Reports, Probate Division

P.D.T.M. Précis des Décisions des Tribunaux du District de Montréal (Montreal Condensed Reports)

(Québec, Can.) 1853–54

P.E.I. Haszard & Walburton's Reports (Prince Edward Island, Can.) 1850–82
Prince Edward Island
Prince Edward Island Reports (Haviland's) 1850–72

P.E.I.J. Prince Edward Island Judgments (unreported decisions available on QL) (Can.) 1986–

P.E.I.L.R.C. Prince Edward Island Law Reform Commission

P.E.I.Rep. Haviland's Prince Edward Island Reports. 1850–72

P.E.I.Rev.Stat. Prince Edward Island Revised Statutes (Can.)

P.E.I.Stat. Prince Edward Island Statutes (Can.)

P.E.L.B. Planning and Environmental Law Bulletin

PEP Projects and Export Policy Division (BOTB)

PER Professional and Executive Recruitment (MSCE)

PERIN Penalty Enforcement Registration of Infringement Notice (Victoria, Aus.)

PES Public Expenditure Survey

PESC Public Expenditure Survey Committee

P.F.S. P.F. Smith's Reports (51–81 Pennsylvania State Reports)

P.F.Smith P.F. Smith's Reports (51–81 Pennsylvania State Reports)

P.G. Procureur Generaal (Neth.) Public Attorney

P.G.R. Liechtensteinisches Zivilgesetzbuch, Personen-und Gesellschaftsrecht

P.H. Parliamentary History

P.-H. Prentice-Hall, Inc.

P.H.A.S. Public Health Advisory Service

P.-H.Am.Lab.Arb.Awards American Labour Arbitration Awards (P.-H.) 1946–

P.-H.Am.Lab.Cas. American Labor Arbitration Awards (P.-H.) 1946–

P.H.B. Parliament House Book (Scot.)

P.H.C.C. Patna High Court Cases (India) 1917–26

P.-H.Cas. American Federal Tax Reports (P.-H.) 1796–

P.-H.Corp. American Corporation Cases (P.-H.) 1868–87

P.-H.Est.Plan. Estate Planning Cases (P-H)

P.-H.Fed.Taxes American Federal Tax Reports (P.-H.) 1796–

P.-H.Fed.Wage & Hour Federal Wage and Hour Cases (P.-H.) 1938–

PHR Convention for the Protection of Human Rights and Fundamental Freedoms. 1950

PHR Prot Protocol to PHR. 1952

P.-H.Tax American Federal Tax Reports (P.-H.) 1796–

P.-H.Tax Ct.Mem. Tax Court Memorandum Decisions (P.-H.) 1928–

P.-H.Tax Ct.Rep.& Mem.Dec. Tax Court Reported and Memorandum Decisions (Prentice-Hall) 1928–

P.H.V. pro hac vice (Lat.) for this purpose or occasion

PI Pensions Intelligence
Performance indicator

P.I.A.C. Public Interest Advocacy Centre (New South Wales, Aus.)

P.I.B. Prices and Incomes Board
Public Information Bulletin (Australian Taxation Office) 1965–
Public Information Bulletin (New Zealand Inland Revenue Department) 1963–

PIB'S Public Information Bulletins (Australian Taxation Office) 1965–

P.I.C.A.O. Provisional International Civil Aviation Organization (UN)

PIE Paedophile Information Exchange

P.I.P.S.C.R. Philippine Islands Public Service Commission Reports

P.I.P.U.C.R. Philippine Islands Public Utility Commission Reports

P.I.Q.R. Personal Injuries and Quantum Reports. 1992–

P.I.Rep. Philippines Island Reports. 1901–46

P.Int. Portfolio International
P.J. ICC Practitioners' Journal (Interstate Commerce Commission, USA) 1933–
Presiding Judge
Printed Judgments, Bombay High Court (India) 1873–1900
P.J.L.B. Lower Burma, Printed Judgments
P.J.T. Prices Justification Tribunal (Aus.)
P.Jr.& H. Patton, Jr., & Heath's Reports (Virginia Special Court of Appeals)
PKG Die Praxis des Kantonsgerichts von Graubunden (Switz.)
P.L. Pamphlet Laws
Poor Law
Public Law
Public Law. 1956–
P/L Proprietary Limited
PLA Port of London Authority
P.L.B. Poor Law Board
Property Law Bulletin. 1981–
P.L.Boards Public Law Boards
PLC Public Limited Company
P.L.C. Practical Law for Companies
P.L.Com. Poor Law Commissioner
P.L.D. All Pakistan Legal Decisions. 1948–
P.L.E. Encyclopedia of Pennsylvania Law
PLF Pacific Legal Foundation
PLI Practising Law Institute (USA)
P.L.I. Product Liability International
P.L.J. Pacific Law Journal (USA) 1970–
Patna Law Journal (India) 1916–21
Pennsylvania Law Journal. 1842–48
Philippine Law Journal. 1914–
Pittsburg Legal Journal. 1853–
P.L.J.N.S. Pittsburg Legal Journal New Series (Pennsylvania)
P.L.M. Pacific Law Magazine (USA) 1867
Poor Law Magazine (Scot.) 1858–1930
P.L.Mag. Poor Law Magazine (Scot.) 1858–1930
P.L.R. Pacific Law Reporter (USA) 1870–77
Pakistan Law Reports
Pakistan Law Review. 1952
Patent Law Review (USA) 1879–80, 1969–
Patna Law Reporter (India) 1923–25
Pennsylvania Law Record (Philadelphia) 1879–80
Planning Law Reports
Private Legislation Reports (Scot.)
Public Lending Right
Punjab Law Reporter (India) 1900–
University of Pittsburgh Law Review. 1935–42, 1947–
P.L.R.Dacca Pakistan Law Reports, Dacca Series. 1951–
P.L.R.J.& K. Punjab Law Reporter, Jammu & Kashmir Series (India)
P.L.R.Kar. Pakistan Law Reports, Karachi Series. 1947–53
P.L.R.Lah. Pakistan Law Reports, Lahore Series. 1947–55
P.L.R.W.P. Pakistan Law Reports, West Pakistan Series. 1956–
P.L.T. Patna Law Times (India) 1920–
Professional Liability Today
Punjab Law Times (India)
P.L.U. Pensions Law Update
P.L.W. Patna Law Weekly (India) 1917
P.M. Pensions Management
Police Magistrate
Prime Minister
PMI Pensions Management Institute
P.N. Professional Negligence
P.N.G.L.R. Papua New Guinea Law Reports
P.N.G.L.R.C. Papua New Guinea Law Reform Commission
P.N.P. Peake's Nisi Prius Reports (170 ER) 1790–94
PNS Private network service
P.O. Patent Office
Post Office
Province of Ontario
Public Officer
P.O.A. Prison Officers' Association
POAC Post Office Advisory Committee
POCL Post Office Counters Limited

P.O.Cas. Perry's Oriental Cases, Bombay (India) 1843–52
P.O.G. Official Gazette, U.S. Patent office
P.O.J. Patent Office Journal (India) 1921–
POS Policy Statement, of the Australian Broadcasting Tribunal (in Durie & Catterns' Broadcasting Law and Practice) 1987–
P.O.U.N.C. Post Office Users' National Council
P.P. Pandectes Périodiques (Belg.) encyclopedia
Parliamentary Papers
Patent of precedence
p.p.a. per power of attorney
P.P.A. Polimeles Protodikion Athinon (Multi-member First Instance Court of Athens)
P.P.C. Pierce's Perpetual Code. 1943
PPELDO Protocol on Privileges and Immunities of ELDO. 1964
PPESRO Protocol concerning the Privileges and Immunities of ESRO. 1963
p.p.i. policy proof of interest
P.P.L.R. Public Procurement Law Review
P.P.M. Professional Practice Management
P.P.P. Polimeles Protodikion Pireos (Multi-member First Instance Court of Piraeus)
P.P.R. Principal Probate Registry
Printed Paper Rate
P.P.S.A.C. Personal Property Security Act Cases (Can.) 1977–
PPSO Convention on the Prevention of Pollution of the Sea by Oil. 1954
P.Q. Parliamentary Question
Province of Quebec
United States Patents Quarterly. 1929–
P.Q.W. Placita de Quo Warranto
P.R. Pacific Reporter (U.S. National Reporter System)
Parliamentary Reports
Patent Roll
Pennsylvania Reports (Penrose & Watts) 1829–32
Philadelphia Reports (Pennsylvania) 1850–51
Philippine Island Reports. 1901–46
Pittsburg Reports (Pennsylvania) 1853–73
Postal Regulations
Press Release
Probate Reports
Proportional Representation
Public Relations
Puerto Rico
Puerto Rico Supreme Court Reports. 1899–
Punjab Record (India) 1866–1919
Pyke's Reports (Can.)
Upper Canada Practice Reports (Ontario) 1850–1900
P.R.B.R. Pension Review Board Reports (Can.) 1972–86
P.R.C. Postal Rate Commission (USA)
P.R.C.P. Practical Register in Common Pleas
P.R.Ch. Practical Register in Chancery
P.R.D. Puerto Rico Decisions. 1899–1906
P.R.F. Puerto Rico Federal Reports. 1900–24
P.R.Fed. Puerto Rico Federal Reports. 1900–24
P.R.I.C.Dec. Puerto Rico Industrial Commission Decisions
P.R.Laws Ann. Laws of Puerto Rico Annotated
PRN Practice Notes, of the Australian Broadcasting Tribunal (in Durie & Catterns' Broadcasting Law and Practice) 1987–
P.R.O. Patent – och Registreringsverket (Swed.) The Patent and Registration Office
Public Record Office
PRO 30/23 Public Record Office, records of Serjeants' Inn, Chancery Lane
PROB 2 Public Record Office, probate inventories

PROB 6 Public Record Office, administrations (Prerogative Court of Canterbury)
PROB 11 Public Record Office, registers of wills (Prerogative Court of Canterbury)
P.R.R. Puerto Rico Supreme Court Reports. 1899–
P.R.S.C.R. Puerto Rico Supreme Court Reports. 1899–
P.R.T. Petroleum Revenue Tax
P.R.T.C.D. Puerto Rico Tax Court Decisions. 1943–
P.R.U. Pay Research Unit (Civil Service)
P.R.U.C. Practice Reports Upper Canada (Ontario) 1850–1900
P.R.& D. Power, Rodwell and Dew's Election Cases. 1847–56
P.R.& D.El.Cas. Power, Rodwell and Dew's Election Cases. 1847–56
P.S. Parliamentary Secretary
Penal Servitude
Permanent Secretary
Personal Secretary
Petty Sessions
Press Secretary
Privy Seal
Public Service
Public Statutes
Purdon's Pennsylvania Statutes
P.S.A. Prices Surveillance Authority (Aus.)
Property Services Agency
Public Service Association (Aus.)
P.S.B. Public Service Board (Aus.)
P.S.B.R. Public Sector Borrowing Requirement
P.S.C. Public Service Commission (USA)
P.S.C.R. Public Service Commission Reports
P.S.C.U.S. Peters' Reports (26–41 U.S.) 1828–42
P.S.D. Petty Session Division
P.S.Q. Political Science Quarterly (USA) 1886–
P.S.R. Pennsylvania State Reports. 1845–
Petty Sessions Review (Aus.) 1967–
P.S.S.R.B. Public Service Staff Relations Board Decisions (Can.) 1982–
PST Profit-sharing trustee
PSTN Public switched telephone network
P.Shaw Patrick Shaw's Justiciary Decisions (Scot.) 1819–31
P.T. Pension Trustee
Pensions Today
Public Trustee
Purchase Tax
PTC Patent, Trademark and Copyright
P.T.O. Patent and Trademark Office (USA)
Public Trustee Office
P.T.P.R. Personal Tax Planning Review
P.T.Rulings Payroll Tax Rulings (CCH)) 1985–
PTT Postal, telegraph and telephone administration
P.Tr. Private Trust
P.U.C. Public Utilities Commission (USA)
P.U.F. Presses Universitaires de France
P.U.Fort. Public Utilities Fortnightly (USA) 1928–
P.U.R. Public Utilities Reports. 1915–33
P.U.R.(N.S.) Public Utilities Reports, New Series. 1934–
P.U.S. Parliamentary Under-Secretary
Permanent Under-Secretary
p.-v. procès-verbal
PVBA Personen Vennootschap met Beperkte Aansprakelijkheid (Belg.) private company
PVG Bundesgesetz betreffend den Postverkehr (Switz.) 1924
P.W. Patent World
Peere Williams' Chancery Reports (24 ER) 1695–1735
Public Welfare
Public Works
PWA Public Works Administration (USA)
P.W.N. Patna Weekly Notes (India)
P.W.R. Punjab Weekly Reporter (India) 1905–23

P.W.T. Public Works and Transportation (USA)
P.Wms. Peere Williams' Chancery Reports (24 ER) 1695–1735
P.& A. Page & Adams' Code. 1912
P.& B. Pugsley & Burbridge's New Brunswick Reports (Can.) 1878–82
P.& C. Prideaux & Cole's Reports (New Session Cases, Vol. 4) 1850–51
P.& C.R. Planning and Compensation Reports. 1949–
Property & Compensation Reports (continuation of above)
P.& D. Perry and Davison's Queen's Bench Reports (48–54 RR) 1838–41
Probate and Divorce
Law Reports, Probate & Divorce. 1865–75
P.& F. Pike & Fischer's Administrative Law (USA)
Pike & Fischer's Federal Rules Service (USA)
Pike & Fischer's OPA Price Service (USA)
P.& F.Radio Reg. Pike & Fischer's Radio Regulation Reporter (USA)
P.& H. Patton, Jr., & Heath's Reports (Virginia Special Court of Appeals) 1855–57
P.& K. Perry & Knapp's Election Cases. 1833
P.& L.Dig.Laws Pepper & Lewis' Digest of Laws (Pennsylvania)
P.& L.Laws Private and Local Laws (USA)
P.& M. Pollock & Maitland's History of English Law
Probate & Matrimonial
P.& M.H.E.L. Pollock & Maitland's History of English Law
P.& N.G.L.R. Papua and New Guinea Law Reports
p.& p. postage and packing
P.& R. Pigott and Rodwell's Reports in Common Pleas. 1843–45
P.& T. Pugsley & Trueman's New Brunswick Reports (Can.) 1882–83
P.& W. Penrose & Watts' Reports (Pennsylvania) 1829–32
Pa. Paine's Circuit Court Reports (USA) 1810–40
Pennsylvania
Pennsylvania Supreme Court Reports. 1845–
Pa.B.A. Pennsylvania Bar Association
Pa.B.A.Q. Pennsylvania Bar Association Quarterly. 1929–
Pa.B.A.Rep. Pennsylvania Bar Association Report
Pa.B.Ass'n.Q. Pennsylvania Bar Association Quarterly. 1929–
Pa.B.Brief. Pennsylvania Bar Brief
Pa.Bar.Asso.Q. Pennsylvania Bar Association Quarterly. 1929–
Pa.Bk.Cas. Pennsylvania Bank Cases
Pa.C. Pennsylvania Commonwealth Court Reports. 1970–
Pa.C.C. Pennsylvania County Court Reports. 1885–1921
Pa.C.Dec.W.C.C. Pennsylvania Courts, Decisions in Workmen's Compensation Cases. 1916–
Pa.C.P. Pennsylvania Common Pleas Reporter. 1879–87
Pa.C.Pl. Pennsylvania Common Pleas Reporter. 1879–87
Pa.Cas. Pennsylvania Supreme Court Cases (Sadler) 1885–88
Pa.Co. Pennsylvania County Court
Pa.Co.Ct. Pennsylvania County Court Reports. 1885–1921
Pa.Co.Ct.R. Pennsylvania County Court Reports. 1885–1921
Pa.Com.Pl. Pennsylvania Common Pleas Reporter. 1879–87
Pa.Commw.Ct. Pennsylvania Commonwealth Court Reports. 1970–
Pa.Cons.Stat. Pennsylvania Consolidated Statutes
Pa.Cons.Stat.Ann. Pennsylvania Consolidated Statutes Annotated
Pa.Corp.R. Pennsylvania Corporation Reporter. 1914–39
Pa.Corp.Rep. Pennsylvania Corporation Reporter. 1914–39

Pa.County Ct. Pennsylvania County Court Reports. 1885–1921

Pa.D.& C. Pennsylvania District & County Reports. 1922–

Pa.D.& C.2d. Pennsylvania District & County Reports, 2nd Series

Pa.Dep.L.& I.Dec. Pennsylvania Department of Labor and Industry Decisions

Pa.Dep.Rep. Pennsylvania Department Reports. 1916–

Pa.Dist. Pennsylvania District Reporter. 1892–1921

Pa.Dist.R. Pennsylvania District Reporter. 1891–1921

Pa.Dist.& C.Rep. Pennsylvania District & County Reports. 1922–

Pa.Dist.& Co. Pennsylvania District & County Reports. 1922–

Pa.Fid. Pennsylvania Fiduciary Reporter. 1951–

Pa.Fiduc. Pennsylvania Fiduciary Reporter. 1951–

Pa.L. Pennsylvania Law Journal. 1842–48
University of Pennsylvania Law Review. 1944–

Pa.L.G. Legal Gazette (Pennsylvania) 1869–76
Legal Gazette Reports (Campell) (Pennsylvania) 1869–71

Pa.L.J. Pennsylvania Law Journal. 1842–48
Pennsylvania Law Journal Reports. 1842–52

Pa.L.J.R. Clark's Pennsylvania Law Journal Reports. 1842–52

Pa.L.Rec. Pennsylvania Law Record. 1879–80

Pa.L.Rev. University of Pennsylvania Law Review. 1944–

Pa.L.S. Pennsylvania Law Series. 1894–96

Pa.Law J. Pennsylvania Law Journal. 1842–48

Pa.Law Jour. Pennsylvania Law Journal. 1842–48

Pa.Law Ser. Pennsylvania Law Series. 1894–96

Pa.Laws Laws of the General Assembly of the Commonwealth of Pennsylvania

Pa.Leg.Gaz. Legal Gazette (Pennsylvania) 1869–76
Legal Gazette Reports (Campbell) (Pennsylvania) 1869–71

Pa.Legis.Serv. Pennsylvania Legislative Service

Pa.Misc. Pennsylvania Miscellaneous Reports

Pa.N.P. Brightly's Nisi Prius Reports (Pennsylvania) 1809–51

Pa.Rec. Pennsylvania Law Record. 1879–80

Pa.Rep. Pennsylvania Reports

Pa.S. Pennsylvania Superior Court Reports. 1895–

Pa.St. Pennsylvania State Reports. 1845–

Pa.St.Tr. Pennsylvania State Trials (Hogan)

Pa.Stat.Ann. Pennsylvania Statutes Annotated

Pa.State. Pennsylvania State Reports. 1845–

Pa.Summary Summary of Pennsylvania Jurisprudence

Pa.Super. Pennsylvania Superior Court Reports. 1895–

Pa.Super.Ct. Pennsylvania Superior Court Reports. 1895–

Pa.W.C.Bd.Dec. Pennsylvania Workmen's Compensation Board Decisions. 1916–

Pa.W.C.Bd.Dec.Dig. Digest of Decisions (Workmen's Compensation Board) (Pennsylvania)

Pac. Pacific
Pacific Reporter (U.S. National Reporter System)

Pac.Coast Int. Pacific Coast International. 1934–46

Pac.Coast L.J. Pacific Coast Law Journal. 1878–83

Pac.L.J. Pacific Law Journal. 1970–

Pac.Law.Mag. Pacific Law Magazine. 1867

Pac.Law Reptr. Pacific Law Reporter, San Francisco. 1870–77
Pac.Leg.N. Pacific Legal News. 1911
Pac.R. Pacific Reporter (U.S. National Reporter System)
Pac.Rep. Pacific Reporter (U.S. National Reporter System)
Pace Envtl.L.Rev. Pace Environmental Law Review (USA)
Pace L.Rev. Pace Law Review (USA)
Pace Y.B.Int'l L. Pace Yearbook of International Law
Pacific Aff. Pacific Affairs
Pacific C.L.J. Pacific Coast Law Journal, San Francisco. 1878–83
Pacific L.J. Pacific Law Journal. 1970–
Pag. Page's Three Early Assize Rolls, County of Northumberland. 1256, 1269, 1279 (Surtees Society) 1811
Pai. Paige's New York Chancery Reports. 1828–45
Paine's Circuit Court Reports (USA) 1810–40
Pai.Ch. Paige's New York Chancery Reports. 1828–45
Paige Paige's New York Chancery Reports. 1828–45
Paige Ch. Paige's New York Chancery Reports. 1828–45
Paine Paine's Circuit Court Reports (USA) 1810–40
Paine C.C. Paine's Circuit Court Reports (USA) 1810–40
Pak. Pakistan
Pak.Bar Council J. Pakistan Bar Council Journal
Pak.Bar.J. Pakistan Bar Journal. 1956–60
Pak.Crim.L.J. Pakistan Criminal Law Journal. 1968–
Pak.L.R. Pakistan Law Reports
Pak.L.Rev. Pakistan Law Review. 1952
Pak.Sup.Ct.Q. Pakistan Supreme Court Quarterly
Pal. Palmer's Assizes at Cambridge, 1260. 1930
Palmer's King's Bench Reports (81 ER) 1619–29
Palmer's Reports (53–60 Vermont)
Pal.Ag. Paley, Principal and Agent. 3ed. 1833
Pal.Conv. Paley, Summary Convictions. 10ed. 1953
Palestine Yrbk.Int.L. The Palestine Yearbook of International Law (Cyprus)
Paley Ag. Paley, Principal and Agent. 3ed. 1833
Paley Princ.& Ag. Paley, Principal & Agent. 3ed. 1833
Palg.Rise & Prog. Palgrave, Rise and Progress of the English Commonwealth. 1832
Palgrave Palgrave's Proceedings in Chancery
Palgrave's Rise and Progress of the English Commonwealth
Palm. Palmer's Assizes at Cambridge, 1260. 1930
Palmer's King's Bench Reports (81 ER) 1619–29
Palmer's Reports (53–60 Vermont)
Palm.Comp.L. Palmer, Company Law. 22ed. 1976
Palm.Comp.Prec. Palmer, Company Precedents. 17ed. 1956–60
Palm.Pr.Comp. Palmer, Private Companies. 41ed. 1950
Palm.Pr.Lords Palmer, Practice in the House of Lords. 1830
Palm.Sh. Palmer, Shareholders. 34ed. 1936
Palm.Wr. Palmer, Law of Wreck. 1843
Palmer Palmer's Assizes at Cambridge, 1260. 1930
Palmer's King's Bench Reports. 1619–29
Palmer's Reports (53–60 Vermont)
Palmer Co.Prec. Palmer's Company Precedents. 17ed. 1956–60
Pamph. Pamphlet
Pan. Panama
Pan-Am.T.S. Pan-American Treaty Series
Pand.Pér. Pandectes périodiques: Recueil de jurisprudence (Belg.)

Panel The Panel, Association of Grand Jurors of New York County Bar. 1924–45
Panst.Prawo Panstwo i Prawo (Poland)
Papua & N.G. Papua and New Guinea Law Reports
Papy Papy's Reports (5–8 Florida)
par. parish
Par. Paragraph
Parker's Exchequer Reports (145 ER) 1743–67
Parker's New York Criminal Reports. 1823–68
Parsons' Reports (65–66 New Hampshire)
Par.Ant. Parochial Antiquities. 1695
Par.Bills & N. Parsons on Bills and Notes
Par.Cont. Parsons on Contracts
Par.Dec. Parsons' Decisions (2–7 Massachusetts)
Par.Eq.Cas. Parsons' Select Equity Cases (Pennsylvania) 1842–51
Par.Part. Parsons, Partnership. 1889
Par.Wills Parsons, Wills. 1854
Para. Paragraph
Paraguay
Parana Jud. Parana Judiciario, doutrina, jurisprudencia e legislacao
Park. Parker's Exchequer Reports (145 ER) 1743–67
Parker's New York Criminal Cases. 1823–68
Parker's New Hampshire Reports (65–66 N.H.)
Park.Arb. Parker, Arbitration. 1820
Park.Cr. Parker's Criminal Reports (New York) 1823–68
Park.Cr.Cas. Parker's New York Criminal Cases. 1823–68
Park.Crim.(N.Y.) Parker's Criminal Cases (New York) 1823–68
Park.Dig. Parker's California Digest
Park.Dow. Park, Dower. 1819
Park.Exch. Parker's Exchequer Reports (145 ER) 1743–67
Park.Hist.Ch. Parkes, History of Court of Chancery. 1828
Park.Ins. Park, Marine Insurance. 8ed. 1842
Park.N.H. Parker's New Hampshire Reports (65–66 N.H.)
Park.Rev.Cas. Parker's Exchequer Reports (Revenue Cases) (145 ER) 1743–67
Parker Parker Exchequer Reports (145 ER) 1743–67
Parker, The Laws of Shipping & Insurance, with digest of cases, 1693–1774, 1775
Parker's New Hampshire Reports (65–66 N.H.)
Parker's New York Criminal Reports. 1823–68
Parker Cr.Cas. Parker's New York Criminal Reports. 1823–68
Parker Cr.Cas.(N.Y.) Parker's New York Criminal Reports. 1823–68
Parker Cr.R. Parker's New York Criminal Reports. 1823–68
Parker Cr.R.(N.Y.) Parker's New York Criminal Reports. 1823–68
Parker Report Report of Home Office Committee on Authorised Procedures for Interrogation of Persons Suspected of Terrorism (Cmnd. 4901) 1972
Parks & Rec. Parks & Recreation
Parks & Wild. Parks & Wildlife
Parl. Parliament
Parliamentarian (Journal of the Parliaments of the Commonwealth of Australia) 1920–
Parliamentary
Parl.Aff. Parliamentary Affairs
Parl.Cas. Parliamentary Cases
Parl.Deb. Parliamentary Debates
Parl.Eur.Doc. Parlement Européen Documents de Séance (European Parliament Working Documents)
Parl.Hist.Eng. Parliamentary History of England
Parl.Reg. Parliamentary Register
Parl.Writs F. Palgrave, Parliamentary Writs and Writs of Military Summons. 1827–34
Parl.& Council (Chancery) Public

Record Office, Parliamentary and Council Proceedings (Chancery) (C.49)
Parliam.Aff. Parliamentary Affairs
Parly Parliamentary
Paroch.Ant. Kennett's Parochial Antiquities. 1695
Pars. Parson's Select Equity Cases (Pennsylvania) 1842–51
Pars.Ans. Parsons, Answer to the Fifth Part of Coke's Reports
Pars.Bills & N. Parsons, Bills and Notes
Pars.Cont. Parsons, Contracts
Pars.Dec. Parsons' Decisions (2–7 Massachusetts)
Pars.Eq.Cas. Parsons' Select Equity Cases (Pennsylvania) 1842–51
Pars.Mar.Ins. Parsons, Marine Insurance
Pars.Mar.Law Parsons, Maritime Law
Pars.Merc.Law Parsons, Mercantile Law
Pars.Sel.Eq.Cas.(Pa.) Parsons' Select Equity Cases (Pennsylvania) 1842–51
Pars.Shipp.& Adm. Parsons, Shipping and Admiralty
Part. Participating
Participation
Partner
Pas. Feast of Easter
Pasicrisie (Belg.) periodical collection of reports
Terminus Paschae (Lat.) Easter Term
Pas.Belge Pasicrisie Belge (Belgium)
Pas.Lux. Pasicrisie Luxembourgeoise (Luxembourg) Law Reports. 1875–
Pasc. Paschal or Easter Term
Paschal's Reports (Supp. to 25; 28–31 Texas)
Pasch. Paschal or Easter Term
Pasch.Dig. Paschal's Texas Digest of Decisions
Paschal Paschal's Reports (28–31 Texas and Supplement to 25)
Paschal's Ann.Const. Paschal's United States Constitution, Annotated
Pasic.Lux. Pasicrisie Luxembourgeoise (Lux.) Law Reports. 1875–
Pasicrisie Pasicrisie Belge: Recueil général de la jurisprudence des cours et tribunaux de Belgique
Pasicrisie int. Pasicrisie internationale
Pasicrisie Lux. Pasicrisie Luxembourgeoise (Lux.) 1875–
Pasin. Pasinomie: collection complète des lois (Belg.) 1833–
Pasin.Lux. Pasinomie luxembourgeoise: recueil des lois (Lux.) 1850–
Pat. All Indian Reporter, Patna. 1916–
Indian Law Reports, Patna. 1922–
Indian Rulings, Patna. 1929–47
Patent
Paterson's Scotch Appeals, House of Lords. 1851–73
Paton's Scotch Appeals, House of Lords. 1726–1821
Public Record Office, patent rolls
Pat.Abr. Paterson's Abridgment of Poor Law Cases. 1857–63
Pat.App. Craigie, Stewart & Paton's Scotch Appeals. 1726–1821
Pat.App.Cas. Paterson's Scotch Appeal Cases. 1851–73
Paton's Scotch Appeal Cases (Craigie, Stewart & Paton) 1726–1821
Pat.Bl. Patentblatt (Ger.) 1877–1945, 1950–
Pat.Cas. Reports of Patent, Design and Trade Mark Cases. 1884–
Pat.Comp. Paterson's Compendium of English and Scotch Law
Pat.Copyright & T.M.Cas. Patent, Copyright & Trade Mark Cases (Baldwin) (USA)
Pat.Dec. Commissioner of Patents Decisions
Pat.Des.& T.M.Rev. Patent, Design and Trade Mark Review (India) 1944–
Pat.Dig. Pattison, Missouri Digest
PatG Patentgesetz (Ger.) Patent Act
Pat.Game L. Paterson, Game Laws. 1861
Pat.H.L.Sc. Paterson's Scotch Appeals. 1851–73
Paton's Scotch Appeals. 1726–1821
Pat.Ins. Paton, Insurance. 1962

Pat.J. Patent Journal, including Trademarks and Models (S.Afr.) 1961–
Pat.L.Ann. Patent Law Annual. 1966–
Pat.L.J. Patna Law Journal (India) 1916–21
Pat.L.R. Patent Law Review (USA) 1969–
Patna Law Reporter (India) 1923–25
Pat.L.Reptr. Patna Law Reporter (India) 1923–25
Pat.L.Rev. Patent Law Review (USA) 1879–80
Patent Law Review (USA) 1969–
Pat.L.T. Patna Law Times (India) 1920–
Pat.L.W. Patna Law Weekly (India) 1917–18
Pat.Law Rev. Patent Law Review (USA) 1879–80
Patent Law Review (USA) 1969–
Pat.Licens. Paterson, Licensing Acts. Annual
Pat.Mort. Patch, Mortgages. 1821
Pat.Off. Patent Office
Pat.Off.Gaz. Official Gazette, U.S. Patent Office
Pat.Off.J. Patent Office Journal (India) 1921–
Pat.Off.Rep. Patent Office Reports
Pat.Off.Soc.J. Patent Office Society Journal (USA) 1918–
Pat.Ser. Indian Law Reports, Patna Series. 1922–
Pat.St.Tr. Paton, Stoppage in Transitu. 1859
Pat.T.M.& Copy.J. Patent, Trademark & Copyright Journal of Research and Education (USA) 1957–64
Pat.& H. Patton, Jr., & Heath's Reports (Virginia Special Court of Appeals) 1855–57
Pat.& Mr. Paterson & Murray's Supreme Court Reports, New South Wales (Aus.) 1870–71
Pat.& Mur. Paterson & Murray's Supreme Court Reports, New South Wales (Aus.) 1870–71
Pat.& T.M.Rev. Patent and Trade Mark Review (USA) 1902–
Pat.& Tr.Mk.Rev. Patent and Trade Mark Review (USA) 1902–
Pater. Paterson's New South Wales Supreme Court Reports (Aus.)
Paterson's Scotch Appeal Cases. 1851–73
Pater.Ap.Cas. Paterson's Appeal Cases (Scot.) 1851–73
Pater.App. Paterson's Appeal Cases (Scot.) 1851–73
Paters.App. Paterson's Appeal Cases (Scot.) 1851–73
Paters.Comp. Paterson, Compendium of English & Scotch Law. 2ed. 1865
Paterson Paterson, Compendium of English & Scotch Law. 2ed. 1865
Paterson, Game Laws of the United Kingdom. 1861
Paterson, Law affecting the Stock Exchange. 1870
Paterson, Liberty of the Press, etc. 1880
Paterson's Scotch Appeal Cases. 1851–73
Paterson's Supreme Court Reports, New South Wales (Aus.)
Paterson Sc.App.Cas. Paterson Scotch Appeal Cases. 1851–73
Patiala Indian Law Reports, Patiala Series. 1953–
Paton Paton's Appeal Cases (Scot.) 1726–1821
Paton App.Cas. Paton's Appeal Cases (Scot.) 1726–1821
Paton Sc.App.Cas. Paton's Appeal Cases (Scot.) 1726–1821
Patr.Elect.Cas. Patrick's Election Cases (Ontario,Can.) 1824–49
Patrick El.Cas. Patrick's Election Cases (Ontario,Can.) 1824–49
Patton & H. Patton,Jr.,& Heath's Reports (Virginia Special Court of Appeals) 1855–57
Patton & H.(Va.) Patton,Jr.,& Heath's Reports (Virginia Special Court of Appeals) 1855–57
Pay.& Iv.Carr. Payne & Ivamy, Carriage by Sea. 10ed. 1976
Pe.R. Pennewill's Delaware Reports (17–23 Del.) 1897–1909

Pea. Peake's Nisi Prius Reports (170 ER) 1790–94

Pea.(2) Peake's Additional Cases (170 ER) 1795–1812

Pea.Add.Cas. Peake's Additional Cases (Vol.2 of Peake) (170 ER) 1795–1812

Pea.M.S. Peachey, Marriage Settlements. 1860

Peab.L.Rev. Peabody Law Review (USA) 1936–41

Peake Peake's Nisi Prius Reports (170 ER) 1790–94

Peake Add.Cas. Peake's Additional Cases (170 ER) 1795–1812

Peake Ev. Peake, Law of Evidence. 5ed. 1822

Peake N.P. Peake's Nisi Prius Reports (170 ER) 1790–94

Peake N.P.Add.Cas. Peake's Additional Cases, Nisi Prius (170 ER) 1795–1812

Peake N.P.Cas. Peake's Nisi Prius Cases (170 ER) 1790–1812

Pearce C.C. Pearce's Reports in Dearsly's Crown Cases (169 ER) 1852–56

Pearce,Inns of Court R.R. Pearce, History of the Inns of Court and Chancery. 1848

Pears. Pearson's Reports (Pennsylvania) 1850–80

Pears.(Pa.) Pearson's Reports (Pennsylvania) 1850–80

Pearson Pearson's Reports (Pennsylvania) 1850–80

Pearson Report Report of Royal Commission on Civil Liability and Compensation for Personal Injury (Cmnd. 7054) 1978

Peck. Peck's Reports (11–22, 24–30 Illinois)
Peck's Reports (7 Tennessee) 1821–24
Peckwell's Election Cases. 1802–06

Peck.El.Cas. Peckwell's Election Cases. 1802–06

Peck.Elec.Cas. Peckwell's Election Cases. 1802–06

Peck(Ill.) Peck's Reports, Illinois Supreme Court Reports (11–22, 24–30 Ill.)

Peck (Tenn.) Peck's Tennessee Reports (7 Tenn.) 1821–24

Peck Tr. Peck's Trial (Impeachment)

Peckw. Peckwell's Election Cases. 1802–06

Peeples Peeples' Reports (78, 79 Georgia)

Peeples & Stevens Peeples' & Stevens' Reports (80–97 Georgia)

Peere Wms. Peere Williams' Chancery & King's Bench Cases (24 ER) 1695–1735

Pelham Pelham's South Australia Reports (Aus.) 1865–66

Pelt. Peltier's Orleans Appeals. 1917–23

Pemb.Eq. Pemberton, Practice in Equity by Way of Revivor & Supplement. 1867

Pemb.Judg. Pemberton, Judgments and Orders. 4ed. 1889

Pen. Pennewill's Delaware Reports (17–23 Del.) 1892–1909
Pennington's Reports (2–3 N.J. Law) 1806–13

Pen.C. Penal Code

Pen.Code Penal Code

Pen.Dec. Pension Decisions U.S. Interior Department

Pen.Laws Penal Laws

Pen.N.J. Pennington's Reports (2–3 N.J. Law) 1806–13

Pen.Ref. Penal Reformer. 1934–39

Pen.Ref.League M.Rec. Penal Reform League Monthly Record. 1909–12

Pen.Ref.League Q.Rec. Penal Reform League Quarterly Record. 1912–20

Pen.World Pensions World

Pen.& W. Penrose & Watts' Pennsylvania Reports. 1829–32

Penn. Pennewill's Delaware Reports (17–23 Del.) 1897–1909
Pennington's New Jersey Reports (2–3 N.J. Law) 1806–13
Pennsylvania
Pennsylvania State Reports. 1845–
Pennypacker's Unreported Pennsylvania Cases. 1881–84

Penn.B.A. Pennsylvania Bar Association
Penn.B.A.Q. Pennsylvania Bar Association Quarterly. 1929–
Penn.Co.Ct.Rep. Pennsylvania County Court Reports. 1885–1921
Penn.Corp.Rep. Pennsylvania Corporation Reporter. 1914–39
Penn.Del. Pennewill's Delaware Reports (17–23 Del.) 1897–1909
Penn.Dist.Rep. Pennsylvania District Reports. 1892–1921
Penn.Dist.& Co.Rep. Pennsylvania District & County Reports. 1921–
Penn.L.G. Pennsylvania Legal Gazette. 1869–76
Pennsylvania Legal Gazette Reports (Campbell) 1869–71
Penn.L.J. Pennsylvania Law Journal. 1842–48
Penn.L.J.R. Pennsylvania Law Journal Reports (Clark) 1842–52
Penn.L.Rec. Pennsylvania Law Record (Philadelphia) 1879–80
Penn.L.Rev. University of Pennsylvania Law Review. 1944–
Penn.Law Jour. Pennsylvania Law Journal. 1842–48
Penn.Rep. Pennsylvania State Reports. 1845–
Penrose & Watts' Pennsylvania Reports. 1829–32
Penn.St. Pennsylvania State Reports. 1845–
Penn.St.R. Pennsylvania State Reports. 1845–
Penna. Pennsylvania
Penne. Pennewill's Delaware Reports (17–23 Del.) 1897–1909
Pennew. Pennewill's Delaware Reports (17–23 Del.) 1897–1909
Pennewill Pennewill's Delaware Reports (17–23 Del.) 1897–1909
Penning. Pennington's Reports (2–3 New Jersey Law) 1806–13
Penny. Pennypacker's Pennsylvania Colonial Cases. 1683–1700
Pennypacker's Unreported Pennsylvania Cases. 1881–84
Penny.Col.Cas. Pennypacker's Pennsylvania Colonial Cases. 1683–1700
Pennyp. Pennypacker's Unreported Pennsylvania Cases. 1881–84
Pennyp.Col.Cas. Pennypacker's Pennsylvania Colonial Cases. 1683–1700
Pennyp.(Pa.) Pennypacker's Unreported Pennsylvania Cases. 1881–84
Penol. Penology
Penr.Anal. Penruddocke, Short Analysis of Criminal Law. 2ed. 1842
Penr.& W. Penrose & Watts' Pennsylvania Reports. 1829–32
Peo.L.Adv. People's Legal Advisor (Utica, N.Y.) 1858
Pep. All India Reporter, Patiala and East Punjab States Union. 1950–57
Pep.L.R. Pepperdine Law Review (USA) 1973–
Pepp.L.Rev. Pepperdine Law Review (USA) 1973–
Pepper & L.Dig.Laws Pepper and Lewis' Digest of Laws (Pennsylvania)
Pepperdine L.R. Pepperdine Law Review (USA) 1973–
Pepperdine L.Rev. Pepperdine Law Review (USA) 1973–
Pepsu. All India Reporter, Patiala and East Punjab States Union. 1950–57
Per. Perera's Select Decisions (Sri.L.)
Per.C.S. Perrault's Conseil Supérieur (Can.) 1727–59
Per.Or.Cas. Perry's Oriental Cases (Bombay, India) 1843–52
Per.P. Perrault's Prévoste de Québec. 1726–59
per pro. per procurationem (Lat.) by proxy
Per.& Dav. Perry & Davison's King's Bench Reports (48–54 RR) 1838–41
Per.& Kn. Perry & Knapp's Election Cases. 1833
Perels Perels, Das internationale öffentliche Seerecht der Gegenwart
Perk. Perkins' Profitable Book (Conveyancing) various editions

Perk.Pr.Bk. Perkins' Profitable Book (Conveyancing)
Perm. Permanent
Perp. Perpetual
Perraud Charmantier Perraud Charmantier, Petit Dictionnaire de Droit
Perrault Parrault's Conseil Supérieur (Can.) 1727–59
Perrault's Prévoste de Québec. 1726–59
Perrault's Quebec Reports
Perry Perry's Notes of Cases (Bombay, India) 1826–47
Perry's Oriental Cases (Bombay, India) 1843–52
Sir Erskine Perry's Reports in Morley's (East) Indian Digest
Perry Ins. Perry's Insolvency Cases. 1831
Perry O.C. Perry's Oriental Cases (Bombay, India) 1843–52
Perry & D. Perry & Davison's King's Bench Reports (48–54 RR) 1838–41
Perry & K. Perry & Knapp's Election Cases. 1833
Perry & Kn. Perry & Knapp's Election Cases. 1833
Pers.Finance L.Q. Personal Finance Law Quarterly Report (USA)
Pers.Inj.Comment'r. Personal Injury Commentator (USA)
Pers.Inj.L.J. Personal Injury Law Journal (USA) 1910–11
Pers.Prop. Personal Property
Pershad Privy Council Judgments (India) 1829–69
Peshawar All India Reporter, Peshawar. 1933–50
Indian Rulings, Peshawar. 1933–47
Pet. Haviland's Prince Edward Island Reports by Peters (Can.) 1850–72
Peters' Admiralty Decisions, District Court (USA) 1780–1807
Peters' Circuit Court Reports (USA) 1803–18
Peters' Supreme Court Reports (26–41 USA) 1828–42
Pet.Ab. Petersdorff's Abridgment of Cases. 1660–1823
Pet.Abr. Petersdorff's Abridgment of Cases. 1660–1823
Pet.Ad. Peters' District Court Reports, Admiralty Decisions (USA) 1780–1807
Pet.Adm. Peter's Admiralty Decisions District Court (USA) 1780–1807
Pet.Bail Petersdorff, Bail. 1824
Pet.Br. Brooke's New Cases (Petit Brooke) (73 ER) 1515–58
Pet.C.C. Peters' Circuit Court Reports (USA) 1803–18
Pet.Cond. Peters' Condensed Reports, Supreme Court (USA) 1791–1827
Pet.Dig. Pefers' United States Digest
Paticolas' Texas Digest
Pet.L.Nat. Petersdorff, Law of Nations
Pet.M.& S. Petersdorff, Master and Servant. 1876
Pet.S.C. Peters' Supreme Court Reports (26–41 U.S.) 1828–42
Pet.Suppl. Supplement to Petersdorff's Abridgment
Peters Haviland's Prince Edward Island Reports by Peters (Can.) 1850–72
Peters' Supreme Court Reports (26–41 U.S.A.) 1828–42
Peters Adm. Peters' Admiralty Decisions, District Court (U.S.A.) 1780–1807
Peters C.C. Peters' Circuit Court Reports (U.S.A.) 1803–13
Petersd.Ab. Petersdorff's Abridgment of Cases. 1660–1823
Petersdorff, Abridgment C. Petersdorff, A Practical and Elementary Abridgment. 1825–30, 1841–44
Petg.Pr.& Ag. Petgrave, Principal and Agent. 1857
Peth.Dis. Petheram, Discovery by Interrogations. 1864
Petit Br. Petit Brooke, or Brooke's New Cases, King's Bench (73 ER) 1515–58
Petn. Petition
Petty S.R. Petty Sessions Review (Aus.) 1967–
Pfd. Preferred

Ph. Phillimore's Ecclesiastical Reports (161 ER) 1809–21
Phillips' Chancery Reports (41 ER) 1841–49
Phillips' Election Cases. 1780–81

Ph.Ch. Phillips' Chancery Reports (41 ER) 1841–49

Ph.Ev. Phillips, Evidence. 10ed. 1852

Ph.St.Tr. Phillips' State Trials. 1826

Ph.& M. Philip and Mary

Phear Wat. Phear, Rights of Water. 1859

Pheney Rep. Pheney's New Term Reports

Phil. Philadelphia Reports. 1850–91
Philippines
Philippine Island Reports. 1901–46
Philips Chancery Reports (41 ER) 1841–49
Philips Election Cases. 1780–81
Phillimore's Ecclesiastical Reports (161 ER) 1809–21
Phillips' Illinois Reports (152–245 Ill.)
Phillips' North Carolina Equity Reports (62 N.C.) 1866–68
Phillips' North Carolina Law Reports (61 N.C.) 1866–68
Philosophy

Phil.Civ.& Can.Law. Phillimore's Civil and Canon Law

Phil.Cop. Philips' Law of Copyright. 1863

Phil.Dom. Phillimore, Domicil. 1847

Phil.Ecc. Phillimore's Ecclesiastical Judgments. 1867–75
Phillimore's Ecclesiastical Law. 2ed. 1895
Phillimore's Ecclesiastical Reports (161 ER) 1809–21

Phil.Ecc.Judg. Phillimore's Ecclesiastical Judgments in Court of Arches. 1867–75

Phil.Ecc.Law Phillimore's Ecclesiastical Law. 2ed. 1895

Phil.Ecc.R. Phillimore's Ecclesiastical Reports (161 ER) 1809–21

Phil.El.Cas. Phillips' Election Cases. 1780–81

Phil.Eq. Phillips' Equity Reports, North Carolina (62 NC) 1866–68

Phil.Ev. Phillips on Evidence. 10ed. 1852

Phil.Ev.Cow.H.& Edw.Notes Phillips' on Evidence, Notes by Cowen, Hill & Edwards

Phil.Fam.Cas. Phillips' Famous Cases in Circumstantial Evidence

Phil.I.L.J. Philippine International Law Journal. 1962–66

Phil.Ins. Phillips, Law of Insurance. 5ed. 1867

Phil.Insan. Phillips, Lunatics. 1858

Phil.Int.L.J. Philippine International Law Journal. 1962–66

Phil.Int.Law Phillimore's International Law. 3ed. 1879–89

Phil.Int.Rom.Law Phillimore's Introduction to the Roman Law

Phil.J.Pub.Admin. Philippine Journal of Public Administration. 1957–

Phil.Jud. Phillimore's Ecclesiastical Judgments. 1867–75

Phil.Judg. Phillimore's Ecclesiastical Judgments. 1867–75

Phil.L.J. Philippine Law Journal. 1914–

Phil.L.Rev. Philippine Law Review. 1911–19

Phil.Lab.Rel.J. Philippine Labour Relations Journal

Phil.Law Phillips' North Carolina Law Reports (61 N.C.) 1866–68

Phil.Mech.Liens Phillips, Mechanics' Liens

Phil.N.C. Phillips' North Carolina Law Reports (61 NC) 1866–68

Phil.Q. Philosophical Quarterly (USA)

Phil.R. Philosophical Review (USA)

Phil.St.Tr. Phillips' State Trials (Prior to 1688) 1826

Phil.Stud. Philippine Studies

Phil.Yb.Int'l L. Philippine Yearbook of International Law

Phil.& M. Philip and Mary

Phil.& Mar. Philip and Mary

Phil.& Publ.Aff. Philosophy and Public Affairs (USA)

Phila. Philadelphia Reports (Pennsylvania) 1850–91

Phila.L.J. Philippine Law Journal. 1914–

Phila.Leg.Int. Philadelphia Legal Intelligencer (Pennsylvania) 1843–

Phila.(Pa.) Philadelphia Reports (Pennsylvania) 1850–91

Philanthrop. The Philanthropist/Le Philanthrope (Can.) 1980–

Philip.L.J. Philippine Law Journal. 1914–

Philip.Yrbk.Intl.L. Philippine Yearbook of International Law

Philippine Philippine Reports. 1901–46

Philippine Co. Philippine Code

Philippine Int'l.L.J. Philippine International Law Journal. 1962–66

Philippine J.Pub.Admin. Philippine Journal of Public Administration. 1957–

Philippine L.J. Philippine Law Journal. 1914–

Philippine L.Rev. Philippine Law Review. 1911–19

Phill. Phillips' Chancery Reports (41 ER) 1841–49
Phillips' Election Cases. 1780–81
Phillips' Equity Reports, North Carolina (62 N.C.) 1866–68
Phillips' Illinois Reports (152–245 Ill.)
Phillips' Law Reports, North Carolina (61 N.C.) 1866–68

Phill.Ch. Phillips' Chancery Reports (41 ER) 1841–49

Phill.Ecc.Judg. Phillimore's Ecclesiastical Judgments. 1867–75

Phill.Ecc.R. Phillimore's Ecclesiastical Reports (161 ER) 1809–21

Phill.Eq.(N.C.) Phillips' Equity Reports, North Carolina (62 N.C.) 1866–68

Phill.Ins. Phillips, Law of Insurance. 5ed. 1867

Phill.L.(N.C.) Phillips' Law Reports, North Carolina (61 N.C.) 1866–68

Phillim. Phillimore's Ecclesiastical Reports (161 ER) 1809–21

Phillim.Dom. Phillimore on the Law of Domicil. 1847

Phillim.Ecc.Law Phillimore's Ecclesiastical Law. 2ed. 1895

Phillim.Eccl. Phillimore's Ecclesiastical Judgments. 1867–75
Phillimore's Ecclesiastical Reports (161 ER) 1809–21

Phillim.Int.Law Phillimore's International Law. 3ed. 1879–89

Phillimore Phillimore, Commentaries upon International Law

Phillimore Report Report of Committee on Contempt of Court (Cmnd. 5794) 1974

Phillips Phillips' Chancery Reports (41 ER) 1841–49
Phillips' Election Cases. 1780–81
Phillips' North Carolina Equity Reports (62 NC) 1866–68
Phillips' North Carolina Law Reports (61 NC) 1866–68
Phillips' Reports (152–245 Illinois)

Phip. Phipson's Digest, Natal Reports (S.Afr.)
Phipson's Reports, Natal Supreme Court (S.Afr.)

Phip.Ev. Phipson, Evidence. 12ed. 1976

Phipson Phipson's Reports, Supreme Court of Natal (S.Afr.)

Pick. Pickering's Massachusetts Supreme Judicial Court Reports (18–41 Mass.) 1822–39

Pick.(Mass.) Pickering's Massachusetts Supreme Judicial Court Reports (18–41 Mass.) 1822–39

Pickle Pickle's Reports (85–108 Tennessee) 1886–1902

Pierce R.R. Pierce on Railroad Law (USA)

Pig. Pigott's Common Recoveries. 3ed. 1792

Pig.Judg. Piggott, Foreign Judgments. 3ed. 1908–09

Pig.Rec. Pigott's Common Recoveries. 3ed. 1792

Pig.& R. Pigott & Rodwell's Registration Appeal Cases. 1843–45

Pike Pike's Reports (1–5 Arkansas)

Pike H.of L. Pike's History of the House of Lords. 1894

Pin. Pinney's Wisconsin Supreme Court Reports. 1839–52

Pinn. Pinney's Wisconsin Supreme Court Reports. 1839–52

Pip.& C.Mil.L. Pipon & Collier, Military Law. 3ed. 1865

Pist. Piston's Mauritius Reports. 1861–62

Piston Piston's Mauritius Reports. 1861–62

Pit.L. University of Pittsburgh Law Review (Pennsylvania) 1935–42, 1947–

Pit.Sur. Pitman, Principal and Surety. 1840

Pitc. Pitcairn's Criminal Trials (Scot.) 1488–1624

Pitc.Crim.Tr. Pitcairn's Criminal Trials (Scot.) 1488–1624

Pitc.Tr. Pitcairn Criminal Trials (Scot.) 1488–1624

Pitm.Prin.& Sur. Pitman, Principal and Surety. 1840

Pitt. Pittsburgh

Pitt.L.J. Pittsburgh Legal Journal. 1853–

Pitts. Pittsburgh
Pittsburgh Reports. 1853–73

Pitts.L.J. Pittsburgh Legal Journal. 1853–

Pitts.L.Rev. University of Pittsburgh Law Review. 1935–42, 1947–

Pitts.Rep. Pittsburgh Reports. 1853–73

Pittsb. Pittsburgh
Pittsburgh Reports. 1853–73

Pittsb.L.Rev. University of Pittsburgh Law Review. 1935–42, 1947–

Pittsb.Leg.J. Pittsburgh Legal Journal (Pennsylvania) 1853–

Pittsb.Leg.J.(Pa.) Pittsburgh Legal Journal (Pennsylvania) 1853–

Pittsb.R.(Pa.) Pittsburgh Reports (Pennsylvania) 1853–73

Pix.Aud. Pixley, Auditors. 8ed. 1901

Pl. Plowden's Commentaries (75 ER) 1550–80

Pl.Ang.–Norm. Bigelow, Placita Anglo-Normannica. 1065–1195

Pl.C. Placita Coronae (Pleas of the Crown)

Pl.Com. Plowden's Commentaries (75 ER) 1550–80

Pl.N. Publications of the Place-Name Society

Pl.Par. Placita Parliamentaria

Pl.Sav. Planned Savings

Pl.& Pr.Cas. Pleading & Practice Cases. 1837–38

Pla. Placitum or Placita

Pla.Par. Placita Parliamentaria

Plac.Abbrev. Placitorum Abbreviatio

Plac.Ang.Nor. Bigelow, Placita Anglo-Normannica. 1065–1195

Plac.Angl.Nor. Bigelow, Placita Anglo-Normannica. 1065–1195

Plac.Gen. Placita Generalia

Plan. Planning

Plan.Zoning & E.D.Inst. Planning, Zoning & Eminent Domain Institute (USA) 1970–

Plan.& Comp. Planning & Compensation Reports. 1949–

Platt Platt on Covenants. 1829
Platt on Leases. 1847

Platt.Cov. Platt on the Law of Covenants. 1829

Platt.Leas. Platt, Leases. 1847

Plaxton Plaxton's Constitutional Decisions of the Privy Council (Can.) 1930–39

plf. plaintiff

Plow. Plowden's Commentaries or Reports (75 ER) 1550–80

Plowd. Plowden's Commentaries or Reports (75 ER) 1550–80

Plt. Peltier's Orleans Appeals Decisions (Louisiana) 1917–23

Plucknett, Concise History T.F.T. Plucknett, Concise History of the Common Law

Plum.Contr. Plumptre, Contracts. 2ed. 1897

Po.Ct. Police Court

Poc.Costs Pocock, Costs. 1881

Pol. Poland
Police
Policy

Political
Politics
Pollexfen's King's Bench Reports (86 ER) 1669–85

Pol.C. Political Code

Pol.Code Political Code

Pol.Cont. Pollock, Principles of Contract. 13ed. 1950

Pol.Dig.Part. Pollock, Digest of the Laws of Partnership. 15ed. 1952

Pol.dir. Politica del diritto (It.)

Pol.Fedn.Newsl. Police Federation Newsletter. 1957–

Pol.Int. Fondo della Polizia internazionale (It.)

Pol.J. Police Journal. 1928–

Pol.L.Q. Police Law Quarterly (USA) 1971–

Pol.Q. Political Quarterly (USA)

Pol.Sci.Q. Political Science Quarterly (USA) 1886–

Pol.Sci.Quar. Political Science Quarterly (USA) 1886–

Pol.Sci.Rev. Political Science Review (India)

Pol.Studies Political Studies

Pol.& Soc'y Politics and Society

Polam.L.J. Polamerican Law Journal (USA) 1938–41

Police Fedn.Newsl. Police Federation Newsletter. 1957–

Police J. Police Journal. 1928–

Police J.Ct. Police Justice's Court (USA)

Police L.Q. Police Law Quarterly (USA) 1971–

PolishYIL Polish Yearbook of International Law

Polish Yrbk.Intl.L. Polish Yearbook of International Law

Poll. Pollack's Ohio Unreported Judicial Decisions. 1807–23
Pollexfen's King's Bench Reports (86 ER) 1669–85

Poll.C.C.Pr. Pollock's Practice of the County Courts. 10ed. 1880

Pollex. Pollexfen's King's Bench Reports (86 ER) 1669–85

Pollexf. Pollexfen's King's Bench Reports (86 ER) 1669–85

Pollexfen Pollexfen's King's Bench Reports (86 ER) 1669–85

Pollock, Essays F. Pollock, Essays in Jurisprudence and Ethics. 1882

Pollock & Maitl. Pollock & Maitland's History of English Law. 2ed. 1898

Pols.Nat. Polson, Law of Nations. 1848

Poly. Polytechnic

Poly.L.Rev. Poly Law Review. 1975–

Polytech. Polytechnic

Pom.Code Rem. Pomeroy on Code Remedies (USA)

Pom.Const.Law Pomeroy's Constitutional Law of the United States

Pom.Eq.Juris. Pomeroy's Equity Jurisprudence

Pom.Rem. Pomeroy on Civil Remedies

Pomeroy Pomeroy's Reports (73–128 California)

Poor L.Mag. Poor Law and Local Government Magazine (Scot.)

Pop. Popham's King's Bench Reports (79 ER) 1592–1626
Popular
Population

Pop.Mo.L.Tr. Popular Monthly Law Tracts. 1877–78

Pope Cust. Pope, Customs and Excise. 11ed. 1828

Pope Lun. Pope, Lunacy. 2ed. 1892

Poph. Popham's King's Bench Reports (79 ER) 1592–1626

Poph.(2) Cases at the end of Popham's Reports

Popham Popham's King's Bench Reports (79 ER) 1592–1626

Popplewell Report Report of the Committee of Inquiry into Crowd Safety and Control at Sports Grounds. Interim Report (Cmnd. 9585) 1985; Final report (Cmnd. 9710) 1986

Port. Porter's Alabama Supreme Court Reports. 1834–39
Porter's Indiana Reports (3–7 Ind.)
Portugal

Port.(Ala.) Porter's Alabama Supreme Court Reports. 1834–39

Port.Ins. Porter's Laws of Insurance. 8ed. 1933
Port.U.L.Rev. Portland University Law Review. 1949–
Porter Porter's Alabama Supreme Court Reports. 1834–39
Porter's Reports (3–7 Indiana)
Porter Report Report of Committee on the Law of Defamation (Cmd.7536) 1948
Portia L.J. Portia Law Journal (USA) 1965–68
Portland U.L.Rev. Portland University Review. 1949–
Pos.Mschr. Juristische Monatsschrift für Posen, West – und Ostpreussen, und Pommern
Posey Posey's Unreported Cases (Texas) 1879–84
Posey Unrep.Cas. Posey's Unreported Cases (Texas) 1879–84
Post Post's Reports (23–26 Michigan)
Post's Reports (42–64 Missouri)
Post.& Ins. Postage and insurance
Post.& Reg. Postage and registration
Poste's Gai. Poste's Translation of Gaius
Poth.Cont. Pothier, Contracts. 1802
Poth.Cont.Sale Pothier, Contract of Sale. 1839
Poth.Contr.Sale Pothier, Contract of Sale. 1839
Poth.Ob. Pothier on the Law of Obligations or Contracts. 1802
Poth.Obl. Pothier on the Law of obligations or Contracts. 1802
Poth.Oblig. Pothier on the Law of Obligations or Contacts. 1802
Poth.Part. Pothier, Partnerships. 1854
Potter Potter's Reports (4–7 Wyoming)
Potts L.D. Potts, Law Dictionary. 3ed. 1815
Pound Festschrift Essays in Jurisprudence in Honour of Roscoe Pound, ed. by R.A. Newman
Pov.L.Rep. Poverty Law Reporter (CCH) (USA)
Pow.App.Proc. Powell's Law of Appellate Proceedings
Pow.Car. Powell, Inland Carriers. 2ed. 1861
Pow.Cont. Powell on Contracts. 1802
Pow.Conv. Powell, Conveyancing. 2ed. 1810
Pow.Dev. Powell, Essay upon the Learning of Devises. 3ed. 1827
Pow.Ev. Powell, Evidence. 10ed. 1921
Pow.Mort. Powell, Mortgages. 6ed. 1826
Pow.Mortg. Powell, Mortgages. 6ed. 1826
Pow.R.& D. Power, Rodwell & Dew's Election Cases. 1847–56
Pow.Surr. Powers' Reports New York Surrogate Court. 1890–94
Powers Powers' Reports, New York Surrogate Court. 1890–94
Powers Sur. Powers' Reports, New York Surrogate Court. 1890–94
Poynt.M.& D. Poynter, Marriage and Divorce. 2ed. 1824
pp. pages
pr. private
proved (date of probate of will)
Pr. Practice Reports
Preamble
Price's Exchequer Reports (145–147 ER) 1814–24
Prior
Private
Pr.Adm.Dig. Pritchard, Admiralty Digest. 3ed. 1887
Pr.C. Prize Cases
Pr.C.K.B. Practice Cases in the King's Bench
Pr.Ch. Precedents in Chancery (Finch) (24 ER) 1689–1722
Pr.Co. Prerogative Court
Pr.Cont. Pratt, Contraband of War. 1861
Pr.Dec. Sneed's Kentucky Decisions (2 Ky.) 1801–05
Pr.Div. Law Reports Probate Division
Pr.Edw.I. Prince Edward Island
Prince Edward Island Reports (Can.)
Pr.Edw.Isl. Prince Edward Island
Prince Edward Island Reports (Can.)

Pr.Exch. Price's Exchequer Reports (145–7 ER) 1814–24
Pr.Falc. Falconer's Decisions, Court of Session Cases (Scot.) 1744–51
Pr.L. Private Laws
Pr.Min. Printed Minutes of Evidence
Pr.R. Practice Reports
Pr.Reg.B.C. Practical Register in the Bail Court
Pr.Reg.C.P. Practical Register of the Common Pleas. 1705–42
Pr.Reg.Ch. Practical Register in Chancery
Pr.Rep. Practice Reports
Pr.Rep.B.C. Lowndes, Maxwell & Pollock's Bail Court Practice Cases (86 RR) 1850–51
Pr.Stat. Private Statutes
Pr.& Div. Law Reports, Probate & Divorce
Pra. Die Praxis des Bundesgerichts (Switz.)
Pra.Cas. Prater, Cases on Conflict between Laws of England and Scotland, Marriage Divorce & Legitimacy. 1835
Pra.H.& W. Prater, Husband and Wife. 2ed. 1836
Praag Praag, Jurisdiction et droit international public. 1915
Praag, Supplement Supplement to Jurisdiction et droit international public. 1935
Prac. Practical
Practice
Practitioners
Prac.Act Practice Act
Prac.Law. Practical Lawyer (Philadelphia) 1955–
Prac.Real Est.Law. The Practical Real Estate Lawyer (USA)
Prac.Tax Law. The Practical Tax Lawyer (USA)
Pract. Practitioner (Baltimore) 1890
Pract.Reg. Practical Register of the Common Pleas. 1705–42
Pract.VAT Practical VAT
Practitioners' J. Practitioners' Journal (Can.)
Pratt Pratt's Contraband of War. 1861
Pratt's Supplement to Bott's Poor Laws. 1833
Pratt Fr.Soc. Pratt, Friendly Societies. 15ed. 1931
Pratt High. Pratt & Mackenzie, Highways. 21ed. 1967
Pratt S.L. Pratt, Sea Lights. 2ed. 1858
Pratt Sav.B. Pratt, Savings Banks. 6ed. 1845
Prav.Stud. Právnické Stúdie (Czechoslovakia)
Prax. Praxis Almae Curiae Cancellariae (Brown)
Prax.Can. Praxis Almae Curiae Cancellariae (Brown)
Praxis Die Praxis des Bundesgerichts (Switz.)
Pre.Ch. Precedents in Chancery (24 ER) 1689–1722
Preb.Dig. Preble, Digest of Patent Cases (USA)
prec. precité (Fr.) supra, cited before
Prec.Ch. Precedents in Chancery (24 ER) 1689–1722
Prec.in Ch. Precedents in Chancery (24 ER) 1689–1722
Pref. Preface
Preference
Preferred
Prefix
Prelim. Preliminary (Incorporated Law Society) 1868–79
Prelim.obj. Preliminary objection
Prem. Premium
Pren.Act. Prentice, Proceedings in an Action. 2ed. 1880
Prep. Preparation
Prer. Prerogative Court
Prerog.Ct. Prerogative Court
Pres. President
Pres.Abs. Preston, Abstracts of Title. 2ed. 1823–24
Pres.Conv. Preston, Conveyancing. 5ed. 1819–29
Pres.Est. Preston, Estates. 3ed. 1829
Pres.Fal. Falconer's Decisions Court of Session (Scot.) 1744–51

Pres.Falc. Falconer's Decisions Court of Session (Scot.) 1744–51

Pres.Leg. Preston, Legacies. 1824

Pres.Mem. Presidential Member

Prest.Conv. Preston, Conveyancing. 5ed. 1819–29

Prest.Est. Preston, Estates. 3ed. 1829

Pret. Pretura (It.) Magistrates' Court

Pri. Price's Exchequer Reports (145–147 ER) 1814–24
Price's Mining Commissioners' Cases (Ontario, Can.) 1906–10

Price Price's Exchequer Reports (145–147 ER) 1814–24
Price's Mining Commissioners' Cases (Ontario, Can.) 1906–10

Price Liens Price, Maritime Liens. 1940

Price Min.Cas. Price's Mining Commissioners' Cases (Ontario, Can.) 1906–10

Price Notes P.C. Price's Notes of Practice Cases in Exchequer. 1830–31

Price P.C. Price's Notes of Practice Cases in Exchequer. 1830–31

Price.Pr.Cas. Price's Notes of Practice Cases in Exchequer. 1830–31

Price & St. Price & Stewart's Trade Mark Cases (USA)

Prickett Prickett's Reports (1 Idaho)

Prid.Ch.W. Prideaux, Directions to Churchwardens. 10ed. 1835

Prid.Conv. Prideaux, Forms and Precedents in Conveyancing. 24ed. 1952

Prid.Judg. Prideaux, Judgments and Crown Debts. 4ed. 1854

Prid.& C. Prideaux and Cole's Reports (New Session Cases, vol. 4) 1850–51

Prid.& Co. Prideaux and Cole's Reports (New Sessions Cases, vol.4) 1850–51

Prin. Principal

Prin.Dec. Sneed's Kentucky Decisions (2 Ky.) 1801–05

Prins & Conderlag Prins and Conderlag's Reports (Sri L.) 1843–52

Prior Report Report of the Committee on the Prison Disciplinary System (Cmnd. 9641) 1985

Prison L.Reptr. Prison Law Reporter (USA)

Prison Serv.J. Prison Service Journal. 1960–

Pritch.M.& D. Pritchard, Divorce & Matrimonial Causes. 3ed. 1874

Pritch.Quar.Sess. Pritchard, Quarter Sessions. 2ed. 1904

Priv. Private

Priv.C.App. Privy Council Appeals

Priv.C.D.I. Indian Privy Council Decisions

Priv.Cond. Privilegia Londini (Lat.) Customs of Privileges of London

Priv.Counc.App. Privy Council Appeals

Priv.Counc.D.I. Privy Council Decisions (India)

PrivExCE Privileges and Exemptions of the Council of Europe. 1949

Priv.Found.Rep. Private Foundations Reporter (CCH) (USA)

Priv.Hous.Fin. Private Housing Finance

Priv.Inv.Abroad Private Investments Abroad

Priv.Laws Private Laws

Priv.St. Private Statutes

Privacy Bull. Privacy Bulletin (Privacy Committee, Sydney) (Aus.) 1985–

Prize C.R. Prize Court Reports (S.Afr.) 1914–18

Pro quer. Pro querante (Lat.) for the plaintiff

pro.tem. pro tempore (Lat.) for the time being

Prob. Law Reports, Pobate Division. 1891–
Probate
Probation
Problem

Prob.C. Probate Code

Prob.Code Probate Code

Prob.Ct. Probate Court

Prob.Ct.Rep. Probate Court Reporter (Ohio)

Prob.Div. Law Reports, Probate Division

Prob.J. Probation Journal. 1974–

Prob.L.J. Probate Law Journal (USA)

Prob.L.T. Probyn, Land Tenure. 4ed. 1881
Prob.Pr.Act Probate Practice Act
Prob.R. Probate Reports (USA) 1875–95
Prob.Rep. Probate Reports (USA) 1875–95
Prob.Rep.Ann. Probate Reports Annotated (USA) 1896–1909
Prob.& Adm.Div. Law Reports, Probate and Admiralty Divisions
Prob.& Div. Law Reports, Probate and Divorce
Prob.& Mat. Probate and Matrimonial Cases
Prob.& Prop. Probate and Property
Probat. Probation
Probat.J. Probation Journal. 1974–
Proc. Procedures
Proceedings
Proclamation
Proc.A.B.A. Proceedings of the American Bar Association
Proc.ASIL Proceedings of the American Society of International Law
Proc.Am.Acad.Pol.Sc. Proceedings of the American Academy of Political Science
Proc.Am.Soc.I.L. Proceedings of the American Society of International Law
Proc.Am.Soc.Society Proceedings of the American Sociological Society
Proc.gén. Procureur général (Fr.) attorney general, district attorney
Proc.Medico-Legal Soc.N.S.W. Proceedings of the Medico-Legal Society of New South Wales (Aus.) 1960–
Proc.Medico-Legal Soc.Vic. Proceedings of the Medico-Legal Society of Victoria (Aus.) 1931–
Proceedings Am.Law Inst. Proceedings of the American Law Institute
Proceedings Am.Soc.Int.Law Proceedings of the American Society of International Law
Procgs. Proceedings
Proctor Proctor: Newsletter of the Queensland Law Society (Aus.) 1982–
Prod. Produced
Product
Production
Prod.Liab.Int. Product Liability International. 1979–
Prod.Liab.Rep. Products Liability Reporter (CCH) (USA)
Prof. Profession
Professional
Professor
Prof.Admin. Professional Administration. 1971–
Professional Administrator
Prof.L. Professional Lawyer
Prom. Promissory
Prop. Property
Proposition (Swed.) A Cabinet Bill to the Riksdag
Prop.Law. Property Lawyer. 1826–30
Prop.Law Bull. Property Law Bulletin. 1980–
Prop.Law.N.S. Property Lawyer, New Series. 1830
Prop.& Comp.R. Property and Compensation Reports
Pros.Atty. Prosecuting Attorney
prosp. prospectively
Prot. Protocol
Prot.C.J. Protocol on the Statute of the European Communities Court of Justice
Prot.P.I. Protocol on Privileges and Immunities
Proudf.Land.Dec. United States Land Decisions (Proudfit)
Prouty Prouty's Reports (61–68 Vermont)
Prov. Province
Prov.Can.Stat. Statutes of the Province of Canada
Prov.J.J. Provincial Judges Journal (Can.) 1977–
Prov.St. Statutes, Laws of the Province of Massachusetts
provns. provisions
Prt.Rep. Practice Reports

Prud. Conseil de prud'hommes (Belg.) labour courts
Przeg.Ustaw.Gospod. Przeglad Ustawodawstwa Gospodarczego (Poland)
Psych. Psychiatry
Psychology
Psych.& M.L.J. Psychological & Medico-Legal Journal
pt. part
pts. parts
Pty. Proprietary
Pty.Ltd. Proprietary Limited
pub. public
publish
published
publisher
publishing
Pub.Acts Public Acts
Pub.Acts N.S.W. Public Acts of New South Wales (Aus.) 1824–1957
Pub.Acts Queensl. Public Acts of Queensland (Reprint) (Aus.) 1828–1936
Pub.Adm. Public Administration. 1926–
Pub.Adm.Rev. Public Administration Review (USA) 1940–
Pub.Adm.& Dev. Public Administration and Development
Pub.Auth. Public Authorities
Pub.Bldgs. Public Buildings
Pub.Cont.L.J. Public Contract Law Journal (USA) 1967–
Pub.Contract L.J. Public Contract Law Journal (USA) 1967–
Pub.Doc. Public Documents
Pub.Ent.Adv.L.Q. Publishing, Entertainment, Advertising and Allied Fields Law Quarterly (USA) 1961–
Pub.Employee Rel.Rep. Public Employee Relations Reports (USA)
Pub.Gen.Acts S.Austl. Public General Acts of South Australia. 1837–1936
Pub.Gen.Laws Public General Laws
Pub.Health Public Health Service, Court Decisions (USA)
Pub.Hous. Public Housing
Pub.L. Public Law. 1956–
Pub.Land L.Rev. The Public Land Law Review (USA)
Pub.Land & Res.L.Dig. Public Land and Resources Law Digest
Pub.Lands Dec. Department of the Interior, Decisions Relating to Public Lands (USA) 1881–
Pub.Law Bull. Public Law Bulletin
Pub.Laws Public Laws
Pub.No. Public Number (assigned to laws passed by the U.S. Congress)
Pub.Rel.Bull. Public Relations Bulletin (A.B.A.) 1953–
Pub.Res.C. Public Resources Code (California)
Pub.Res.No. Public Resolution Number (assigned to public resolutions passed by the U.S. Congress)
Pub.Ser.Comm. Public Service Commission (USA)
Pub.Serv. Public Service
Pub.St. Public Statutes
Pub.U.Rep. Public Utilities Reports (USA) 1915–
Pub.Util. Public Utilities
Pub.Util.C. Public Utilities Code (California)
Pub.Util.Comm. Public Utilites Commission (USA)
Pub.Util.Fort. Public Utilites Fortnightly (USA) 1928–
Pub.Util.L.Anthol. Public Utilites Law Anthology (USA) 1974–
Pub.& Loc.Laws Public and Local Laws
publ. publication
published
Publ.Adm.& Dev. Public Administration and Development
Publ.Contract L.J. Public Contract Law Journal (USA)
Publ.Finance Public Finance (Neth.)
Publ.Finance Q. Public Finance Quarterly
Publ.Interest Public Interest (USA)
Publ.L. Public Law. 1956–
Publ.L.Forum Public Law Forum
Publ.& Entertainm. Publishing, Entertainment, Advertising and Allied Fields Law Quarterly (USA)

pubn. publication
Puerto Rico F. Puerto Rico Federal Reports. 1900–24
Puerto Rico Fed. Puerto Rico Federal Reports. 1900–24
Puerto Rico Rep. Puerto Rico Supreme Court Reports. 1899–
Pufendorf Pufendorf, De Jure Naturae et Gentium. 1688
Pug. Pugsley's New Brunswick Reports (Can.) 1872–77
Pugs. Pugsley's New Brunswick Reports (Can.) 1872–77
Pugs.& Bur. Pugsley & Burbridge's New Brunswick Reports. 1878–82
Pugs.& Burb. Pugsley & Burbridge's New Brunswick Reports. 1878–82
Pugs.& Tru. Pugsley & Trueman's New Brunswick Reports (Can.) 1882–83
Pull.Acc. Pulling, Mercantile Accounts. 1846
Pull.Accts. Pulling, Mercantile Accounts. 1846
Pull.Att. Pulling, Attorneys & Solicitors. 3ed. 1862
Pull.Laws & Cust.Lond. Pulling, Laws, Customs, Regulations and Usages of the City & Port of London. 1842
Pull.Port of London Pulling, Laws, Customs, Regulations and Usages of the City & Port of London. 1842
Pulling A. Pulling, The Order of the Coif. 1884
Pulsifer(Me.) Pulsifer's Reports (35–68 Maine)
Pump Ct. Pump Court. 1883–91
Pun. All India Reporter, Punjab. 1951–
Indian Law Reports, Punjab. 1949–
Punj. All India Reporter, Punjab. 1951–
Punj.Ind. Punjab, India
Punj.Pak. Punjab, Pakistan
Punj.Rec. Punjab Record (India) 1866–1919
Pur. Feast of the Purification of the Blessed Virgin Mary
Purchase
Purd.Dig. Purdon, Digest of Pennsylvania Laws
Purd.Dig.Laws Purdon, Digest of Pennsylvania Laws
Pvt. Private
Py.R. Pyke, Lower Canada King's Bench Reports (Quebec, Can.) 1809–10
Pyke Pyke, Lower Canada King's Bench Reports (Quebec, Can.) 1809–10
Pyke L.C. Pyke, Lower Canada King's Bench Reports (Quebec, Can.) 1809–10
Pyke's R. Pyke, Lower Canada King's Bench Reports (Quebec, Can.) 1809–10

Q

Q. Quadragesms (Year Books, Part IV)
Quarterly
Quebec
Queen
Queensland
Question
Questioned
Quorum

Q.A.C. Quebec Appeal Cases (Can.) 1986–

Q.B. Law Reports, Queen's Bench. 1891–1901, 1952–
Queen's Bench
Queen's Bench Reports (Adolphus & Ellis, New Series) (113–118 ER) 1841–52
Queen's Bench Reports (Quebec, Can.) 1892–1900
Queen's Bench Reports, Upper Canada. 1844–82

Q.B.A. Queensland Bar Association (Aus.)

Q.B.D. Law Reports Queen's Bench Division. 1875–90
Queen's Bench Division

Q.B.Div'l.Ct. Queen's Bench Divisional Court

Q.B.L.C. Queen's Bench Reports, Lower Canada (Quebec) 1892–1900

Q.B.R. Queen's Bench Reports (Adolphus & Ellis, New Series) (113–118 ER) 1841–52

Q.B.U.C. Queen's Bench Reports, Upper Canada. 1844–82

Q.Bar News Queensland Bar News (Aus.) 1980–

Q.C. Queen's Counsel

Q.C.A.R. Queensland Criminal Reports (Aus.) 1860–1907

Q.C.L.C. Quebec Common Law Cases (Can.) 1990–

Q.C.L.E. Queensland Continuing Legal Education (Aus.)

Q.C.L.L.R. Queensland Crown Lands Law Reports (Aus.) 1859–

Q.C.L.R. Queensland Criminal Reports (Aus.) 1860–1907

Q.C.R. Queensland Criminal Reports (Aus.) 1860–1907

Q.Case Note Queensland Law Reporter Case Note (Aus.)

Q.Conv.R. Queensland Conveyancing Reports (in Queensland Law and Practice) (Aus.) 1982–

Q.Ct.of Cr.App. Queensland Court of Criminal Appeal (Aus.)

q.d. quasi dicat (Lat.) as if one should say
quais dictum (Lat.) as if said

q.e.n. quare executionem non (Lat.) wherefore execution should not be issued

Q.G.G. Queensland Government Gazette (Aus.)

Q.G.I.G. Queensland Government Industrial Gazette

Q.Gov.Indus.Gaz. Queensland Government Industrial Gazette

Q.I.C. Queensland Industrial Commission (Aus.)

Q.I.Ct. Queensland Industrial Court (Aus.)

Q.I.T.L.J. Queensland Institute of Technology Law Journal (Aus.) 1985–

Q.I.T.School of Law Queensland

Institute of Technology School of Law (Aus.)

Q.J.Econ. Quarterly Journal of Economics

Q.J.Lib.Congress The Quarterly Journal of the Library of Congress

Q.J.P. Queensland Justice of the Peace and Local Authorities' Journal (Aus.) 1907–72

Q.J.P.Mag.Cas. Queensland Justice of the Peace. Magisterial Cases (Aus.) 1907–72

Q.J.P.R. Queensland Justice of the Peace Reports (Aus.) 1907–72

Q.L. Quebec Law
Queensland Lawyer. 1973–

Q.L.Beor Beor's Queensland Law Reports (Aus.) 1876–78

Q.L.C.R. Queensland Land Court Reports (Aus.)

Q.L.J. Queens Law Journal (Can.) 1971–
Queensland Law Journal. 1878–1901

Q.L.J.(N.C.) Queensland Law Journal (Notes of Cases) (Aus.) 1878–1901

Q.L.R. Quebec Law Reports (Can.) 1874–91
Queensland Law Reporter
Queensland Law Reports (Aus.) 1876–78

Q.L.R.(Beor) Beor's Queensland Law Reports (Aus.) 1876–78

Q.L.R.C. Queensland Law Reform Commision

Q.L.S.J. Queensland Law Society Journal (Aus.) 1971–

Q.Law Soc.J. Queensland Law Society Journal (Aus.) 1971–

Q.Local Govt.Sci. Quarterly of Local Government Science (Finland)

Q.N. Quarterly Newsletter (ABA) 1974–
Quarterly Notes (Mal.) 1926–27

Q.N.T.J.B. Queensland and Northern Territory Judgments Bulletin (Aus.) 1987–

Q.O.R. Quebec Official Reports. 1892–

Q.P.C.A.I.Rep. Queensland Parliamentary Commissioner for Administration Investigations Report (Aus.) 1975–

Q.P.L.R. Queensland Planning Law Reports (Aus.) 1982–

Q.P.R. Quebec Practice Reports. 1896–1943
Queensland Practice Reports

Q.R. Quebec Official Reports. 1892–

Q.R.Ec.Bus. Quarterly Review of Economics and Business

Q.R.K.B. Quebec King's Bench Reports (Can.) 1901–41, 1942–

Q.R.Q.B. Quebec Queen's Bench Reports (Can.) 1892–1900

Q.R.S.C. Quebec Official Reports, Superior Court. 1892–

Q.R.& A.I. The Queen's Regulations and Admiralty Instructions for the Government of Her Majesty's Naval Service. 1953–

Q.Rev.Juris. Quarterly Review of Jurisprudence. 1887–88

Q.S. Quarter Sessions
Queen's Serjeant at Law

Q.S.C. Rapports Judiciaires de Québec, Cour Supérieure (Can.)

Q.S.C.R. Queensland Supreme Court Reports. 1860–81

Q.S.R. Queensland State Reports (Aus.) 1902–57

q.t. qui tam (Lat.) who as well

Q.U.L.J. Queensland University Law Journal. 1948–

q.v. quod vide (Lat.) which see

Q.Vic. Statutes of Québec in the reign of Victoria

QW Qualifying Week

Q.W.N. Queensland Law Reporter & Weekly Notes. 1908–72

Q.War. Quo Warranto

Qd.L. Queensland Lawyer (Aus.) 1973–

Qd.R. Queensland Reports. 1958–

Qld. Queensland

Qld.Inst.Tecnol.L.J. Queensland Institute of Technology Law Journal (Aus.) 1985–

Qly.Land.R. Fitzgibbon's Irish Land Reports. 1895–1920

Qu.Jour.Int–Amer.Rel. Quarterly Journal of Inter-American Relations. 1939
Qu.L.J. Quarterly Law Journal (USA) 1856–59
Qu.L.Rev. Quarterly Law Review (USA) 1860–61
Quadr. Quadragesms (Year Books, Part IV)
Quart. Quarterly Review
Quart.Bull.of Polish Inst.Arts & Science Quarterly Bulletin of the Polish Institute of Arts and Sciences of America
Quart.L.J.(Va.) Quarterly Law Journal (Virginia, USA) 1856–59
Quart.L.Rev.(Va.) Quarterly Law Review (Virginia, USA) 1860–61
Quart.Newsl. Quarterly Newsletter (ABA) 1974–
Quat.Journ.of Econ. Quarterly Journal of Economics
Quat.Rev.Econ.& Bus. Quarterly Review of Economics and Business
Que. Québec
Que.C.A. Rapports Judiciares Officiels, Cour du Banc du Roi (de la Reine), Cour d'Appel (Can.) 1892–
Que.C.B.R. Rapports Judiciares Officiels, Cour du Banc du Roi (de la Reine), Cour d'Appel (Can.) 1892–
Que.C.S. Rapports Judiciares Officiels, Cour Supérieure (Can.) 1892–
Que.K.B. Quebec Official Reports, King's bench (Can.) 1901–42, 1942–
Que.L.R. Quebec Law Reports (Can.) 1874–91
Que.P.R. Quebec Practice Reports. 1897–1943
Que.Pr. Quebec Practice Reports. 1897–1943
Que.Q.B. Quebec Official Reports Queen's Bench. 1892–1900
Que.Rev.Stat. Quebec Revised Statutes (Can.)
Que.S.C. Quebec Offical Reports, Superior Court (Can.) 1892–
Que.Stat. Quebec Statutes (Can.)
Queb.K.B. Quebec Official Reports, King's Bench (Can.) 1942–
Queb.Pr. Quebec Practice Reports. 1897–1943
Queb.S.C. Quebec Official Reports, Superior Court (Can.)
Quebec C.C.R.O. Quebec Civil Code Revision Office
Quebec L.(Can.) Quebec Law Reports. 1874–91
Quebec Pr.(Can.) Quebec Practice Reports. 1897–1943, 1944–
Queens B.Bull. Queens Bar Bulletin (USA) 1928–
Queens C.B.A.Bull. Queens County Bar Association Bulletin
Queens Intra.L.J. Queens Intramural Law Journal (Can.) 1968–70
Queens.J.P. & Loc.Auth.Jo. Queensland Justice of the Peace and Local Authorities' Journal. 1907–
Queens L.J. Queens Law Journal (Can.) 1971–
Queens.L.J. Queensland Law Journal (Aus.) 1879–1901
Queens.L.R. Queensland Law Reports (Aus.) 1876–78
Queens.St.R. Queensland State Reports
Queensl. Queensland
Queensland Law Reports (Aus.) 1876–78
Queensl.J.P.(Aus.) Queensland Justice of the Peace and Local Authorities' Journal. 1907–
Queensl.L.J.(Aus.) Queensland Law Journal (Aus.) 1879–1901
Queensl.L.J. & R. Queensland Law Journal & Reports (Aus.) 1879–1901
Queensl.L.R. Queensland Law Reports (Aus.) 1876–78
Queensl.L.S.J. Queensland Law Society Journal. 1971–
Queensl.S.C.(Aus.) Queensland Supreme Court Reports. 1860–81
Queensl.S.Ct.R. Queensland Supreme Court Reports. 1860–81
Queensl.St.(Austr.) Queensland State Reports

Queensl.Stat. Queensland Statutes (Aus.)

Queensl.W.N.(Aus.) Queensland Law Reporter & Weekly Notes. 1908–

Queensland L.Soc'y J. Queensland Law Society Journal (Aus.)

Quin. Quincy's Massachusetts Reports. 1761–72

Quin Bank. Quin, Banking. 1833

Quincy Quincy's Superior Court of Judicature Reports (Massachusetts) 1761–72

Quinti, Quinto Year Book 5 Henry 5

quot. quotation
quoted
quoting

R

r. repeal
repealed
repealing
rule

R. All India Reporter, Rajasthan. 1950
Kentucky Law Reporter. 1880–1908
King Richard
Railroad
Railway
Rawle's Reports (Pennsylvania) 1828–35
Receuil de la Jurisprudence de la Court (European Court Reports) 1954–
Recht (Ger.) Law
Regina (Queen)
Repealed
Report(s)
The Reports. 1893–95
Rescinded
Resolved
Rettie's Session Cases, 4th Series (Scot.) 1873–98
Reversed
Revision
Revoked
Rex (King)
Rhodesia (Zimbabwe) High Court
Rolls
Roscoe's Reports of the Supreme Court (Cape, S.Afr.) 1861–78
Rule
Russian

R.1 Cro. Croke's King's Bench Reports tempore Elizabeth. 1582–1603

R.2 Cro. Croke's King's Bench Reports tempore James I. 1603–25

R.3 Cro. Croke's King's Bench Reports tempore Charles I. 1625–41

RA Regeringsrattens arsbok (Swed.) The annual Supreme Administrative Court reporter. 1909–
Riksaklagare (Swed.) Chief Crown Prosecutor

R.A. Ratepayers' Association
Rating Appeals
Registration Appeals
Regulation Appeals
La Revue administrative (Fr.) 1948–
Rhodesia (Zimbabwe) Appellate Division
Rules and Administration
Rules on Appeal

R(A) Decisions of the Commissioner under the Social Security and Child Benefit Acts (Attendance allowance)

RAC Rent Assessment Committee

R.A.C. Ramsay's Appeal Cases (Quebec, Can.) 1873–86

RAD Research and Analysis Department

R.A.D.I.C. African Journal of International and Comparative Law

RAGBens Entscheidungen des Reichsarbeitsgerichts und der Landersarbeitsgerichte (Ger.) Labour Court Reports

R.A.I. Recueil des arbitrages internationaux

RAP Radical Alternatives to Prison

R.A.P. Règlement d'administration publique (Fr.) administrative regulation
Rules for Admission to Practice

RArb Recht der Arbeit (Ger.) 1948–
RB Rättegångsbalk (Swed.) The Code of Judicial Procedure
R.B. La Revue du Barreau (Québec, Can.) 1941–
R.B.D.I. Revue Belge de Droit International (Belg.)
RBFM Reglement van het Beamtenfonds voor het Mijnbedrijf (Neth.) Social Security (Mines) Regulations
R.B.G. British Guiana Reports of Opinions
RBP Restrictive Business Practices
RBTC Register of Burials at the Temple Church, 1628–1853. 1905
RBelDI Revue Belge de droit International
R.C. Nicholl, Hare & Carrow's Railway Cases. 1835–55
Railway Cases
Record Commissioners
Registration Cases
Registre de commerce (Switz.)
Remington's Code (USA)
Revised Code
La Revue Critique (Québec, Can.) 1870–75
Rolls Court
Ruling Cases, ed. Campbell 1894–1908
R.C.A.D.I. Recueil des Cours de l'Académie de Droit International
R.C.D.A. Revue canadienne du droit d'auteur
R.C.D.I. Revue critique de droit international (Fr.) 1934–46
R.C.D.I.P. Revue critique de droit international privé (Fr.) 1947
R.C.de l'E. Rapports de la Cour de Echiquier (Exchequer Court Reports) (Can.) 1875–1922
R.C.J. Reports of Certain Judgments of the Supreme Court, Vice-Admiralty Court and Full Court of Appeal, Lagos (Nig.) 1884–92
Royal Courts of Justice
RC(J) Rettie, Crawford & Melville, Session Cases, 4th Series (Scot.) 1873–98
R.C.L. Ruling Case Law
R.C.L.J. Revue critique de législation et jurisprudence (Fr.) 1851–1914, 1924–
RCM Resolution of the Council of Ministers
R.C.M.P.Q. Royal Canadian Mounted Police Quarterly. 1933–
R.C.N. Rating Case Notes
R.C.S. Remington's Compiled Statutes (USA) 1922
Supreme Court Reports (Can.) 1876–
R.C.S.Supp. Remington's Compiled Statutes Supplement
R.C.W.A. Revised Code of Washington Annotated
R.C. & C.R. Revenue, Civil & Criminal Reporter, Calcutta (India) 1866–68
R.(Ct.of Sess.) Rettie, Crawford & Melville, Session Cases, 4th Series (Scot.) 1873–98
rd Royal Decree (It.)
R.D. Indian Revenue Decisions, United Provinces. 1883–
Regio Decreto (It.) Royal Decree
R.D.A. République démocratique allemande
Rules for the Discipline of Attorneys (USA)
R.D.A.T. Registered Designs Appeal Tribunal (USA)
R.d.agr. Rivista di diritto agrario (It.)
R.d.C. Recueil des Cours de l'Académie de Droit International (Neth.)
R.D.C. Rural District Council
R.d.civ. Rivista di diritto civile (It.)
R.d.comm. Rivista di diritto commerciale (It.)
RDEur Rivista de diritto europeo (It.)
R.D.F.Q. Recueil de droit fiscal québecois (Can.) 1977–
R.D.H. Revue des droits de l'homme
R.D.I. Recueil de droit immobilier (Québec, Can.) 1986–
Revue de droit international et de législation comparée (Belg.) 1869–
R.D.I.(égyptienne) Revue égyptienne de droit international

R.D.I.(española) Revista española de derecho internacional (Sp.)
R.D.I.(Geneva) Revue de droit international, de sciences diplomatiques, politiques et sociales (Switz.)
R.D.I.(héllenique) Revue héllenique de droit international
R.D.I.L.C. Revue de droit international et de législation comparée (Belg.) 1869–
R.D.I.M.O. Revue de droit international pour le Moyen-Orient
R.D.I.P. Revue de droit international privé (Fr.) 1922–33
R.D.I.P.D.P.I. Revue de droit international privé et de droit pénal international (Fr.) 1905–21
R.D.I.P.P. Rivista di diritto internazionale privato e processuale (It.) 1965–
R.D.I.(Paris) Revue de droit international (Fr.)
R.D.I.S.D.P. Revue de droit international, de sciences diplomatiques et politiques (Switz.)
RDL Regio Decreto Legge (It.) Royal Legislative Decree
R.D.P. Recueil des Décisions du Conseil des Prises (Fr.) 1947
Receuil de droit pénal (Fr.) 1947–74
Revue du droit public (Fr.) 1894–
R.D.P.S.P. Revue du droit public et de la science politique en France et à l'étranger
R.d.proc. Rivista di diritto processuale (It.)
R.D.S. Revue de droit suisse (Switz.)
R.D.Sup. Revenue Decisions, United Provinces, Supplement (India)
R.D.T. Revue de droit du travail (Québec, Can.)
R.D.U.N.B. Revue de droit de l'Université du Nouveau-Brunswick (Can.) 1951–
R.D.U.S. Revue de droit (Faculté de droit, Université de Sherbrooke, Québec) (Can.) 1970–
R.de D. Revue de droit, Université de Sherbrooke, Québec (Can.) 1970–
R.de d.McGill Revue de droit de Macgill – McGill Law Journal (Can.) 1955–
R.de D.Pen. Revue de droit pénal (Can.)
R.de droit comp. Revue de droit comparatif (Can.)
R.de J. Revue de jurisprudence (Québec) 1895–
R.de Jur. Revue de jurisprudence (Québec) 1895–
R.de L. Revue de législation et de jurisprudence (Can.) 1845–48
R.de Legis. Revue de la législation (Can.)
R.du B. La revue du Barreau (Québec) 1941–
R.du B.can. Revue de Barreau canadien – Canadian Bar Review. 1923–
R.du D. La revue du droit (Québec) 1922–39
R.du N. Revue du Notariat (Québec) 1898–
R.du Not. Revue du Notariat (Québec) 1898–
R.E. Revised Edition
R.E.C.I.E.L. Review of European Community and International Environmental Law
R.E.Code I/no. Selected Decisions of the Umpire on Reinstatement in Civil Employment. 1944–
R.E.D. A'Beckett's New South Wales Reserved & Equity Decisions. 1845
Russell's Equity Decisions, Nova Scotia (Can.) 1873–82
REG Rückerstattungsgesetz (Ger.) Restitution Law
R.E.L.R. Revised and Expurgated Law Reports (India) up to 1906
REgDI Revue égyptienne de droit international
REspDI Revista Española de Derecho Internacional (Sp.)
R.et I. Regina et Imperatrix (Queen and Empress)
Rex et Imperator (King and Emperor)
RF Regeringsform (Swed.) The Instrument of Government

R(F) Decisions of the Commissioner under the Social Security and Child Benefit Acts (Child benefit)
R.F.A. République fédérale d'Allemagne
RFH Reichsfinanzhof (Ger.) Reich Finance Court
R.F.L. Reports of Family Law (Can.)
R.F.S. Registry of Friendly Societies
RG Rechtsgeschichte (Ger.)
Reichsgericht (Ger.) Reich Supreme Court
Rettens Gang (Norway) law reports
R.G. Regula generalis (General Rule or Order of Court) (Can.)
Revue générale de droit international public
R(G) Decisions of the Commissioner under the National Insurance Acts (maternity benefit, widow's benefit, guardian's allowance, child's special allowance) 1948–
RGA Revue générale de l'air
R.G.A.T. Revue générale des assurances terrestres (Fr.) 1929–
RGBL Reichsgesetzblatt (Ger.) Reich Law Gazette
RGBl Reichsgesetzblatt (Ger.) Reich Law Gazette
R.G.C.R. Renner's Gold Coast Reports (Ghana) 1868–1914
R.G.D. Revue générale de droit (Québec, Can.) 1970–
R.G.D.I. Revue générale de droit international public (Fr.) 1894–
R.G.D.I.P. Revue générale de droit international public (Fr.) 1894–
R.G.J.B. Répertoire général de la jurisprudence belge (Belg.) law report. 1926–
R.G.L. Review of Ghana Law. 1969–
RGR Komm. Reichsgerichtskommentar
RGSt. Entscheidungen des Reichsgerichts in Strafsachen (Ger.) Reports of the Reich Supreme Court in Criminal Matters. 1880–1944
RGW Rat für Gegenseitige Wirtschaftshilfe
RGZ Entscheidungen des Reichsgerichts in Zivilsachen (Ger.) Reports of Decisions of the Reich Supreme Court in Civil Cases. 1880–1945
R.Gen. Revue générale de droit (Québec, Can.) 1970–
R.H. Rotuli Hundredorum. 1218–1307
R.H.C. Road Haulage Cases. 1950–
R.H.D.I. Revue héllenique de droit international
RHFE Entscheidungen des Reichsfinanzhofs (Ger.) law reports on Fiscal Court
R.H.L. Rettie, Crawford & Melville, Session Cases, 4th Series (Scot.) 1873–98
R.(H.L.) Rettie, Crawford & Melville, Session Cases, 4th Series (Scot.) 1873–98
R.I. Regina et Imperatrix (Queen and Empress)
Reinsurance
Revue de droit international (Fr.)
Revue de droit international, de sciences diplomatiques, politiques et sociales (Switz.)
Revue de droit international et de la législation comparée (Belg.)
Rex et Imperator (King and Emperor)
Rhode Island
Rhode Island Supreme Court Reports. 1928–
R(I) Decisions of the Commissioner under the National Insurance (Industrial Injuries) Acts. 1948–
R.I.A. Research Institute of America
R.I.A.A. Reports of International Arbitral Awards (UN) 1948–
R.I.B.J. Rhode Island Bar Journal (USA) 1952–
R.I.Bd.R.C. Rhode Island Board of Railroad Commission Reports
R.I.C.R. Revue international de la Croix Rouge
R.I.C.S. Royal Institution of Chartered Surveyors
R.I.Ct.Rec. Rhode Island Court Records

RID International Regulations Concerning the Carriage of Dangerous Goods by Rail
Rechtswissenschaftlicher Informationsdienst (Ger.) 1952–59

R.I.D.A. Revue Internationale du Droit d'Auteur (Fr.)

R.I.D.C. Revue internationale de droit comparé (Fr.) 1949–

R.I.D.P. Revue international de droit pénal (Fr.) 1924–40.1946–

R.I.Dec. Rhode Island Decisions (USA)

R.I.F. Revue internationale français du droit des gens (Fr.)

RIFD Rivista internazionale di filosofia del diritto (It.)

R.I.F.D.G. Revue internationale français du droit des gens (Fr.)

R.I.Gen.Laws General Laws of Rhode Island

R.I.(Geneva) Revue de droit international, de sciences diplomatiques, politiques et sociales

R.I.I.A. Royal Institute of International Affairs

R.I.P.A. Royal Institute of Public Administration

R.I.P.U.C. Rhode Island Public Utilities Commission

R.I.(Paris) Revue de droit international

R.I.Pub.Laws Public Laws of Rhode Island

R.I.R.C. Rhode Island Railroad Commission

RISG Rivista italiana delle scienze giuridiche

R.I.T.D. Revue internationale de la théorie du droit

RIW Recht der Internationalen Wirtschaft (Ger.)

R.Int'l.Arb.Awards United Nations Reports of International Arbitral Awards

R.J. A'Beckett's Reserved Judgments, Port Phillip (N.S.W., Aus.) 1846–51
La Revue de Jurisprudence (Québec) 1895–
Revue Judiciaire, by Bruzard (Mauritius) 1843–44

R.(J.) Justiciary Cases in vols. of Session Cases. 1873–98

R.J.P.I.C. Revue juridique et politique, indépendance et coopération

R.J.P.U.F. Revue juridique et politique de l'union française

R.J.O. Rapports Judiciaires Officiels de Québec (Quebec Official Law Reports)

R.J.O.Q.(B.R.) Rapports Judiciaires Officiels de Québec, Cour du Banc du Roi (Quebec Official Reports, King's Bench)

R.J.O.Q.,C.S. Rapports Judiciaires Officiels de Québec, Cour Supérieure (Quebec Official Reports, Superior Court)

R.J.Q. Rapports Judiciaires de Québec (Can.) 1892–
Recueils de jurisprudence du Québec (Can.) 1986–

R.J.Q.,B.R. Rapports Judiciaires de Québec, Cour de Banc du Roi (Quebec Official Reports, King's Bench)

R.J.Q.,C.S. Rapports Judiciaires de Québec, Cour Supérieure (Quebec Official Reports, Superior Court)

R.J.R. Mathieu's Quebec Revised Reports (Can.) 1726–1891

R.J.R.Q. Mathieu's Quebec Revised Reports (Can.) 1726–1891

R.J.T. La Revue Juridique Thémis (Can.) 1951–

R.J.& P.J. Revenue, Judicial & Police Journal (Calcutta, India) 1863–65

RKG Reichsknappsschaftsgesetz (Ger.) Act on Miners' Insurance Premiums

RL Richtlinien (Ger.) instructions, directions

R.L. Recent Law (N.Z.) 1966–74
Revised Laws
Revue Légale (Can.) 1869–
Roman Law

R.L.B.Dec. Railroad Labor Board Decisions (USA)

RLG Bundesgesetz über Rohrleitungsanlagen zur Beförderung flüßiger und gasformiger Brenn–

oder Treibstoffe (Switz.) 1963
Research Libraries Group

R.L.J. Rhodesian Law Journal. 1961–

R.L.N.S. Revue Légale, New Series (Can.) 1895–1942

R.L.O.S. Revue Légale, Old Series (Can.) 1869–92

R.L.Q.B. Revue Légale Reports, Queen's Bench (Can.)

R.L.R. Rhodesian Law Reports
Rutgers Law Review (USA) 1947–

R.L.S.C. Revue Légale Reports, Supreme Court (Can.)

R.L.W. Rajasthan Law Weekly (India)

R.L.& S. Ridgway, Lapp and Schoales' Irish King's Bench Reports. 1793–95

R.L.& W. Roberts, Leaming & Wallis' New Court Cases. 1849–51

R.M. Rechtsgeleerd Magazijn (Neth.) 1882–1938

R(M) Decisions of the Commissioner under the Social Security and Child Benefit Acts (mobility allowance)

RMBl. Reichsministerialblatt (Ger.) Imperial Official Gazette

RMC Revue du Marché Commun

R.M.C.C. Ryan & Moody's Crown Cases. 1824–44

R.M.C.C.R. Ryan & Moody's Crown Cases. 1824–44

RMCE European Agreement on Regulations governing the Movement of Persons between member states of the Council Europe

R.M.Ch. P.M. Charlton's Reports (Georgia) 1811–37

R.M.Charlt.(Ga.) P.M. Charlton's Reports (Georgia) 1811–37

R.M.L.R. Rocky Mountain Law Review (USA) 1928–62

R.M.R. Rocky Mountain Law Review (USA) 1928–62

R.M.Th. Rechtsgeleerd magazijn Themis (Neth.) 1939–

R.M.Themis Rechtsgeleerd magazijn Themis (Neth.) 1939–

R.N.C.A. Rhodesia and Nyasaland Court of Appeal Law Reports. 1939–

R.N.L.J. Rhodesia and Nyasaland Law Journal. 1961–63

R.N.R.E. Application for writ of error refused, no reversible error

RO Recueil des lois fédérales (Switz.) collection of enactments
Recuei officiel des lois et ordonnances de la Confédération suisse
Rent Officer
Riksdagsordning (Swed.) Riksdag Act

R.O.a.s. Recueil officiel des lois et ordonnances de la Confédération suisse, ancienne serie. 1848–74

ROI Return on investment

ROLF Recueil officiel des lois fédérales (Switz.)

R.O.N.W.T. Revised Ordinances, North West Territories (Can.)

ROSET Register of Solicitors Employing Trainees

ROW Rights of Women

R.P. Lag om inforande av nya rattegangsbalken 1946
Rapports de Pratique de Québec (Can.) 1898–
Rotuli Parliamentorum. 1278–1533
Rules and Precedents (British Columbia Practice) (Can.)
Rules of Procedure
Rules of Procedure of the Court of Justice

R(P) Decisions of the Commissioner under the National Insurance Acts (Retirement Pension) 1948–

RPB Recognised professional body

R.P.C. Canadian Patent Reporter. 1941–
Real Property Cases. 1843–48
Real Property Commissioner's Report. 1832
Reports of Patent, Design & Trade Mark Cases. 1884–
Restrictive Practices Court

R.P.C.Rep. Real Property Commissioners' Report. 1832

R.P.Ct. Restrictive Practices Court

R.P.D. Repatriation Pension Decisions (Aus.) 1985–

R.P.D.B. Répertoire Pratique de Droit Belge (Belg.) encyclopedia

R.P.D.T.M.C. Reports of Patent, Design and Trade Mark Cases. 1884–

RPI Retail Price Index

RPOA Recognised Private Operating Agency

R.P.P. Revue politique et parlementaire

R.P.P.P. Rules of Pleading Practice and Procedure

R.P.Q. Rapports de Pratique de Québec (Quebec Practice Reports) (Can.) 1897–1943, 1944–

R.P.R. Real Property Reports (Can.) 1977–

R.P.S. Revue pratique des societés

R.P.W. Rawle, Penrose & Watts' Reports (Pennsylvania) 1828–40

R.P.& W. Rawle, Penrose & Watts' Reports (Pennsylvania) 1828–40

R.Pat.Cas. Reports of Patent, Design and Trade Mark Cases. 1884–

R.R. Pike and Fischer's Radio Regulations (USA)
Railroad
Revised Reports. 1785–1866

R.R.2d. Pike & Fischer's Radio Regulations, Second Series (USA)

R.R.C. Ryde's Rating Cases. 1956–

R.R.Cr.R. Revised Reports, Criminal Rulings (India) 1862–75

R.R.L.R. Rent Review & Lease Renewal

RRM Registre des régimes matrimoniaux (Switz.)

R.R.Rep. Railroad Reports (USA) 1902–13

R.R.S. Remington's Revised Statutes

R.R.T. Repatriation Review Tribunal (Aus.)
Resource Rent Tax (Aus.)

R.R.& Cn.Cas. Railway & Canal Cases. 1835–54

R.S. Recueil officiel des lois et ordonnances de la confédération suisse (Switz.) collection of enactments
Recueil systematique des lois fédérales (Switz.) 1848–1947
Reprinted Statutes of New Zealand. 1979–
Revenue Solicitors Act 1828
Revised Statutes
Revue des societés (Fr.) 1883–
Rolls Series

R(S) Decisions of the Commissioner under the National Insurance Acts (Sickness Benefit) 1948–

R.S.A. Arbitration Services Reporter (Can.) 1977–
Revised Statutes Annotated
Revised Statutes of Alberta (Can.)

RSANU Nation Unies, Recueil des sentences arbitrales

R.S.B.C. Revised Statutes of British Columbia (Can.)

R.S.C. Revised Statutes of Canada
Rules of the Supreme Court

R.S.C.O. Rules of the Supreme Court, Order (Number)

R.S.Comp. Statutes of Connecticut, Compilation of 1854

RSFSR Russian Soviet Federated Socialist Republic

R.S.G. Republic of the Sudan Gazette

R.S.J. Revue suisse de jurisprudence

R.S.M. Revised Statutes of Manitoba (Can.)

R.S.N. Revised Statutes of Newfoundland (Can.)

R.S.N.B. Revised Statutes of New Brunswick (Can.)

R.S.N.S. Revised Statutes of Nova Scotia (Can.)

RSNT Revised Single Negotiating Text

R.S.O. Revised Statutes of Ontario (Can.)

R.S.Q. Revised Statutes of Quebec (Can.)

R.S.S. Revised Statutes of Saskatchewan (Can.)

R.S.Supp. Supplement to Revised Statutes

R.T. Round Table: the Commonwealth Journal of International Affairs (Aus.) 1910–

R.T.A. Road Traffic Act

R.T.D.E. Revue trimestrielle de droit européen (Fr.) 1965–

RTDEur Revue trimestrielle de droit européen (Fr.) 1965–

R.t.F. Reports tempore Finch, Chancery Cases (23 ER) 1673–81

RTG Agreement for International Rail Transport of Goods

R.t.H. Cases tempore Hardwicke, King's Bench (95 ER) 1733–38
Reports of Cases Concerning Settlements tempore Holt (90 ER) 1688–1710

R.t.Hardw. Cases tempore Hardwicke King's Bench (95 ER) 1733–38

R.t.Holt. Reports tempore Holt, King's Bench (90 ER) 1688–1710

RTLB Road Traffic Law Bulletin. 1984–

R.T.P.I. Royal Town Planning Institute

R.t.Q.A. Reports tempore Queen Anne (11 Modern) (88 ER) 1702–10

R.T.R. Road Traffic Reports. 1970–

R.t.W. Manitoba Reports tempore Wood. 1875–83

R(U) Decisions of the Commissioner under the National Insurance Acts (Unemployment Benefit) 1948–

RVO Reichsversicherungsordnung (Ger.) Imperial Insurance Act

R.V.R. Rating and Valuation Reporter. 1965–

RW Rechtskundig Weekblad (Belg.) 1931–40, 1946–
Rechtswissenschaft (Ger.)

R.W. Right of Way
Royal Warrant

R.& B. Remington & Ballinger's Code. 1910

R.& B.Supp. Remington & Ballinger's Code. 1913 Supplement

R.& C. Russell & Chesley's Nova Scotia Reports. 1875–79

R.& C.C. Railway & Canal Cases. 1835–54

R.& C.Ca. Railway & Canal Cases. 1835–54

R.& C.Cas. Railway & Canal Cases. 1835–54

R.& C.N.Sc. Russell & Chesley's Nova Scotia Reports. 1875–79

R.& C.Tr.Cas. Railway & Canal Traffic Cases. 1855–1949

R.& Can.Cas. Railway & Canal Cases. 1835–54

R.& Can.Tr.Cas. Railway & Canal Traffic Cases. 1855–1949

R.& D. Research & Development

R.& G. Russell & Geldert's Nova Scotia Reports (NSR 13–27) 1879–95

R.& G.N.Sc. Russell & Geldert's Nova Scotia Reports (NSR 13–27) 1879–95

R.& H.Bank. Roche & Hazlitt, Bankruptcy. 2ed. 1873

R.& H.Dig. Robinson & Harrison's Digest (Ontario, Can.)

R.& I.T. Rating & Income Tax Reports. 1924–60

R.& J. Rabkin & Johnson, Federal Income, Gift & Estate Taxation (USA)
Rafique & Jackson's Privy Council Decisions (India)

R.& J.Dig. Robinson & Joseph's Digest (Ontario,Can.)

R.& J.P.C. Russian and Japanese Prize Cases

R.& L.L.& T. Redman & Lyon, Landlord and Tenant. 8ed. 1924

R.& M. Russell & Mylne's Chancery Reports (39 ER) 1829–31
Ryan & Moody's Nisi Prius Reports (171 ER) 1823–26
Law Reporter, Montreal (Can.) 1853–54

R.& M.Dig. Rapalje & Mack's Digest of Railway Law (USA)

R.& M.N.P. Ryan & Moody's Nisi Prius Reports (171 ER) 1823–26

R.& McG. Income Tax Decisions of Australasia, Ratcliffe & M'Grath. 1891–1930

R.& McG.Ct.of Rev. Court of Review Decisions, Ratcliffe & M'Grath, New South Wales (Aus.) 1913–27

R.& My. Russell & Mylne's Chancery Reports (39 ER) 1829–31

R.& N. Rhodesia and Nyasaland Law Reports. 1956–64

R.& N.L.R. Rhodesia and Nyasaland Law Reports. 1956–64

R.& R. Russell & Ryan's Crown Cases Reserved (168 ER) 1799–1823

R.& R.C.C. Russell & Ryan's Crown Cases Reserved (169 ER) 1799–1823

R.& Ry.C.C. Russell & Ryan's Crown Cases Reserved (168 ER) 1799–1823

R.& V.R. Rating and Valuation Reports. 1960–

Ra.Ca. Railway & Canal Cases. 1835–54

RabelsZ. Rabels Zeitschrift für ausländisches und internationales Privatrecht

Raccolta Raccolta della Giurisprudenza della Corte (It.) Official reports of the judgments of the European Court

Rad.Reg. Radio Regulation (P–H) (USA)

Rader Rader's Reports (138–163 Missouri)

Rag. Ragland California Superior Court Decisions. 1921–26

Rag.Super.Ct.Dec.(Calif.) Ragland California Superior Court Decisions. 1921–26

Rail.Ca. Railway and Canal Cases. 1835–54

Rail.& Can.Cas. Railway & Canal Cases. 1835–54
Railway and Canal Traffic Cases. 1855–1949

Railw.Cas. Railway & Canal Cases. 1835–54

Railway & Corp.L.J. Railway & Corporation Law Journal (USA) 1887–92

Railway & Corp.Law.J. Railway & Corporation Law Journal (USA) 1887–92

Raj. All India Reporter, Rajasthan. 1950–
Rajaratam Revised Reports (Sri L.)

Raj.Ind. Rajasthan. India

Rajasthan Indian Law Reports, Rajasthan Series. 1952–

Ram. Ramanathan's Reports (Sri L.) 1820–77
Ramsey's Quebec Appeal Cases. 1873–86

Ram.Ass. Ram, Assets, Debts and Incumbrances. 2ed. 1837

Ram.Cas.P.& E. Ram, Cases of Pleading & Evidence

Ram.F. Ram, Treatise on Facts. 1861

Ram.Leg.J. Ram, Science of Legal Judgment. 2ed. 1834

Ram.Rep. Ramanathan's Supreme Court Reports (Sri L.) 1820–77

Ram.S.C. Ramanathan's Supreme Court Reports (Sri L.) 1820–77

Ram.W. Ram, Exposition of Wills of Landed Property. 1827

Ram.& Mor. Ramsey & Morin's Montreal Law Reporter (Can.) 1853–54

Ramachandrier A. Ramachandrier's Cases on Adoption (India) 1892

Ramachandrier D.G. Ramachandrier's Cases on Dancing Girls (India) 1892

Ramachandrier H.M.L. Ramachandrier's Cases on Hindu Marriage Law (India) 1891

Ramanathan Ramanathan's Supreme Court Reports (Sri L.) 1820–77

Rams.App. Ramsey's Appeal Cases, Quebec (Can.) 1873–86

Rand. Randall's Reports (62–71 Ohio State)
Randolph's Reports (21–56 Kansas) 1895–96
Randolph's Reports (7–11 Louisiana)
Randolph's Reports (22–27 Virginia) 1821–28

Rand.Perp. Randell, Perpetuity. 1822

Raney Raney's Reports (16–20 Florida)

Rang.Cr.L.J. Rangoon Criminal Law Journal (Burma) 1931

Rang.Dec. Sparks' Rangoon Decisions (Burma)

Rang.L.R. Rangoon Law Reports (Burma)

Rank.P. Rankin, Patents. 1824

Rank.S.& P.Exec. Ranking, Spicer Pegler, Executorship. 21ed. 1971

Rank.& S.Comp.L. Ranking & Spicer, Company Law. 11ed. 1970
Rao D.H.L. Rao's Decisions on Hindu Law (India) 1893
Rap.Fed.Ref.Dig. Rapalje's Federal Reference Digest (USA)
Rap.Jud.Q.B.R. Rapport Judiciaires de Québec, Cour du Banc de la Reine
Rap.Jud.Q.C.S. Rapport Judiciaires de Québec, Cour Supérieure
Rap.Jud.Québec C.S.(Can.) Rapports Judiciaires de Québec, Cour Supérieure
Rap.Jud.Québec K.B.(Can.) Rapports Judiciaires de Québec, King's Bench
Rap.Jud.Québec Q.B.(Can.) Rapports Judiciaires de Québec, Queen's Bench
Rap.N.Y.Dig. Rapalje's New York Digest
Rap.& L. Rapalje & Lawrence, American and English Cases
Rap.& L.Law Dict. Rapalje and Lawrence, Law Dictionary (USA)
Rap.& Law Rapalje & Lawrence, American & English Cases
Rapal.& L. Rapalje & Lawrence, American & English Cases
Rapp.gest. Rapport du Conseil fédérale à l'Assemblée fédérale sur sa gestation (Switz.)
Rass.Arb. Rassegua dell'arbitrata (It.)
Rass.dir.comm. Rassegne di diretto commerciale italiano e straniero (It.) 1883–89
Rass.dir.leg. Rassegna di diritto legislazione e medicina legale veterinaria (It.) 1967–
Rass.dir.pubbl. Rassegna di diritto pubblico (It.) 1946–
Rass.prop.indust. Rassegna della proprieta industriale, letteraria ed artistica (It.) 1934–42, 1946–
Rass.stud.pen. Rassegna di studi penitenziari (It.) 1951–
Rast. Rastell's Entries. 1566
Rastell's Statutes. 1066–1557
Rast.Abr. Rastell, Abreviamentum Statutorum
Rast.Ent. Rastell's Entries. 1566
Rat.Sel.Cas. Rattigan's Unreported Cases in Hindu Law (India) 1869–71
Rat.Unrep.Cr. Ratanlal's Unreported Criminal Cases (India)
Ratt.L.C. Rattigan's Select Hindu Law Cases (India) 1869–71
Rattigan Rattigan's Select Hindu Law Cases (India) 1869–71
Raw. Rawle's Pennsylvania Reports. 1828–35
Raw.Eq. Rawle, Equity in Pennsylvania
Rawl.Mun.Corp. Rawlinson, Municipal Corporations. 10ed. 1910
Rawle Rawle's Pennsylvania Supreme Court Reports. 1828–35
Rawle, Const.U.S. Rawle on the Constitution of the United States
Rawle Pen.& W. Rawle, Penrose & Watts' Pennsylvania Reports. 1828–40
Ray Med.Jur. Ray's Medical Jurisprudence of Insanity. 1839
Ray.Sir T. Sir T. Raymond's King's Bench Reports (83 ER) 1660–84
Ray.Ti.Cas. Rayner's Tithe Cases. 1575–1782
Rayden Rayden on Divorce
Raym. Lord Raymond's King's Bench Reports (91–2 ER) 1694–1732
Sir Thomas Raymond's King's Bench Reports (83 ER) 1660–84
Raym.Ent. Lord Raymond's Entries. 1765
Raym.Ld. Lord Raymond's King's Bench Reports (91–2 ER) 1694–1732
Raym.Sir T. Sir Thomas Raymond's King's Bench Reports (83 ER) 1660–84
Raym.T. Sir Thomas Raymond's King's Bench Reports (83 ER) 1660–84
Raymond Raymond's Reports (81–99 Iowa)
Rayn. Rayner's Tithe Cases. 1575–1782
Rayn.Ti.Cas. Rayner's Tithe Cases. 1575–1782
Rb. District Court (Neth.)
Rd. Road
RdC Recueil des Cours de l'Académie de Droit International de La Haye
rd.-l. regio decreto legge

Rdagr. Rivista di diritto agrario (It.)
Rdciv. Rivista di diritto civile (It.)
Rdcomm. Rivista di diritto comerciale (It.)
Rdproc. Rivista di diritto processuale
Re-af. Re-affirmed
Re.de J. Revue de Jurisprudence (Québec,Can.) 1895–
Re.de L. Revue de Législation et de Jurisprudence (Québec,Can.) 1845–58
Re.L.R. Reinsurance Law Reports. 1991–
Reading Report Committee on Consolidation of Highway Law Report (Cmnd.630) 1958–9
Real Est.Rec. Real Estate Record (New York)
Real Estate L.J. Real Estate Law Journal (USA) 1972–
Real Pr.Cas. Real Property Cases. 1843–47
Real Prop. Real Property
Real Prop.Cas. Real Property Cases. 1843–47
Real Prop.Prob.& Tr.J. Real Property Probate & Trust Journal (USA) 1966–
Rec. American Law Record. 1872–87
Ceylon Law Recorder. 1919–
Receipt
Record(s)
Recorder
Recueil (Fr.) collection
Recueil des arrêts du Conseil d'État
Rec.Ass'n.Bar City of N.Y. Record of the Association of the Bar of the City of New York. 1946–
Rec.Comm. Record Commission
Rec.Cons.d'Ét. Recueil des arrêts du Conseil d'État (Lebon) (Fr.) Collection of the decisions of the Conseil d'État
Rec.Dal. Recueil Dalloz Sirey (Fr.)
Rec.Dec. Vaux' Recorders Decisions (Pennsylvania) 1841–45
Rec.des Cours (La Haye) Recueil des Cours, Académie de Droit International de la Haye (Neth.)
Rec.L. Recent Law (N.Z.) 1966–74
Rec.Laws Recent Laws in Canada
Rec.Lebon Recueil des décisions du Conseil d'État (Fr.)
Rec.NU Recueil des traités, Nations Unies
Rec.Penant Recueil Penant (Fr.)
Rec.SdN Recueil des traités, Societe des Nations
Rec.Somm. Recueil des sommaires de la jurisprudence française
Rec.TAM Recueil des décisions des tribunaux arbitraux mixtes
Recd. Received
Rechtsk.Weekbl. Rechtskundig Weekblad (Belg.)
Record Record of the Association of the Bar of the City of New York. 1946–
Record of N.Y.C.B.A. Record of the Association of the Bar of the City of New York. 1946–
Recueil Recueil des cours de l'Académie de droit international de la Haye
Recueil general Recueil general périodique et critique des décisions, conventions et lois relatives au droit international public et privé. 1924–38
Recueil Geny Recueil d'études sur les sources du droit en l'honneur de Francois Geny. 1936
Red. Reddington's Reports (31–35 Maine)
Redfield's New York Surrogate Reports. 1857–82
Redwar's Comments on Ordinances of the Gold Coast Colony (Ghana) 1889–1909
Red.Am.R.R.Cas. Redfield's Leading American Railway Cases
Red.Cas.R.R. Redfield's Leading American Railway Cases
Red.Cas.Wills Redfield's Leading Cases on Wills (USA)
Red.Int.L. Reddie, Inquiries in International Law. 2ed. 1851
Red.Mar.Com. Reddie, Law of Maritime Commerce. 1841
Red.Mar.Int.L. Reddie, Researches in Maritime International Law. 1844–45

Red.R.R.Cas. Redfield's Leading American Railway Cases

Red.Sc.L. Reddie, Science of Law. 2ed.

Red.Wills Redfield's Leading Cases on Wills

Red.& Big.Cas.B.& N. Redfield & Bigelow's Leading Cases on Bills and Notes

Redcliffe-Maud Report Royal Commission on Local Government in England & Wales Report (Cmnd. 4040) 1969

Redem. Redemption

Redf. Redfield's New York Surrogate Reports. 1857–82

Redf.Am.Railw.Cas. Redfield's Leading American Railway Cases

Redf.(N.Y.) Redfield's New York Surrogate Reports. 1857–82

Redf.R.Cas. Redfield's Leading American Railway Cases

Redf.Railways Redfield's Leading American Railway Cases

Redf.Sur.(N.Y.) Redfield's New York Surrogate Reports. 1857–82

Redf.Surr. Redfield's New York Surrogate Reports. 1857–82

Redf.Wills Redfield's Leading Cases on Wills (USA)

Redf.& B. Redfield & Bigelow's Leading Cases on Bills and Notes

Redington Redington's Reports (31–35 Maine)

Redwar Redwar's Comments on Ordinances of the Gold Coast (Ghana) 1889–1909

Reed Reed, Bill of Sale Acts. 14ed. 1926

Reese 5 & 11 Heiskell's Tennessee Reports

Reeves Eng.Law Reeves' History of the English Law

Reeves H.E.L. Reeves' History of the English Law

Reeves Hist.Eng.Law Reeves' History of the English Law

Ref. Referee
Reference
Referred
Refining
Reform

Ref.Dec. Referee's Decision

Ref.J. Referees' Journal (Journal of National Association of Referees in Bankruptcy)

Ref.n.r.e. Refused, not reversible error

Ref.w.m. Refused, want of merit

Reform Reform (Australian Law Reform Commission) 1976–

Reg. Regina (Queen)
Register
Registered
Registrar
Registration
Registry
Regulation

Reg.App. Registration Appeals

RegBl. Regierungsblatt (Ger.) Government gazette

Reg.Brev. Registrum Brevium (Register of Writs)

Reg.Cas. Registration Cases

Reg.Deb. Gales & Seaton's Register of Debates in Congress. 1824–37

Reg.Deb.(G.& S.) Gale & Seaton's Register of Debates in Congress. 1824–37

Reg.Deb.(Gales) Gales' Register of Debates in Congress. 1789–91

Reg.-Gen. Registrar-General

Reg.Lib. Register Book
Registrar's Book, Chancery

Reg.Maj. Books of Regiam Majestatem (Scot.)

Reg.Om.Brev. Registrum Omnium Brevium

Reg.Orig. Registrum Originale

Reg.Pl. Regular Placitandi

RegRL Lag om Kungl. Maj:ts regeringsratt (Swed.) Law on the Supreme Administrative Court. 1909

Reg.T.M. Registered Trade Mark

Reg.Writ Register of Writs

Regd. Registered

Regl. Règlement (Fr.) adminstrative ordinance or rule of procedure

Regr. Registrar

Regs. Regulations
Reh.allowed Rehearing allowed
Reh.den. Rehearing denied
Reh'g Rehearing
Reilly Reilly's Arbitration Cases
Reilly E.A. Reilly, European Arbitration, Lord Westbury's Decisions
Rein. Reinstated
rel. relatore (It.) reporter
Rel. Relations
Religion
Rel.Ind. Relations industrielle – Industrial Relations (Can.)
Rem. Remittance
Remitted
Rem.Cr.Tr. Remarkable Criminal Trials
Rem.Tr. Remarkable Trials
Rem.Tr.No.Ch. Benson's Remarkable Trials & Notorious Characters
Rem'd. Remanded
Rem'g Remanding
Remy Remy's Reports (145–162 Indiana;15–33 Indiana Appellate)
Ren. Renner, Reports, Notes of Cases Gold Coast Colony and Colony of Nigeria. 1861–1914
Renn. Renner, Reports, Notes of Cases Gold Coast Colony and Colony of Nigeria. 1861–1914
Renton Report Committee on the Preparation of Legislation. Report (Cmnd. 6053) 1975
Reorg. Reorganisation
Rep. Coke's King's Bench Reports (76–77 ER) 1572–1616
Knapp's Privy Council Reports
Repeal
Repealed
Répertoire (Fr., Belg.) encylopedia
Repertorio di giurisprudenza patria (It.)
Report
Reporter
The Reporter, Boston, Mass.
The Reporter, Washington & New York
Reports
Representative
Representing
Reprint
Republic(an)
Wallace, The Reporters. 4ed. 1882
Rep.Ass.Y. Clayton's Reports of Assizes at York. 1631–50
Rep.Atty.Gen. Attorney General's Reports (USA)
Rep.Att'y.Genl. Attorney General's Reports (USA)
Rep.Cas.Eq. Gilbert's Equity Reports (25 ER) 1705–27
Rep.Cas.Inc.Tax Reports of Cases relating to Income Tax. 1875
Rep.Cas.Madr. Sudder Dewanny Adawlut Reports (Madras, India) 1805–62
Rep.Cas.Pr. Cooke's Practice Cases, Common Pleas (125 ER) 1706–47
Rep.Ch. Reports in Chancery (21 ER) 1615–1712
Rep.Ch.Pr. Reports in Chancery Practice
Rép.civ. Répertoire de droit civil (Encyclopédie juridique Dalloz) (Fr.) Encyclopedia of civil law
Rep.Com.Cas. Commercial Cases, Small Cause Court (Bengal, India) 1851–60
Reports of Commercial Cases. 1895–1941
Rep.Const.Ct. South Carolina Constitutional Court Reports
Rep.Cr.L.Com. Reports of Criminal Law Commissioners
Rép.crim. Répertoire de droit criminel et de procédure pénale (Encylopedia juridique Dalloz) (Fr.) Encylopedia of criminal law and procedure
Rep.Eq. Gilbert's Equity Reports (25 ER) 1705–27
RepFI Repertorio generale del Foro italiano
Rep.Fam.L. Reports of Family Law
RepGciv. Repertorio generale della Giustzia civile (It.)
RepGI Repertorio generale della Giurisprudenza italiana
Rep.in C.A. Court of Appeal Reports (N.Z.) 1883–87

Rep.in Can. Reports in Chancery (21 ER) 1615–1712
Rep.in Ch. Reports in Chancery (21 ER) 1615–1712
Rep.in Cha. Bittleston's Chamber Cases. 1883–84
Rep.Jur. Repertorium Juridicum
Rep.M.C. Reports of Municipal Corporations (USA)
Rep.of Sel.Cas.in Ch. Kelynge's Select Cases in Chancery (125 ER) 1730–36
Rep.Pat.Cas. Reports of Patent, Design and Trade Mark Cases. 1884–
Rep.Pat.Des.& Tr.Cas. Reports of Patent, Design & Trademark Cases. 1884–
Rép.proc. Répertoire de procédure civile et commerciale (Encylopédie juridique Dalloz) (Fr.) Encylopedia of civil and commercial procedure
Rep.Q.A. Reports tempore Queen Anne (11 Modern Reports) (88 ER) 1702–10
Rep.Sel.Cas.Ch. Kelynge's Select Cases in Chancery (125 ER) 1730–36
Rep.t.F. Finch's Reports, Chancery (23 ER) 1673–81
Rep.t.Finch Finch's Reports, Chancery (23 ER) 1673–81
Rep.t.Hard. Lee's Reports tempore Hardwicke, King's Bench (95 ER) 1733–38
Rep.t.Hardw. Lee's Reports tempore Hardwicke, King's Bench (95 ER) 1733–38
Rep.t.Holt Reports tempore Holt (Cases of Settlement) (90 ER) 1688–1710
Rep.t.O.Br. Carter's Common Pleas Reports tempore O. Bridgmen (124 ER) 1644–73
Rep.t.Talb. Reports tempore Talbot, Chancery. 1730–37
Rep.t.Wood Manitoba Reports tempore Wood (Can.) 1875–83
Rep.Yorke Ass. Clayton's Reports & Pleas of Assizes at Yorke. 1631–50
Répertoire S.D.N. Répertoire des questions de droit international général posées devant la Societé des Nations. 1942
repl. replacement
Repl. Replevin
Reporter Reporter: Australian Institute of Criminology Quarterly. 1979–
Reports Coke's King's Bench Reports (76–77 ER) 1572–1616
Repr. Representing
Reprint(ed)
Repr.Acts W.Austl. Reprinted Acts of Western Australia
Repr.Stat.N.Z. Reprint of the Statutes of New Zealand
Rept.on Bkptcy. Reports on Bankruptcy by the Minister for Business and Consumer Affairs (Aus.) 1968–
Reptr. Reporter
Repub. Republic(an)
Req. La Chambre des requêtes de la Cour de Cassation (Fr.) Chamber of Requests of the Cour de Cassation
res. resolu (Fr.) resolved, decided
Res. Reserve(d)
Residence
Resigned
Resolution
Resolved
Resources
Res.B. Home Office Research Bulletin
Res.Cas. Reserved Cases (Ire.) 1860–64
Rés.Dél.Ass.féd. Résumés des délibérations de l'Assemblée fédérale (Switz.)
Res.Gamma Eta Gamma Rescript of Gamma Eta Gamma (USA) 1912–1942
Res Ipsa Res Ipsa Loquitur (USA) 1936–41
Res Jud. Res Judicatae (Victoria, Aus.) 1935–57
Res pub. Res publica (Belg.) 1959–
Res.& E.J. A'Beckett's Reserved Judgments, New South Wales (Aus.) 1845
Res.& Eq.J. A'Beckett's Reserved Judgments, New South Wales (Aus.) 1845
Res.& Eq.Jud. A'Beckett's Reserved

Judgments, New South Wales (Aus.) 1845

Res.& Eq.Judg. A'Beckett's Reserved Judgments, New South Wales (Aus.) 1845

Research Dir.Newsl. Research Director's Newsletter (Can.)

Reserv.Cas. Reserved Cases (Ire.) 1860–64

Resn.Coee.Min. Resolution of the Committee of Ministers (European Communities)

Resources Resources: Newsletter of the Canadian Institute of Resources Law. 1982–

resp. respectively
respondent

Resp.Merid. Responsa Meridiana (S.Afr.) 1964–

Responsa Merid. Responsa Meridiana (S.Afr.)

restr. restricted

Restric.Prac. Reports of Restrictive Practices Cases. 1957–72

Ret. Retired

retrosp. retrospectively

Rett. Rettie's Court of Session Cases. 4th Series (Scot.) 1873–98

Rettie Rettie's Court of Session Cases. 4th Series (Scot.) 1873–98

rev. revenue
review
revise(d)

Rev. Cour de Révision (Monaco)
Revenue
Reversed in
Reversing
Review
Revise(d)
Revision
Statutory Rules and Orders and Statutory Instruments Revised. 1948 (Edition)

Rev.1903 Statutory Rules and Orders Revised. 1903 (Edition)

Rev.adm. La Revue adminstrative (Fr.) 1948–

Rev.admin. La Revue administrative (Fr.) 1948–

Rev.admin.publ. Revista de administracion publica (Sp.)

Rev.Algér.Sci.Jur. Revue algérienne des sciences juridiques, économiques et politiques (Algeria)

Rev.Arb. Revue de l'arbitrage

Rev.ass.terr. Revue des assurances terrestres (Fr.)

Rev.Bar. Revue du Barreau du Québec. 1967–
Revue du Barreau de la Province de Québec. 1941–66

Rev.Bd. Review Board

Rev.Belge D.I. Revue Belge de droit international

Rev.Belge Dr.Intern. Revue Belge de droit international

Rev.Burkinabe Dr. Revue Burkinabe de droit (Burkina Faso)

Rev.C.& C.Rep. Revenue, Civil & Criminal Reporter (Calcutta, India) 1866–68

Rev.Can. Revue Canadienne (Québec) 1864–1922

Rev.can.d.comm. Revue canadienne du droit de commerce – Canadian Business Law Journal. 1976–

Rev.can.d.fam. Revue canadienne de droit familial – Canadian Journal of Family Law. 1980–

Rev.can.de crim. Revue canadienne de criminologie – Canadian Journal of Criminology. 1959–

Rev.Cas. Revenue Cases

Rev.Cas.(Ind.) Revised Cases (India) 1809–1909

Rev.Civ.Code Revised Civil Code

Rev.Civ.St. Revised Civil Statutes

Rev.Code Revised Code

Rev.Code Civ.Proc. Revised Code of Civil Procedure

Rev.Code Cr.Proc. Revised Code of Criminal Procedure

Rev.Col.Abog. Revista del Colegio del Abogados

Rev.Congo Dr. Revue congolaise de droit (Congo)

Rev.Cont.L. Review of Contemporary Law (Belg.)
Rev.Cr.Code Revised Criminal Code
Rev.Cr.D.I.P. Revue critique de droit international privé (Fr.) 1905–
Rev.crit. Revue critique de législation et de jurisprudence (Québec) 1871–75
Rev.Crit.de Legis et Jur. Revue critique de législation et de jurisprudence (Québec) 1871–75
Rev.crit.dr.intl.priv. Revue critique de droit international privé (Fr.) 1905–
Rev.crit.juris.belge Revue critique de jurisprudence belge (Belg.) 1947–
Rev.Cub.Der. Revista Cubana de derecho (Cuba)
Rev.D.P.R. Revista de Derecho Puertorriqueno. 1961–
Rev.de Der.y Juris. Revista de Derecho y Jurisprudencia (Chile)
Rev.de Droit Unif. Revue de droit uniforme (It.) Uniform Law Review
Rev.de Jur. Revue de Jurisprudence (Québec) 1895–1942
Rev.de l'adm. Revue de l'administration et du droit administratif de la belgique (Belg.) 1854–
Rev.de la Fac.de Derecho de la U.N.A.M. Revista de la Facultad de Derecho de la Universidad Autonoma de Mexico
Rev.de Lég. Revue de législation et de jurisprudence (Québec) 1845–58
Rev.de Légis. Revue de législation et de jurisprudence (Québec) 1845–48
Rev.de Légn. Revue de législation et de jurisprudence (Québec) 1845–48
Rev.Der.Juris.Adm. Revista de Derecho, Jurisprudencia y Administracion (Uruguay)
Rev.Der.Merc. Revista de derecho mercantil (Sp.)
Rev.Der.Priv. Revista de derecho privado (Sp.)
Rev.Der.Proc.Dirig.Iberoam. Revista de derecho procesal: dirigida a Iberoamericana (Sp.)
Rev.Der.& Cienc.Soc. Revista de derecho y ciencias sociales (Chile)
Rev.Der.& Jurisp.(Chile) Revista de derecho y jurisprudencia y gaceta de los tribunales (Chile)
Rev.Dir.Est.Soc. Revista de Direito e de Estudos Sociais (Port.)
Rev.dir.int. Revue du droit international (Belg.)
Rev.dos Trib. Revista dos Tribunais (Brazil)
Rev.Dr.Aff.Intern. Revue de droit des affaires internationales (Fr.)
Rev.Dr.Banc. Revue du droit bancaire
Rev.Dr.Canon. Revue du droit canonique (Fr.)
Rev.Dr.Intern.& Comp. Revue de droit international et de droit comparé (Belg.)
Rev.Dr.Milit. Revue de droit militaire et de droit de la guerre (Belg.)
Rev.Dr.Pen. Revue de droit pénal et de criminologie (Belg.)
Rev.Dr.Publ.& Sci.Pol. Revue du droit public et de la science politique en France et a l'étranger (Fr.)
Rev.Dr.Sherbrooke Revue de droit/Université de Sherbrooke (Can.)
Rev.Dr.Uniforme Revue de droit uniforme
Rev.drt.intern.et drt.comp. Revue de droit international et de droit comparé (Belg.) 1908–14, 1922–39, 1949–
Rev.drt.intern.et lég.comp. Revue de droit international et de législation comparée (Belg.) 1869–1940
Rev.drt.pén. Revue de droit pénal et de criminolgie (Belg.) 1907–
Rev.du B. Revue du Barreau de la Province de Québec. 1941–66
Rev.du Dr. Revue du droit (Québec) 1922–39
Rev.du Not. Revue du notariat (Québec) 1898–
Rev.du not.belg. Revue du notariat belge (Belg.) 1971–
rev.ed. revised edition
Rev.Eg. Revue égyptienne de droit international (Egypt)

Rev.Egypt.Dr.Intern. Revue égyptienne de droit international (Egypt)

Rev.Enreg. Revue de l'enregistrement

Rev.Esp.Der.Intern. Revista Española de Derecho Internacional (Sp.)

Rev.Euro.Dr.Pub. Revue européenne de droit public

Rev.Fac.Der.(Mexico) Revista de la Facultad de Derecho de Mexico

Rev.Fac.Dir.Sao Paulo Revista da Faculdade de Direito, Universidade de Sao Paulo (Brazil)

Rev.Fac.Dir.Univ.Lisboa Revista da Faculdade de Direito da Universidade de Lisboa (Port.)

Rev.Forense Revista Forense (Brazil)

Rev.Foro Lima Revista de Foro, Organo del Colegio de Abogados de Lima (Peru)

Rev.Fr.Dr.Admin. Revue française de droit administratif (Fr.)

Rev.Fr.Dr.Aérien Revue française de droit aérien et spatial (Fr.)

Rev.Gén.D.I.Publ. Revue général de droit international public

Rev.Gen.Der. Revista General de Derecho (Sp.)

Rev.Gén.Dr.Com. Revue générale de droit commercial

Rev.Gén.Dr.Intern.Pub. Revue générale de droit international public (Fr.)

Rev.Gén.Dr.Ottawa Revue générale de droit/Université de Ottawa (Can.)

Rev.Gen.Leg.y Jur. Revista General de Legislacion y Jurisprudencia (Sp.)

Rev.Gen.Legis.Jurisp. Revista General de Legislacion y Jurisprudencia (Sp.)

Rev.Ghana L. Review of Ghana Law

Rev.Héllen.Dr.Intern. Revue héllenique de droit international (Gr.)

Rev.Hist.Dr.Fr.& Etran. Revue historique de droit français et étranger (Fr.)

Rev.Inst.Belge Revue de l'Institut de Droit Comparé (Belg.)

Rev.Int.de Phil. Revue internationale de philosophie

Rev.Int.T.du Droit Revue internationale de la théorie du droit

Rev.Intern.Dr.Antiq. Revue internationale des droits de l'antiquité (Belg.)

Rev.Intern.Dr.Auteur Revue internationale du droit de l'auteur (Fr.)

Rev.Intern.Dr.Comp. Revue internationale de droit comparé (Fr.)

Rev.Intern.Dr.Econ. Revue internationale de droit économique (Belg.)

Rev.Intern.Dr.Pen. Revue internationale de droit pénal (Fr.)

Rev.Int'l Comm.Jurists Review of the International Commission of Jurists (Switz.)

Rev.Investigac.Jur. Revista de Investigaciones Juridicas (Mexico)

Rev.J.& P.J. Revenue, Judicial & Police Journal (Bengal, India) 1863–65

Rev.Jur.Als.-Lor. Revue juridique d'Alsace-Lorraine

Rev.Jur.de B.A. Revista Juridica de Buenos Aires

Rev.Jur.Environ. Revue juridique de l'environnement (Fr.)

Rev.Jur.Peru Revista Juridica del Peru

Rev.Jur.Pol.& Econ.Maroc Revue juridique politique et économique de Maroc (Morocco)

Rev.Jur.Rwanda Revue juridique du Rwanda

Rev.Jur.Thémis La revue juridique Thémis (Can.)

Rev.Jur.U.I. Revista Juridica de la Universidad Interamericana de Puerto Rico

Rev.Jur.Zaire Revue juridique de Zaire

Rev.Jur.& Pol. Independ.& Coop. Revue juridique et politique, independence et coopération (Fr.)

Rev.Jurisp. Revista de Jurisprudencia (Port.)

Rev.Laws Revised Laws

Rev.Lég. La Revue Légale (Québec) 1869–92, 1895–

Rev.Lég.N.S. La Revue Légale, New Series (Québec) 1895–

Rev.Lég.(O.S.) La Revue Légale, Old Series (Québec) 1869–92
Rev.Légale La Revue Légale (Québec) 1869–92, 1895–
Rev.Legisl.Jurispr. Revista de Legislacao e de Jurisprudencia (Port.)
Rev.Litig. The Review of Litigation
Rev.Marché Com. Revue du Marché Commun (Fr.)
Rev.Mun.Code Revised Municipal Code (USA)
Rev.Not. Revue du Notariat (Québec) 1898–
Rev.not.belge Revue du Notariat belge (Belg.) 1971–
Rev.Ord. Revised Ordinances
Rev.Ord.Advog. Revista da Ordem dos Advogados (Port.)
Rev.Ord.N.W.T. Revised Ordinances, Northwest Territories (Can.) 1888
Rev.Peruana Der.Intern. Revista Peruana de Derecho Internacional (Peru)
Rev.Proc. Revenue Procedure (USA)
Rev.Québec.Dr.Intern. Revue québecoise de droit international (Can.)
Rev.R. Revised Reports. 1785–1866
Rev.reh. Reversed on rehearing
Rev.Rep. Revised Reports. 1785–1866
Rev.Rul. Revenue Ruling (USA)
Rev.Sci.Crim.& Dr.Pén. Revue de science criminelle et de droit pénal comparé (Fr.)
Rev.Sénégal Dr. Revue sénégalaise de droit (Senegal)
Rev.Soc.L. Review of Socialist Law (Neth.) 1975–
Revue des societés
Rev.Socialist L. Review of Socialist Law (Neth.) 1975–
Rev.St. Revised Statutes
Rev.Stat. Revised Statutes
Rev.Tax'n Individ. The Review of Taxation of Individuals (USA)
Rev.Trib. Revista dos Tribunais (Port.)
Rev.Tribunais Revista dos Tribunais (Brazil)
Rev.trim.civ. Revue trimestrielle de droit civil (Fr.) 1902–
Rev.trim.com. Revue trimestrielle de droit commercial (Fr.) 1948–
Rev.trim.dr.civ. Revue trimestrielle de droit civil (Fr.) 1902–
Rev.trim.dr.com. Revue trimestrielle de droit commercial (Fr.) 1948–
Rev.trim.dr.comm.& écon. Revue trimestrielle de droit commercial et de droit économique (Fr.)
Rev.trim.dr.euro. Revue trimestrielle de droit européen (Fr.)
Rev.trim.dr.homme Revue trimestrielle des droits de l'homme (Belg.)
Rev.trim.droit civil Revue trimestrielle de droit civil (Fr.) 1902–
Rev.trim.droit eur. Revue trimestrielle de droit européen (Fr.) 1965–
Rev.Tunis Dr. Revue tunisienne de droit (Tunisia)
Rev.& T.C. Revenue and Taxation Code
Rev.& Tax. Revenue and Taxation
rev'd. reversed
rev'g. reversing
Revised R. Revised Reports. 1785–1866
Revista del Foro La Revista del Foro: organo del Colegio de Abogados (Peru)
Revista Der.Int. Revista de Derecho Internacional
Revista Der.Priv. Revista de Derecho Privado (Sp.)
Revista Dir.Civ. Revista de Direito Civil, Commercial e Criminal (Brazil)
Revista Españ.Der.Int. Revista Española de Derecho Internacional (Sp.)
Revue internationale Revue internationale de la théorie du droit
Reyn. Reynolds Reports (40–42 Mississippi)
Reynolds Reynolds Reports (40–42 Mississippi)
rgl. regolamento (It.)
Rh.C.A. Rhodesian Court of Appeal Law Reports. 1939–46
Rh.L.J. Rhodesian Law Journal. 1961–
Ri.DI Rivista de diritto internazionale (It.)
Ri.DP Rivista de diritto pubblico (It.)

Ri.SPI Rivista di studi politici internazionali (It.)
Ric. Richard (King)
Rice Rice's South Carolina Law Reports (24 SCL) 1838–39
Rice Ch. Rice's South Carolina Equity Reports (14 SCEq.) 1838–39
Rice Dig. Rice, Digest of Patent Office Decisions (USA)
Rice Eq. Rice's South Carolina Equity Reports (14 SCEq.) 1838–39
Rice Ev. Rice's Law of Evidence (USA)
Rice L.(S.C.) Rice's South Carolina Law Reports (24 SCL) 1838–39
Rice's Code Rice's Code of Practice (Colorado)
Rich. Richard (King)
Richardson's Reports (18 US Court Claims)
Richardson's South Carolina Law Reports (30–31 SCL) 1844–46; (37–49 SCL) 1850–68
Richardson's Reports (3–5 New Hampshire)
Rich.C.P. Richardson's Chancery Practice. 1838
Richardson's Practice in the Court of Common Pleas. 7ed. 1792
Rich.Cas. Richardson's South Carolina Equity Cases (9 SC Eq.) 1831–32
Rich.Cas.(S.C.) Richardson's South Carolina Equity Cases (9 SC Eq.) 1831–32
Rich.Ch. Richardson's South Carolina Equity Reports (18–19 SCEq.) 1844–46; (24–31 SCEq.) 1850–68
Rich.Ch.Pr. Richardson, Chancery Practice. 1838
Rich.Ct.Cl. Richardson's Court of Claims Reports (18 U.S. Court of Claims)
Rich.Eq. Richardson's South Carolina Equity Reports (18–19 SCEq.) 1844–46; (24–31 SCEq.) 1850–68
Rich.Eq.Cas. Richardson's South Carolina Equity Cases (9 SCEq.) 1831–32
Rich.Eq.Ch. Richardson's South Carolina Equity Reports (18–19 SC Eq.) 1844–46; (24–31 SCEq.) 1850–68
Rich.L.(S.C.) Richardson's South Carolina Law Reports (30–31 SCL) 1844–46; (37–49 SCL) 1850–68
Rich.Land.A. Richey, Irish Land Act
Rich.Law(S.C.) Richardson's South Carolina Law Reports (30–31 SCL) 1844–46; (37–49 SCL) 1850–58
Rich.N.H. Richardson's Reports (3–5 New Hampshire)
Rich.N.S. Richardson's South Carolina Reports, New Series. 1850–68
Rich.Pr.C.P. Richardson, Attorney's Practice in the Court of Common Pleas. 7ed. 1792
Rich.Pr.K.B. Richardson, Attorney's Practice in the Court of King's Bench. 8ed. 1792
Rich.& H. Richardson & Hook's Street Railway Decisions (USA)
Rich.& S. Richardson & Sayles' Select Cases of Procedure without Writ
Rich.& W. Richardson & Woodbury's Reports (2 New Hampshire)
Rick.& M. Rickards & Michael's Locus Standi Reports. 1885–89
Rick.& S. Rickards & Saunders' Locus Standi Reports. 1890–94
Rid.Sup.Proc. Riddle, Supplementary Proceedings, New York
Ridg. Ridgeway's Reports tempore Hardwicke, Chancery (27 ER) 1744–46
Ridg.Ap. Ridgeway's Parliamentary Reports (Ire.) 1784–96
Ridg.Cas. Ridgeway's Reports tempore Hardwicke, Chancery (27 ER) 1744–46
Ridg.L.& S. Ridgeway, Lapp & Schoales' Irish Term Reports. 1793–95
Ridg.P.C. Ridgeway's Parliamentary Reports (Ire.) 1784–96
Ridg.Parl.Rep. Ridgeway's Parliamentary Reports (Ire.) 1784–96
Ridg.Pr.Rep. Ridgeway's Parliamentary Reports (Ire.) 1784–96
Ridg.Rep. Ridgeway's Individual Reports of State Trials (Ire.)

Ridg.St.Tr. Ridgeway's Individual Reports of State Trials (Ire.)

Ridg.t.H. Ridgeway's Reports tempore Hardwicke, Chancery (27 ER) 1744–46

Ridg.t.Hard. Ridgeway's Reports tempore Hardwicke, Chancery (27 ER) 1744–46

Ridg.temp.H. Ridgeway's Reports tempore Hardwicke Chancery (27 ER) 1744–46

Ridgew. Ridgeway's Reports tempore Hardwick Chancery (27 ER) 1744–46

Ridgew.Ir.P.C. Ridgeway's Parliamentary Reports (Ire.) 1784–96

Ridgew.L.& S.(Ire.) Ridgeway, Lapp & Schoales Irish Term Reports. 1793–95

Ridgew.t.Hardw. Ridgeway's Reports tempore Hardwicke, Chancery (27 ER) 1744–46

Ridley,Civil & Ecc.Law Ridley's Civil & Ecclesiastical Law. 4ed. 1675

Ried. Riedell's Reports (68, 69 New Hampshire)

Rigg Calendar of the Plea Rolls of the Exchequer of the Jews preserved in the Public Record Office, 1218–77 (Jewish Hist. Soc.)
Select Pleas, Starrs, and other Records from the Rolls of the Exchequer of the Jews (Selden Society Publication 15)

Ril. Riley's South Carolina Chancery Reports (12 SCEq.) 1836–37
Riley's South Carolina Law Reports (22 SCL) 1836–37
Riley's West Virginia Reports (37–42 W.Va.)

Ril.Harp. Riley's edition of Harper's South Carolina Reports

Riley Riley's South Carolina Chancery Reports (12 SCEq.) 1836–37
Riley's South Carolina Law Reports (22 SCL) 1836–37
Riley's West Virginia Reports (37–42 West Va.)

Riley Ch. Riley's South Carolina Chancery Reports 912 SCEq.) 1836–37

Riley Eq. Riley's South Carolina Equity Reports (12 SCEq.) 1836–37

Riley Eq.(S.C.) Riley's South Carolina Equity Reports (12 SCEq.) 1836–37

Riley L.(S.C.) Riley's South Carolina Law Reports (22 SCL) 1836–37

Rin. Riner's Reports (2 Wyoming)

Riner Riner's Reports (2 Wyoming)

Ring.Bank. Ringwood, Principles of Bankruptcy. 18ed. 1947

Ritch. Bacon's Decisions by Ritchie. 1617–21
Ritchie's Equity Reports (Nova Scotia) 1872–82

Ritch.Eq.Dec. Ritchie's Equity Reports (Nova Scotia) 1872–82

Ritch.Eq.Rep. Ritchie's Equity Reports (Nova Scotia) 1872–82

Ritchie Ritchie's Equity Reports (Nova Scotia) 1872–82

Rits.Int. Ritso, Introduction to the Science of Law. 1815

Riv.Ann.Reg. Rivington's Annual Register

Riv.di dir.civ. Rivista di diritto civile (It.) 1955–

Riv.dir.civ. Rivista di diritto civile (It.) 1955–

Riv.dir.comm. Rivista del diritto commerciale (It.) 1903–

Riv.dir.europeo Rivista di diritto europeo (It.) 1961–

Riv.dir.ind. Rivista di diritto industriale (It.) 1952–

Riv.dir.int.e comp.del lavoro Rivista di diritto internazionale e comparato del lavoro (It.) 1953–

Riv.dir.intern.priv.& proc. Rivista di diritto internazionale privato e processuale (It.)

Riv.dir.internaz. Rivista di diritto internazionale (It.) 1906–42, 1953–

Riv.dir.internaz.comp.lav. Rivista di diritto internazionale e comparato del lavoro (It.) 1953–

Riv.dir int'le Rivista di diritto internazionale (It.) 1906–42, 1953–

Riv.dir.int'le priv.& proc. Rivista di diritto internazionale privato e processuale (It.)

Riv.dir.lav. Rivista di diritto del lavoro (It.) 1926–31, 1949–
Riv.dir.matr. Rivista del diritto matrimoniale e dello stato delle persone (It.) 1958–68
Riv.dir.priv. Rivista di diritto privato (It.) 1931–39
Riv.dir.proc. Rivista di diritto processuale (It.) 1946–
Riv.fil Rivista di filosofia (It.)
Riv.Int.di Fil.del Dir. Rivista internazionale di filosofia del diritto (It.) 1921–
Riv.internaz.fil.dir. Rivista internazionale di filisofia del diritto (It.) 1921–
Riv.int'le fil.dir. Rivista internazionale di filosofia del diritto (It.) 1921–
Riv.it.dir.proc.pen. Rivista italiana di diritto e procedure penale (It.) 1929–
Riv.it.scienze giur. Rivista italiana per le scienze guiridiche (It.) 1886–1921, 1926–40, 1947–
Riv.not. Rivista notartato (It.)
Riv.pen. Rivista penale (It.) 1930–
Riv.soc. Rivista delle societa (It.) 1956–
Riv.tr.dir.pub. Rivista trimestrale di diritto pubblico (It.) 1951–
Riv.trim.dir.proc.civ. Rivista trimestrale di diritto e procedura civile (It.) 1947–
Riv.trim.dir.pubbl. Rivista trimestrale di diritto pubblico (It.) 1951–
Rivista Rivista di diritto internazionale (It.) 1906–42, 1953–
Rivista Dir.Int.di Napoli Rivista di diritto internazionale e di legislazione comparata (it.)
Rivista Dir.Priv. Rivista di diritto privato (It.) 1931–39
Rivista Italiana Rivista italiana di diritto internazionale privato e processuale (It.)
Rmdr. Remainder
Ro. Rolle's Abridgment. 1668
Ro.Abr. Rolle's Abridgment. 1668
Ro.Rep. Robards' Conscript Cases (Texas) 1862–65
Rolle's King's Bench Reports (81 ER) 1614–25
Road L. Road Law
Rob. Robards' Conscript Cases (Texas 1862–65)
Robards' Reports (12, 13 Missouri)
Roberts' Reports (29–31 Louisiana Annual)
Robertson's Ecclesiastical Reports (163 ER) 1844–53
Robertson's Reports (1 Hawaii)
Robertson's Reports (24–30 New York Superior) 1863–68
Robertson's Scotch Appeal Cases. 1707–27
(Christopher) Robinson's Admiralty Reports (165 ER) 1799–1808
(William) Robinson's Admiralty Reports (166 ER) 1838–1852
Robinson's Reports (38 California)
Robinson's Reports (2–9, 17–23 Colorado Appeals)
Robinson's Reports (1–4 Loiusiana Annual) 1841–46
Robinson's Reports (1 Nevada)
Robinson's Reports (1–8 Ontario)
Robinson's Reports (40,41 Virginia) 1842–44
Robinson's Scotch Appeal Cases. 1840–41
(Christopher) Robinson's Upper Canada Reports
(J.L.) Robinson's Upper Canada Reports
Rob.Ad. C. Robinson's Admiralty Reports (165 ER) 1799–1808
Rob.Adm. C. Robinson's Admiralty Reports (165 ER) 1799–1808
W. Robinson's Admiralty Reports (166 ER) 1838–52
Rob.Adm.& Pr. Roberts on Admiralty & Prize
Rob.App. Robertson's Scotch Appeal Cases. 1707–27
Robinson's Scotch Appeal Cases. 1840–41
Rob.Bank. Robertson, Handbook of Bankers' Law

Robson, Law and Practice in Bankruptcy. 7ed. 1894

Rob.Cal. Robinson's Reports (38 California)

Rob.Cas. Robertson's Scotch Appeal Cases. 1707–27

Rob.Chr. Christopher Robinson's Admiralty Reports. 1799–1808

Rob.Colo. Robinson's Reports (2–9, 17–23 Colorado Appeals)

Rob.Cons.Cas.(Tex.) Robards' Conscript Cases (Texas) 1862–65

Rob.Consc.Cas. Robards' Conscript Cases (Texas) 1862–65

Rob.E. Robertson's Ecclesiastical Reports (163 ER) 1844–53

Rob.Ecc. Robertson's Ecclesiastical Reports (163 ER) 1844–53

Rob.Eccl. Robertson's Ecclesiastical Reports (163 ER) 1844–53

Rob.Eq. Roberts, Principles of Equity. 3ed. 1877

Rob.Fr. Roberts, Frauds. 1805

Rob.Gav. Robinson, Common Law of Kent, or Custom on Gavelkind. 5ed. 1897

Rob.Hawaii Robertsons' Reports (1 Hawaii)

Rob.Jun. William Robinson's Admiralty Reports (166 ER) 1838–52

Rob.Jus. Robinson, Justice of the Peace. 1836

Rob.L.& W. Roberts, Leeming & Wallis' New Court Cases. 1849–51

Rob.La. Robinson's Supreme Court Reports (1–4 Loiusiana Annual)

Rob.Leg. Robertson, Legitimation by Subsequent Marriage. 1829

Rob.Mar.(N.Y.) Robertson & Jacob's New York Marine Court Reports. 1874–79

Rob.Mo. Robards' Reports (12,13 Missouri)

Rob.N.Y. Robertson's Reports (24–30 New York Superior Court) 1863–68

Rob.Nev. Robinson's Reports (1 Nevada)

Rob.Ont. Robinson's Reports (1–8 Ontario)

Rob.Per.Suc. Robertson, Law of Personal Succession. 1836

Rob.S.I. Robertson's Sandwich Island Reports (1 Hawaii)

Rob.Sc.App. Robertson's Scotch Appeal Cases. 1707–27
Robinson's Scotch Appeal Cases. 1840–41

Rob.Sr.Ct. Robertson's Reports (24–30 New York Superior Court) 1863–68

Rob.Super.Ct. Robertson's Reports (24–30 New York Superior Court) 1863–68

Rob.U.C. Robinson's King's Bench Reports (Upper Canada) 1831–44, 1844–82

Rob.Va. Robinson's Reports (40,41 Virginia) 1842–44

Rob.W. Roberts, Wills and Codicils. 3ed. 1826

Rob.Wm.Adm. William Robinson's Admiralty Reports (166 ER) 1838–52

Rob.& J. Robards' & Jackson's Reports (26, 27 Texas)

Robards Robards' Conscript Cases (Texas) 1862–65
Robards' Reports (12, 13 Missouri)

Robards & Jackson Robards & Jackson's Reports (26–27 Texas)

Robb. Robbins' Reports (67–70 New Jersey Equity) 1904–05
Robb's United States Patent Cases

Robb.(N.J.) Robbins' New Jersey Equity Reports (67–70 NJ Eq.) 1904–05

Robb.Pat.Cas. Robb's United States Patent Cases

Robert. Robertson's Scotch Appeal Cases. 1707–1727

Robert.App. Robertson's Scotch Appeal Cases. 1707–27

Robert.App.Cas. Robertson's Scotch Appeal Cases. 1707–27

Roberts Divorce Cases (Ire.) 1816–1905
Roberts' Reports (29–31 Louisiana Annual)

Robertson Robertson's Ecclesiastical Reports (163 ER) 1844–53

Robertson's Reports (1 Hawaii)
Robertson's Reports, New York Marine Court. 1874–79
Robertson's Reports (24–30 New York Superior) 1863–68
Robertson's Scotch Appeal Cases. 1707–27

Robin.App. Robinson's Scotch Appeal Cases. 1840–41

Robin.Sc.App. Robinson's Scotch Appeal Cases. 1840–41

Robinson Christopher Robinson's Admiralty Reports (165 ER) 1799–1808
W. Robinson's Admiralty Reports (166 ER) 1838–52
Robinson's Reports (38 California)
Robinson's Reports (2–9, 17–23 Colorado Appeals)
Robinson's Reports (1–4 Louisiana Annual) 1841–46
Robinson's Reports (1 Nevada)
Robinson's Reports (1–8 Ontario)
Robinson's Reports (40–41 Virginia) 1842–44
Robinson Scotch Appeal Cases. 1840–41
J.L. Robinson's Upper Canada Reports

Robinson Report Report of the Interdepartmental Committee on Conciliation (P.D. Robinson, chairman) (Lord Chancellor's Department) 1983

Robinson Sc.App.Cas. Robinson's Scotch Appeal Cases. 1840–41

Robs.Bank. Robson, Bankruptcy Practice. 7ed. 1894

Robs.Bankr. Robertson's Handbook of Bankers' law

Robson Robson, Bankruptcy Practice. 7ed. 1894

Robt.Eccl. Robertson's Ecclesiastical Reports (163 ER) 1844–53

Robt.(N.Y.) Robertson's Reports (24–30 New York Superior Court) 1863–68

Robt.Sc.App.Cas. Robertson's Scotch Appeal Cases. 1707–27

Rocc. Roccus' de Navibus et Naulo (Maritime Law)

Roche D.& K. Roche, Dillon & Kehoe's Irish Land Reports. 1881–82

Roche & H.Bank. Roche & Hazlitt, Bankruptcy Practice. 2ed. 1873

Rocky Mt.L.Rev. Rocky Mountain Law Review. 1928–62

Rocky Mt.M.L.Inst. Rocky Mountain Mineral Law Institute. 1955–

Rocky Mtn.Min.L.Inst. Rocky Mountain Mineral Law Institute. 1955–

Rodm. Rodman's Reports (78–82 Kentucky) 1879–83

Rodman Rodman's Reports (78–82 Kentucky) 1879–83

Rog.C.H.R. Rogers' City Hall Recorder (New York) 1816–22

Rog.Ecc.L. Rogers, Ecclesiastical Law. 5ed. 1857

Rog.Ecc.Law Rogers, Ecclesiastical Law. 5ed. 1857

Rog.Elec. Rogers, Elections and Registrations. 21ed. 1935

Rog.Jud.Acts. Rogers, Judicature Acts. 1876

Rog.Min. Rogers, Mines, Minerals and Quarries. 2ed. 1876

Rog.Rec. Rogers' New York City Hall Recorder. 1816–22

Rogers Rogers' Reports (47–51 Louisiana Annual)

Rol. Rolle's Abridgment. 1668
Rolle's King's Bench Reports (81 ER) 1614–25

Rol.Ab. Rolle's Abridgment. 1668

Rolin, Principes A. Rolin, Principes de droit international privé belge. 1897

Roll. Roll of the Term
Rolle's Abridgment. 1668
Rolle's King's Bench Reports (81 ER) 1614–25

Roll.Abr. Rolle's Abridgment. 1668

Roll.Rep. Rolle's King's Bench Reports (81 ER) 1614–25

Rolle Rolle's Abridgment. 1668
Rolle's King's Bench Reports (81 ER) 1614–25

Rolle Abr. Rolle's Abridgment. 1668

Rolle R. Rolle's King's Bench Reports (81 ER) 1614–25

Rolls Ct.Rep. Rolls' Court Reports
Rom. Roman
Romilly's Notes of Chancery Cases. 1767–87
Rom.Cas. Romilly's Notes of Chancery Cases. 1767–87
Rom.Cr.Law Romilly, Observations on the Criminal Law. 3ed. 1813
Rom.Law Roman Law
Romano, Ordinamento S. Romano, L'Ordinamento Giuridico (It.) 2ed. 1946
Romano, Principi S. Romano, Principi di Diritto Constituzionale Generale (It.) 1945
Romilly N.C. Romilly's Notes of Chancery Cases. 1767–87
Root Root's Connecticut Supreme Court Reports. 1789–98 (with a variety of cases 1774–89)
Root Bt.Laws Root, Digest of Law and Practice in Bankruptcy. 1818
Rop. Roper, Legacies. 4ed. 1847
Rop.H.& W. Roper, Law of Property between Husband and Wife. 2ed. 1826
Rop.Husb.& Wife Roper, Law of Property between Husband and Wife. 2ed. 1826
Rop.Leg. Roper, Legacies. 4ed. 1847
Rop.Prop. Roper, Property between Husband and Wife. 2ed. 1826
Rosc. Roscoe's Reports of the Supreme Court (Cape. S.Afr.) 1861–78
Rosc.Act. Roscoe, Actions. 1825
Rosc.Adm. Roscoe, Admiralty Jurisdiction and Practice. 5ed. 1931
Rosc.Bdg.Cas. Roscoe, Digest of Building Cases. 4ed. 1900
Rosc.Bills Roscoe, Bills of Exchange. 2ed. 1843
Rosc.Civ.Pr. Roscoe, Outlines of Civil Procedure. 2ed. 1880
Rosc.Cr. Roscoe, Criminal Evidence and Practice. 16ed. 1952
Rosc.Crim.Ev. Roscoe, Criminal Evidence and Practice. 16ed. 1952
Rosc.Ev. Roscoe, Nisi Prius Evidence. 20ed. 1934
Rosc.Jur. Roscoe's Jurist
Rosc.Light Roscoe, Law of Light. 4ed. 1904
Rosc.N.P. Roscoe, Law of Evidence Nisi Prius. 20ed. 1934
Rosc.P.C. Roscoe's Prize Cases. 1745–1858
Rosc.Pl. Roscoe, Pleading. 1845
Roscoe Roscoe's Reports of Supreme Court of Cape of Good Hope (S.Afr.) 1861–78
Roscoe Bldg.Cas. Roscoe, Digest of Building Cases. 4ed. 1900
Roscoe Cr.Ev. Roscoe, Criminal Evidence and Practice. 16ed. 1952
Roscoe's B.C. Roscoe, Digest of Building Cases. 4ed. 1900
Rose Rose's Bankruptcy Reports. 1810–16
Rose B.C. Rose's Bankruptcy Reports. 1810–16
Rose Bankr. Rose's Bankruptcy Reports. 1810–16
Rose-Innes L.A. Rose-Innes, Judicial Review of Administrative Tribunals in South Africa
Rose Notes Rose's Notes on United States Reports
Rosenberger Pock.L.J. Rosenberger's Pocket Law Journal (USA) 1894–1900
Roskill Report Report of the Fraud Trials Committee. 1986
Ross Conv. Ross, Lectures on Conveyancing (Scot.)
Ross L.C. Ross's Leading Cases in Commercial Law. 1853–57
Ross's Leading Cases in the Law of Scotland (Land Rights) 1638–1849
Ross Ldg.Cas. Ross's Leading Cases in Commercial Law. 1853–57
Ross's Leading Cases in the Law of Scotland (Land Rights) 1638–1849
Ross Lead.Cas. Ross's Leading Cases in Commercial Law. 1853–57
Ross's Leading Cases in the Law of Scotland (Land Rights) 1638–1840
Ross V.& P. Ross, Vendors & Purchasers. 2ed. 1826

Rot.Chart. Rotulus Chartarum (The Charter Roll)

Rot.Claus. Rotuli Clausi (Close Rolls)

Rot.Cur.Reg. Rotuli Curiae Regis by Palgrove. 1194–99

Rot.Cur.Regis. Rotuli Curiae Regis by Palgrove. 1194–99

Rot.Flor. Rotae Florentine Reports of the Supreme Court, or Rota, of Florence

Rot.Lit.Claus. Rotuli Literarum Clausarum (Record Commission) 1833–44

Rot.Lit.Pat. Rotuli Literarum Patentium (Record Commission) 1835

Rot.Parl. Rotuli Parliamentorum. 1278–1553

Rot.Pat. Rotuli Patentes (Patent Rolls)

Rot.Plac. Rotulus Placitorum (the Plea Roll)

Rothschild Report Royal Commission on Gambling. Report (Cmnd. 7200) 1978

Rotuli Curiae Reg. Rotuli Curiae Regis. 1194–99

Round Dom. Round, Law of Domicil. 1861

Round L.& A. Round, Right to Light and Air. 1868

Round Lien Round, Law of Lien. 1863

Rouse Conv. Rouse, Practical Conveyancer. 3ed. 1867

Rouse Cop. Rouse, Copyhold Enfranchisement Manual. 3ed. 1866

Rouse Pr.Mort. Rouse, Precedents and Conveyances of Mortgaged Property.

Rousseau C.H. Rousseau, Principes généraux du droit international public. 1944

Row.Eng.Const. Rowland, Manual of the English Constitution. 1859

Rowe Rowe's Interesting Cases (England and Ireland) 1798–1823

Rowe Rep. Rowe's Interesting Cases (England & Ireland) 1798–1823

Rowell Rowell's Reports (45–52 Vermont)

Rowell,El.Cas. Rowell's Contested Election Cases, U.S. House of Representatives

Roxburgh Report Committee on Land Charges (Cmd. 9825) 1956

Roy.Asiatic Soc'y J. Royal Asiatic Society Journal

Roy.Dig. Royall's Digest of Virginia Reports

Roy.Hist.Soc'y Trans. Royal Historical Society Transactions

rspr. rechtspraak (Neth.) case law, judicial decisions

Rspr. Rechtsprechung (Ger.) court practice

RsprArb. Rechtsprechung in Arbeitssachen (Ger.) Labour Court Reports

rt. right

Rt.Law Rep. Rent Law Reports (India)

Rts. Rights

Rub.Conv. Rubinstein, Conveyancing. 5ed. 1884

Rucker Rucker's Reports (43–46 West Virginia)

Ruegg Emp.L. Ruegg, Employer's Liability. 9ed. 1922

Ruff. Ruffhead's edition of the Statutes by Serjeant Runnington. 1235–1785
Ruffin & Hawks' Reports (8 North Carolina) 1820–21
Statutes at Large, Ruffhead's Edition. 1235–1764

Ruff.& H. Ruffin & Hawks' Reports (8 North Carolina) 1820–21

Rul.Cas. Ruling Cases edited by Campbell. 1894–1908

Rules Sup.Ct. Rules of the Supreme Court

Runn. Runnell's Reports (38–56 Iowa)
Statutes at Large, Runnington's Edition. 1235–1785

Runn.Eject. Runnington, Ejectment. 2ed. 1820

Runnell Runnell's Reports (38–56 Iowa)

Rus. Russell's Chancery Reports tempore Eldon (38 ER) 1823–29
Russell's Election Cases (Nova Scotia, Can.) 1874

Rus.E.C. Russell's Contested Election Cases (Massachusetts)
Russell's Election Cases (Nova Scotia, Can.) 1874

Rus.E.R. Russell's Election Cases (Nova Scotia, Can.) 1874

Rus.Elec.Rep. Russell's Election Cases (Nova Scotia, Can.) 1874

Rus.Eq.Rep. Russell's Equity Decisions (Nova Scotia, Can.)

Rus.& C.Eq.Cas. Russell & Chesley's Equity Cases (Nova Scotia, Can.) 1875–79

Rushcliffe Report Committee on Legal Aid and Advice in England & Wales. Report (Cmd. 6641) 1948
Land Transfer Committee. Report (Cmd. 6467) 1942/3

Russ. Russell's Chancery Reports (38 ER) 1823–29
Russell's Election Cases (Nova Scotia, Can.) 1874

Russ.Arb. Russell, Arbitration. 19ed. 1978

Russ.Ch. Russell's Chancery Reports (38 ER) 1823–29

Russ.Con.El.(Mass.) Russell's Contested Elections, Massachusetts

Russ.Cr. Russell on Crime. 12ed. 1964

Russ.Crim. Russell on Crime. 12ed. 1964

Russ.Crimes. Russell on Crime. 12ed. 1964

Russ.El.Cas. Russell's Election Cases (Nova Scotia,Can.) 1874

Russ.Elect.Cas. Russell's Contested Election Cases, Massachusetts (USA)
Russell's Election Cases (Nova Scotia, Can.) 1874

Russ.Eq. Russell's Equity Cases (Nova Scotia, Can.)

Russ.Eq.Cas. Russell's Equity Cases (Nova Scotia, Can.)

Russ,Eq.Rep. Russell's Equity Decisions (Nova Scotia, Can.)

Russ.Fact. Russell, Factors and Brokers. 1844

Russ.Merc.Ag. Russell, Mercantile Agency. 2ed. 1873

Russ.N.Sc. Russell's Equity Cases (Nova Scotia,Can.)

Russ.t.Eld. Russell's Chancery Reports tempore Eldon (38 ER) 1823–29

Russ.& C. Russell & Chesley's Nova Scotia Reports (NSR 10–12) 1875–79

Russ.& Ches. Russell & Chesley's Nova Scotia Reports (NSR 10–12) 1875–79

Russ.& Ches.Eq. Russell & Chesley's Nova Scotia Equity Reports (NSR 10–12) 1875–79

Russ.& Eq. Russell & Chesley's Nova Scotia Equity Reports (NSR 10–12) 1875–79

Russ.& G. Russell & Geldert's Nova Scotia Reports (NSR 13–27) (Can.) 1879–95

Russ.& Geld. Russell & Geldert's Nova Scotia Reports (NSR 13–27) (Can.) 1879–95

Russ.& M. Russell & Mylne's Chancery Reports (39 ER) 1829–31

Russ.& My. Russell & Mylne's Chancery Reports (39 ER) 1829–31

Russ.& R. Russell & Ryan's Crown Cases Reserved (168 ER) 1799–1824

Russ.& R.C.C. Russell & Ryan's Crown Cases Reserved (168 ER) 1799–1824

Russ.& R.Cr.Cas. Russell & Ryan's Crown Cases Reserved (168 ER) 1799–1824

Russ.& Ry. Russell & Ryan's Crown Cases Reserved (168 ER) 1799–1824

Russell Russell's Equity Decisions (Nova Scotia, Can.)

Russell N.S. Russell's Nova Scotia Equity Decisions (Can.)

Russell Report Lord Chancellor's Office Report on the Law of Succession in relation to Illegitimate Persons (Cmnd. 3051) 1966

Russian Rev. Russian Review (USA)

Rut.-Cam.L.J. Rutgers-Camden Law Journal (USA) 1969–

Rutg.Cas. Rutger-Waddington Case, New York. 1784

Rutg.L.R. Rutgers Law Review (USA) 1947–

Rutg.L.Rev. Rutgers Law Review (USA) 1947–

Rutgers-Camden L.J. Rutgers-Camden Law Journal (USA) 1969–

Rutgers J.Comp.& L. Rutgers Journal of Computers and the Law (USA) 1970–

Rutgers J.Computers & Law Rutgers Journal of Computers and the Law (USA) 1970–

Rutgers L.J. Rutgers Law Journal (USA)

Rutgers L.Rev. Rutgers Law Review (USA) 1947–

Rutgers U.L.Rev. Rutgers University Law Review (USA) 1947–48

Rv. Wetboek van Burgerlijke Regtsvordering (Neth.)

Ry. Railway

Ry.Cas. Reports of Railway & Canal Cases. 1835–54

Ry.Corp.Law Jour. Railway & Corporation Law Journal (USA) 1887–92

Ry.F. Rymer's Foedera. 1704–35

Ry.M.C.C. Ryan & Moody's Crown Cases Reserved. 1824–44

Ry.Med.Jur. Ryan, Medical Jurisprudence. 1831

Ry.& C.Cas. Railway & Canal Cases. 1835–54

Ry.& C.Traffic Cas. Railway & Canal Traffic Cases. 1855–1949

Ry.& Can.Cas. Railway & Canal Cases. 1835–54

Ry.& Can.Tr.Cas. Reports of Railway and Canal Traffic Cases. 1855–1949

Ry.& Can.Traf.Cas. Reports of Railway and Canal Traffic Cases. 1855–1949

Ry.& Can.Traffic Cas. Reports of Railway and Canal Cases. 1855–1949

Ry.& Corp.Law J. Railway and Corporation Law Journal (USA) 1887–92

Ry.& Corp.Law Jour. Railway and Corporation Law Journal (USA) 1887–92

Ry.& M. Ryan & Moody's Nisi Prius Reports (171 ER) 1823–26

Ry.& M.C.C. Ryan & Moody's Crown Cases Reserved. 1824–44

Ry.& M.N.P. Ryan & Moody's Nisi Prius Reports (171 ER) 1823–26

Ry.& Moo. Ryan and Moody's Reports. 1823–26

Ryan & M. Ryan and Moody's Nisi Prius Reports (171 ER) 1823–26

Ryde Ryde's Rating Appeals. 1871–93

Ryde Rat.App. Ryde's Rating Appeals. 1871–1893

Ryde & K. Ryde and Konstam's Reports of Rating Appeals. 1894–1904

Ryde & K.Rat.App. Ryde and Konstam's Reports of Rating Appeals. 1894–1904

Ryl.Plac.Parl. Ryley's Placita Parliamentaria. 1290–1307

RzW Rechtspechung zum Wiedergutmachungsrecht (Ger.) Reports on Restitution Law. 1949/50–

S

s. same case
section
seguente (It.) and following (section paragraph, etc.)

S. New York Supplement
Recueil Sirey (Fr.)
Saskatchewan
Scotland
Scottish
Searle's Cases in the Supreme Court (Cape, S.Afr) 1850–67
Section
Seite (Ger.) page
Senate
Senate Bill (USA)
Shaw's Session Cases (Scot.) 1st Series. 1821–38
Shaw's House of Lords Appeal Cases (Scot.) 1821–24
Solicitor's Opinion
South
Southeastern Reporter (properly S.E.)
Southern
Southern Reporter
Southwestern Reporter (properly S.W.)
Spanish
Statute
Superseded
Supreme Court Reporter (USA)
Wetboek van Strafrecht (Neth.) criminal code

S.2d. New York Supplement, Second Series
Southern Reporter, Second Series (USA)

s.a. see also
sub anno (Lat.) under the year
subject to approval

SA Sveriges advokatsamfund (Swedish Lawyers' Association)

S.A. Shops Act
Société anonyme (Belg. & Fr.) share or stock company, corporation
South Africa
South African Law Reports. 1947–
South Australia

S.A.A. Standards Association of Australia

S.A.B.I.C. Saudi Arabia Basic Industries Corporation

S.A.C.L.R.C. South Australian Criminal Law Reform Committee

SACO Sveriges akademikers centralorganisation (The Central Organisation of Swedish University Graduates)

S.A.D.Beng. Select Cases, Sudder Dewanny Adawlut by Macnaghten and others (Bengal, India) 1791–1858

S.A.D.Bom. Sudder Dewanny Adawlut Reports (Bombay, India)

S.A.D.Mad. Madras Sudder Dewanny Adawlut Reports (India) 1805–62

S.A.D.N.W.F. Sudder Dewanny Adawlut Cases, North West Frontier (Pak.) 1846–63

S.A.Dept.of A-G South Australia Department of the Attorney–General

S.A.Dept.of A-G L.R.C.Rep. South Australia Department of the Attorney–General, Law Reform Committee Report

s.a.e. stamped addressed envelope

SAF Svenska Arbetsgivareföreningen (Swed.) The Confederation of Employers' Associations

SAG Schweizerische Aktiengesellschaft (Switz.)
S.A.I. Societa Anonima Italiana (It.) Incorporated Company
S.A.I.C. South Australian Industrial Commission
S.A.I.Ct. South Australian Industrial Court
S.A.I.G. South Australian Industrial Gazette
S.A.I.R. South Australian Industrial Reports. 1916–
S.A.J.H.R. South African Journal on Human Rights
S.A.L.C.R. South Australian Licensing Court Reports. 1967–78
S.A.L.J. South African Law Journal. 1901–
S.A.L.L.B. South Australian Law Librarians' Bulletin. 1986–
S.A.L.L.G. South Australian Law Librarians Group
S.A.L.R. South African Law Reports. 1947–
South Australian Law Reports. 1865–1892, 1899–1921
S.A.L.R.C. South Australian Law Reform Committee
S.A.L.R.C.P. South African Law Reports, Cape Provincial Division. 1910–46
S.A.L.R.S.W.A. South African Law Reports, South West African Reports. 1920–46
S.A.L.T. South African Law Times. 1932–36
Strategic Arms Limitation Talks
S.A.Law Reports,C.P. South African Law Reports, Cape Provincial Division. 1910–46
S.A.Law Reports,C.P.D. South African Law Reports, Cape Provincial Division. 1910–46
S.A.Law Reports,N.P.D. South African Law Reports, Natal State Province Division. 1910–46
S.A.Law Reports,S.W.A. Reports of the High Court of South-West Africa (S.Afr.) 1920–46
S.A.Law Soc.Bull. South Australia Law Society Bulletin. 1979–
S.A.M.A. Saudi Arabia Monetary Agency
SAO School Attendance Order
S.A.P.L. South African Public Law
S.A.P.R. South Australian Planning Reports. 1967–
Suid Afrikaanse Publiek Reg (South African Public Law)
S.A.R. South African Republic
South African Republic Supreme Court Reports. 1881–92
South Australian Industrial Reports. 1916–
S.a.r.l. Societé à responsabilité limitée (Fr.) Limited liability company
S.A.R.L. Societé à responsabilité limitée (Fr.) Limited liability company
S.A.S.R. South Australian State Reports (Continuation of South Australian Law Reports) 1921–71, 1971–
S.A.T.C. South African Tax Cases. 1921–
S.A.Tax Cas. South African Tax Cases. 1921–
SAYIL South African Yearbook of International Law
S.Afr. South Africa
S.Afr.J.Crim.L. South African Journal of Criminal Law and Criminology. 1977–
S.Afr.J.Hum.Rts. South African Journal on Human Rights
S.Afr.L.J. South African Law Journal. 1901–
S.Afr.L.R. South African Law Reports. 1884–
S.Afr.L.R.App. South African Law Reports Appeals
S.Afr.Tax Cas. South African Tax Cases. 1921–
S.Afr.Y.I.L. South African Yearbook of International Law. 1975–
S.Afr.Yrbk.Intl.L. South African Yearbook of International Law. 1975–

S.App. Shaw's Scottish House of Lords Appeal Cases. 1821–24
S.Aust. South Australia
S.Aust.L.R. South Australian Law Reports. 1865–1892, 1899–1920
S.Austl.L.R. South Australian Law Reports. 1865–1892, 1899–1920
S.Austl.St.R. South Australian State Reports. 1921–71, 1971–
S.Austr. South Australia
S.Austrl.L.R. South Australian Law Reports. 1865–92, 1899–1921
S.B. Senate Bill (in state legislation) (USA)
Small Business
Statute Book
Supplementary Benefit
Supreme Bench
SBA Small Business Administration (USA)
SBAC Society of British Aerospace Companies
SBAT Supplementary Benefit Appeal Tribunal
S.B.C. Statutes of British Columbia
Supplementary Benefits Commission
SBLI Southeastern Bankruptcy Law Institute (USA)
SBM State Bar of Montana
SBT State Bar of Texas
SBTC Sino British Trade Council (BOTB)
S.Bar.J. State Bar Journal of California. 1926–
S.Bell Bell's House of Lords Appeals (Scot.) 1842–50
s.c. self contained
single column
small capital(s)
S.C. All India Reporter, Supreme Court Reports. 1950–
Juta's Supreme Court Reports (Cape, S.Afr.) 1880–1910
Quebec Official Reports, Superior Court (Can.) 1892–
Same Case
Security Council (UN)
Select Cases. Oudh (India)
Senior Counsel
Session Cases (Scot.)
Slavery Convention. 1926
South Carolina
South Carolina Reports. 1868–
Special Constable
Standing Committee
Stated Cases (British Columbia Assessment Authority) (Can.) 1965–
Statutory Committee
Stubbs, Select Charters and Other Illustrations of English Constitutional History. 9ed. 1913
Superior Court
Supreme Court
Supreme Court Reporter (National Reporter System) (USA)
United Nations Security Council
SCA Scottish Court Administration
Supreme and Exchequer Courts Act (Can.)
Supreme Court Appeals (India) 1905–
SC(ACT) Supreme Court (Australian Capital Territory)
S.C.A.G. Standing Committee of Attorney-Generals
SCAP Supreme Command Allied Powers
S.C.Acts Acts and Joint Resolutions of South Carolina
SCB South Carolina Bar
S.C.Bar Assn. South Carolina Bar Association
S.C.C. Cameron's Supreme Court Cases (Can.)
Scottish Consumer Council
Select Cases in Chancery tempore King, ed. Macnaghten (25 ER) 1724–33
Small Causes Court (India)
Supreme Court Cases (India)
Supreme Court Circular (Sri L.) 1878–91
Supreme Court of Canada
S.C.C.R. Scottish Criminal Case Reports
S.C.Cas. Supreme Court Cases
S.C.Code South Carolina Code

S.C.D.C. Supreme Court Reports, District of Columbia (USA)
S.C.D.C.N.S. Supreme Court Reports, District of Columbia, New Series
S.C.D.(St.V.) Supreme Court Decisions (St.Vincent) 1928–36
S.C.Dig. Cassell's Supreme Court Digest
S.C.E. Strange's Select Cases Relating to Evidence. 1698–1732
S.C.Eq. South Carolina Equity Reports. 1784–1868
S.C.(H.L.) Session Cases, House of Lords (Scot.) 1850–
S.C.in Banco Supreme Court in Banco (Can.)
S.C.Is. Selected Judgments of the Supreme Court of Israel. 1948–
S.C.J. Justiciary Cases, Session Cases (Scot.) 1907–16
Supreme Court Journal (India) 1950–
Supreme Court of Canada Judgments (unreported decisions available on QL) 1986–
S.C.(J.) Session Cases, Justiciary (Scot.) 1907–16
S.C.J.B. Jamaica Supreme Court Judgment Books
S.C.L. Santa Clara Lawyer. 1961–65
Select Cases in Chancery, tempore King (25 ER) 1724–33
Society for Computers and Law
Society of Conservative Lawyers
South Carolina Law Reports. 1783–1868
S.C.L.J. South Carolina Law Journal. 1884–
S.C.L.Q. South Carolina Law Quarterly. 1948–62
S.C.L.R. Santa Clara Law Review. 1975–
Scottish Civil Law Reports
Southern Carolina Law Review. 1962–
S.C.L.Rev. Southern Carolina Law Review. 1962–
S.C.M. Summary Court-Martial
S.C.(Nig.) Judgments of the Supreme Court of Nigeria
SCOLAG Scottish Legal Action Group Bulletin. 1975–
S.C.O.N.U.L. Standing Conference of National and University Libraries
SCOR Security Council Official Records (UN)
S.C.of A.G. Standing Committee of Commonwealth and State Attorneys-General
S.C.Oudh. Oudh Select Cases (India)
SCP Simplified Clearance Procedure
S.C.P.S.C. South Carolina Public Service Commission Reports
S.C.R. Canada Law Reports, Supreme Court (Can.) 1923–
Juta's Supreme Court Cases (Cape, S.A.) 1880–1910
Law Reports of Supreme Court of Sarawak, North Borneo and Brunei. 1954–
South Carolina Reports. 1868–
Supreme Court Reports (Can.) 1876–1922
Supreme Court Reports (India) 1950–
Supreme Court Reports (N.S.W., Aus.) 1862–76
Supreme Court Reports (Queensland, Aus.) 1860–81
Supreme Court Reports (Sarawak) 1928–41, 1946–51
Supreme Court Reports (Sri L.) 1892–93
S.C.R.(N.S.)(N.S.W.) Supreme Court Reports (New Series) (N.S.W., Aus.) 1878–79
S.C.R.(N.S.W.) Supreme Court Reports, New South Wales. 1862–76
S.C.R.(N.S.W.)Eq. Supreme Court Reports, Equity (N.S.W., Aus.) 1862–79
S.C.R.(N.S.W.)(L.) Supreme Court Reports, Law (N.S.W.,Aus.) 1862–79
S.C.R.(Q) Queensland Supreme Court Reports (Aus.) 1860–81
S.C.R.R. Securities and Corporate Regulation Review (Can.) 1986–
S.C.Rep. Juta's Supreme Court Cases (Cape, S.A.) 1880–1910
S.C.Res. Senate Concurrent Resolution (USA)

S.C.S. Society of Civil Servants
Supplementary Convention on the Abolition of Slavery, the Slave Trade and Institutions and Practices Similar to Slavery. 1956

S.C.S.S. Scottish Council of Social Service

S.C.(W.A.) Supreme Court (Western Australia)

S.Ca.L.R. Southern California Law Review. 1927–

S.Cal.L.Rev. Southern California Law Review. 1927–

S.Car. South Carolina
South Carolina Reports. 1868–

S.Con.Res. Senate Concurrent Resolution (USA)

S.Ct. Supreme Court
Supreme Court Reporter (USA) 1882–

S.Ct.Rev. Supreme Court Review (USA) 1960–

S.Ct.Vict. Reports of Cases, Supreme Court of Victoria (Aus.) 1861–69

s.d. semi-detached
senza data (It.)

S.D. Decisions of the Sudder Court (Bengal, India) 1845–62
South Dakota
South Dakota Reports. 1890–
Southern District
State Department (USA)

S.D.A. Decisions of the Sudder Dewanny Adawlut Court (Bengal, India) 1845–62

SDB Sex Discrimination Board (South Australia)
State Bar of South Dakota

S.D.B.Jo. South Dakota Bar Journal. 1932–

S.D.C. Supreme Court, District of Columbia Reports

S.D.Compiled Laws Ann. South Dakota Compiled Laws Annotated

S.D.K. Si-De-Ka Quarterly (USA) 1917–

S.D.L.Rev. South Dakota Law Review. 1956–

S.D.N. Societé des Nations

S.d.N.A.C. Societé des Nations, Assemblée, Commissions

S.d.N.A.P. Societé des Nations, Assemblée plénière

S.d.N.J.O. Societé des Nations, Journal Officiel

S.d.N.Rec. Recueil des traités et des engagements internationaux enregistres par le Sécretariat de la Societé des Nations

S.D.N.Y. Southern District of New York

S.D.R. New York State Department Reports. 1913–14
Special Drawing Rights (IMF)
Special Duties Reports (Can.) 1946–

S.D.Rulings Stamp Duties Rulings (in New South Wales Revenue Rulings) (CCH) 1985–

S.D.Sess.Laws South Dakota Sessional Laws

S.D.St.B.J. South Dakota State Bar Journal. 1932–

S.D.Uniform Prob.Code South Dakota Uniform Probate Code

S.D.& B. Shaw, Dunlop & Bell's Session Cases. 1st series (Scot.) 1821–38

S.D.& B.Supp. Shaw, Dunlop & Bell's Supplement, containing House of Lords Decisions (Scot.)

S.Dak. South Dakota
South Dakota Reports. 1890–

S.Doc. Senate Document (USA)

S.E. Societaas Europea (The European Company)
Southeastern Reporter, National Reporter System (USA) 1887–1939

S.E.2d. Southeastern Reporter, Second Series. 1939–

SEATAG South East Asia Trade Advisory Group (BOTB)

S.E.A.T.O. South-East Asia Treaty Organisation

S.E.C. Securities and Exchange Commission Decisions and Reports (USA) 1934–

S.E.C.Jud.Dec. Securities & Exchange Commission Judicial Decisions

S.E.G.J. Law Society Solicitors' European Group Journal
SELA Latin American Economic System
SEMO Societé Belgo-Française d'Énergie Nucléaire Mosane
S.E.R. Sociaal Economische Raad (Neth.) Social and Economic Council
S.E.T. Selective Employment Tax
S.E.W. Sociaal-economische Wetgeving (Neth.) 1952–
S.F. San Francisco
Senior Fellow
Sinking Fund
Sinn Fein (Ire.)
S.F.A. Sudder Foujdaree Adawlut Reports (India) 1826–50
SFEC State Foreign Economic Commission (USSR)
S.F.I. Societé Financière Internationale (Banque Mondiale)
S.F.L.J. San Francisco Law Journal. 1877–78
S.F.L.R. University of San Francisco Law Review. 1966–
SFO Serious Fraud Office
SFS Svensk författningssamling (The official journal of Swedish legislation) 1825–
S.F.S. Sine fraude sua (Lat.) without fraud on his part
SG Sozialgericht (Ger.) Social Security Court
s.g. senza giorno (It.)
S.G. Solicitor General
s.h. senza ora (It.)
SHAC London Housing Aid Centre
S.H.A.P.E. Supreme Headquarters, Allied Powers in Europe
S.H.D. Scottish Home Department
S.H.E.& P.G. Stephenson Harwood Employment and Pensions Group
S.H.H.D. Scottish Home & Health Department
S.I. Statutory Instrument
SIA Studies in International Affairs
SICJ Statute of the International Court of Justice
SICL Serjeants' Inn, Chancery Lane
SIDS Sudden infant death syndrome (cot death)
S.I.D.S. Societé internationale de droit du travail et de la sécurité sociale (International Society for Labour Law and Social Legislation)
SIFS Serjeants' Inn, Fleet Street
SIR Wet Selectieve Investeringsregeling (Neth.) Act on Selective Investments
SITC Standard International Trade Classification
SITPRO Simplification of International Trade Procedures
S.Ill.U.L.J. Southern Illinois University Law Journal. 1976–
s.j. sub judice (Lat.) under consideration
SJ Sveriges juristforbund (The Swedish Federation of Jurists)
S.J. Saskatchewan Judgments (unreported decisions available on QL) (Can.) 1986–
Scottish Jurist. 1829–73
La Semaine Judiciaire (Switz.)
Solicitors' Journal. 1857–
S.J.C. Standing Joint Committee
S.J.D. Scientiae Juridicae Doctor (Doctor of Juridical Science)
S.J.F. Semanario Judicial de la Federacion (Suprema Corte de Justicia) (Mexico)
SJIR Schweizerisches Jahrbuch fflr Internationales Recht (Switz.)
S.J.L.B. Selected Judgments, Lower Burma
Solicitors' Journal Lawbrief
S.J.L.R. St John's Law Review (USA) 1926–
S.J.L.S. Singapore Journal of Legal Studies (previously Malaya Law Review)
S.J.Res. Senate Joint Resolution (USA)
S.J.Suppl. Supplement to the Solicitors' Journal
SJZ Schweizerische Juristen-Zeitung (Switzerland) 1904–
Suddeutsche Juristenzeitung (Ger.) 1946–50

S.J.Z. Selected Judgments of Zambia
S.Jur. Sirey, Jurisprudence (Fr.)
S.Jur.I Sirey, Jurisprudence, Cour de Cassation (Fr.)
S.Jur.II Sirey, Jurisprudence, Other Courts (Fr.)
S.Jur.III Sirey, Jurisprudence, Jurisprudence administrative (Fr.)
S.Just. J. Shaw's Justiciary Reports (Scot.) 1848–52
P. Shaw's Justiciary Decisions (Scot.) 1819–31
SK Systematischer Kommentar zum Strafgesetzbuch (Ger.)
SKK Veröffentlichungen der Schweizerischen Kartellkommission (Switz.) cartel reports
SL Strafflag (Swed.) penal code. 1864
s.l. senza luogo (It.)
S.L. Salvage Loss
Serjeant-at-Law
Session Laws
Solicitor-at-Law
SLA Senior Legal Assistant
Statutory Licensing Authority
S.L.A.C. Suburban Law Association Convention (Victoria, Aus.)
S.L.A.G. Scottish Legal Action Group
S.L.C. Scottish Land Courts
Scottish Land Court Reports. 1913–
Scottish Law Commission
Smith's Leading Cases. 13ed. 1929
Statute Law Committee
Stuart's Appeal Cases (Quebec, Can.) 1810–53
Subscriber Line Charge
S.L.C.App. Stuart's Appeal Cases (Quebec) 1810–53
S.L.C.R. Scottish Land Court Reports. 1913–
S.L.C.R.App. Scottish Land Court Reports (Appendix)
S.L.Co.R. Appendices of Proceedings of the Scottish Land Court
S.L.F.C. Sierra Leone Full Court Reports
S.L.G. Scottish Law Gazette. 1933–
S.L.G.B. Society of Local Government Barristers
SLIC Scottish Library and Information Council
S.L.J. Scottish Law Journal. 1858–61
Southwestern Law Journal (USA) 1947–
Straits Law Journal (Mal.) 1888–92
S.L.J.R. Sudan Law Journal and Reports. 1956–
S.L.L. Society of Labour Lawyers
S.L.L.R. Sierra Leone Law Reports
s.l.p. sine legitima prole (Lat.) without lawful issue
S.L.R. Saskatchewan Law Reports (Can.) 1907–31
Scottish Land Court Reports. 1913–
Scottish Law Reporter. 1865–1925
Scottish Law Review and Sheriff Court Reports. 1885–1963
Seychelles Law Reports. 1921–23
Sind Law Reporter (Pak.) 1907–
Singapore Law Reports. 1946–49, 1953–56
Southern Law Review (St Louis, Mo.) 1875–83
Special Leave Refused
Stanford Law Review. 1948–
Statute Law Reform
Statute Law Revision
Student Law Review
Sudan Law Reports
Sydney Law Review (Aus.) 1953–
S.L.R.Act Statute Law Reform Act
S.L.R.Leic. Leicester's Straits Law Reports (Mal.) 1827–77
S.L.R.Leicester Leicester's Straits Law Reports (Mal.) 1827–77
S.L.R.N.S. Straits Law Reports, New Series (Mal.) 1891–92
S.L.Rev. Scottish Law Review & Sheriff Court Reports. 1885–1963
S.L.S. Statute Law Society
S.L.S.D.R.S.G. Special Legislative Supplement to the Democratic Republic of the Sudan Gazette
S.L.T. Scots Law Times (Scot.) 1893–
Scots Law Times Reports. 1950–
S.L.T.(Land Ct.) Scots Law Times Land Court Reports. 1950–

S.L.T.(Lands Tr.) Scots Law Times Lands Tribunal Reports
S.L.T.(Lyon Ct.) Scots Law Times Lyon Court Reports. 1950–
S.L.T.(News) Scots Law Times, News section
S.L.T.(Notes) Scots Law Times Notes of Recent Decisions. 1946–
S.L.T.(Sh.Ct.) Scots Law Times, Sheriff Court Reports. 1893–
S.L.U.L.J. Saint Louis University Law Journal
S.M. Senior Magistrate
Stipendiary Magistrate
S.M.A. Sociaal Maandblad Arbeid (Neth.)
S.M.C.D. Supreme Military Council Decree (Ghana) 1975
SMGS Agreement on International Rail Transport of Goods
S.M.H. Sydney Morning Herald (Aus.) 1831–
SMIL Statistics and Market Intelligence Library (BOTB)
S.M.L.J. St. Mary's Law Journal (USA) 1969–
S.M.M.& T. Society of Motor Manufacturing & Traders
s.m.p. sine mascula prole (Lat.) without male issue
SMP Statutory Maternity Pay
SMPS Agreement on International Passenger Traffic
S.N. Session Notes (Scot.) 1925–48
Statutes of Newfoundland
S.N.A. Sudder Nizamat Adawlut Reports (Bengal, India) 1805–50
S.N.A.Beng. Sudder Nizmut Adawlut Reports (Bengal, India) 1805–50
S.N.A.Beng.(N.S.) Sudder Nizamut Adawlut Reports, New Series (Bengal, India) 1851–59
SNHAT Shelter National Housing Aid Trust
SNIP Scottish National Information Plan
SNK Council of People's Commissars (USSR)
SNOP Statement of National Objectives and Priorities
s.o. siehe oben (Ger.) see above
SO Successionsordning (Swed.) Fundamental law on succession to the throne. 1810
Sveriges overenskommelser med frammande makter (Swed.) Agreements with foreign powers. 1912–
S.O. Scottish Office
Solicitor's Opinion
Standing Order
Stationery Office
Statistical Office
S.O.A.S. School of Oriental & African Studies (London University)
S.O.A.S.Bull. SOAS Bulletin
S.O.E. State Owned Enterprise (N.Z.)
S.O.G.A.T. Society of Graphical and Allied Trades
S.O.L.Rev. School of Law Review (Can.) 1942–55
SOU Statens Offentliga Utredningar (Swedish Committee reports)
S.of C. Statutes of Canada
S.of S. Secretary of State
s.p. same point
same principle
senza pagina (It.)
sine prole (Lat.) without issue
SP Single Payment
SP 4 Public Record Office, state papers of Henry VIII signed by stamp
S.p.A. Public company (It.)
S.P.C. South Pacific Commission (UN)
S.P.G. Special Patrol Group
SPIDR Society of Professionals for Dispute Resolution (USA)
S.P.J. Senior Puisne Judge
s.p.l. sine prole legitime (Lat.) without legitimate issue
S.P.L.P. Scottish Planning Law and Practice
s.p.m. sine prole mascula (Lat.) without male issue
s.p.m.s. sine prole mascula superstite (Lat.) without surviving male issue
S.p.O. Sociedade por Quotas (Port.)

S.P.O. Statutory Publications Office

s.p.s. sine prole superstite (Lat.) without surviving issue

S.P.T.L. Society of Public Teachers of Law

S.P.U.C. Society for the Protection of Unborn Children

S.Pac.L.R. South Pacific Law Review (Aus.) 1948–50

S.Q.R. State Reports (Queensland, Aus.) 1905–

S.R. Liechtensteinisches Zivilgesetzbuch, Sachenrecht

New South Wales State Reports. 1901–

New York State Reporter. 1886–96

Senate Resolution (USA)

Southern Rhodesia

Southern Rhodesia Law Reports. 1911–

Statutes of the Realm. 1810–24

Statutes Revised

Statutory Regulations (N.Z.) 1936–

Statutory Rules (Aus.) 1901–

Summary Record

Supreme Court of Quebec Reports

S.R.C. Stuart's Appeal Cases (Québec) 1810–53

S.R.C.C. strikes, riots and civil commotions

S.R.H.C.R. Southern Rhodesia High Court Reports. 1911–

SRL Private company (It.)

Sveriges Rikes Lag (Swed.) statute book

S.R.(N.S.W.) New South Wales State Reports. 1901–70

S.R.(N.S.W.)B.& P. State Reports, Bankruptcy and Probate (N.S.W., Aus.) 1901–70

S.R.(N.S.W.)Eq. State Reports, Equity (N.S.W., Aus.) 1901–70

SRO Self regulating organisation

S.R.O.& S.I.Rev. Statutory Rules and Orders and Statutory Instruments Revised

S.R.Q. State Reports Queensland (Aus.) 1905–

S.R.R. Scots Revised Reports

S.R.(W.A.) State Reports (Western Australia) 1980–

S.R.& O. Statutory Rules and Orders

S.Rept. Senate Committee Reports (USA)

S.Res. Senate Resolution (USA)

s.s. sworn statement

S.S. Secretary of State

Selden Society

Silvernail's New York Supreme Court Reports. 1889–90

Social Security

Steamship

Straits Settlements

Synopsis Series of the United States Treasury Decisions

SSAC Social Security Advisory Committee

S.S.B. Scots Styles Book

S.S.C. Sandford's Superior Court Reports, New York (3–7 N.Y.S.Ct.) 1847–52

Sarawak Supreme Court Reports

Scots Session Cases

State Services Commission (N.Z.)

S.S.C.R. Sind Sudder Court Reports (India)

SSG Bundesgesetz flber die Seeschiffahrt unter der Schweizerflagge (Switz.) 1953

S.S.L. Scandinavian Studies in Law

S.S.L.R. Straits Settlements Law Reports (Mal.) 1867–1942

S.S.L.R.Supp. Straits Settlements Law Reports, Supplement (Mal.) 1897–99

SSP Statutory Sick Pay

S.S.R. Social Security Reporter (Aus.) 1981–

S.S.R.C. Social Science Research Council

SS&D Soviet Statutes and Decisions

S.T. State Trials. 1163–1820

STARS Settlement Transfer and Registration Scheme

S.T.C. Sales Tax Cases (India) 1950–

Simon's Tax Cases. 1973–

Society for Technical Communication (USA)

State Tax Cases (CCH) (USA) 1918–44

S.T.D. Synopsis Decisions, U.S. Treasury
STEP Selective Temporary Employment Programme
STEur Série des Traités Européens (Council of Europe)
S.T.L.J. South Texas Law Journal. 1955–
S.T.U.C. Scottish Trades Union Congress
S.Teind Shaw's Teind Court Decisions (Scot.) 1821–31
S.Tex.L.J. South Texas Law Journal. 1955–
s.u. siehe unten (Ger.) see below
S.U.L.Rev. Southern University Law Review (USA)
SUVA Schweizerische Unfallversicherungsanstalt (Switz.)
S.V.A.R. Stuart's Vice-Admiralty Reports (Quebec) 1836–74
SVG Bundesgesetz flber den Strassenverkehr (Switz.) 1958
s.v.p. s'il vous plaît (Fr.) please
S.W. South Western Reporter (National Reporter System (USA) 1887–
S.W.2d. South Western Reporter, Second Series
S.W.A. Reports of the High Court of South West Africa. 1920–46
South West Africa
SWAT Special Weapons and Tactics
SWIFT Society for Worldwide Interbank Financial Telecommunications
S.W.L.J. South Western Law Journal & Reporter (Nashville, USA) 1844
S.W.L.Rev. Southwestern Law Review (USA) 1916–18
S.W.Law J. Southwestern Law Journal & Reporter (Nashville, USA) 1844
S.W.Poli.Sci.Q. Southwestern Political and Social Science Quarterly (USA)
S.W.Rep. South Western Reporter (cited S.W.) (USA) 1887–
SZ. Sammlung der Entscheidungen des Österreichischen Obersten Gerichtshofes in Zivil- und Justizverwaltungssachen (Austria)
S.& A. Saunders and Austin's Locus Standi Reports. 1895–1904
S.& B. Saunders and Bidder's Locus Standi Reports. 1905–19
Smith and Batty's Irish King's Bench Reports. 1824–25
S.& C. Saunders & Cole's Bail Court Reports (82 RR) 1846–48
Swan & Critchfield's Revised Statutes (Ohio)
S.& C.Rev.St. Swan and Critchfield's Revised Statutes (Ohio)
S.& D. Shaw & Dunlop's Session Cases. 1st Series (Scot.) 1821–38
S.& G. Smale & Giffard's Reports (65 ER) 1852–71
Stone & Graham's Court of Referees Reports
Stone & Graham's Private Bills Reports. 1865
S.& L. Schoales and Lefroy's Irish Chancery Reports. 1802–06
S.& L.S. Social and Legal Studies
S.& M. Shaw & Maclean's Scotch Appeals (Scot.) 1835–38
Smedes & Marshall's Chancery Reports (Mississippi) 1840–43
Smedes & Marshall's Reports (9–22 Mississippi) 1843–50
S.& M.Ch. Smedes & Marshall's Mississippi Chancery Reports. 1840–43
S.& M.Chy. Smedes & Marshall's Mississippi Chancery Reports. 1840–43
S.& Mar. Smedes & Marshall's Mississippi Reports (9–22 Miss.) 1843–50
S.& S. Sausse & Scully's Irish Rolls Court Reports. 1837–40
Schip en Schade
Searle & Smith's Probate & Divorce Reports. 1859–60
Simons & Stuart's Vice-Chancellor's Reports (57 ER) 1822–26
Swan and Sayer, Revised Statutes of Ohio
S.& Sc. Sausse & Scully's Irish Rolls Court Reports. 1837–40

S.& Sm. Searle & Smith's Probate & Divorce Reports. 1859–60
S.& T. Swabey & Tristram's Probate and Divorce Reports (164 ER) 1858–65
Sächs.Arch. Sächsisches Archiv für Rechtsflege
Sachse N.M. Sachse's Minutes, Norwich Mayoralty Court
Sad.Pa.Cas. Sadler's Cases (Pennsylvania) 1885–88
Sad.Pa.Cs. Sadler's Cases (Pennsylvania) 1885–88
Sadler(Pa.) Sadler's Cases (Pennsylvania) 1885–88
Saint Saint's Digest of Registration Cases. 5ed. 1910
Sal. Salinger's Reports (88–117 Iowa)
Sal.Comp.Cr. Salaman, Liquidation and Composition with Creditors. 2ed. 1882
Salk. Salkeld's King's Bench Reports (91 ER) 1689–1712
Sales. Salesianum (It.) 1939–
Salm.Abr. Salmon's Abridgment of State Trials. 2ed. 1741
Salm.St.Tr. Salmon's Edition of the State Trials
San. Sanford's Reports (59 Alabama)
San D.L.R. San Diego Law Review. 1964–
San Diego L.Rev. San Diego Law Review. 1964–
San F.L.J. San Francisco Law Journal. 1877–78
San Fr.L.B. San Francisco Law Bulletin
San Fr.L.J. San Francisco Law Journal. 1964–
San Fran.L.B. San Francisco Law Bulletin
San Fran.L.J. San Francisco Law Journal. 1877–78
San Fran.Law Bull. San Francisco Law Bulletin
San.Just. Sanders' Edition of Justinian's Institutes
Sanb.& B.Ann.St. Sanborn and Berryman's Annotated Statutes (Wisconsin)
Sand. Sandford New York Superior Court Reports (3–7 N.Y.S.Ct.) 1847–52
Sand.Ch. Sandford's New York Chancery Reports. 1843–47
Sand.Chy. Sandford's New York Chancery Reports. 1843–47
Sand.Essays Sanders, Essays on Uses and Trusts. 5ed. 1844
Sand.I.Rep. Sandwich Islands (Hawaii) Reports
Sand.Uses and Trusts Sanders on Uses and Trusts. 5ed. 1844
Sand.& H.Dig. Sandels & Hill's Digest of Statutes (Arkansas)
Sandf. Sandford's Reports (3–7 New York Superior) 1847–52
Sandf.Ch. Sandford's New York Chancery Reports. 1843–47
Sandf.Ch.(N.Y.) Sandford's New York Chancery Reports. 1843–47
Sandf.(N.Y.) Sandford's Reports (3–7 New York Superior) 1847–52
Sandf.Suc. Sandford, Heritable Succession in Scotland
Sandl.St.Pap. Sandler's State Papers
Sanf. Sanford's Reports (59 Alabama)
Sanken Sangyo Mondai Kenkyukai (Japan) Council on Industrial Policy
Santa Clara L.R. Santa Clara Law Review. 1975–
Santa Clara Law. Santa Clara Lawyer (USA) 1961–75
Sanyal Sanyal's Criminal Cases between Natives and Europeans (India) 1796–1895
Sar. Saraswathi's Privy Council Judgments (India) 1825–1910
Sar.Ch.Sen. Saratoga Chancery Sentinel (New York) 1841–47
Sar.F.C.L. Sarbah, Fanti Customary Laws (Ghana) 2ed. 1904
Sar.F.L.R. Sarbah's Fanti Law Cases (Ghana) 1845–1903
Sar.F.N.C. Sarbah, Fanti National Constitution (Ghana)
Sarat.Ch.Sent. Saratoga Chancery Sentinel (New York) 1841–47
Sarbah Sarbah's Fanti Law Reports (Ghana) 1845–1903

Sarbah F.C. Sarbah, Fanti Customary Laws (Ghana) 2ed. 1904

Sask. Saskatchewan
Saskatchewan Law Reports (Can.) 1908–31

Sask.B.R. Saskatchewan Bar Review (Can.) 1936–66

Sask.B.Rev. Saskatchewan Bar Review (Can.) 1936–66

Sask.Bar Rev. Saskatchewan Bar Review (Can.) 1936–66

Sask.Dec. Saskatchewan Decisions (Can.) 1975–

Sask.Gaz. Saskatchewan Gazette (Can.)

Sask.L.R. Saskatchewan Law Reports (Can.) 1908–31

Sask.L.R.C. Saskatchewan Law Reform Commission

Sask.L.Rev. Saskatchewan Law Review (Can.) 1967–

Sask.Rev.Stat. Saskatchewan Revised Statutes (Can.)

Sask.Stat. Saskatchewan Statutes (Can.)

Sau. All India Reporter, Saurashtra. 1950–57

Sau.L.R. Saurashtra Law Reports (India) 1952–55

Sau.& Sc. Sausse & Scully's Irish Rolls Court Reports. 1837–40

Sauls. Reports in the time of Saulsbury (5–6 Delaware)

Saund. Saunders' King's Bench Reports (85 ER) 1666–73

Saund.Ass. Saunders, Assault and Battery. 1842

Saund.B.C. Saunders & Cole's Bail Court Reports (82 RR) 1846–48

Saund.Bast. Saunders, Affiliation and Bastardy. 11ed. 1915

Saund.Mag.Pr. Saunders, Magistrates' Court Practice. 6ed. 1902

Saund.Mil.L. Saunders, Militia Law. 4ed. 1855

Saund.Mun.Reg. Saunders, Municipal Registration. 2ed. 1873

Saund.Neg. Saunders, Negligence. 2ed. 1878

Saund.Pl.& Ev. Saunders, Pleading & Evidence in Civil Actions. 2ed. 1851

Saund.Prec. Saunders, Precedents of Indictments. 3ed. 1904

Saund.War. Saunders, Warranties and Representations. 1874

Saund.& A. Saunders & Austin's Locus Standi Reports. 1805–1904

Saund.& Aust. Saunders & Austin's Locus Standi Reports. 1895–1904

Saund.& B. Saunders and Bidder's Locus Standi Reports. 1905–19

Saund.& C. Saunders and Cole's Bail Court Reports (82 RR) 1846–48

Saund.& M. Saunders & Macrae's County Courts & Insolvency Cases. 1852–58

Saund.& Mac. Saunders & Macrae's County Court & Insolvency Cases. 1852–58

Sausse & Sc. Sausse & Scully's Irish Rolls Court Reports. 1837–40

Sav. Savile's Common Pleas Reports (123 ER) 1580–94

Sav.Conf.Law Savigny, Conflict of Laws. 2ed. 1880

Sav.Pos. Savigny, Possessions. 6ed. 1848

Sav.Priv. Trial of the Savannah Privateers

Savigny,Hist.Rom.Law Savigny's History of the Roman Law

Savile Savile's Common Pleas Reports (123 ER) 1580–94

Saw. Sawyer's Circuit Court Reports (USA) 1870–91

Sax. Saxton's New Jersey Chancery Reports (1 N.J.Eq.) 1830–32

Saxt. Saxton's New Jersey Chancery Reports (1 N.J.Eq.) 1830–32

Saxt.Ch. Saxton's Chancery Reports (1 N.J.Eq.) 1830–32

Say. Sayer's King's Bench Reports (96 Er) 1751–56

Sayer Sayer's King's Bench Reports (96 ER) 1751–56

Sayles'Ann.Civ.St. Sayles' Annotated Civil Statutes (Texas)

Sayles' Civ.St. Sayles' Revised Civil Statutes (Texas)

Sayles'Rev.Civ.St. Sayles' Revised Civil Statutes (Texas)
Sayles'St. Sayles' Revised Civil Statutes (Texas)
Sayles'Supp. Supplement to Sayles' Annotated Civil Statutes (Texas)
Sc. Scaccaria (Exchequer)
Scammon's Illinois Reports (2–5 Ill.) 1832–43
Scandinavia(n)
Scotland
Scots
Scottish
Scott's Reports Common Pleas (41–54 RR) 1834–40
Sc.Costs Scott, A.B.C. Guide to Costs. 2ed. 1910
Sc.Cts. Scottish Courts
Sc.Jur. Scottish Jurist. 1829–73
Sc.L.J. Scottish Law Journal and Sheriff Court Record. 1858–61
Sc.L.M. Scottish Law Magazine and Sheriff Court Reporter. 1862–67
Sc.L.R. Scottish Law Reporter. 1865–1925
Scottish Law Review and Sheriff Court Reports. 1885–1963
Sc.L.Rep. Scottish Law Reporter. 1865–1925
Sc.L.Rev. Scottish Law Review and Sheriff Court Reports. 1885–1963
Sc.L.T. Scots Law Times. 1893–
Sc.La.R. Scottish Land Court Reports (Supplement to the Scottish Law Review) 1913–
Sc.La.Rep.App. Appendices to Scottish Land Court Reports
Sc.Mun.App.Rep. Scotch Munitions Appeals Reports
Sc.N.R. Scott's New Reports Common Pleas (56–66 RR) 1840–45
Sc.Pos. Scuola Positiva (It.) 1891–1972
Sc.R.R. Scots Revised Reports Superior Courts. 1707–1873, 1898–1908
Sc.Rev.Rept. Scots Revised Reports. 1707–1873, 1898–1908
Sc.Sess.Cas. Scotch Court of Session Cases
Sc.Stud.Criminol. Scandinavian Studies in Criminology. 1965–
Sc.Stud.Law Scandinavian Studies in Law. 1957–
Sc.& Div. Law Reports, Scotch and Divorce Appeals. 1866–75
Sc.& Div.App. Law Reports, Scotch and Divorce Appeals. 1866–75
Scac. Scaccaria Curia (Court of Exchequer)
Scam. Scammon's Illinois Reports (2–5 Ill.) 1832–44
Scan.Studies Scandinavian Studies in Law. 1957–
Scand.Stud.Criminol. Scandinavian Studies in Criminology. 1965–
Scand.Stud.Law Scandinavian Studies in Law. 1957–
Scarman Report Home Office Report of Inquiry into Red Lion Square Disorders of June 15, 1974 (Cmnd. 5919) 1975
Northern Ireland Report of the Tribunal of Inquiry into Violence and Civil Disturbances in 1969 (Cmd. 566) 1972
Sch. schedule
school
Sch.Aq.R. Schultes, Aquatic Rights. 1811
SchG Schiedsgericht (Ger.) arbitration court
Sch.L.R. Schuylkill Legal Record (Pennsylvania) 1879–
Sch.Reg. Schuylkill Register (Pennsylvania) 1933–45
Sch.& Lef. Schoales & Lefroy's Irish Chancery Reports. 1802–06
Schalk Schalk's Jamaica Law Reports. 1855–76
Sched. Schedule
Scher. Scherer, New York Miscellaneous Reports (22–47 N.Y. Misc.)
Schlesw.-Holst.Anz. Schleswig-Holstein Anzeiger
Schm.Exp. Schmitthoff, Export Trade. 7ed. 1980

Schm.L.J. Schmidt, Law Journal (New Orleans)
Schoales & L. Schoales and Lefroy's Irish Chancery Reports. 1802–06
School of L.R. School of Law Review, Toronto University (Can.) 1942–55
Schuy.Leg.Rec.(Pa.) Schuylkill Legal Record (Pennsylvania) 1879–
Schuy.Reg.(Pa.) Schuylkill Register (Pennsylvania) 1933–45
Schuyl.Leg.Rec. Schuylkill Legal Record (Pennsylvania) 1879–
Schuyl.Leg.Reg. Schuylkill Legal Register (Pennsylvania) 1933–45
Schw.Jb.Int.R. Schweizerisches Jahrbuch für internationales Recht (Switz.)
Schw.Z.Str. Schweizerische Zeitschrift für Strafrecht (Switz.)
Schwarz.Int.L. Schwarzenberger, International Law
Schwarz.Man.Int. Schwarzenberger, Manual of International Law. 6ed. 1976
Schwz.Jahrb Schweizer Jahrbuch für internationales Recht (Switz.)
Sci. Science(s)
Sci.Fa. Scire facias (revival of judgment)
Sci.Iur.(Portugal) Scientia Iuridica, Revista de Direito Comparado Portugues e Brasileiro (Port.)
Sci.Jur.(Romania) Sciences Juridiques – Legal Sciences (Romania)
Sco. Scott's Common Pleas Reports (41–54 RR) 1834–40
Sco.Bankers Mag. The Scottish Bankers Magazine
Sco.Costs Scott, Costs in the High Court. 4ed. 1880
Sco.N.R. Scott's New Reports, Common Pleas (56–66 RR) 1840–45
Scot. Scotland
Scots
Scottish
Scot.App.Rep. Scottish Appeal Reports
Scot.Jur. Scottish Jurist. 1829–73
Scot.L.J. Scottish Law Journal & Sheriff Court Record. 1858–61
Scot.L.M. Scottish Law Magazine & Sheriff Court Reporter. 1862–67
Scot.L.Mag. Scottish Law Magazine & Sheriff Court Reporter. 1862–67
Scot.L.R. Scottish Law Reporter. 1865–1925
Scottish Law Review and Sheriff Court Reports. 1885–1963
Scot.L.Rep. Scottish Law Reporter. 1865–1925
Scot.L.Rev. Scottish Law Review and Sheriff Court Reports. 1885–1963
Scot.L.T. Scots Law Times. 1893–
Scot.Law.Com. Scottish Law Commission
Scot.Law.J. Scottish Law Journal and Sheriff Court Record. 1858–61
Scots L.T. Scots Law Times. 1893–
Scots L.T.R. Scots Law Times Reports
Scots R.R. Scots Revised Reports. 1707–1873, 1898–1908
Scott Scott's Common Pleas Reports (41–54 RR) 1834–40
Scott's Reports (25, 26 New York Civil Procedure)
Scott Festschrift Perspectives of Law, ed. by R. Pound, E.N. Griswold & A.E. Sutherland. 1964
Scott J. Scott's Common Pleas Reports (41–54 RR) 1834–40
Scott N.R. Scott's New Common Pleas Reports (56–66 RR) 1840–45
Scott, Reports, vol.I J.B. Scott, The Hague Court Reports. 1916
Scott, Reports, vol.II J.B. Scott, The Hague Court Reports, Second Series. 1932
Scr.L.T. Scranton Law Times (Pennsylvania) 1873–85
Scrat.Bdg.Soc. Scratchley, Building Societies. 5ed. 1883
Scrat.Life Ass. Scratchley, Life Assurance. 13ed. 1887
Scrat.& Bra. Scratchley & Brabook, Building Societies. 2ed. 1882
Scriv.Cop. Scriven, Copyholds. 7ed. 1896
Scriven Scriven, Copyholds. 7ed. 1896
Scrut.Charter. Scrutton, Charterparties. 18ed. 1974

Scrutton Scrutton, Charterparties. 18ed. 1974
Sea.Vend. Seaborne, Vendors & Purchasers. 9ed. 1926
Sea.& Sm. Searle & Smith's Probate & Divorce Reports. 1859–60
Searle Searle's Supreme Court Reports (Cape, S.A.) 1850–67
Searle Dig. Searle, Minnesota Digest
Searle & Sm. Searle & Smith's Probate & Divorce Reports. 1859–60
Seb.Tr.M. Sebastian, Trade Marks. 5ed. 1911
Sec. Secretary
Section
Secundum (Lat.) According to
Securities
Secus (Lat.)
Sec.Bk.Judg. Huxley's Second Book of Judgments. 1675
Sec.L.Rev. Securities Law Review (USA) 1969–
Sec.Leg. Secundum Legum (Lat.) according to law
Sec.of State Secretary of State
Sec.reg. Secundum regulam (Lat.) according to rule
Sec.Reg.Guide Securities Regulation Guide (P–H) (USA)
Sec.Reg.L.J. Securities Regulation Law Journal (USA) 1973–
Sec.Reg.& L.Rep. Securities Regulation & Law Reports (USA)
Secd.pt.Edw.III Year Books, Part III
Secd.pt.H.VI Year Books, Part VIII
Secy. Secretary
Sedg.L.Cas. Sedgwick's Leading Cases on Damages
Sedgwick's Leading Cases on Real Property
Sedg.Stat.Law Sedgwick on Statutory and Constitutional Law
Sedg.& W.Tit. Sedgwick and Wait on the Trial of Title to Land
Seign.Rep. Lower Canada Seignorial Reports (Quebec) 1856
Sel.App.Beng. Selected Appeals, Sudder Dewanny Adawlut (Bengal, India) up to 1804
Sel.Ca.t.King Select Cases in Chancery tempore King (25 ER) 1724–33
Sel.Cas. Select Cases, Central Provinces (India)
Sel.Cas.Ch. Select Cases in Chancery. 1685–1698
Sel.Cas.Ch.(t.King) Select Cases in Chancery tempore King (25 ER) 1724–33
Sel.Cas.d.A. Select Cases, Sudder Dewanny Adawlut (India)
Sel.Cas.Ev. Select Cases in Evidence (Strange) 1698–1732
Sel.Cas.K.B.Edw.I. Select Cases in King's Bench under Edward I (Sayles)
Sel.Cas.N.F. Select Cases, Newfoundland. 1817–28
Sel.Cas.N.W.P. Select Cases, North West Province (India)
Sel.Cas.N.Y. Yates' Select Cases (New York) 1809
Sel.Cas.S.D.A. Select Cases, Sudder Dewanny Adawlut (India)
Sel.Cas.t.Br. Cooper's Select Cases tempore Brougham. 1833–34
Sel.Cas.t.King Select Cases in Chancery tempore King (25 ER) 1724–33
Sel.Cas.t.Nap. Select Cases tempore Napier (Ire.) 1858–59
Sel.Cas.with Opin. Select Cases with Opinions, by a Solicitor
Sel.Ch.Cas. Select Cases in Chancery tempore King ed Macnaghten (25 ER) 1724–33
Sel.Com. Select Committee
Sel.Dec.Bomb. Morris' Sudder Dewanny Adawlut Reports (Bombay, India) 1847–54
Sel.Dec.Madr. Select Decrees, Sudder Dewanny Adawlut (Madras, India) 1805–47
Sel.N.P. Selwyn's Law of Nisi Prius. 13ed. 1869
Sel.Off.Ch. Selden, Office of Lord Chancellor. 1671
Sel.Pr. Sellon's Practice of the Courts

of King's Bench and Common Pleas. 2ed. 1798

Seld. Selden's Reports (5–10 new York) 1851–54

Seld.Fl. Selden, Dissertation annexed to Fleta

Seld.J. Selden, Jani Anglorum. 1610

Seld.J.P. Selden, Judicature in Parliaments. 1681

Seld.Mar.Cl. Selden, Mare Clausum. 1635

Seld.Notes Selden's Notes, New York Court of Appeals. 1852–54

Seld.Soc. Selden Society Yearbook

Seld.Tit.Hon. Selden's Titles of Honour. 1614

Sell.Pr. Sellon's Practice of the Courts of King's Bench and Common Pleas. 2ed. 1798

Sell.Prac. Sellon's Practice of the Courts of King's Bench and Common Pleas. 2ed. 1798

Selw.N.P. Selwyn, Law of Nisi Prius. 13ed. 1869

Selw.& Barn. Barnewall & Alderson's King's Bench Reports, 1st Part (106 ER) 1817–22

Sem.Jud. La Semaine Judiciaire (Switz.)

Sem.Jur. La Semaine Juridique (Jurisclasseur périodique) (Fr.) 1926–

Sem.Jur.Cahiers Entr. Semaine Juridique. Cahiers de Droit de l'Enterprise (Fr.)

Sem.Jurid. La Semaine Juridique (Jurisclasseur périodique) (Fr.) 1926–

Seman.Jud. Semanario Judicial de la Federación. Sentencias dictadas por la Suprema Corte (Mexico)

Sen. Senate
Senator
Senior

Sen.Doc. Senate Document (USA)

Sen.J. Senate Journal (USA)

Sen.Jo. Senate Journal (USA)

Sen.Rep. Senate Report (USA)

sent. sentenza (It.) decision, judgment

Seoul L.J. Seoul Law Journal (S. Korea)

Sep.Op. Separate Opinion

Ser. Series

Serg.& Lowb. English Common Law Reports, American Reprint edited by Sergeant & Lowber

Serg.& Lowb.Rep. English Common Law Reports, American Reprint edited by Sergeant & Lowber

Serg.& R. Sergeant & Rawle's Pennsylvania Reports. 1814–28

Serg.& Raw. Sergeant & Rawle's Pennsylvania Reports. 1814–28

Serg.& Rawl. Sergeant & Rawle's Pennsylvania Reports. 1814–28

Serv. Service

Sess. Session

Sess.Acts Session Acts

Sess.Ca. Session Cases (Scotland) 1821–
Session Cases touching Settlements (93 ER) 1710–48

Sess.Cas. Session Cases (Scotland) 1821–
S. 1st series (Shaw) 1821–38
D. 2nd Series (Dunlop) 1838–62
M. 3rd Series (Macpherson) 1862–73
R. 4th Series (Rettie) 1873–98
F. 5th Series (Fraser) 1898–1906
(6 Ser.) 6th Series. 1906–
Session Cases touching Settlements (93 ER) 1710–48

Sess.Cas.K.B. Session cases touching Settlements (93 ER) 1710–48

Sess.Cas.Sc. Court of Session Cases (Scotland)

Sess.Laws Session Laws

Sess.N. Session Notes (Scot.) 1925–48

Sess.Pap.C.C. Central Criminal Court Sessional Papers. 1834–1913

Sess.Pap.C.C.C. Central Criminal Court Sessional Papers. 1834–1913

Sess.Pap.O.B. Central Criminal Court Sessional Papers. 1834–1913

Seton Seton, Forms of Decrees, Judgments and Orders in Equity. 7ed. 1912

Seton Dec. Seton, Forms of Decrees, Judgments and Orders in Equity. 7ed. 1912

Seton Hall L.Rev. Seton Hall Law Review (USA) 1970–

Seton Hall Legis.J. Seton Hall Legislative Journal (USA)

Sett.Cas. Burrow's Settlement Cases. 1733–76
Cases of Settlements & Removals, King's Bench. 1710–42

Sett.& Rem. Burrows' Settlement Cases. 1733–76
Cases of Settlements & Removals, King's Bench. 1710–42

Seuff.Arch. J.A. Seuffert, Archiv für Entscheidungen der obersten Gerichte in den deutschen Staaten (Ger.)

Sev.App.Cas. Sevestre's Appeal Cases, High Court (Bengal, India) 1864–68

Sev.H.C. Sevestre's Appeal Cases, High Court (Bengal, India) 1864–68

Sev.S.D.A. Sevestre's Sudder Dewanny Adawlut Reports (Bengal, India) 1834–72

Sevestre Sevestre's Appeal Cases, High Court (Bengal, India) 1864–68

Sew.Cor. Sewell, Coroners. 1843

Sew.Sh. Sewell, Sheriff. 1842

Sex.L.Rep. Sexual Law Reporter (USA) 1975–

Sey.Merch.Sh. Seymour, Merchant Shipping Acts. 2ed. 1857

Seych.L.R. Seychelles Law Reports

sez. sezione (It.) division

Sez.Un. Full court (It.)

Sh. Shadforth's Reserved Judgments, Victoria (Aus.) 1846–51
Shand's Reports (11–41 South Carolina)
Shaw's Appeal Cases (Scot.) 1821–24
Shaw's Justiciary Cases (Scot.) 1848–52
Shaw's Session Cases (Scot.) 1821–38
Shaw's Teind Court Decisions (Scot.) 1821–31
G.B. Shaw's Vermont Reports (10, 11 Vt.)
W.G. Shaw's Vermont Reports (30–35 Vt.)
Sheil's Cape Times Law Reports (S.Afr.) 1891–1910
Sheldon's Reports (Buffalo, New York Superior Court) 1854–75
Shepherd's Reports (19–21, 24–41, 49–51,60, 63, 64 Alabama)
Shepherd's Select Cases (Alabama) 1861–63
Shepley's Reports (13–18, 21–30 Maine)
Sheriff
Shipp's Reports (66, 67 North Carolina)
Shirley's Reports (49–55 New Hampshire)
Shower's King's Bench Reports (89 ER) 1678–95
Shower's Parliamentary Cases (1 ER) 1694–99

Sh.App. Shaw's Appeals (Scot.) 1821–24

Sh.C. Sheriff's Court

Sh.Crim.Cas. Shaw's Justiciary Court Criminal Cases (Scot.) 1848–52

Sh.Ct. Sheriff Court (Scot.)

Sh.Ct.of Sess. Shaw's Session Cases (Scot.) 1821–38

Sh.Ct.Rep. Sheriff Court Reports (Scot.) 1885–1963

Sh.Dig. Shaw's Digest of Decisions (Scot.)

Sh.Jus. J. Shaw's Justiciary Cases (Scot.) 1848–52

Sh.Just. P. Shaw's Justiciary Decisions (Scot.) 1919–31

Sh.Litt. Shortt, Works of Literature. 2ed. 1884

Sh.Sc.App. Shaw's Scotch Appeals Cases. 1821–24

Sh.Teind Ct. Shaw's Teind Court Decisions (Scot.) 1821–31

Sh.W.& C. Shaw, Wilson & Courtenay's Scotch Appeals Reports (Wilson & Shaw's Reports) 1825–35

Sh.& Dunl. Shaw & Dunlop's Scotch Court of Session Reports, 1st Series. 1821–38

Sh.& Macl. Shaw & Maclean's Scotch Appeal Cases. 1835–38

Shad. Shadforth's Reports (Victoria, Aus.) 1846–51

Shan. Shannon's Unreported Tennessee Cases (Tenn.) 1847–94

Shan.Cas. Shannon's Unreported Tennessee Cases (Tenn.) 1847–94

Shand Shand's Reports (11–41 South Carolina)

Shand Pr. Shand, Practice of the Court of Session (Scot.)

Shannon Cas.(Tenn.) Shannon's Unreported Tennessee Cases. 1847–94

Shannon's Code Shannon's Annotated Code (Tennessee)

Shark.Elec. Sharkey, Practice of Election Committees. 2ed. 1866

Sharpe Calendar of Coroners Rolls of the City of London. 1350–70

Shars.Bl.Comm. Sharswood's Edition of Blackstone's Commentaries

Shars.Black. Sharswood's Edition of Blackstone's Commentaries

Shars.Tab.Ca. Sharswood's Table of Cases, Connecticut (USA)

Shaw Shaw's Appeal Cases (Scot.) 1821–24
Shaw's Justiciary Cases (Scot.) 1848–52
Shaw's Session Cases, 1st Series (Scot.) 1821–38
Shaw's Teind Court Decisions (Scot.) 1821–31
G.B. Shaw's Vermont Reports (10, 11 Vt.)
W.G. Shaw's Vermont Reports (30, 35 Vt.)

Shaw App. Shaw's Appeal Cases (Scot.) 1821–24

Shaw Crim.Cas. Shaw's Criminal Cases, Justiciary Court (Scot.) 1848–52

Shaw,D.& B. Shaw, Dunlop & Bell's Session Cases (1st Series) (Scot.) 1821–38

Shaw,D.& B.Supp. Shaw, Dunlop & Bell's Supplement, House of Lords Decisions (Scot.)

Shaw Dec. Shaw's Decisions, Session Cases, 1st Series (Scot.) 1821–38

Shaw Dunl.& B. Shaw, Dunlop & Bell, Session Cases (Scot.) 1821–38

Shaw(G.B.) G.B. Shaw's Reports (10, 11 Vermont)

Shaw H.L. Shaw's Appeal Cases, House of Lords (Scot.) 1821–24

Shaw J. John Shaw's Justiciary Cases (Scot.) 1848–52

Shaw Jus. John Shaw's Justiciary Cases (Scot.) 1848–52

Shaw P. Patrick Shaw's Teind Court Decisions (Scot.) 1821–31

Shaw P.L. Shaw's Parish Law. 8ed. 1895

Shaw Sc.App.Cas. Shaw's Scotch Appeal Cases, House of Lords. 1821–24

Shaw T.Cas. Shaw's Teind Court Decisions. 1821–31

Shaw Teind Shaw's Teind Court Decisions. 1821–31

Shaw.(Vt.) G.B. Shaw's Vermont Reports (10,11 Vt.)
W.G. Shaw's Vermont Reports (30,35 Vt.)

Shaw(W.G.) W.G. Shaw's Vermont Reports (30,35 Vt.)

Shaw,W.& C. Shaw, Wilson & Courtenay's Scotch Appeal Reports, House of Lords. 1825–35

Shaw & D. Shaw & Dunlop's Court of Session Reports, 1st Series (Scot.) 1821–38

Shaw & Dunl. Shaw & Dunlop's Court of Session Reports, 1st Series (Scot.) 1821–38

Shaw & M. Shaw & Maclean's Scotch Appeal Cases. 1835–38

Shaw & M.Sc.App.Cas. Shaw & Maclean's Scotch Appeal Cases. 1835–38

Shaw & Macl. Shaw & Maclean's Scotch Appeal Cases. 1835–38

Shear.Cont. Shearwood, Contract. 1897

Shear.Pers.Pr. Shearwood, Personal Property. 1882

Shear.R.Pr. Shearwood, Real Property. 3ed. 1885

Shear.& R.Neg. Shearman & Redfield on Negligence

Shearm.& Red.Neg. Shearman & Redfield on Negligence

Sheil Cape Times Reports edited by Sheil (S.Afr.) 1891–1910

Sheil Ir.Bar Sheil, Sketches of the Irish Bar

Shel.Bank. Shelford, Bankrupt and Insolvency Law. 3ed. 1862

Shel.Ca. Shelley's Cases in Coke's Reports, vol. 1

Shel.High. Shelford, Highways. 4ed. 1869

Shel.J.St.Com. Shelford, Joint Stock Companies. 2ed. 1870

Shel.Lun. Shelford, Lunatics. 2ed. 1847

Shel.M.& D. Shelford, Marriage and Divorce. 1841

Shel.Mort. Shelford, Mortmain and Charitable Uses. 1836

Shel.Prob. Shelford, Probate, Legacy etc. 2ed. 1861

Shel.R.Pr.St. Sheldon, Real Property Statutes. 9ed. 1893

Shel.Ry. Shelford, Railways. 4ed. 1869

Shel.Wills Shelford, Wills. 1838

Sheld. Sheldon's Reports, Superior Court of Buffalo (New York) 1854–75

Sheldon Sheldon's Reports, Superior Court of Buffalo (New York) 1854–75

Shelf.Lun. Shelford, Lunatics. 2ed. 1847

Shelf.Mar.& Div. Shelford, Marriage and Divorce. 1841

Shep. Shepherd's Reports (19–21, 24–41, 49–51, 60, 63, 64 Alabama)
Shepherd's Alabama Select Cases. 1861–73
Shepley's Reports (13–18, 21–30 Maine)

Shep.Prec. Sheppard, Precedent of Precedents. 9ed. 1825

Shep.Touch. Sheppard, Touchstone of Common Assurance. 8ed. 1826

Sheph.Sel.Cas. Shepherd's Select Cases (Alabama) 1861–63

Shepherd Shepherd's Reports (19–21, 24–41, 49–51, 60, 63, 64 Alabama)

Shepley Shepley's Reports (13–18, 21–30 Maine)

Sher.Ct.Rep. Sheriff Court Reporter
Sheriff Court Reporter (Scot.) 1885–

Shill.W.C. Shillman's Workmen's Compensation Cases (Ire.) 1934–38

Ship.Gaz. Shipping Gazette, London

Shipp Shipp's Reports (66–67 North Carolina)

Shir.Cr.L. Shirley, Sketch of the Criminal Law. 2ed. 1889

Shir.Mag.L. Shirley, Magisterial Law. 2ed. 1896

Shirl. Shirley's Reports (49–55 New Hampshire)

Shirl.L.C. Shirley's Leading Cases in the Common Law. 11ed. 1931

Shirley Shirley's Reports (49–55 New Hampshire)

Shoji Homu Shoji Homu (Commercial Law) (Japan)

Shome L.R. Shome's Law Reporter (India) 1877–81

Shortt.Inf. Shortt, Informations. 1887

Shortt Inform. Shortt, Informations. 1887

Shortt Lit. Shortt, Literature and Art. 2ed. 1884

Show. Shower's King's Bench Reports, ed. Butt (89ER) 1768–95
Shower's Parliamentary Cases (1 ER) 1694–99

Show.K.B. Shower's King's Bench Reports, ed. Butt (89 ER) 1678–95

Show.P.C. Shower's Parliamentary Cases (1 ER) 1694–99

Show.Parl.Cas. Shower's Parliamentary Cases (1 ER) 1694–99

Shower K.B. Shower's King's Bench Reports (89 ER) 1678–95

Shower P.C. Shower's Parliamentary Cases (1 ER) 1694–99

Sibert Sibert, Traité de droit international public. 1951

Sick. Sickels' Reports (46–85 New York Court of Appeals)

Sick.Min.Dec. Sickels' U.S. Mining Law and Decisions

Sick.Op. Sickels' Opinions of the New York Attorney-Generals

Sid. Siderfin's King's Bench Reports (82 ER) 1657–70

Siderfin, Reports T. Siderfin, Les reports des divers special cases argue et adjudge en le Court del Bank le Roy. 1683–84

Sierra Leone L.R. Law Reports (Sierra Leone) 1912–24

Sierra Leone L.Rec. Law Recorder (Sierra Leone) 1922–45
Silv. Silvernail's Court of Appeals Reports (New York) 1886–92
Silvernail's Reports (9–14 New York Criminal Reports)
Silvernail's Supreme Court Reports. 1889–90
Silv.A. Silvernail's Court of Appeals Reports (New York) 1886–92
Silv.App. Silvernail's Court of Appeals Reports (New York) 1886–92
Silv.Cit. Silvernail's New York Citations
Silv.Ct.App.(N.Y.) Silvernail's Court of Appeals Reports (New York) 1886–90
Silv.Sup. Silvernail's Supreme Court Reports (New York) 1889–90
Silv.Unrep. Silvernail's Unreported Cases (New York)
Sim. Simmons' Reports (95–97, 99 Wisconsin)
Simons' Vice Chancellor's Reports (57–60 ER) 1826–50
Sim.Dig. Simmons, Wisconsin Digest
Sim.Dig.Pat.Dec. Simonds, Digest of Patent Office Decisions (USA)
Sim.N.S. Simons' Vice-Chancellor's Reports, New Series (61 ER) 1850–52
Sim.Ry.Acc. Simon, Law Relating to Railway Accidents. 1862–
Sim.& C. Simmons & Conover's Reports (99–100 Wisconsin)
Sim.& S. Simons & Stuart's Vice-Chancellor's Reports (57 ER) 1822–26
Sim.& St. Simons & Stuart's Vice Chancellor's Reports (57 ER) 1822–26
Sim.& Stu. Simons & Stuart's Vice-Chancellor's Reports (57 ER) 1822–26
Simla All India Reporter, Simla. 1951
Simp.Inf. Simpson, Infants. 4ed. 1926
Sinclair Sinclair's Manuscript Decisions, Session Cases (Scot.)
Sinclair Report Review of Scottish child care law (Child Care Law Group) 1990
Sind All India Reporter, Sind. 1914–50
Indian Rulings, Sind. 1929–47
Sind,Pak. Sind, Pakistan
Sing.L.R. Singapore Law Review
Singapore J.Legal Stud. Singapore Journal of Legal Studies
Singapore L.Rev. Singapore Law Review
Singer Prob.Cas.(Pa.) Singer's Probate Cases (Pennsylvania) 1901–04
Singers Singer's Probate Cases (Pennsylvania) 1901–04
Sir J.S. Sir John Strange's Reports, 1716–49
Sir L.Jenk. Wynne's Life of Sir Leoline Jenkins. 1724
Sir T.J. Sir Thomas Jones' Reports, King's Bench & Common Pleas (84 ER) 1667–85
Sir T.Ray Sir T. Raymond's King's Bench & Common Pleas Reports (83 ER) 1660–84
Sirey Recueil général des lois et des arrêts (founded by Sirey)
Six Circ. Cases on the Six Circuits (Ire.) 1841–43
SjoL Sjolag (Swed.) maritime law
Skene Sir John Skene's De Verborum Significatione. 7ed. 1683
Skene de Verb.Sig. Sir John Skene's De Verborum Significtione. 7ed. 1683
Skill.Pol.Rep. Skillman's New York Police Reports. 1828–29
Skin. Skinner's King's Bench Reports (90 ER) 1681–98
Skinker Skinker's Reports (65–79 Missouri)
Skinner Skinner's King's Bench Reports (90 ER) 1681–98
SkmL Lag om skiljeman (Swed.) arbitration law
Slade Slade's Reports (15 Vermont)
Slg. Sammlung
Sloan Leg.Reg. Sloan's Legal Register (New York)
Sm. Smith's King's Bench Reports (7–8 RR) 1803–06
Sm.Act. Smith, Action at Law. 12ed. 1876
Sm.Adm.Pr. Smith, Admiralty Practice. 4ed. 1892

Sm.C.C.M. Smith's Circuit Court Martial Reports (Maine) 1831

Sm.Ch.Pr. Smith, Chancery Practice. 7ed. 1862

Sm.Com.L. Smith, Manual of Common Law. 12ed. 1905

Sm.Con. Smith, Contracts. 8ed. 1885

Sm.Cond.Ala. Smith's Condensed Alabama Reports

Sm.E.D. E.D. Smith's Common Pleas Reports (New York) 1850–58

Sm.Ecc.Cts. Smith, Ecclesiastical Courts. 7ed. 1920

Sm.Eq. Smith, H.A. Principles of Equity. 5ed. 1914
Smith, J.S. Principles of Equity. 1856
Smith, J.W. Manual of Equity Jurisprudence. 15ed. 1900

Sm.For.Med. Smith, Forensic Medicine. 10ed. 1955

Sm.Ind. Smith's Reports (in 1–4 Indiana) 1848–49

Sm.K.B. Smith's King's Bench Reports (7–8 RR) 1803–06

Sm.L.C. Smith's Leading Cases in Various Branches of the Law. 13ed. 1929

Sm.L.J. Smith's Law Journal. 1804–06

Sm.M.& S. Smith, Master and Servant. 8ed. 1931

Sm.Me. Smith's Reports (61–84 Maine)

Sm.Merc.L. Smith, Mercantile Law. 13ed. 1931

Sm.Neg. Smith, Negligence. 2ed. 1884

Sm.Pat. Smith, Patents. 2ed. 1854

Sm.Pl. Somersetshire Pleas Civil & Criminal (Somerset Record Society Publications, vols. 11, 36, 41, 44)

Sm.& B.R.R.Cas. Smith & Bates' American Railway Cases

Sm.& Bat. Smith & Batty's King's Bench Reports (Ire.) 1824–25

Sm.& G. Smale & Giffard's Chancery Reports (65 ER) 1852–57
Smith & Guthrie's Reports (81–101 Missouri Appeals)

Sm.& M. Smedes & Marshall's Reports (9–22 Mississippi) 1843–50

Sm.& M.Ch. Smedes & Marshall's Chancery Reports (Mississippi) 1840–43

Sm.& S. Smith & Sager's Drainage Cases (Ontario, Can.) 1904–16

Sm.& Sod.L.& T. Smith & Soden, Lanlord and Tenant. 2ed. 1878

Sma.& Giff. Smale & Giffard's Chancery Reports (65 ER) 1852–57

Smale & G. Smale & Giffard's Chancery Reports (65 ER) 1852–57

Smed.& M. Smedes & Marshall's Mississippi Reports (9–22 Miss.) 1843–50

Smed.& M.Ch. Smedes & Marshall's Mississippi Chancery Reports. 1840–43

Smedes & M.Ch. Smedes & Marshall's Mississippi Chancery Reports (Miss.) 1840–43

Smedes & M.(Miss.) Smedes & Marshall's Mississippi Reports (9–22 Miss.) 1843–50

Smeth.L.S. Smethurst on Locus Standi. 1867

Smi.& Bat. Smith and Batty's King's Bench Reports (Ire.) 1824–25

Smith C.L. Smith's Registration Cases. 1895–1914
E.B. Smith's New York Common Pleas Reports. 1850–58
E.H. Smith's Reports (147–162 New York Court of Appeals)
E.P. Smith's Reports (15–27 New York Court of Appeals)
J.P. Smith's King's Bench Reports (7–8 RR) 1803–06
P.F. Smith's Pennsylvania State Reports (51–81 Pa.State)
Smith's California Reports (54–62 California)
Smith's Indiana Reports (1–4 Ind.) 1848–49
Smith's New Hampshire Reports. 1796–1816
Smith's Reports (61–64 Maine)
Smith's Reports (81–101 Missouri Appeals)
Smith's Reports (2–4 South Dakota)

Smith's Reports (1–11 Wisconsin)
Smith's Tennessee Reports (154–164 Tenn.) 1925–32

Smith Act. Smith, Action at Law. 12ed. 1876

Smith C.C.M. Smith's Circuit Courts Martial Reports (Maine) 1831

Smith C.P. Smith's Common Pleas Reports (New York) 1850–58

Smith,Ch.Pr. Smith, Chancery Practice. 7ed. 1862

Smith Com.Law Smith, Manual of Common Law. 12ed. 1905

Smith Cond.Rep. Smith's Condensed Reports (Alabama)

Smith Cont. Smith, Contracts. 8ed. 1885

Smith Ct.App. E.P.Smith's Reports (15–27 New York Court of Appeals)

Smith de Rep.Angl. Smith (Sir Thomas) De Republica Anglorum. 1583

Smith E.D. E.D. Smith's New York Common Pleas Reports. 1850–58

Smith E.H. E.H. Smith's Reports (147–162 New York Court of Appeals)

Smith E.P. E.P. Smith's Reports (15–27 New York Court of Appeals)

Smith Ex.Int. Smith on Executory Interest. 1844

Smith-Hurd Smith-Hurd's Illinois Annotated Statutes (USA)

Smith-Hurd Ann.St. Smith-Hurd's Illinois Annotated Statutes (USA)

Smith Ind. Smith's Indiana Reports (1–4 Ind.) 1848–49

Smith J.P. J.P.Smith's King's Bench Reports (7–8 RR) 1803–06

Smith K.B. J.P.Smith's King's Bench Reports (7–8 RR) 1803–06

Smith L.C. Smith's Leading Cases. 13ed. 1929

Smith L.J. Smith's Law Journal. 1804–06

Smith Laws Pa. Smith's Laws of Pennsylvania

Smith Lead Cas. Smith's Leading Cases. 13ed. 1929

Smith Man.Eq.Jur. Smith's Manual of Equity Jurisprudence. 15ed. 1900

Smith Me. Smith's Reports (61–64 Maine)

Smith Merc.Law Smith, Mercantile Law. 13ed. 1931

Smith N.H. Smith's New Hampshire Reports. 1796–1816

Smith N.Y. E.H. Smith's Reports (147–162 New York Court Appeals)
E.P. Smith's Reports (15–27 New York Court of Appeals)

Smith P.F. P.F. Smith's Pennsylvania State Reports (51–81 Pa. State)

Smith Pa. P.F. Smith's Pennsylvania State Reports (51–81 Pa. State)

Smith Reg. C.L. Smith's Registration Cases. 1895–1914

Smith Wis. Smith's Reports (1–11 Wisconsin)

Smith & B. Smith & Batty's King's Bench Reports (Ire.) 1824–25
Smith & Bates' American Railway Cases

Smith & B.R.R.C. Smith & Bates' American Railway Cases

Smith & Bat. Smith & Batty's King's Bench Reports (Ire.) 1824–25

Smith & G. Smith & Guthrie's Missouri Appeals Reports (81–101 Mo.)

Smith & H. Smith & Heiskell's Tennessee Reports

Smith's Lead.Cas. Smith's Leading Cases in Various Branches of the Law. 13ed. 1929

Smoult Smoult's Supreme Court Reports (Bengal, India) 1774–98

Smy. Smythe's Irish Common Pleas Reports (Ire.) 1839–40

Smy.& B. Smythe & Bourke's Irish Marriage Cases. 1842

Smythe Smythe's Irish Common Pleas Reports (Ire.) 1839–40

Sn.& W.Ch. Snow & Winstanley, Chancery Practice

snc The ordinary partnership (It.)

Sneed Sneed's Kentucky Decisions (2 Ky.) 1801–05
Sneed's Reports (33–37 Tennessee) 1853–58

Sneed Dec. Sneed's Kentucky Decisions (2 Ky.) 1801–05
Snell Eq. Snell, Principles of Equity. 27ed. 1973
Snow Snow's Reports (3 Utah)
So. Southern
Southern Reporter, National Reporter System (USA) 1887–1941
So.2d Southern Reporter, Second Series (USA) 1941–
So.Afr.J.Crim.L.& Criminol. South African Journal of Criminal Law and Criminology
So.Afr.L.J. South African Law Journal. 1901–
So.Afr.L.R. South African Law Reports. 1947–
So.Afr.L.T. South African Law Times. 1932–36
So.Afr.Prize Cas. South African Prize Cases (Juta)
So.African L. South African Law Reports. 1947–
So.African L.J. South African Law Journal. 1901–
So.Aus.L.R. South Australian Law Reports. 1865–92, 1899–1920
So.Austr.L. South Australian Law Reports. 1865–92, 1899–1920
So.Austr.St. South Australian State Reports. 1921–
So.C. South Carolina Reports. 1868–
So.Cal.L.R. Southern California Law Review. 1927–
So.Calif.L.Rev. Southern California Law Review. 1927–
So.Car. South Carolina
South Carolina Reports. 1868–
So.Car.B.A.Rep. South Carolina Bar Association Reports
So.Car.Const. South Carolina Constitutional Reports
So.Car.L.J. South Carolina Law Journal
So.Car.L.Q. South Carolina Law Quarterly. 1948–62
So.Car.L.Rev. South Carolina Law Review. 1962–
So.Carol.L.R. South Carolina Law Review. 1962–
So.Dak.B.Jo. South Dakota Bar Journal. 1932–
So.Dak.L.Rev. South Dakota Law Review. 1956–
So.East.Rep. Southeastern Reporter (USA) usually cited S.E.
So.Ill.U.L.J. Southern Illinois University Law Journal. 1976–
So.Jersey L.S.Dictum South Jersey Law School Dictum. 1928–30
So.L.J. Southern Law Journal & Reporter (USA) 1878–81
So.L.J.& Rep. Southern Law Journal & Reporter (USA) 1878–81
So.L.Q. Southern Law Quarterly. 1916–18
So.L.R. Southern Law Review (Nashville, Tenn.) 1872–74
So.L.R.N.S. Southern Law Review, New Series (St. Loius, Mo.) 1875–83
So.L.Rev. Southern Law Review (Nashville, Tenn.) 1872–74
Southern Law Review (St. Louis, Mo.) 1875–83
So.L.Rev.N.S. Southern Law Review, New Series (St.Louis,Mo.) 1875–83
So.L.T. Southern Law Times (USA) 1885–86
So.Law. Southern Lawyer (USA) 1937
So.Rep. Southern Reporter (USA) usually cited South or So.
So.Sec.Rep. Social Security Reporter (Aus.) 1981–
So.Tex.L.J. South Texas Law Journal. 1955–
So.Univ.L.Rev. Southern University Law Review (USA) 1974–
So.West.L.J. Southwestern Law Journal (USA) 1947–
So.West.Rep. Southwestern Reporter (USA) usually cited S.W.
Soc. Social
Society
Sociological
Sociology
La section sociale de la Cour de

Cassation (Fr.) Social security and Labour division of the Cour de Cassation
Soc.Csewrk. Social Casework (Can.)
Soc.dir. Sociologia del diritto (It.) 1974–
Soc.Econ. Social Economics
Soc.L. Socialist Lawyer
Soc.Lab.Bull. Social and Labour Bulletin (ILO) 1974–
Soc.Mean.Leg.Con. Social Meaning of Legal Concepts (USA) 1948–53
Soc.Problems Social Problems
Soc.Research Social Research: an International Quarterly of Political and Social Science
Soc.Sci.Assn. Social Science Association
Soc.Sci.Bull. Social Science Bulletin
Soc.Sci.Q. Social Science Quarterly
Soc.Sec. Social Security
Soc.Sec.Bull. Social Security Bulletin
Soc.Ser. Social Services
Soc.Serv. Social Services
Soc.Theory & Pract. Social Theory and Practice
Soc.Wkr. Social Worker (Can.)
Soc.Work Social Work (Can.)
Social-Econ.Wetgeving Sociaal-Economische Wetgeving (Neth.)
Soc'y. Society
Sohyo Nihon Rodo Kumiai So-hyog-kai (Japan) General Council of Labour Unions
Sol. Solicitor
The Solicitor. 1934–61
Soloman's Court of Request Appeals (Sri L.)
Sol.Cl.Gaz. Solicitors' Clerks' Gazette. 1921–40
Sol.G. Solicitor General
Sol.Gen. Solicitor General
Sol.J. Solicitor's Journal (& Reporter) 1857–
Sol.J.& R. Solicitors' Journal & Reporter. 1857–
Sol.Jo. Solicitors Journal (& Reporter) 1857–
Sol.Man.Cl.Gaz. Solictors' Managing Clerks' Gazette. 1941–62
Sol.Op. Solicitors' Opinion
Sol.Q. Solicitor Quarterly. 1962–65
Solar L.Rep. Solar Law Reporter
Solic.J. Solicitor's Journal. 1857–
Solrs. Solicitors
Som. Somerset Legal Journal (Pennsylvania) 1920–
Som.L.R. Somalia Law Reports
Som.L.J. Somerset Legal Journal (Pennsylvania) 1920–
Som.Leg.J.(Pa.) Somerset Legal Journal (Pennsylvania) 1920–
Som.Pl. Somersetshire Pleas
Somerset L.J. Somerset Legal Journal (Pennsylvania) 1920–
Somm. Sommaires (Fr., Belg.) summaries, digests
Sotsial.Zakon. Sotsialisticheskaia Zakonnost (USSR)
Sou.Aus.L.R. South Australian Law Reports. 1865–92, 1899–1920
South. Southern Reporter (National Reporter System) (USA)
South Afr.Yb.Int'l L. South African Yearbook of International Law
South.Aus.L.R. South Australian Law Reports. 1865–92, 1899–1921
South Car. South Carolina
South Carolina Reports. 1868–
South Dak.L.Rev. South Dakota Law Review
South.Ill.U.L.J. Southern Illinois University Law Journal. 1976–
South.L.J. Southern Law Journal. 1878–81
South.L.J.& Rep. Southern Law Journal & Reporter (USA) 1878–81
South.L.Rev. Southern Law Review (USA) 1872–74
South.L.Rev.N.S. Southern Law Review, New Series (USA) 1875–83
South.Law J. Southern Law Journal (Tuscaloosa, Ala.) 1878–81
South.Law J.& Rep. Southern Law Journal & Reporter. 1878–81
South.Law Rev. Southern Law Review (USA) 1872–74
South.Law Rev.N.S. Southern Law

Review, New Series (USA) 1875–83

South Texas L.J. South Texas Law Journal

South.U.L.Rev. Southern University Law Review (USA) 1974–

Southard Southard's New Jersey Law Reports (4–5 N.J. Law) 1816–20

Southw.L.J. Southwestern Law Journal (Texas) 1947–
Southwestern Law Journal & Reporter (USA) 1844

Southwest.J.Philosoph. Southwestern Journal of Philosophy

Southwest.U.L.Rev. Souhwestern University Law Review

Southwestern L.J. Southwestern Law Journal (Texas) 1947–

Southwood Commission Royal Commission on Environmental Pollution

Sov.Stat.& Dec. Soviet Statutes and Decisions

Sovet.Gosud.Prav. Sovetskoe Gosudarstvo i Pravo (USSR)

Sovet.Iustit. Sovetskaia Iustitsiia (USSR)

Soviet L.& Govt. Soviet Law and Government (USA) 1962–

Sp. Spain
Spalte (Ger.) column
Special
Speer's South Carolina Law Reports (28–29 S.C.L.) 1842–44
Spinks' Ecclesiastical & Admiralty Reports (164 ER) 1853–55
Spinks' Prize Cases (164 ER) 1854–56

SpA public company (It.)

Sp.Ch. Speers' South Carolina Chancery Reports (17 S.C.Eq.) 1842–44

Sp.Cr.Ct. Special Criminal Court

Sp.Ecc.& Ad. Spinks' Ecclesiastical and Admiralty Reports (164 ER) 1853–55

Sp.Eq. Speers' South Carolina Equity Reports (17 S.C.Eq.) 1842–44

Sp.Glos. Spelman's Glossary. 1626

Sp.Laws Montesquieu, Spirit of the Laws

SpO Sociedade por Quotas (Port.)

Sp.Pr.Cas. Spinks' Prize Cases (164 ER) 1854–56

SpR. Spruchrepertorium des Obersten Gerichtshofes (Austria)

Sp.& Sel.Cas. Special and Selected Law Cases. 1648

Sparks. Sparks' Reports (Burma)

Spaulding Spaulding's Reports (71–80 Maine)

Spear Ch. Spears' (or Speers') South Carolina Equity Reports (17 S.C.Eq.) 1842–44

Spear Eq. Spears' (or Speers') South Carolina Equity Reports (17 S.C.Eq.) 1842–44

Spear.High. Spearman, Highways. 1881

Spears Spears' (or Speers') South Carolina Equity Reports (17 S.C.Eq.) 1842–44
Spears' South Carolina Law Reports (28–29 S.C.L.) 1842–44

Spears Eq. Spears' (or Speers') South Carolina Reports (17 S.C.Eq.) 1842–44

spec. special
specification

Speers Speers' South Carolina Equity Reports (17 S.C.Eq.) 1842–44
Spears' (or Speers') South Carolina Law Reports (28–29 S.C.L.) 1842–44

Speers Eq. Spears' (or Speers') South Carolina Equity Reports (17 S.C.Eq.) 1842–44

Speers Eq.(S.C.) Speers' (or Spears') South Carolina Equity Reports (17 S.C.Eq.) 1842–44

Speers L.(S.C.) Speers' South Carolina Law Reports (28–29 S.C.L.) 1842–44

Spel.Feuds. Spelman on Feuds. 1698

Spel.Gl. Spelman's Glossary. 1626

Spel.L.T. Spelman's Law Terms. 1684

Spel.Rep. Spelman's Reports, Manuscript, King's Bench

Spelm. Spelman's Glossary. 1626

Spelman Spelman's Glossary. 1626

Spen.(N.J.) Spencer's Reports (20 New Jersey Law) 1842–46

Spenc. Spencer's Reports (10–20 Minnesota)
Spencer's Reports (20 New Jersey Law) 1842–46

Spence Ch. Spence's Equitable Jurisdiction of the Court of Chancery. 1846–49

Spenc.Eq.Jur. Spence's Equitable Jurisdiction of the Court of Chancery. 1846–49

Spence Pat.Inv. Spence, Patentable Inventions. 1851

Spencer Spencer's Reports (10–20 Minnesota)
Spencer's Reports (20 New Jersey Law) 1842–46

Spens.Sel.Cas. Spens' Select Cases (Bombay, India)

Spike M.& S. Spike, Master and Servant. 3ed. 1872

Spinks Spinks' Ecclesiastical & Admiralty Reports (164 ER) 1853–55
Spinks' Prize Court Cases (164 ER) 1854–56

Spinks Eccl.& Adm. Spinks' Ecclesiastical & Admiralty Reports (164 ER) 1853–55

Spinks P.C. Spinks' Prize Cases (164 ER) 1854–56

Spinks Prize Cas. Spinks' Prize Cases (164 ER) 1854–56

Spoon. Spooner's Reports (12–15 Wisconsin)

Spooner Spooner's Reports (12–15 Wisconsin)

Spott.Eq.Rep. Spottiswoode's Equity Reports

Spottis. R. Spottiswoode's Court of Session Reports (Scot.)

Spottis.C.L.& Eq.Rep. Common Law and Equity Reports, published by Spottiswoode

Spottis.Eq. Spottiswoode, Equity (Scot.)

Spottis.Pr. Spottiswoode, Practicles (Scot.)

Spottis.St. Spottiswoode, Styles (Scot.)

Spottisw. Spottiswoode, Equity (Scot.)

Spottisw.Eq. Spottiswoode, Equity (Scot.)

Spr. Sprague's United States District Court (Admiralty) Decisions. 1841–64

Squibb Auc. Squibb, Auctioneers. 2ed. 1891

Sri.L. Sri Lanka

ss. et pages suivantes (and following pages)
sections
seguenti (It.) the following (plural)

St. Stair's Decisions, Court of Session (Scot.) 1661–81
Stair's Institutes. 5ed. 1832
State
Statute(s)
Storey's Circuit Court Reports (USA) 1839–45
Street
Stuart, Milne & Peddie's Session Cases (Scot.) 1851–53
United States Statutes at Large

StAZ. Zeitschrift für Standesamtwesen (Ger.)

St.Ab. Statham's Abridgment

St.Adm.N.S. Stuart's Lower Canada Vice-Admiralty Reports, New Series

St.AnoG Steueranpassungsgesetz (Ger.) Taxation Adaptation Act

St.at Large Statutes at Large (USA)

St.Bar.Rev. State Bar Review (Washington) 1934–36

St.Brown Stewart-Brown's Cases in the Court of the Star Chamber. 1455–1547

St.C. Stephen, Commentaries on the Laws of England. 21ed. 1950

St.Cas. Stillingfleet, Ecclesiastical cases. 1698–1704

St.Ch.Cas. Star Chamber Cases. 1477–1648

St.Dept. State Department Reports (USA)

St.Eccl.Cas. Stillingfleet's Ecclesiastical Cases. 1698–1704

StGB Strafgesetzbuch (Ger.) Criminal Code

St.Gloc. Statute of Gloucester

St.Inst. Stair's Institutes. 5ed. 1832
Statutory Instrument

St.John's L.Rev. St John's Law Review (Brooklyn, N.Y.) 1926–

St.L.U.Intra.L.Rev. St Louis University Intramural Law Review. 1949

St.Law Loughborough's Digest of Statute Law (Kentucky)
St.Lim. Statute of Limitations
St.Louis L.Rev. St Louis Law Review. 1915–36
St.Louis U.L.J. St Louis University Law Journal. 1949–
St.Louis U.Pub.L.Rev. St Louis University Public Law Review
St.M.& P. Stuart, Milne & Peddie's Court of Session Cases (Scot.) 1851–53
St.Mary's L.J. St Mary's Law Journal (Texas) 1969–
St.N. Staatsblad der Nederlanden (Neth.) statute series
StO Steuerordnung (Ger.) tax law
St.P. State Papers
StPO Strafprozessordnung (Ger.) Code of criminal procedure
St.Pl.Cr. Staunford's Pleas of the Crown. 1557
St.Pr.Reg. Style's Practical Register. 4ed. 1707
St.R. Stuart's Appeal Cases (Quebec) 1810–53
St.R.Q. Queensland State Reports (Aus.) 1902–57
St.R.Qd. Queensland State Reports (Aus.) 1902–57
St.R.Queensl. Queensland State Reports (Aus.) 1902–57
St.R.& O. Statutory Rules and Orders
St.Rep. State Reports
State Reporter
St.Rep.N.S.W. State Reports (New South Wales)
St.Rep.Queensl.(Austr.) Queensland State Reports (Aus.) 1902–57
St.Ry.Rep. Street Railway Reports (USA) 1903–13
St.Tr. Howell's State Trials. 1163–1820
St.Tr.N.S. State Trials New Series, Macdonnell's. 1820–58
St.Tri. State Trials. 1163–1820
StW Steuer und Wirtschaft (Ger.) 1922–44, 1947–
St.Westm. Statute of Westminster
St.& R. Staat und Recht (Ger.)
Stafford Stafford's Reports (69–71 Vermont)
Stainton Report Committee on Local Land Charges Report (Cmd. 8440) 1951
Stair Stair's Decisions, Court of Session (Scot.) 1661–81
Stair I. Stair's Institutes. 5ed. 1832
Stair Inst. Stair's Institutes. 5ed. 1832
Stair Prin. Stair, Principles of the Laws of Scotland
Stair Rep. Stair's Decisions, Court of Session (Scot.) 1661–81
Stal.Elect. Stalman, Election and Satisfaction. 1827
Stan. Stanford
Stan.Dig. Stanton's Kentucky Digest
Stan.Envtl.L.J. Stanford Environmental Law Journal
Stan.J.Int'l L. Stanford Journal of International Law
Stan.J.Int'l.Stud. Stanford Journal of International Studies. 1968–
Stan.L.R. Stanford Law Review. 1948–
Stan.L.Rev. Stanford Law Review. 1948–
Stanford Stanford's Pleas of the Crown. 1557
Stanford L.Rev. Stanford Law Review. 1948–
Stanton Stanton's Reports (11–13 Ohio)
Stanton's Rev.St. Stanton's Revised Statutes (Kentucky)
Star. Starkie's Nisi Prius Reports (171 ER) 1814–22
Star Ch.Ca. Star Chamber Cases. 1477–1648
Star Ch.Cas. Star Chamber Cases. 1477–1648
Star S.C. Star Session Cases. 1824–25
Stark. Starkie's Nisi Prius Reports (171 ER) 1814–22
Stark.C.L. Starkie's Criminal Law. 3ed. 1828
Stark.Cr.Pl. Starkie, Criminal Pleadings. 3ed. 1828
Stark.Ev. Starkie, Evidence. 4ed. 1853
Stark.Jury Tr. Starkie on Trial by Jury

Stark.Lib. Starkie, Slander & Libel. 7ed. 1908
Stark.N.P. Starkie's Nisi Prius Reports (171 ER) 1814–22
Stark.Sl.& L. Starkie, Slander & Libel. 7ed. 1908
Starkie Starkie's Nisi Prius Reports (171 ER) 1814–22
Starkie Ev. Starkie, Evidence. 4ed. 1853
Starkie,Sland.& L. Starkie, Slander & Libel. 7ed. 1908
Starkie's Starkie's Nisi Prius Reports (171 ER) 1814–22
Starr & C.Ann.St. Starr and Curtis' Annotated Statutes (Illinois)
Stat. Statistic(s)
Stationery
Statute(s)
Statutes at Large (USA)
Stat.at L. Statutes at Large
Stat.Dec. Statutory Declaration
Stat.Def. Statutory Definition(s)
Stat.Glo. Statute of Gloucester
Stat.Inst. Statutory Instrument(s)
Stat.jud. Statistiques judiciares (Belg.) 1955–
Stat.L.R. Statute Law Review. 1980–
Stat.Law Com. Statute Law Committee
Stat.Law Soc. Statute Law Society
Stat.Marl. Statute of Marlbridge
Stat.Mer. Statute of Merton
Stat.N.S.W. Statutes of New South Wales (Aus.)
Stat.N.Z. Statutes of New Zealand
Stat.O.& R. Statutory Orders and Regulations (Can.)
Stat.R.& O. Statutory Rules and Orders. 1890–1947
Stat.R.& O.N.I. Statutory Rules and Orders of Northern ireland
Stat.R.& O.& Stat.Inst.Rev. Statutory Rules and Orders and Statutory Instruments Revised, to December 31, 1948
Stat.Realm Statutes of the Realm
Stat.Reg.N.Z. Statutory Regulations (N.Z.)
Stat.Rev. Statutes Revised
Stat.Westm. Statute of Westminster
Stat.Winch. Statute of Winchester
State Fin. State Finance
State Gov't. State Government
State Tax Cas. State Tax Cases (CCH) (USA) 1918–44
State Tax Cas.Rep. State Tax Cases Reporter (CCH)
State Tr. Howell's State Trials. 1163–1820
State Tr.N.S. State Trials, New Series (Macdonnell) 1820–58
Stath.Abr. Statham's Abridgment
Statute L.Rev. Statute Law Review. 1980–
Staund.Pl. Staunford's Pleas of the Crown. 1557
Staundf.Prerog. Staunford's Exposition of the King's Prerogative. 1567
Stb. Staatsblad (Neth.) Official Bulletin
Der Steuerberater (Ger.) 1931–44, 1951–
Stbl. Staatsblad (Neth.) Official Bulletin
Stbl.v.N.I. Staatsblad van Nederlandsch Indië
Stc. Nederlandse Staatscourant
Ste. Societe
Steer P.L. Steer, Parish Law. 6ed. 1899
Stenton Stenton, Rolls of the Justices in Eyre
Stenton G. Rolls of the Justices in Eyre for Gloucestershire, Worcestershire and Staffordshire. 1221–22
Stenton Y. Rolls of the Justices in Eyre in Yorkshire. 1218–21
Steph. Stephens' Supreme Court Decisions (Jamaica) 1774–1923
Steph.Cl. Stephens, Clergy. 1848
Steph.Com. Stephen, Commentaries on the Laws of England. 21ed. 1950
Steph.Comm. Stephen, Commentaries on the Laws of England. 21ed. 1950
Steph.Cr.L. Stephen, General View of the Criminal Law. 2ed. 1890
Steph.Dig. Stephen's New Brunswick Digest (Can.)
Steph.Dig.Cr.L. Stephen, Digest of the Criminal Law. 9ed. 1950

Steph.Dig.Ev. Stephen, Digest of the Law of Evidence. 12ed. rev.1946
Steph.Elect. Stephens, Elections. 1840
Steph.N.P. Stephens, Nisi Prius. 1842
Steph.Pl. Stephen, Pleading. 7ed. 1866
Stephen, H.C.L. Stephen's History of Criminal Law. 1883
Stephens Supreme Court Decisions (Jamaica) 1774–1923
Stetson L.Rev. Stetson Law Review (USA)
Stev.Arb. Stevens, Arbitration. 2ed. 1835
Stev.Av. Stevens, Average. 5ed. 1835
Stev.Dig. Steven's New Brunswick Digest
Stevens & G. Stevens & Graham's Reports (98–139 Georgia)
Stew. Stewart's Alabama Reports. 1827–31
Stewart's New Jersey Equity Reports (28–45 N.J.Eq.) 1877–89
Stewart's Reports (1–10 South Dakota)
Stewart's Vice Admiralty Reports (Nova Scotia) 1803–13
Stew.Adm. Stewart's Vice Admiralty Reports (Nova Scotia) 1803–13
Stew.Admr Stewart's Vice Admiralty Reports (Nova Scotia) 1803–13
Stew.Ans. Stewart, Answer to Dirleton's Doubts (Scot.) 3ed. 1762
Stew.Dig. Stewart's Digest of Decisions of Law and Equity (New Jersey)
Stew.Eq. Stewart's New Jersey Equity Reports (28–45 N.J.Eq.) 1877–89
Stew.N.Sc. Stewart's Nova Scotia Vice Admiralty Reports (Can.) 1803–13
Stew.V.A. Stewart's Vice-Admiralty Reports (Nova Scotia) 1803–13
Stew.& P. Stewart & Porter's Alabama Supreme Court Reports. 1831–34
Stewart Stewart's Alabama Reports. 1827–31
Stewart's New Jersey Equity Reports (28–45 N.J.Eq.) 1877–89
Stewart's Reports (1–10 South Dakota)
Stewart's Vice Admiralty Reports (Nova Scotia) 1803–13
Stewart-Brown Stewart-Brown's Cases in the Court of Star Chamber. 1455–1547
Stewart Committee Committee on Alternatives to Prosecution. Report 2 (Cmnd. 8958) (Scot.) 1983
Stewart Vice–Adm.(Nov.Sc.) Stewart's Nova Scotia Vice Admiralty Reports. 1803–13
Sth.Afr.Rep. South African Republic Supreme Court Cases. 1881–92
Stil. Stillingfleet's Ecclesiastical Cases. 1698–1704
Stiles Stiles' Reports (22–29 Iowa)
Stiles(Ia.) Stiles' Reports (22–29 Iowa)
Still.Eccl.Cas. Stillingfleet's Ecclesiastical Cases. 1698–1704
Stim.Gloss. Stimson's Law Glossary
Stim.Law.Gloss. Stimson's Law Glossary
Stiness Stiness' Reports (20–34 Rhode Island)
stk. stock
Stmt. Statement
Stn.L. Stanford Law Review. 1948–
Sto. Storey's Reports (Delaware)
Story's United States Circuit Court Reports. 1839–45
Sto.Ag. Story on Agency. 9ed. 1882
Sto.Att.Lien Stokes, Lien of Attorneys and solicitors. 1860
Sto.Bailm. Story on Bailment. 9ed. 1878
Sto.Bills Story on Bills. 4ed. 1860
Sto.C.C. Story's United States Circuit Court Reports. 1839–45
Sto.Conf.Law Story on Conlict of Laws. 8ed. 1883
Sto.Const. Story's Commentaries on the Constitution of the United States. 5ed. 1891
Sto.Eq.Jur. Story on Equity Jurisprudence. Numerous eds. 1836–1920
Sto.Eq.Pl. Story on Equity Pleadings. 10ed. 1892
Sto.Part. Story on Partnership. 7ed. 1881
Sto.& G. Stone and Graham's Private Bills Decisions. 1865

Stock. Stockton's New Jersey Equity Reports (9–11 N.J.Eq.) 1852–58
Stockton's Vice-Admiralty Reports, New Brunswick. 1879–91

Stock.Adm. Stockton's Vice-Admiralty Reports (New Brunswick) 1879–91

Stockett Stockett's Reports (27–79 Maryland)

Stockt. Stockton's New Jersey Equity Reports (9–11 N.J.Eq.) 1852–58

Stockt.Vice-Adm. Stockton's Vice Admiralty Reports (New Brunswick) 1879–91

Stockton Stockton's Vice Admiralty Reports (New Brunswick) 1879–91

Stockton Adm.(New Br.) Stockton's Vice-Admiralty Reports (New Brunswick) 1879–91

Stone Stones' Justices Manual (Annual)

Stone Ben.Bdg.Soc. Stone, Benefit Building Societies. 1851

Stone Just.Man. Stone, Justices' Manual (Annual)

Stonham Reports Home Office. Report of the Joint Working Party on the Constitutional Relationship between the Isle of Man and the United Kingdom. 1969

Story Story, Equity Jurisprudence. Numerous eds. 1836–1920
Story's United States Circuit Court Reports. 1839–45

Story Ag. Story on Agency. 9ed. 1882

Story Bailm. Story on Bailment. 9ed. 1878

Story,Bills Story on Bills. 4ed. 1860

Story Comm.Const. Story's Commentaries on the Constitution of the United States. 5ed. 1891

Story Confl.Laws Story on Conflict of Laws. 8ed. 1883

Story Const. Story's Commentaries on the Constitution of the United States. 5ed.

Story Eq.Jur. Story on Equity Jurisprudence. Numerous eds. 1836–1920

Story Eq.Pl. Story's Equity Pleadings. 10ed. 1892

Story Partn. Story on Partnership. 7ed. 1881

Story Prom.Notes Story on Promissory Notes. 7ed. 1878

Str. Strange's Cases of Evidence. 1698–1732
Strange's King's Bench Reports (93 ER) 1716–49

Str.8vo. Strange's Cases of Evidence. 1698–1732

Str.Cas.Ev. Strange's Cases of Evidence. 1698–1732

Str.Ev. Strange's Cases of Evidence. 1698–1752

Str.N.C. Strange's Notes of Cases (Madras, India) 1798–1816

Str.& H.C. Streets and Highways Code

Stra. Strange's King's Bench Reports (93 ER) 1716–49

Strahan Strahan's Reports (19 Oregon)

Stran. Strange's King's Bench Reports (93 ER) 1716–49

Strange Strange's King's Bench Reports (93 ER) 1716–49

Strange,Madras Strange's Notes of Cases (Madras, India) 1898–1816

Stratton Stratton's Reports (12–14 & 19 Oregon)

Street Ry.Rep. Street Railway Reports (USA) 1903–13

Strick.Ev. Strickland, Evidence. 1830

Striethorst Archiv für Rechtsfalle die zur Entscheidung des königlichen Obertribunals gelangt sind (Prussia) 1851–80

Stringf. Stringfellow's Reports (9–11 Missouri Appeals)

Stringfellow Stringfellow's Reports (9–11 Missouri Appeals)

Strob. Strobhart's South Carolina Equity Reports (20–23 S.C.Eq.) 1846–50

Strob.Eq. Strobhart's South Carolina Equity Reports (20–23 S.C.Eq.) 1846–50

Strobh.Eq.(S.C.) Strobhart South Carolina Equity Reports (20–23 S.C.Eq.) 1846–50

Strobh.L.(S.C) Strobhart's South Carolina Law Reports (32–36 S.C.L.) 1846–50

Strupp, Elements Strupp, Elements du droit international public, universel, européen et americain. 2ed. 1930

Strupp, Wort. Strupp, Wörterbuch des Völkerrechts und der Diplomatie. 1924–29

Struve Struve's Reports (Washington Territory) 1854–88

Stu.Adm. Stuart's Lower Canada Vice-Admiralty Reports (Quebec) 1836–74

Stu.Adm.N.S. Stuart's Lower Canada Vice-Admiralty Reports, New Series

Stu.Adm.V.A. Stuart's Lower Canada Vice-Admiralty Reports (Quebec) 1836–74

Stu.Ap. Stuart's Lower Canada King's Bench Reports, Appeal Cases (Quebec) 1810–53

Stu.K.B. Stuart's Lower Canada King's Bench Reports (Quebec) 1810–53

Stu.L.C. Stuart's Lower Canada Reports (Quebec) 1810–53

Stu.M.& P. Stuart, Milne & Peddie's Court of Session Cases (Scot.) 1851–53

Stu.Mil.& Ped. Stuart, Milne & Peddie's Court of Session Cases (Scot.) 1851–53

Stu.V.A. Stuart's Lower Canada Vice-Admiralty Reports (Quebec) 1836–74

Stuart Stuart, Milne & Peddie's Court of Session Cases (Scot.) 1851–53
Stuart's Lower Canada Reports (Quebec) 1810–53
Stuart's Lower Canada Vice-Admiralty Reports (Quebec) 1836–74

Stuart Adm.N.S. Stuart's Lower Canada Vice-Admiralty Reports, New Series

Stuart Beng. Stuart's Select Cases (Bengal, India) 1860

Stuart K.B. Stuart's Lower Canada King's Bench Reports (Quebec) 1810–53

Stuart K.B.(Quebec) Stuart's Lower Canada King's Bench Reports (Quebec) 1810–53

Stuart L.C.K.B. Stuart's Lower Canada King's Bench Reports (Quebec) 1810–53

Stuart L.C.V.A. Stuart's Lower Canada Vice-Admiralty Reports (Quebec) 1836–74

Stuart M.& P. Stuart, Milne and Peddie's Court of Session Cases (Scot.) 1851–53

Stuart Vice-Adm. Stuart's Lower Canada Vice-Admiralty Reports (Quebec) 1836–74

Stuart's Adm. Stuart's Lower Canada Vice-Admiralty Reports (Quebec) 1836–74

Stuart's R. Stuart's Lower Canada King's Bench Reports, Appeal Cases (Quebec) 1810–53

Stubbs,C.H. Stubb's Constitutional History. rev. ed. 1951

Stud. Studies

Stud.Cercet.Jur. Studii si Cercetari Juridice (Romania)

Stud.Comp.Int'l Develop. Studies in Comparative International Development

Stud.Doc.Hist.& Iuris Studia et Documenta Historiae et Iuris (It.)

Stud.in Comp.Local Govt. Studies in Comparative Local Government (Neth.)

Stud.Transnatl.Econ.L. Studies in Transnational Economic Law (Neth.)

Stud.& Doc.His.Jur. Studia et Documenta Historiae et Juris (It.)

Student L.Rev. Student Law Review (USA)

Student Law. Student Lawyer (USA) 1951–

Student Law J. Student Lawyer Journal (USA) 1934

Studi pavia Studi nelle scienze giuridiche e sociali dell'Universita di Pavia (It.) 1912–

Studi sass. Studi sassaresi (It.) 1901–

Studi sen. Studi senesi nel Circolo giuridico della R. Universita (It.) 1884–

Sturg.B.L. Sturgeon, Bankrupt Acts. 2ed. 1832
Sturg.Ins.D. Sturgeon, Insolvent Debtors Act. 1842
Stuyt A.M. Stuyt, Survey of International Arbitrations, 1794–1938. 1939
Sty. Style's King's Bench Reports (82 ER) 1646–55
Sty.Pr.Reg. Style's Practical Register. 1657–1710
Style Style's King's Bench Reports (82 ER) 1646–55
Style Pr.Reg. Style's Practical Register
Su. Superior Court
Supreme Court
Su.Ct.Cir. Supreme Court Circular
Su.Ct.Rev. Supreme Court Review (USA) 1960–
Su.L.R. Suffolk University Law Review (USA) 1967–
Suarez Suarez, Tratado de derecho internacional publico. 1916
sub. subordinate
subscription
substitute(d)
sub.nom. sub nomine (Lat.) under the name
subd. subdivision
subj. subject
subs. subscription
subsidiary
substitute(d)
Subs.Leg.Austl.Cap.Terr. Subsidiary Legislation of the Australian Capital Territory
subsc. subscription
subsec. subsection
subst. substitute(d)
suc. successor
Sud.Dew.Ad. Sudder Dewanny Adawlut Reports (India)
Sud.Dew.Rep. Sudder Dewanny Adawlut Reports (India)
Sudan L.J.& Rep. Sudan Law Journal and Reports
Suffolk U.L.Rev. Suffolk University Law Review (USA) 1967–
Suffolk Transnat'l L.J. Suffolk Transnational Law Journal (USA)
Sug.Hd.Bk. Sugden, Handy Book on Property Law. 8ed. 1869
Sug.Pow. Sugden, Powers. 8ed. 1861
Sug.Pr. Sugden, Property. 1849
Sug.Pr.St. Sugden, Real Property Statutes. 2ed. 1862
Sug.Prop. Sugden, Property. 1849
Sug.V.& P. Sugden on Vendors and Purchasers. 14ed. 1862
Sug.Vend. Sugden, Vendors & Purchasers. 14ed. 1862
Sugd.Powers Sugden, Powers. 8ed. 1861
Sugd.Vend. Sugden, Vendors & Purchasers. 14ed. 1862
Sull.Lect. Sullivan's Lectures on Constitution and Laws of England. 2ed. 1790
Sum. Sumner's Circuit Court Reports (USA) 1829–39
Hale's Summary of Pleas of the Crown
Sum.Dec. Summary Decisions, Sudder Dewanny Adawlut (Bengal, India) 1834–57
Sum.Ves. Sumner's Edition of Vesey's Reports
Summ.Dec. Summary Decisions, Sudder Dewanny Adawlut (Bengal, India) 1834–57
Summa St Thomas Aquinas, Summa Theologica. 1267
Summerfield Summerfield's Reports (21 Nevada)
Summerfield S. S. Summerfield's Reports (21 Nevada)
Sumn. Sumner's United States Circuit Court Reports (USA) 1829–39
Sumn.Ves. Sumner's Edition of Vesey's Reports
Sumner Sumner's United States Circuit Court Reports (USA) 1829–39
Sup. Superior
Supra (Lat.) above
Supreme
Sup.Ct. Supreme Court
Supreme Court Reporter (National Reporter System) (USA) 1882–

Sup.Ct.App. Supreme Court Appeals (India) 1937–
Sup.Ct.G.B. Supreme Court, Grand Bench (Japan) Saiko Saibansho, Daihotei
Sup.Ct.J. Supreme Court Journal (India) 1950–
Sup.Ct.M.R. Supreme Court Monthly Review (India) 1968–
Sup.Ct.Pr. Supreme Court Practice
Sup.Ct.R. Supreme Court Reports (India) 1950–
Sup.Ct.Rep. Supreme Court Reporter (USA) 1882–
Sup.Ct.Rev. Supreme Court Review (USA) 1960–
Sup.Jud.Ct. Supreme Judicial Court
Sup.Trib.Fed. Supremo Tribunal Federal (Brazil)
Super. Superior Court
Superior Court Reports
Super.Ct. Superior Court
Super.Ct.App.Div. Superior Court Appelate Division
Super.Ct.Ch.Div. Superior Court Chancery Division
Super.Ct.Law Div. Superior Court Law Division
Super.Ct.Rep. Superior Court Reports
Supp. New York Supplement Reports. 1888–1937
Supplement
Supp.Code Supplement to Code
Supp.Gen.St. Supplement to the General Statutes
Supp.Ves.Jun. Supplement to Vesey, Jr., Reports. 1789–1817
suppl. supplement
supplementary
supplemented
Supr. Superior
Supreme
Supr.Ct.Rep. Supreme Court Reporter (USA) 1882–
Supreme Court L.R. Supreme Court Law Review (Can.) 1979–
Sur. Surety
Sur.Ct. Surrogate's Court
Surr. Surrogate
Surr.Ct. Surrogate's Court
Survey Calif.L. Survey of California Law. 1953–
Sus.Leg.Chron. Susquehanna Legal Chronical (Pennsylvania) 1878–79
susp. suspended
Susq.L.C. Susquehanna Legal Chronical (Pennsylvania) 1878–79
Susq.L.Chron. Susquehanna Legal Chronical (Pennyslvania) 1878–79
Susquehanna Leg.Chron.(Pa.) Susquehanna Legal Chronical (Pennsylvania) 1878–79
Suth. Sutherland's High Court Reports (Bengal, India) 1864
Sutherland's Weekly Reports (India) 1864–76
Suth.App. Sutherland's Appeal Reports, Small Causes Court (Bengal, India) 1861–65
Suth.Bengal Sutherland's Bengal High Court Reports (Bengal, India) 1864
Suth.F.B.R. Sutherland's Full Bench Reports (Bengal, India) 1862–64
Suth.Mis. Sutherland's Weekly Reports, Miscellaneous Appeals (India) 1864–76
Suth.P.C.A. Sutherland Privy Council Appeals (India) 1831–80
Suth.P.C.J. Sutherland Privy Council Appeals (India) 1831–80
Suth.Sp.N. Sutherland's Full Bench Reports (Bengal,India) 1862–64
Sutherland's Special Number of Weekly Reports
Suth.W.R. Sutherland's Weeekly Reports (India) 1864–76
Suth.W.R.Mis. Sutherland's Weekly Reports, Miscellaneous Appeals (India) 1864–76
Sutton Sutton, Personal Actions at Common Law. 1929
Sv. Wetboek van Strafvordering (Neth.) code of criminal procedure
SvJT Svensk Juristtidning (Swed.) 1916–
Svensk Juristtid. Svensk Juristtidning (Sweden)

Sver.Advok. Tidskrift for Sveriges Advokatsamfund (Swed.)

Sw. Southwest(ern)
Swabey's Admiralty Reports (166 ER) 1855–59
Swan's Reports (31–32 Tennessee) 1851–53
Swanston's Chancery Reports (36 ER) 1818–19
Sweeny's New York Superior Court Reports (31–32 N.Y.S. Ct.) 1869–70
Swinton's Justiciary Reports (Scot.) 1835–41

Sw.L.J. Southwestern Law Journal (USA) 1947–

Sw.U.L.Rev. Southwestern University Law Review (USA) 1916–

Sw.& Tr. Swabey & Tristram's Ecclesiastical Reports (164 ER) 1858–65

Swab.Admr. Swabey's Admiralty Reports (166 ER) 1855–59

Swab.Div. Swabey, Divorce and Matrimonial Causes. 3ed. 1859

Swab.& T. Swabey & Tristram's Ecclesiastical Reports (164 ER) 1858–65

Swab.& Tr. Swabey & Tristram's Ecclesiastical Reports (164 ER) 1858–65

Swabey Adm. Swabey's Admiralty Reports (166 ER) 1855–59

Swabey & T. Swabey & Tristram's Ecclesiastical Reports (164 ER) 1858–65

Swan Swan's Tennessee Supreme Court Reports (31–32 Tenn.) 1851–53
Swanston's Chancery Reports (36 ER) 1818–19

Swan.Ch. Swanston's Chancery Reports (36 ER) 1818–19

Swan Eccl.C. Swan, Ecclesiastical Courts. 1830

Swan Pl.& Pr. Swan, Pleading and Practice (Ohio)

Swan Pr. Swan, Practice (Ohio)

Swan & C.R.St. Swan and Critchfield's Revised Statutes (Ohio)

Swan & S.St. Swan and Sayler's Supplement to the Revised Statutes (Ohio)

Swans. Swanston's Chancery Reports (36 ER) 1818–19

Swan's St. Swan's Statutes (Ohio)

Swanst. Swanston's Chancery Reports (36 ER) 1818–19

Swed. Sweden

Sween. Sweeny's New York Superior Court Reports (31–32 N.Y.S. Ct.) 1869–70

Sweeney Sweeny's New York Superior Court Reports (31–32 N.Y.S. Ct.) 1869–70

Sweeny Sweeny's New York Superior Court Reports (31–32 N.Y.S. Ct.) 1869–70

Sweet Sweet, Law Dictionary. 1882
Sweet, Marriage Settlement Cases
Sweet, Precedents in Conveyancing. 4ed. 1886
Sweet, Wills. 1837

Sweet L.D. Sweet, Dictionary of English Law. 1882

Sweet M.Sett.Cas. Sweet's Marriage Settlement Cases

Sweet Pr.Conv. Sweet, Precedents in Conveyancing. 4ed. 1886

Swift Dig. Swift's Digest (Connecticut)

Swin. Swinburne on Wills. 10ed. 1803
Swinton's Justiciary Reports (Scot.) 1835–41

Swin.Jus.Cas. Swinton's Justiciary Cases (Scot.) 1835–41

Swin.Reg.App. Swinton's Registration Appeal Cases (Scot.) 1835–41

Swinb.Desc. Swinburne, Descents. 1825

Swinb.Mar. Swinburne, Married Women. 1846

Swinb.Wills Swinburne on Wills. 10ed. 1803

Swint. Swinton's Justiciary Cases (Scot.) 1835–41

Swiss RWA Swiss Review of World Affairs

Switz. Switzerland

Sy.J.Int.L. Syracuse Journal of International Law and Commerce (USA) 1972–

Sy.L.R. Syracuse Law Review (USA) 1949–

Syd.App. Sydney Appeals (Aus.)
Sydney, Jurisdiction and Modern Practice in Appeals. 1824

Syd.Inst.Crim.Proc. University of Sydney Faculty of Law Proceedings of the Institute of Criminology (Aus.) 1967–

Syd.L.R. Sydney Law Review (Aus.) 1953–

Syd.L.Rev. Sydney Law Review (Aus.) 1953–

Sydney L.Rev. Sydney Law Review (Aus.) 1953–

Syl. The Syllabi (USA) 1876–77

Sym.Code Syms, Code of English Law. 1870

Syme Syme's Justiciary Reports (Scot.) 1826–30

Symp. Symposium

syn. synonym
synopsis

Syn.Ser. Synopsis Series of Treasury Decisions (USA)

Syracuse J.Int'l L. Syracuse Journal of International Law (USA)

Syracuse J.Int'l.L.& Com. Syracuse Journal of International Law and Commerce (USA) 1972–

Syracuse L.Rev. Syracuse Law Review (USA) 1949–

syst. system

T

t. tempore (Lat.) in the time of
tome (Fr.) volume
tomo (It.) volume

T. Tappan's Common Pleas Reports (Ohio) 1816–19
Taxes
Teil (Ger.) part
Tempore (Lat.) in the time of
Term
Territory
Title
Traffic Cases. 1874–
Traité de Droit Civil du Québec
Transvaal Provincial Division Reports (S.Afr.) 1910–46
Trinity

T.A. Board of Tax Appeals (USA)
Tithe Annuity
Tribunal administratif (Fr.) Administrative court (of first instance)

T/A Trading as

T.A.B. Technical Assistance Board (U.N.)

TACC Telecom Australia Consumer Council

T.A.M. Tribunaux arbitraux mixtes

TAR Tribunale amministrativo regionale (It.) Regional Administrative Tribunal

T.Ad. The Tax Adviser (New York) 1970–

TBA Tennessee Bar Association

TBDF Transborder Data Flows

T.B.Mon. T.B. Monroe's Kentucky Supreme Court Reports (17–23 Ky.) 1824–28

T.B.Mon.(Ky.) T.B. Monroe's Kentucky Supreme Court Reports (17–23 Ky.) 1824–28

T.B.R.D. Taxation Board of Review Decisions (Aus.) 1925–51

T.B.R.D.(N.S.) Taxation Board of Review Decisions (New Series) (Aus.) 1950–69

T.B.& M. Tracewell, Bowers & Mitchell's U.S. Comptroller's Decisions

T.C. All India Reporter, Travancore-Cochin. 1950–57
Reports of Tax Cases. 1875–
Tariff Commission (USA)
Tax Court of the United States Reports. 1942–
Town Clerk
Town Council(lor)
Trade Cases (CCH) (USA)
Tribunal des conflits (Fr.) tribunal of conflicts
Trusteeship Council (U.N.)

T.C.B. Title Certificate Book

TCDC Technical Co-operation amongst Developing Countries (UN/ODA)

T.C.L. The Capital Letter (N.Z.) 1978–

T.C.L.R. Trade and Competition Law Reports (N.Z.) 1986–

T.C.Leaflet Tax Case Leaflet

TCM Draft Convention for the International Combined Carriage of Goods
Tax Court Memorandum Decisions (CCH) 1942–
Tax Court Memorandum Decisions (P–H) 1928–

T.C.M.(CCH) Tax Court Memorandum Decisions (CCH) 1942–

T.C.M.(P–H) Tax Court Memorandum Decisions (P–H) 1928–

T.C.Memo Tax Court Memorandum Decisions (P–H) 1928–

TCO Tjanstemannens Centralorganisation (Swed.) The Confederation of Unions of Salaried Employees

T.C.Q. Tax Counsellor's Quarterly (USA) 1957–

T.C.R. Transit Commission Reports (New York)

T.C.T. Canadian Trade and Commodity Tax Cases. 1989–

T.C.V. Common International Tariff International Convention for Transport of Goods

T.Ct. Tax Court of the United States Reports. 1942–

T.Ct.Mem. Tax Court of U.S. Memorandum

T.Cv. Tax Convention

T.D. Tealto Dail (Ire.) Member of the Dail Treasury Decisions (U.S. Treasury Dept)

TDAD Trade Development Assistance Division (US Department of Commerce)

T.D.B. Total Disability Benefit
Trade and Development Board (U.N.)

TDRef Agreement relating to the Issue of a Travel Document to Refugees who are the Concern of the Intergovernmental Committee on Refugees. 1946

T e C Fondo Trattati e Convenzioni (It.)

TECO Technical Co-operation Committee (OECD)

T.E.S. The Times Educational Supplement

T.Ev. Taylor, Evidence. 12ed. 1931

TF Tryckfrihetsforordning (Swed.) Freedom of the Press Act. 1949

T.F. Tribunal fédéral suisse (Switz.)

T.F.M. Testators Family Maintenance

TFP Total factor productivity

TG Testamentsgesetz (Ger.) Law on Wills

T.G.W.U. Transport and General Workers' Union

T.H. Reports of the Witwatersrand High Court (Transvaal, S.Afr.) 1902–10

THE Technical Help to Exporters (BSI)

T.H.E.S. The Times Higher Educational Supplement

THRHR Tydskrif vir Heedendaagse Romeins-Hollandse Reg (S.Afr.) 1948–

T.I.A. Taxation in Australia. 1963–
Taxation Institute of Australia

T.I.A.Conv.Papers Taxation Institute of Australia Convention Papers. 1945–

T.I.A.S. Treaties and Other International Acts Series (USA)

T.I.C. Tasmanian Industrial Commission (Aus.)

T.I.R. Transit international routier (Customs Convention on the International Transport of Goods Under Cover of TIR Carnets)

T.J. Recueils de Jurisprudence, Tribunal de la Jeunesse (Québec, Can.) 1979–

T.Jo. T. Jones King's Bench Reports (84 ER) 1667–85

T.Jones T. Jones King's Bench Reports (84 ER) 1667–85

T.L. Reports of the Witwatersrand Local Division of the Supreme Court (S.Afr.) 1910–46
Rastell's Termes de la Ley

TLA Skadestandslagen (Swed.) The Tort Liability Act

T.L.I. Trust Law International

T.L.J. Travancore Law Journal (India) 1910–48
Trent Law Journal

T.L.N. Tasmanian Law Newsletter (Aus.)
T.L.O. Total Loss Only
T.L.Q. Temple Law Quarterly (USA) 1927–
T.L.R. Tanganyika Law Reports. 1921–52
Tanzania Gazette Law Reports
Tasmanian Law Reports (Aus.) 1905–40
Tax Law Review (USA) 1945–
Times Law Reports. 1884–1952
Travancore Law Reports (India) 1884–1948
Tulane Law Review (USA) 1929–
T.L.R.(R.) Tanganyika Law Reports (Revised) 1921–52
T.L.S. The Times Literary Supplement
T.L.T. Travancore Law Times (India) 1926–
T.L.W. The Lawyers' Weekly (Can.) 1986–
T.L.& P. Trust Law and Practice
T.Lawyr. The Tax Lawyer (USA) 1967–
T.M. Tax Magazine (USA) 1930–38
Tax Management
Tax Memo (Can.) 1954–
Trademark
T.M.Bull. Trade Mark Bulletin, New Series (USA)
TMC Asser Verzameling Jurisprudentie en Annotaties Europees Recht (Neth.)
T.M.J. Trade Marks Journal. 1876–
T.M.L. Three Mile Limit
T.M.N. Tax Matters Newsletter (Aus.) 1981–
T.M.Rec. Trade Mark Record (USA) 1886–1914
T.M.Rep. Trade Mark Reporter (USA) 1911–
T.Marshall L.Rev. Thurgood Marshall Law Review
TNC Transnational Corporation
TNPNW Treaty on the Non-proliferation of Nuclear Weapons. 1968
T.N.S. Tax News Service (Neth.)
T.O.L. Ticket of Leave (Macquarie University Law Society) (Aus.) 1984–
T.O.P. Temporarily Out of Print
TOPS Training Opportunities Scheme (Manpower Services Commission)
TORG Protocol on the Termination of the Occupational Regime in the FRD. 1954
ToT Transfer of Technology
T.P. Tax Planning
Transvaal Supreme Court Reports (S.Afr.) 1910–46
T.P.C. Trade Practices Cases (Aus.) 1977–82
Trade Practices Commission (Aus.)
T.P.C.Bull. Trade Practices Commission Bulletin (Aus.) 1978–
T.P.C.D. Trade Practices Commission Decisions and Determinations (Aus.) 1977–82
T.P.C.D.D. Trade Practices Commission Decisions and Determinations (Aus.) 1977–82
T.P.D. South African Law Reports, Transvaal Provincial Division (S.Afr.) 1910–46
T.P.G. Town Planning and Local Government Guide (Aus.) 1956–
T.P.I. Town Planning Institute
T.P.L.G.G. Town Planning and Local Government Guide (Aus.) 1956–
T.P.R. Trade Practices Reports (Aus.) 1982–83
T.P.R.S. Trade Practices Reporting Service (Aus.) 1976–82
T.P.T. Tolley's Practical Tax
T.P.V. Tolley's Practical VAT
TQM Total Quality Management
TR Tydskrif vir Regswetenskap (S.Afr.) 1976–
T.R. Caines' Term Reports (New York) 1803–05
Durnford & East's Term Reports (99–101 ER) 1785–1800
Taxation Reports. 1939–
T.R.A. Taxation Review Authority (N.Z.)
T.R.C. Tithe Rent Charge
T.R.E. Tempore Regis Edwardi (in the time of King Edward)

T.R.H.S. Transactions of the Royal Historical Society
TRIPS Trade-Related Aspects of Intellectual Property
T.R.N.S. Term Reports, New Series (East's Reports) (102–104 ER) 1801–1812
T.R.(N.Y.) Caines' Term Reports (New York) 1803–05
T.R.N.Z. Tax Reports (N.Z.) 1974–
T.R.R. Trade Regulation Reporter (USA)
Trade Regulation Review (USA) 1936–38
TRW Treaty providing for the Renunciation of War as an Instrument of National Policy. 1928
Tydskrif vir Regswetenskap (S.Afr.) 1976–
T.Ray. Sir T. Raymond's King's Bench Reports (83 ER) 1660–84
T.Raym. Sir T. Raymond's King's Bench Reports (83 ER) 1660–84
T.S. Transvaal Supreme Court Reports (S.Afr.) 1902–10
Treasury Solicitor
Treaty Series
TSA Tidskrift for Sveriges advokatsamfund (Journal of the Swedish Lawyers' Association) 1937–
Tydskrif vir die Suid-Afrikaanse Reg (S.Afr.) 1976–
TSAR Tydskrif vir die Suid-Afrikaanse Reg (S.Afr.) 1976–
T.S.T. Canada Trade and Sales Tax Cases. 1989–
T.T. Tobacco Tax Ruling (USA)
Tribunal du Travail (Québec, Can.)
Trinity Term
T.T.I. Tolley's Tax Investigations
Tulane Tax Institute (USA) 1951–
T.T.L.R. Tanganyika Territory Law Reports. 1921–47
T.T.R. Tarleton's Term Reports (New South Wales, Aus.) 1881–3
t.u. testo unico (It.) consolidated statutes
TUAC Trade Union Advisory Committee
T.U.C. Temporary Unemployment Compensation
Trades Union Congress
T.U.C.C. Transport Users' Consultative Council
TUCP The Consolidated Law on the Communes and Provinces (It.)
T.U.P.Charl. T.U.P. Charlton's Reports (Georgia) 1805–11
TUPS The Consolidated Law on Public Safety (It.)
T.V.A. Taxe sur la valeur ajoutée (Fr.)
Value added tax
Tennessee Valley Authority
TVG Tarifvertragsgesetz (Ger.)
Collective Agreements Act
T.v.S. Tijdschrift voor Strafrecht (Neth.) 1886–1943, 1946–
TVVS Tijdschrift voor Vennootschappen, Verenigingenen Stichtingen (Neth.) 1958–
T.W. Trademark World
T.W.U. Transport Workers' Union of Australia
T.& B. Taylor & Bell's Supreme Court Reports (Bengal, India) 1849–53
T.& C. Thompson & Cook's New York Supreme Court Reports. 1873–75
T.& G. Tyrwhitt & Granger's Exchequer Reports (46 RR) 1835–36
T.& M. Temple & Mew's Crown Cases (169 ER) 1848–51
T.& P. Turner & Phillips' Chancery Reports
T.& R. Turner & Russell's Chancery Reports (37 ER) 1822–24
T.& S. Thomson & Steger's Tennessee Statutes
T.& T.Sup. Trinidad & Tobago Supreme Court Judgments
Table Table: Journal of the Society of Clerks-at-the-Table in the Commonwealth Parliament (Aus.) 1933–
Tait Tait's Index to Morison's Dictionary (Scot.)
Tait's Index to Scottish Session Cases. 1823

Tait's Manuscript Decisions, Session Cases (Scot.)

Tal. Talbot's Cases in Equity, ed. Williams (25 ER) 1733–38

Talb. Talbot's Cases in Equity, ed. Williams (25 ER) 1733–38

Tam. Tamlyn's Rolls Court Reports (48 ER) 1829–30

Tamb. Tambyah's Reports (Sri L.) 1899–1911

Taml. Tamlyn's Rolls Court Reports (48 ER) 1829–30

Taml.Ev. Tamlyn, Evidence in Chancery. 2ed. 1846

Taml.T.Y. Tamlyn, Terms of Years. 1825

Tamlyn Tamlyn's Rolls Court Reports (48 ER) 1829–30

Tamlyn Ch. Tamlyn's Rolls Court Reports (48 ER) 1829–30

Tan. Taney's United States Circuit Reports. 1836–61

Tan.L.R. Tanganyika Territory Law Reports. 1921–47

Tanc.Q.W. Tancred, Quo Warranto. 1830

Taney Taney's United States Circuit Court Reports. 1836–61

Tann. Tanner's Reports (8–14 Indiana) Tanner's Reports (13–17 Utah)

Tap. Tappan's Ohio Common Pleas Reports. 1816–19

Tap.Man. Tapping, Writ of Mandamus. 1848

Tapp. Tappan's Ohio Common Pleas Reports. 1816–19

Tapp M.& Ch. Tapp, Maintenance and Champerty. 1861

Tappan Tappan's Ohio Common Pleas Reports. 1816–19

Tappan (Ohio) Tappan's Ohio Common Pleas Reports. 1816–19

Tapping Tapping, Writ of Mandamus. 1848

Tarl. Tarleton's Term Reports (New South Wales, Aus.) 1881–83

Tarl.Term R. Tarleton's Term Reports (New South Wales, Aus.) 1881–83

Tas. Tasmania

Tas.Bldg.App.R. Tasmanian Building Appeals Reports (Aus.)

Tas.Irreg.Notes Tasmanian Irregular Notes (Aus.)

Tas.L.N. Tasmanian Law Newsletter

Tas.L.R. Tasmanian Law Reports (Aus.) 1905–40

Tas.L.R.C. Tasmanian Law Reform Commission

Tas.L.Rev. University of Tasmania Law Review (Aus.) 1958–

Tas.R. Tasmanian Reports (Aus.) 1979–

Tas.S.R. Tasmanian State Reports. 1941–78

Tas.Univ.L.Rev. Tasmanian University Law Review. 1958–

Tasm. Tasmanian State Reports. 1941–

Tasm.L.R. Tasmanian Law Reports (Aus.) 1905–40

Tasm.St.R. Tasmanian State Reports (Aus.) 1941–

Tasm.Stat. Tasmanian Statutes (Aus.)

Tasm.Stat.R. Tasmanian Statutory Rules with Tables (Aus.)

Tasm.U.L.Rev. Tasmanian University Law Review. 1958–63

Tasmania L.R. University of Tasmania Law Review. 1964–

Tasmanian U.L.Rev. Tasmanian University Law Review. 1958–63

Tasw.Lang.Hist. Taswell-Langmead, English Consitutional History. 10ed. 1946

Tate's Dig. Tate's Digest of Laws (Virginia)

Taun. Taunton's Common Pleas Reports (127–129 ER) 1808–19

Taunt. Taunton's Common Pleas Reports (127–129 ER) 1808–19

Tax. Taxation. 1927–

Tax A.B.C. Tax Appeal Board Cases (Can.) 1949–

Tax Ad. The Tax Adviser (New York) 1970–

Tax Adm'rs.News Tax Administrator's News (USA) 1937–41

Tax Cas. Reports of Tax Cases. 1875–

Tax Coun.Q. Tax Counsellor's Quarterly (USA) 1957–
Tax Counsellor's Q. Tax Counsellor's Quarterly (USA) 1957–
Tax Ct.Mem.Dec. Tax Court Memorandum Decisions (CCH) 1942–
Tax Court Memorandum Decisions (P–H) 1928–
Tax Ct.Rep. Tax Court Reporter (CCH) (USA)
Tax Ct.Rep.Dec. Tax Court Reported Decisions (P–H) (USA) 1952–
Tax.in Aust. Taxation in Australia. 1963–
Tax.Int. Taxation International
Tax J. Tax Journal
Tax L.R. Tax Law Reporter (USA)
Tax L.Rep. Tax Law Reporter (USA)
Tax L.Rev. Tax Law Review (New York) 1945–
Tax Law. The Tax Lawyer (USA) 1967–
Tax Law Rep. Tax Law Reporter (USA)
Tax Mag. Tax Magazine (USA) 1930–38
Tax Man.Intl.J. Tax Management International Journal (USA)
Tax P. Taxation Practitioner
Tax Pl.Int. Tax Planning International. 1976–
Tax Pl.Rev. Tax Planning Review. 1979–
Tax.R. Taxation Reports. 1939–
Tax Rev. Tax Review
Tax & Inv. Tax and Investment
Tax.& Rev. Taxation and Revenue
Taxes Taxes – The Tax Magazine (USA) 1923–
Taxn. Taxation
Taxation. 1927–
Taxn.in Aust. Taxation in Australia. 1963–
Tay. Taylor
Taylor's Reports (1 North Carolina) 1798–1802
Taylor's Supreme Court Reports (Bengal, India) 1847–48
Taylor's Upper Canada King's Bench Reports (Ontario, Can.) 1823–27
Tay.Bk.R. Taylor, Book of Rights. 1833
Tay.Ev. Taylor, Evidence. 12ed. 1931
Tay.Glos. Taylor, Law Glossary. 2ed. 1823
Tay.J.L. J.L. Taylor's North Carolina Reports (1 N.C.) 1798–1802
Tay.Med.Jur. Taylor, Medical Jurisprudence. 12ed. 1966
Tay.N.C. Taylor's North Carolina Reports (1 N.C.) 1798–1802
Tay.Poi. Taylor, Poisons. 3ed. 1875
Tay.Tit. Taylor, Tithe Commutation. 1876
Tay.U.C. Taylor's Upper Canada King's Bench Reports (Ontario, Can.) 1823–27
Tay.& B. Taylor & Bell's Supreme Court Reports (Bengal, India) 1849–53
Tayl.Ev. Taylor, Evidence. 12ed. 1931
Tayl.Gloss. Taylor's Law Glossary. 2ed. 1823
Tayl.Hist.Gav. Taylor (Silas) History of Gavelkind. 1663
Tayl.Med.Jur. Taylor, Medical Jurisprudence. 12ed. 1966
Tayl.N.C. Taylor's North Carolina Reports (1 N.C.) 1798–1802
Tayl.St. Taylor's Revised Statutes (Wisconsin)
Taylor Taylor's Customary Laws of Rembau (Mal.) 1903–28
Taylor's North Carolina Reports (1 N.C.) 1798–1802
Taylor's Supreme Court Reports (Bengal, India) 1847–48
Taylor's Term Reports (4 North Carolina) 1816–18
Taylor's Upper Canada King's Bench Reports (Can.) 1823–27
Taylor K.B.(Can.) Taylor's Upper Canada King's Bench Reports (Can.) 1823–27
Taylor(Malaya) Taylor's Customary Laws of Rembau (Mal.) 1903–28
Taylor U.C. Taylor's Upper Canada King's Bench Reports (Ontario) 1823–27
Tbr. Tractatenblad (Neth.) treaty series
Tchr. Teacher

Teasdale Report Football spectator violence: report of an official working group (DOE) 1984

Tech. Technical
Technique
Technology

Tech.Inst. Technical Institution

Teiss. Teissier's Court of Appeal, Parish of Orleans Reports. 1903–17

Teissier Teissier's Court of Appeal, Parish of Orleans Reports. 1903–17

Tel. Telephone
Telegram
Telegraph

Tel Aviv Univ.Stud.L. Tel Aviv University Studies in Law (Israel)

Telecom. Telecommunications

Telecom.Policy Telecommunication Policy (USA)

Tem. The Templar. 1788–89

Temp. Temple
Temporary
Tempore (Lat.) in the time of

Temp.Emer.Ct.App. Temporary Emergency Court of Appeals (USA)

Temp.Envtl.L.& Tech.J. Temple Environmental Law and Technology Journal

Temp.L.Q. Temple Law Quarterly (USA) 1927–

Temp.L.Rev. Temple Law Review

Temp.Univ.L.Q. Temple University Law Quarterly (USA) 1938–45

Temp.Wood. Manitoba Reports tempore Wood (Can.) 1875–83

Temp.& M. Temple & Mew's Crown Cases (169 ER) 1848–51

Temple L.Q. Temple Law Quarterly (USA) 1927–

Temple & M. Temple & Mew's Crown Cases (169 ER) 1848–51

Ten. Tennessee
Tennessee Reports. 1791–

Ten.Cas. Shannon's Unreported Cases (Tennessee) 1847–94
Thompson's Unreported Cases (Tennessee) 1847–69

Tenn. Tennessee
Tennessee Supreme Court Reports. 1791–

Tenn.App. Tennessee Appeals Reports. 1925–

Tenn.App.Bull. Tennessee Appellate Bulletin

Tenn.B.A. Tennessee Bar Association

Tenn.C.C.A. Tennessee Court of Civil Appeals

Tenn.Cas. Shannon's Unreported Cases (Tenn.) 1847–94
Thompson's Unreported Cases (Tennessee) 1847–69

Tenn.Ch. Cooper's Tennessee Chancery Reports. 1872–1878

Tenn.Ch.A. Tennessee Chancery Appeals (Wright) 1901–04

Tenn.Ch.App. Tennessee Chancery Appeals (Wright) 1901–04

Tenn.Ch.App.Dec. Tennessee Chancery Appeals Decisions. 1895–1907

Tenn.Civ.A. Tennessee Civil Appeals (Higgins) 1910–18

Tenn.Civ.App. Tennessee Civil Appeals (Higgins) 1910–18

Tenn.Code Ann. Tennessee Code Annotated

Tenn.L.R.C. Tennessee Law Revision Commission

Tenn.L.Rev. Tennessee Law Review. 1922–

Tenn.Leg.Rep. Tennessee Legal Reporter

Tenn.Pub.Acts Public Acts of the State of Tennessee

Ter. Terry's Reports (Delaware) 1939–

Ter.Laws Territorial Laws

Term Durnford & East's Term Reports (99–101 ER) 1785–1800
Taylor's North Carolina Term Reports (4 N.C.) 1816–18

Term.de la L. Rastell's Termes de la Ley

Term N.C. Taylor's North Carolina Term Reports (4 N.C.) 1816–18

Term R. Durnford & East's Term Reports (99–101 ER) 1785–1800

Term Rep. Durnford & East's Term Reports (99–101 ER) 1785–1800

Term Rep.(N.C.) Taylor's Term Reports North Carolina (4 N.C.) 1816–18
Terr. Terrell's Reports (52–71 Texas)
Territories
Territory
Terr.L. Territories Law (Northwest Territories)
Terr.L.(Can.) Territories Law Reports (N.W.T., Can) 1885–1907
Terr.L.J. Territory Law Journal (Northern Territory Law Society) (Aus.) 1975–
Terr.L.R. Territories Law Reports (N.W.T., Can.) 1885–1907
Terr.Sea J. Territorial Sea Journal
Terr.& Walk. Terrell & Walker's Reports (38–51 Texas)
Teruv. Teruvenkatachariar's Railway Cases (India) 1864–1911
Test. Testamentary
Testator
Testimonial
Tex. Texas
Texas Supreme Court Reports. 1846–
Tex.A. Texas Court of Appeals
Tex.A.Civ. White & Willson's Texas Civil Appeals Cases. 1876–92
Tex.A.Civ.Cas. White & Willson's Texas Civil Appeal Cases. 1876–92
Tex.App. Texas Civil Appeals Cases. 1876–92
Texas Court of Appeals Reports (Criminal Cases) 1876–
Tex.B.J. Texas Bar Journal. 1938–
Tex.Bus.Corp.Act Ann. Texas Business Corporation Act Annotated
Tex.Civ.App. Texas Civil Appeals Reports. 1892–1911
Tex.Civ.Cas. Texas Court of Appeals Decisions, Civil Cases (White & Willson) 1876–92
Tex.Civ.Rep. Texas Civil Appeals Reports. 1892–1911
Tex.Code Ann. Texas Codes Annotated
Tex.Code Crim.Proc.Ann. Texas Code of Criminal Procedure Annotated
Tex.Com.App. Texas Commission of Appeals
Tex.Cr.App. Texas Criminal Appeals Reports. 1876–
Tex.Cr.R. Texas Criminal Appeals Reports. 1876–
Tex.Crim. Texas Criminal Appeals Reports. 1876–
Tex.Crim.Rep. Texas Criminal Appeals Reports. 1876–
Tex.Ct.App.Dec.Civ. Texas Court of Appeals Decisions, Civil Cases (White & Willson) 1876–92
Tex.Ct.Rep. Texas Court Reporter. 1900–08
Tex.Dec. Texas Decisions
Tex.Elec.Code Ann. Texas Election Code Annotated
Tex.Gen.Laws General and Special Laws of the State of Texas
Tex.Ins.Code Ann. Texas Insurance Code Annotated
Tex.Int.L.Forum Texas International Law Forum. 1965–71
Tex.Int.L.J. Texas International Law Journal. 1971–
Tex.Jur. Texas Jurisprudence
Tex.Jur.2d. Texas Jurisprudence, 2d series
Tex.L.J. Texas Law Journal (Austin) 1882–96
Texas Law Journal (Tyler) 1877–82
Tex.L.Rep. Texas Law Reporter. 1882–84
Tex.L.Rev. Texas Law Review. 1883–86
Tex.Law & Leg. Texas Law and Legislation. 1947
Tex.Prob.Code Ann. Texas Probate Court Annotated
Tex.Rev.Civ.Stat.Ann.(Vernon) Texas Revised Civil Statutes Annotated
Tex.S. Texas Supreme Court Reports, Supplement
Tex.S.Ct. Texas Supreme Court Reports. 1846–
Tex.So.Intra.L.Rev. Texas Southern Intramural Law Review. 1970–71
Tex.So.U.L.Rev. Texas Southern University Law Review. 1971–
Tex.Stat.Ann. Texas Statutes Annotated

Tex.Supp. Texas Supplement
Tex.Tech.L.Rev. Texas Tech Law Review. 1969/70–
Tex.Unrep.Cas. Posey's Unreported Cases (Texas) 1879–84
Texas B.J. Texas Bar Journal
Texas Dig. Texas Digest
Texas Int'l.L.J. Texas International Law Journal. 1971–
Texas L.Rev. Texas Law Review. 1883–86, 1922–
Texas South U.L.Rev. Texas Southern University Law Review. 1971–
Texas Tech L.Rev. Texas Tech Law Review. 1969/70–
Th.br. Thesaurus Brevium. 2ed. 1687
Th.C.C. Thacher's Criminal Cases (Massachusetts) 1823–42
Th.C.Const.Law Thomas' Leading Cases in Constitutional Law. 8ed. 1947 (later Phillips)
Th.& C. Thompson & Cook's Supreme Court Reports (New York) 1873–75
Thac.Cr.Cas. Thacher's Criminal Cases (Massachusetts) 1823–42
Thach.Cr. Thacher's Criminal Cases (Massachusetts) 1823–42
Thacher,Cr.Cas. Thacher's Criminal Cases (Massachusetts) 1823–42
Thacher Crim.Cas.(Mass.) Thacher's Criminal Cases (Massachusetts) 1823–42
Thai.Yrbk.Intl.& Comp.L. Thailand Yearbook of International and Comparative Law
Thayer Thayer's Reports (18 Oregon)
Thayer,Prelim.Treatise Ev. Thayer's Preliminary Treatise on Evidence. 1898
Thel. Theloall, Le digest des Briefes. 2ed. 1687
Them. American Themis (New York) 1844
Revue juridique Thémis de l'Université de Montréal. 1966
Thémis: ou, Bibliothèque du jurisconsulte (Fr., Belg.) 1824–31
La Thémis: Revue de législation, de droit et de jurisprudence (Montréal, Can.) 1879–84
Thémis: Revue juridique (Montréal, Can.) 1951–65
Themis: Verzameling van bijdragen tot de kennis van het publiek en privaatrecht (Neth.) 1839–1938
Themis: Zeitschrift für Doctrin und Praxis des romischen Rechts (Ger.) 1838–41
Themis: Zeitschrift für praktische Rechtswissenschaft (Ger.) 1827–30
Themis American Themis (New York) 1844
Revue juridique Thémis de l'Université de Montréal. 1966–
Thémis: ou, Bibliotèque du jurisconsulte (Fr., Belg.) 1824–31
La Thémis: Revue de législation, de droit et de jurisprudence (Montréal, Can.) 1879–84
Thémis: Revue juridique (Montréal, Can.) 1951–65
Themis: Verzameling van bijdragen tot de kenniis van het publiek en privaatrecht (Neth.) 1839–1938
Themis: Zeitschrift für Doctrin und Praxis des romischen Rechts (Ger.) 1838–41
Themis: Zeitschrift für praktische Rechtswissenschaft (Ger.) 1827–30
Theo.Pr.& S. Theobald, Principal and Surety. 1832
Theo.Wills Theobald, Wills. 13ed. 1971
Theobald Theobald, Wills. 13ed. 1971
Thes. Thesawaleme (Sri L.)
Thes.Acroasium Thesaurus Acroasium (Gr.)
Thes.Brev. Thesaurus Brevium. 2ed. 1687
Third World L.J. Boston College Third World Law Journal
Third World Leg.Stud. Third World Legal Studies
Thom. Thomas' Reports (1 Wyoming) 1870
Thomson's Nova Scotia Reports (Can.) (1 N.S.) 1834–51; (3 N.S.) 1856–59

Thom.B.B.S. Thompson, Benefit Building Societies. 1850

Thom.Co.Lit. Thomas' Edition of Coke upon Littleton

Thom.Co.Litt. Thomas' Edition of Coke upon Littleton

Thom.Const.L. Thomas' Leading Cases in Constitutional Law. 8ed. 1947 (later eds. Phillips)

Thom.Dec. Thomson's Nova Scotia Reports (1 N.S.) 1834–51

Thom.L.C. Thomas' Leading Cases on Constitutional Law

Thom.N.Sc. Thomson's Nova Scotia Reports (Can.) 1834–51, 1856–59

Thom.Rep. Thomson's Nova Scotia Reports (Can.) 1834–51,56–59

Thom.Sel.Dec. Thomson, Select Decisions (Nova Scotia)

Thom.Un.Jur. Thomas, Universal Jurisprudence. 2ed. 1829

Thom.& Fr. Thomas & Franklin Reports (1 Maryland Chancery) 1847

Thomas Thomas' Reports (1 Wyoming) 1870

Thomp.Cal. Thompson's Reports (39–40 California)

Thomp.Cit. Thompson's Citations (Ohio)

Thomp.Dig. Thompson's Digest of Laws (Florida)

Thomp.N.B.Cas. Thompson's National Bank Cases (USA) 1864–78

Thomp.Pat. Thompson, Patent Laws of all Countries. 13ed. 1905

Thomp.Tenn.Cas. Thompson's Unreported Tennessee Cases. 1847–69

Thomp.& C. Thompson & Cook's New York Supreme Court Reports. 1873–75

Thomp.& St.Code Thompson and Steger's Code (Tennessee)

Thomps.Cas. Thompson's Tennessee Cases (128–153 Tenn.) 1913–26

Thompson Thompson's Reports (39–40 California)

Thompson Unrep.(Pa.) Thompson's Unreported Cases (Pennsylvania)

Thompson's Fla.Dig. Thompson's Digest of Laws, Florida

Thor. Thorington's Reports (107 Alabama)

Thorn. Thornton, Notes of Ecclesiastical and Maritime Cases. 1841–50

Thorpe Thorpe's Reports (52 Louisiana Annual) 1900

Thos.Co.Litt. Thomas' edition of Coke upon Littleton

Thring J.St.Com. Thring, Joint Stock Companies. 5ed. 1889

Thring.L.D. Thring, Land Drainage Act. 1862

Tichb.Tr. Report of the Tichborne Trial (London)

Tidd Tidd's Costs in Civil Actions. 1792–

Tidd's Practice of the Court of King's Bench and Common Pleas. 9ed. 1833

Tidd.App. Appendix to Tidd's Practice

Tidd Pr. Tidd, Practice of the Courts of King's Bench and Common Pleas. 9ed. 1833

Tidd Prac. Tidd, Practice of the Courts of King's Bench and Common Pleas. 9ed. 1833

Tids.Jur.Foren. Tidskrift, utgiven av Juridiska Föreningen (Finland)

Tids.Rettsviten. Tidskrift for Rettsvitenskap (Norway)

Tiff. Tiffany's Reports (28–39 New York Court of Appeals) 1867–68

Tiffany Tiffany's Reports (28–39 New York Court of Appeals) 1867–68

Tijd.v.Rechtsg. Tijdschrift voor Rechtsgeschiedenis (Neth.)

Tijds.Antill.R-Jus. Tijdschrift voor Antilliaans Recht-Justicia (Neth. Antilles)

Tijds.Arbit. Tijdschrift voor Arbitrage (Neth.)

Tijds.Belg.Burger.R. Tijdschrift voor Belgisch Burgerlijk Recht (Belg.)

Tijds.Rgeschied. Tijdschrift voor Rechtsgeschiedenis (Neth.)

Tijdsch.v.Privaatr. Tijdschrift voor Privaatrecht (Belg.)

Til.& Sh.Pr. Tillinghast & Shearman, New York Practice
Till.& Yates App. Tillinghast & Yates on Appeals
Tillman Tillman's Reports (68, 69, 71, 73, 75 Alabama)
Tils.St.L. Tilsley, Stamp Laws. 3ed. 1871
Times Times Law Reports (Sri L.) Old Series. 1922–39; New series. 1940–
Times L.R. Times Law Reports. 1884–1952
Times Law Reports (Sri L.) Old Series. 1922–39; New Series. 1940–
Times L.Rep. Times Law Reports. 1884–1952
Times Law Reports (Sri L.) (O.S.) 1922–39; (N.S.) 1940–
Tinw. Tinwald's Reports, Court of Session (Scot.)
Tit. Tithe
Title
Tn. Tennessee
Tennessee Reports. 1791–
Tn.A. Tennessee Appeals Reports. 1925–
Tn.Cr. Tennessee Criminal Appeals Reports
Tn.L. Tennessee Law Review. 1922–
Tn.L.R. Tennessee Law Review. 1922–
To.Jo. Sir Thomas Jones' King's Bench Reports (84 ER) 1677–85
Tobey Tobey's Reports (9–10 Rhode Island)
Todai Tokyo Daigaku (Japan) Tokyo University
Tol. Toledo
Tol.L.R. University of Toledo Law Review. 1969–
Toledo L.Rev. University of Toledo Law Review
Toll.Ex. Toller, Executors. 7ed. 1838
Toller Toller, Executors. 7ed. 1838
Tolst.Div. Tolstoy, Divorce and Matrimonial Causes
Toml. Tomlins' Supplement to Brown's Parliamentary Cases (Tomlins' Election Cases) 1689–1795
Toml.Cas. Tomlins' Election Cases. 1689–1795
Toml.L.D. Tomlin, Law Dictionary. 4ed. 1835
Toml.Law Dict. Tomlin, Law Dictionary. 4ed. 1835
Toml.Supp.Br. Tomlins' Supplement to Brown's Parliamentary Cases (Tomlins' Election Cases) 1689–1795
Tomlin Report Report of the Land Transfer Committee (Cmd. 4776) 1934–5
Tomlins Tomlins' Law Dictionary. 4ed. 1835
Top.L. Topical Law
Toronto U.Faculty L.Rev. Toronto University Faculty Law Review (Can.)
Tort & Ins.L.J. Tort and Insurance Law Journal
Tot. Tothill's Transactions in Chancery (21 ER) 1559–1646
Toth. Tothill's Transactions in Chancery (21 ER) 1559–1646
Touch. Sheppard's Touchstone. 8ed. 1826
Tourg.Dig. Tourgee, North Carolina Digest
Touro L.Rev. Touro Law Review
Town.St.Tr. Townsend, Modern State Trials. 1850
Tr. Transaction
Transcript
Translated
Translation
Treaty
Trial
Trinidad
Tristram's Consistory Judgments. 1872–90
Trust
Trustee
Tr.App. Transcript Appeals (New York) 1867–68
Tr.Ch. Transactions in Chancery (Tothill's Reports) (21 ER) 1559–1646
Tr.Consist.J. Tristram's Consistory Judgments. 1872–90
Tr.Ind.Act Trust Indenture Act
Tr.Judge J. Trial Judges' Journal (USA) 1962–71
Tr.L. Trading Law

Tr.L.R. Trading Law Reports
Trinidad Law Reports. 1893–
Tr.Law Guide Trial Lawyer's Guide (USA) 1957–
Tr.Law.Q. Trial Lawyer's Quarterly (USA) 1964–
TrP. Transpatent (Ger.) 1949–
Tr.Ser. Treaty Series
Tr.& Est. Trusts & Estates
Tr.& H.Pr. Troubat & Haly's Pennsylvania Practice
Trace.& M. Tracewell & Mitchell, Unites States Comptroller's Decisions
Trad.L. Trading Law
Trade Cas. Trade Cases (CCH) 1944–
Trade L.Topics Trade Law Topics (Can.) 1985–
Trade Mark R. Trademark Reporter (USA) 1911–
Trade Reg.Rep.(Trade Cas.) Trade Regulation Reporter, Trade Cases (USA)
Trademark Bull. Bulletin of United States Trademark Association
Trademark Rep. Trademark Reporter (USA) 1911–
Trademark Rptr. Trademark Reporter (USA) 1911–
Traff.Cas. Traffic Cases. 1874–
trans. transaction
transcript
transfer
transferred
translation
translator
Trans.Ap. Transcript Appeals (New York) 1867–68
Trans.App. Transcript Appeals (New York) 1867–68
Trans.Grotius Soc. Transactions of the Grotius Society
Trans.I.L.A. Transactions of the International Law Association. 1873–1924
Trans.& Wit. Transvaal & Witwatersrand Reports (S.Afr.)
Transc.A. Transcript Appeals (New York) 1867–68
Transcr.A. Transcript Appeals (New York) 1867–68
transf. transferred
transl. translated
translation
translator
Transnat'l. Transnational
Transnat'l Immigration L.Rep. Transnational Immigration Law Reporter (USA)
Transnat'l.Rep. Transnational Reporter
Transp. Transport
Transportation
Transp.L.J. Transportation Law Journal (USA) 1969–
Transp.L.Sem. Transportation Law Seminar (USA) 1971–
Transp.Prac.J. Transportation Practitioners Journal (USA)
transtl. transitional
Trav.Ass.Capitant Travaux de l'Association Henri Capitant des Amis de la Culture Juridique Française (Fr.)
Trav.-Cochin Indian Law Reports, Kerala Series. 1950–
Trav.Com.Fr.D.I.P. Travaux du Comité Français de Droit International Privé (Fr.)
Trav.comité franc.dr.int.pr. Travaux du Comité Français de Droit International Privé (Fr.)
Trav.Ind. Travancore, India
Trav.L.J. Travancor Law Journal (India) 1910–47
Trav.L.R. Travancore Law Reports (India) 1910–47
Trav.L.T. Travancore Law Times (India) 1926–38
Tray.Lat.Max. Trayner, Latin Maxims and Phrases. 4ed. 1894
Tray.Leg.Max. Trayner, Latin Maxims and Phrases. 4ed. 1894
Trb. Tractatenblad van het Koninkrijk der Nederlanden (Neth.)
Tread. Treadway's South Carolina Constitutional Reports
Treadway's South Carolina Law Reports (6–7 S.C.L.) 1812–16

Tread.Const. Treadway's South Carolina Constitutional Reports

Treadway Const.(S.C.) Treadway's South Carolina Constitutional Reports

Treas. Treasurer
Treasury

Treas.Dec. Treasury Decisions Under Customs and Other Laws (USA) 1943–

Treas.Dec.Int.Rev. Treasury Decisions Under Internal Revenue Laws (USA) 1942–

Treas.Dept. Treasury Department (USA)

Treas.Regs. United States Treasury Regulations

Treby, Reports Reports of cases by Sir George Treby. 1700 (MS in Middle Temple Library)

Tred. Tredgold's Cape Colony Reports (S.Afr.)

Trehern British & Colonial Prize Cases. 1914–22

Trem. Tremaine's Pleas of the Crown. 1723

Trem.P.C. Tremaine's Pleas of the Crown. 1723

Trent L.J. Trent Law Journal. 1977–

tres in three weeks (return)

Trev.Tax.Suc. Trevor, Taxes on Succession. 4ed. 1881

Trf. Transfer

Tri.Bish. Trial of the Seven Bishops

Tri.E.of Cov. Trial of the Earl of Coventry

Trial Law.Guide Trial Lawyer's Guide (USA) 1957–

Trial Law.Q. Trial Lawyers' Quarterly (USA) 1964–

Trib. Tribunal
Tribunale (It.) ordinary court of first instance

Trib.admin. Tribunal adminstratif (Fr.) Administrative Court

Trib.civ. Tribunal civil (Fr.) Civil Court

Trib.com. Tribunal de commerce (Fr.) Commercial Court

Trib.Comm.Bruxelles Tribunal de commerce de Bruxelles (Belg.)

Trib.con. Tribunal des conflits (Fr.)

Trib.corr. Tribunal correctionnel (Fr.) criminal court

Trib.gde.inst. Tribunal de grande instance (Fr.)

Trib.gr.inst. Tribunal de grande instance (Fr.)

Trib.inst. Tribunal d'instance (Fr.)

Trib.paix Tribunal de paix (Fr.) petty court

Trib.simple pol. Tribunal de simple police (Fr.) police court

Trib.Supr. Tribunal Suprème

Trim. Rivista trimestrale di diritto e procedura civile (It.)

Trim.pubbl. Rivista trimestrale di diritto pubblico

Trin. Trinity Term

Trinidad L.R. Trinidad Law Reports. 1893–

Trint.T. Trinity Term

Trip. All India Reporter, Tripura. 1952–

Tripp Tripp's Reports (5, 6 Dakota)

Tris.Pr.Pr. Tristram, Probate Practice

Trist. Tristram's Consistory Judgments. 1872–90
Tristram's Probate Practice

Tristram Tristram's Consistory Judgments. 1872–90
Tristram's Probate Practice

Troub.& H.Prac. Troubat & Haly's Practice (Pennsylvania)

Trow.D.& Cr. Trower, Debtor and Creditor. 1860

Trow.Eq. Trower, Manual of the Prevalance of Equity. 1876

Tru. Trueman's Equity Cases (New Brunswick) (Can.) 1876–93

Tru.L.I. Trust Law International

Tru.Railw.Rep. Truman's American Railway Reports. 1872–81

True. Trueman's Equity Cases (New Brunswick) (Can.) 1876–93

Truem.Eq.Cas. Trueman's Equity Cases (New Brunswick) 1876–93

Truemans Eq.Cas. Trueman's Equity Cases (New Brunswick) 1876–93

Trust Bull. Trust Bulletin, American Bankers Association. 1921–70
Trust Co.Mag. Trust Companies Magazine. 1904–38
Trust L.& P. Trust Law and Practice
Trust Lett. Trust Letter, American Bankers Association. 1971–
Trust Terr. Trust Territory
Trusts & Est. Trusts & Estates (USA) 1904–
Trye Jus Filiz. Trye's Jus Filizarii. 1684
Ts.L.J. Tulsa Law Journal. 1964–
Tu.Civ.L.F. Tulane Civil Law Forum. 1973–
Tu.L. Tulane Law Review (Orleans, La.) 1929–
Tu.L.R. Tulane Law Review (Orleans, La.) 1929–
Tuck. Tucker & Clephan's Reports (21 District of Columbia) 1892–93
Tucker's Reports (156–175 Massachusetts)
Tucker's Select Cases (Newfoundland) 1817–28
Tucker's Surrogate Reports (New York) 1864–69
Tuck.Sel.Cas. Tucker's Select Cases (Newfoundland) 1817–28
Tuck.Sur. Tucker's Surrogate Reports (New York) 1864–69
Tuck.Surr. Tucker's Surrogate Reports (New York) 1864–69
Tuck.& C. Tucker & Clephan's District of Columbia Reports (21 D.C.) 1892–93
Tuck.& Cl. Tucker & Clephan's District of Columbia Reports (21 D.C.) 1892–93
Tucker(N.Y.) Tucker's New York Surrogate Reports. 1864–69
Tucker Report Report of the Committee on the Limitation of Actions (Cmd. 7740) 1949
Tud.Cas.Merc.Law Tudor's Leading Cases on Mercantile Law. 3ed. 1884
Tud.Cas.R.P. Tudor, Leading Cases on Real Property. 4ed. 1898
Tud.Char.Tr. Tudor, Charitable Trusts. 2ed. 1871
Tudor Lead.Cas.Real Prop. Tudor, Leading Cases on Real Property. 4ed. 1898
Tudor's L.C.M.L. Tudor's Leading Cases on Mercantile Law. 3ed. 1884
Tudor's L.C.R.P. Tudor's Leading Cases on Real Property. 4ed. 1898
Tul. Tulane
Tul.Civ.L.F. Tulane Civil Law Forum. 1973–
Tul.L.Rev. Tulane Law Review
Tul.Mar.L.J. Tulane Maritime Law Journal
Tul.Tax Inst. Tulane Tax Institute. 1951–
Tulane L.Rev. Tulane Law Review. 1929–
Tulsa L.J. Tulsa Law Journal. 1964–
Tup.App. Tupper's Appeal Reports (Ontario, Can.) 1876–1900
Tupp. Tupper's Appeal Reports, (Ontario, Can.) 1876–1900
Tupper's Upper Canada Practice Reports. 1850–1900
Tupper Tupper's Appeals Reports, (Ontario, Can.) 1876–1900
Tupper's Upper Canada Practice Reports (Can.) 1850–1900
Tur. Turner's Reports (35–48 Arkansas)
Turner's Reports (99–101 Kentucky)
Tur.& R. Turner & Russell's Chancery Reports (37 ER) 1822–24
Tur.& Ru. Turner & Russell's Chancery Reports (37 ER) 1822–24
Tur.& Rus. Turner & Russell's Chancery Reports (37 ER) 1822–24
Turkish Yb.Int'l L. Turkish Yearbook of International Law
Turkish Yb.Int'l Rel. Turkish Yearbook of International Relations
Turn. Turner's Reports (35–48 Arkansas)
Turner's Reports (99–101 Kentucky)
Turner Select Pleas of the Forest (Selden Society Publication 13) 1901
Turn.Ch.Pr. Turner, Practice of the Court of Chancery. 4ed. 1821
Turn.Cop. Turner, Copyright in Designs. 1849

Turn.Pat. Turner, Patents. 1851

Turn.& R. Turner & Russell's Chancery Reports (37 ER) 1822–24

Turn.& Rus. Turner and Russell's Chancery Reports (37 ER) 1822–24

Turn.& Russ. Turner and Russell's Chancery Reports (37 ER) 1822–24

Turnour, Reports Reports of cases by Arthur Turnour. 1651

Tutt.& C. Tuttle & Carpenter's Reports (52 California)

Tutt.& Carp. Tuttle & Carpenter's Reports (52 California)

Tuttle Tuttle & Carpenter's Reports (52 California)

Tuttle & Carpenter Tuttle & Carpenter's Reports (52 California)

Tvl.S.A. Transvaal, South Africa

Tw.Nat.P. Twiss, Law of Nations in Time of Peace. 2ed. 1884

Tw.Nat.W. Twiss, Law of Nations in Time of War. 2ed. 1875

Twiss Twiss, The Law of Nations

Tx. Tax
Texas
Texas Reports. 1846–

Tx.Ci. Texas Civil Appeals Reports. 1892–1911

Tx.Cr. Texas Criminal Appeals Reports. 1876–

Tx.L. Texas Law Review. 1922–

Tx.L.J. Texas Law Journal (Tyler) 1877–82; (Austin) 1882–96

Tx.L.R. Texas Law Review. 1922–

Tyds.Heden.Rom-Holland R. Tydskrift vir Hedendaagse Romeins-Hollandse Reg (S.Afr.)

Tyds.S.Afr.R. Tydskrift vir die Suid-Afrikaanse Reg (S.Afr.)

Tydskr.v.Hedend.R.H. Tydskrift vir Hedendaagse Romeins-Hollandse Reg (S.Afr.)

Tydskr.vir die Sud.-Afr. Reg. Tydskrift vir die Suid–Afrikaanse Reg (S.Afr.)

Tydskrif Tydskrif vir Hedendaagse Romeins-Hollandse Reg (S.Afr.) 1937–46, 1948–

Tyl. Tyler's Vermont Supreme Court Reports. 1800–03

Tyler Tyler's Vermont Supreme Court Reports. 1800–03

Tyng Tyng's Reports (2–17 Massachusetts) 1806–20

Tyr. Tyrwhitt's Exchequer Reports (35–40 RR) 1830–35

Tyr.& Gr. Tyrwhitt & Granger's Exchequer Reports (46 RR) 1835–36

Tyrw. Tyrwhitt's Exchequer Reports (35–40 RR) 1830–35

Tyrw.& G. Tyrwhitt & Granger's Exchequer Reports (46 RR) 1835–36

Tyt.Mil.L. Tytler, Military Law and Courts Martial. 3ed. 1812

Tytler,Mil.Law. Tytler, Military Law and Courts Martial. 3ed. 1812

U

U. Ugeskrift for Retsvaesen (Den.) 1867–
University
Utah
Utah Reports. 1855–

U.2d. Utah Reports, Second Series

ua unit of account

U/A Under Agreement
Underwriting Account

U.A.R. Uniform Aanbestedingsreglement (Neth.) Standard Conditions for Uniform Tenders

UASt. Umsatzaugleichsteuer (Ger.) Sales Equalisation Tax

U.A.V. Uniforme Administratieve Voorwaarde (Neth.) Standard Contruction Conditions

U.Ark.Little Rock L.J. University of Arkansas at Little Rock Law Journal

UB Unemployment Benefit

U.B. Upper Bench

UBA-FB Umweltbundesamt Forschungsbericht

U.B.C.L.R. University of British Columbia Law Review (Can.) 1959–

U.B.C.L.Rev. University of British Columbia Law Review (Can.) 1959–

U.B.C.Legal N. University of British Columbia Legal Notes (Can.) 1949–58

U.B.L.R. University of Baltimore Law Review. 1971–

U.B.L.S.L.J. University of Botswana, Lesotho and Swaziland Law Journal. 1970–

U.B.Pr. Upper Bench Precedents tempore Car. I

U.B.R. Upper Burma Rulings

U.Balt.L.R. University of Baltimore Law Review. 1971–

U.Bridgeport L.Rev. University of Bridgeport Law Review (USA)

U.Brit.Col.L.Rev. University of British Columbia Law Review (Can.) 1959–

U.C. Unité de Compte Européenne
Upper Canada

UCA Uniform Companies Act 1961 (Aus.)

U.C.App. Upper Canada Appeal Reports

U.C.App.(Can.) Upper Canada Appeal Reports

U.C.App.Rep. Upper Canada Appeal Reports

U.C.C. Uniform Commercial Code (USA)
Universal Copyright Convention. 1952

U.C.C.L.J. Uniform Commercial Code Law Journal

U.C.C.P. Upper Canada Common Pleas Reports. 1850–82

U.C.C.P.(Can.) Upper Canada Common Pleas Reports. 1850–82

U.C.C.P.D. Upper Canada Common Pleas Division Reports (Ontario)

U.C.C.R. Upper Canada Court Records (Report of Ontario Bureau of Archives)

U.C.C.Rep.Serv. Uniform Commercial Code Reporting Service

U.C.Ch. Grant's Upper Canada Chancery Reports. 1849–82

U.C.Ch.(Can.) Grant's Upper Canada Chancery Reports. 1849–82

U.C.Cham. Upper Canada Chambers Reports. 1846–52

U.C.Chamb. Upper Canada Chambers Reports. 1846–52
U.C.Chan. Grant's Upper Canada Chancery Reports. 1849–82
U.C.D.L.Rev. University of California, Davis Law Review. 1969–
U.C.Davis L.R. University of California, Davis Law Review
U.C.E. Unité de compte européenne (Fr.)
U.C.E.& A. Grant's Ontario Error and Appeal Reports (Can.) 1846–66
U.C.Err.& App. Upper Canada Error and Appeal Reports (Ontario) 1846–66
U.C.Err.& App.(Can.) Upper Canada Error and Appeal Reports (Ontario) 1846–66
UCHILS The University of Chicago Law School
U.C.Jur. Upper Canada Jurist. 1844–48
U.C.Jur.(Can.) Upper Canada Jurist. 1844–48
U.C.K.B. Upper Canada King's Bench Reports, Old Series. 1831–44
U.C.K.B.(Can.) Upper Canada King's Bench Reports, Old Series. 1831–44
U.C.L. University College London
U.C.L.A. University of California at Los Angeles
U.C.L.A.–Alaska L.Rev. University of California at Los Angeles – Alaska Law Review (USA) 1971–
U.C.L.A.Intra.L.Rev. U.C.L.A. Intramural Law Review. 1952–53
U.C.L.A.J.Envtl.L.& Pol'y U.C.L.A. Journal of Environmental Law and Policy
U.C.L.A.L.Rev. U.C.L.A. Law Review. 1953–
U.C.L.A.Law Rev. University of California at Los Angeles Law Review. 1953–
U.C.L.A. P.B.L.J. University of California at Los Angeles, Pacific Basin Law Journal (USA) 1982–
U.C.L.A.Pac.Basin L.J. University of California at Los Angeles, Pacific Basin Law Journal (USA) 1982–
U.C.L.J. Upper Canada Law Journal. 1855–1922
U.C.L.J.N.S. Upper Canada Law Journal, New Series. 1865–1922
U.C.L.J.N.S.(Can.) Upper Canada Law Journal, New Series. 1865–1922
U.C.L.J.O.S. Canada Law Journal, Old Series. 1855–1864
U.C.L.R. University of Ceylon Law Review. 1958
University of Chicago Law Review. 1933–
University of Cincinnati Law Review. 1927–42, 1948–
University of Colorado Law Review. 1962–
U.C.O.S. Upper Canada King's Bench Reports, Old Series. 1831–44
U.C.P.R. Upper Canada Practice Reports. 1850–1900
U.C.Pr. Upper Canada Practice Reports. 1850–1900
U.C.Pr.(Can.) Upper Canada Practice Reports. 1850–1900
U.C.Pr.R. Upper Canada Practice Reports. 1850–1900
U.C.Pract. Upper Canada Practice Reports. 1850–1900
U.C.Q.B. Upper Canada Queen's Bench Reports. 1844–81
U.C.Q.B.O.S. Upper Canada Queen's Bench Reports, Old Series. 1831–44
U.C.Q.B.O.S.(Can.) Upper Canada Queen's Bench Reports, Old Series. 1831–44
U.C.R. University of Cincinnati Law Review (Ohio) 1927–42, 1948–
Upper Canada Reports
U.C.Rep. Upper Canada Reports
U.Ceylon L.R. University of Ceylon Law Review. 1958
U.Chi.L.Rec. University of Chicago Law School Record. 1951–
U.Chi.L.Rev. University of Chicago Law Review. 1933–
U.Chi.L.S.Rec. University of Chicago Law School Record. 1951–
U.Chi.Legal F. University of Chicago Legal Forum

U.Chicago L.Rev. University of Chicago Law Review. 1933–

U.Cin.L.Rev. University of Cincinnati Law Review. 1927–42, 1948–

U.Colo.L.Rev. University of Colorado Law Review. 1962–

U.D.C. Universal Decimal Classification
Urban District Council

UDHR Universal Declaration of Human Rights. 1948

U.D.I. Unilateral Declaration of Independence

U.Dayton L.Rev. University of Dayton Law Review

U.Det.J.Urb.L. University of Detroit Journal of Urban Law. 1976–

U.Det.L.J. University of Detroit Law Journal. 1931–66

U.Det.L.Rev. University of Detroit Law Review

U.Detroit J.Urban L. University of Detroit Journal of Urban Law

U.Detroit L.J. University of Detroit Law Journal. 1931–66

UEAC Union of Central African States

UE.Law J. University of the East Law Journal (Philippines)

U.F.A.W. Universities Federation of Animal Welfare

U.f.R. Ugeskrift for Retsvaesen (Denmark)

U.Fla.J.L.& Pub.Pol'y University of Florida Journal of Law and Public Policy

U.Fla.L.Rev. University of Florida Law Review. 1948–

U.G.C. University Grants Committee

U.G.L.J. University of Ghana Law Journal. 1964–

U.Ghana L.J. University of Ghana Law Journal

U.Haw.L.Rev. University of Hawaii Law Review

U.I.A. Union Internationale des Avocats (International Association of Lawyers)
Union of International Associations

UIC Unemployment Insurance Commission

U.I.D. Selected Decisions by Umpire for Northern Ireland, respecting Claims to Benefit

U.Ill.L.B. University of Illinois Law Bulletin. 1918

U.Ill.L.Bull. University of Illinois Law Bulletin. 1918

U.Ill.L.F. Univesity of Illinois Law Forum. 1949–

U.Ill.L.Forum University of Illinois Law Forum. 1949–

U.Ill.L.Rev. University of Illinois Law Review

U.Iowa L Rev. University of Iowa Law Review. 1915–

U.J. Uganda Journal

U.K. United Kingdom

UKIAS United Kingdom Immigrants Advisory Service

U.K.L.R. University of Kansas Law Review. 1952–

UKREP United Kingdom Permanent Representative (EEC)

U.K.T.S. United Kingdom Treaty Series. 1892–

U.Kan.City L.Rev. University of Kansas City Law Review. 1938–63

U.Kan.L.R. University of Kansas Law Review. 1952–

UL Utsokningslag (Swed.) Code of Execution

U.L.A. Uniform Laws Annotated

U.L.C. Uniform Law Cases (UNIDROIT, Rome)

U.L.C.J. University Law College Journal, Rajputana University (India) 1954–

U.L.R. Uganda Protectorate Law Reports. 1904–51
Uniform Law Review (It.) 1973–
Union Law Review (S.Afr.) 1910–11
University Law Review (USA) 1893–97
Utah Law Review. 1949–
Utilities Law Reporter (USA)
Utilities Law Review

U.M.E. Unité Monétaire Européenne

UMKCLR University of Missouri at Kansas City Law Review. 1964–

UMKC L.Rev. University of Missouri at Kansas City Law Review. 1964–

U.M.L.R. University of Malaya Law Review. 1959–61
University of Miami Law Review. 1957–

U.Maine L.Rev. University of Maine Law Review

U.Malaya L.Rev. University of Malaya Law Review

U.Mary.L.Forum University of Maryland Law Forum

U.Miami Ent.& Sports L.Rev. University of Miami Entertainment and Sports Law Review

U.Miami Inter–Am.L.Rev. University of Miami Inter-American Law Review

U.Miami L.Rev. University of Miami Law Review. 1957–

U.Mich.J.Law Reform University of Michigan Journal of Law Reform. 1970–

U.Missouri at K.C.L.Rev. University of Missouri at Kansas City Law Review. 1964–

U.Mo.B.,Law Ser. University of Missouri Bulletin, Law Series. 1913–35

U.Mo.Bull.L.Ser. University of Missouri Bulletin, Law Series. 1913–35

U.Mo.K.C.L.Rev. University of Missouri at Kansas City Law Review. 1964–

U.Mo.L.Bull. University of Missouri Law Bulletin. 1913–35

U.N. United Nations

U.N.A. United Nations Association

U.N.A.A.R. United Nations Arbitral Awards Reports

U.N.B.L.J. University of New Brunswick Law Journal (Can.) 1952–

U.N.B.L.S.J. University of New Brunswick Law School Journal. 1947–51

U.N.B.Law Journal University of New Brunswick Law Journal (Can.) 1952–

U.N.Bull. United Nations Bulletin (USA) 1946–

UNCDD United Nations Convention on the Declaration of Death of Missing Persons. 1950

U.N.C.I.O. United Nations Conference on International Organisation

U.N.C.I.P. United Nations Commission on India and Pakistan

UNCITRAL United Nations Commission on International Trade Law

UNCLOS United Nations Conference on the Law of the Sea

UNCTAD United Nations Conference on Trade and Development

UNDP United Nations Development Programme

UNDRO United Nations Disaster Relief Office

U.N.Doc. United Nations Documents

U.N.E.C.A. United Nations Economic Commission for Africa

U.N.E.D.A. United Nations Economic Development Administration

U.N.E.F. United Nations Emergency Force

U.N.E.P. United Nations Environment Programme

U.N.E.P./R.O.L.A.C. UNEP Regional Office for Latin America and the Caribbean

UNESCO United Nations Educational, Scientific and Cultural Organisation

U.N.E.S.C.O.R. United Nations Economic and Social Council Official Record

U.N.F.A.O. United Nations Food and Agriculture Organisation

U.N.F.P.A. United Nations Fund for Population Activities

U.N.G.A. United Nations General Assembly

U.N.G.A.O.R. United Nations General Assembly Official Record

U.N.H.C.R. United Nations High Commissioner for Refugees

U.N.H.Q. United Nations Headquarters

UNICEF United Nations Children's Emergency Fund
UNIDF United Nations Industrial Development Fund
U.N.I.D.O. United Nations Industrial Development Organisation
UNIDROIT International Institute for the Unification of Private Law
UNIFIL United Nations Interim Force in Lebanon
UNISCAN Anglo-Scandinavian Economic Committee
U.N.I.T.A.R. United Nations Institute for Training and Research
U.N.J.Y. United Nations Juridical Yearbook. 1962–
U.N.Juridical Y.B. United Nations Juridical Year Book. 1962–
U.N.L.L. United Nations League of Lawyers
U.N.L.O.S. United Nations Law of the Sea (Conference)
U.N.L.R. United Nations Law Reports. 1966–
U.N.L.S. United Nations Legislative Series
UNMC United Nations Monthly Chronicle
UN Mo.Chron. U.N. Monthly Chronicle
U.N.O. United Nations Organisation
U.N.R.E.F. United Nations Refugee Emergency Fund
U.N.R.I.A.A. United Nations Reports of International Arbitral Awards
UNRISD United Nations Research Institute for Social Development
U.N.R.R.A. United Relief and Rehabilitation Administration
U.N.R.W.A. United Nations Relief and Works Agency
U.N.Rev. United Nations Review (USA) 1941–45
U.N.S.C.C.U.R. United Nations Scientific Conference on the Conservation & Utilisation of Resources
U.N.S.D.D. United Nations Social Development Division
U.N.S.G. United Nations Secretary General
U.N.S.W.L.J. University of New South Wales Law Journal (Aus.)
U.N.T.C. United Nations Trusteeship Council
U.N.T.C.O.R. United Nations Trusteeship Council Official Record
U.N.T.D.I.D. United Nations Trade Data Interchange Directory
U.N.T.E.A. United Nations Temporary Executive Authority
U.N.T.F.D.P.P. United Nations Trust for Development Planning and Projections
U.N.T.F.D.S. United Nations Trust Fund for Social Development
U.N.T.S. United Nations Treaty Series
U.N.T.S.O. United Nations Truce Supervisory Organisation
U.N.T.T. United Nations Trust Territory
U.N.Y.B. United Nations Year Book
U.N.Y.B.I.L.C. United Nations Yearbook of the International Law Commission
U.New Brunswick L.J. University of New Brunswick Law Journal (Can.)
U.New South Wales L.J. University of New South Wales Law Journal (Aus.)
U.Newark L.Rev. University of Newark Law Review (USA) 1936–42
U.O P.L.Rev. University of Pennsylvania Law Review. 1944–
U.of Chi.L.Rev. University of Chicago Law Review
U.of Cin.L.Rev. University of Cincinnati Law Review
U.of Detroit L.J. University of Detroit Law Journal
U.of Fla.L.Rev. University of Florida Law Review
U.of Kans.City L.Rev. University of Kansas City Law Review
U.of M.L.B. University of Missouri Law Bulletin. 1913–35

U.of Omaha Bull. Night Law School Bulletin, University of Omaha. 1923–27
U.of P.L.R. University of Pennsylvania Law Review. 1944–
U.of Pa.L.Rev. University of Pennsylvania Law Review. 1944–
U.of Pitt.L.Rev. University of Pittsburgh Law Review
U.of T.School of L.R. School of Law Review, Toronto University (Can.) 1942–55
U.of Toronto L.J. University of Toronto Law Journal
U.P.Ind. Uttar Pradesh (India)
U.P.L.R. Uganda Protectorate Law Reports. 1904–51
United Provinces Law Reports (India) 1919–22
U.P.L.T. United Provinces Law Times (India) 1937–
U.P.News Unauthorised Practice News (USA) 1934–
UPU Universal Postal Union
U.Pa.L.Rev. University of Pennsylvania Law Review. 1944–
U.Pitt.L.Rev. University of Pittsburgh Law Review. 1935–42, 1947–
U.Puget Sound L.Rev. University of Puget Sound Law Review
U.Q.L.J. University of Queensland Law Journal (Aus.) 1948–
U.Queens.L.J. University of Queensland Law Journal (Aus.) 1948–
URG Urheberrechtsgesetz (Ger.) Copyright Act
U.Rich.L.N. University of Richmond Law Notes (USA) 1958–67
U.Rich.L.Rev. University of Richmond Law Review (USA) 1968–
U.Richmond L.Rev. University of Richmond Law Review (USA) 1968–
u.s. ut supra (Lat.) as above
U.S. United States Supreme Court Reports. 1790–
U.S.A. United States of America
USAA United States Arbitration Act
U.S.Ap. United States Appeals Reports. 1892–99
U.S.App. United States Appeals Reports. 1892–99
U.S.App.D.C. United States Court of Appeals Reports, District of Columbia. 1941–
U.S.Av. United States Aviation Reports. 1822–
U.S.Av.R. United States Aviation Reports. 1822–
U.S.Aviation Rep. United States Aviation Reports. 1822–
U.S.C. United States Code
U.S.C.A. United States Code Annotated
U.S.C.App. United States Code Appendix
U.S.C.C. United States Circuit Court
United States Court of Claims
U.S.C.C.A. United States Circuit Court of Appeals Reports. 1892–1919
U.S.C.C.P.A. United States Court of Customs and Patent Appeals
U.S.C.Govt'l.Rev. University of South Carolina Governmental Review
U.S.C.S. United States Code Service
U.S.C.Supp. United States Code Supplement
U.S.cert.den. Certiorari denied by U.S. Supreme Court
U.S.cert.dis. Certiorari dismissed by U.S. Supreme Court
U.S.Comp.St. United States Compiled Statutes
U.S.Comp.St.Supp. United States Compiled Statutes Supplement
U.S.Cong.& Adm.Serv. U.S. Congressional and Administrative Service
U.S.Ct.Cl. United States Court of Claims
U.S.D.C. United States District Court
United States District of Columbia
U.S.Daily United States Daily, Washington, D.C. 1926–33
U.S.Dept.Int. United States Department of the Interior
U.S.Dig. United States Digest
U.S.Dist.Ct. United States District Court

U.S.E. Encyclopedia of United States Reports
U.S.F.L.Rev. University of San Francisco Law Review
U.S.F.V.L.Rev. University of San Fernando Valley Law Review. 1967–
U.S.G. United States Government
U.S.I.C.C.Rep. United States Interstate Commerce Commission Reports. 1887–
U.S.I.C.C.V.R. U.S. Interstate Commerce Commission Valuation Reports. 1918–
USIS United States Information Service
U.S.Jur. United States Jurist. 1871–73
U.S.L.Ed. Lawyers' Edition, United States Supreme Court Reports. 1790–
U.S.L.Ed.2d. Lawyers' Edition, United States Supreme Court Reports, Second Series
U.S.L.J. United States Law Journal and Civilian's Magazine. 1822–23, 1826
U.S.L.Mag. United States Monthly Law Magazine. 1850–52
U.S.L.Rev. United States Law Review. 1929–40
U.S.L.W. United States Law Week. 1933–
U.S.Law Ed. United States Supreme Court Reports, Lawyers' Edition. 1790–
U.S.Law Int. United States Law Intelligencer and Review (Providence and Philadelphia) 1829–31
U.S.Law Jour. United States Law Journal and Civilian's Magazine. 1822–23, 1826
U.S.Law Mag. United States Monthly Law Magazine. 1850–52
U.S.Month.Law Mag. United States Monthly Law Magazine. 1850–52
U.S.P.Q. United States Patents Quarterly (USA) 1929–
U.S.Pat.Q. United States Patents Quarterly (USA) 1929–
U.S.Pat.Quar. United States Patents Quarterly. 1929–
U.S.Pat.Quart. United States Patents Quarterly. 1929–
U.S.R. United States Supreme Court Reports. 1790–
U.S.R.R.Lab.Bd.Dec. Decisions of the United States Railroad Labor Board. 1920–26
U.S.R.S. United States Revised Statutes
U.S.Reg. United States Register (Philadelphia)
U.S.reh.den. Rehearing denied by U.S. Supreme Court
U.S.Rep. United States Reports. 1875–
U.S.Rep.(L.Ed.) United States Reports, Lawyers' Edition. 1790–
U.S.Rev.St. United States Revised Statutes
U.S.S.C.Rep. United States Supreme Court Reports. 1790–
U.S.S.R. Union of Soviet Socialist Republics
U.S.St.at L. United States Statutes at Large
U.S.St.Tr. United States State Trials (Wharton)
U.S.Stat. United States Statutes at Large
U.S.Sup.Ct. United States Supreme Court Reporter. 1882–
UST United States Treaties & Other International Agreements. 1950–
U.S.T.C. United States Tax Cases (CCH) 1935–
U.S.T.D. United States Treaty Development
U.S.T.I.A. United States Treaties and International Agreements
U.S.Tax Cas. United States Tax Cases (CCH) (USA) 1935–
U.S.Treas.Reg. United States Treasury Regulations
U.S.Treaty Ser. United States Treaty Series
u.s.w. und so weiter (Ger.) and so forth
U.S.& Can.Av. United States and Canadian Aviation Reports
U.San Fernando V.L.Rev. University of San Fernando Valley Law Review. 1967–
U.San Fernando Valley L.Rev. University of San Fernando Valley Law Review

U.San.Fran.L.Rev. University of San Francisco Law Review. 1966–
U.San Francisco L.Rev. University of San Francisco Law Review. 1966–
U.So.Cal.Tax Inst. University of Southern California Tax Institute
UStG Umsatzsteuergesetz (Ger.) Turnover Tax Act
UStandG Umsatzsteueränderungsgesetz (Ger.) Turnover Tax (Amendment) Act
U.T. Unit Trust
U.T.Fac.L.Rev. Faculty of Law Review, University of Toronto (Can.) 1973–
U.T.Faculty L.R. Faculty of Law Review, University of Toronto (Can.) 1973–
U.T.L.J. University of Toronto Law Journal (Can.) 1935–
U.T.L.R. University of Tasmania Law Review (Aus.) 1958–
U.Tas.L.R. University of Tasmania Law Review (Aus.) 1958–
U.Tasm.L.Rev. University of Tasmania Law Review (or Tasmania University Law Review) 1958–
U.Tol.L.Rev. University of Toledo Law Review. 1969–
U.Toledo Intra.L.R. University of Toledo Intramural Law Review. 1967–68
U.Toledo L.Rev. University of Toledo Law Review. 1969–
U.Tor.Fac.L.R. University of Toronto Faculty of Law Review. 1973–
U.Tor.L.Rev. University of Toronto School of Law Review. 1942–55
U.Toronto Fac.L.Rev. University of Toronto Faculty of Law Review. 1973–
U.Toronto L.J. University of Toronto Law Journal (Can.) 1935–
U/w Underwriter
U/W Under Will
U.W.A.L.R. University of Western Australia Law Review. 1948–
U.W.A.L.Rev. University of Western Australia Law Review. 1948–
U.W.Austl.L.Rev. University of Western Australia Law Review. 1948–
UWG Gesetz gegen den unläuteren Wettbewerb (Ger.) Law against Unfair Competition
UWI University of the West Indies
U.W.L.A.L.Rev. University of West Los Angeles Law Review. 1969–
U.W.L.A.Rev. University of West Los Angeles Law Review. 1969–
U.W.O.L.Rev. University of Western Ontario Law Review. 1976–
U.W.Ont.L.Rev. University of Western Ontario Law Review. 1976–
U.Wash.L.Rev. University of Washington Law Review. 1919–
U.West.Aust.Ann.L.Rev. University of Western Australia Annual Law Review. 1960–
U.West.Aust.L.Rev. University of Western Australia Law Review. 1960–
U.West L.A.L.Rev. University of West Los Angeles Law Review
U.Western Aust.L.Rev. University of Western Australia Law Review. 1960–
U.Western Ont.L Rev. University of Western Ontario Law Review. 1976–
U.Windsor L.Rev. University of Windsor Law Review (USA)
U/wrs Underwriters
U.Zambia L.B. University of Zambia Law Bulletin. 1970–
Üb Übereinkommen (Ger.) agreement
überarb.Aufl. überarbeitete Auflage
Udal Udal's Fiji Law Reports. 1875–97
UfR Ugeskrift för Retsvaesen (Den.) 1867–
Ug.L.F. Uganda Law Focus. 1972–
Ug.L.R. Uganda Protectorate Law Reports. 1904–51
Ug.Pr.L.R. Uganda Protectorate Law Reports. 1904–51
Uganda L.F. Uganda Law Focus. 1972–
Uganda L.R. Uganda Protectorate Law Reports. 1904–51
Uganda Leg.Focus Uganda Legal Focus
Uges.Retsv. Ugeskrift för Retsvaesen (Den.)
uitg. uitgave (Neth.) edition
Ukrainian Q. Ukrainian Quarterly

Ulm.L.Rec. Ulman's Law Record (New York)
Un.of Gh.L.J. University of Ghana Law Journal. 1964–
Un.Prac.News Unauthorised Practice News (USA) 1934–
Un.Trav.Dec. Unreported Travancore Decisions (India)
Unauth. Unauthorised
Unconsol.Laws Unconsolidated Laws
Und. Undivided
Und.Ch.Pr. Underhill, Chancery Procedure. 1881
Und.Conv. Underhill, New Conveyancing. 1925
Und.Part. Underhill, Partnership. 10ed. 1975
Und.Sher. Under Sheriff
Und.Torts Underhill, Torts. 16ed. 1949
Und.Tr. Underhill, Trusts and Trustees
Unemp.Ins. Unemployment Insurance
Unempl.Ins.Rep. Unemployment Insurance Reporter (CCH) (USA)
Unidroit Yb. International Institute for the Unification of Private Law, Yearbook (It.)
Unif. Unified
Uniform
Uniform City Ct.Act. Uniform City Court Act
Uniform Dist.Ct.Act. Uniform District Court Act
Uniform L.Rev. Uniform Law Review/Revue de Droit Uniforme (It.)
Union Pac.L.D.B. Union Pacific Law Department Bulletin. 1911–29
Univ. Universal
University
Univ.Chicago Law Rev. University of Chicago Law Review
Univ.Ghana L.J. University of Ghana Law Review
Univ.Hum.Rts. Universal Human Rights (USA) 1979–
Univ.Ill.L.Forum University of Illinois Law Forum
Univ.L.Coll.J. University Law College Journal, Rajputana University (India) 1954–
Univ.L.R. University Law Review (USA) 1893–97
Univ.L.Rev. University Law Review (USA) 1893–97
Univ.of Chic.L.R. Iniversity of Chicago Law Review
Univ.of Cin.L.R. University of Cincinnati Law Review
Univ.of Fla.L.R. University of Florida Law Review
Univ.of Malaya L.R. University of Malaya Law Review
Univ.of Pa.L.R. University of Pennsylvania Law Review
Univ.of Tas.L.R. University of Tasmania Law Review (Aus.) 1958–
Univ.of Toronto L.J. University of Toronto Law Journal
Univ.of W.A.L.R. University of Western Australia Law Review
Univ.Q.L.J. University of Queensland Law Journal (Aus.) 1948–
Univ.Qld.L.J. University of Queensland Law Journal (Aus.) 1948–
Univ.S.Inst.of Crim.Proc. University of Sydney Faculty of Law Institute of Criminology Proceedings (Aus.) 1967–
Univ.T.L.R. University of Tasmania Law Review. 1958–
Univ.Tasmania L.Rev. University of Tasmania Law Review. 1958–
Univ.W.A.Ann.L.Rev. University of Western Australia Annual Law Review. 1948–59
Univ.W.A.L.Rev. University of Western Australia Law Review. 1948–
Unof. Unofficial
Unrep.Cr.C. Bombay Unreported Criminal Cases (India) 1862–98
Unrep.N.Y.Est.T.C. Unreported New York Estate Tax Cases (P–H)
Unrep.Wills Cas. Unreported Wills Cases (P–H)
unverand.Aufl. unveranderte Auflage
Up.Ben.Pr. Upper Bench Precedents tempore Car. I

Up.Ben.Pre. Upper Bench Precedents tempore Car. I
Up.Can. Upper Canada
Urb. Urban
Urb.Aff.Rep. Urban Affairs Reporter (CCH) (USA)
Urb.Law. The Urban Lawyer (USA)
Urb.Law Pol. Urban Law & Policy (Neth.) 1978–
Urban L.Ann. Urban Law Annual (USA) 1968–
Urban L.& Policy Urban Law and Policy
Urban Law. The Urban Lawyer (USA) 1969–
Urban Law Ann. Urban Law Annual (USA) 1968–
Urblaw Urban Law and Policy (Neth.) 1978–
Urk. Urkunde (Ger.) document, deed, instrument
Urt. Urteil (Ger.) judgment, decision
Ut. Utah
Utah Reports. 1855–
Ut.B.J. Utah Bar Journal. 1973–
Ut.L.R. Utah Law Review. 1949–
Utah Utah Supreme Court Reports. 1855–
Utah 2d Utah Reports, Second Series
Utah B.Bull. Utah Bar Bulletin. 1931–
Utah B.J. Utah Bar Journal. 1973–
Utah Code Ann. Utah Code Annotated
Utah L.Rev. Utah Law Review. 1949–
Utah S.B.A. Utah State Bar Association
Uthwatt Report Leasehold Committee Report (Cmd. 7706) 1949
Util. Utility
Utilities
Util.L.Rep. Utilities Law Reporter (CCH) (USA)

V

v. vedi (It.) see
versus
voir (Fr.) see
volume
V. Vacated
Verb
Verfassung (Ger.) constitution
Verfügung (Ger.) order, decree
Vermont
Vermont Reports. 1826–
Verordnung (Ger.) decree, regulation, ordinance
Version
Vice
Victoria
Vide (Lat.) see
Virginia
Virginia Reports. 1880–
Viscount
Voce (Lat.) word
Void
Volume
VAAP Soviet Copyright Agency (USSR)
VACLE Joint Committee on Continuing Legal Education of the Virginia State Bar and The Virginia Bar Association
V.A.D. Vermogens Aanwas Deling (Neth.) Equity Increase Participation
Veterans' Affairs Decisions, Appealed Pension & Civil Service Retirement Cases (U.S.) 1930–32
VADS Value-added data service
V.A.M.S. Vernon's Annotated Missouri Statutes
V.A.R. Victorian Administrative Reports (in Kyrou's Victorian Administrative Law) (Aus.) 1985–
V.A.S.C.A.R. Visual Average Speed Computer and Recorder
VAS Value-added service
V.A.T. Value Added Tax
VAT Int. VAT Intelligence
V.A.T.S. Vernon's Annotated Texas Statutes
V.A.T.T.R. Value Added Tax Tribunal Reports. 1973–
V.A.T.Trib.Rep. Value Added Tax Tribunal Reports. 1973–
VBl. Verordnungsblatt (Ger.) official gazette
V.B.N. Victorian Bar News (Aus.) 1977–
v.c. valuation clause
V.-C. Vice-Chancellor
Vice-Chancellor's Court
V.C.Adm. Victoria Reports, Admiralty
V.-C.C. Vice-Chancellor's Court
VCCR Vienna Convention on Consular Relations. 1963
VCDR Vienna Convention on Diplomatic Relations. 1961
V.C.Eq. Victoria Reports, Equity
V.C.J.C. Chief Justices Law Reform Committee, Victoria (Aus.)
VCLD Vienna Convention on Civil Liability for Nuclear Damage. 1963
VCLOT Vienna Convention on the Law of Treaties. 1969
V.C.Rep. Vice-Chancellor's Reports
V.Conv.R. Victorian Conveyancing Reports (in Victorian Conveyancing Law and Practice) (Aus.) 1981–
v.d. various dates
V.D. Valuation Decisions
VEB Volkseigener Betrieb
VEL Validated export licence

V.G. Verbi gratia (Lat.) for the sake of example

VGH Verwaltungsgerichtshof (Ger.) District Administrative Court of Appeal

VGKO Verwaltungsgerichtskostenordnung (Ger.) Administratice Courts Costs Regulations

VGO Verwaltungsgerichtsordnung (Ger.) Administrative Court Act

V.G.P.O. Victorian Government Printing Office (Aus.)

V.H.Eq.Dr. Van Heythuysen, Equity Draftsman. 2ed. 1828

v.i. vide infra (Lat.) see below

V.I. Virgin Islands
Virgin Island Reports. 1917–

V.I.A.C. Victorian Industrial Appeals Court (Aus.)

V.I.B.J. Virgin Islands Bar Journal. 1967–

V.I.Code Ann. Virgin Islands Code Annotated

V.I.N. Victorian Industrial Notes (in Alley's Industrial Law Victoria) (Aus.) 1982–

V.I.R. Victoria Imperatrix Regina (Victoria Empress and Queen)
Victorian Industrial Reports (in Alley's Industrial Law Victoria) (Aus.) 1982–

V.J.B. Victorian Judgments Bulletin (Aus.) 1985–

VL Vattenlag (Swed.) Water Code

V.L. Vestre Landsret (Den.) Western Court of Appeal

V.L.D. Victorian Licensing Decisions (in Bourke's Liquor Laws of Victoria) (Aus.) 1976–

V.L.E. Victorian Legal Executive (Aus.) 1977–

V.L.L.G. Victorian Law Librarians' Group (Aus.)

V.L.R. Vanderbilt Law Review (Tenn.) 1947–
Victorian Law Reports (Aus.) 1875–1956

V.L.R.(Adm.) Victorian Law Reports, Admiralty (Aus.) 1875–1884

V.L.R.C. Victorian Law Reform Commission (Aus.)

V.L.R.C.W.P. Victorian Law Reform Commission Working Paper (Aus.)

V.L.R.(E.) Victorian Law Reports, Equity (Aus.) 1875–84

V.L.R.(Eq.) Victorian Law Reports, Equity (Aus.) 1875–84

V.L.R.(I.P.& M.) Victorian Law Reports, Insolvency, Probate and Matrimonial (Aus.) 1875–84

V.L.R.(L.) Victorian Law Reports, Law (Aus.) 1875–84

V.L.R.(M.) Victorian Law Reports, Mining (Aus.) 1875–84

V.L.R.(P.& M.) Victorian Law Reports, Probate & Matrimonial (Aus.) 1875–84

V.L.T. Victorian Law Times (Aus.) 1856–57

V.N. Van Ness' Prize Cases (USA) 1814

VNIIGPE All-Union Scientific Research Institute of State Patent Examination (USSR)

V.N.O. Vereniging van Nederlandse Ondernemers (Neth.) Federation of Netherlands Enterprises

VO Verordnung (Ger.) decree

VOBL BZ Verordnungsblatt für die Britische Zone (Ger.) Official Gazette of former British Zone of Occupation

v.o.f. vennootschap onder firma (Neth.) limited partnership

V.P. All India Reporter, Vindhya Pradesh. 1951–57
Vice President

V.P.A. Victorian Planning Appeal Decisions (Aus.) 1969–82

VPC Vardepapperscentralen (Swed.) The Securities Register Centre

VR Verkeersrecht (Neth.)

V.R. Valuation Reports, Interstate Commerce Commission (USA) 1918–
Vermont Reports. 1826–
Victorian Reports (Aus.) 1870–72
Victorian Reports (Aus.) 1957–
Villanova Law Review (USA) 1956–
Webb, A'Beckett & Williams' Victorian Reports (Aus.) 1870–72

V.R.Adm. Victorian Reports, Admiralty (Aus.) 1870–72
V.R.B. Veterans' Review Board (Aus.)
V.R.(E.) Webb, A'Beckett and Williams' Equity Reports (Victoria, Aus.) 1870–72
V.R.(Eq.) Webb A'Beckett and Williams' Equity Reports (Victoria, Aus.) 1870–72
V.R.(I.E.& M.) Webb, A'Beckett and Williams' Insolvency, Ecclesiastical and Matrimonial Reports (Victoria, Aus.) 1870–72
V.R.(L.) Victorian Reports, Law
V.R.(Law) Victorian Reports, Law (Aus.)
v.s. vide supra (Lat.) see above
voorschrift (Neth.) rule, order
V.S. Vermont Statutes
V.S.L.R.C. Victorian Statute Law Revision Committee (Aus.)
VSO Voluntary Service Overseas
VTAK Foreign Trade Arbitration Commission (USSR)
V.T.B.R.Case Victorian Taxation Board of Review Case (Aus.)
VTsIK All-Russian Central Executive Committee
VTsSPS All-Union Central Trade Union Council (USSR)
V.U.C.L.R. Victoria University College Law Review (N.Z.) 1953–57
V.U.L.R. Valparaiso University Law Review. 1966–
V.U.W. Victoria University of Wellington (N.Z.)
V.U.W.L.R. Victoria University of Wellington Law Review (N.Z.) 1957–
V.U.W.L.Rev. Victoria University of Wellington Law Review (N.Z.) 1957–
VV Voorlopig Verslag (Neth.)
VVB Vereinigung volkseigener Betriebe (Ger.) Association of State Enterprises
VVDStRL Veröffentlichungen der Vereinigung der Deutschen Staatsrechtslehrer (Ger.) Proceedings of the Society of German Teachers of Public Law. 1924–
VVS SSSR Vedomosti Verkhovnogo Soveta SSSR (USSR) Official Gazette of the Supreme Soviet
V.& B. Vesey & Beames' Chancery Reports (35 ER) 1812–14
V.& S. Vernon & Scriven's Irish King's Bench Reports. 1786–88
Va. Gilmer's Virginia Reports (21 Va.) 1820–21
Virginia
Virginia Reports. 1880–
Va.Acts Acts of the General Assembly of the Commonwealth of Virginia
Va.B.A. Virginia State Bar Association
Va.B.A.J. Virginia Bar Association Journal. 1975–
Va.Bar Assn. Virginia State Bar Association
Va.Bar News Virginia Bar News
Va.Cas. Virginia Cases (by Brockenbrough & Holmes)
Virginia Criminal Cases, Virginia Reports (3–4 Va.) 1789–1826
Va.Ch.Dec. Wythe's Chancery Decisions (Virginia) 1788–99
Va.Code Code of Virginia
Va.Col.Dec. Virginia Colonial Decisions (Raldolph & Barradall) 1728–53
Va.Dec. Virginia Decisions (Unreported) 1870–1900
Va.Envtl.L.J. Virginia Environmental Law Journal
Va.J.I.L. Virginia Journal of International Law. 1963–
Va.J.Int'l.L. Virginia Journal of International Law. 1963–
Va.L. Virginia Law Review. 1913–
Va.L.Dig. Virginia Law Digest. 1928–33
Va.L.J. Virginia Law Journal. 1877–93
Va.L.Reg. Virginia Law Register. 1895–1928
Va.L.Reg.N.S. Virginia Law Register, New Series. 1915–1928
Va.L.Rev. Virginia Law Review. 1913–
Va.L.Wk.Dicta Comp. Virginia Law Weekly; Dicta; Compilation. 1948–
Va.Law J. Virginia Law Journal. 1877–93

Va.R. Gilmer's Virginia Reports (21 Va.) 1820–21

Va.S.B.A. Virginia State Bar Association Virginia State Bar Association Reports

Vaizey Vaizey's Law of Settlements. 1887

Val. Valparaiso

Val.Com. Valin's Commentaries. 1760

Val.Rep. Valuation Reports, Interstate Commerce Commission (USA) 1918–

Val.Rep.I.C.C. Valuation Reports, Interstate Commerce Commission (USA) 1918–

Val.U.L.Rev. Valparaiso University Law Review. 1966–

Valparaiso Univ.L.Rev. Valparaiso University Law Review. 1966–

Van K. Van Koughwet's Reports, Upper Canada Common Pleas. 1864–71

Van.K.& H. Upper Canada Common Pleas Reports. 1864–71

Van.L. Vander Linden's Practice, Cape Colony (S.Afr.)

Van N. Van Ness' Prize Cases, U.S. District Court, District of New York. 1814

Van Ness,Prize Cas. Van Ness' Prize Cases, U.S. District Court, District of New York. 1814

Van.Rep. Vanderstraaten's Decisions in Appeal, Supreme Court (Sri L.) 1869–71

Vand. Vanderbilt

Vand.Int. The Vanderbilt International. 1967/8–71

Vand.J.Transnat'l.L. Vanderbilt Journal of Transnational Law. 1971–

Vand.L.Rev. Vanderbilt Law Review. 1947–

Vanderb.L.R. Vanderbilt Law Review. 1947–

Vanderbilt J.Transnatl.L. Vanderbilt Journal of Transnational Law (USA)

Vanderstr. Vanderstraaten's Decisions, Supreme Court Appeal (Sri L.) 1869–71

Vanderstraaten Vanderstraaten's Decisions in Appeal, Supreme Court (Sri L.) 1869–71

var. various

Varney Report Criminal injuries compensation – a statutory scheme: report of an interdepartmental working party. 1986

Vatt. Vattel, Law of Nations. 4ed. 1872

Vattel Vattel, Law of Nations. 4ed. 1872

Vaug. Vaughan's Common Pleas Reports (124 ER) 1665–73

Vaugh. Vaughan's Common Pleas Reports (124 ER) 1665–73

Vaughan Vaughan's Common Pleas Reports (124 ER) 1665–73

Vaux Vaux's Recorder's Decisions, Philadelphia, Pa. 1841–45

Vaux(Pa.) Vaux's Recorder's Decisions, Philadelphia,Pa. 1841–45

Vaux Rec.Dec. Vaux's Recorder's Decisions, Philadelphia, Pa. 1841–45

Ve. Vesey, Senior's Chancery Reports (27–28 ER) 1747–56

Ve.& B. Vesey & Beames' Chancery Reports (35 ER) 1812–14

Veazey Veazey's Reports (36–44 Vermont)

Veh.C. Vehicle Code

Veh.& Traf. Vehicle and Traffic

Vent. Ventris' King's Bench Reports (86 ER) 1668–88

Ventr. Ventris' King's Bench Reports (86 ER) 1668–88

ver. vereniging (Neth.) association

Ver. Vermont Reports. 1826–

VerfGH Verfassungsgerichtshof (Ger.) Provincial Constitutional Court

Verf.u.R.Übersee Verfassung und Recht in Übersee (Ger.) Law and Politics in Africa, Asia and Latin America

Verh. Verhandlungen (Ger.) Minutes of parliamentary proceedings

Verm. Vermont Reports. 1826–

Vermont L.Rev. Vermont Law Review

Vern. Vernon's Chancery Reports (23 ER) 1680–1719

Vern.& S. Vernon & Scriven's Irish King's Bench Reports (Ire.) 1786–88

Vern.& Scr. Vernon & Scriven's Irish King's Bench Reports (Ire.) 1786–88

Vern.& Scriv. Vernon & Scriven's Irish King's Bench Reports (Ire.) 1786–88
Vernon's Ann.C.C.P. Vernon's Annotated Texas Code of Criminal Procedure
Vernon's Ann.Civ.St. Vernon's-Annotated Texas Civil Statutes
Vernon's Ann.P.C. Vernon's Annotated Texas Penal Code
Veröffentl.Komm.Europarecht Veröffent lichungen der Kommission für Europarecht (Austria)
VerwArch Verwaltungsarchiv (Ger.)
VerwG Verwaltungsgericht (Ger.) administrative court or tribunal
VerwGH Verwaltungsgerichtshof (Ger.) Administrative Court of Appeal
VerwPr Die Verwaltungspraxis (Ger.) 1927–
Ves. Vesey Junior's Chancery Reports (30–4 ER) 1789–1817
Vesey Senior's English Chancery Reports (27–28 ER) 1747–56
Ves.Jr. Vesey Junior's Chancery Reports (30–34 ER) 1789–1817
Ves.Jr.Suppl. Hovenden's Supplement to Vesey Junior's Reports, Chancery (34 ER) 1789–1817
Ves.Jun. Vesey Junior's Chancery Reports (30–34 ER) 1789–1817
Ves.Jun.Supp. Hovenden's Supplement to Vesey Junior's Reports (34 ER) 1789–1817
Ves.Sen. Vesey Senior's Chancery Reports (27–28 ER) 1747–56
Ves.Sen.Supp. Supplement to Vesey Senior's Chancery Reports by Belt (28 ER) 1747–56
Ves.Sr. Vesey Senior's Chancery Reports (27–28 ER) 1747–56
Ves.Sr.Supp. Supplement to Vesey Senior's Chancery Reports (28 ER) 1747–56
Ves.Supp. Supplement to Vesey Junior's Chancery Reports by Hovenden (34 ER) 1789–1817
Ves.& B. Vesey & Beames' Chancery Reports (35 ER) 1812–14
Ves.& Bea. Vesey & Beames' Chancery Reports (35 ER) 1812–14
Ves.& Beam. Vesey & Beames' Chancery Reports (35 ER) 1812–14
Vest.Moskov.U.Prav. Vestnik Moskovskogo Universiteta, Seriia Pravo (USSR)
Vet.N.Br. Old Natura Brevium
Vet.Na.B. Old Natura Brevium
Vez. Vezey's (Vesey's) Chancery Reports
VfGH Verfassungsgerichthof (Ger.) Constitutional Court
Vic. (Queen) Victoria
Victoria, Australia
Vic.A.C.R. Victorian Accident Compensation Reports (in Boyes & O'Loughlin's Accident Compensation Victoria) (Aus.) 1987–
Vic.Bar News Victorian Bar News (Aus.) 1977–
Vic.C.C. County Court Reports (Victoria, Aus.)
Vic.Legal Exec. Victorian Legal Executive (Aus.) 1977–
Vic.Rep. Webb, A'Beckett & Williams' Victoria Reports (Aus.) 1870–72
Vic.Sup.Ct.F.C. Victorian Supreme Court, Full Court (Aus.)
vice pres. vice president
Vict. (Queen) Victoria
Victoria, Australia
Victorian Reports (Aus.)
Vict.Admr. Victorian Reports, Admiralty. 1870–72
Vict.C.S. Victorian Consolidated Statutes
Vict.Eq. Victorian Reports Equity. 1870–72
Vict.L. Victorian Reports, Law. 1870–72
Vict.L.(Austr.) Victorian Reports, Law (Aus.) 1870–72
Vict.L.J. Victorian Law Journal (Aus.) 1932–33
Vict.L.R. Victorian Law Reports (Aust.) 1875–1956
Vict.L.R.Min. Victorian Law Reports Mining (Aus.) 1875–84

Vict.L.T. Victorian Law Times (Aus.) 1856–57
Vict.Rep. Webb, A'Beckett & Williams' Victoria Reports (Aus.) 1870–72
Vict.Rep.(Adm.) Victorian Reports, Admiralty (Aus.) 1870–72
Vict.Rep.(Austr.) Victorian Reports (Aus.) 1870–72
Vict.Rep.(Eq.) Victorian Reports, Equity (Aus.) 1870–72
Vict.Rep.(Law) Victorian Reports, Law (Aus.) 1870 72
Vict.Rev. Victorian Review
Vict.St.Tr. Victorian State Trials (Aus.)
Vict.Stat. Victorian Statutes (Aus.)
Vict.Stat.R.,Regs.& B. Victorian Statutory Rules, Regulations and By-Laws (Aus.)
Vict.U.C.L.Rev. Victoria University College Law Review (N.Z.) 1953–57
Vict.U.of Wellington L.Rev. Victoria University of Wellington Law Review (N.Z.) 1957–
Vict.U.Well.L.Rev. Victoria University of Wellington Law Review (N.Z.) 1957–
Vict.W.C.R. Workers Compensation Board Decisions (in Boyes & O'Loughlin's Accident Compensation Victoria) (Aus.) 1982–
Vid. Vidian's Exact Pleader. 1684
vig. vigente (It.) in force
Vil.& Br. Vilas & Byrant's Edition of the Wisconsin Reports
Vilas Vilas' Reports (1–5 New York Criminal Reports)
Vill.L.Rev. Villanova Law Review (USA) 1956–
Villanova L.Rev. Villanova Law Review (USA) 1956–
Vin.Abr. Viner's Abridgment of Law and Equity. 1741–53
Vin.Supp. Supplement to Viner's Abridgment of Law and Equity
Viner,Abr. Viner's Abridgment of Law & Equity. 1741–53
Vir. Virginia
Virginia Cases. 1880–
Virgin's Reports (52–60 Maine)
Vir.L.J. Virginia Law Journal. 1877–93
Virg. Virginia
Virginia Cases. 1880–
Virgin's Reports (52–60 Maine)
Virg.Cas. Virginia Cases (by Brockenbrough & Holmes)
Virg.J.I.L. Virginia Journal of International Law
Virg.L.J. Virginia Law Journal. 1877–93
Virgin Virgin's Reports (52–60 Maine)
Virginia J.Intl.L. Virginia Journal of International Law
virt. virtually
viz. videlicet (Lat.) namely
Vo.L.R. Villanova Law Review. 1956–
Vo. Verso
vol. volume
voluntary
volunteer
vols. volumes
Vorw. Vorwort (Ger.) Foreword
Vr. Vroom's Reports (30–85 New Jersey Law)
Vroom Vroom's Reports (30–85 New Jersey Law Reports) 1862–72, 1872–1914
Vroom(G.D.W.) G.D.W. Vroom's Reports (36–85 New Jersey Law Reports) 1872–1914
Vroom(P.D.) P.D. Vroom's Reports (30–35 New Jersey Law Reports) 1862–72
Vt. Vermont
Vermont Reports. 1826–
Vt.Acts Laws of Vermont
Vt.B.A. Vermont Bar Association
Vermont Bar Association Reports
Vt.L.Rev. Vermont Law Review
Vt.Stat.Ann. Vermont Statutes Annotated
VwGO Verwaltungsgerichtsordnung (Ger.) Administrative Court Act

W

w. wet (Neth.) act or statute

W. Wales
Washington Reports. 1890–1939
Watermayer's Reports of the Supreme Court (Cape, S.Afr.) 1857–
Watts Pennsylvania Reports. 1832–40
Weekblad van het Recht (Neth.)
Welsh
Wendell's Reports (New York) 1826–41
West
Western
Westminster
Wheaton's Reports (14–25 U.S.) 1816–27
William (King)
Willson's Reports (Texas Civil Cases, Court of Appeals) 1876–92
Wisconsin Reports. 1853–
Witwatersrand Local Division Reports (S.Afr.) 1910–46
Wright's Ohio Reports. 1831–34
Wyoming Reports. 1870–

W.2d Washington State Reports, Second Series. 1939–

W.A. West Africa
Western Australia
With Average

W.A.A.F. Women's Auxiliary Air Force

W.A.A.R. Western Australia Arbitration Reports. 1901–20

W.A.Ann.L.R. University of Western Australia Annual Law Review

W.A.Arb.R. Western Australia Arbitration Reports. 1901–20

W.A'B.& W. Webb, A'Beckett & Williams' Reports (Victoria, Aus.) 1870–72

W.A'B.& W.Eq. Webb, A'Beckett & Williams' Equity Reports (Victoria, Aus.) 1870–72

W.A'B.& W.I.E.& M. Webb, A'Beckett & Williams' Insolvency, Ecclesiastical and Matrimonial Reports (Victoria, Aus.) 1870–72

W.A'B.& W.Min. Webb, A'Beckett & Williams' Mining Cases (Victoria, Aus.) 1870–72

W.A.C.A. West African Court of Appeal Reports. 1930–55

W.A.G.G. Western Australia Government Gazette

W.A.I.A.Ct. Western Australia Industrial Appeal Court

W.A.I.G. Western Australian Industrial Gazette. 1921–

W.A.I.R.C. Western Australian Industrial Relations Commission

W.A.Indus.Gaz. Western Australia Industrial Gazette. 1921–

W.A.L.C. West African Lands Committee Report (Cd. 1047, 1048)

W.A.L.R. University of Western Australia Law Review. 1948–
West African Law Reports (Gambia, Ghana & Sierra Leone) 1955–
Western Australian Law Reports. 1899–1959

W.A.L.R.C. Western Australia Law Reform Commission

W.A.L.R.C.Bull. Western Australia Law Reform Commission Bulletin

W.A.L.R.C.W.P. Western Australia Law Reform Commission Working Paper

W.A.R. Western Australian Reports. 1960–
Women Against Rape
WATTC World Administrative Telegraph and Telephone Conference
W.A.U.L.R. Western Australia University Law Review. 1948–
W.Af.L.R. West African Law Reports. 1955–
W.Afr.App. West African Court of Appeal Reports
W.Ap. Washington Appellate Reports. 1869–
W.Aus. Western Australia
W.Aust. Western Australia
W.Austl. Western Australia
W.Austl.Acts Western Australian Acts
W.Austl.Ind.Gaz. Western Australia Industrial Gazette. 1921–
W.Austl.J.P. Western Australia Justice of the Peace
W.Austl.L.R. Western Australia Law Reports. 1898–
WBR Wetboek van Burgerlijke Regtsvordering (Neth.) code of civil procedure
W.Beng.Ind. West Bengal, India
W.Bl. Sir William Blackstone's King's Bench Reports (96 ER) 1746–80
W.Bla. Sir William Blackstone's King's Bench Reports (96 ER) 1746–80
W.Black. Sir William Blackstone's King's Bench Reports (96 ER) 1746–80
W.C. Watch Committee
W.C.A. Workmen's Compensation Act
W.C.A.T.R. Workers' Compensation Appeals Tribunal Reporter (Can.) 1985–
W.C.B. Weekly Criminal Bulletin (Can.) 1976–
Workmen's Compensation Bureau (USA)
W.C.B.D.(Vic.) Workers' Compensation Board Decisions (Victoria, Aus.) 1938–
W.C.B.D.(W.A.) Workers' Compensation Board Decisions (W. Aus.) 1950–
W.C.C. Washington's Circuit Court Reports (USA)
Welsh Consumer Council
Workers' Compensation Cases (in Victorian Workers Compensation Practice) (Aus.) 1981–
Workmen's Compensation Cases. 1898–1907
W.C.C.(N.Z.) Workers' Compensation Cases (N.Z.) 1901–40
W.C.C.R.(N.S.W.) Workers' Compensation Commission Reports of Cases (N.S.W., Aus.) 1926–
W.C.D. Western Charter Digest (Can.) 1983–4
W.C.Ins.Rep. Workmen's Compensation & Insurance Reports. 1912–33
W.C.L. World Confederation of Labour
W.C.L.A. Workers' Compensation Legislation in Australia. 1980–
W.C.L.J. Workmen's Compensation Law Journal (USA) 1918–22
W.C.L.R. Workmen's Compensation Law Review (USA) 1974–
W.C.Ops. Workmen's Compensation Opinions, U.S. Department of Commerce
W.C.R. Workers' Compensation Commission Reports of Cases (N.S.W., Aus.) 1926–
W.C.R.(N.S.W.) Workers' Compensation Reports (New South Wales, Aus.) 1926–
W.C.R.(Qld.) Workers' Compensation Reports (Queensland, Aus.) 1919–
W.C.R.(Qn.) Worker's Compensation Reports (Queensland, Aus.) 1919–
W.C.R.(W.A.) Workers' Compensation Reports (Western Australia) 1981–
W.C.Rep. Workmen's Compensation Reports (N.S.W., Aus.) 1926–
W.C.& I.R. Workmen's Compensation and Insurance Reports. 1912–33
W.C.& I.Rep. Workmen's Compensation and Insurance Reports. 1912–33
W.C.& Ins. Workmen's Compensation and Insurance Reports. 1912–33
W.C.& Ins.Rep. Workmen's

Compensation and Insurance Reports. 1912–33
W.Coast Rep. West Coast Reporter (USA) 1884–86
W.Ct.S.A. Water Courts Decisions (S.Afr.)
W/D Withdrawal
Withdrawn
W.D.C.P. Weekly Digest of Civil Procedure (Ontario, Can.) 1986–
W.D.F.L. Weekly Digest of Family Law (Can.) 1982–
W.D.P.M. Wrongful Dismissal Practice Manual (Can.) 1984–
w.e. week ending
w.e.f. with effect from
W.E.U. Western European Union
W.E.U. I Protocol modifying and completing the Brussels (Western European Union) Treaty. 1954
W.E.U. II Protocol No. II on the Forces of the Western European Union. 1954
W.E.U. III Protocol No. III on the Control of Armaments. 1954
W.E.U. IV Protocol No. IV on the Agency of Western European Union. 1954
WEUS Agreement on the Status of the Western European Union, National Representatives and International Staff. 1955
W.Ent. Winch's Book of Entries
WFC World Food Council
WFP World Food Programme (UN)
WFR Weekblad voor fiscaal recht (Neth.) 1872–
W.F.T.U. World Federation of Trade Unions
W.F.U.N.A. World Federation of United Nations Associations
WGO WGO, Monatshefte für Osteuropäisches Recht (Ger.)
W.Ger. West Germany
W.H. Wage & Hour Cases (USA) 1938–
W.H.C. South African Law Reports, Witwatersrand Supreme Court. 1910–46
W.H.Cas. Wage & Hour Cases (USA) 1938–
W.H.Chron. Westminster Hall Chronicle and Legal Examiner. 1835–36
WHO World Health Organization (UN)
W.H.R. Wage & Hour Reporter (USA)
W.H.& G. Welsby, Hurlstone and Gordon's Exchequer Reports (154–156 ER) 1847–56
W.I. West India(n)
West Indies
W.I.C.A. Judgments of the West Indian Court of Appeal. 1920–
WICLIP West Indian Case Law Indexing Project
W.I.Fed. West Indies Federation
W.I.H. Work in hand
WILIP West Indian Legislation Indexing Project
W.I.L.J. West Indian Law Journal (Jam.) 1977–
WIPO World Intellectual Property Organization
W.I.P.R. World Intellectual Property Reports. 1987–
WIR Wet Investeringsrekening (Neth.) Investment Account Act
W.I.R. West Indian Reports. 1959–
W.I.S.A.L.R. Western Indian States Agency Law Reports. 1924–
W.I.S.A.Law Rep. Western Indian States Agency Law Reports. 1924–
W.I.S.A.Law Reports Western Indian States Agency Law Reports. 1924–
WJ Wet op de Jaarrekening van Ondernemingen (Neth.) Annual Accounts Act
W.J. Western Jurist (USA) 1867–83
W.Jo. Sir William Jones' King's Bench Reports (82 ER) 1620–41
W.Jones Sir William Jones' King's Bench Reports (82 ER) 1620–41
WK Wetboek van Koophandel (Neth.) commercial code
W.Kel. William Kelynge's Chancery Reports (25 ER) 1730–36

W.Kelynge William Kelynge's Chancery Reports (25 ER) 1730–36
W.L. Water Law
W.L.A.C. Western Labour Arbitration Cases (Can.) 1966–
W.L.B. Weekly Law Bulletin (Ohio) 1880–84
W.L.Bull.(Ohio) Weekly Law Bulletin (Ohio) 1880–84
W.L.D. South African Law Reports, Witwatersrand Local Division. 1910–46
W.L.G. Weekly Law Gazette (Ohio) 1858–60
W.L.Gaz.(Ohio) Weekly Law Gazette (Ohio) 1858–60
W.L.J. Washburn Law Journal (USA) 1960–
Western Law Journal (USA) 1843–53
Willamette Law Journal (USA) 1959–
Wyoming Law Journal. 1946–65
W.L.Jour. Washburn Law Journal (USA) 1960–
Western Law Journal (USA) 1843–53
Willamette Law Journal (USA) 1959–
Wyoming Law Journal. 1946–65
W.L.L.R. Washington & Lee Law Review (USA) 1939–
W.L.M. Western Law Monthly (Ohio) 1859–63
W.L.Q. Washington University Law Quarterly (Missouri) 1936–
W.L.R. Washington Law Reporter (D.C.) 1874–
Washington Law Review (Seattle) 1919–
Weekly Law Reports. 1953–
Western Law Reporter (Can.) 1905–16
Wisconsin Law Review. 1920–
World Law Review (USA) 1970–
W.L.R.P. Wandsworth Legal Resource Project
W.L.S. Weekly Law Sheets (Butterworths) (Can.)
W.L.T. Western Law Times (Can.) 1889–95
W.M.L. Willamette Law Journal (Oregon) 1959–
W.M.L.R. William & Mary Law Review (USA) 1957–
W.M.O. World Meteorological Organisation (U.N.)
W.M.R. William and Mary Review of Virginia Law. 1949–
W.N. Calcutta Weekly Notes (India) 1896–1941
Weekly Notes. 1866–1952
W.N.(Calc.) Calcutta Weekly Notes (India) 1896–1941
W.N.C. Weekly Notes of Cases (Pennsylvania) 1874–99
W.N.C.(Pa.) Weekly Notes of Cases (Pennsylvania) 1874–99
W.N.Cas. Weekly Notes of Cases (Pennsylvania) 1874–99
W.N.L.N. Western Nigeria Legal Notice. 1961–
W.N.L.R. Western Nigeria Law Reports. 1956–
W.N.Misc. Weekly Notes, Miscellaneous. 1866–1952
W.N.(N.S.W.) Weekly Notes, New South Wales. 1884–1970
W.O.C. Woods' Oriental Cases (Mal.) 1842–69
W.Ont.L.Rev. Western Ontario Law Review. 1967–75
W.P. Pakistan Law Reports, West Pakistan Series. 1956–
Working Paper
W.P.C. Webster's Patent Cases (Bail Court Reports) 1840–41
Wollaston's Practice Cases (Bail Court Reports) 1840–41
W.P.Cas. Webster's Patent Cases. 1601–1855
Wollaston's Practice Cases (Bail Court Reports) 1840–41
W.P.H.C. Western Pacific High Commission
w.p.m. words per minute
WPNR Weekblad voor privaatrecht, notariaat en registratie (Neth.) 1975–
Weekblad voor privaatrecht, notaris-ambt en registratie (Neth.) 1870–1974

W.P.R. Webster's Patent Cases. 1601–1855

WPTLC World Peace Through Law Conference

W.R. Sutherland's Weekly Reports (Bengal, India) 1864–77
Weekly Reporter. 1853–1906
Weekly Reporter (Cape, S.Afr.) 1912–14
Wendell's Reports (New York) 1826–41
Western Region
West's Chancery Reports temp. Hardwicke (24 ER) 1736–39
Willelmus Rex (King William)
Wisconsin Reports. 1853–

W.R.Calc. Sutherland's Weekly Reporter (India) 1864–77

W.R.L. Western Reserve Law Review (Ohio) 1949–67

W.R.N.L.R. Western Region of Nigeria Law Reports. 1955–

W.R.N.S. Womens Royal Naval service

WRP Wettbewerb in Recht und Praxis (Ger.) 1955–

WRRC Women's Research and Resources Centre

W.R.T.L.B. Wilkinson's Road Traffic Law Bulletin. 1983–

WRvS/R Weekoverzicht Raad van State, Afdeling Rechtspraak (Neth.)

W.Rep. West's Chancery Reports tempore Hardwicke (25 ER) 1736–39

W.Res.L.Rev. Western Reserve Law Review (Ohio) 1949–67

W.Rob. W. Robinson's Admiralty Reports (166 ER) 1838–52

W.Rob.Adm. W. Robinson's Admiralty Reports (166 ER) 1838–52

W.S. Wagner's Statutes (Missouri)
Writer to the Signet

W.S.A. Wisconsin Statutes Annotated

WSBA Washington State Bar Association

WStG Wehrstrafgesetz (Ger.) Military criminal law

W.T. Washington Territory Reports. 1854–88

WTI The World Trade Institute

W.T.R. Weekly Transcript Reports (New York) 1861
World Tax Report. 1984–

W.Ty.R. Washington Territory Reports. 1854–55

W.u.R. Wirtschaft und Recht (Switz.)

W.V. West Virginia Reports. 1864–

W.V.Bar West Virginia Bar. 1894–95

W.V.L. West Virginia Law Review. 1949–

W.V.L.Q. West Virginia Law Quarterly. 1917–49

W.V.L.R. West Virginia Law Review. 1949–

W.V.R. Wörterbuch des Völkerrechts und der Diplomatie. 1924–29

W.V.R. II Wörterbuch des Völkerrechts. 2ed. 1960–62

W.Va. West Virginia
West Virginia Supreme Court Reports. 1864–

W.Va.Acts Acts of the Legislature of West Virginia

W.Va.Bar West Virginia Bar. 1894–95

W.Va.Code West Virginia Code

W.Va.L.Q. West Virginia Law Quarterly. 1917–49

W.Va.L.Rev. West Virginia Law Review. 1949–

W.W. Wyatt and Webb's Reports (Victoria, Aus.) 1861–63

W.W.D. Western Weekly Digest (Can.) 1975–6

W.W.H. W.W. Harrington's Reports (31–39 Delaware) 1919–39

W.W.Harr. W.W. Harrington's Reports (31–39 Delaware) 1919–39

W.W.Harr.Del. W.W. Harrington's Reports (31–39 Delaware) 1919–39

W.W.R. Western Weekly Law Reports (Can.) 1911–50, 1955–

W.W.R.(N.S.) Western Weekly Reports, New Series (Can.) 1951–5

W.W.& A'B. Wyatt, Webb & A'Beckett's Reports (Victoria, Aus.) 1864–69

W.W.& A'B.(E.) Wyatt, Webb & A'Beckett's Equity Reports (Victoria, Aus.) 1864–69

W.W.& A'B.Eq. Wyatt, Webb & A'Beckett's Equity Reports (Vict., Aus.) 1864–69

W.W.& A'B.(I.E.& M.) Wyatt, Webb & A'Beckett's Reports, Insolvency, Ecclesiastical & Matrimonial (Vict., Aus.) 1864–69

W.W.& A'B.(M.) Wyatt, Webb & A'Beckett's Reports, Mining (Vict., Aus.) 1864–69

W.W.& A'B.Min. Wyatt, Webb & A'Beckett's Reports, Mining (Vict., Aus.) 1864–69

W.W.& D. Willmore, Wollaston and Davison's Queen's Bench Reports (52 RR) 1837

W.W.& H. Willmore, Wollaston and Hodges' Queen's Bench Reports (52 RR) 1838–39

WZG Warenzeichengesetz (Ger.) Trade Marks Act

W.& B. Wolferstan & Bristowe's Election Cases. 1859–64

W.& B.Dig. Walker & Bates, Ohio Digest

W.& C. Wilson & Courtenay's Appeal Cases (Scot.)

W.& C.Conv. Wolstenholme & Cherry, Conveyancing Statutes. 13ed. 1972

W.& D. Wolferstan & Dew's Election Cases. 1856–58

W.& L. Washington and Lee Law Review (Virginia) 1939–

W.& L.Dig. Wood & Long, Illinois Digest

W.& M. William & Mary Law Review (USA) 1957–
Woodbury & Minot's United States Circuit Court Reports. 1845–47

W.& S. Watts & Sergeant's Pennsylvania Reports. 1841–45
Wilson & Shaw's Appeal Cases, House of Lords (Scot.) 1825–35

W.& S.App. Wilson & Shaw's Appeal Cases (Scot.) 1825–35

W.& T.Eq.Ca. White & Tudor's Leading Cases in Equity. 9ed. 1928

W.& T.L.C. White & Tudor's Leading Cases in Equity. 9ed. 1928

W.& W. de Witt & Weeresinghe's Appeal Court Reports (Sri L.)
White & Wilson's Texas Civil Cases, Court of Appeals. 1876–92
Wyatt & Webb's Victorian Reports (Aus.) 1861–63

W.& W.(E.) Wyatt & Webb's Reports, Equity (Victoria, Aus.) 1861–63

W.& W.(Eq.) Wyatt & Webb's Reports, Equity (Victoria, Aus.) 1861–63

W.& W.(I.E.& M.) Wyatt & Webb's Reports, Insolvency, Ecclesiastical & Matrimonial (Victoria, Aus.) 1861–63

W.& W.(L.) Wyatt & Webb's Reports, Law (Victoria, Aus.) 1861–63

W.& W.Vict. Wyatt & Webb's Victorian Reports (Aus.) 1861–63

W.& W.& A'B. Wyatt, Webb & A'Beckett's Reports (Victoria, Aus.) 1864–69

W.& W.& A'B.(E.) Wyatt, Webb & A'Beckett's Reports, Equity (Victoria, Aus.) 1864–69

W.& W.& A'B.(Eq.) Wyatt, Webb & A'Beckett's Reports, Equity (Victoria, Aus.) 1864–69

W.& W.& A'B.(I.E.& M.) Wyatt, Webb & A'Beckett's Reports, Insolvency, Ecclesiastical and Matrimonial (Victoria, Aus.) 1864–69

W.& W.& A'B.(M.) Wyatt, Webb & A'Beckett's Reports, Mining (Victoria, Aus.) 1864–69

W.& W.& A'B.(Min.) Wyatt, Webb & A'Beckett's Reports, Mining (Victoria, Aus.) 1864–69

Wa. Washington
Washington Reports. 1890–1939
Watts' Reports (Pennsylvania) 1832–40

Wa.2d Washington State Reports, Second Series. 1939–

Wa.A. Washington Appellate Reports

Wa.L.R. Washington Law Review. 1919–

Wad.Dig. Waddilove, Digest of Ecclesiastical Cases. 1849–

Wad.Mar.& Div. Waddilove, Marriage & Divorce. 1864
Wade & Phillips Constitutional Law
Wag.St. Wagner's Statutes (Missouri)
Wage and Hour Cas. Wage and Hour Cases (USA) 1938–
Wage-Pr.L. Wage-Price Law and Economics Review (USA) 1975–
Wait Co. Wait's Annotated Code (New York)
Wait Dig. Wait's Digest (New York)
Wait.Pr. Wait's New York Practice
Wait St.Pap. Wait's State Papers of the United States
Wait Tab.Ca. Wait's New York Table of Cases
Wait's Prac. Wait's New York Practice
Wake For.L.Rev. Wake Forest Law Review (USA) 1970–
Wake Forest Inra.L.Rev. Wake Forest Intramural Law Review (USA) 1968–70
Wal.by L. Wallis' Irish Reports by Lyne. 1766–91
Wal.Jr. J.W. Wallace's United States Circuit Court Reports. 1842–62
Wal.Prin. Wallace, Principles of the Scottish Law
Wal.Sr. J.B. Wallace's United States Circuit Court Reports. 1801
Walf.Cust. Walford, Laws of the Customs. 1846
Walf.Part. Walford, Parties to Actions. 1842
Walf.Railw. Walford, Railways. 2ed. 1846
Walk. Walker's Michigan Chancery Reports. 1842–45
Walker's Reports (96, 109 Alabama)
Walker's Reports (1 Mississippi) 1818–32
Walker's Reports (Pennsylvania) 1855–85
Walker's Reports (22–25, 38–51, 72–88 Texas; 1–10 Civil Appeals Texas)
Walk.Bank.L. Walker, Banking Law. 2ed. 1885
Walk.Ch. Walker's Michigan Chancery Reports. 1842–45
Walk.Ch.Cas. Walker's Michigan Chancery Reports. 1842–45
Walk.Ch.Mich. Walker's Michigan Chancery Reports. 1842–45
Walk.Exec. Walker & Elgood, Executors and Administrators. 6ed. 1926
Walk.La.Dig. Walker, Louisiana Digest
Walk.Miss. Walker's Reports (1 Mississippi) 1818–32
Walk.Pa. Walker's Reports (Pennsylvania) 1855–85
Walk.Tex. Walker's Reports (22–25, 38–51, 72–88 Texas; 1–10 Civil Appeals Texas)
Walker Walker's Michigan Chancery Reports. 1842–45
Walker's Reports (96, 109 Alabama)
Walker's Reports (1 Mississippi) 1818–32
Walker's Reports (Pennsylvania) 1855–85
Walker's Reports (22–25, 38–51, 72–88 Texas; 1–10 Civil Appeals Texas)
Wall. Wallace's Circuit Court Reports (USA) 1801, 1842–62
Wallace's Nova Scotia Reports (Can.) 1884–1907
Wallace's Supreme Court Reports (68–90 U.S.) 1863–74
Wallis' Irish Chancery Reports. 1766–91
Wallis' Philadelphia Reports. 1850–91
Wall.C.C. J.B. Wallace's Circuit Court Reports (USA) 1801
J.W. Wallace's Circuit Court Reports (USA) 1842–62
Wall.Jr. J.W. Wallace's Circuit Court Reports (USA) 1842–62
Wall.Jr.C.C. J.W.Wallace's Circuit Court Reports (USA) 1842–62
Wall.Lyn. Wallis' Irish Chancery Reports by Lyne. 1766–91
Wall.Pr. Wallace, Principles of the Laws of Scotland
Wall.Rep. Wallace, The Reporters
Wallace's Supreme Court Reports (68–90 U.S.) 1863–74

Wall.S.C. Wallace's Supreme Court Reports (68–90 U.S.) 1863–74
Wall.Sen. J.B. Wallace's United States Circuit Court Reports (USA) 1801
Wallis Wallis' Irish Chancery Reports by Lyne. 1766–91
Wallis by L. Wallis' Irish Chancery Reports by Lyne. 1766–91
Wallis by Lyne Wallis' Irish Chancery Reports by Lyne. 1766–91
Wallis(Ir.) Wallis' Irish Chancery Reports by Lyne. 1766–91
Walp.Rub. Walpole's Rubric of the Common Law. 2ed. 1891
Walsh Walsh, Registry Cases (Ire.)
Walt.H.& W. Walton, Husband and Wife (Scot.)
Walt.Lim. Walter, Statute of Limitations. 4ed. 1883
Walter Walter's Reports (14–16 New Mexico)
War. Warrants
War.Prof.Dut. Warren, Moral, Social and Professional Duties of Attorneys and Solicitors. 2ed. 1851
War.Op. Warwick's Opinions (City Solicitor of Philadelphia)
Ward. Warden's Reports (2,4 Ohio State)
Ward.Leg. Ward, Legacies. 1826
Ward, Notebook Judicial Notebooks of Sir Edward Ward (Lincoln's Inn MS) 1714
Ward, Reports Reports of Cases by Sir Edward Ward while at the Bar (Lincoln's Inn MS) 1673–97
Ward.& Sm. Warden & Smith's Reports (3 Ohio State Reports)
Warden Warden's Reports (2, 4, Ohio State Reports)
Warden & Smith Warden & Smith's Reports (3 Ohio State)
Ware Ware's United States District Court Reports. 1822–66
Warn.Rspr. Die Rechtsprechung des Reichsgerichts auf dem Gebiete des Zivilrechts, herausgegeben von O. Warneyer (Ger.)
Warnock Report Report of the Committee of Inquiry into Human Fertilisation and Embryology (DHSS) (Cmnd. 9314) 1984
Warth Code West Virginia Code. 1899
Warwick's Op. Warwick's Opinions (City Solicitor of Philadelphia)
Wash. Washburn's Reports (16–23 Vermont)
Washington
Washington Reports. 1889–
Washington Territory Reports. 1854–88
Washington's Circuit Court Reports (USA) 1803–27
Washington's Reports (1, 2 Virginia) 1790–96
Wash.2d Washington Reports, Second Series. 1939–
Wash.App. Washington Appellate Reports. 1969–
Wash.C.C. Washington's Circuit Court Reports (USA) 1803–27
Wash.Co. Washington County Reports (Pennsylvania) 1920–
Wash.Co.(Pa.) Washington County Reports (Pennsylvania) 1920–
Wash.Dec. Washington Decisions
Wash.Dig. Washburn, Vermont Digest
Wash.Jur. Washington Jurist
Wash.L.R. Washington Law Review. 1919–
Wash.L.R.(Dist.Col.) Washington Law Reporter (Washington, D.C.) 1874–
Wash.L.Rep. Washington Law Reporter (Washington, D.C.) 1874–
Wash.L.Rev. Washington Law Review. 1919–
Wash.Law.Rep. Washington Law Reporter (Washington, D.C.) 1874–
Wash.Laws Laws of Washington
Wash.Legis.Serv. Washington Legislative Service (West)
Wash.P.U.R. Washington Public Utility Commission Reports
Wash.Rev.Code Revised Code of Washington

Wash.Rev.Code Ann. Washington Revised Code Annotated

Wash.S.B.A. Washington State Bar Association
Washington State Bar Association Proceedings

Wash.St. Washington State Reports. 1889–

Wash.T. Washington Territory Opinions. 1854–64
Washington Territory Reports. 1854–88

Wash.Ter. Washington Territory Opinions. 1854–64
Washington Territory Reports. 1854–88

Wash.Ter.N.S. Allen's Washington Territory Reports, New Series. 1854–88

Wash.Terr. Washington Territory Opinions. 1854–64
Washington Territory Reports. 1854–88

Wash.Ty. Washington Territory Opinions. 1854–64
Washington Territory Reports. 1854–88

Wash.U.L.Q. Washington University Law Quarterly (Missouri) 1936–

Wash.Va. Washington's Reports (1, 2 Virginia) 1790–96

Wash.& Haz.P.E.I. Washburton & Hazard's Reports (Prince Edward Island, Canada)

Wash.& Lee L.Rev. Washington & Lee Law Review (Virginia) 1939–

Washbourne L.J. Washbourne Law Journal

Washburn Washburn's Reports (16–23 Vermont)

Washburn L.J. Washburn Law Journal (Kansas) 1960–

Wasserman Report Report of the Working Party on Forensic Pathology (Home Office) 1989

Wat. Watermeyer's Supreme Court Reports, Cape of Good Hope (S.Afr.) 1857

Wat.C.G.H. Watermeyer's Supreme Court Reports, Cape of Good Hope (S.Afr.) 1857

Wat.Con. Watkins, Conveyancing. 9ed. 1845

Wat.Cop. Watkins, Copholds. 6ed. 1829

Wat.Cr.Dig. Waterman's Criminal Digest (USA)

Water C. Water Code

Watermeyer Watermeyer's Supreme Court Reports, Cape of Good Hope (S.Afr.) 1857

Watk.Con. Watkins, Conveyancing. 9ed. 1845

Watk.Conv. Watkins, Conveyancing. 9ed. 1845

Watk.Cop. Watkins, Copyholds. 6ed. 1829

Watk.Copyh. Watkins, Copyholds. 6ed. 1829

Watk.Des. Watkins, Descents. 1798

Wats.Arb. Watson, Arbitration. 3ed. 1846

Wats.Comp.Eq. Watson, Compendium of Equity. 2ed. 1886

Wats.Part. Watson, Partnership. 2ed. 1807

Wats.Sher. Watson, Office and Duty of Sheriff. 2ed. 1848

Watson Watson, Bristol Pleas of the Crown. 1902
Watson, Compendium of Equity. 2ed. 1886

Watson Eq. Watson, Compendium of Equity. 2ed. 1886

Watts. Watts' Pennsylvania Reports. 1832–40
Watts' Reports (16–24 West Virginia)

Watts.(Pa.) Watt's Pennsylvania Reports. 1832–40

Watts & S. Watts & Sergeant's Reports (Pennsylvania) 1841–45

Watts & S.(Pa.) Watts & Sergeant's Reports (Pennsylvania) 1841–45

Watts & Serg. Watts & Sergeant's Reports (Pennsylvania) 1841–45

Wayne L.Rev. Wayne Law Review (Michigan) 1954–

We. West's Chancery Reports (25 ER) 1736–39
West's Reports, House of Lords (9 ER) 1839–41
Western's Tithe Cases. 1535–1822

Web.P.C. Webster's Patent Cases. 1601–1855

Web.Pat. Webster, New Patent Law. 4ed. 1854

Web.Pat.Cas. Webster's Patent Cases. 1601–1855

Webb Webb's Reports (6–20 Kansas)
Webb's Reports (11–20 Texas Civil Appeals)

Webb,A'B.& W. Webb, A'Beckett & Williams's Reports (Victoria, Aus.) 1870–72

Webb,A'B.& W.Eq. Webb, A'Beckett, & Williams' Equity Reports (Victoria, Aus.) 1870–72

Webb,A'B.& W.I.E.& M. Webb, A'Beckett & Williams' Insolvency, Ecclesiastical & Matrimonial Reports (Victoria, Aus.) 1870–72

Webb,A'B.& W.Min. Webb, A'Beckett & Williams' Mining Cases (Victoria, Aus.) 1870–72

Webb & D. Webb & Duval's Reports (1–3 Texas)

Webb & Duval Webb & Duval's Reports (1–3 Texas)

Webs. Webster's Patent Cases. 1601–1855

Webs.Pat.Cas. Webster's Patent Cases. 1601–1855

Webster Pat.Cas. Webster's Patent Cases. 1601–1855

Week.Cin.L.B. Weekly Cincinnati Law Bulletin. 1879–83

Week.Dig. New York Weekly Digest. 1876–88

Week.Dig.(N.Y.) New York Weekly Digest. 1876–88

Week.Jur. Weekly Jurist (Bloomington, Ill.) 1874–81

Week.L.Gaz. Weekly Law Gazette (USA) 1858–60

Week.L.Mag. Weekly Law Magazine. 1842–43

Week.L.R. Weekly Law Reports. 1953–

Week.L.Rev. Weekly Law Review (San Francisco) 1885

Week.Law Bull. Weekly Law Bulletin & Ohio Law Journal. 1885–1901

Week.Law Gaz. Weekly Law Gazette (Ohio) 1858–60

Week.Law & Bk.Bull. Weekly Law & Bank Bulletin (Cincinnati) 1858

Week.No. New South Wales Weekly Notes (Aus.) 1884–
Weekly Notes of Cases. 1866–1952
Weekly Notes of Cases (Pennsylvania) 1874–99

Week.No.Cas. Weekly Notes of Cases. 1866–1952
Weekly Notes of Cases (Pennsylvania) 1874–99

Week.R. Weekly Reporter. 1853–1906

Week.Rep. Weekly Reporter. 1853–1906

Week.Reptr. Weekly Reporter, London. 1853–1906
Weekly Reporter, Bengal, (India)

Week.Trans.Rep. Weekly Transcript Reports (New York) 1861

Week.Trans.Repts. Weekly Transcript Reports (New York) 1861

Weeky Cin.Law Bull. Weekly Cincinnati Law Bulletin. 1879–83

Weekly L.R. Weekly Law Reports. 1953–

Weekly Notes Weekly Notes of Cases. 1866–1952

Weer. Weerakoon's Appeal Court Reports (Sri L.)

Weight.M.& L. Weightman, Marriage and Legitimacy. 1871

Weight.Med.Leg.Gaz. Weightman's Medico-Legal Gazette

Weir Weir's Criminal Rulings (India) 1879–1905

Wel. Welsh's Irish Registry Cases. 1832–40

Welf. Welfare

Welf.Eq. Welford, Equity Pleadings. 1842

Welf.R.Bull. Welfare Rights Bulletin

Welf.& Inst. Welfare & Institutions

Welf.& Inst.C. Welfare & Institutions Code

Welfare L.Bull. Welfare Law Bulletin

Welfare L.News Welfare Law News

Well.High. Wellbeloved, Highways. 1829

Welsb.H.& G. Welsby, Hurlstone and Gordon's Exchequer Reports (154–6 ER) 1847–56

Welsb.Hurl.& G. Welsby, Hurlstone and Gordon's Exchequer Reports (154–6 ER) 1847–56

Welsby H.& G. Welsby, Hurlstone and Gordon's Exchequer Reports (154–6 ER) 1847–56

Welsh Welsh's Case of James Feighny (Ire.) 1838
Welsh's Irish Cases at Sligo. 1838
Welsh's Registry Cases (Ire.) 1832–40

Welsh Reg.Cas. Welsh's Registry Cases (Ire.) 1832–40

Wend. Wendell's Reports (New York) 1826–41

Wend.Bl. Wendell's Blackstone

Wend.(N.Y.) Wendell's Reports (New York) 1826–41

Wendell Wendell's Reports (New York) 1826–41

Wendt. Wendt's Reports of Cases (Sri L.) 1882–84

Wendt.Mar.Leg. Wendt, Maritime Legislation. 3ed. 1888

Wenz. Wenzell's Reports (60–72 Minnesota)

Wes.C.L.J. Westmoreland County Law Journal (Pennsylvania) 1911

Wes.Res.Law Jo. Western Reserve Law Journal (Ohio) 1895–1901

West. West's Chancery Reports tempore Hardwicke (25 ER) 1736–39
West's Reports House of Lords (9 ER) 1839–41
Western's London Tithe Cases. 1535–1822
Westmoreland County Law Journal (Pennsylvania) 1911–
Weston's Reports (11–14 Vermont)

West A.U.L.R. University of Western Australia Law Review. 1948–

West.Aus. Western Australia

West.Aust.L.Rev. University of Western Australia Law Review. 1948–

West.Austl. Western Australian Reports

West.Austr.L. Western Australia Law Reports

West Ch. West's Chancery Reports tempore Hardwicke (25 ER) 1736–39

West Chy. West's Chancery Reports tempore Hardwicke (25 ER) 1736–39

West Co.Rep. West Coast Reporter (USA) 1884–86

West Coast Rep. West Coast Reporter (USA) 1884–86

West Ext. West, Extents. 1817

West H.L. West's Reports, House of Lords (9 ER) 1839–41

West.Jur. Western Jurist (Des Moines, Iowa) 1867–83

West L.J. Western Law Journal (Ohio) 1843–53

West.L.M. Western Law Monthly (Ohio) 1859–63

West.L.Mo. Western Law Monthly (Ohio) 1859–63

West.L.R. Western Law Reporter (Can.) 1905–16

West.L.R.(Can.) Western Law Reporter (Can.) 1905–16

West.L.Rev. Western Law Review (San Francisco) 1885
Western Law Review (Can.) 1961–66

West.L.T. Western Law Times (Can.) 1889–95

West.Law J. Western Law Journal (Cincinnati, Ohio) 1843–53

West.Law Month. Western Law Monthly (Ohio) 1859–63

West.Law Rev. Western Law Review (Can.) 1961–66

West.Leg.Obs. Western Legal Observer (Illinois) 1849

West.New Engl.L.Rev. Western New England Law Review (USA)

West.Ont.L.Rev. Western Ontario Law Review (Can.)

West.Pr.Int.Law Westlake, Private International Law. 7ed. 1925

West.Res.L.J. Western Reserve Law Journal (USA)

West.Res.Law Rev. Western Reserve Law Review (USA) 1949–62

West.State U.L.Rev. Western State University Law Review (USA)

West t.H. West's Chancery Reports tempore Hardwicke (25 ER) 1736–39

West.t.Hard. West's Chancery Reports tempore Hardwicke (25 ER) 1736–39

West t.Hardw. West's Chancery Reports tempore Hardwicke (25 ER) 1736–39

West temp.Hard. West's Chancery Reports tempore Hardwicke (25 ER) 1736–39

West.Ti.Cas. Western's London Tithe Cases. 1535–1822

West.Tithe Cas. Western's London Tithe Cases. 1535–1822

West Va. West Virginia
West Virginia Reports. 1864–

West Va.B.A. West Viginia Bar Association

West.Va.L.Rev. Western Virginia Law Review (USA)

West.Week.(Can.) Western Weekly Reports (Can.) 1912–50

West.Week.N. Western Weekly Notes (Can.)

West.Week.N.S.(Can.) Western Weekly Reports New Series (Can.) 1951–

West.Week.Rep. Western Weekly Reports (Can.) 1912–50

Western L.Rev. Western Law Review (Can.) 1961–66

Western Ont.L.Rev. Western Ontario Law Review. 1967–75

Western Pol.Q. Western Political Quarterly (USA)

Western Res.L.J. Western Reserve Law Journal (USA)

Western Res.L.Rev. Western Reserve Law Review (USA) 1949–62

Western Reserve L.N. Western Reserve Law Notes (USA) 1941–42

Western Rev. Western Review (USA)

Westl.Priv.Int.Law Westlake, Private International Law. 7ed. 1925

Westm. Statute of Westminster
Westmoreland County Law Journal (Pennsylvania) 1911–

Westm.Hall.Chron. Westminster Hall Chronicle and Legal Examiner. 1835–36

Westm.L.J. Westmoreland County Law Journal (Pennsylvania) 1911–

Westm.Rev. Westminster Review

Westmore.Co.L.J.(Pa.) Westmoreland County Law Journal (Pennsylvania) 1911–

Westmoreland Co.L.J. Westmoreland County Law Journal (Pensylvania) 1911–

Weston Weston's Reports (11–14 Vermont)

West's Op. West's Opinions (City Solicitor of Philadelphia, Pa.)

Weth. Wethey's Reports, Upper Canada Queen's Bench

Weth.U.C. Wethey's Reports, Upper Canada Queen's Bench

Wethey Wethey's Reports, Upper Canada Queen's Bench

WettbRuPr. Wettbewerb in Recht und Praxis (Ger.) 1955–

Wetter J.G. Wetter, The international arbitral process. 1979

Wh. Warton's Reports (Pennsylvania) 1835–41
Wheaton's International Law. 7ed. 1944
Wheaton's Reports (14–25 U.S.) 1816–27
Wheeler's New York Criminal Cases. 1791–1825

Wh.Cr.Cas. Wheeler's New York Criminal Cases. 1791–1825

Wh.& T.L.C. White & Tudor, Leading Cases in Equity. 9ed. 1928

Wh.& Tud. White & Tudor, Leading Cases in Equity. 9ed. 1928

Whar. Wharton's Reports (Pennsylvania) 1835–41

Whar.Conv. Wharton, Principles of Conveyancing. 1851

Whar.Dig. Wharton, Pennsylvania Digest

Whar.Innk. Wharton, Innkeepers. 1876

Whar.Law Dic. Wharton, Law Lexicon. 14ed. 1938

Whar.Leg.Max. Wharton, Legal Maxims. 3ed. 1903

Whar.St.Tr. Wharton's State Trials (USA)

Whar.& St.Med.Jur. Wharton & Stille, Medical Jurisprudence

Whart. Wharton's Reports (Pennsylvania) 1835–41

Whart.Pa. Wharton's Reports (Pennsylvania) 1835–41

Whart.St.Tr. Wharton's State Trials (USA)

Whart.State Tr. Wharton's State Trials (USA)

Wharton Wharton, Law Lexicon. 14ed. 1938
Wharton's Reports (Pennsylvania) 1835–41

Wheat. Wheaton's Supreme Court Reports (14–25 U.S.) 1816–27

Wheat.El.Int.Law Wheaton, Elements of International Law. 7ed. 1944

Wheat.Int.Law Wheaton, Elements of International Law. 7ed. 1944

Wheaton Wheaton's Supreme Court Reports (14–25 U.S.) 1816–27

Wheel. Wheeler's Criminal Cases (New York) 1791–1825
Wheelock's Reports (32–37 Texas)

Wheel.Br.Cas. Wheeling Bridge Case

Wheel.Cr.Cas. Wheeler's Criminal Cases (New York) 1791–1825

Wheel.Cr.Rec. Wheeler's Criminal Recorder (New York) 1822–23

Wheel.(Tex.) Wheelock's Reports (32–37 Texas)

Wheeler Abr. Wheeler's Abridgment of American Common Law

Wheeler C.C. Wheeler's Criminal Cases (New York) 1791–1825

Wheeler Cr.Cas. Wheeler's Criminal Cases (New York) 1791–1825

Whish L.D. Whishaw, New Law Dictionary. 1829

Whishaw Whishaw, New Law Dictionary. 1829

Whit.Eq.Pr. Whitworth, Equity Precedents. 1848

Whit.Lien Whitaker, Rights of Lien and Stoppage in Transitu. 1812

Whit.Pat.Cas. Whitman's Patent Cases (USA) 1810–74

White White's Justiciary Reports (Scot.) 1886–93
White's Reports (31–44 Texas Court of Appeals) 1876–92
White's Reports (10–15 West Virginia)

White.Char. Whiteford, Charities. 1878

White New Coll. White, New Collection of the Laws, etc. of Great Britain, France and Spain

White.W.& M. Whiteley, Weights, Measures and Weighing Machines. 1879

White & Civ.Cas.Ct.App. White & Willson's Civil Cases Court of Appeals (Texas) 1876–92

White & T.L.Cas. White & Tudor, Leading Cases in Equity. 9ed. 1928

White & T.Lead.Cas.Eq. White & Tudor, Leading Cases in Equity. 9ed. 1928

White & Tud.L.C. White & Tudor, Leading Cases in Equity. 9ed. 1928

White & Tudor White & Tudor, Leading Cases in Equity. 9ed. 1928

White & W. White & Willson's Reports (Texas Civil Cases of Court of Appeals) 1876–92

White & W.Civ.Cas.Ct.App. White & Willson's Civil Cases, Court of Appeals (31–44 Texas) 1876–92

White & W.(Tex.) White & Willson's Civil Cases, Court of Appeals (31–44 Texas) 1876–92

Whiteacre Whiteacre: Newsletter of the Sydney University Law Graduates' Association (Aus.) 1967–75

Whiteman Digest M.M. Whiteman, Digest of International Law. 1963–

White's Ann.Pen.Code White's Annotated Penal Code, Texas
White's Rep. White's Reports (31–44 Texas Appeals) 1876–92
White's Reports (10–15 West Virginia)
Whitford Report Report of the Committee to Consider the Law of Copyright and Designs (Cmnd. 6732) 1977
Whitm.B.L. Whitmarsh, Bankrupt Law. 2ed. 1817
Whitm.Pat.Cas. Whitman's Patent Cases (USA) 1810–74
Whitm.Pat.Law Rev. Whitman, Patent Law Review (Washington, D.C.) 1879–80
Whitman Pat.Cas.(U.S.) Whitman's Patent Cases (USA) 1810–74
Whitt. Whittlesey's Reports (32–41 Missouri)
Whittier Law Rev. Whittier Law Review (USA)
Whittlesey Whittlesey's Reports (32–41 Missouri)
Wi. Wisconsin
Wi.L.R. Wisconsin Law Review. 1920–
Wig.Disc. Wigram, Discovery. 2ed. 1840
Wight. Wightwick's Exchequer Reports (145 ER) 1810–11
Wight El.Cas. Wight, Scottish Election Cases. 1784–96
Wightw. Wightwick's Exchequer Reports (145 ER) 1810–11
Wiht. Wihtred
Wilb.Stat. Wilberforce, Construction and
Operation of Statutes. 1881
Wilberforce Wilberforce, Construction and Operation of Statutes. 1881
Wilc.Cond. Wilcox's Condensed Ohio Reports (1–7 Ohio Reprint) 1821–31
Wilc.Cond.Rep. Wilcox's Condensed Ohio Reports (1–7 Ohio Reprint) 1821–31
Wilcox Wilcox's Reports (10 Ohio)
Wilcox's Lackawanna County Reports (Pennsylvania) 1887–89
Wildm.Int.L. Wildman, International Law. 1849–50
Wildm.Search Wildman, Search, Capture and Prize. 1854
Wilk. Wilkinson, Owen, Paterson & Murray's New South Wales Reports. 1862–65
Wilkinson's Texas Court of Appeals & Civil Appeals Reports
Wilk.Funds Wilkinson, Public Funds. 1839
Wilk.Lim. Wilkinson, Limitation of Actions. 1829
Wilk,P.& M. Wilkinson, Owen, Paterson & Murray's Reports, New South Wales (Aus.) 1862–65
Wilk.Prec. Wilkinson, Precedents in Conveyancing. 4ed. 1890
Wilk.Repl. Wilkinson, Replevin. 1825
Wilk.Ship. Wilkinson, Shipping. 1843
Wilk.& Mur. Wilkinson, Owen, Paterson & Murray's New South Wales Reports (Aus.) 1862–65
Wilk.& Ow. Wilkinson, Owen, Paterson & Murray's New South Wales Reports (Aus.) 1862–65
Wilk.& Pat. Wilkinson, Owen, Paterson & Murray's New South Wales Reports (Aus.) 1862–65
Will. Willes' Common Pleas Reports (ed. Durnford) (125 ER) 1737–60
William
Williams' Massachusetts Reports (1 Mass.) 1804–05
Williams' Vermont Reports (27–29 Vt.)
Willson's Reports (29–30 Texas Appeals, 1,2 Texas Civil Appeals)
Will.Abr. Williams, Abridgment of Cases. 1798–1803
Will.Ann.Reg. Williams Annual Register, New York
Will.Auct. Williams, Auctions. 5ed. 1829
Will.Bankt. William, Law and Practice of Bankruptcy
Will.Com. Williams, Rights of Common. 1880
Will.Eq.Pl. Willis, Equity Pleading. 1820
Will.Ex. Williams, Executors
Will.L.J. Willamette Law Journal

(USA) 1959–

Will.Mass. Williams' Reports (1 Massachusetts) 1804–05

Will.P. Peere-Williams' Chancery Reports (24 ER) 1695–1735

Will.Per.Pr. Williams, Personal Property. 18ed. 1926

Will.Pet.Ch. Williams, Petitions in Chancery. 1880

Will.Real Ass. Williams, Real Assets. 1861

Will.Saund. Williams' Notes to Saunders' Reports (85 ER) 1666–73

Will.Seis. Williams, Seisin of the Freehold. 1878

Will.Vt. Williams Reports (27–29 Vermont)

Will.Woll.& D. Willmore, Wollaston & Davison's Queen's Bench Reports (52 RR) 1837

Will.Woll.& Dav. Willmore, Wollaston & Davison's Queen's Bench Reports (52 RR) 1837

Will.Woll.& H. Willmore, Wollaston and Hodges' Queen's Bench Reports (52 RR) 1838–39

Will.Woll.& Hodg. Willmore, Wollaston and Hodges' Queen's Bench Reports (52 RR) 1838–39

Will.& Mar. William and Mary

Willamette L.J. Willamette Law Journal (USA) 1959–

Willc.Const. Willcock, Office of Constable. 1827

Willc.Med.Pr. Willcock, Medical Profession. 1830

Willc.Mun.Corp. Willcock, Municipal Corporations. 1827

Willes Willes Common Pleas Reports ed. Durnford (125 ER) 1737–60

William Mitchell L.Rev. William Mitchell Law Review (USA)

William & Mary L.Rev. William and Mary Law Review (USA)

Williams Peere Williams' Chancery Reports (24 ER) 1695–1735
Williams' Reports (1 Massachusetts) 1804–05
Williams' Reports (10–12 Utah)
Williams' Reports (27–29 Vermont)

Williams B.Pr. Williams' Bankruptcy Practice

Williams,Common Williams, Rights of Common. 1880

Williams,Ex'rs. Williams, Executors

Williams P. Peere Williams' Chancery Reports (24 ER) 1695–1735

Williams,Pers.Prop. Williams, Personal Property. 18ed. 1926

Williams,Saund. Williams' Notes to Saunders' Reports (85 ER) 1666–73

Williams,Seis. Williams, Seisin of the Freehold. 1878

Williams & B.Adm.Jur. Williams and Bruce's Admiralty Practice. 3ed. 1902

Williams & Bruce Ad.Pr. Williams and Bruce's Admiralty Practice. 3ed. 1902

Willis Eq. Willis, Equity Pleadings. 1820

Williston Williston on Contracts (USA)
Williston on Sales (USA)

Willm.W.& D. Willmore, Wollaston & Davison's Queen's Bench Reports (52 RR) 1837

Willm.W.& H. Willmore, Wollaston & Hodges' Queen's Bench Reports (52 RR) 1838–39

Wills.Circ.Ev. Wills, Circumstantial Evidence. 7ed. 1937

Wills.Est.Tr. Wills, Estates Trusts (P–H) (USA)

Willson Willson's Reports (29–30 Texas Appeals, 1, 2 Texas Court of Appeals Civil Cases)

Willson Civ.Cas.Ct.App. White & Willson's Civil Cases of Texas Court of Appeals. 1876–92

Wilm. Wilmot's Notes and Opinions, King's Bench (97 ER) 1757–70

Wilm.Judg. Wilmot's Notes and Opinions, King's Bench (97 ER) 1757–70

Wilm.Op. Wilmot's Notes and Opinions, King's Bench (97 ER) 1757–70

Wilmot's Notes Wilmot's Notes and Opinions, Kings Bench (97 ER) 1757–70

Wils. Wilson's Chancery Reports (37 ER) 1818–19
Wilson's King's Bench Reports (95 ER) 1742–74

Wils.Ch. Wilson's Chancery Reports (37 ER) 1818–19

Wils.Ent. Wilson's Entries & Pleading (3 Lord Raymond's Reports)

Wils.Ex. Wilson's Exchequer Reports (159 ER) 1805–17

Wils.Exch. Wilson's Exchequer Reports (159 ER) 1805–17

Wils.Ind. Wilson's Reports, Indiana Superior Court. 1871–74

Wils.K.B. Wilson's King's Bench Reports (95 ER) 1742–74

Wils.Minn. Wilson's Reports (48–59 Minnesota)

Wils.Oreg. Wilson's Reports (1–2 Oregon)

Wils.Super.(Ind.) Wilson's Reports, Indiana Superior Court. 1871–74

Wils.& Court. Wilson & Courtenay's Scotch Appeals Cases

Wils.& S. Wilson & Shaw's Scottish Appeal Cases. 1825–35

Wils.& Sh. Wilson & Shaw's Scottish Appeal Cases. 1825–35

Wilson Wilson's Chancery Reports (37 ER) 1818–19
Wilson's Exchequer Reports (159 ER) 1805–17
Wilson's King's Bench Reports (95 ER) 1742–74
Wilson's Reports, Indiana Superior Court. 1871–74
Wilson's Reports (48–59 Minnesota)
Wilson's Reports (1–3 Oregon)

Wilson & Shaw Wilson & Shaw's Scottish Appeals Cases. 1825–35

Wilson's Rev.& Ann.St. Wilson's Revised and Annotated Statutes, Oklahoma

Win. Winch's Common Pleas Reports (124 ER) 1621–25
Winer's Unreported Opinions (New York Supreme Court) 1912–40
Winston's North Carolina Reports (60 N.C.) 1863–64

Win.Eq. Winston's Equity Reports North Carolina (60 N.C.) 1863–64

Winch Winch's Common Pleas Reports (124 ER) 1621–25

Windsor Yearb.Access Justice The Windsor Yearbook of Access to Justice – Recueil Annuel de Windsor d'Accès à la Justice (Can.) 1981–

Windsor Yrbk. Acc.Jus. The Windsor Yearbook of Access to Justice – Annuel de Windsor d'Accès à la Justice (Can.)

Wing. Wingate's Maxims. 1658

Wing.Max. Wingate's Maxims. 1658

Winn Report Reports of the Committee on Personal Injuries Litigation (Cmnd. 3691) 1968

Winst. Winston's Equity Reports, North Carolina (60 N.C.) 1863–64

Winst.Eq.(N.C) Winston's Equity Reports, North Carolina (60 N.C.) 1863–64

Winst.L.(N.C.) Winston's Law Reports, North Carolina. 1863–64

Wis. Wisconsin
Wisconsin Reports. 1853–

Wis.2d. Wisconsin Reports, Second Series

Wis.B.A.Bull. Wisconsin State Bar Association Bulletin. 1927–48

Wis.B.Bull. Wisconsin Bar Bulletin. 1948–

Wis.Bar Assn. Wisconsin State Bar Association

Wis.I.C. Wisconsin Industrial Commission (Workmen's Compensation) Reports

Wis.L.N. Wisconsin Legal News. 1878–84

Wis.L.Rev. Wisconsin Law Review. 1920–

Wis.Leg.N. Wisconsin Legal News. 1878–84

Wis.Legis.Serv. Wisconsin Legislative Services (West)

Wis.P.S.C. Wisconsin Public Service Commission Reports

Wis.P.S.C.Ops. Wisconsin Public Service Commission Opinions & Decisions
Wis.R.C.R. Wisconsin Railroad Commission Reports
Wis.S.B.A. Wisconsin State Bar Association
Wis.S.B.A.Bull. Wisconsin State Bar Association Bulletin. 1927–48
Wis.Stat. Wisconsin Statutes
Wis.Stat.Ann.(West) West's Wisconsin Statutes Annotated
Wistra Zeitschrift für Wirtschaft, Steuer, Strafrecht (Ger.)
With.Corp.Cas. Withrow, American Corporation Cases
Withrow Withrow's American Corporation Cases
Withrow's Reports (9–11 Iowa)
Witkin,Cal.Summary Witkin's Summary of California Law
Wkly.L.Bul. Weekly Law Bulletin (Ohio) 1880–84
Wkly.L.Gaz. Weekly Law Gazette (Ohio) 1858–60
Wkly.Law Gaz. Weekly Law Gazette (Ohio) 1858–60
Wkly.N.C. Weekly Notes of Cases (Pennsylvania) 1874–99
Wkly.Rep. Weekly Reporter. 1853–1906
Wm. William
Wm.Bl. William Blackstone's King's Bench Reports (96 ER) 1746–80
Wm.L.J. Willamette Law Journal (USA) 1959–
Wm.Rob. William Robinson's Admiralty Reports (166 ER) 1838–52
Wm.Rob.Adm. William Robinson's Admiralty Reports (166 ER) 1838–52
Wm.& M. William and Mary
Wm.& Mary William and Mary
Wm.& Mary L.Rev. William & Mary Law Review (USA) 1957–
Wms.Ann.Reg. Williams' Annual Register, New York
Wms.Bank. Williams on Bankruptcy
Wms.Ex. Williams, Executors
Wms.Exors. Williams on Executors
Wms.Ex'rs. Williams on Executors
Wms.Exs. Williams on Executors
Wms.Mass. Williams' Massachusetts Reports (1 Mass.) 1804–05
Wms.Notes Williams' Notes to Saunders' Reports (85 ER) 1666–73
Wms.P. Peere Williams' Chancery Reports (24 ER) 1695–1735
Wms.P.P. Williams, Personal Property. 18ed. 1926
Wms.Peere Peere Williams' Chancery Reports (24 ER) 1695–1735
Wms.R.P. Williams (J.) Real Property. 24ed. 1926
Wms.Saund. Williams' Notes to Saunders' Reports (85 ER) 1666–73
Wms.Vt. Williams' Reports (27–29 Vermont)
Wms.& Bruce Williams & Bruce, Admiralty Practice. 3ed. 1902
Wn. Washington Reports. 1890–1939
Wn.2d. Washington Reports, Second Series. 1939–
Wn.L. Waynes Law Review (Mich.) 1954–
Wn.L.R. Washington Law Review (Seattle) 1919–
Wayne Law Review (Michigan) 1954–
Wn.T. Washington Territory Reports. 1854–88
Wol. Wolcott's Reports (7 Delaware Chancery)
Wollaston's Bail Court Reports. 1840–41
Wolf.& B. Wolferstan & Bristow's Election Cases. 1859–64
Wolf.& D. Wolferstan & Dew's Election Cases. 1856–58
Wolfenden Report Report of Department Committee on Homosexual Offences and Prostitution (Cmnd.247) 1956–57
Woll. Wollaston's Bail Court Reports. 1840–41
Women L.Jour. Women Lawyers Journal (USA) 1911–
Women Law.J. Women Lawyers Journal (USA) 1911–

Women Lawyer's J. Women Lawyers Journal (USA) 1911–

Women's L.J. Women's Law Journal (USA)

Women's Rights L.Reptr. Women's Rights Law Reporter

Wont.Land Reg. Wontner, Land Registry Practice. 12ed. 1975

Wood Wood, Mercantile Agreements. 1886
Wood's Tithe Cases. 1650–1798
Woods, United States Circuit Court Reports. 1870–83

Wood Conv. Wood on Conveyancing. 6ed. 1800

Wood Decr. Wood's Tithe Cases. 1650–1798

Wood H. Hutton Wood's Tithe Cases. 1650–1798

Wood.Inst. Wood's Institute of the Laws of England. Various eds. 1720–72

Wood.Lect. Wooddeson's Lectures on Laws of England. 2ed. 1834

Wood Ti.Cas. Wood's Tithe Cases. 1650–1798

Wood Tit.Cas. Wood's Tithe Cases. 1650–1798

Wood Tr.M. Wood, Trade Marks. 1876

Wood.& M. Woodbury & Minot's United States Circuit Court Reports. 1845–47

Woodb.& M. Woodbury & Minot's United States Circuit Court Reports. 1845–47

Woodd.Lect. Wooddeson's Lectures on the Laws of England. 2ed. 1834

Wooddeson,Lect. Woodeson's lectures on the Laws of England. 2ed. 1834

Woodf. Woodfall, Landlord and Tenant. 28ed. 1978

Woodf.L.& T. Woodfall, Landlord and Tenant. 28ed. 1978

Woodf.Landl.& T. Woodfall, Landlord and Tenant. 28ed. 1978

Woodf.Landl.& Ten. Woodfall, Landlord and Tenant. 28ed. 1978

Wooding Committee The Report of the Committee on Legal Education (in the Caribbean). 1964

Woodman Cr.Cas. Woodman's Reports of Thacher's Criminal Cases (Massachusetts) 1823–42

Woods Woods' United States Circuit Court Reports. 1870–83

Woods C.C. Wood's United States Circuit Court Reports. 1870–83

Wood's Civ.Law Wood's New Institute of the Imperial or Civil Law. 1685

Wood's Dig. Wood's Digest of Laws (California)

Woods,Ins. Wood's Institute of the Law of England

Wood's R. Wood's Manitoba Reports. 1875–83

Woodw.Dec. Woodward's Decisions (Pennsylvania) 1861–74

Woodw.Dec.Pa. Woodward's Decisions (Pennsylvania) 1861–74

Wool. Woolworth's Circuit Court Reports (USA) 1863–69
Woolworth's Reports (1 Nebraska)

Wool.C.C. Woolworth's Reports United States Circuit Court (Miller's Decisions) 1863–69

Wool.Int. Woolsey, Introduction to International Law. 6ed. 1888

Woolf.Adult. Woolf, Adulterations. 1874

Woolr.Cert. Woolrych, Certificates. 1826

Woolr.Com. Woolrych, Rights of Common. 2ed. 1850

Woolr.Cr.L. Woolrych, Criminal Law. 1862

Woolr.L.W. Woolrych, Law of Waters. 2ed. 1851

Woolr.P.W. Woolrych, Party Walls. 1845

Woolr.Sew. Woolrych, Sewers. 3ed. 1864

Woolr.Waters Woolrych, Law of Waters. 2ed. 1851

Woolr.Ways Woolrych, Law of Ways. 2ed. 1847

Woolr.Wind.L. Woolrych, Window Lights. 2ed. 1864

Wools.Int.L. Woolsey, Introduction to Study of International Law. 6ed. 1888

Woolw. Woolworth's Reports (1 Nebraska)
Woolworth's United States Circuit Court Reports. 1863–69

Woolw.Rep. Woolworth's Reports (1 Nebraska)
Woolworth's United States Circuit Court Reports. 1863–69

Words.Elect. Wordsworth, Law of Elections. 6ed. 1868

Words.Elect.Cas. Wordsworth's Election Cases. 1834

Work.Comp. Workmen's Compensation

Workmen's Comp.L.Rep. Workmen's Compensation Law Reporter (CCH) (USA)

World Aff. World Affairs

World L.Rev. World Law Review

World Trade L.J. World Trade Law Journal

Worth.Jur. Worthington, Power of Juries. 1825

Worth.Prec.Wills Worthington, General Precedent for Wills. 5ed. 1852

Wr. Wright
Wright's Pennsylvania Reports (37–50 Pa. state)

Wr.Ch. Wright's Ohio Reports. 1831–34

Wr.Ohio Wright's Ohio Reports. 1831–34

Wr.Pa. Wright's Pennsylvania Reports (37–50 Pa. State)

Wright Wright's Ohio Reports. 1831–34
Wright's Pennsylvania Reports (37–50 Pa.State)

Wright Ch. Wright's Reports (Ohio) 1831–34

Wright Cr.Cons. Wright, Criminal Conspiracies. 1873

Wright N.P. Wright's Nisi Prius Reports (Ohio)

Wright Ten. Wright on Tenures. 4ed. 1792

Writ of error den. Writ of error denied

Ws.L. Washington Law Review (Seattle) 1919–
Washington Law Review and State Bar Journal. 1936–61

Wsb. Washburn Law Journal (Kansas) 1960–

Wsh. Washington State Reports. 1890–

WuM Wohnungswirtschaft und Mietrecht (Ger.)

WuR Die Wirtschaft und das Recht (Ger.)

WuW Wirtschaft und Wettbewerb (Ger.) 1951–

Wy. Wyoming
Wyoming Reports. 1870–1959
Wythe's Chancery Reports (Virginia) 1788–99

Wy.Dic. Wyatt's Dickens' Chancery Reports. 1559–1798

Wy.Dic. Wyatt's Dickens' Chancery Reports. 1559–1798

Wy.L.J. Wyoming Law Journal. 1946–65

Wy.Pr.R. Wyatt's Practical Register in Chancery. 1800

Wy.W.& A'Beck. Wyatt, Webb & A'Beckett's Reports (Victoria, Aus.) 1864–69

Wy.& W. Wyatt & Webb's Victorian Reports (Victoria, Aus.) 1861–63

Wyat.& W.Eq. Wyatt & Webb's Equity Reports (Victoria, Aus.) 1861–63

Wyatt Pr,R. Wyatt's Practical Register in Chancery. 1800

Wyatt,Prac.Reg. Wyatt's Practical Register in Chancery. 1800

Wyatt,W.& A'B Wyatt, Webb & A'Beckett's Reports (Victoria, Aus.) 1864–69

Wyatt,W.& A'B.Eq. Wyatt, Webb & A'Beckett's Equity Reports (Victoria, Aus.) 1864–69

Wyatt,W.& A'B.I.E.& M. Wyatt, Webb & A'Beckett's Insolvency, Ecclesiastical & Matrimonial Reports (Victoria, Aus.) 1864–69

Wyatt,W.& A'B.Min. Wyatt, Webb & A'Beckett's Mining Cases (Victoria, Aus.) 1864–69

Wyatt & W. Wyatt & Webb's Reports (Victoria, Aus.) 1861–63

Wyatt & W.(Eq.) Wyatt & Webb's Reports, Equity (Victoria, Aus.) 1861–63

Wyatt & W.I.E.& M. Wyatt & Webb's Insolvency, Ecclesiastical & Matrimonial Reports (Victoria, Aus.) 1861–63

Wyatt & W.Min. Wyatt & Webb's Mining Cases (Victoria, Aus.) 1861–63

Wyatt & Webb Wyatt & Webb's Reports (Victoria, Aus.) 1861–63

Wylie Report The Final Report of the Land Law Working Group (Northern Ireland) 1991

Wyman Wyman's Civil & Criminal Reports (India)

Wynne Edward Wynne (ed.), Observations touching the Antiquity and Dignity of the Degree of Serjeant at Law. 1765

Wyo. Wyoming
Wyoming Reports. 1870–1959

Wyo.B.A. Wyoming Bar Association

Wyo.L.J. Wyoming Law Journal. 1946–65

Wyo.P.S.C. Wyoming Public Service Commission Reports

Wyo.S.B.A. Wyoming State Bar Association
Wyoming State Bar Association, Proceedings

Wyo.Sess.Laws Session Laws of Wyoming

Wyo.Stat. Wyoming Statutes

Wyo.T. Wyoming Territory

Wythe Wythe's Chancery Reports (Virginia)

Wythe Ch.(Va.) Wythe's Chancery Reports (Virginia) 1788–1799

Wythe(Va.) Wythe's Chancery Reports (Virginia) 1788–99

X

x. unknown quantity
x.d. not including right to dividend
x.div. not including right to dividend
x.ref. cross reference
X.W. Without warrants
Xian Dai Faxue Xian Dai Faxue (Modern Law Science) (China)

Y

y. year
youngest

Y. Yeates Pennsylvania Reports. 1791–1808

Y.A. York-Antwerp Rules

Y.A.D. Young's Admiralty Decisions (Nova Scotia, Can.) 1865–80

Y.B. Year Books. 1292–1537
Year Books (ed. Dieser) 1388–89
Year Books (ed. Maynard) 1367–1537

Y.B.Air & Space L. Yearbook of Air & Space Law (Can.) 1965–67

Y.B.C.A. Yearbook, Commercial Arbitration (Neth.) 1976–

Y.B.Commercial Arbitration Yearbook, Commercial Arbitration (Neth.) 1976–

Y.B.Ed.I. Year Books of Edward I

Y.B.Eur.Conv.On Human Rights Year Book of the European Convention of Human Rights (Neth.) 1959–

Y.B.Eur.L. Yearbook of European Law

Y.B.Hum.Rts. Yearbook on Human Rights (USA) 1947–

Y.B.I.C.J. Yearbook of the International Court of Justice. 1947–

Y.B.I.L. Yearbook of International Law

Y.B.I.L.C. Yearbook of the International Law Commission (UN)

Y.B.Int'l.L.Comm'n. Yearbook of the International Law Commission. 1949–

Y.B.Rich.II Bellewe's Les Ans du Roy Richard le Second (72 ER) 1378–1400

Y.B.(R.S.) Year Books, Rolls Series. 1292–1546
Year Books, Rolls Series, ed. Horwood. 1292–1307
Year Books, Rolls Series, ed. Horwood & Pike. 1337–46

Y.B. (Rolls Ser.) Year Books, Rolls Series. 1292–1546

Y.B.S.C. Year Books, Selected Cases

Y.B.(S.S.) Year Books, Selden Society. 1307–19

Y.B.U.N. Yearbook of the United Nations

Y.B.W.A. Yearbook of World Affairs

Y.B.World Aff. Yearbook of World Affairs

Y.J. Yukon Judgments (unreported decisions available on QL) (Can.) 1986–

Y.L.C.T. Yearbook of Law, Computers and Technology

Y.L.J. Yale Law Journal. 1891–

Y.L.R. York Legal Record (Pennsylvania) 1880–

Y.L.S.N. Young Lawyers Section Newsletter (Law Society of New South Wales, Aus.) 1982–

YOP Youth Opportunities Programme

Y.R. Yukon Reports (Can.) 1986–

Y.T. Yukon Territory, Canada

Y.U.N. Yearbook of the United Nations

Y.& C. Younge & Collyer's Chancery Reports (62–63 ER) 1841–43
Younge & Collyer's Exchequer Reports (160 ER) 1834–42

Y.& C.C.C. Younge & Collyer's Chancery Cases (62–63 ER) 1841–43

Y.& C.Ch. Younge & Collyer's Chancery Cases (62–63 ER) 1841–43

Y.& C.Ch.Cas. Younge & Collyer's Chancery Cases (62–3 ER) 1841–43

Y.& C.Ex. Younge & Collyer's Exchequer Reports (160 ER) 1834–42
Y.& C.Exch. Younge & Collyer's Exchequer Reports (160 ER) 1834–42
Y.& Coll. Younge & Collyer's Chancery Reports (62–63 ER) 1841–43
Younge & Collyer's Exchequer Reports (160 ER) 1834–42
Y.& J. Younge & Jervis' Exchequer Reports (148 ER) 1826–30
Yale J.Int'l L. The Yale Journal of International Law
Yale J.on Reg. Yale Journal on Regulation
Yale L.J. Yale Law Journal. 1891–
Yale L.& Pol'y Rev. Yale Law and Policy Review
Yale Rev.Law & Soc.Act'n. Yale Review of Law and Social Action. 1970–
Yale St.Wld.Pub.Ord. Yale Studies in World Public Order. 1974–
Yale Stud.World P.O. Yale Studies in World Public Order
Yates-Lee Yates-Lee on Bankruptcy. 3ed. 1887
Yates Sel.Cas. Yates' Select Cases (New York) 1809
Yates Sel.Cas.(N.Y.) Yates' Select Cases (New York) 1809
Yea. Yeates' Reports (Pennsylvania) 1791–1808
Yearb. Year Book
Yeates Yeates' Pennsylvania Reports. 1791–1808
Yel. Yelverton's King's Bench Reports (80 ER) 1602–13
Yelv. Yelverton's King's Bench Reports (80 ER) 1602–13
Yer. Yerger's Tennessee Supreme Court Reports (9–18 Tenn.) 1828–37
Yerg. Yerger's Tennessee Supreme Court Reports (9–18 Tenn.) 1828–37
Yerg.(Tenn.) Yerger's Tennessee Supreme Court Reports (9–18 Tenn.) 1828–37
Yo. Younge's Exchequer in Equity Reports (159 ER) 1830–32
Yool Waste Yool, Waste, Nuisance and Trespass. 1863
York York Legal Record (Pennsylvania) 1880–
York Ass. Clayton's Reports (York Assizes) 1631–50
York Leg.Rec. York Legal Record (Pennsylvania) 1880–
York Leg.Rec.(Pa.) York Legal Record (Pennsylvania) 1880–
Yorke Ass. Clayton's Reports (York Assizes) 1631–50
You. Younge's Exchequer in Equity Reports (159 ER) 1830–32
You.& Coll.Ch. Younge & Collyer's Chancery Reports (62–63 ER) 1841–43
You.& Coll.Ex. Younge & Collyer's Exchequer Reports (160 ER) 1834–42
You.& Jerv. Younge & Jervis' Exchequer Reports (148 ER) 1826–30
Young Young's Reports (21–47 Minnesota)
Young Adm. Young's Admiralty Decisions (Nova Scotia, Can.) 1865–80
Young Adm.Dec.(Nov.Sc.) Young's Admiralty Decisions (Nova Scotia, Can.) 1865–80
Young M.L.Cas. Young's Maritime Law Cases. 1837–60
Young V.A.Dec. Young's Nova Scotia Vice-Admiralty Decisions. 1865–80
Younge Younge's Exchequer in Equity Reports (159 ER) 1830–32
Younge Exch. Younge's Exchequer in Equity Reports (159 ER) 1830–32
Younge & C.Ch. Younge & Collyer's Chancery Reports (62–63 ER) 1841–43
Younge & C.Ch.Cas. Younge & Collyer's Chancery Reports (62–63 ER) 1841–43
Younge & C.Exch. Younge & Collyer's Exchequer Reports (160 ER) 1834–42
Younge & Coll.Ch. Younge & Collyer's Chancery Reports (62–63 ER) 1841–43
Younge & Coll.Ex. Younge & Collyer's Exchequer Reports (160 ER) 1834–42
Younge & J. Younge & Jervis's Exchequer Reports (148 ER) 1826–30

Younge & Je. Younge & Jervis's Exchequer Reports (148 ER) 1826–30
Younge & Jerv. Younge & Jervis's Exchequer Reports (148 ER) 1826–30
Younger Report Report of the Committee on Privacy (Cmnd. 5012) 1972
Youth Ct. Youth Court (USA)
Yr.Bk. Year Book
Yrbk.Euro.L. Yearbook of European Law
Yrbk.Socialist Leg.Sys. Yearbook on Socialist Legal Systems (USA)
Yugoslav L. Yugoslav Law
Yuk. Yukon Territory
Yuk.Ord. Yukon Ordinances (Can.)
Yuk.Rev.Ord. Yukon Revised Ordinances (Can.)
Yukon Terr. Yukon Territory

Z

Z. Zeitschrift (Ger.) review
Zeitung (Ger.) newspaper, review
Zentralblatt (Ger.) Official gazette
Zimbabwe High Court
Zoll (Ger.) customs duty

Z.A. Zimbabwe Appellate Division

ZAGS Registry for Acts of Civil Status (USSR)

Z.ai.Arbeits–& Sozial R Zeitschrift für ausländisches und internationales Arbeits- und Sozialrecht (Ger.)

Z.aö.RV Zeitschrift für ausländisches öffentliches Recht und Völkerrecht (Ger.)

Z.aö.R.u.V.R. Zeitschrift für ausländisches öffentliches Recht und Völkerrecht (Ger.)

Z.ausl.PR. Zeitschrift für ausländisches und internationales Privatrecht

ZBGR Zeitschrift für Beurkundungs- und Grundbuchrecht (Switz.)

ZBJV Zeitschrift des Bernischen Juristenvereins (Switz.)

ZBernJurV Zeitschrift des Bernischen Juristenvereins (Switz.)

Z.ev.KR Zeitschrift für Evangelisches Kirchenrecht (Ger.)

Z.f.a.ö.R.u.V. Zeitschrift für ausländisches öffentliches Recht und Völkerrecht

Z.f.a.u.i.P. Zeitschrift für ausländisches und internationales Privatrecht

ZFL Zeitschrift für Luftrecht (Ger.) 1952–

Z.f.Ostrecht Zeitschrift für Ostrecht (Ger.)

Z.f.RV. Zeitschrift für Rechtsvergleichung (Ger.)

Z.f.V. Zeitschrift für Völkerrecht (Ger.)

ZGB Schweizerisches Zivilgesetzbuch (Switz.)

ZG Zollgesetz (Ger.) Customs Act

ZG Fa Xue Zhong Guo Fa Xue (China)

ZGR Zeitschrift für Unternehmens- und Gesellschaftsrecht (Ger.)

ZG She Hui ZYJS Zhong Guo She Hui Zhui Yi Jian She (China)

ZHR Zeitschrift für das gesamte Handelsrecht und Wirtschaftsrecht (Ger.)

ZIP Zeitschrift für Wirtschaftsrecht (Ger.)

Z.int.R. Niemeyer's Zeitschrift für internationales Recht (Ger.)

Z.L.J. Zambia Law Journal. 1969–

Z.L.R. Zanzibar Protectorate Law Reports. 1868–1950
Zanzibar Law Reports. 1919–50

ZLuftR Zeitschrift für Luft- und Weltraumrecht (Ger.)

Z.ö.R. Österreichische Zeitschrift für öffentliches Recht (Austria)

Z.osteurop.R. Zeitschrift für osteuropäisches Recht

ZPO Zivilprozessordnung (Ger.) code of civil procedure

ZR Blätter für zürcherische Rechtsprechung (Switz.)

ZRGGermAbt Zeitschrift der Savigny-Stiftung für Rechtsgeschichte, Germanistische Abteilung (Ger.)

ZRGKanAbt Zeitschrift der Savigny-Stiftung für Rechtsgeschichte, Kanonistische Abteilung (Ger.)

ZRGRomAbt Zeitschrift der Savigny-Stiftung für Rechtsgeschichte, Romanistische Abteilung (Ger.)
ZRP Zeitschrift für Rechtspolitik (Ger.)
ZRSoz Zeitschrift für Rechtssoziologie (Ger.)
ZRV Zeitschrift für Rechtsvergleichung, Internationales Privatrecht und Europarecht Austria)
Z.Rechtspflege Bayern Zeitschrift für Rechtspflege in Bayern (Switz.)
ZS. Zeitschrift (Ger.) review
ZSR Zeitschrift für schweizerisches Recht (Switz.)
ZSSt Zeitschrift der Savigny-Stiftung für Rechtsgeschichte
ZSchwR Zeitschrift für schweizerisches Recht (Switz.)
Z.Schweiz.R. Zeitschrift für schweizerisches Recht (Switz.)
ZStW Zeitschrift für die gesamte Strafrechtswissenschaft (Ger.) 1881–1944, 1950–
ZStrW Zeitschrift für die gesamte Strafrechtswissenschaft (Ger.) 1881–1944, 1950–
ZVersWes Zietschrift für Versicherungswesen (Ger.) 1950–
ZVglRWiss Zeitschrift für vergleichende Rechtswissenschaft (Ger.)
ZVölkR Zeitschrift für Völkerrecht (Ger.) 1906–44
ZVormO Zollvormerkordnung (Ger.) Customs Booking Regulations
ZWallRspr Zeitschrift für Walliser Rechtsprechung – Revue valaisanne de jurisprudence (Switz.)
ZZP Zeitschrift für Zivilprozess (Ger.) 1879–1943, 1950–
Z.Ziv.Proz. Zeitschrift für Zivilprozess (Ger.) 1879–1943, 1950–
Za. Zabriskie's Reports (21–24 New Jersey Law) 1847–55
Zab.(N.J.) Zabriskie's Reports (21–24 New Jersey Law) 1847–55
Zambia L.J. Zambia Law Journal. 1969–
Zane Zane's Reports (4–9 Utah)
Zanzib.Prot.L.R. Zanzibar Protectorate Law Reports. 1868–1950
ZaöRV Zeitschrift für ausländisches öffentliches Recht und Völkerrecht (Ger.)
ZaörV Zeitschrift für ausländisches öffentliches Recht und Völkerrecht (Ger.)
ZbJV Zeitschrift des bernischen Juristenvereins (Switz.)
ZblDDR Zentraltblatt der Deutschen Demoktratischen Repuplic (Ger.) Official Gazette of the German Democratic Republic. 1953–
ZblSozVers. Zentralblatt für Sozialversicherung und Versorgung (Ger.) 1947–
Zbor.Prav.Fak.Zagreb Zbornik Pravnog Fakulteta u Zagreb (Yugoslavia)
Zbor.Rad.Prav.Fak.Split Zbornik Radova Pravnog Fakulteta Splitu (Yugoslavia)
Zeit.geschicht.Rechtsw. Zeitschrift für geschichtliche Rechtswissenschaft (Ger.)
ZfL Zeitschrift für Luftraumrecht und Weltraumfragen (Ger.)
ZfR Zeitschrift für Rechtsvergleichung (Austria)
ZfV Zeitschrift für Versicherungswesen (Ger.) 1950–
ZfZ Zeitschrift für Zolle und Verbrauchssteuern (Ger.)
Zilla C.D. Zilla Court Decisions (Bengal, Madras, North West Provinces) (India)
Zimbabwe L.J. The Zimbabwe Law Journal
Zimbabwe L.Rev. Zimbabwe Law Review
ZivA Archiv für civilistische Praxis (Ger.) 1818–1944, 1948–
Zsarb. Zusammenarbeit
Zschft.f.ausl.öffentl.Recht Zeitschrift für ausländisches öffentliches Recht und Völkerrecht (Ger.)
Zschft.f.ausl.u.intl.Prvätr. Zeitschrift für ausländisches und internationales

Privatrecht (Ger.)

Zschft.f.gesamte Staatwiss. Zeitschrift für die gesamte Staatwissenschaft (Ger.)

Zschft.f.vergl.Rechtwissenschaft Zeitschrift für vergleichende Rechtswissenschaft (Ger.)

Zschft.für Rechtssoziol. Zeitschrift für Rechtssoziologie (Ger.)

Zschft.Luft-u.Weltr.-recht Zeitschrift für Luftrecht-und Weltraumrechtsfragen (Ger.)

Zschft.Rechtsvergl. Zeitschrift für Rechtsvergleichung (Austria)

Zschft.Savigny–Germ. Zeitschrift der Savigny Stiftung für Rechtsgeschichte, Germanischtische Abteilung (Ger.)

Zschft.Savigny–Kanon. Zeitschrift der Savigny Stiftung für Rechtsgeschichte, Kanonistische Abteilung (Ger.)

Zschft.Savigny–Rom. Zeitschrift der Savigny Stiftung für Rechtsgeschichte, Romanistische Abteilung (Ger.)

zsgest. zusammengestellt

Ztg. Zeitung (Ger.) newspaper, review

Zululand Zululand Commissioner's Court Cases (S.Afr.)